Arguing About Language

Arguing About Language presents a comprehensive selection of key readings on fundamental issues in the philosophy of language. It offers a fresh and exciting introduction to the subject, addressing both perennial problems and emerging topics.

Classic readings from Frege, Russell, Kripke, Chomsky, Quine, Grice, Lewis and Davidson appear alongside more recent pieces by philosophers or linguists such as Robyn Carston, Crispin Wright, Timothy Williamson and Nathan Salmon. Organised into clear sections, readings have been chosen that engage with one another and often take opposing views on the same question, helping students to get to grips with the key areas of debate in the philosophy of language, including:

- Sense and reference
- Definite descriptions
- Linguistic conventions
- Language and behaviour
- Descriptivism and rigidity
- Contextualism
- Vagueness
- Rule-following and normativity
- Fictional discourse

Each article selected is clear, thought-provoking and free from unnecessary jargon. The editors provide lucid introductions to each section in which they give an overview of the debate and outline the arguments of the papers.

Arguing About Language is an ideal reader for students looking for a balanced yet up-to-date introduction to the philosophy of language.

Darragh Byrne is Lecturer in Philosophy at the University of Birmingham, UK.

Max Kölbel is ICREA Research Professor at the University of Barcelona, Spain. He is the author of *Truth without Objectivity* (Routledge, 2002) and co-editor of *Wittgenstein's Lasting Significance* (Routledge, 2004) with Bernhard Weiss, as well as *Relative Truth* (2008) with Manuel Garcia-Carpintero.

Arguing About Philosophy

This exciting and lively series introduces key subjects in philosophy with the help of a vibrant set of readings. In contrast to many standard anthologies which often reprint the same technical and remote extracts, each volume in the *Arguing About Philosophy* series is built around essential but fresher philosophical readings, designed to attract the curiosity of students coming to the subject for the first time. A key feature of the series is the inclusion of well-known yet often neglected readings from related fields, such as popular science, film and fiction. Each volume is edited by leading figures in their chosen field and each section carefully introduced and set in context, making the series an exciting starting point for those looking to get to grips with philosophy.

Arguing About Knowledge
Edited by Duncan Pritchard and Ram Neta

Arguing About Law
Edited by John Oberdiek and Aileen Kanvanagh

Arguing About Metaethics
Edited by Andrew Fisher and Simon Kirchin

Arguing About the Mind
Edited by Brie Gertler and Lawrence Shapiro

Arguing About Art 3rd Edition
Edited by Alex Neill and Aaron Ridley

Arguing About Metaphysics
Edited by Michael Rea

Arguing About Political Philosophy
Edited by Matt Zwolinski

Arguing About Religion
Edited by Kevin Timpe

Forthcoming titles:

Arguing About Bioethics
Edited by Steven Holland

Arguing About Language

Edited by

Darragh Byrne and Max Kölbel

Routledge
Taylor & Francis Group

LONDON AND NEW YORK

First published 2010
by Routledge
2 Park Square, Milton Park, Abingdon, Oxon OX14 4RN

Simultaneously published in the USA and Canada
by Routledge
711 Third Avenue, New York, NY 10017, USA

Routledge is an imprint of the Taylor & Francis Group, an informa business

Typeset in Joanna and Bell Gothic by
RefineCatch Limited, Bungay, Suffolk

British Library Cataloguing in Publication Data
A catalogue record for this book is available from the British Library

Library of Congress Cataloging-in-Publication Data
Arguing about language / edited by Darragh Byrne and Max Kölbel.
    p. cm.
  Includes bibliographical references and index.
  1. Language and languages—Philosophy.   2. Language and culture.
    I. Byrne, Darragh.   II. Kölbel, Max.
  P107.A76 2009
  401—dc22

                                                        2009014383

ISBN10: 0–415–46243–6 (hbk)
ISBN10: 0–415–46244–4 (pbk)

ISBN13: 978–0–415–46243–3 (hbk)
ISBN13: 978–0–415–46244–0 (pbk)

Contents

Contents   vii

Acknowledgements

Part one: A Homeric struggle: communication and truth

Grice, H. Paul 1957: 'Meaning', *Philosophical Review* 66, pp. 377–88. Copyright, 1957, Sage School of Philosophy of Cornell University. All rights reserved. Used by permission of the publisher, Duke University Press and Mrs K. Grice.

Strawson, Peter F. 2004 [1970]: Extract from *Meaning and Truth* (Inaugural Lecture), Oxford: Oxford University Press; reprinted in Peter F. Strawson, *Logico-Linguistic Papers*, Aldershot, UK: Ashgate, pp. 171–89. Copyright P. F. Strawson (1971, 2004). Reprinted here by permission of the Estate of P. F. Strawson and Ashgate Publishing.

Dummett, Michael 1989: Extract from 'Language and Communication', in A. George (ed.), *Reflections on Chomsky*, Oxford: Blackwell, pp. 192–9; reprinted in M. Dummett, *The Seas of Language*, Oxford: Oxford University Press (1993).

Part two: Sense and reference

Frege, Gottlob 1892: Extract from 'Über Sinn und Bedeutung', *Zeitschrift für Philosophie und philosophische Kritik*, NF, 100, pp. 25–50. Translation by Max Kölbel.

Salmon, Nathan 1986: Extracts from *Frege's Puzzle*, Cambridge, MA: MIT Press. Reprinted by kind permission of the publisher.

Part three: Definite descriptions: quantifiers or singular terms?

Russell, Bertrand 1919: Extract from chapter 16 of *Introduction to Mathematical Philosophy* ('Descriptions'), London: Allen and Unwin. By permission of The Bertrand Russell Peace Foundation Ltd.

Strawson, Peter F. 1950: 'On Referring', *Mind* 59, pp. 320–44. Reprinted by permission of the Estate of P. F. Strawson

Russell, Bertrand 1956: 'Mr. Strawson on Referring', *Mind* 66, pp. 385–9.

Part four: Rigidity vs descriptivism

Kripke, Saul 1980: Lecture 2 of *Naming and Necessity*, Oxford: Blackwell, pp. 71–105. Reproduced by permission of Blackwell Publishing Ltd.

Jackson, Frank 1998: Excerpt from 'Reference and Description Revisited', *Philosophical Perspectives* 12, *Language, Mind and Ontology*, pp. 201–18. Reproduced by permission of Blackwell Publishing Ltd.

Part five: Analyticity

Quine, W. V. 1953: 'Two Dogmas of Empiricism', reprinted by permission of the publisher from *From a Logical Point of View: Nine Logico-Philosophical Essays*, pp. 20–46, Cambridge, MA: Harvard University Press. Copyright 1953, 1961, 1980 by the President and Fellows of Harvard College, renewed 1989 by W. V. Quine.

Grice, H. P., and P. F. Strawson 1956: 'In Defense of a Dogma', *Philosophical Review* 65, pp. 141–58. Copyright, 1956, Sage School of Philosophy of Cornell University. All rights reserved. Used by permission of the publisher, Duke University Press and the Estate of P. F. Strawson and Mrs K.Grice.

Part six: Truth and meaning

Davidson, Donald 1967: 'Truth and Meaning', *Synthese* 17, no. 3, pp. 304–23, with kind permission of Springer Science and Business Media and Marcia Cavell.

Foster, John 1976: Extract from 'Meaning and Truth Theory', in G. Evans and J. McDowell (eds), *Truth and Meaning*, Oxford: Oxford University Press, pp. 7–23. By permission of Oxford University Press.

Part seven: Meaning, intention and convention

Lewis, David 1975: 'Languages and Language', in K. Gunderson (ed.), *Minnesota Studies in the Philosophy of Science* VII, Minneapolis: University of Minnesota Press; reprinted in D. Lewis, *Philosophical Papers*, Oxford: Oxford University Press (1983), pp. 163–88. Reprinted here by kind permission of Stephanie R. Lewis.

Hawthorne, John 1990: 'A Note on "Languages and Language"', *Australasian Journal of Philosophy* 68, pp. 116–18. Taylor & Francis, http://www.informaworld.com; reprinted by permission of the author and publisher.

Laurence, Stephen 1996: 'A Chomskian Alternative to Convention-Based Semantics', *Mind* 105, pp. 269–301. Reprinted by kind permission of the author.

Part eight: Knowledge of language

Chomsky, Noam, 1986: Chapter 1 of *Knowledge of Language: Its Nature, Origin and Use*, New York: Praeger. Reproduced with permission of Greenwood Publishing, Inc., Westport, CT.

Evans, Gareth, 1981: 'Semantic Theory and Tacit Knowledge', in S. Holtzman and C. Leich (eds), *Wittgenstein: To Follow a Rule*, London: Routledge, 118–37. Reproduced by permission of Taylor and Francis Books UK.

Wright, Crispin 1986: Section III of 'Theories of Meaning and Speakers' Knowledge', in Crispin Wright, *Realism, Meaning and Truth*, Oxford: Blackwell, pp. 217–37; 2nd edn (1993). Reproduced by permission of the author and Blackwell Publishing Ltd.

Part nine: Meaning, holism and inferential role

Lepore, Ernest, and Jerry Fodor 1993: 'Why Meaning (Probably) Isn't Conceptual Role', *Philosophical Issues* 3, pp. 15–35. Reproduced by permission of Blackwell Publishing Ltd.

Pagin, Peter 1997: 'Is Compositionality Compatible with Holism?', *Mind & Language* 12, pp. 11–33. Reproduced by permission of Blackwell Publishing Ltd.

Part ten: Implicature

Grice, H. Paul 1975: 'Logic and Conversation', in P. Cole and J. Morgan (eds), *Syntax and Semantics*, vol. 3: *Speech Acts*, New York: Academic Press, pp. 41–58; reprinted in H. Paul Grice, *Studies in the Ways of Words*, pp. 22–40, Cambridge, MA: Harvard Univesity Press (1989). Reprinted here by permission of the publisher and Mrs K. Grice.

Carston, Robyn 2002: 'Linguistic Meaning, Communicated Meaning and Cognitive Pragmatics', *Mind & Language* 17, pp. 127–48. Reproduced by permission of Blackwell Publishing Ltd.

Part eleven: Compositionality and context

Lahav, Ran 1989: 'Against Compositionality: The Case of Adjectives', *Philosophical Studies* 57, pp. 261–79. With kind permission of Springer Science and Business Media and the author.

Szabó, Zoltán 2001: 'Adjectives in Context', in R. Harnish and I. Kenesei (eds), *Perspectives on Semantics, Pragmatics, and Discourse*, Amsterdam: John Benjamins, pp. 119–46. With kind permission by John Benjamins Publishing Company, Amsterdam/Philadelphia, www.benjamins.com

Part twelve: Rule-following and normativity

Wright, Crispin 1984: 'Kripke's Account of the Argument against Private Language', *Journal of Philosophy* 81, pp. 759–78. Reproduced by kind permission of the author and journal.

Wikforss, Åsa Maria 2001: 'Semantic Normativity', *Philosophical Studies* 102, pp. 203–26. With kind permission of Springer Science and Business Media and the author.

Part thirteen: Metaphor

Davidson, Donald 1978: 'What Metaphors Mean', *Critical Enquiry* 5, pp. 31–47. Reprinted in *Essays on Truth and Meaning*, Oxford: Oxford University Press (1984). Reprinted by kind permission of Marcia Cavell.

Black, Max 1979: 'How Metaphors Work: A Reply to Donald Davidson', *Critical Enquiry* 6, pp. 131–43.

Part fourteen: Language and vagueness

Varzi, Achille 2001: 'Vagueness, Logic and Ontology', in *The Dialogue: Yearbooks for Philosophical Hermeneutics* 1, pp. 135–54.

Williamson, Timothy 1992: 'Vagueness and Ignorance', *Proceeding of the Aristotelian Society Supplementary Volume* 66, pp. 145–62. Reprinted courtesy of the Editor of the Aristotelian Society; copyright 1992.

Fara, Delia Graff 2000: Extracts from 'Shifting Sands: An Interest-Relative Theory of Vagueness', *Philosophical Topics*, 28, no. 1, pp. 45–81. Used with the permission of the author and the University of Arkansas Press, www.uapress.com

Part fifteen: Fictional discourse

Lewis, David 1978: 'Truth in Fiction', *American Philosophical Quarterly* 15, pp. 37–46; reprinted in David Lewis, *Philosophical Papers*, vol. 1, Oxford: Oxford University Press (1983), pp. 261–80. Reprinted here by kind permission of Stephanie R. Lewis and *American Philosophical Quarterly*.

Predelli, Stefano 1997: 'Talk about Fiction', *Erkenntnis* 46, pp. 69–77. With kind permission of Springer Science and Business Media and the author.

Thomasson, Amie L. 2003: 'Speaking of Fictional Characters', *Dialectica* 57, pp. 207–26. Reproduced by permission of Blackwell Publishing Ltd.

Every effort has been made to trace and contact copyright holders. The publishers would be pleased to hear from any copyright holder not acknowledged here so that this section may be amended at the earliest opportunity.

We have had some very generous help at various stages of preparing the book. We would like to thank Alex Barber, John Collins, Manuel García-Carpintero, Guy Longworth, Gideon Makin, Peter Pagin, Chiara Panizza, Mark Sainsbury and Rob Stainton. For their patience, help and support throughout what turned out to be a rather lengthy and sometimes frustrating process, we would like to thank Tony Bruce and other members of the Routledge editorial team.

GENERAL INTRODUCTION

THE DISTINCTIVE FEATURE of this anthology in the philosophy of language is that it is organized around points of debate, both long-standing and recent. When one is new to a topic in philosophy, it is often difficult to read original work, i.e. work written by the researchers themselves. Without background knowledge, it is hard to see the wood for the trees: hard to gauge the significance of claims, hard to separate widely shared background assumptions from controversial claims, and hard to recognize consequences and connections between related issues. A classic solution to this problem is the introductory lecture or textbook, which offers a digest of the issues and thereby provides orientation. Such digests are no doubt necessary, but they run the risk of homogenizing and streamlining the material. The effects of this can be to compromise the autonomy of the student and to detach her from the real academic debate, thus making it more difficult for her to come to engage in it seriously and actively for herself. This reader attempts a different solution. It compiles pairs and triples of texts which defend opposing views on successive issues, and which in many cases engage directly with one another. Our hope is that this organization into thematic groups will make the texts more accessible and increase the number of students who read originals as opposed to digests.

In selecting texts, we pursued two main aims. First, we undertook to collect a representative core of classic texts, covering a spectrum of topics wide enough to make the book suitable for use in traditional philosophy of language courses. Secondly, we wanted to expand on the range of topics that are usually compiled in anthologies, for the debate among researchers has moved on in ways we felt ought to be reflected.

These aims constrained our selection of texts and topics. Additional constraints were engendered by spatial and financial considerations. This has led to omissions of key authors and key topics. Among the candidate parts of the book which these constraints led us to remove was, for example, one containing papers on indexicals, content and context. Readers should not infer too quickly from the omission of a favourite author or topic to the editors' lack of appreciation of these authors or topics.

The anthology contains 15 parts, each one containing two or three articles on a specific topic. Each of the parts begins with an introduction, in which we attempt to explain aspects of the philosophical background which may not be explicitly explained by the readings which follow, and in which we very briefly summarize the readings' main conclusions. We then suggest a number of questions and tasks for the student that we hope will help her to study the texts and to acquire a critical understanding of the topic at issue. These questions and tasks would, we suggest, also be highly suitable for discussion between students, in seminars or elsewhere. The introductions end with bibliographical references and suggestions for further reading.

Part One contains Paul Grice's classic paper 'Meaning' as well as P. F. Strawson's inaugural lecture 'Meaning and Truth' and an extract from Michael Dummett's paper 'Language and Communication'. Grice here defines his influential notion of *speaker-meaning* ('meaning$_{NN}$') in terms of speakers' intentions. Strawson contrasts the approach exemplified by Grice, of explicating linguistic meaning in terms of communicative intentions, with the approach of 'theorists of formal semantics' who aim to explicate meaning in terms of notions like *reference* and *truth*, and who place great emphasis on the idea that meanings are compositional: i.e. that the meanings of complex expressions (such as sentences) are determined by the meanings of their constituent expressions. Strawson objects to the formal semanticists' account, but attempts to show how theorists of communication-intention may appropriate some of their results and analytical devices (e.g. compositionality) and in doing so, overcome the tension between the two approaches. Dummett advocates the formal semantics approach, and in the third reading, criticizes the communication-intention view.

The 'Homeric' struggle Strawson perceives between the communicative approach and formal semantics is perhaps no longer perceived in this way by contemporary philosophers of language. Nevertheless, even today a broad divide remains between those who emphasize the cognitive or psychological aspects of communication and find formal semantics incapable of doing them justice, and those who, on the other hand, believe that the approach of formal semantics is fundamentally on the right track and needs merely to be refined in various ways.

This theme is taken up later, in Parts Ten and Eleven. In Part Ten (Implicature), we pit Grice, with his epoch-making paper 'Logic and Conversation' against a much younger critic, Robyn Carston, who – while herself firmly embedded in the tradition founded by that paper – criticizes several aspects of Grice's model of non-literal communication. In Part Eleven (Compositionality and Context), Ran Lahav's paper exemplifies a group of theorists (including Travis, Sperber and Wilson, Carston and Recanati) who are sceptical about the possibility of providing compositional semantics for natural languages. Lahav argues that the semantic contributions made by adjectives in various contexts cannot be anticipated by a general semantic rule. Zoltán Szabó defends the possibility of compositional semantics for adjectives against the sorts of worries raised by Lahav and the others.

In Part Two (Sense and Reference), we reproduce an extract from Gottlob Frege's article 'On Sense and Reference' in a new translation. This is probably the most influential paper ever written in the philosophy of language. Much of contemporary semantics is still, in one way or another, an attempt to come to grips with the problems Frege raised, such as the problem of non-extensional contexts. Our second text in this Part is good evidence for the continuing importance of Frege's paper. Opposition to Frege is represented here by extracts from Nathan Salmon's book, *Frege's Puzzle*, which was published 94 years after Frege's 'On Sense and Reference', but which is nonetheless a direct response to Frege's paper.

Part Three (Definite Descriptions: Quantifiers or Singular Terms?) reproduces another classic debate that every philosophy of language course should cover: Bertrand Russell's argument (against Frege) that sentences containing definite descriptions (roughly, expressions of the form 'the *F*') express general rather than singular propositions. The main readings here are chapter 16 of Russell's *Introduction to Mathematical Philosophy*, which is perhaps more accessible than his original 1905 presentation in 'On Denoting', and P. F. Strawson's 'On Referring', which criticizes Russell and defends a position more like Frege's. Finally, we reproduce Russell's reply to Strawson, 'Mr. Strawson on Referring'.

Part Four (Rigidity vs Descriptivism) opens with a text by Saul Kripke, another influential critic of Frege. Frege believed that proper names have a descriptive sense, i.e. they are semantically associated with some information about the bearer of the name, and that it is this sense which determines who or what the name refers to. In his *Naming and Necessity*, Kripke attacks this descriptivist view, which he attributes not only to Frege but also to Russell. His alternative, 'causal picture' of the reference of names enjoyed the status of near-orthodoxy for several decades. However, in recent years descriptivist dissent has become more vociferous. It is here represented by Frank Jackson's article 'Reference and Description Revisited'.

Like Kripke's rejection of descriptivism about names, W. V. Quine's rejection of the distinction between analytic and synthetic sentences was widely accepted for many years. In Part Five (Analyticity), we reproduce Quine's classic 'Two Dogmas of Empiricism' and Strawson and Grice's contemporary reply, 'In Defense of a Dogma'.

Parts Six–Nine all concern certain foundational worries about semantic theorising. In Part Six, Donald Davidson spells out his Quinean programme for a purely extensional semantics in 'Truth and Meaning'. According to Davidson, a certain form of theory that merely specifies materially necessary and sufficient conditions for the truth of each sentence of a natural language can contain information sufficient for interpreting all the sentences in it, and in this sense can serve as a theory of meaning for that language. John Foster's reply 'Meaning and Truth Theory' spells out one of the central problems for Davidson's programme – one which Davidson and his followers have had to address, although they have addressed it in various different ways.

Part Seven (Meaning, Intention and Convention) takes us back to Grice's 'Meaning' from Part One. Grice believed that the meaning of sentence types, i.e. what semantic theories are in the business of describing, could ultimately be explained in terms of what speakers of the language 'speaker-mean' ('mean$_{NN}$') when they use the sentences. In his book *Convention* and in his article 'Languages and Language', which is here reproduced, David Lewis elaborates on Grice's idea. His concern is with the key foundational question for natural language semantics: what could it mean to say that a language in the abstract sense, as described by a formal semantic theory, is the language actually used by a population of language users? Lewis's answer is that the population uses the language just if its members conform to a convention of 'truthfulness and trust' in the language, where such a convention is spelled out in terms of the mutual beliefs and preferences (intentions) of the language users. Lewis is here opposed, in one way by John Hawthorne, and in another by Stephen Laurence. Hawthorne argues that there are languages that are not, in an intuitive sense, used by a population, yet which are implausibly accredited that status by Lewis's definition. Laurence's complaint is that the conventions Lewis discusses lack psychological reality. He adduces evidence from psychology to argue that the instrumental reasoning capabilities invoked by Lewis are in fact independent of linguistic abilities, and he proposes an alternative, Chomskian account.

Part Eight (Knowledge of Language) continues the theme of the psychological reality of semantic theorizing by examining whether and in what sense a semantic theory is known by language users. First, Noam Chomsky argues that language acquisition should be viewed as the acquisition of a systematic 'generative grammar', rather than merely as habituation in a practical ability. Gareth Evans, in 'Semantic Theory and Tacit Knowledge' argues further that semantic theories should be viewed as systematic representations of 'tacit knowledge' states enjoyed by language users, and so reflect not only their knowledge of the meanings of sentences, but also the cognitive routes by which this knowledge is generated by the language faculties of language users. Empiricist philosophers like Quine have traditionally questioned the empirical respectability of such proposals: Evans addresses this concern, arguing that data concerning patterns of acquisition and loss of linguistic competence can help to select between structurally distinct semantic theories that deliver equivalent predictions about sentence meanings. In the extract we reproduce from Crispin Wright's paper, 'Theories of Meaning and Speakers' Knowledge', Wright criticizes the attribution of tacit knowledge states to speakers, and offers several objections to Evans's approach.

In Part Nine (Meaning, Holism and Conceptual Role) we examine a debate which, like those considered in Parts One and Six, concerns a fundamental *metaphysical* question – this time that of what kinds of properties *determine* the meanings of expressions. In an influential paper, Jerry Fodor and Ernie Lepore contrast two kinds of views: those which maintain that meanings depend on relations between expressions and the objects, properties etc. they pick out; and those according to which meanings are determined by *roles* which expressions play in thinking, and in particular, by the patterns of *inferences* which speakers are disposed to make between sentences containing them. Fodor and Lepore criticize the latter approach, arguing that it conflicts with the widely accepted thesis that meanings are compositional. Advocates of inferential role theories hold that meanings are *holistic*, i.e. that the meanings of different expressions are determined together in an interdependent way, and this thesis plays an important role in Fodor and Lepore's argument. In the subsequent reading, Peter Pagin examines holism in detail, and argues that the compositionality thesis is compatible with reasonable versions of it, and with inferential role theories.

The topic of Part Twelve (Rule-Following and Normativity) is also metaphysical in character, and begins with a discussion by Crispin Wright of a notorious 'sceptical' argument suggested by Wittgenstein, and developed in different ways in Saul Kripke's 1982 book, *Wittgenstein on Rules and Private Language*, and in roughly contemporary work of Wright's. The striking conclusion of Kripke's version of this argument is that there are 'no facts about meanings'. Here, Wright argues that we can resist this conclusion, but that to do so we must revise various aspects of an intuitively natural conception of the epistemology and metaphysics of language. A prominent role in the Wittgensteinian arguments is played by the assumption that meaning is *normative:* i.e. that understanding a meaning involves grasping a *rule* concerning how an expression ought to be used. In her paper, Åsa Wikforss undertakes to defend the conceptions of meaning threatened by the Wittgensteinian arguments by examining this assumption in detail, and arguing that we should reject it.

Parts Thirteen–Fifteen concern three more specific problem areas. Part Thirteen, on metaphorical communication, begins with Davidson's attack on 'cognitive' theories of metaphor in 'What Metaphors Mean'. Davidson argues that metaphors do not encode a special figurative meaning in addition to their literal meaning, and that what metaphors convey is not a propositional message that could have been literally expressed. Max Black, himself a cognitivist about metaphor, analyses and rejects every step of Davidson's argument, and subjects Davidson's own proposal to criticism.

Part Fourteen (Language and Vagueness) concerns an area of intense recent debate: vagueness and sorites paradoxes. We here provide a glimpse of those aspects of the debate that are most relevant to the philosophy of language. We begin with a comprehensive statement by Achille Varzi of the position known as 'supervaluationism'. Supervaluationism is the view that vague expressions are associated with a range of extensions – 'admissible sharpenings' – and that the truth of a vague sentence consists in its truth relative to all admissible sharpenings, and its falsity in lack of truth in all admissible sharpenings. Although this results in truth-value gaps, the supervaluationist claims as a great advantage that she can retain most of classical logic. In the second paper, Timothy Williamson argues precisely against non-bivalent solutions (i.e. those that allow certain indicative sentences to be neither true nor false) and instead promotes 'epistemicism', the view that in fact vague expressions do have precise extensions, albeit extensions whose precise boundaries we cannot come to know because of certain principles governing knowledge. In the third paper, Delia Graff Fara (formerly Delia Graff) propounds a third type of approach, an 'interest-relative theory of vagueness', according to which the difficulty of recognizing the boundaries of vague predicates is a result of the characteristic way in which they shift from one context to another.

Finally, Part Fifteen considers problems specifically raised by fictional discourse. In part, these problems take us back to the early parts of this book, in that they concern the reference, or lack of reference, of fictional names. But there are also separate problems that arise from the fact that we evaluate fictional sentences differently depending on whether we are engaging in 'internal' fictional discourse or in 'external' discourse about the fiction. Lewis's 'Truth in Fiction' proposes the postulation of implicit operators in 'internal' occurrences of fictional sentences. The account explains how it is that we can sometimes truly utter the sentence 'Sherlock Holmes lives in 221B Baker Street'. Stefano Predelli, in 'Talking about Fiction', agrees with the assessment that these utterances should be regarded as true, but offers an objection to Lewis's account. He proposes an alternative, which manages to avoid postulating implicit operators in selected contexts. Amie Thomasson disagrees with both Lewis and Predelli in that she does not regard internal discourse utterances like the above as genuinely true. She argues that fictional names refer to abstract artefacts, and such entities do not tend to live in terraced London houses.

PART ONE

A Homeric struggle: meaning, communication and truth

INTRODUCTION TO PART ONE

PHILOSOPHY OF LANGUAGE in the analytic tradition (and indeed, 'analytic philosophy' itself) is widely agreed to have begun at the end of the nineteenth century and the beginning of the twentieth, with the work of Gottlob Frege and Bertrand Russell. Parts Two and Three of this collection, respectively, concern two of the most important controversies instigated by these pioneers, but we begin with a more general issue, to set the scene for these finer-grained debates.

What is language? What is it for a linguistic expression to have meaning? One intuitive answer – or beginning of an answer – to these questions is liable to appear almost platitudinous, and was endorsed e.g. by Hobbes and Locke (and perhaps even Aristotle). The basic idea is that the defining characteristic of language is that it enables users to *communicate* with one another. In the first reading below, Paul Grice develops this intuition in detail. Grice's fundamental suggestion is that a speaker's meaning something by a sentence consists in his or her uttering it with the *intention* 'to produce some effect in an audience' – e.g. that of getting the audience to believe something. As it stands, this basic idea is too simple: that intention cannot be a sufficient condition because there are ways of getting people to believe things which do not involve language or do not do so in the right way. So Grice refines his specification of the intention: the speaker must intend his or her audience not only to form the belief, but to do so *on the basis of the speaker's utterance*, in a sense that involves *recognizing* that it was made with the relevant intention.

Grice's label for the semantic property characterized here is 'speaker-meaning' (sometimes known as 'utterer's meaning') and as he explains, it is a species of a genus he labels 'nonnatural' meaning. Speaker-meaning concerns 'what a speaker or writer means by a sign on a particular occasion', and may be contrasted with another species of nonnatural meaning which he labels 'timeless' meaning. An expression's timeless meaning is the literal, objective meaning which, as it were, it carries with it from one occasion of use to another. Towards the end of the paper Grice suggests that the timeless meaning of an expression might be explained in terms of the communicative intentions with which people generally use it, and in later work, he develops an analysis of sentences' timeless meanings (here often termed 'sentence' or 'expression' meanings) in terms of the speaker-meanings which speakers *conventionally* use them to effect. We consider this part of Grice's project in Part Seven below; for now our main interest is in his suggestion that we can analyse a suitable notion of speaker-meaning in terms of that of speakers' *communicative intentions*.

P. F. Strawson's interest, in the second reading, is in the 'Homeric struggle' he identifies between advocates of this Gricean conception of meaning – the 'theorists of communication-intention' – and those he labels 'theorists of formal semantics'. Strawson characterizes the latter group as committed to analysing linguistic meaning in terms that make no essential allusion to the notion which the Griceans consider fundamental: that of *communication*. The formal semanticists' fundamental explanatory notion is, instead, that of a sentence's *truth condition:* the condition under which it would be true.

The formal semanticists' guiding aspiration is to characterize the meanings of linguistic expressions in terms of relations which hold between the expressions and objects, properties, etc. which they 'pick out'. The most intuitive case is that of *reference:* the relation which holds most paradigmatically between a proper name, such as 'Barack Obama', and its *referent*, the object (in this case, a man) it denotes. Intuition has, perhaps, less to say about relations of this kind involving expressions of other types – e.g. *predicates*, such as 'is tired', and declarative sentences, such as 'Barack Obama is tired'. However, formal semanticists find 'items' – often abstract or theoretical in character – to play these roles. A guiding assumption here is that meanings are *compositional* – the meaning of a complex expression (e.g. a sentence) is determined by (or even consists in) the meanings of the sub-sentential expressions it contains and the way in which they are arranged – and one reason why the notion of a truth condition emerges as a leading contender for the role of 'item' in terms of which to explicate the meaning of a sentence is that it is feasible to think of truth conditions as determined by the 'items' assigned to sub-sentential components. E.g., the truth conditions of the sentence 'Barack Obama is tired' are those in which the referent of the name 'Barack Obama' exhibits the property or satisfies the condition we might assign to the predicate, 'is tired'.

Strawson's worry about formal semantics concerns whether the notion of a truth condition – or indeed, that of *truth* – can be satisfactorily 'explained or understood' in terms that do not allude essentially to communication. He suggests that a plausible analysis of truth will incorporate the observation that 'one who makes a statement or assertion makes a true statement if and only if things are as, in making that statement, he takes them to be'. If this is right, then to explicate the notion of a truth condition, a formal semanticist would have to invoke that of an *assertion*. An assertion is a type of *action* (more specifically, a type of what theorists call a *speech act*) and Strawson's concern is that to specify what kind of action it is, we may need to invoke the notion of a *communicative intention*. Prima facie, an assertion just is an action performed with an intention of the kind to which a Gricean analysis of speaker-meaning appeals.

In our third reading, Michael Dummett attacks the Gricean account, by arguing that it is vulnerable to the same objection as a less 'sophisticated' view which he labels the 'code theory of meaning'. According to the code theory, the primary function of language is to facilitate the *communication of speakers' thoughts*, and what makes this possible is that speakers associate linguistic expressions with psychological entities: *constituents* of their thoughts. Thus, e.g., suppose you think that Barack Obama is tired, and undertake to communicate this to me by uttering the sentence, 'Barack Obama is tired'. According to the code theory, what makes this possible is that you associate (encode) the expressions, 'Barack Obama' and 'is tired' with constituents of your thought: your communicative intention will be satisfied if I associate (encode) the words with appropriate thought constituents of my own, so that hearing the sentence brings to (my) mind a thought that Barack Obama is tired.

Dummett's discussion is complicated by an ambiguity in the noun, 'thought', which he notes, but does not always take as much care to disambiguate as he might. 'Thought' can denote a subjective component of someone's *thinking*, as it does in the paragraph above, and in the sentence, 'Sarah's thought was impeded by her hangover'. Alternatively (and this is the sense of the word Dummett attributes to Frege) the word can denote an entity more commonly called a *proposition:* an 'object' of a kind which is *grasped* or *entertained* in the course of typical thinking, and which is objective in the sense that other thinkers can grasp the same one. For an example of this latter meaning, consider the sentence, 'Sarah's first thought on waking was that tequila is dangerous'. Philosophers of language disagree over how precisely propositions should be characterized – the issue will arise at various points in this book – but most agree that we need some such notion. For the remainder of this introduction, we shall try to minimize misunderstanding by using the words 'thinking' and 'proposition' respectively.

Dummett's objection to the code theory is that it rests on an untenable conception of thinking. Code theorists are conspicuously committed to the view that there can be 'unarticulated' or 'naked' thinking: i.e. thinking which is not mediated by language, does not have a linguistic 'vehicle'. If what gives your sentences their meanings is your associating their component expressions with constituents of your thinking, then on pain of circularity, the content of your thinking cannot depend on the possibility of its linguistic articulation. Now, Dummett does not deny that unverbalized thinking occurs – indeed, he offers some plausible examples. His objection, rather, is to the conception of such thinking – and so of thinking in general – to which the code theorist seems committed. Suppose, he suggests, that just as you leave your house it occurs to you that you have forgotten something you meant to take along. You might articulate this with a sentence such as, 'I've forgotten Bob's book'; but it is also possible to do the same thinking without articulating it linguistically.[1] The code theorists' conception of the relation between the sentence and the thinking entails that when you codify the latter with a sentence, the sentence's constituents (words) and structure mirror those of the thinking; and since the thinking is the same even when it is not articulated, it seems it must have these constituents and structure, even in the unarticulated case. Dummett argues that this consequence – in effect, that unarticulated thinking, and so thinking in general, takes place in a sort of 'mental language private to the thinker' – is implausible. Something must serve as the vehicle of a piece of unarticulated thinking, he concedes, but it is a mistake to assume that this vehicle must have a composition and structure like those of a sentence which would express it. Depending on the context in which your remembering Bob's book occurs, the vehicle could be a mental image of Bob or Bob's name coming to mind, or it could be your action of suddenly turning around, going back inside, and fetching the

---

[1] By 'the same thinking' we of course mean thinking of the same *type:* no implausible identity of *tokens* is intended. We omit this qualification below.

book. Thinking is 'embodied in (inner and outer) *reactions,* which, in the whole context, are intelligible only as embodying those thoughts'.[2]

It's a good question whether communication-intention theorists like Grice and Strawson are committed to a conception of thinking which is sufficiently similar to the code theorist's to render them vulnerable to the same objection. Dummett argues that they are, and his reason seems to be that their conception of the communicative *intentions* in terms of which their analysis proceeds is similar to the code theorists' conception of unarticulated thinking. Both are conceptions of a kind of thinking which can occur without linguistic articulation, yet whose vehicle is assumed, implausibly, always to be essentially language-like. A more promising approach, Dummett suggests, is to be found in Frege's contribution to the project of formal semantics. On Frege's account, sentences do not *encode* constituents of thinking: they *express propositions.*

[2] The view that all thinking occurs in a language-like medium is explicitly endorsed in the philosophy of mind by advocates of the 'language of thought hypothesis'. See e.g. Fodor, 1975, 1987; and for a useful recent survey, Aydede 2008.

Questions and tasks

1   In your own words, explain Grice's distinction between 'natural' and 'non-natural' meaning. What are the essential characteristics of the latter?
2   Explain and evaluate Strawson's response to the objection made against Gricean accounts, that 'certain communication-intentions presuppose the existence of language' (p. 25 below).
3   Do you think it is possible to explicate the notion of truth conditions in terms that do not invoke the notion of communication?
4   Compare Strawson's analysis of speaker-meaning with Grice's. Which is best? (Evaluate Dummett's appraisal of the distinctive feature of Strawson's version.)
5   What is Dummett's account of unverbalized thinking? Is it plausible?
6   Do you agree with Dummett that the Gricean approach is 'essentially no more than a sophisticated version of the code conception of language'?

References and further reading

Avramides, A. 1997: 'Intention and Convention', in B. Hale and C. Wright (eds), *A Companion to the Philosophy of Language,* Oxford: Blackwell, pp. 60–86.

Aydede, M. 2008: 'The Language of Thought Hypothesis', in Edward N. Zalta (ed.), *The Stanford Encyclopedia of Philosophy* (Fall 2008 edn), http://plato.stanford.edu/archives/fall2008/entries/language-thought/

Blackburn, S. 1984: *Spreading the Word: Groundings in the Philosophy of Language,* Oxford: Oxford University Press.

Fodor, J. 1975: *The Language of Thought,* Cambridge, MA: Harvard University Press.

Fodor, J. 1987: *Psychosemantics: The Problem of Meaning in the Philosophy of Mind*, Cambridge, MA: MIT Press.

Grice, P. 1989: *Studies in the Ways of Words*, Cambridge, MA: Harvard University Press.

McDowell, J. 1980: 'Meaning, Communication and Knowledge', in Z. van Straaten (ed.), *Philosophical Subjects: Essays Presented to P.F. Strawson*, pp. 117–39, Oxford: Oxford University Press; reprinted in J. McDowell, *Meaning, Knowledge and Reality*, Cambridge, MA: Harvard University Press (1998).

Neale, S. 1992: 'Paul Grice and the Philosophy of Language', *Linguistics and Philosophy* 15, pp. 509–59.

Rumfitt, I. 1995: 'Truth Conditions and Communication', *Mind* 104, pp. 827–62.

Schiffer, S. 1972: *Meaning*, Oxford: Oxford University Press.

Searle, J. 1969: *Speech Acts: An Essay in the Philosophy of Language*, Cambridge: Cambridge University Press.

Chapter 1

H. Paul Grice

MEANING

Consider the following sentences:

"Those spots mean (meant) measles."
"Those spots didn't mean anything to me, but to the doctor they meant measles."
"The recent budget means that we shall have a hard year."

(1) I cannot say, "Those spots meant measles, but he hadn't got measles," and I cannot say, "The recent budget means that we shall have a hard year, but we shan't have." That is to say, in cases like the above, *x meant that p* and *x means that p* entail *p*.

(2) I cannot argue from "Those spots mean (meant) measles" to any conclusion about "what is (was) meant by those spots"; for example, I am not entitled to say, "What was meant by those spots was that he had measles." Equally I cannot draw from the statement about the recent budget the conclusion "What is meant by the recent budget is that we shall have a hard year."

(3) I cannot argue from "Those spots meant measles" to any conclusion to the effect that somebody or other meant by those spots so-and-so. *Mutatis mutandis*, the same is true of the sentence about the recent budget.

(4) For none of the above examples can a restatement be found in which the verb "mean" is followed by a sentence or phrase in inverted commas. Thus "Those spots meant measles"

cannot be reformulated as "Those spots meant 'measles' " or as "Those spots meant 'he has measles.' "

(5) On the other hand, for all these examples an approximate restatement can be found beginning with the phrase "The fact that . . ."; for example, "The fact that he had those spots meant that he had measles" and "The fact that the recent budget was as it was means that we shall have a hard year."

Now contrast the above sentences with the following:

"Those three rings on the bell (of the bus) mean that the 'bus is full.' "
"That remark, 'Smith couldn't get on without his trouble and strife,' meant that Smith found his wife indispensable."

(1) I can use the first of these and go on to say, "But it isn't in fact full—the conductor has made a mistake"; and I can use the second and go on, "But in fact Smith deserted her seven years ago." That is to say, here *x means that p* and *x meant that p* do not entail *p*.

(2) I can argue from the first to some statement about "what is (was) meant" by the rings on the bell and from the second to some statement about "what is (was) meant" by the quoted remark.

(3) I can argue from the first sentence to the conclusion that somebody (viz., the conductor)

meant, or at any rate should have meant, by the rings that the bus is full, and I can argue analogously for the second sentence.

(4) The first sentence can be restated in a form in which the verb "mean" is followed by a phrase in inverted commas, that is, "Those three rings on the bell mean 'the bus is full.' " So also can the second sentence.

(5) Such a sentence as "The fact that the bell has been rung three times means that the bus is full" is not a restatement of the meaning of the first sentence. Both may be true, but they do not have, even approximately, the same meaning.

When the expressions "means," "means something," "means that" are used in the kind of way in which they are used in the first set of sentences, I shall speak of the sense, or senses, in which they are used, as the *natural* sense, or senses, of the expressions in question. When the expressions are used in the kind of way in which they are used in the second set of sentences, I shall speak of the sense, or senses, in which they are used, as the *nonnatural* sense, or senses, of the expressions in question. I shall use the abbreviation "means$_{NN}$" to distinguish the nonnatural sense or senses.

I propose, for convenience, also to include under the head of natural senses of "mean" such senses of "mean" as may be exemplified in sentences of the pattern "A means (meant) *to do* so-and-so (by x)," where A is a human agent. By contrast, as the previous examples show, I include under the head of nonnatural senses of "mean" any senses of "mean" found in sentences of the patterns "A means (meant) something by x" or "A means (meant) by x that. . . ." (This is overrigid; but it will serve as an indication.)

I do not want to maintain that *all* our uses of "mean" fall easily, obviously, and tidily into one of the two groups I have distinguished; but I think that in most cases we should be at least fairly strongly inclined to assimilate a use of "mean" to one group rather than to the other.

The question which now arises is this: "What more can be said about the distinction between the cases where we should say that the word is applied in a natural sense and the cases where we should say that the word is applied in a nonnatural sense?" Asking this question will not of course prohibit us from trying to give an explanation of "meaning$_{NN}$" in terms of one or another natural sense of "mean."

This question about the distinction between natural and nonnatural meaning is, I think, what people are getting at when they display an interest in a distinction between "natural" and "conventional" signs. But I think my formulation is better. For some things which can mean$_{NN}$ something are not signs (e.g., words are not), and some are not conventional in any ordinary sense (e.g., certain gestures); while some things which mean naturally are not signs of what they mean (cf. the recent budget example).

I want first to consider briefly, and reject, what I might term a causal type of answer to the question, "What is meaning$_{NN}$?" We might try to say, for instance, more or less with C. L. Stevenson,[1] that for x to mean$_{NN}$ something, x must have (roughly) a tendency to produce in an audience some attitude (cognitive or otherwise) and a tendency, in the case of a speaker, to *be* produced *by* that attitude, these tendencies being dependent on "an elaborate process of conditioning attending the use of the sign in communication."[2] This clearly will not do.

(1) Let us consider a case where an utterance, if it qualifies at all as meaning$_{NN}$ something, will be of a descriptive or informative kind and the relevant attitude, therefore, will be a cognitive one, for example, a belief. (I use "utterance" as a neutral word to apply to any candidate for meaning$_{NN}$; it has a convenient act-object ambiguity.) It is no doubt the case that many people have a tendency to put on a tail coat when they think they are about to go to a dance, and it is no doubt also the case that many people, on seeing someone put on a tail coat, would conclude that the person in question was about to go to a dance.

Does this satisfy us that putting on a tail coat means$_{NN}$ that one is about to go to a dance (or indeed means$_{NN}$ anything at all)? Obviously not. It is no help to refer to the qualifying phrase "dependent on an elaborate process of conditioning. . . ." For if all this means is that the response to the sight of a tail coat being put on is in some way learned or acquired, it will not exclude the present case from being one of meaning$_{NN}$. But if we have to take seriously the second part of the qualifying phrase ("attending the use of the sign in communication"), then the account of meaning$_{NN}$ is obviously circular. We might just as well say, "X has meaning$_{NN}$ if it is used in communication," which, though true, is not helpful.

(2) If this is not enough, there is a difficulty—really the same difficulty, I think—which Stevenson recognizes: how we are to avoid saying, for example, that "Jones is tall" is part of what is meant by "Jones is an athlete," since to tell someone that Jones is an athlete would tend to make him believe that Jones is tall. Stevenson here resorts to invoking linguistic rules, namely, a permissive rule of language that "athletes may be nontall." This amounts to saying that we are not prohibited by rule from speaking of "nontall athletes." But why are we not prohibited? Not because it is not bad grammar, or is not impolite, and so on, but presumably because it is not meaningless (or, if this is too strong, does not in any way violate the rules of meaning for the expressions concerned). But this seems to involve us in another circle. Moreover, one wants to ask why, if it is legitimate to appeal here to rules to distinguish what is meant from what is suggested, this appeal was not made earlier, in the case of groans, for example, to deal with which Stevenson originally introduced the qualifying phrase about dependence on conditioning.

A further deficiency in a causal theory of the type just expounded seems to be that, even if we accept it as it stands, we are furnished with an analysis only of statements about the *standard* meaning, or the meaning in general, of a "sign." No provision is made for dealing with statements about what a particular speaker or writer means by a sign on a particular occasion (which may well diverge from the standard meaning of the sign); nor is it obvious how the theory could be adapted to make such provision. One might even go further in criticism and maintain that the causal theory ignores the fact that the meaning (in general) of a sign needs to be explained in terms of what users of the sign do (or should) mean by it on particular occasions; and so the latter notion, which is unexplained by the causal theory, is in fact the fundamental one. I am sympathetic to this more radical criticism, though I am aware that the point is controversial.

I do not propose to consider any further theories of the "causal-tendency" type. I suspect no such theory could avoid difficulties analogous to those I have outlined without utterly losing its claim to rank as a theory of this type.

I will now try a different and, I hope, more promising line. If we can elucidate the meaning of

"x meant$_{NN}$ something (on a particular occasion)" and
"x meant$_{NN}$ that so-and-so (on a particular occasion)"

and of

"A meant$_{NN}$ something by x (on a particular occasion)" and
"A meant$_{NN}$ by x that so-and-so (on a particular occasion),"

this might reasonably be expected to help us with

"x means$_{NN}$ (timeless) something (that so-and-so),"
"A means$_{NN}$ (timeless) by x something (that so-and-so),"

and with the explication of "means the same as," "understands," "entails," and so on. Let us for the moment pretend that we have to deal only with utterances which might be informative or descriptive.

A first shot would be to suggest that "x $meant_{NN}$ something" would be true if x was intended by its utterer to induce a belief in some "audience" and that to say what the belief was would be to say what x $meant_{NN}$. This will not do. I might leave B's handkerchief near the scene of a murder in order to induce the detective to believe that B was the murderer; but we should not want to say that the handkerchief (or my leaving it there) $meant_{NN}$ anything or that I had $meant_{NN}$ by leaving it that B was the murderer. Clearly we must at least add that, for x to have $meant_{NN}$ anything, not merely must it have been "uttered" with the intention of inducing a certain belief but also the utterer must have intended an "audience" to recognize the intention behind the utterance.

This, though perhaps better, is not good enough. Consider the following cases:

(1)   Herod presents Salome with the head of St. John the Baptist on a charger.
(2)   Feeling faint, a child lets its mother see how pale it is (hoping that she may draw her own conclusions and help).
(3)   I leave the china my daughter has broken lying around for my wife to see.

Here we seem to have cases which satisfy the conditions so far given for $meaning_{NN}$. For example, Herod intended to make Salome believe that St. John the Baptist was dead and no doubt also intended Salome to recognize that he intended her to believe that St. John the Baptist was dead. Similarly for the other cases. Yet I certainly do not think that we should want to say that we have here cases of $meaning_{NN}$.

What we want to find is the difference between, for example, "deliberately and openly letting someone know" and "telling" and between "getting someone to think" and "telling."

The way out is perhaps as follows. Compare the following two cases:

(1)   I show Mr. X a photograph of Mr. Y displaying undue familiarity to Mrs. X.
(2)   I draw a picture of Mr. Y behaving in this manner and show it to Mr. X.

I find that I want to deny that in (1) the photograph (or my showing it to Mr. X) $meant_{NN}$ anything at all; while I want to assert that in (2) the picture (or my drawing and showing it) $meant_{NN}$ something (that Mr. Y had been unduly unfamiliar), or at least that I had $meant_{NN}$ by it that Mr. Y had been unduly familiar. What is the difference between the two cases? Surely that in case (1) Mr. X's recognition of my intention to make him believe that there is something between Mr. Y and Mrs. X is (more or less) irrelevant to the production of this effect by the photograph. Mr. X would be led by the photograph at least to suspect Mrs. X even if instead of showing it to him I had left it in his room by accident; and I (the photograph shower) would not be unaware of this. But it will make a difference to the effect of my picture on Mr. X whether or not he takes me to be intending to inform him (make him believe something) about Mrs. X, and not to be just doodling or trying to produce a work of art.

But now we seem to be landed in a further difficulty if we accept this account. For consider now, say, frowning. If I frown spontaneously, in the ordinary course of events, someone looking at me may well treat the frown as a natural sign of displeasure. But if I frown deliberately (to convey my displeasure), an onlooker may be expected, provided he recognizes my intention, still to conclude that I am displeased. Ought we not then to say, since it could not be expected to make any difference to the onlooker's reaction whether he regards my frown as spontaneous or as intended to be informative, that my frown (deliberate) does not mean$_{NN}$ anything? I think this difficulty can be met; for though in general a deliberate frown may have the same effect (as regards inducing belief in my displeasure) as a spontaneous frown, it can be expected to have the same effect only *provided* the audience takes it as intended to convey displeasure. That is, if we take away the recognition of intention, leaving the other circumstances (including the recognition of the frown as deliberate), the belief-producing tendency of the frown must be regarded as being impaired or destroyed.

Perhaps we may sum up what is necessary for *A* to mean$_{NN}$ something by *x* as follows. *A* must intend to induce by *x* a belief in an audience, and he must also intend his utterance to be recognized as so intended. But these intentions are not independent; the recognition is intended by *A* to play its part in inducing the belief, and if it does not do so something will have gone wrong with the fulfillment of *A*'s intentions. Moreover, *A*'s intending that the recognition should play this part implies, I think, that he assumes that there is some chance that it will in fact play this part, that he does not regard it as a foregone conclusion that the belief will be induced in the audience whether or not the intention behind the utterance is recognized. Shortly, perhaps, we may say that "*A* meant$_{NN}$ something by *x*" is roughly equivalent to "*A* uttered *x* with the intention of inducing a belief by means of the recognition of this intention." (This seems to involve a reflexive paradox, but it does not really do so.)

Now perhaps it is time to drop the pretense that we have to deal only with "informative" cases. Let us start with some examples of imperatives or quasi-imperatives. I have a very avaricious man in my room, and I want him to go; so I throw a pound note out of the window. Is there here any utterance with a meaning$_{NN}$? No, because in behaving as I did, I did not intend his recognition of my purpose to be in any way effective in getting him to go. This is parallel to the photograph case. If on the other hand I had

pointed to the door or given him a little push, then my behavior might well be held to constitute a meaningful$_{NN}$ utterance, just because the recognition of my intention would be intended by me to be effective in speeding his departure. Another pair of cases would be (1) a policeman who stops a car by standing in its way and (2) a policeman who stops a car by waving.

Or, to turn briefly to another type of case, if as an examiner I fail a man, I may well cause him distress or indignation or humiliation; and if I am vindictive, I may intend this effect and even intend him to recognize my intention. But I should not be inclined to say that my failing him meant$_{NN}$ anything. On the other hand, if I cut someone in the street I do feel inclined to assimilate this to the cases of meaning$_{NN}$, and this inclination seems to me dependent on the fact that I could not reasonably expect him to be distressed (indignant, humiliated) unless he recognized my intention to affect him in this way. (Cf., if my college stopped my salary altogether I should accuse them of ruining me; if they cut it by 2/6d I might accuse them of insulting me; with some intermediate amounts I might not know quite what to say.)

Perhaps then we may make the following generalizations.

(1) "*A* meant$_{NN}$ something by *x*" is (roughly) equivalent to "*A* intended the utterance of *x* to produce some effect in an audience by means of the recognition of this intention"; and we may add that to ask what *A* meant is to ask for a specification of the intended effect (though, of course, it may not always be possible to get a straight answer involving a "that" clause, for example, "a belief that . . .").

(2) "*x* meant something" is (roughly) equivalent to "Somebody meant$_{NN}$ something by *x*." Here again there will be cases where this will not quite work. I feel inclined to say that (as regards traffic lights) the change to red meant$_{NN}$ that the traffic was to stop; but it would be very unnatural to say, "Somebody (e.g., the Corporation) meant$_{NN}$ by the red-light change that the

traffic was to stop." Nevertheless, there seems to be *some* sort of reference to somebody's intentions.

(3) "x means$_{NN}$ (timeless) that so-and-so" might as a first shot be equated with some statement or disjunction of statements about what "people" (vague) intend (with qualifications about "recognition") to effect by x. I shall have a word to say about this.

Will any kind of intended effect do, or may there be cases where an effect is intended (with the required qualifications) and yet we should not want to talk of meaning$_{NN}$? Suppose I discovered some person so constituted that, when I told him that whenever I grunted in a special way I wanted him to blush or to incur some physical malady, thereafter whenever he recognized the grunt (and with it my intention), he did blush or incur the malady. Should we then want to say that the grunt meant$_{NN}$ something? I do not think so. This points to the fact that for x to have meaning$_{NN}$, the intended effect must be something which in some sense is within the control of the audience, or that in some sense of "reason" the recognition of the intention behind x is for the audience a reason and not merely a cause. It might look as if there is a sort of pun here ("reason for believing" and "reason for doing"), but I do not think this is serious. For though no doubt from one point of view questions about reasons for believing are questions about evidence and so quite different from questions about reasons for doing, nevertheless to recognize an utterer's intention in uttering x (descriptive utterance), to have a reason for believing that so-and-so, is at least quite like "having a motive for" accepting so-and-so. Decisions "that" seem to involve decisions "to" (and this is why we can "refuse to believe" and also be "compelled to believe"). (The "cutting" case needs slightly different treatment, for one cannot in any straightforward sense "decide" to be offended; but one can refuse to be offended.) It looks then as if the intended effect must be something within the control of the audience, or

at least the *sort* of thing which is within its control.

One point before passing to an objection or two. I think it follows that from what I have said about the connection between meaning$_{NN}$ and recognition of intention that (insofar as I am right) only what I may call the primary intention of an utterer is relevant to the meaning$_{NN}$ of an utterance. For if I utter x, intending (with the aid of the recognition of this intention) to induce an effect E, and intend this effect E to lead to a further effect F, then insofar as the occurrence of F is thought to be dependent solely on E, I cannot regard F as in the least dependent on recognition of my intention to induce E. That is, if (say) I intend to get a man to do something by giving him some information, it cannot be regarded as relevant to the meaning$_{NN}$ of my utterance to describe what I intend him to do.

Now some question may be raised about my use, fairly free, of such words as "intention" and "recognition." I must disclaim any intention of peopling all our talking life with armies of complicated psychological occurrences. I do not hope to solve any philosophical puzzles about intending, but I do want briefly to argue that no special difficulties are raised by my use of the word "intention" in connection with meaning. First, there will be cases where an utterance is accompanied or preceded by a conscious "plan," or explicit formulation of intention (e.g., I declare how I am going to use x, or ask myself how to "get something across"). The presence of such an explicit "plan" obviously counts fairly heavily in favor of the utterer's intention (meaning) being as "planned"; though it is not, I think, conclusive; for example, a speaker who has declared an intention to use a familiar expression in an unfamiliar way may slip into the familiar use. Similarly in nonlinguistic cases: if we are asking about an agent's intention, a previous expression counts heavily; nevertheless, a man might plan to throw a letter in the dustbin and yet take it to the post; when lifting his hand he might "come to" and say *either* "I didn't intend to do this at all" or "I suppose I must have been intending to put it in."

Explicitly formulated linguistic (or quasi-linguistic) intentions are no doubt comparatively rare. In their absence we would seem to rely on very much the same kinds of criteria as we do in the case of nonlinguistic intentions where there is a general usage. An utterer is held to intend to convey what is normally conveyed (or normally intended to be conveyed), and we require a good reason for accepting that a particular use diverges from the general usage (e.g., he never knew or had forgotten the general usage). Similarly in nonlinguistic cases: we are presumed to intend the normal consequences of our actions.

Again, in cases where there is doubt, say, about which of two or more things an utterer intends to convey, we tend to refer to the context (linguistic or otherwise) of the utterance and ask which of the alternatives would be relevant to other things he is saying or doing, or which intention in a particular situation would fit in with some purpose he obviously has (e.g., a man who calls for a "pump" at a fire would not want

a bicycle pump). Nonlinguistic parallels are obvious: context is a criterion in settling the question of why a man who has just put a cigarette in his mouth has put his hand in his pocket; relevance to an obvious end is a criterion in settling why a man is running away from a bull.

In certain linguistic cases we ask the utterer afterward about his intention, and in a few of these cases (the very difficult ones, like a philosopher asked to explain the meaning of an unclear passage in one of his works), the answer is not based on what he remembers but is more like a decision, a decision about how what he said is to be taken. I cannot find a nonlinguistic parallel here; but the case is so special as not to seem to contribute a vital difference.

All this is very obvious; but surely to show that the criteria for judging linguistic intentions are very like the criteria for judging nonlinguistic intentions is to show that linguistic intentions are very like nonlinguistic intentions.

Notes

1 *Ethics and Language* (New Haven, 1944), ch. iii.
2 *Ibid.*, p. 57.

Chapter 2

P. F. Strawson

MEANING AND TRUTH

[. . .]

What is it for anything to have a *meaning* at all, in the way, or in the sense, in which words or sentences or signals have meaning? What is it for a particular sentence to have the meaning or meanings it does have? What is it for a particular phrase, or a particular word, to have the meaning or meanings it does have? These are obviously connected questions. Any account we give of meaning in general (in the relevant sense) must square with the account we give of what it is for particular expressions to have particular meanings; and we must acknowledge, as two complementary truths, first, that the meaning of a sentence in general depends, in some systematic way, on the meanings of the words that make it up and, second, that for a word to have a particular meaning is a matter of its making a particular systematic contribution to the meanings of the sentences in which it occurs.

I am not going to undertake to try to answer these so obviously connected questions. That is not a task for one lecture; or for one man. I want rather to discuss a certain conflict, or apparent conflict, more or less dimly discernible in current approaches to these questions. For the sake of a label, we might call it the conflict between the theorists of communication-intention and the theorists of formal semantics. According to the former, it is impossible to give an adequate account of the concept of meaning without reference to the possession by speakers of audience-directed intentions of a certain complex kind. The particular meanings of words and sentences are, no doubt, largely a matter of rule and convention; but the general nature of such rules and conventions can be ultimately understood only by reference to the concept of communication-intention. The opposed view, at least in its negative aspect, is that this doctrine simply gets things the wrong way round or the wrong way up, or mistakes the contingent for the essential. Of course we may expect a certain regularity of relationship between what people intend to communicate by uttering certain sentences and what those sentences conventionally mean. But the system of semantic and syntactical rules, in the mastery of which knowledge of a language consists – the rules which determine the meanings of sentences – is not a system of rules for communicating at all. The rules can be exploited for this purpose; but this is incidental to their essential character. It would be perfectly possible for someone to understand a language completely – to have a perfect linguistic competence – without having even the implicit thought of the function of communication; provided, of course, that the language in question did not contain words explicitly referring to this function.

A struggle on what seems to be such a central issue in philosophy should have something of a Homeric quality; and a Homeric struggle calls for gods and heroes. I can at least, though tentatively, name some living captains and benevolent shades: on the one side, say, Grice, Austin, and the later Wittgenstein; on the other, Chomsky, Frege, and the earlier Wittgenstein.

First, then, as to the theorists of communication-intention. The simplest, and most readily intelligible, though not the only way of joining their ranks is to present your general theory of meaning in two stages: first, present and elucidate a primitive concept of *communication* (or communication-intention) in terms which do not presuppose the concept of *linguistic meaning*; then show that the latter concept can be, and is to be, explained in terms of the former.[1] For any theorist who follows this path, the fundamental concept in the theory of meaning is that of a speaker's, or, generally, an utterer's, *meaning something by* an audience-directed utterance on a particular occasion. An utterance is something produced or executed by an utterer; it need not be vocal; it could be a gesture or a drawing or the moving or disposing of objects in a certain way. What an utterer means by his utterance is incidentally specified in specifying the complex intention with which he produces the utterance. The analysis of the kind of intention in question is too complex to be given in detail here, so I shall confine myself to incomplete description. An utterer might have, as one of his intentions in executing his utterance, that of bringing his audience to think that he, the utterer, believes some proposition, say the proposition that *p*; and he might intend this intention to be wholly overt, to be clearly recognized by the audience. Or again he might have the intention of bringing his audience to think that he, the utterer, wants his audience to perform some action, say *a*; and he might intend this intention of his to be wholly overt, to be clearly recognized by the audience. Then, provided certain other conditions on utterer's intention are fulfilled, the utterer may be said, in the relevant sense, to mean something by his utterance: specifically, to mean that *p*, in the declarative mode,

in the first case and to mean, in the imperative mode, that the audience is to perform action *a* in the second case. Grice, for one, has given us reason to think that, with sufficient care, and far greater refinement than I have indicated, it is possible to expound such a concept of communication-intention or, as he calls it, utterer's meaning, which is proof against objection and which does not presuppose the notion of linguistic meaning.

Now a word about how the analysis of linguistic meaning in terms of utterer's meaning is supposed to proceed. Here again I shall not go into details. The details would be very complex. But the fundamental idea is comparatively simple. We are accustomed, and reasonably, to think of linguistic meaning in terms of rules and conventions, semantic and syntactic. And when we consider the enormous elaboration of these rules and conventions – their capacity, as the modern linguists stress, to generate an infinite number of sentences in a given language – we may feel infinitely removed from the sort of primitive communication situation which we naturally think of when trying to understand the notion of utterer's meaning in terms which clearly do not presuppose linguistic meaning. But rules or conventions govern human practices and purposive human activities. So we should ask what purposive activities are governed by *these* conventions. What are *these* rules rules for doing? And the very simple thought I spoke of which underlies the suggested type of analysis is that these rules are, precisely, rules for communicating, rules by the observance of which the utterer may achieve his purpose, fulfil his communication-intention; and that this is their *essential* character. That is, it is not just a fortunate fact that these rules allow of use for this purpose; rather, the very nature of the rules concerned can be understood only if they are seen as rules whereby this purpose can be achieved.

This simple thought may seem too simple; and in several ways. For it is clear that we can, and do, communicate very complicated things by the use of language; and if we are to think of language as, fundamentally, a system of rules for facilitating the achievement of our communication-intentions, and if the analysis is not to be circular, must we not credit ourselves with extremely complicated communication-intentions (or at least desires) independently of having at our disposal the linguistic means of fulfilling those desires? And is not this absurd? I think this is absurd. But the programme of analysis does not require it. All that the analysis requires is that we can explain the notion of conventions of communication in terms of the notion of pre-conventional communication at a rather basic level. Given that we can do this, then there is more than one way in which we can start pulling ourselves up by our own linguistic boot-straps. And it looks as if we can explain the notion of conventions of communication in terms of the notion of pre-conventional communication at a rather basic level.

We can, for example, tell ourselves a story of the analytic-genetic variety. Suppose an utterer achieves a pre-conventional communication success with a given audience by means of an utterance, say x. He has a complex intention, vis-à-vis the audience, of the sort which counts as a communication-intention and succeeds in fulfilling that intention by uttering x. Let us suppose that the primary intention was such that the utterer *meant* that p by uttering x; and, since, by hypothesis, he achieved a communication-success, he was so *understood* by his audience. Now if the same communication-problem presents itself later to the same utterer in relation to the same audience, the fact, known to both of them, that the utterer meant that p by uttering x before, gives the utterer a reason for uttering x again and the audience a reason for interpreting the utterance in the same way as before. (The reason which each has is the knowledge that the other has the knowledge which he has.) So it is easy to see how the utterance of x could become established as between this utterer and this audience as a means of meaning that p. Because it has

worked, it becomes established; and then it works *because* it is established. And it is easy to see how this story could be told so as to involve not just a group of two, but a wider group. So we can have a movement from an utterer pre-conventionally meaning that p by an utterance of x to the utterance-type x conventionally meaning that p within a group and thence back to utterer-members of the group meaning that p by a token of the type, but now *in accordance with the conventions*.

Now of course this explanation of conventional meaning in terms of utterer's meaning is not enough by itself. For it only covers the case, or only obviously covers the case, of utterance-types without structure – i.e. of utterance-types of which the meaning is not systematically derived from the meanings of their parts. But it is characteristic of linguistic utterance-types to have structure. The meaning of a sentence is a syntactic function of the meanings of its parts and their arrangement. But there is no reason in principle why a pre-conventional utterance should not have a certain complexity – a kind of complexity which allowed an utterer, having achieved one communication-success, to achieve another by repeating one part of the utterance while varying the other part, what he means on the second occasion having something in common with, and something which differentiates it from, what he meant on the first occasion. And if he does thus achieve a second success, the way is open for a rudimentary *system* of utterance-types to become established, i.e. to become conventional within a group.

A system of conventions can be modified to meet needs which we can scarcely imagine existing before the system existed. And its modification and enrichment may in turn create the possibility of thoughts such as we cannot understand what it would be for one to have, without supposing such modification and enrichment to have taken place. In this way we can picture a kind of alternating development. Primitive communication-intentions and successes give rise to the emergence of a limited conventional meaning-system, which makes possible its own enrichment and development which in turn makes possible the enlargement of thought and of communication-needs to a point at which there is once more pressure on the existing resources of language which is in turn responsive to such pressure. . . . And of course there is an element of mystery in this; but so there is in human intellectual and social creativity anyway.

All the foregoing is by way of the roughest possible sketch of some salient features of a communication-intention theory of meaning and of a hint as to how it might meet the obvious objection that certain communication-intentions presuppose the existence of language. It has all been said before, and with far greater refinement. But it will serve, I hope, as a sufficient basis for the confrontation of views that I wish to arrange.

Now, then, for the at least apparently opposed view, which I have so far characterized only in its negative aspect. Of course the holders of this view share some ground with their opponents. Both agree that the meanings of the sentences of a language are largely determined by the semantic and syntactic rules or conventions of that language. Both agree that the members of any group or community of people who share knowledge of a language – who have a common linguistic competence – have at their disposal a more or less powerful instrument or means of communicating, and thereby of modifying each other's beliefs or attitudes or influencing each other's actions. Both agree that these means are regularly used in a quite conventional way, that what people intend to communicate by what they say is regularly related to the conventional meanings of the sentences they utter. Where they differ is as to the relations between the meaning-determining rules of the language, on the one hand, and the function of communication, on the other: one party insists, and the other (apparently) refuses to allow, that the general nature of those rules can be understood only by reference to this function.

The refusal naturally prompts a question, viz. What is the general character of those rules which must in some sense have been mastered by anyone who speaks and understands a given language? The rejected answer grounds their general character in the social function of communicating, for example, beliefs or wishes or instructions. If this answer is rejected, another must be offered. So we ask again: What is the general character of these meaning-determining rules?

It seems to me that there is only one type of answer that has ever been seriously advanced or developed, or needs to be seriously considered, as providing a possible alternative to the thesis of the communication-theorist. This is an answer which rests on the motion of truth-conditions. The thought that the sense of a sentence is determined by its truth-conditions is to be found in Frege and in the early Wittgenstein, and we find it again in many subsequent writers. I take, as an example, a recent article by Professor Davidson. Davidson is rightly concerned with the point that an adequate account of the meaning-rules for a language L will show how the meanings of sentences depend on the meanings of words in L; and a theory of meaning for L will do this, he says, if it contains a recursive definition of truth-in-L. The 'obvious connection', he says, between such a definition of truth and the concept of meaning is this: 'the definition works by giving the necessary and sufficient conditions for the truth of every sentence, and *to give truth-conditions is a way of giving the meaning of a sentence*. To know the semantic concept of truth for a language is to know what it is for a sentence – any sentence – to be true, and *this amounts, in one good sense we can give to the phrase, to understanding the language*'.[2]

Davidson, in the article I quote from, has a limited concern. But the concern finds its place inside a more general idea; and the general idea, plainly enough, is that the syntactic and semantic rules together determine the meanings of all the sentences of a language and do this by means, precisely, of determining their truth-conditions.

Now if we are to get at the root of the matter, to isolate the crucial issue, it seems to me important to set aside, at least initially, one class of objections to the adequacy of such a conception of meaning. I say one class of objections; but it is a class which admits of subdivisions. Thus it may be pointed out that there are some kinds of sentences – e.g. imperatives, optatives, and interrogatives – to which the notion of truth-conditions seems inappropriate, in that the conventional utterance of such sentences does not result in the saying of anything true or false. Or again it may be pointed out that even sentences to which the notion of truth-conditions does seem appropriate may contain expressions which certainly make a difference to their conventional meaning, but not the sort of difference which can be explained in terms of their truth-conditions. Compare the sentence 'Fortunately, Socrates is dead' with the sentence 'Unfortunately, Socrates is dead'. Compare a sentence of the form 'p and q' with the corresponding sentence of the form 'p but q'. It is clear that the meanings of the members of each pair of sentences differ; it is far from clear that their truth-conditions differ. And there are not just one or two expressions which give rise to this problem, but many such expressions.

Obviously both a comprehensive general theory of meaning and a comprehensive semantic theory for a particular language must be equipped to deal with these points. Yet they may reasonably be regarded as peripheral points. For it is a truth implicitly acknowledged by communication-theorists themselves[3] that in almost all the things we should count as sentences there is a substantial central core of meaning which is explicable either in terms of truth-conditions or in terms of some related notion quite simply derivable from that of a truth-condition, for example the notion, as we might call it, of a compliance-condition in the case of an imperative sentence or a fulfilment-condition in the case of an optative. If we suppose, therefore, that an account can be given of the notion of a truth-condition itself, an account which is indeed independent of reference to communication-intention, then we may reasonably think that the greater part of the task of a general theory of meaning has been accomplished without such reference. And by the same token, on the same supposition, we may think that the greater part of the particular theory of meaning of a particular language L can also be given, free of any such, even implicit, reference; for it can be given by systematically setting out the syntactic and semantical rules which determine truth-conditions for sentences of L.

Of course, as already admitted, something will have to be added to complete our general theory and to complete our particular theories. Thus for a particular theory an account will have to be added of the transformations that yield sentences with compliance-conditions or fulfilment-conditions out of sentences with truth-conditions; and the general theory will have to say what sort of thing, semantically speaking, such a derived sentence in general is. But this, though yielding a large harvest in sentences, is in itself a relatively small addition to either particular or general theory. Again, other additions will be necessary in connection with the other objections I mentioned. But, heartened by his hypothesized success into confidence, the theorist may reckon on dealing with some of these additions without essential reference to communication-intention; and, heartened by his hypothesized success into generosity, he may be happy to concede rights in some small outlying portion of the *de facto* territory of theoretical semantics to the theorist of communication-intention, instead of confining the latter entirely to some less appetizing territory called theoretical pragmatics.

I hope it is now clear what the central issue is. It consists in nothing other than the simple-seeming question whether the notion of truth-conditions can itself be explained or understood without reference to the function of communication. One minor clarification is called for before I turn to examine the question directly. I have freely used the phrase 'the truth-conditions of sentences' and I have spoken of these truth-conditions as determined by the semantical and syntactical rules of the language to which the sentences belong. In such a context we naturally understand the word 'sentence' in the sense of a 'type-sentence'. (By a sentence in the sense of a type I mean the sense in which there is just one English sentence, say, 'I am feeling shivery', or just one English sentence, say, 'She had her sixteenth birthday yesterday', which one and the same sentence may be uttered on countless different occasions by different people and with different references or applications.) But for many type-sentences, such as those just mentioned, the question whether they, the *sentences*, are true or false is one that has no natural application: it is not the invariant type-sentences themselves that are naturally said to be true or false, but rather the systematically varying things that people say, the propositions they express, when they utter those sentences on different particular occasions. But if the notion of truth-*values* is in general inappropriate to type-sentences, how can the notion of truth-*conditions* be appropriate? For presumably the truth-conditions of something are the conditions under which it is true.

The difficulty, however, is quite easily resolved. All that needs to be said is that the statement of truth-conditions for many type-sentences – perhaps most that are actually uttered in ordinary conversation – has to be, and can be, relativized in a systematic way to contextual conditions of utterance. A general statement of truth-conditions for such a sentence will then be, not a statement of conditions under which that sentence is a truth, but a general statement of a type of conditions under which different particular utterances of it will issue in different particular truths. And there are other more or less equivalent, though rather less natural, ways of resolving the difficulty.

So now, at last, to the central issue. For the theorists of formal semantics, as I have called

them, the whole weight, or most of the weight, both of a general theory of meaning and of particular semantic theories, falls on the notion of truth-conditions and hence on the notion of truth. We agree to let it rest there. But we still cannot be satisfied that we have an adequate general understanding of the notion of meaning unless we are satisfied that we have an adequate general understanding of the notion of truth.

There is one manoeuvre here that would completely block all hope of achieving adequate understanding; and, if I am not mistaken, it is a manoeuvre which has a certain appeal for some theorists of formal semantics. This is to react to a demand for a general explication of the notion of truth by referring us back to a Tarski-like conception of truth-in-a-given-language, L, a conception which is elucidated precisely by a recursive statement of the rules which determine the truth-conditions for sentences of L. This amounts to a refusal to face the general philosophical question altogether. Having agreed to the general point that the meanings of the sentences of a language are determined, or largely determined, by rules which determine truth-conditions, we then raise the general question what sort of thing truth-conditions are, or what truth-conditions are conditions *of*; and we are told that the concept of truth for a given language is defined by the rules which determine the truth-conditions for sentences of that language.

Evidently we cannot be satisfied with this. So we return to our general question about truth. And immediately we feel some embarrassment. For we have come to think there is very little to say about truth *in general*. But let us see what we can do with this very little. Here is one way of saying something uncontroversial and fairly general about truth. One who makes a statement or assertion makes a true statement if and only if things are as, in making that statement, he states them to be. Or again: one who expresses a supposition expresses a true supposition if and only if things are as, in expressing that supposition, he expressly supposes them to be. Now let us inter-weave with such innocuous remarks as these the agreed thoughts about meaning and truth-conditions. Then we have, first: the meaning of a sentence is determined by those rules which determine how things are stated to be by one who, in uttering the sentence, makes a state-ment; or, how things are expressly supposed to be by one who, in uttering the sentence, expresses a supposition. And then, remembering that the rules are relativized to contextual condi-tions, we can paraphrase as follows: the meaning of a sentence is determined by the rules which determine *what* statement is made by one who, in uttering the sentence in given conditions, makes a statement; or, which determine *what* suppos-ition is expressed by one who, in uttering the sentence in given conditions, expresses a suppos-ition; and so on.

Thus we are led, by way of the notion of truth, back to the notion of the *content* of such speech acts as stating, expressly supposing, and so on. And there the theorist of communication-intention sees his chance. There is no hope, he says, of elucidating the notion of the content of such speech acts without paying some attention to the notions of those speech acts themselves. Now of all the speech acts in which something true or false may, in one mode or another, be put forward, it is reasonable to regard that of statement or assertion as having an especially central position. (Hot for certainties, we value speculation primarily because we value informa-tion.) And we cannot, the theorist maintains, elucidate the notion of stating or asserting except in terms of audience-directed intention. For the fundamental case of stating or asserting, in terms of which all variants must be understood, is that of uttering a sentence with a certain intention – an intention wholly overt in the sense required by the analysis of utterer's meaning – which can be incompletely described as that of letting an audience know, or getting it to think, that the speaker has a certain belief; as a result of which there may, or may not, be activated or produced

in the audience that same belief. The rules determining the conventional meaning of the sentence join with the contextual conditions of its utterance to determine what the belief in question is in such a primary and fundamental case. And in determining what the belief in ques-tion is in such a case, the rules determine what statement is made in such a case. To determine the former is to determine the latter. But this is precisely what we wanted. For when we set out from the agreed point that the rules which determine truth-conditions thereby determine meaning, the conclusion to which we were led was precisely that those rules determined what statement was made by one who, in uttering the sentence, made a statement. So the agreed point, so far from being an alternative to a communica-tion theory of meaning, leads us straight in to such a theory of meaning.

The conclusion may seem a little too swift. So let us see if there is any way of avoiding it. The general condition of avoiding it is clear. It is that we should be able to give an account of the notion of truth-conditions which involves no essential reference to communicative speech acts. The alternative of refusing to give any account at all – of just resting on the notion of truth-conditions – is, as I have already indicated, simply not open to us if we are concerned with the philosophical elucidation of the notion of meaning: it would simply leave us with the con-cepts of meaning and truth each pointing blankly and unhelpfully at the other. Neither would it be helpful, though it might at this point be tempting, to retreat from the notion of truth-conditions to the less specific notion of correlation in general; to say, simply, that the rules which determine the meanings of sen-tences do so by correlating the sentences, envis-aged as uttered in certain contextual conditions, with certain possible states of affairs. One reason why this will not do is that the notion of correl-ation in general is simply too unspecific. There are many kinds of behaviour (including verbal behaviour) – and many more kinds could be imagined – which are correlated by rule with possible states of affairs without its being the case that such correlation confers upon them the kind of relation to those possible states of affairs that we are concerned with.

Another reason why it will not do is the following. Consider the sentence 'I am tired'. The rules which determine its meaning are indeed such as to correlate the sentence, envisaged as uttered by a particular speaker at a particular time, with the possible state of affairs of the speaker's being tired at that time. But this feature is not peculiar to that sentence or to the members of the class of sentences which have the same meaning as it. For consider the sentence 'I am not tired'. The rules which determine its meaning are also such as to correlate the sentence, envisaged as uttered by a certain speaker at a certain time, with the possible state of affairs of that speaker's being tired at that time. Of course the kinds of correlation are different. They are respectively such that one who uttered the first sentence would normally be understood as affirming, and one who uttered the second sentence would normally be understood as denying, that the state of affairs in question obtained; or again they are such that one who utters the first sentence when the state of affairs in question obtains has made a true statement and one who utters the second sentence in these circumstances has made a false statement. But to invoke these differences would be precisely to give up the idea of employing only the unspecific notion of correlation in general. It is not worth labouring the point further. But it will readily be seen not only that sentences different, and even opposed, in meaning are correlated, in one way or another, with the same possible state of affairs, but also that one and the same unambiguous sentence is correlated, in one way or another, with very many different and in some cases mutually incompatible states of affairs. The sentence 'I am tired' is correlated with the possible state of affairs of the speaker's being at the point of total exhaustion and also with the state of affairs of his being as fresh as a daisy. The sentence 'I am over 40' is correlated with any possible state of affairs whatever regarding the speaker's age; the sentence 'Swans are white' with any state of affairs whatever regarding the colour of swans.

The quite unspecific notion of correlation, then, is useless for the purpose in hand. It is necessary to find some way of specifying a particular correlation in each case, viz. the correlation of the sentence with the possible state of affairs the obtaining of which would be necessary and sufficient for something *true* to have been said in the uttering of the sentence under whatever contextual conditions are envisaged. So we are back once more with the notion of truth-conditions and with the question, whether we can give an account of this notion which involves no essential reference to communicative speech acts, i.e. to communication-intention.

I can at this point see only one resource open, or apparently open, to the theorist of meaning who still holds that the notion of communication-intention has no essential place in the analysis of the concept of meaning. If he is not to swallow his opponent's hook, he must take some leaves out of his book. He sees now that he cannot stop with the idea of truth. That idea leads straight to the idea of *what is said*, the content of what is said, when utterances are made; and that in turn to the question of what is being *done* when utterances are made. But may not the theorist go some way along this path without going as far along it as his opponent? Might it not be possible to *delete* the reference to communication-intention while *preserving* a reference to, say, belief-expression? And will not this, incidentally, be more realistic in so far as we often voice our thoughts to ourselves, with no communicative intention?

The manoeuvre proposed merits a fuller description. It goes as follows. First, follow the communication-theorist in responding to the challenge for an elucidation of the notion of truth-conditions by invoking the notion of, e.g. and centrally, statement or assertion (accepting the uncontroversial point that one makes a true statement or assertion when things are as, in making that assertion, one asserts them to be). Second, follow the communication-theorist again in responding to the challenge for an elucidation of the notion of asserting by making a connection with the notion of belief (conceding that to make an assertion is, in the primary case, to give expression to a belief; to make a true assertion is to give expression to a correct belief; and a belief is correct when things are as one who holds that belief, in so far as he holds that belief, believes them to be). But third, part company with the communication-theorist over the nature of this connection between assertion and belief; deny, that is, that the analysis of the notion of asserting involves essential reference to an intention, for example, to get an audience to think that the maker of the assertion holds the belief; deny that the analysis of the notion of asserting involves *any* kind of reference to audience-directed intention; maintain, on the contrary, that it is perfectly satisfactory to accept as fundamental here the notion of simply voicing or expressing a belief. Then conclude that the meaning-determining rules for a sentence of the language are the rules which determine *what* belief is conventionally articulated by one who, in given contextual conditions, utters the sentence. As before, determining what this belief is, is the same thing as determining what assertion is made. So all the merits of the opponent's theory are preserved while the reference to communication is extruded.

Of course, more must be said by this theorist, as by his opponent. For sentences which can be used to express beliefs need not always be so used. But the point is one to be made on both sides. So we may neglect it for the present.

Now will this do? I do not think it will. But in order to see that it will not, we may have to struggle hard against a certain illusion. For the notion of expressing a belief may seem to us

perfectly straightforward; and hence the notion of expressing a belief in accordance with certain conventions may seem equally straightforward. Yet, in so far as the notion of expressing a belief is the notion we need, it may borrow all its force and apparent straightforwardness from precisely the communication-situation which it was supposed to free the analysis of meaning from depending on. We may be tempted to argue as follows. Often we express beliefs with an audience-directed intention; we intend that our audience should take us to have the belief we express and perhaps that that belief should be activated or produced in the audience as well. But then what could be plainer than this: that what we can do with an audience-directed intention we can also do without any such intention? That is to say, the audience-directed intention, when it is present, is something added on to the activity of expressing a belief and in no way essential to it – or to the concept of it.

Now what a mixture of truth and falsity, of platitude and illusion, we have here! Suppose we reconsider for a moment that analysis of utterer's meaning which was roughly sketched at the beginning. The utterer produces something – his utterance x – with a complex audience-directed intention, involving, say, getting the audience to think that he has a certain belief. We cannot detach or extract from the analysis an element which corresponds to his expressing a belief with no such intention – though we could indeed produce the following description and imagine a case for it: he acts *as if* he had such an intention though as a matter of fact he has not. But here the description depends on the description of the case in which he has such an intention.

What I am suggesting is that we may be tempted, here as elsewhere, by a kind of bogus arithmetic of concepts. Given the concept of Audience Directed Belief Expression (ADBE), we can indeed think of Belief Expression (BE) without Audience Direction (AD), and find cases of this. But it does not follow that the concept of

ADBE is a kind of logical compound of the two simpler concepts of AD and BE and hence that BE is conceptually independent of ADBE.

Of course these remarks do not show that there is no such thing as an independent concept of belief-expression which will meet the needs of the anti-communication-theorist. They are only remarks directed against a too simple argument to the effect that there is such a concept.

This much is clear. If there is such an essentially independent concept of belief-expression which is to meet the needs of the analysis of the notion of meaning, we cannot just stop with the phrase 'expressing a belief'. We must be able to give some *account* of this concept, to tell ourselves some intelligible story about it. We can sometimes reasonably talk of a man's actions or his behaviour as expressing a belief when, for example, we see those actions as directed towards an end or goal which it is plausible to ascribe to him in so far as it is also plausible to ascribe to him that belief. But this reflection by itself does not get us very far. For one thing, on the present programme, we are debarred from making reference to the end or goal of communication an essential part of our story. For another, the sort of behaviour we are to be concerned with must be, or be capable of being, formalized or conventionalized in such a way that it can be regarded as subjected to, or performed in observance of, rules; and of rules, moreover, which regulate the behaviour precisely in its aspect as expression of belief. It will not do to say simply: we might suppose a man to find *some* satisfaction (unspecified) or *some* point (unspecified) in performing certain formalized (perhaps vocal) actions on some occasions, these actions being systematically related to his having certain beliefs. For suppose a man had a practice of vocalizing in a certain way whenever he saw the sun rise and in another, partly similar, partly different, way whenever he saw it set. Then this practice would be regularly related to certain beliefs, i.e. that the sun was rising or that it was

setting. But this description gives us no reason at all for saying that when the man indulged in this practice he was *expressing the belief* that the sun was rising or setting, in accordance with a rule for doing so. We really have not enough of a description to know *what* to say. As far as we could tell, we might say, he just seems to have this ritual of *saluting* the rising or the setting sun in this way. What need of his it satisfies we don't know.

Let us suppose, however – for the sake of the argument – that we can elaborate some relevant conception of expressing a belief which presupposes nothing which, on the present programme, we are debarred from presupposing; and that we draw on this concept of expressing a belief in order to give an account, or analysis, on the lines indicated, of the notion of linguistic meaning. Then an interesting consequence ensues. That is, it will appear as a quite contingent truth about language that the rules or conventions which determine the meanings of the sentences of a language are public or social rules or conventions. This will be, as it were, a natural fact, a fact of nature, in no way essential to the concept of a language, and calling for a natural explanation which must not be allowed to touch or modify that concept. There must be nothing in the *concept* to rule out the idea that every individual might have his own language which only he understands. But then one might ask: Why should each individual observe his own rules? or any rules? Why shouldn't he express any belief he likes in any way he happens to fancy when he happens to have the urge to express it? There is one answer at least which the theorist is debarred from giving to this question, if only in the interests of his own programme. He cannot say: Well, a man might wish to *record* his beliefs so that he could refer to the records later, and then he would find it convenient to have rules to interpret his own records. The theorist is debarred from giving this answer because it introduces, though in an attenuated form, the concept of communication-intention: the earlier man communicates with his later self.

There might be one way of stilling the doubts which arise so rapidly along this path. That would be to offer possible natural explanations of the supposed natural fact that language is public, that linguistic rules are more or less socially common rules; explanations which successfully avoided any suggestion that the connection of public rules with communication was anything but incidental and contingent. How might such an explanation go? We might say that it was an agreed point that the possession of a language enlarges the mind, that there are beliefs one could not express without a language to express them in, thoughts one could not entertain without a rule-governed system of expressions for articulating them. And it is a fact about human beings that they simply would not acquire mastery of such a system unless they were exposed, as children, to conditioning or training by adult members of a community. Without concerning ourselves about the remote origins of language, then, we may suppose the adult members of a community to wish their successors to have this mind-enlarging instrument at their disposal – and evidently the whole procedure of training will be simplified if they all teach the same, the common language. We may reasonably suppose that the learners, to begin with, do not quite appreciate what they will ultimately be doing with language; that it is for them, to begin with, a matter of learning to do the right thing rather than learning to say the true thing, i.e. a matter of responding vocally to situations in a way which will earn them reward or avoid punishment rather than a matter of *expressing their beliefs*. But later they come to realize that they have mastered a system which enables them to perform this (still unexplained) activity whenever they wish to; and *then* they are speaking a language.

Of course it must be admitted that in the process they are liable also to acquire the *secondary* skill of communicating their beliefs. But this is simply something added on, an extra and conceptually uncovenanted benefit, quite incidental to the description of what it is to have mastered the meaning-rules of the language. If, indeed, you pointedly direct utterances, of which the essential function is belief-expression, to another member of the community, he will be apt to take it that you hold whatever beliefs are in question and indeed that you intend him to take this to be so; and this fact may give rise, indeed, it must be admitted, does give rise, to a whole cluster of social consequences; and opens up all sorts of possibilities of kinds of linguistic communication other than that which is based on belief-expression. This is why, as already acknowledged, we may have ultimately to allow some essential reference to communication-intention into outlying portions of our semantic theory. But this risk is incurred only when we go beyond the central core of meaning, determined by the rules which determine truth-conditions. As far as the central core is concerned, the function of communication remains secondary, derivative, conceptually inessential.

I hope it is clear that any such story is going to be too perverse and arbitrary to satisfy the requirements of an acceptable theory. If this is the way the game has to be played, then the communication-theorist must be allowed to have won it.

But must the game, finally, be played in this way? I think, finally, it must. It is indeed a generally harmless and salutary thing to say that to know the meaning of a sentence is to know under what conditions one who utters it says something true. But if we wish for a philosophical elucidation of the concept of meaning, then the dictum represents, not the end, but the beginning, of our task. It simply narrows, and relocates, our problem, forcing us to inquire what is contained in the little phrase '. . . says something true'. Of course there are many ways in which one can say something which is in fact true, give expression, if you like, to a true proposition, without thereby expressing belief in it, without asserting that proposition: for example when the words in question form certain sorts of subordinate or co-ordinate clauses, and when one is quoting or play-acting and so on. But when we come to try to explain in general what it is to say something true, to express a true proposition, reference to belief or to assertion (and thereby to belief) is inescapable. Thus we may harmlessly venture: Someone says something true if things are as he says they are. But this 'says' already has the force of 'asserts'. Or, to eschew the 'says' which equals 'asserts', we may harmlessly venture: Someone propounds, in some mode or other, a true proposition if things are as anyone who believed what he propounds would thereby believe them to be. And here the reference to belief is explicit.

Reference, direct or indirect, to belief-expression is inseparable from the analysis of saying something true (or false). And, as I have tried to show, it is unrealistic to the point of unintelligibility – or, at least, of extreme perversity – to try to free the notion of the linguistic expression of belief from all essential connection with the concept of communication-intention.

Earlier I hinted that the habit of some philosophers of speaking as if 'true' were a predicate of type-sentences was only a minor aberration, which could readily enough be accommodated to the facts. And so it can. But it is not a simple matter of pedantry to insist on correcting the aberration. For if we are not careful, it is liable to lead us totally wrong. It is liable, when we inquire into the nature of meaning, to make us forget what sentences are for. We connect meaning with truth and truth, too simply, with sentences; and sentences belong to language. But, as theorists, we know nothing of human *language* unless we understand human *speech*.

Notes

1 Not the *only* way; for to say that a concept ϕ cannot be adequately elucidated without reference to a concept ψ is not the same thing as to say that it is possible to give a classical analysis of ϕ in terms of ψ. But the *simplest* way; for the classical method of analysis is that in terms of which, in our tradition, we most naturally think.

2 'Truth and Meaning' (*Synthese*, 1967, p. 310) [this volume, Chapter 13]. My italics.

3 This acknowledgement is probably implicit, though not very clearly so, in Austin's concept of *locutionary meaning* (see *How to Do Things with Words*, Oxford, 1962); it is certainly implicit in Grice's distinction between what speakers *actually say*, in a favoured sense of 'say', and what they imply (see 'Utterer's Meaning, Sentence-Meaning and Word-Meaning', in *Foundations of Language*, 1968); and again in Searle's distinction between the *proposition* put forward and the illocutionary mode in which it is put forward (see *Speech Acts*, Cambridge, 1969).

Chapter 3

Michael Dummett

LANGUAGE AND COMMUNICATION

Language, it is natural to say, has two principal functions: that of an instrument of communication, and that of a vehicle of thought. We are therefore impelled to ask which of the two is primary. Is it because language is an instrument of communication that it can also serve as a vehicle of thought? Or is it, conversely, because it is a vehicle of thought, and can therefore express thoughts, that it can be used by one person to communicate his thoughts to others?

A view that might claim to represent common sense is that the primary function of language is to be used as an instrument of communication, and that, when so used, it operates as a code for thought. On this view, it is only because we happen to lack a faculty for directly transmitting thoughts from mind to mind that we are compelled to encode them in sounds or marks on paper. If we had the faculty, therefore, we should have no need of language. But the corollary conflicts with common sense: namely that language is not a vehicle of thought at all. Common sense exclaims against this that surely we often think in words: but the advocate of the code theory of language, if he has his wits about him, will reply that we never do any such thing, indeed, that the very notion is unintelligible. Rather, words, spoken aloud or rehearsed in the imagination, often *accompany* our thoughts, but in no way embody them. For, if we should not need language but for the need to communicate our thoughts, we must be capable of having *naked*

thoughts (to vary the metaphor once again) – thoughts devoid of linguistic or other representational clothing: thoughts may represent the world, but, to have thoughts, we need nothing that represents *them*. Thus thoughts do not *need* a representation, although, for purposes of communication, they may be verbally represented; and from this it follows that a thought cannot exist – cannot be present to the mind – merely through some verbal or other symbolic representation, which is what it would be for the representation to be the vehicle or embodiment of the thought. The whole substance of the code theory of language is that the speaker encodes his thought as a sentence and the hearer decodes the sentence as that thought: but, if language could be the vehicle of thought, the hearer would not need to decode the utterance nor the speaker to have encoded the thought in the first place. Either no thoughts have vehicles or all thoughts must have them.

What we call 'thinking in words' is, then, according to the code theory of language, one of two things. It may be thinking *about* how to express our thoughts in words, as with someone rehearsing a speech or lecture or writing a book or article. On this view, we should resist the illusion that the thought is not fully formed until it is articulated in words: it need no more be so than it is for the translator who is considering how to express in a sentence of one language the thought expressed in one of another language.

More usually, the code theorist maintains, the relation of the words to the thought is that of the sound to the written letters. Someone who is fluent in reading a given script, say Roman script, cannot see a written or printed word, for instance a name at a railway station, without mentally attaching a pronunciation to it. If it belongs to a language of whose pronunciation he is uncertain, he may have no confidence that he is mentally pronouncing it correctly; but he is as unable to read it dissociated from any phonetic value as he is unable to see it as one illiterate in that script would do (or as he himself would see a word in a script of which he was ignorant). Likewise, according to the code theorist, we are so overwhelmingly accustomed to speech in our mother-tongue, or sometimes in other languages, that, except in moments of emergency, we are unable to entertain thoughts in the forefront of our minds without putting them into words: and so we fall victims to the illusion that the words embody the thought, whereas they merely adorn it. But, he urges, try repeatedly going over, aloud or silently, some familiar words – a well-known quotation or an often-used formula – not abstractedly, but with attention. However hard you try to fasten your attention on the words, you will keep having, in the background or, as it were, skimming between the words, wisps of thought, which you could without difficulty express: and ask yourself whether these background thoughts are also in words. Surely you will agree that they are naked thoughts, he says: the whole conception of thinking 'in' words is spurious. An amusing example occurred in a novel I recently read, in which a character remarked that she was interested to note, while she was thinking through some question, that she did so entirely verbally, thus confirming her long-held opinion that all our thinking is in words: her interlocutor failed to ask her whether her thought, 'I am thinking in words', was itself in words.

The question was one which exercised Wittgenstein, as illustrated by the following quotation from the *Philosophical Investigations*, in which I thought it best to replace the word 'pen' by 'pencil'.

> Speak the line, 'Yes, the pencil is blunt: oh, well, it will do', first thinking it; then without thought; and then just think the thought without the words. (1, 330.)

Wittgenstein goes on to describe a case in which someone would naturally be described as having had just that thought without words; but remarks that 'what constitutes thought here is not some process which has to accompany the words if they are not to be spoken without thought'. His idea is surely that, if it were, it would not be difficult to obey the instruction, 'Just think the thought without the words', whereas it needs a quite special kind of background to make sense of saying of someone that he had such a thought, but not in words. We could say – although Wittgenstein himself does not expressly say this – that thought needs a vehicle of some kind, although this may not consist of words, but of something quite different like actions.

The difficulty of obeying the instruction to think the thought without the words is, however, due, in part, to the ambiguity of the term 'thinking'. When Wittgenstein speaks of someone's uttering the sentence, 'The pencil is blunt', thinking it, he does not mean his doing what would ordinarily be described as thinking that the pencil is blunt: there may be no pencil around, or, if there is, it may be quite evidently sharp. Wittgenstein means, rather, that he utters the sentence aware of what the words mean. In Frege's terminology, he grasps the thought expressed by the sentence, without necessarily judging it to be true; or, rather, since no definite thought will be expressed in the absence of any salient pencil, he attends to the meanings of the words, considered independently of any occasion of utterance. Now suppose someone were to say to me, 'Think that the pencil is blunt', or, 'Think the thought that the pencil is blunt', without raising the question whether I am to think in words or without them: even if it is obvious which pencil is being referred to, what am I to do? If 'think' is to be taken in its most usual sense, as in contexts like, 'I suddenly thought that this would be my last chance of getting a meal that night', then it means 'judge' rather than merely 'grasp', and I might answer, 'I cannot have thoughts to order: the pencil just isn't blunt at all'. If, on the other hand, 'think' is being used to mean 'entertain the thought', with no implication that it is to be taken as true, then again I am in difficulties, this time because I cannot help but have obeyed the command as soon as it was given: for just understanding the command involved grasping the thought that the pencil was blunt.

It is plain that having a thought is something of a quite different kind from uttering a sentence: it is not merely in a different medium, as it were, but of a different character. A policeman shows me a photograph, and asks, 'Have you ever seen this man?': I study the photograph, perhaps trying and failing to evoke a feeling of familiarity, perhaps running through in my mind the facial appearance of a range of slight acquaintances, decide I have never seen the man, and answer, 'No'. In the context of the question, the word 'No' expresses the thought, 'I have never seen this man'. I may have had that thought just before answering, or my answer may have been the first embodiment of my thought. In neither case, however, would it be natural to say that I thought, 'No': only that I thought, 'I have never seen him'. For all that, the thought came to me with no greater articulation than the one-word answer. This is because the content of a thought is much *more* determined by context than that of an utterance. If, for example, I am walking out of my house, the coming to mind of a single personal name, or of an image of the person's face, may constitute my having the thought, 'I've left the book I promised So-and-so behind'. Thoughts, when not framed in

sentences, are not framed in some mental language private to the thinker: they are, rather, embodied in (inner or outer) *reactions* which, in the whole context, are intelligible only as embodying those thoughts. We give verbal reports of such thoughts, at the time or later: asked by my companion, 'Why are you turning back?' I will say, 'I've left So-and-so's book behind'; recounting my day hours afterwards, I may say, 'Just as I was leaving the house, I thought, "I've left So-and-so's book behind" '. Such a report may be called an *interpretation*: it is not read off from an inner tape recorder, but is, as it were, *ascribed* to oneself on the basis of the remembered stimuli and reactions to them. This ponderous terminology, of interpretation and ascription, is not intended to suggest that there is anything dubious about a report of this kind. On the contrary, although my inner reactions, or the inner stimuli that prompted them, may have been hidden from view, anyone who knew what they were, and knew enough about my background, would put the same interpretation on them.

This fact is sufficient to show that, when someone reports his unverbalised or unarticulated thoughts, he is not recalling some inner utterance in a language of the mind: on a few occasions, he may contradict an interpretation suggested by another in favour of a different one, but he cannot intelligibly lay claim to a thought that fails to make sense of his actions and reactions. It is for this reason that the code conception of language is untenable. For language to be a code for thought, thoughts have to be like sentences, and have constituents analogous to words, and the thought-constituents must be matched to the words by some process of association. A word will then evoke the associated thought-constituent in the mind of the hearer, and, for one who wishes to communicate his thought, its constituents will evoke the corresponding words. But this fantasy will not serve as an account of our understanding of language, because there is no such thing as a thought-constituent's coming to mind, independently of any word or symbol that expresses it. To suppose that such a mental event can occur is to have an altogether primitive picture of the character of thinking.

The point is obscured when the term 'thought' is used in Frege's way: for Fregean thoughts indeed have constituents, and, for a sentence to *express* such a thought, there must be a certain match between its composition and that of the thought. For instance, no one could have the thought that Venus has an elliptical orbit without possessing the concept of an ellipse; and, in accordance with Gareth Evans's 'Generality Constraint' (1982, pp. 100–5) this requires that he be able to think of other things as elliptical. Moreover, to grasp a thought involves an apprehension of its complexity: one could not think that the orbit of Venus is an ellipse without being aware that one could judge other shapes to be or not to be ellipses. What does not, in general, have an analogous structure is the thinking of the thought – the inner or outer process that, against the necessary background, constitutes having that thought. This is why Frege rightly held that thoughts, in his sense, and their component concepts or senses, are not contents of the mind, as a mental image is: a mental content, as here understood, must be something whose presence does not depend upon there being any particular background.

Were the code theory of language tenable, it would be easy to explain how the words and sentences of a language have the meanings that they do; but it would still be necessary to give a philosophical explanation of what a thought is. For a thought does not resemble a mental image or a sensation: it has the distinctive feature of being, or at least of being capable of being, true or false, and thus relating to reality external to the mind. The same may, of course, be said of a mental image, in so far as it is apprehended as an image of a particular thing, and even of a sensation, in so far as it is taken as engendered by some non-mental object or event. A mental image or sensation, considered as such, does not,

however, *have* to be so apprehended: it can exist simply as a constituent of inner experience, unintegrated with an awareness of external reality. For this reason, it is highly plausible that what renders an image the image of a certain object is nothing intrinsic to it as an image, but a concomitant *thought* to the effect that it represents that object, and similarly for sensations: hence, if this is right, thought remains unique in its representative character. This representative character requires philosophical explanation. Mental images and sensations are sufficiently explained when a description has been given of what it is like to have them: but a description of what it is like to have a thought, were it possible to give such a thing, would be quite inadequate as a philosophical account of thoughts, since it could not encompass what makes them capable of possessing a truth-value.

The failure of the code theory of language leaves us without an explanation of what it is for an expression of a language to have a meaning. But, if that cannot be explained in terms of a coding of thoughts into sentences by means of an association between words and thought-constituents, it must be explained in such a way as to make manifest how sentences serve to express thoughts, without taking as given a prior understanding of what a thought is. Just such an explanation was in effect essayed by Frege. He insisted that the important thing was the thought, not the sentence; he claimed that the existence of the thought did not depend upon its being grasped or expressed by any rational being; and he also claimed that there might exist beings who could grasp the very same thoughts as we do without needing to conceive them as clothed in language. But his semantic theory made no appeal to an antecedent conception of thoughts: the theory itself sought to explain what it is for a sentence to express a thought without invoking any conception, given in advance, of the thought that it expresses.

That is why Frege is rightly regarded as the grandfather of analytical philosophy, whose distinctive methodology, until quite recently, was to approach the philosophy of thought via the philosophy of language. From such a standpoint, the most important feature of language is that it serves as a vehicle of thought. It is not necessary, in order to adopt this standpoint, to deny that unverbalised thought is in principle possible, nor even to deny, as Frege did, that it is in practice possible for human beings. It is not necessary, either, to deny that thought is possible for creatures who have no language in which to express it. It is necessary only to believe that thought, by its nature, cannot occur without a vehicle, and that language is the vehicle whose operation is the most perspicuous and hence the most amenable to a systematic philosophical account. This is so for two reasons. First, the ascription to a subject of his having a given thought at a particular time can be justified only by the presence of an often extensive background to the occurrence of whatever served as the vehicle of the thought. In the ideal case when the vehicle is a fully explicit verbal expression of the thought, however, the only background to which appeal is needed is the existence of the language and the subject's knowledge of it – an immensely complex but structured phenomenon, relatively isolable from other circumstances. And, secondly, a fully explicit verbal expression is the only vehicle whose structure must reflect the structure of the thought.

From this standpoint, to analyse linguistic meaning along Gricean lines is to pursue an altogether misconceived strategy. When the utterance is an assertoric one, Strawson's version of such an analysis is given in terms of the hearer's recognition of the speaker's intention to communicate that he has a certain belief. McDowell's emendation, that what the speaker wishes to communicate is a piece of information, which may be about anything, rather than only about his own doxastic condition, is undoubtedly an improvement, for language is certainly used primarily as contributing to our transactions with the world, rather than

as conveying to one another how it is with us in our thinking parts (McDowell, 1980, pp. 117–39). It is essential to our most basic acquisition of the practice of using a language that we learn to act on what others tell us; only as a more sophisticated by-product do we learn to use their utterances as revealing their beliefs, and, even then, their intention is still typically to inform us that what they say is so rather than to allow us a glimpse of their private convictions. Were it otherwise, it would be, as it were, an afterthought that we could, by making an unintended use of them, gain information from the assertions of others; and we should accept those assertions as true only on occasions on which we had particular reason to trust the speaker's veracity, rather than, as now, whenever we have no particular reason to doubt it.

McDowell's formulation and Strawson's both suffer, however, from an awkwardness in generalising them to utterances of all kinds, rather than merely assertoric ones: more importantly, both go astray by in effect helping themselves to the specific content of the utterance instead of explaining what confers that content upon it. Their formulations, in their ungeneralised forms, are candidates for being characterisations of *assertions*, as opposed to questions, requests, and so on: they purport to explain what it is to make an assertion with a certain content, given that we already grasp the notion of something's having that content. That is to say, they aim to characterise asserting that something is the case, on the assumption that we already know what it is to have the information that it is the case (McDowell), or to ascribe to someone a belief that it is the case (Strawson). However, being informed that such-and-such is so and believing that such-and-such is so both obviously involve having the *thought* that such-and-such is so: and thus this strategy of explanation takes as already given the conception of the thought expressed by a sentence and, at most, explains what it is to assert that that thought is true.

The Gricean line of explanation is hence

essentially no more than a sophisticated version of the code conception of language. To understand an assertoric utterance, I must understand two things: that it *is* assertoric, that is, serves to voice an assertion; and what, specifically, it is used to assert. Any explanation of linguistic meaning must, among other things, explain what features of such an utterance enable a hearer to recognise these two aspects of its significance. An explanation of what constitutes a grasp of the concept of being informed that something is so, or of that of believing that something is so, is certainly called for; but let us suppose that such an explanation is to hand. Assume, now, that I, as hearer, do grasp these concepts, and, further, that I am able to recognise the utterance in question as assertoric. What matters, much more than *how* I recognise this — what feature of the utterance indicates to me that this is its character — is what it is for me to take it, rightly or wrongly, as assertoric. Given that I have the general concept of information or of belief, this is at least arguably explicable in the manner of Grice, as amended by McDowell or otherwise. On any account of language, there remains to be explained which features of the utterance convey to me what, specifically, is being asserted: the content of the assertion or, in Frege's terminology, the thought asserted to be true. This formulation, however, makes it appear that we already have a clear conception of what it is for me to grasp the thought, and are concerned only to explain how I identify it as that which the sentence expresses; but, when the philosophy of language is treated as supplying the only route to a philosophical account of thinking, the formulation is misleading. Rather, we need to explain what it is for me to grasp what thought is being asserted in such a manner as thereby to explain what it is for me to grasp that thought at all. By contrast, the Grice/Strawson/McDowell theory assumes that, by some conventional means, I am able to recognise which thought it is that the utterance serves to assert as true; but, in assuming this, it takes my ability to grasp this thought

as given antecedently to my recognising it to be that which is asserted. It thus treats the sentence as *encoding* the thought, rather than as *expressing* it.

The fundamental point made by Frege (1923, p. 36) and slightly earlier by Wittgenstein (1921, 4.027, 4.03) that language enables us to grasp *new* thoughts, is often sneered at by those too impatient to stop to reflect upon it. In Chomsky's writings it reappears, heavily emphasised, both in the form that we are able to understand new *sentences*, and more importantly, in the form stated by Frege (see in particular Chomsky 1988, pp. 170 and 184). If it was merely that we could understand a new way of conveying a familiar thought, a language could be simply a code for thoughts. According to the appropriate version of the code conception of language, we can grasp a large range of thoughts, independently of their formulation in language, and can apprehend relations between them by means of which they may be located in logical space: sentences then serve to pick them out by their co-ordinates in this space, enabling us to identify the thoughts so conveyed; and a certain redundancy in the co-ordinate system allows distinct sentences to convey the same thought. This picture of language depends upon taking our grasp of the thoughts that can be conveyed by language as antecedent to our understanding of the language: it is therefore exposed as false by the fact that such an understanding suffices to enable us to grasp quite new thoughts when they are expressed in that language. There is a fundamental difference between expressing a thought and using some conventional means to identify it. Given an invalid argument, the phrase 'the weakest additional assumption needed to render the argument valid' picks out a unique thought; but it does not *express* that thought, since it is possible to understand the phrase without knowing which thought it picks out. A sentence expressing the thought, on the other hand, cannot be understood without knowing what thought it expresses. It is an essential feature of anything properly called a 'language' that its phrases and sentences genuinely *express* their meanings. That is the difference between a language and a code; and that is why the mastery of a language enables a speaker to grasp new thoughts expressed in it.

The Grice/Strawson/McDowell theory may, then, conceivably be on the right track to an explanation of a restricted facet of linguistic meaning, namely the assertoric force attached to certain utterances, as contrasted with the interrogative, optative, imperatival, or other type of force attached to others. Here it is unimportant that the overt indicators of the force attached are, in most languages, unreliable and insufficient in number: what matter are the distinctions that a hearer needs to draw if he is to have understood what has been said. Someone who mistakes a request for a question is not in error merely about the *point* of the utterance, that is, about why the speaker said what he did: he is mistaken about what it was that was said. But a theory of the Gricean type is powerless to explain any other aspect of meaning. For that, an approach along Fregean lines is required: one, namely, that, by explaining what, in general, the specific content of a sentence is, and by displaying the contributions made by particular words to determining the content of sentences that contain them, shows what it is for a sentence to express a thought, and, thereby, what thoughts are.

So far, then, the contest between the view that the primary function of language is that of an instrument of communication and the view that it is that of a vehicle of thought appears to be going decisively in favour of the latter. This was the contest staged by Strawson in his celebrated inaugural lecture 'Meaning and Truth', in which he dubbed proponents of the former view 'communication-intention theorists' and proponents of the latter 'theorists of formal semantics' (repr. 1971, pp. 170–89) [this volume, Chapter 1]. If the foregoing argument has been right, communication-intention theories, that is, Gricean theories, at best contribute to that part of a theory of meaning which, in Fregean terms, constitutes the theory of force.

[. . .]

References

Chomsky, Noam 1988: *Language and Problems of Knowledge*, (Cambridge, Mass.: MIT Press).

Evans, Gareth 1982: *The Varieties of Reference*, (Oxford: Oxford University Press).

Frege, Gotlob 1923: 'Gedankengefuge', in G. Frege, *Collected Papers on Mathematics, Logic and Philosophy*, B. McGuinness (ed.), (Oxford: Blackwell, 1984).

McDowell, John 1980: 'Meaning, communication and knowledge', in Z. van Straaten (ed.), *Philosophical Subjects*, (Oxford: Oxford University Press).

Strawson, Peter F. 1971: *Logico-Linguistic Papers*, (London: Methuen).

Wittgenstein, Ludwig 1921: *Traaatus Logico-Philosophicus*, trans. D. Pears and B.F. McGuinness, (London and New York: Routledge & Kegan Paul).

Wittgenstein, Ludwig 1953: *Philosophical Investigations*. Trans. E. Anscombe (Oxford: Blackwell).

PART TWO

Sense and reference

INTRODUCTION TO PART TWO

GOTTLOB FREGE, who is widely considered to have been one of the founders of analytic philosophy of language, and indeed, of analytic philosophy, favoured the kind of approach to meaning characterized in Part One by Strawson as 'formal semantics'. He argued that the meanings of expressions are *objective* in the sense that different people can 'grasp' the same ones – in a way that they cannot share psychological items, 'ideas' – and he undertook to characterize expressions' meanings in terms of relations in which they stand to the extra-linguistic, extra-mental items they 'pick out'.

If we begin with singular terms – i.e. expressions such as 'Bob Dylan' and 'the Moon' which denote individual objects – then the most obvious candidates for the role of objective meanings are the objects the terms denote. The relation between a singular term and the object it denotes is known as *reference*, and (to avoid ambiguity) many contemporary philosophers use the word 'referents' for the objects denoted. Everyone agrees that singular terms typically *have* referents, but not everyone agrees that these objects are the *meanings* of the terms. The view that names have no meanings in addition to their referents was articulated and defended in the nineteenth century by J.S. Mill, and is sometimes labelled the Millian theory. It is also widely known as the *direct reference* theory.

In earlier work, Frege had endorsed something like the Millian view, but early in the reading below he explains why he has come to reject it. An object can be the referent of several singular terms, e.g. 'Bob Dylan' and 'Robert Zimmerman' refer to the same man, 'the morning star' and 'the evening star' refer to the same planet (Venus), etc. Now consider a pair of sentences such as the following:

(1) Bob Dylan is Robert Zimmerman
(2) Bob Dylan is Bob Dylan.

If the Millian accepts that meanings are compositional – i.e. that the meaning of a complex expression (e.g. a sentence) is determined by (or composed of) the meanings of its constituent expressions and mode of composition – then she ought to regard these sentences as having the same meaning, and so as apt to express the same information. But, as Frege points out, such pairs do not seem to express the same information. (1) is *informative* in a way that (2) is not: anyone who understands the sentence can *know* what is expressed by (2) *a priori*, whereas knowledge of what is expressed by (1) can only be known *a posteriori*. (1) and (2) appear to differ in what Frege calls 'cognitive value'. And if that is so, then by compositionality again, what the name 'Bob Dylan' contributes to the information expressed by a sentence cannot be the same as what is contributed by 'Robert Zimmerman'.

Hence, what a name contributes to the information content of a sentence is not just its referent.[1]

One might expect these considerations to drive Frege back towards the ideational conception of meaning, since it is plausible that the co-referential terms featured in informative identity sentences such as (1) are associated with different ideas. But Frege's conviction that what the sentences express is *objective* leads him in a different direction, and he endeavours instead to explain the (apparent) cognitive difference in terms of a new semantic notion: that of the '*sense*' of an expression. Frege tells us that the sense of a singular term is a '*mode of presentation*' of its referent. His examples of 'the morning star' and 'the evening star' help to illustrate what he may have in mind. The first of these terms is associated with one way (one 'mode') in which the planet Venus may be 'presented' to one – (i.e. in the morning, perhaps in a certain region of the sky, etc.) while the second is associated with another way. Grasping the sense of the term 'the morning star', Frege seems to be suggesting, involves the first of these ways in which Venus may be presented, while grasping the sense of 'the evening star' involves the second. And Frege insists that associating a term with a sense is not a matter of associating it with an *idea*. While ideas are essentially subjective and private, senses are available for different speakers to share. Like referents, they are objective.

The main topic of this Part of this book is Frege's argument for his contention that singular terms have senses distinct from their referents, but before setting the scene for Nathan Salmon's critique of that argument, we should briefly introduce Frege's views on the meanings of expressions of other kinds, and in particular, those of declarative sentences. He suggests that a sentence of this sort 'contains a thought', and in a footnote, immediately explains that by this he does not understand 'the subjective act of thinking but [rather] its objective content, which is capable of being the common property of many'. Suppose that you believe that cycling is dangerous, and I believe that it is not. It is natural to describe this as a case in which you believe the very 'thing' which I disbelieve; and it is 'things' of this sort – more usually called 'propositions' – which Frege intends his term, 'thoughts', to denote. His investigation into the relation between a sentence and the thought it expresses is usefully constrained by the thesis of compositionality, which he assumes to be true of senses as well as referents. Thus, he assumes, if a sentence has a sense or a reference, then this must be the kind of thing that can be determined by (or composed of) the senses or referents of its constituent expressions and the way in which they are composed. Now, if sentences have referents, then since the components of pairs of sentences like (1) and (2) are co-referential, so the sentences must also be co-referential; but the thoughts they express are, apparently, distinct. Thus the thought expressed by a sentence is not its referent: it is its sense.

---

[1] Note that for Frege, the phrase 'proper name' covers definite descriptions (e.g. 'the furthest celestial body away from the Earth') as well as ordinary names (such as 'Bob Dylan'). Also, he uses the word 'reference' where (as noted above) contemporary philosophers would often use 'referent'.

Frege's next question is whether, like singular terms, declarative sentences have referents as well as senses. In fact, Frege allows that *some* singular terms – e.g. names in fiction such as 'Ulysses' – lack referents, and this concession informs his treatment of the issue whether sentences typically have referents. Frege reasons that if a name like 'Ulysses' lacks a referent, then by compositionality (about referents) sentences containing it also lack referents. However, he says, 'someone who seriously considers the sentence true or false' will *presuppose* that all of the singular terms it contains have referents. And what's more, '[t]he fact that we take trouble over the [referent] of a sentence part at all is a sign that we recognize and require a [referent] also for the sentence itself'. Moreover, Frege argues, since our 'serious' interest in a sentence just is an interest in whether it is true or false, the natural candidate for the referent of a sentence which has one, is its *truth value:* 'the fact that it is true or that it is false'.

Another merit of the idea that the referent of a declarative sentence is its truth value is that it helps us explain the semantic contribution which such a sentence makes to a more complex sentence in which it is embedded – at least in canonical cases. Consider e.g. a sentence formed by conjoining two simpler sentences with a *sentence connective* such as 'and':

(3)   The Moon is full and Bob Dylan is singing.

If we assume that sentences have referents, and that these are determined by (or composed of) the referents of their components, than we must allow that we can replace any of (3)'s component expressions – including those which are themselves sentences – with co-referring expressions, without changing the referent of the whole complex sentence. Not all prima facie candidates for the role of sentence-referents satisfy this constraint, but truth values do so. E.g. if the referent of (3) is the value, *true*, then the referent of each of the simpler sentences it contains must also be *true*, and we can replace either of those with another true sentence without changing the referent/truth value of the complex.[2]

Notice, however, that the assignment of truth values to sentences does not seem to explain the contribution made by sentences to *all* complex sentences in which they occur. Frege touches on this problem about one-third of the way through the extract below, but in this section of the paper he does not elaborate in detail. Paradigmatic exceptional cases are sentences utilizing 'direct speech' to specify the words used by a third-party speaker, and sentences utilizing 'indirect speech' to specify information expressed or believed by a third-party. E.g.:

(4)   Sarah says, 'Bob Dylan is singing'
(5)   Sarah says that Bob Dylan is singing
(6)   Sarah believes that Bob Dylan is singing.

Let's assume that each of these sentences is true. In that case, considerations similar to those rehearsed above imply that all of the sentences that result from replacing

---

[2] This is a basic version of an argument which is nowadays known as 'the slingshot'. See the Introduction to Part Six for a little more discussion.

expressions embedded in the sentences with co-referring expressions are also true. But this seems wrong: e.g. if we replace the name 'Bob Dylan' in any of (1)–(3) with the co-referring, 'Robert Zimmerman', the result is a sentence that looks as though it could very easily be false. Even more worryingly, it seems easy to make any of the sentences into a false one by replacing the *sentence* embedded in it (in each case, the sentence 'Bob Dylan is singing') with another with the same truth value, but which Sarah does not say/believe.

Frege begins with the case of 'direct speech', observing plausibly that here, 'what one wants to talk about' are the words themselves rather than what the words signify or express. Thus in a case like (4), the referent of the embedded sentence is not its 'ordinary' or 'customary' referent – i.e. its truth value – but rather the sentence itself. In sentences like (5), Frege suggests, the embedded sentence also has an atypical, 'indirect' referent, in this case, the *thought/proposition* which that sentence expresses, the *sense* of the sentence. In a section of the paper not reprinted below, he develops a similar treatment of sentences like (6), proposing that here too, the referent of the embedded sentence is its customary sense. Whether this proposal suffices to deal adequately with all of the issues engendered by these problematic, 'intensional' constructions is controversial, but there is surely no doubting its *prima facie* appeal. Intuitively, (5) and (6) are not really *about* Bob Dylan: they're about Sarah and what she says and believes.

Hopefully, we have now said enough to give a taste of some of the more important components of Frege's influential theory. Chapter 5 below comprises excerpts from a book in which Nathan Salmon develops a very detailed critique of a central one of these elements: the argument for the contention that singular terms have senses distinct from their referents. In the passages reprinted here, Salmon identifies the most important considerations underwriting Frege's argument, and indicates in outline how he thinks an advocate of the Millian or direct reference view should respond to it.[3]

Salmon begins his discussion by clarifying the semantic notion in which he is interested, what he calls the 'information content' of a sentence. Like Frege's notion of the *sense* or *thought* expressed by a sentence, this is intended to account for differences in cognitive value. Following David Kaplan, Salmon labels the broadly Millian view which he aims to defend against Frege's attack, the 'naïve theory'. We have omitted much of Salmon's nuanced discussion of the naïve theory, and of the 'modified naïve theory' which he regards as the most plausible version of it. For our purposes here, it suffices to characterize it as committed to the claim that the contribution which a singular term makes to the information content of a declarative sentence (in effect, the proposition expressed by the sentence) is simply its referent.

According to Salmon, the premise of Frege's argument which advocates of the naïve theory should reject is the one according to which sentences like (1) and (2) differ in respect of information content. The key to making this rejection palatable is a distinction between the information content of a sentence and what Salmon calls the '*information imparted*' by a particular utterance of the sentence. Suppose, to borrow

---

[3] For a fuller defence of this response to Frege, we recommend the rest of Salmon's book.

a famous example from Grice, that a professor is asked to provide a letter of recommendation for a student contemplating an academic career, and writes, 'Jones has beautiful handwriting and is always very punctual'. The information content of this sentence is a proposition about Jones's handwriting and timekeeping, but given the context at issue, the sentence serves to *impart* distinct information about Jones's suitability for academic work. Another, less obvious, kind of information which sentences can impart on occasion is 'meta-linguistic' information: information about the *expressions* they contain. E.g., Salmon suggests, the sentence '5 = V' can be used to impart the meta-linguistic information that the Roman numeral 'V' denotes the number 5. In a similar spirit, advocates of the naïve theory should argue that (1) and (2) have the same information content: the difference between them is that (1) can, while (2) cannot, be used to impart the meta-linguistic information that 'Bob Dylan' and 'Robert Zimmerman' are co-referring terms.[4]

---

[4] Salmon's claim that (1) and (2) express the same information does not imply that the *beliefs* attributed by sentences like (6) are the same as those attributed by the sentences that result from replacing singular terms in them with co-referring singular terms (i.e., it does not imply e.g. that the belief that Bob Dylan is Bob Dylan is the same as the belief that Bob Dylan is Robert Zimmerman). Indeed, Salmon himself rejects this latter claim, and elsewhere in *Frege's Puzzle* he develops a theory of belief on which such pairs may be distinct. On Salmon's account, belief is a three-place relation which holds between persons, propositions/information contents and *'guises'* – i.e. *ways in which* propositions are grasped. Debate continues over whether Salmon's treatment of propositional attitudes is substantially different from that of 'neo-Fregean' philosophers such as Evans, McDowell and Peacocke (or indeed from that of Frege).

Questions and tasks

1   At the beginning of 'On Sense and Reference', Frege considers his earlier view, that what is expressed by the sentence, 'a = b' is information concerning only the *names* involved, rather than also information about their referents. Explain and evaluate the argument Frege offers against this.

2   Frege maintains that expressions such as 'Ulysses' and 'the least converging series' are singular terms with senses but no referents. Is this consistent with his characterization of senses as *modes of presentation* of referents?

3   Explain and evaluate Frege's arguments for the claims that sentences have referents, and that these are truth values.

4   Frege proposes that the senses of singular terms are *modes of presentation* of their referents, and that the (ordinary) referents of sentences are their *truth values*. Do you think he also holds that the (ordinary) senses of sentences are *modes of presentation* of their truth values? Is this a helpful way to think about sense?

5   Explain why sentences attributing propositional attitudes (e.g. (6)) are problematic, and explain the Fregean solution. Finally, consider whether the sentence 'Necessarily, 3 + 4 = 7' gives rise to similar problems, and if so, whether they can be solved in the same way.

6   How plausible is Salmon's suggestion that pairs of sentences such as (1) and
     (2) express the same information content?

References and further reading

Chalmers, D. 2002: 'On Sense and Intension', in J. Tomberlin (ed.), *Philosophical
     Perspectives*, 16: *Language and Mind*, Oxford: Blackwell, pp. 135–82.
Dummett, M. 1981: *Frege. Philosophy of Language*, 2nd edn, London: Duckworth.
Dummett, M. 1978: 'Frege's Distinction between Sense and Reference', in Dummett,
     M., *Truth and Other Enigmas*, London: Duckworth, pp. 116–44.
Dummett, M. 1981: *The Interpretation of Frege's Philosophy*, London: Duckworth.
Evans, G. 1982: *The Varieties of Reference*, Oxford: Oxford University Press.
Frege, G. 1956: 'The Thought: A Logical Inquiry', *Mind* 65, pp. 289–311.
Frege, G. 1980: *The Foundations of Arithmetic*, J. L. Austin (trans.), Oxford:
     Blackwell.
Frege, G. 1984: 'Function and Concept', in G. Frege, *Collected Papers on Mathematics,
     Logic and Philosophy*, B. McGuinness (ed.), Oxford: Blackwell, 137–56.
Heck, R., and R. May 2006: 'Frege's Contribution to Philosophy of Language', in
     E. Lepore and B. Smith (eds), *The Oxford Handbook of Philosophy of Language*,
     Oxford: Oxford University Press, pp. 3–39.
May, R. 2006: 'The Invariance of Sense', *Journal of Philosophy* 103, pp. 111–44.
McDowell, J. 1977: 'On the Sense and Reference of a Proper Name', *Mind* 86,
     pp. 159–85; reprinted in J. McDowell, *Meaning, Knowledge and Reality*,
     Cambridge, MA: Harvard University Press (1998).
Noonan, H. 2001: *Frege: A Critical Introduction*, Cambridge, UK: Polity Press.
Salmon, N. 1986: *Frege's Puzzle*, Cambridge, MA: MIT Press.

Chapter 4

Gottlob Frege

ON SENSE AND REFERENCE[1]

based on a random choice.

Equality[2] challenges our capacity to think, because it gives rise to questions that are not quite easy to answer. Is it a relation? a relation between objects? or between names or signs for objects? I had assumed the latter in my *Begriffs-schrift*. The reasons that seem to favour it are the following: $a = a$ and $a = b$ are obviously sentences of different cognitive value: $a = a$ holds a priori, and, following Kant, should be called analytic, while sentences of the form $a = b$ often contain valuable extensions of our knowledge and cannot always be justified a priori. The discovery that a new sun does not rise every morning but always the same one has probably been one of the most consequential discoveries in astronomy. Even now we cannot always take for granted that we will recognise a small planet or comet. Now, if we wanted to view equality as a relation between that which the names "a" and "b" mean,[3] then it would seem that $a = b$ could not be different from $a = a$, in case $a = b$ is true. It would express a relation of a thing to itself, namely such a relation in which each thing stands to itself, but none stands to another. What one wants to say by $a = b$ seems to be that the signs or names "a" and "b" mean[4] the same, so that one would be talking precisely about those signs, and asserting a relation between them. But this relation would hold between the names or signs only in so far as they name or designate[5] something. The relation would be one that is mediated by the connection of each of the signs

with the same object designated. But this [connection] is arbitrary. One cannot prevent anyone from accepting any arbitrarily producible procedure or object as a sign for anything. Thus a sentence $a = b$ would no longer concern the issue itself, but only our way of using signs; we would not express any proper knowledge with it. However, in many cases that is precisely what we want to do. If sign "a" differs from sign "b" merely as an object (in this case by its shape), but not as a sign—this is supposed to mean: not in the way in which it designates something—then the cognitive value of $a = a$ would be essentially equal to that of $a = b$, if $a = b$ is true. A difference can only come about because the difference of the sign corresponds to a difference in the way in which what is signified is given. Let a, b, c be the lines that connect the vertices of a triangle with the midpoints of the opposite sides.[6] Then the intersection of a and b is the same as the intersection of b and c. Thus we have different designations of the same point, and these names ("intersection of a and b", "intersection of b and c") indicate at the same time the mode of presentation,[7] so that real knowledge is contained in the sentence.

It is thus natural to view as tied to a sign (name, combination of words, written sign) not just what is designated by the sign (which may be called the Reference[8] of the sign), but also what I would like to call the Sense of the sign, which contains the way of being given. In our example, then, while the Reference of the expressions "the intersection of *a* and *b*" and "the intersection of *b* and *c*" would be the same, their Sense would not. The Reference of "Evening Star" and "Morning Star" would be the same, but not the Sense.[9]

It follows from the context that by "sign" and "name" I have here been meaning any designation that takes the place of a proper name, the Reference of which is thus a determinate object (taking this word in the widest extension), but not a concept or relation, which will be discussed in another essay.[10] The designation of a particular object can also consist of several words or other signs. For brevity, any such designation may be called proper name.

The Sense of a proper name is grasped by anyone who has sufficient knowledge of the language or set of designations to which it belongs;[11] but this only ever illuminates the Reference, if there is one, on one side. All-round knowledge of the Reference would involve our being able to specify immediately for any given Sense, whether it belongs to that Reference. We never reach that point.

The regular association between a sign, its Sense and its Reference is such that to the sign corresponds a determinate Sense, and to it in turn corresponds a determinate Reference, while it is not just one sign that belongs to a Reference (to an object). The same Sense has different expressions in different languages, even in the same language. Exceptions to this regular behaviour do of course occur. Certainly, in a perfect System of signs, a determinate Sense should correspond to each expression; but popular languages often fail to fulfil this demand, and one has to be content if at least in the same context the same word always has the same Sense. Perhaps one might concede that a grammatically correctly formed expression that stands in for a proper name always has a Sense. But that does not settle whether there is also a Reference that corresponds to the Sense. The words "the celestial body furthest away from the Earth" do have a

Sense; but it is very doubtful whether they also have a Reference. The expression "the least convergent series" has a Sense; but one proves that it has no Reference, because for each convergent series one can find a less convergent one that is still convergent. Thus grasping a Sense does not yet guarantee having a Reference.

When one uses words in the ordinary way, their Reference is that about which one wants to speak. But occasionally one wants to talk about the words themselves or about their Sense. This occurs, e.g., when one cites the words of another in direct speech. In this case one's own words first Refer to the words of the other, and it is only these that have the ordinary Reference. Then we have signs of signs. In writing one encloses the word images [Wortbilder] in quotation marks in this case. Therefore a word image that is enclosed in quotation marks must not be taken as having the ordinary Reference.

• If one wants to talk about the Sense of an expression "A", one can do so simply by using the phrase "the Sense of expression 'A' ". In indirect speech one speaks about the Sense of, for example, the speech of another. It is clear from this that in this form of speech the words do not have their ordinary Reference either, but Refer to what is ordinarily their Sense. In order to have a short expression, let us say: in indirect speech, the words are used indirectly, or have their indirect Reference. Thus we distinguish the ordinary Reference of a word from its indirect Reference and its ordinary Sense from its indirect Sense. So the indirect Reference of a word is its ordinary Sense. One should always keep an eye on such exceptions, if one is to understand correctly the way in which sign, Sense and Reference are associated.

The Reference and Sense of a sign is to be distinguished from the idea [Vorstellung] associated with it. If the Reference of a sign is an object that can be perceived by the senses, then my idea of it is an inner image brought about by memories of sense impressions that I have had, and of activities, internal as well as external, that

I have carried out.[12] This is often soaked in feelings; the clarity of its individual parts varies and vacillates. The same idea is not always tied to the same Sense, not even in the same person. The idea is subjective: one person's idea is not that of another. By virtue of this alone, there are many differences among the ideas that are associated with the same Sense. A painter, a horseman, a zoologist will associate very different ideas with the name "Bucephalus". In this, the idea differs essentially from the Sense of a sign, which can be common property of many and is not a mode of an individual soul. For one can hardly deny that humanity has a common treasure of thoughts that it transmits from one generation to another.[13]

Thus, while there are no misgivings about speaking of the Sense without further qualification, one must, strictly speaking add in the case of the idea, whom it belongs to at what time. One might say: just as one person connects this idea and another that idea with the same word, similarly one may associate this Sense with it, and another that Sense. But in that case the difference does consist merely in the kind of association. This is no obstacle to both grasping the same Sense; while they cannot have the same idea. *Si duo idem faciunt, non est idem* [= if two do the same, it is not the same]. If two people have an idea of the same, then each still has their own idea. Even though it is on occasion possible to discover differences between the ideas, or even feelings, of different people, a precise comparison is not possible because we can't have these ideas together in one consciousness.

The Reference of a proper name is the object itself that we thereby designate; the idea we have when we do so is wholly subjective. In-between is the Sense, which is no longer subjective, like the idea, but which is not the object itself either. The following simile might be suitable for clarifying these interrelations. Someone is looking at the moon through a telescope. I compare the moon itself with the Reference, it is the object of observation which is mediated through the real

image which is projected from the lens inside the telescope and through the observer's retinal image. I compare the former with the Sense, the latter with the idea or intuition. The image inside the telescope is only one-sided, it depends on the location of the observer, but it is still objective in so far as it can serve several observers. In any case, it would be possible to set things up in such a way that several people can use it simultaneously. As far as retinal images are concerned, each person would still have their own. Even geometrical congruence would be hard to achieve because of the differences in the way the eyes have developed. Real coincidence would be out of the question. Perhaps one could elaborate the simile further by assuming that the retinal image of A can be made visible for B; or that A himself could see his own retinal image in a mirror. This might be good for showing that an idea can itself be taken as the object, but that as such it is to the observer not what it is immediately to the one who has the idea. However, to pursue this would lead too far astray.

We can now recognize three levels of difference among words, expressions and whole sentences. Either the difference concerns at most the ideas; or it concerns the Sense but not the Reference; or, finally, it concerns the Reference as well. With respect to the first level one should note that, because of the insecure connection of ideas with words, there may occur a difference for one person that another person cannot find. The difference between translation and original should not go beyond the first level. The differences that are still possible here include the colourings and illuminations with which poetry and eloquence seek to endow Sense. These colourings and illuminations are not objective, but each listener or reader must create these for himself according to the hints of the poet or orator. Without some kinship between human ideas art would of course not be possible; however, it can never be established to what extent the intentions of the poet are complied with. In what follows there shall be no more talk of ideas and intuitions; they have only been mentioned here so that the idea a word triggers in a hearer is not confused with its Sense or its Reference.

In order to enable short and precise expression, let us stipulate the following turns of phrase:

A proper name (word, sign, string of signs, expression) expresses its Sense but Refers to, or designates, its Reference. With a sign we express its Sense and designate with it its Reference.

Perhaps an idealist or sceptic would have objected long ago: "You are speaking without further ado of the moon as an object; but how do you know that the name 'the moon' has a Reference at all? How do you know that anything has a Reference?" I reply that it is not our intention to speak about our idea of the moon, and that we do not content ourselves with the Sense, when we say "the moon", but we presuppose a Reference. It would be to miss the Sense completely, if one were to assume that in the sentence "the moon is smaller than the Earth" one is talking about an idea of the moon. If the speaker wanted this, he or she would use the phrase "my idea of the moon". Now, we might of course be mistaken in that presupposition, and such mistakes have occurred. However, the question whether we are perhaps always mistaken in this may be left unanswered here; in order to justify speaking about the Reference of a sign, it suffices for now to point to our intention in speaking or thinking, even if with the proviso: in case there is such a Reference.

Until now, only the Sense and Reference of those expressions have been considered that we have called proper names. We shall now enquire into the Sense and Reference of a whole assertoric sentence. Such a sentence contains a thought.[14] Should this thought be seen as its Sense or as its Reference? Let us suppose for a moment that the sentence has a Reference! If we now replace a word in it by another word with the same Reference but a different Sense, then this cannot have an influence on the Reference of the sentence. But we do see that the thought changes in such a case; for the thought of the sentence "the Morning Star is a body illuminated by the sun" is different from that of the sentence "the Evening Star is a body illuminated by the sun". Someone who didn't know that the Evening Star is the Morning Star might regard the one thought as true, the other as false. Therefore the thought cannot be the Reference of the sentence. Rather, we have to view it as the Sense. But what about the Reference then? May we ask what it is at all? Perhaps a sentence as a whole has a Sense but no Reference? In any case it is to be expected that such sentences occur, just as there are sentence parts that do have a Sense but no Reference. And sentences that contain proper names without Reference will be of this kind. The sentence "Ulysses was fast asleep when he was put to shore on Ithaca" obviously has a Sense. But because it is doubtful whether the name "Ulysses" that occurs in it has a Reference, it is therefore also doubtful whether the whole sentence has one. But it is surely certain that someone who seriously considers the sentence true or false will also admit that the name "Ulysses" has a Reference, not just a Sense, for it is the Reference of this name of which the predicate is affirmed or denied. He who does not recognize a Reference cannot affirm or deny a predicate of it. Now, advancing to the Reference of the name would be superfluous; one could be content with the Sense, if one wanted to come to a halt at the thought. If only the Sense of the sentence, the thought, mattered, it would be unnecessary to care about the Reference of a sentence part; for the Sense of the sentence only the Sense of a part, not the Reference, is taken into consideration. The thought remains the same, whether the name "Ulysses" has a Reference or not. The fact that we take trouble over the Reference of a sentence part at all is a sign that we recognize and require a Reference also for the sentence itself. The thought loses in value as soon as we realize that one of its parts lacks a Reference. We are therefore within our rights not to rest content with the Sense of a sentence, but to enquire also after its Reference. But why do we want it to be, then, that each proper name has not only a Sense but also a Reference? Why isn't the thought enough for us? Because, and in so far as, its truth-value matters to us. This is not always the case. For example when listening to an epic, we are gripped—besides the pleasant sound of the language—only by the Sense of the sentences and the ideas and feelings thereby aroused. In asking after the truth we would be leaving behind the enjoyment of art and be turning to a scientific contemplation. That's also why we do not care whether, for example, the name "Ulysses" has a Reference, as long as we take up the poem as a work of art.[15] It is therefore our striving for truth which drives us everywhere to advance from Sense to Reference.

We have seen that a Reference corresponding to a sentence is to be sought whenever the Reference of the constituents matters; and this is the case when, and only when, we ask after the truth-value.

We are therefore pushed into recognizing the truth-value of a sentence as its Reference. By the truth-value of a sentence I mean the fact that it is true or that it is false. There are no further truth-values. For brevity's sake, I call the one the True, and the other the False. Every assertoric sentence in which the Reference of the words matters should therefore be viewed as a proper name, and furthermore its Reference, if there is one, is either the True or the False. These two objects are recognised, even if tacitly, by anyone who judges at all, or who takes something to be true, thus by the sceptic, too. To describe the truth-values as objects may at this point seem an arbitrary idea and possibly a mere play with words, from which no profound inferences should be drawn. What I call object can be explained in more detail only in connection with concept and relation. I want to reserve this for another essay. But may that much be clear at this point: that in every judgement—be it as obvious as it may—the step from the level of thoughts to the level of References (the objective) has already happened.

One might be tempted to think of the relation of thought to the True not as that of Sense to Reference, but as that of subject to predicate. After all one can say directly: "the thought that 5 is a prime number is true". But if one looks more in detail, one notices that no more has been said in this than in the simple sentence "5 is a prime number". In both cases, the assertion of truth lies in the form of an assertoric sentence, and where this form does not have its usual force, e.g. in the mouth of an actor on stage, the sentence "the thought that 5 is a prime number is true" also contains just one thought, namely the same thought as the simple "5 is a prime number". One can take from this that the relation of the thought to the truth-value must not, after all, be compared to that of subject to predicate. For subject and predicate are (in the logical sense) parts of a thought; they stand on the same level for cognition. By compounding subject and predicate one only ever gets to a thought, never from a Sense to its truth-value. One is moving on the same level, but one does not advance from one level to the next. A truth-value cannot be a part of a thought, just as, say, the sun can't, because it [the truth-value] is not a Sense but an object.

If our conjecture that the Reference of a sentence is its truth-value is correct, then the latter must remain unchanged if a sentence part is replaced by an expression of the same Reference but different Sense. And this is in fact the case. Leibniz states directly: "Eadem sunt, quae sibi mutuo substitui possunt, salva veritate" [= the same are those which can be mutually replaced under preservation of truth]. What else but the truth-value could be found, which belongs generally to every sentence in which the Reference of constituents matters, which remains unchanged under a substitution of the kind indicated?

If, now, the truth-value of a sentence is its Reference then on the one hand all true sentences have the same Reference, and so on the other hand all the false ones. We see from this that in the sentence's Reference everything particular is blurred. Therefore it will never be the

Reference of a sentence alone that matters to us; but neither does the mere thought provide knowledge, but only the thought together with its Reference, i.e. its truth-value. Judging can be captured as the advancement from a thought to its truth-value. Of course this is not supposed to be a definition. Judging is after all something entirely unique and beyond comparison. One could even say that judging is distinguishing parts within the truth-value. This distinction occurs by recourse to the thought. Each Sense that corresponds to a truth-value would correspond to its own manner of dissection. I did, though, use the word "part" in a special way here. For I employed the sentence's whole-part relation in the case of its Reference by calling the Reference of a word part of the Reference of the sentence, when that word is itself part of the sentence—a manner of speaking that is of course open to criticism, because in the case of Reference the whole and a part do not determine the remaining part, and because in the case of bodies the word part is already used in a different sense. A separate expression should be created for this.

We shall now further test the hypothesis that the truth-value of a sentence is its Reference. We found that the truth-value of a sentence remains untouched if we replace one expression in it by another with the same Reference: however, we have not yet considered the case where the expression to be replaced is itself a sentence. Now, if our view is correct, then the truth-value of a sentence that contains another sentence as part should remain unchanged if we substitute for the subsentence another sentence whose truth-value is the same. Exceptions are to be expected if the whole or the subsentence were direct or indirect speech; for, as we have seen, the Reference of words is not the ordinary one in that case. Again, in direct speech, a sentence refers to a sentence and in indirect speech to a thought.

[. . .]

Let us now return to our point of departure! If we found the cognitive value of "$a = a$" and

"$a = b$" generally to be different, then this is explained by the fact that the Sense of the sentence, namely the thought expressed in it, is to be taken into account no less than its Reference, that is its truth-value. Now, if $a = b$ then the Reference of "b" is the same as that of "a", and therefore the truth-value of "$a = b$" also the same as that of "$a = a$". Nevertheless the Sense of "b" can be different from the Sense of "a", and thus the thought expressed in "$a = b$" also different from the one expressed in "$a = a$". Then the two sentences do not have the same cognitive value. If, as above, we mean by "judgement" the advancement from the thought to its truth-value, then we will also say that the judgements are different.

Notes

1   [Translator's note: There are already two published English translations of Frege's "Über Sinn und Bedeutung", so why are we providing a third one? There were several considerations: First, the only translation we regarded as acceptable was that by Black. However, this translation has already been revised twice, and we did not want to add to this chaos of versions of the Black translation. Secondly, it seemed to us that the Black translation, which is on the whole very good, sometimes departs unnecessarily from the original. Thirdly, the cost for a licence to re-use the Black translation would have entailed cuts in other places in this volume, which we found difficult, given that we were already having to make cuts.]

2   I am using this word in the sense of Identity and I mean "$a = b$" in the sense of "a is the same as b" or "a and b coincide".

3   [Translator's note: The verb "to mean" here translates Frege's "bedeuten". Later in this article, Frege introduces a special stipulated sense for the verb "bedeuten", which will be translated here as "to refer to". See note 8 below where the translation of the special technical use of "bedeuten" is explained.]

4   [Translator's note: See note 3.]

5   [Translator's note: The German verb "bezeichnen", the participle "Bezeichnetes", and the noun

"Bezeichnung", have been uniformly translated as "to designate", "thing designated" and "Designation".]

6 [Translator's note: This diagram illustrates Frege's example:]

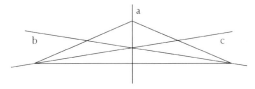

7 [Translator's note: "Mode of presentation" has become the standard translation for Frege's "Art des Gegebenseins", which literally means *way of being given*. This translation adopts the standard translation in order to avoid confusion.]

8 [Translator's note: At this point, Frege explictly introduces the terms "Bedeutung" and "Sinn" in their special technical sense. From this point on, these terms and their cognates—when used with the special technical sense Frege gives them—will be translated as "Reference" and "Sense", each time indicating the technical use by capitalization. It seems best to translate the term "Bedeutung" in this way because the terms "reference" or "referent" are almost uniformly used nowadays for the object a singular term stands for. "Meaning" may have been a better translation initially, as it has more or less the same non-technical connotations as "Bedeutung" in German (and this is no doubt the reason why the revised Black translation uses it); however, this would now be misleading.]

9 [Translator's note: The German names "Abendstern" and "Morgenstern", here translated as "Evening Star" and Morning Star", which are alternative names for Venus, are sometimes translated as "Hesperus" and "Phosphorus".]

10 [Translator's note: Frege's essay "On Concept and Object" discusses concepts and relations.]

11 In the case of an actual proper name [i.e. a proper name in the usual sense, not in the sense just defined] such as "Aristotle", opinions may of course diverge as to its Sense. One might, for example, assume as its Sense: Plato's pupil and teacher of Alexander the Great. He who does this will associate a different Sense with the sentence "Aristotle was born in Stagira" from someone who assumed as Sense of this name: the teacher of Alexander the Great, who was born in Stagira. As long as at least the Reference remains the same, these vacillations of sense can be tolerated, even though they are to be avoided in the edifice of knowledge of a demonstrative science, and would not be allowed to occur in a perfect language.

12 We can bring the idea under one head with intuitions [Anschauungen]. In the case of intuitions, the sense impressions and activities themselves take the place of the traces they have left behind in the soul. For our purpose, the difference is of no consequence, given that presumably besides sensations and activities, memories of them help complete the intuitive image. But one can also understand "intuition" to mean an object in so far as it is perceptible through the senses or is spatial.

13 That is why it is unhelpful to use the word "idea" to designate things that are so fundamentally different.

14 By thought I do not mean the subjective act of thinking but its objective content, which is capable of being the common property of many.

15 It would be desirable to have a special expression for signs that are meant to have only a Sense. If we call such expressions images, then the actor's words on stage would be images, even the actor would be an image.

Chapter 5

Nathan Salmon

FREGE'S PUZZLE

Frege's Puzzle and the naive theory

Frege's Puzzle and information content

[. . .] How can $\ulcorner a = b \urcorner$, if true, differ in "cognitive value"—that is, in cognitive information content—from $\ulcorner a = a \urcorner$? Clearly they differ, since the first is informative and a posteriori where the latter is uninformative and a priori. But, assuming that $\ulcorner a = b \urcorner$ predicates the relation of identity between the referent of the name a and the referent of the name b, and that $\ulcorner a = a \urcorner$ predicates the relation of identity between the referent of a and the referent of a, then if $\ulcorner a = b \urcorner$ is true, it predicates the same relation between the same pair of objects as does $\ulcorner a = a \urcorner$. It would seem, then, that $\ulcorner a = b \urcorner$ and $\ulcorner a = a \urcorner$ ought to convey the same piece of information. But clearly they do not. So what gives here?

A number of philosophers have found the identity relation, taken as the relation that "each thing stands in to itself, but no thing stands to another," curious, mysterious, or bogus. In the *Tractatus* (sections 5.53–5.535), Wittgenstein denies that there is any such relation.[1] Earlier, in *Begriffsschrift* (section 8), Frege took a similar tack, proposing an analysis of identity sentences according to which singular terms "display their own selves [appear in propria persona] when they are combined by means of the sign ['='] for identity of content [referent], for this expresses the circumstance of two names [singular terms] having the same content [referent]." Thus the

early Frege and Wittgenstein attempted to rid themselves of the puzzle. More recent philosophy has followed Frege's later characterization of the origins of the puzzle as one arising from reflection on the concept of the identity by the use of such epithets as 'Frege's puzzle about identity' or 'Frege's identity problem'. The first point I wish to emphasize about 'Frege's puzzle about identity' is that, pace Frege, it is not a puzzle about identity. It has virtually nothing to do with identity. Different versions of the very same puzzle, or formally analogous puzzles that pose the very same set of questions and philosophical issues in the very same way, arise with certain constructions not involving the identity predicate or the identity relation. For example, the sentence 'Shakespeare wrote *Timon of Athens*' is informative, whereas 'The author of *Timon of Athens* wrote *Timon of Athens*' is not. The same question arises: How can that be? Given that the first sentence is true, it would seem that both sentences contain the same piece of information; they both attribute the same property (authorship of *Timon of Athens*) to the same individual (Shakespeare). This kind of example is unlike Frege's version of the puzzle in that it involves a definite description, whereas Frege's can involve two proper names and consequently applies pressure against a wider range of semantic theories. It is not difficult, however, to construct further puzzling examples involving two names without using the identity predicate; the sentence

'Hesperus is a planet if Phosphorus is' is informative and apparently a posteriori, whereas the sentence 'Phosphorus is a planet if Phosphorus is' is uninformative and a priori. However, both sentences attribute the same property, *being a planet if Phosphorus is*, to the same entity, the planet Venus. Looked at another way, both sentences attribute the same relation, *x is a planet if y is*, to the same (reflexive) pair of objects. In either case, the two sentences seem to contain the very same information.

It is easy to see from these examples that versions of Frege's Puzzle can be constructed in connection with any predicate whatsoever, not just with the identity predicate. What, then, is the general puzzle about if it is not a puzzle about identity? These same examples provide the answer. The general problem is a problem concerning pieces of information (in a nontechnical sense), such as the information that Socrates is wise or the information that Socrates is wise if Plato is. The various versions of Frege's Puzzle are stated in terms of declarative sentences rather than in terms of information. This is because there is an obvious and intimate relation between pieces of information (such as the information that Socrates is wise) and declarative sentences (such as 'Socrates is wise'). Declarative sentences have various semantic attributes: they are true, or false, or neither; they have semantic intentions (i.e., correlated functions from possible worlds to truth values); they involve reference to individuals, such as Socrates; and so on. But the fundamental semantic role of a declarative sentence is to encode information.[2] I mean the term 'information' in a broad sense to include misinformation (that is, inaccurate or incorrect pieces of information), and even pieces of information that are neither true nor false. Pragmatically, we use declarative sentences to communicate or convey information to others (generally, not just the information encoded by the sentence), but we may also use declarative sentences simply to record information for possible future use, and perhaps even to record

information with no anticipation of any future use. If for some reason I need to make a record of the date of my marriage, say to recall that piece of information on a later occasion, I can simply write the words 'I was married on August 28, 1980', or memorize them, or repeat them to myself. Declarative sentences are primarily a means of encoding information, and they are a remarkably efficient means at that. Many of their other semantic and pragmatic functions follow from or depend upon their fundamental semantic role of encoding information.

This statement of the semantic relation between declarative sentences and information is somewhat vague, but it is clear enough to convey one of the fundamental presuppositions of Frege's Puzzle. Vague though it may be, it is also obviously correct. Any reasonable semantic theory for declarative sentences ought to allow for some account of declarative sentences as information encoders, at least to the extent of not contradicting it. A conception of sentences as information encoders will be assumed throughout this book. A declarative sentence will be said to *contain* the information it encodes, and that piece of information will be described as the *information content* of the sentence.

Pieces of information are, like the sentences that encode them, abstract entities. Many of their properties can be "read off" from the encoding sentences. Thus, for instance, it is evident that pieces of information are not ontologically simple, but complex. The information that Socrates is wise and the information that Socrates is snub-nosed are both, in the same way, pieces of information directly about Socrates; hence, they must have some component in common. Likewise, the information that Socrates is wise has some component in common with the information that Plato is wise, and that component is different from what it has in common with the information that Socrates is snub-nosed. Correspondingly, the declarative sentence 'Socrates is wise' shares certain syntactic components with the sentences 'Socrates is snub-nosed' and

'Plato is wise'. These syntactic components—the name 'Socrates' and the predicate 'is wise'—are separately semantically correlated with the corresponding component of the piece of information encoded by the sentence. Let us call the information component semantically correlated with an expression the *information value* of the expression. The information value of the name 'Socrates' is that which the name contributes to the information encoded by such sentences as 'Socrates is wise' and 'Socrates is snub-nosed'; similarly, the information value of the predicate 'is wise' is that entity which the predicate contributes to the information encoded by such sentences as 'Socrates is wise' and 'Plato is wise'. As a limiting case, the information value of a declarative sentence is the piece of information it encodes, its information content.

[. . .]

The structure of Frege's Puzzle

Compositionality

I have claimed that Frege's Puzzle concerns the nature and structure of pieces of information (the sort of information semantically contained in a declarative sentence), and that an adequate solution must address this issue directly. It is important for this purpose to focus on the principles and assumptions involved in the derivation of Frege's Puzzle.

Preliminary investigation into the nature and structure of pieces of information uncovered that a piece of information is a complex abstract entity whose components are the information values of the components of a sentence that contains the information [. . .]. There are two components of the information that Socrates is wise: what is had in common between the information that Socrates is wise and the information that Socrates is snub-nosed, and what is had in common between the information that Socrates is wise and the information that Plato is wise. It is natural to suppose that the first component is

precisely the individual whom that information is about, i.e., the man Socrates. Frege's Puzzle challenges this natural idea by proposing two purportedly distinct pieces of information that have the very same predicative component and are about the very same individual. The implicit assumption is a principle of compositionality for pieces of information: If pieces of information are complex abstract entities, and two pieces of information p and q having the same structure and mode of composition are numerically distinct, then there must be some component of one that is not a component of the other; otherwise p and q would be one and the very same piece of information. (Compare the principle of extensionality for classes or sets.)

This compositionality principle for pieces of information might be challenged. Complex entities having the very same components and mode of composition cannot always be identified with one another. The clipboard on which I am now writing has the very same component molecules as the matter that now constitutes it, but, for familiar philosophical reasons, the clipboard is not identical with its present matter. The clipboard came into existence long after its present matter did, and it will cease to exist long before its present matter does (if the matter ever ceases to exist). Moreover, strictly speaking, the clipboard is constituted by different (albeit largely overlapping) matter at different times, and is only briefly constituted by its present molecules, though the present matter is forever constituted by these very molecules. Similarly, to use an example due to Richard Sharvy, the Supreme Court of the United States has the very same membership as the set of its present justices, but the Court and the set of its present justices are distinct complex entities, since the Court changes its membership over time whereas no set can change its membership.[3] Even complex entities of the very same kind having the same constituents and mode of composition cannot always be identified. Different ad hoc committees within a university department can coincide exactly in membership though they remain different committees with different functions and responsibilities.

In contrast with these examples, it would seem that pieces of information do obey the principle of compositionality implicit in Frege's Puzzle. For each of the complex entities mentioned above as violators of a corresponding compositionality principle, there is some significant aspect of the entity, some crucial feature of it, that differentiates it from any distinct entity composed of the very same constituents in the very same way. The Supreme Court and the set of its present justices differ in their flexibility with respect to change in membership. Any two distinct ad hoc committees differ in at least some of their functions or purposes. But pieces of information having the very same structure and components, combined in the very same way, cannot change in constitution, and they fulfill the same purposes and perform the same functions. In any event, if two pieces of information, p and q, are composed of the very same components in the very same way but are distinct, it would seem that there must also be some important aspect in which they differ, some significant property had by p and not by q or vice versa. This, however, raises the same challenging question posed by Frege, or at least a philosophically important question similar to Frege's original question: What in the world is this mysterious feature or aspect of pieces of information in which two pieces of information composed of the same components in the same way can yet differ? Even if the principle of compositionality for pieces of information fails, some variant of Frege's Puzzle remains a pressing philosophical problem for semantic theory.

In order to produce two distinct pieces of information that are about the same individuals and that have the same predicative component, Frege offers a pair of declarative sentences involving the same predicate but different singular terms for the same object and argues that these sentences must be seen as containing different

pieces of information. To this end, Frege's Puzzle, in its original form, tacitly invokes the following principle concerning information content:

> If a declarative sentence S has the very same cognitive information content (Erkenntniswerte) as a declarative sentence S′, then S is informative ("contains an extension of our knowledge") if and only if S′ is (does).

I shall call this principle *Frege's Law*. It is an exceedingly plausible principle connecting the concepts of *information content* and *informativeness*. Still, it might be thought that it is precisely the unquestioning acceptance of this principle that is the source of the puzzle. It might even be argued that the puzzle should be recast as a reductio ad absurdum of the principle. "What independent reason can there be," one might ask, "for holding this principle to be true? In fact, isn't it clear that the informativeness or uninformativeness of a sentence depends on more factors than just the information content of the sentence, so that two sentences having the same content may yet differ in their informativeness?"[4]

This line of attack against Frege's Puzzle is sorely mistaken. Given the sense of 'informative' that is relevant to the puzzle, Frege's Law is unassailable. Properly understood, Frege's Law should be seen as a special instance of Leibniz's Law, the Indiscernibility of Identicals. This is because, on a proper understanding of 'informative', the informativeness or uninformativeness (a posteriority or a priority, etc.) of a sentence is a *derivative* semantic property of the sentence, one that the sentence has only by virtue of encoding the information that it does encode. That is, to say that a sentence, on a particular occasion of use, is (as the term is used in the context of Frege's Puzzle) *informative* (or that it is *a posteriori*) is to say something about the *information content* of the sentence: It is to say that the information content is not somehow already given, or that the content is nontrivial, or that it is knowable only by recourse to experience and not merely by reflection on the concepts involved, or that it is an "extension of our knowledge," or something along these lines. There is some such property P of pieces of information such that a sentence is informative, in the sense relevant to Frege's Puzzle, if and only if its information content has the property P.

Of course, there are other senses of 'informative' on which even a trivial identity statement may be described as "informative". For example, if you do not speak a word of French but you have it on good authority that Jean-Paul's next inscription will be of a true French sentence, and you observe Jean-Paul then write the words 'Cicéron est identique à Cicéron', the sentence in question, on this occasion of use, may be said to be "informative" on several counts. By way of its inscription, you are given a great deal of non-trivial information; you are thereby given that a certain sequence of marks is a meaningful and grammatical expression of French, that it is in fact a French sentence, and that it is a true sentence. If you also know even a minimum about the grammar of Romance or Indo-European languages, and you know that 'Cicéron' is a name, you are also thereby given the information that the words 'est identique à' probably signify some relation in French, a relation that the relevant person called 'Cicéron' in French bears to himself. However, all this is quite irrelevant to Frege's Puzzle.

It is extremely important in dealing with Frege's Puzzle and related philosophical problems to distinguish the notion of the *information content* of a sentence on a particular occasion of its use from the notion of the *information imparted* by the particular utterance of the sentence. The first is a semantic notion, the second a pragmatic notion. Failure to make this distinction has led many a well-meaning philosopher astray. I have already discussed the notion of semantically encoded information at some length in the previous chapter [see original reading for references to other chapters]. In claiming that it is a basic function of sentences to encode information,

I invoke the notion of semantically encoded information. To illustrate the quite different notion of pragmatically imparted information, it is best to begin with a nonlinguistic and uncontroversial example. Consider some of the ways in which one might receive or learn the information that Smith has a cold. One way, of course, is for someone (perhaps Smith) to produce with assertive intent a conventional symbol that semantically encodes that information; for example, Smith may utter the sentence 'I have a cold' in conversation. Under certain circumstances, another way to learn that Smith has a cold—one not involving language—is simply to observe Smith sneeze and then blow his nose. In this sense, Smith's blowing his nose imparts, or can impart, the information that he has a cold. Though the blowing of a nose may thus impart certain information, it would be utterly ridiculous to suppose that nose blowing has any semantic content. One can imagine a society in which blowing one's nose is a linguistic gesture—a move in the language game—much like shaking one's head 'no' is in our society; fortunately, however, we do not live in such a society. In our society, nose blowing has no semantic significance whatsoever. It is an entirely nonlinguistic act.

Now, just as Smith's nose blowing may impart the information that Smith has a cold, without itself having any semantic attributes and hence without semantically encoding any information, so any observable event typically imparts some information to the astute observer—hence the saying "Actions speak louder than words." Utterances are no exception. In uttering a sentence, one produces a symbol that semantically encodes a piece of information, and in so doing one performs an action (indeed, several actions) that, like any other action, may impart information in the nonsemantic way that even nose blowing may impart information. Of course, typically the information semantically encoded by a sentence will be pragmatically imparted by utterances of the sentence. But the two notions may diverge and often do. In addition to (sometimes instead of) the information semantically encoded by a sentence, an utterance of the sentence may impart further information concerning the speaker's beliefs, intentions, and attitudes, information concerning the very form of words chosen, or other extraneous information. The further information thus imparted can often be of greater significance than the information actually encoded by the sentence itself. Such is the case with Jean-Paul's inscription of 'Cicéron est identique à Cicéron'. In this sense, even utterances can "speak louder than words." In particular, one piece of information typically imparted by the utterance of a sentence S is the information that S is true with respect to the context of the utterance. It is rarely the case, however, that a sentence semantically encodes the information about itself that it is true (or, for that matter, that it is not true—such is the stuff of which paradoxes are made).

Frege himself was aware of the distinction between semantically encoded and pragmatically imparted information. Using his word 'thought' (Gedanke) for what I am calling 'information', Frege explicitly drew the distinction, or something very similar to it, in a section entitled "Separating a Thought from its Trappings" of an essay entitled "Logic," estimated to have been composed in 1897:

> . . . we have to make a distinction between the thoughts that are expressed and those which the speaker leads others to take as true although he does not express them. If a commander conceals his weakness from the enemy by making his troops keep changing their uniforms, he is not telling a lie; for he is not expressing any thoughts, although his actions are calculated to induce thoughts in others. And we find the same thing in the case of speech itself, as when one gives a special tone to the voice or chooses special words. (In *Posthumous Writings*, ed. Hermes et al., at p. 140)

Frege's Puzzle concerns only the information content of Jean-Paul's sentence—the nature and structure of the information semantically contained in or encoded by the sentence with respect to the particular context of use—and not the information pragmatically imparted by the particular utterance. When Frege claims that sentences of the form $\ulcorner a = a \urcorner$ are a priori and do not "contain very valuable extensions of our knowledge," and are in this respect different from sentences of the form $\ulcorner a = b \urcorner$, there is no question but that he is concerned only with the "thought expressed" by this form of sentence, i.e. its information content, and not with the unexpressed "thoughts" that the utterance "leads us to take as true." The information content of Jean-Paul's sentence is utterly trivial. It is in this essentially semantic sense of 'informative', having to do with the character of the information encoded by a sentence, that this French sentence is quite definitely uninformative. Its information content is a *given*, and does not "extend our knowledge."

To take another example due to Carnap, consider the numerical equation '5 = V', using both the Arabic and the Roman numeral for five.[5] To someone familiar with one but not both of these numeral systems, an inscription of this equation pragmatically imparts nontrivial information, e.g. the information concerning one of the numerals that it is a numeral for the number five. But the information semantically encoded by the equation is precisely the same as that encoded by '5 = 5'. This is an instance of the trivial law of reflexivity of equality. The encoded information is not a "valuable extension of knowledge," or anything of the sort. In the relevant sense, the equation is utterly uninformative. A similar situation obtains with respect to sentences like 'Opthalmologists are oculists' and 'Alienists are psychiatrists'. To someone unfamiliar with the grammatical subject term but familiar with the grammatical predicate term, an utterance or inscription of one of these sentences pragmatically imparts nontrivial linguistic information concerning the meaning of the grammatical subject term, though the semantically encoded information is utterly trivial. Indeed, it is just this feature of these sentences—the fact that their semantic information content is trivial—that suits them to the task of conveying the meanings of 'ophthalmologist' and 'alienist'. This is unlike the examples that give rise to Frege's Puzzle (e.g. 'Hesperus is Phosphorus'), in which we are to suppose that the audience has complete mastery of both terms and finds the utterance or inscription informative nevertheless.

Properly understood, then, Frege's Law is not merely a plausible principle connecting the concepts of information content and informativeness, or even a fundamental law of semantics. It is a truth of logic. Hence, it is no solution to the puzzle to challenge Frege's Law.

[. . .]

The crux of Frege's Puzzle

The minor premise

There are three main elements in Frege's Puzzle, and in the corresponding strategy: Frege's Law, the compositionality principle, and the further premise that $\ulcorner a = b \urcorner$ is informative and a posteriori whereas $\ulcorner a = a \urcorner$ is not. I have argued that there is nothing to be gained by challenging the compositionality principle, and that Frege's Law is beyond challenge, since properly understood it is simply a special instance of Leibniz's Law. Still to be considered is the minor premise that $\ulcorner a = b \urcorner$ is informative whereas $\ulcorner a = a \urcorner$ is not.

Historically, philosophers who have had some inclination toward something like the naive theory, including Frege, Mill, and Russell, have allowed that $\ulcorner a = b \urcorner$ is informative and a posteriori whereas $\ulcorner a = a \urcorner$ is not. This was thought too obvious to be denied, and other means for coming to grips with Frege's Puzzle were sought and devised. In contemporary philosophy, direct-reference theorists—who should find the naive theory particularly congenial—have typic-

ally conceded this point, or something tantamount to it, and have therefore abstained from outright, unequivocal endorsement of the naive theory or any modification of the naive theory. Consider the following remarks:

> [You] see a star in the evening and it's called 'Hesperus'. . . . We see a star in the morning and call it 'Phosphorus'. Well, then we find . . . that Hesperus and Phosphorus are in fact the same. So we express this by 'Hesperus is Phosphorus'. Here we're certainly not just saying of an object that it's identical with itself. This is something that we discovered. (Saul Kripke, *Naming and Necessity*, pp. 28–29)

> [We] do not know *a priori* that Hesperus is Phosphorus, and are in no position to find out . . . except empirically. (ibid., p. 104; see also the disclaimer on pp. 20–21)

> Before appropriate empirical discoveries were made, men might have failed to know that Hesperus was Phosphorus, or even to believe it, even though they of course knew and believed that Hesperus was Hesperus. (Kripke, "A Puzzle About Belief," p. 243—but see p. 281, note 44; see also the disclaimer at p. 273, note 10)

> Certainly Frege's argument shows meaning cannot just *be* reference. . . . (Hilary Putnam, "Comments," p. 285)

> If we distinguish a sentence from the proposition it expresses then the terms 'truth' and 'necessity' apply to the proposition expressed by a sentence, while the terms 'a priori' and 'a posteriori' are sentence relative. Given that it is true that Cicero is Tully (and whatever we need about what the relevant sentences express) 'Cicero is Cicero' and 'Cicero is Tully' express the same *proposition*. And the proposition is necessarily true. But looking at

the proposition through the lens of the *sentence* 'Cicero is Cicero' the proposition can be seen *a priori* to be true, but through 'Cicero is Tully' one may need an *a posteriori* investigation. (Keith Donnellan, "Kripke and Putnam on Natural Kind Terms," note 2 on p. 88)

Faced with Frege's identity puzzle, it is difficult indeed to maintain that the names 'Hesperus' and 'Phosphorus' make precisely the same contribution to the information content of sentences that contain either one. Such a claim would be extremist. (Nathan Salmon, *Reference and Essence*, p. 13)

Here is where well-intentioned philosophers have been led astray. It is precisely the seemingly trivial premise that $\ulcorner a = b \urcorner$ is informative whereas $\ulcorner a = a \urcorner$ is not informative that should be challenged, and a proper appreciation for the distinction between semantically encoded and pragmatically imparted information points the way. Recall that Frege's Law is erected into a truth of logic by understanding the word 'informative' in such a way that to say that a sentence is informative is to say something about its information content. By the same token, however, with 'informative' so understood, and with a sharp distinction between semantically encoded information and pragmatically imparted information kept in mind, it is not in the least bit obvious, as Frege's Puzzle maintains, that $\ulcorner a = b \urcorner$ is, whereas $\ulcorner a = a \urcorner$ is not, informative *in the relevant sense*. To be sure, $\ulcorner a = b \urcorner$ *sounds* informative, whereas $\ulcorner a = a \urcorner$ does not. Indeed, an utterance of $\ulcorner a = b \urcorner$ genuinely imparts information that is more valuable than that imparted by an utterance of $\ulcorner a = a \urcorner$. For example, it imparts the nontrivial linguistic information about the sentence $\ulcorner a = b \urcorner$ that it is true, and hence that the names a and b are co-referential. But that is pragmatically imparted information, and presumably not semantically encoded information. (See the discussion in section 3.2 of the "Begriffsschrift" solution to Frege's Puzzle.) It is by no means

clear that the sentence $\ulcorner a = b \urcorner$, stripped naked of its pragmatic impartations and with only its properly semantic information content left, is any more informative in the relevant sense than $\ulcorner a = a \urcorner$. Abstracting from their markedly different pragmatic impartations, one can see that these two sentences may well semantically encode the very same piece of information. I believe that they do. At the very least, it is by no means certain, as Frege's Puzzle pretends, that the difference in "cognitive significance" we seem to hear is not due entirely to a difference in pragmatically imparted information. Yet, until we can be certain of this, Frege's law cannot be applied and Frege's Puzzle does not get off the ground. In effect, then, Frege's Strategy begs the question against the modified naive theory. Of course, if one fails to draw the distinction between semantically encoded and pragmatically imparted information, as so many philosophers have, it is small wonder that information pragmatically imparted by (utterances of) $\ulcorner a = b \urcorner$ may be mistaken for semantically encoded information.[6] If Frege's Stategy is ultimately to succeed, a further argument must be made to show that the information imparted by $\ulcorner a = b \urcorner$ that makes it sound informative is, in fact, semantically encoded. In the meantime, Frege's Puzzle by itself is certainly not the final and conclusive refutation of the modified naive theory that the orthodox theorists have taken it to be. For all that Frege's Strategy achieves, the modified naive theory remains the best and most plausible theory available concerning the nature and structure of the information encoded by declarative sentences.

Ironically, as was noted in section 4.2 [p. 61 above], Frege was not unaware of the distinction between semantically encoded and merely pragmatically imparted information. He did not fully appreciate the significance of this distinction for his theory of information content. In particular, he failed to notice that the distinction undermines his main argument against the naive theory.

Substitutivity

The general puzzle, however, is not so easily put to rest. Although the premise that $\lceil a = b \rceil$ is informative whereas $\lceil a = a \rceil$ is not facilitates the derivation of Frege's Puzzle, this premise is not an essential element in the general puzzle. The premise is invoked in conjunction with Frege's Law to establish the result that there are pairs of sentences of the form f_a and f_b that differ in information content from one another—i.e., that encode different pieces of information—even though a and b are co-referential (genuine) proper names, demonstratives, single-word indexical singular terms, or any combination thereof. This is the crux of Frege's Puzzle. One might attempt to establish this result in some more general way, without invoking the suspect premise that $\lceil a = \rceil b$ is informative. As Michael Dummett has stressed, and as Frege's formulation of the puzzle clearly indicates, the notion of *information content* relevant to Frege's Puzzle is closely tied to the ordinary, everyday notions of *knowledge* and *belief*. One intuitively appealing picture that is entrenched in philosophical tradition depicts belief as a type of inward assent, or a disposition toward inward assent, to a piece of information. To believe that r is to concur covertly with, to endorse mentally, to nod approval to, the information that r when r occurs to you. At the very least, to believe that r one must adopt some sort of favorable disposition or attitude toward the information that r. In fact, the adoption of some such favorable attitude toward a piece of information is both necessary and sufficient for belief. That is just what belief is.[7] To believe that r is, so to speak, to include that piece of information in one's personal inner "data bank." It is to have that information at one's disposal to rely upon, to act upon, to draw inferences from, or to do nothing with. Belief is thus a relation to pieces of information.

These observations suggest the following principal schema, where the substituends for S and S′ are declarative English sentences:

If the information that S = the information that S′, then someone believes that S if and only if he or she believes that S′.

Analogous schemata may be written for assertion and the other so-called propositional attitudes of knowledge, hope, and so forth. Like Frege's Law, each of these schemata may be regarded as (formal mode renderings of) so many instances of Leibniz's Law. In fact, Frege's Law can be viewed as a minor variation of one such schema:

If the information that S = the information that S′, then it is informative (knowable only a posteriori, a valuable extension of our knowledge, etc.) that S if and only if it is informative (a posteriori, etc.) that S′.

The thesis of the substitutivity of co-informational sentences in propositional attitude contexts is the thesis that every proper instance of any of these schemata is true. This may be separated into the thesis of the substitutivity of co-informational sentences in assertion contexts and so on for each of the attitudes. The thesis, or theses, is virtually a logical consequence of the idea that the object or content of a given belief, piece of knowledge, etc., is a piece of information, or a "proposition", and that a sentence encoding that information thereby gives the content of the belief. This idea, or something like it, is a commonplace in the philosophy of language; it is usually taken for granted without challenge by both sides in philosophical disputes over related issues (such as the question of the logical form of belief attributions). Some philosophers, in an effort to rescue a favored theory of propositions from the pitfalls of propositional attitude contexts, have rejected the thesis of substitutivity of co-informational (or co-propositional) sentences in propositional attitude contexts. But doing so seems both extreme and ad hoc. If the favored theory of propositions conflicts with the thesis, it would be more plausible to reject the theory.[8]

Insofar as some of the substitutivity theses are accepted as plausible principles concerning the relation between the pieces of information contained in a sentence and the content of an attitude (belief, knowledge, etc.) thereby expressed, they yield an important procedure for establishing that two given pieces of information are distinct. One may simply rely on our ordinary, everyday criteria, whatever they happen to be, for correctly saying that someone believes or knows something or does not believe or know it. We do not have to be able to specify these criteria; we need only to be able to apply them correctly in certain paradigm cases.

Now, there is no denying that, given the proper circumstances, we say things like 'Lois Lane does not realize (know, believe) that Clark Kent is Superman' and 'There was a time when it was not known that Hesperus is Phosphorus'. Such pronouncements are in clear violation of the modified naive theory taken together with the thesis of substitutivity of co-informational sentences in doxastic and epistemic contexts. When we make these utterances, we typically do not intend to be speaking elliptically or figuratively; we take ourselves to be speaking literally and truthfully. Of course, one could intentionally utter such sentences in a metaphorical vein, or as an ellipsis for something else, but such circumstances are quite different from the usual circumstances in which such utterances are made, which are so familiar to teachers and students of contemporary analytic philosophy. The crucial question, however, is whether when we say such things we are correctly applying the criteria that govern the correct use of propositional-attitude locutions.

Recently a number of philosophers, mostly under the influence of the direct reference theory, have expressed doubt about the literal truth of such utterances in ordinary usage. If someone believes that Hesperus is a planet, they claim, then, strictly speaking, he or she also believes that Phosphorus is a planet, regardless of what the philosophically untutored or unenlightened

say about his or her belief state. Whatever fact such speakers are attempting to convey by denying the belief ascription, the fact is not the lack of the ascribed belief but something else—perhaps the lack of a corresponding metalinguistic belief to the effect that a certain sentence is true. It is my view that this general approach to these problems is essentially correct, as far as it has been developed. The major problem with this approach is that it has not been developed far enough. I shall say more about this in due course. First, however, it is important to note a glaring philosophical difficulty inherent in this approach.

It is easy nowadays to get caught up in direct-reference mania, but one should never be blinded to possible departures from standard and generally reliable philosophical method and practice. What is ordinarily said in everyday language about a certain set of circumstances—where we take ourselves to be speaking literally and truthfully, and where the circumstances are judged to constitute a paradigm case of what we are saying, etc.—is often regarded as an important datum, sometimes the only possible datum, relevant to a certain philosophical or conceptual question about the facts in the matter. Of course, what we ordinarily say in everyday language is sometimes misleading, sometimes irrelevant, sometimes just plain wrong, but in cases where the issue concerns the applicability or inapplicability of a certain concept or term ordinary usage is often the best available guide to the facts. Consider, for example, the sorts of considerations invoked by epistemologists in deciding that Edmund Gettier's celebrated examples constitute genuine counterexamples to the traditional analysis of knowledge as justified true belief, or the sorts of considerations invoked by philosophers of perception in deciding that the state of experiencing a visual impression that is in fact caused by and resembles a certain external object is not the same thing as *seeing* the object. In the familiar problem cases, we simply do not say that the subject *knows* the relevant piece of information,

or that he or she *sees* the relevant object. That is
not the way we speak. Our forbearance in attributing knowledge or visual perception in these
cases is rightly taken as conclusive evidence that
such attributions are strictly false, given the
actual and ordinary meanings of 'know' and
'see'. Philosophical programs such as that of analyzing knowledge or that of analyzing perception are, in a significant sense, at least partly an
attempt to specify and articulate the implicit criteria or principles that govern the correct application of such terms as 'know' and 'see'. It is
precisely for this reason that philosophers so
often consult linguistic intuition in doing epistemology or metaphysics. Ordinary language is
relevant because it is, at least to some extent,
ordinary language that is under investigation.
And ordinary usage is a reliable guide to the
principles governing the correct use of ordinary
language. When the traditional analyses of
knowledge or perception are challenged
through thought experiments concerning what
we would say in certain problem cases, philosophers are rightly skeptical of the reply that
ordinary usage is incorrect and that the subject
does indeed know the proposition in question,
or see the object in question, even though we
typically say that he or she does not. Anyone
maintaining this position may well by suspected
of protecting an invested interest in the theory
being challenged, rather than pursuing in good
faith the philosopher's primary purpose of seeking truth no matter where the facts may lead.
This is not to disparage such concepts as *justified*
true belief and *experiencing a visual impression caused by*
and resembling an external object. Such concepts may be
epistemologically important. However, they
demonstrably do not correspond—at least, they
do not correspond exactly—to the everyday criteria that are implicit in ordinary usage for
knowing or seeing. These criteria are, in a significant sense, *what are in question.*

Similarly, the claim that Lois Lane does,
strictly speaking, believe and even know that
Clark Kent is Superman (since she knows that he

is Clark Kent) must not be made lightly, lest
he or she who makes it be placed under the
same suspicion. For here the question concerns,
at least partly, the tacit principles governing
the correct use of ordinary-language words such
as 'believe', and the ordinary-usage evidence
against the claim is strong indeed. The plain fact
is that we simply do not speak that way. Perhaps
we should learn to use a language in which
propositional-attitude idioms function in strict
accordance with the modified naive theory
across the board, including the troublesome
'Hesperus'–'Phosphorus' and 'Cicero'–'Tully'
cases, since ordinary language already agrees
with the modified naive theory in the other,
more commonplace sorts of cases. But that is a
question for prescriptive philosophy of language, not one for descriptive philosophy of
language. The more immediate and pressing
philosophical question concerns the actual criteria that are implicitly at work in the everyday
notion of belief, and the other attitudes, in their
crude form, as they arise in real life without
theoretical or aesthetic alteration.

I maintain that, according to these very criteria (in the standard sort of circumstance), it
is, strictly speaking, correct to say that Lois Lane
does know that Clark Kent is Superman, and that
when ordinary speakers deny this they are typically operating under a linguistic confusion, systematically misapplying the criteria that govern
the applicability or inapplicability of their own
doxastic and epistemic terms and concepts.
Similarly, anyone who knows that Hesperus is
Hesperus knows that Hesperus is Phosphorus,
no matter how strongly he or she may deny
the latter. Moreover, anyone who knows that
he or she knows that Hesperus is Hesperus
also knows that he or she knows that Hesperus
is Phosphorus, no matter how self-consciously
he or she may disbelieve that Hesperus is
Phosphorus.[9]

These claims clash sharply with ordinary
usage. Whereas it is (as I have argued) extremely
important not to lose sight of the tried and true

philosophical tool of looking to ordinary usage in such matters, it is equally important to recognize the limitations of that test. Ordinary usage is a reliable guide to correct usage, but it is only a guide. Ordinary usage can sometimes be incorrect usage. Even when the ordinary usage of a certain locution is systematic, it can be systematically incorrect—if, for example, the language is deficient in ways that compel speakers to violate its rules in order to convey what they intend, or if the principles and social conventions governing the appropriateness of certain utterances require certain systematic violations of the principles and rules governing correct and incorrect applications of the terms used. My claim is that ordinary usage with regard to such predicates as 'is aware that Clark Kent is Superman' and 'believes that Hesperus is Phosphorus' conflicts with the criteria governing their correct application in just this way. However inappropriate it may be in most contexts to say so, Lois Lane is (according to the myth) fully aware that Clark Kent is Superman, and anyone who believes that Hesperus is Hesperus does in fact believe that Hesperus is Phosphorus. We do not speak this way; in fact, it is customary to say just the opposite. But if we wish to utter what is true, and if we care nothing about social convention, we should speak this way. The customary way of speaking involves us in uttering falsehoods.

Of course, it is no defense of the modified naive theory simply to make these bold claims. It is incumbent on the philosopher who makes these claims (i.e., me) to offer some reason for supposing that ordinary speakers, in the normal course of things, would be led to distort the rules of language systematically, so that ordinary usage cannot be relied upon in these cases as a guide to the correct-applicability conditions of the relevant terms and concepts. The account I shall offer is complex. The main part of this account will be given in section 8.4 [see original reading]. For now, a tentative account is provided by repeating the distinction between semantically encoded and pragmatically

imparted information. If one is not careful to keep this distinction in mind, it is altogether too easy to confuse information pragmatically imparted by (utterances of) 'Hesperus is Phosphorus' for semantically encoded information. In saying that A believes that Hesperus is Phosphorus, taken literally, we are merely attributing to A a relation (belief) to a certain piece of information (the information semantically encoded by 'Hesperus is Phosphorus'). The 'that'-clause 'that Hesperus is Phosphorus' functions here as a means for referring to that piece of information. Since the form of words 'Hesperus is Phosphorus' is considerably richer in pragmatic impartations than other expressions having the same semantic information content (e.g. 'Hesperus is Hesperus'), if one is not careful one cannot help but mistake the 'that'-clause as referring to this somewhat richer information—information which A may not believe. (See note 1.) Utterances of the locution $\ulcorner a$ believes that $S\urcorner$ may even typically involve a Gricean implicature to the effect that the person referred to by a believes the information that is typically pragmatically imparted by utterances of S. Even so, that is not part of the literal content of the belief attribution. The general masses, and most philosophers, are not sufficiently aware of the effect that an implicature of this kind would have on ordinary usage. It is no embarrassment to the modified naive theory that ordinary speakers typically deny literally true belief attributions (and other propositional-attitude attributions) when these attributions involve a 'that'-clause whose utterance typically pragmatically imparts information which the speaker recognizes not to be among the beliefs (or other propositional attitudes) of the subject of the attribution. In fact, it would be an embarrassment to the modified naive theory if speakers did not do this. With widespread ignorance of the significance of the distinction between semantically encoded and pragmatically imparted information, such violation of the rules of the language is entirely to be expected.

Notes

1   See also Wittgenstein, *Philosophical Grammar* (Berkeley: University of California Press, 1974), at pp. 315–318; *Philosophical Investigations* (New York: Macmillan), at p. 216. For a more recent endorsement of the general strategy see Ian Hacking, "Comment on Wiggins," in *Philosophy of Logic*, ed. S. Körner (Berkeley: University of California Press, 1976).

2   A word of clarification is needed concerning my use of the semantic predicates 'encode' and 'information'. Throughout this book I am concerned with discrete units of information that are specifiable by means of a 'that'-clause, e.g. the information that Socrates was wise. These discrete units are *pieces of information*. I shall generally use the mass noun 'information' as if it were shorthand for the count noun phrase 'piece of information', i.e., as a general term whose extension is the class of pieces of information. Thus, I write 'information that is such-and-such' to mean "pieces of information that are such-and-such," 'the same information' to mean "the same pieces of information," 'different information' to mean "different pieces of information," and so on. I use the verb 'encode' in such a way that an unambiguous declarative sentence encodes (with respect to a given possible context c) a *single* piece of information, which is referred to (with respect to c) by the result of prefixing 'the information that' to the sentence and which is to be called 'the information content' of the sentence (with respect to c). A declarative sentence may encode (with respect to a given context) two or more pieces of information, but if it does so it is ambiguous. Pieces of information encoded by the logical consequences of an unambiguous sentence are not themselves encoded, in this sense, by the sentence. The (piece of) information that snow is white and grass is green is different information (a different piece of information) from the (piece of) information that snow is white, though intuitively the latter is included as part of the former. The sentence 'Snow is white and grass is green' encodes only the former, not the latter. This constitutes a departure from at least one standard usage, according to which the information content of a sentence is perhaps something like a class of pieces of information, closed under logical consequence.

I am not concerned in this book with a notion of an *amount* of information, which arises in the mathematical theory of communication or information. The information *that snow is white and grass is green and Socrates is Socrates* may be no more or less information than the information *that both snow is white if and only if grass is green and either snow is white or grass is green*. Nevertheless, general considerations involving Leibniz's Law strongly suggest that they are numerically distinct pieces of information. For instance, the first concerns Socrates whereas the second does not.

3   R. Sharvy, "Why a Class Can't Change Its Members," *Noûs* 2, no. 4 (1968): 303–314.

4   One pair of sentences proposed to me as a counterinstance to Frege's Law in correspondence by a prominent philosopher of logic and semantics is ' 'Hesperus' refers to Hesperus' (uninformative) and ' 'Hesperus' refers to Phosphorus' (informative). I shall criticize the claim that Frege's Law *could be* (let alone that it is) subject to counterexample, but perhaps a special caveat is called for in connection with this particular example. These two sentences are equally informative, in the sense of the term 'informative' that is relevant to Frege's Puzzle. In particular, even the first sentence is informative—and not simply because it entails the nontrivial fact that 'Hesperus' is not nonreferring. The sentence 'If 'Hesperus' refers to anything, it refers to Hesperus' is equally informative, in the relevant sense. (In this connection, see Kripke, *Naming and Necessity*, pp. 68–70.) These sentences are not only informative, they (or, more accurate, their information contents) are the subject of serious dispute among semanticists. Richard Montague denied that 'Hesperus' refers to Hesperus, as did Russell. (See note 2 to chapter 3 [of the original reading].) If a semantic oracle were to have pronounced the truth that 'Hesperus' does indeed refer to Hesperus, these philosophers should have found the pronouncement only too painfully informative. (More probably, they might have denounced the oracle as a fraud.) The sentence ' 'Hesperus' refers to Hesperus' is, by itself and in abstraction from context, incomplete. Reference is a relation among expressions, objects, and linguistic systems; names refer to things (or fail to refer to things) in this or that language, or in this or that idiolect. There are (possible) languages in which 'Hesperus' refers to

nothing, and still others in which it refers to the Milky Way. The information that 'Hesperus' refers to Hesperus in English is a nontrivial piece of information about English. Things might have been otherwise, and it is not "given" or known a priori what the expression 'Hesperus' refers to in English.

One sentence that might be correctly regarded as uninformative, in the relevant sense, and is easily confused with ' 'Hesperus' refers to Hesperus', is the following: 'The sentence ' 'Hesperus' refers to Hesperus in English' is true 'in English*', where 'English*' refers to the extension of English into a metalanguage for English. The apparent triviality of this meta-metatheoretic sentence is no doubt the source of the erroneous claim that ' 'Hesperus' refers to Hesperus' is uninformative. But, as we shall see, it is crucial in discussing Frege's Puzzle to maintain a sharp distinction between the information content of a sentence S and the further and separate metalinguistic information that S is true. Frege's Puzzle concerns the former, and not generally the latter. The reasons behind the apparent triviality of the meta-metatheoretic sentence mentioned above are complex (see Kripke, *Naming and Necessity*, pp. 68–70), but in no way does this sentence present a problem for Frege's Law. That the two original sentences are equally informative does not entail that they semantically encode the same piece of information. It does entail that the modified-naive-theorist, in claiming that they encode the same information, has nothing to fear from Frege's Law.

5 R. Carnap, "Reply to Leonard Linsky," *Philosophy of Science* 16, no. 4 (1949): 347–350, at pp. 347–348.

6 In claiming that Frege and Russell and their followers have mistaken pragmatically imparted information for semantically encoded information, I do not mean that they would assent to such things as 'The sentence 'Hesperus is Phosphorus' expresses in English the information about itself that it is true'. Clearly they would not; in any case, they need not. Nor would someone who mistakes a particular celebrity impersonator for the president of the United States assent to 'The president is the celebrity impersonator'. Philosophers mistake pragmatically imparted information for semantically encoded information in failing to keep the two sharply distinct and consequently judging whether a sentence

S is informative partly on the basis of information pragmatically imparted by utterances of S.

Other writers have drawn distinctions similar to the one drawn here between semantically encoded and pragmatically imparted information as part of a defense of something like the original or the modified naive theory, though I came upon the idea independently. See Michael Tye, "The Puzzle of Hesperus and Phosphorus," *Australasian Journal of Philosophy* 56, no. 3 (1978): 219–224, at p. 224; Raymond Bradley and Norman Swartz, *Possible Worlds: An Introduction to Logic and Its Philosophy* (Indianapolis: Hackett, 1979), at pp. 191–192; Tom McKay, "On Proper Names in Belief Ascriptions," *Philosophical Studies* 39 (1981): 287–303, at pp. 294–295; R. M. Sainsbury, "On a Fregean Argument for the Distinctness of Sense and Reference," *Analysis* 43 (January 1983): 12–14; Takashi Yagisawa, Meaning and Belief, Ph.D. diss., Princeton University, 1981; J. Paul Reddam, Pragmatics and the Language of Belief, Ph.D. diss., University of Southern California, 1982. However, there are subtleties involved in Frege's Puzzle that these writers do not discuss. These subtleties will be developed in chapter 7 of this book [of the original reading] with a new and stronger version of the puzzle, for which the solution presented here is simply irrelevant. (McKay comes very close to recognizing some of the finer aspects of the puzzle in his note 17, wherein he discusses an example (due to David Kaplan) involving a case of change of mind to suspension of judgment similar to the example to be presented in section 7.2 of this book. McKay's brief discussion of the example does not bring out the moral of my chapter 8.)

7 I am not talking here about overt verbal assent to a *sentence*, but about *mental* assent to a proposition.

The conception of belief as inward assent is apparently advanced by Saint Augustine in chapter 5 of *Predestination of the Saints*, where belief is analyzed as "to think with assent." For an illuminating contemporary discussion of the analysis of belief as assent to an entertained proposition, see H. H. Price, *Belief* (London: Allen and Unwin, 1969), especially series I, lectures 8 and 9, and series II, lectures 1–3.

In suggesting that belief might be understood in terms of inward assent, concurrence, or approval, I am not suggesting a reduction of belief to a phenomenological episode (in the style of Hume). By 'inward assent', etc., I do not mean merely a private, subjective experience directed toward or involving the relevant piece of information (such as the experience one typically has when reading or saying the words 'yes, I agree' to oneself, together with a "feeling of understanding" of these words, etc.). Such an analysis would be unacceptable for familiar philosophical reasons: In unusual circumstances someone could have these experiences without believing, and without even grasping, the proposition. By 'inward assent', etc., I mean a state of *cognition*, with everything that this entails.

Furthermore, in speaking of a *disposition* to inward assent, or other favorable *dispositions*, I do not mean merely an inclination, tendency, or propensity to assent, etc. (the usual philosophical use of 'disposition' as in, e.g., 'dispositional property'). Here again, it is possible for someone to have such inclinations without believing the proposition, and vice versa. In saying that someone is favorably "disposed" toward something, I mean that the person harbors a positive, favorable attitude (e.g. agreement, as opposed to disagreement or indifference) toward the thing. Typically, the harboring of this attitude will result in certain inclinations or propensities, but that is not part of the analysis of the attitude, and in extraordinary circumstances the harboring of the favorable attitude may not result in the typical inclinations. Conversely, the inclinations may be present in the absence of the favorable attitude. It is probably best to speak of 'attitudes' rather than 'dispositions'. So understood, the suggested analysis may appear unilluminating, but then at least it is not controversial.

I use the term 'believe', and its cognates, in such a way that one believes that S if one is convinced that S, of the opinion that S, confident that S, persuaded that S, etc., but it is not sufficient that one merely thinks it likely that S, guesses that S, suspects that S theorizes that S, assumes that S, or supposes that S.

8   I have in mind theories like that given by Robert Stalnaker in "Assertion," in *Syntax and Semantics 9: Pragmatics*, ed. P. Cole (New York: Academic, 1978). See also Stalnaker, "Indexical Belief," *Synthèse* 49, no. 1 (1981): 129–151; David Lewis, "What Puzzling Pierre Believes," *Australasian Journal of Philosophy* 59, no. 3 (1981): 283–289. The favored theory of

propositions here is one that identifies propositions with sets of possible worlds—a theory on which propositions are even more coarse-grained than on the modified naive theory—though that is largely irrelevant to the main idea behind Stalnaker's account. Stalnaker claims that, in at least some propositional-attitude contexts, a 'that'-clause, ⌜that S⌝, will sometimes refer not to the proposition expressed by the sentence S but instead to a related proposition, which Stalnaker calls 'the diagonal proposition of the propositional concept for S'. This so-called diagonal proposition, if it is a proposition at all, is best identified as the singular proposition about S that it is true—or, more accurate, as the proposition *that the proposition semantically encoded by S, as uttered in a context, is true*. (Stalnaker shows reluctance to so identify the diagonal proposition. The coarse-grainedness of his favored theory of propositions enables him to avoid specifying the relevant proposition in this way; however, from the point of view of a more fine-grained theory (such as the modified naive theory or the Fregean theory), the metatheoretic proposition that S is true is the most plausible candidate for being the diagonal proposition.) I shall not argue the point fully here. For present purposes, it is sufficient that this be one way of understanding what Stalnaker means by 'the diagonal proposition'. In effect, then, on Stalnaker's theory a 'that'-clause ⌜that S⌝ may be ambiguous. It sometimes refers to the proposition encoded by S, and it sometimes refers to a different, metatheoretic proposition about S itself. Rather than postulate this sort of complexity or ambiguity in connection with 'that'-clauses, it would be more plausible to claim that, in some cases, the speaker reporting a propositional attitude strictly speaking misspoke and, for complete accuracy, should have used a more complicated formal-mode 'that'-clause in place of the material-mode 'that'-clause used.

9   This consequence of the modified naive theory concerning nesting of propositional-attitude operators often goes unnoticed. In an attempt to soften the blow of the modified naive theory, it is sometimes argued that, for example, though the ancients strictly speaking did believe the proposition that Hesperus is Phosphorus, since this is just the trivial proposition that Hesperus is Hesperus, they did not realize that the proposition that Hesperus is

Phosphorus is really the very same proposition as the trivial proposition that Hesperus is Hesperus, and hence they did not realize that they believed that Hesperus is Phosphorus. Similarly, it is sometimes argued that, since the name 'Hamlet' from Shakespeare's fiction actually refers to no one, there is no such thing as a proposition that Hamlet does not exist, and hence the sentence 'Hamlet does not exist' strictly speaking has no information content, but still there is a proposition that there exists no proposition that Hamlet does not exist, and it is true. All of this is inconsistent with the modifed naive theory. On the modified naive theory, if a is a single-word singular term (individual constant), then for any sentence ϕ_a containing a, barring quotation marks and other such aberrant devices, the 'that'-clause $\ulcorner$that $\phi_a\urcorner$ refers to the singular proposition that is the information content of the sentence. It is tempting to think of the 'that'-term as a sort of description of the proposition by specifying its components, like $\ulcorner$the proposition made up of a and the property of being $\phi\urcorner$, analogous to a set-theoretic abstraction term $\ulcorner\langle a$, the property of being $\phi\rangle\urcorner$. But this is incorrect. A set-abstraction term $\ulcorner(\hat{x})\phi_x\urcorner$ may be regarded as a special sort of definite description, since it is equivalent to $\ulcorner(\imath y)[Set(y)$ & $(x)(x \in y \; \Xi \; \phi_x)]\urcorner$. Thus, a set-abstraction term is descriptional—specifically, descriptional in terms of the property of being a set with such-and-such membership. The 'that'-operator attaches to a sentence to form a singular term referring to the sentence's information content. Since 'that Plato is wise' refers to a different proposition from 'that the author of The Republic is wise', however, one cannot see the 'that'-term as referring to its referent proposition by mentioning the components of the referent proposition. Plato is not a component of the proposition that the author of The Republic is wise, though he is referred to by the component term 'the author of The Republic'. In a word, the 'that'-operator is nonextensional. One should think of the 'that'-operator as analogous to quotation marks, and of a 'that'-term $\ulcorner$that $S\urcorner$ as analogous to a quotation name, only referring to the information content of S rather than S itself. (See the introduction on the 'that'-operator.) A 'that'-clause $\ulcorner$that $\phi_a\urcorner$, then, is a singular term whose information value is the ordered pair of the information value of the 'that'-operator and the information content of ϕ_a, the letter being a singular

proposition p about the referent of a. A sentence involving this 'that'-clause, $\ulcorner\psi[$that $\phi_a]\urcorner$, encodes a singular proposition about the proposition p, to wit, that (the proposition identical with) it is ψ, and the 'that'-clause formed from this sentence, $\ulcorner$that $\psi[$that $\phi_a]\urcorner$, refers to this singular proposition about p. If b is any proper name or other single-word singular term co-referential with a, then $\ulcorner$that $\phi_b\urcorner$ refers to the very same proposition p, and $\ulcorner\psi[$that $\phi_b]\urcorner$ encodes the same singular proposition about p that (the proposition identical with) it is ψ, so that $\ulcorner$that $\psi[$that $\phi_a]\urcorner$ and $\ulcorner$that $\psi[$that $\phi_b]\urcorner$ are co-referential. In particular, if the sentence 'Jones realizes that he believes that Hesperus is Hesperus' is true, then what Jones realizes is a certain singular proposition about the proposition that Hesperus is Hesperus, to the effect that he believes it. Since the proposition that Hesperus is Hesperus is, according to the modified naive theory, the same proposition as the proposition that Hesperus is Phosphorus, another way of specifying what Jones realizes, according to the modified naive theory, is 'that Jones believes that Hesperus is Phosphorus'. Hence, on the modified naive theory, if the original sentence is true, so is 'Jones realizes that he believes that Hesperus is Phosphorus'. The proposition that Jones believes that Hesperus is Hesperus is the same proposition as the proposition that Jones believes that Hesperus is Phosphorus, and thus if Jones realizes the former he realizes the latter. Similarly, if the nonexistence of Hamlet means that there is no such proposition as the proposition that Hamlet does not exist, then it also means that there is no such proposition as the proposition that the proposition that Hamlet does not exist does not itself exist. Few philosophers—even direct-reference theorists who accede to the modified-naive-theoretical claim that the ancients strictly speaking believed that Hesperus is Phosphorus—have been willing to endorse these further consequences of the modified naive theory. Properly seen, however, they are no more unacceptable than the better-known controversial consequences of the modified naive theory.

These points concerning nested occurrences of 'that'-clauses are important in connection with the modified naive theory's account of Mates's problem concerning nested propositional attitude contexts. See appendix B [in original reading].

PART THREE

Definite descriptions: quantifiers or singular terms?

INTRODUCTION TO PART THREE

SINGULAR TERMS ARE EXPRESSIONS whose role it is to pick out, or denote, individual objects, and whose contributions to the meanings of sentences in which they feature may be isolated as single 'units of significance'. As we saw in Part Two, direct reference theorists think of these units as the terms' *referents*, while Fregeans maintain that they are the terms' *senses:* i.e. (objective, mind-independent) *modes* under which the referents are *presented* (to speakers). As also emerged in Part Two, Frege's main reason for attributing senses to proper names and other singular terms was that it allowed him to explain apparent differences in *cognitive value* between pairs of sentences which differ only in respect of co-referring singular terms. Another motivation for the invocation of senses is that it allows Frege to explain the meaningfulness of sentences containing singular terms which lack referents – e.g. 'Ulysses', 'the least converging series', etc.

Bertrand Russell agreed with Frege that pairs of sentences like those Frege used to defend his invocation of sense differ in cognitive value, and he accepted that many terms which appear to denote individual objects are meaningful whether or not the objects exist. However, Russell was deeply suspicious of Frege's notion of sense. In his most celebrated contribution to the philosophy of language – the 1905 paper, 'On Denoting' – he undertook to explain these and other data without recourse to anything like it. In the piece we present below – a chapter from his 1919 book, *Introduction to Mathematical Philosophy* – he does not discuss Fregean sense, but he reprises much of the argument of 'On Denoting', and he does so in what most commentators agree to be neater and more accessible terms.

Russell uses the word 'name' for what we have been describing as a singular term, and as you might expect given his scepticism about sense, the account he favours of the semantics of such expressions is the direct reference view. In these works, however, Russell's principal focus is on singular *definite descriptions* – complex expressions such as 'the capital city of France', which pick out individual objects by specifying properties they uniquely exhibit. Frege and others assumed that definite descriptions are singular terms. Grammatically, they play the same kinds of roles in sentences as proper names, and like names they are usually associated with – or as we shall say, *satisfied by* – particular individual objects. Against this, Russell maintains that definite descriptions are not names – i.e. (in our terms) are not singular terms. He accepts that definite descriptions occupy name-like positions in sentences, but he contends that the structure of the proposition expressed by a sentence containing a definite description does not mirror that of the sentence. In particular, the proposition expressed by such a sentence does not 'contain a constituent' corresponding to the definite description. Thus it does not incorporate anything which might be characterized as the description's *referent*, or indeed for that matter, as its *sense*.[1]

So what, according to Russell, is the structure of a proposition expressed by a sentence containing a definite description? To introduce Russell's answer to this question we need to say a little about *quantification*. Compare the following sentences:

(1)   Bertrand Russell is bald
(2)   A man is bald.

Sentence (1) contains a proper name: 'Bertrand Russell'. As we saw in Part Two above, philosophers disagree over the analysis of the semantics of names (e.g. over whether names have senses as well as referents). But notwithstanding such differences, most agree that the proposition expressed by a sentence such as (1) incorporates a constituent corresponding to the name. Sentence (2) contains what Russell terms an 'indefinite' or 'ambiguous' description: the phrase 'a man'. As that phrase seems to occupy the same position in (2) as is occupied by the name in (1), it may be tempting to expect an analysis of the proposition expressed by (2) to disclose a constituent corresponding to that phrase. At the beginning of the chapter below, Russell rebuts this, by arguing that sentences like (2) are not about particular objects. (2) does not express a proposition which predicates baldness of a particular man. What it expresses, rather, is a proposition about the *quantity* of objects which exhibit certain features or properties: it says that *at least one object is human and bald*.

Next consider a similar-looking sentence featuring a singular definite description in place of the name:

(3)   The present king of France is bald.

Russell's contention is that here, the phrase 'the present king of France' operates semantically much like 'a man' in (2), as a device of quantification, and so (3) expresses a proposition which is more perspicuously expressed by something like the following:

(4)   *Exactly one* object is a present king of France, and any object which is a king of France is bald.[2]

Because this analysis does not posit within the proposition expressed by (3) a constituent corresponding to the definite description, it is not hampered by the fact that in this case the description is not satisfied by any object.

Notice that (although Russell does not discuss this explicitly below) the analysis would also allow Russell to explain the difference in cognitive value between pairs

---

[1] Beware: a confusing aspect of Russell's writing is his use of the word 'proposition'. Sometimes he seems to use this term to mean *sentence*, and at other times he seems to mean *what is expressed* by a sentence, or the meaning of a sentence. We use the term in the second of these ways.

[2] Russell's formulation is in fact more complicated than this. Readers should consider whether there are any significant differences between the two formulations.

of sentences which differ only in respect of co-referring definite descriptions. Consider, e.g.:

(5)   The capital of France has nearly 12 million inhabitants
(6)   The city which hosted the 1924 Olympic Games has nearly 12 million inhabitants.

Russell would say that to believe the proposition expressed by (5) is to believe that there is exactly one object which is a capital city of France, and that any such object has nearly 12 million inhabitants; and that to believe the proposition expressed by (6) is to believe that there is exactly one object which hosted the 1924 Olympic Games, and that any such object has nearly 12 million inhabitants. One could have one of these beliefs without having the other.

It is plausible, then, that Russell's analysis of definite descriptions explains (at least some of) the data that Frege sought to account for in terms of the notion of sense, at least insofar as those data involve sentences featuring definite descriptions. However, a Fregean would observe that sentences featuring proper names give rise to analogous problems: e.g. 'Ulysses', lacks a referent, 'Bob Dylan' and 'Robert Zimmerman' are co-referring, etc. We shall postpone discussion of this issue until Part Five, but here we observe that towards the end of the first reading below, Russell appears to endorse a proposal that bears on it: i.e. that – appearances not-withstanding – such expressions are not really names (i.e. not really singular terms) but are 'abbreviated description[s]'.

In the second reading below, P. F. Strawson mounts an influential critique of Russell's theory of definite descriptions. Since there is currently no king of France, sentence (3) is not true. Russell inferred from this that it is false, and his theory is designed (inter alia) to accommodate this. According to Strawson, the error here is the assumption that sentences – considered, as it were, in the abstract – are true or false, and that expressions – considered in the abstract – refer. Consider a sentence containing an indexical expression, e.g.:

(7)   He is bald.

(7) can be used to express a truth on certain occasions, and on others it can be used to express a falsehood. Plausibly, there are also occasions – those on which the speaker has nobody in particular 'in mind' – on which the indexical expression, 'He', refers to nobody, and in which the sentence expresses neither a truth nor a falsehood. Strawson maintains that in general it is not *sentences* which are true or false, but particular *uses* that speakers make of them. Moreover, he argues, although a seventeenth-century use of (3) might have been true or false, a contemporary use is neither.

Strawson also argues that Russell's claim that definite descriptions are quantificational devices misrepresents the occasions on which sentences such as (3) are used truly or falsely. That exactly one object is a king of France is *presupposed* or 'implied' by someone who uses (3) to say something true or false; it is not part of what she *says*.

Our final selection is Russell's entertainingly bad-tempered reply to Strawson. In response to Strawson's first point, Russell concedes, in effect, that sentences featuring indexical (or 'egocentric') expressions such as 'he' in (7) and 'present' in (3) can be used to say different things on different occasions. However he insists that sentences featuring definite descriptions do not *in general* exhibit this characteristic, and he offers some examples of descriptions which appear not to.

Questions and tasks

1   How does Russell argue that 'no actual man enters into' what is asserted by the sentence, 'I met a man'?
2   How, according to Russell, do logicians such as Meinong attempt to deal with definite descriptions which aren't satisfied by anything, by positing 'unreal objects'? Are Russell's objections to this approach compelling?
3   Which part or parts (if any) of the proposition expressed by 'The king of France is bald' correspond to the expression 'The king of France'?
4   Why do you think Russell suggests that when we ask whether Homer existed, we use the word 'Homer' as an 'abbreviated description'?
5   Although he rejects Russell's assumption that sentences – opposed to *uses* of sentences – are true or false, Strawson concedes that sentences are *meaningful*. Explain and evaluate his account of sentence meaning.
6   Consider a conversational situation in which you say to a friend, 'The car in which I learned to drive was a Ford'. Do you think the proposition that a particular car exists (or existed) is part of what you *said*, or is that proposition merely something 'implied' by what you said – something which the two of you *presupposed*?
7   In the third reading below, does Russell address (whether explicitly or implicitly) the most serious of Strawson's objections? If so, is his response convincing?

References and further reading

Bezuidenhout, A., and M. Reimer (eds) 2003: *Descriptions and Beyond: An Inter-disciplinary Collection of Essays on Definite and Indefinite Descriptions*, Oxford: Oxford University Press.

Donnellan, K. 1966: 'Reference and Definite Descriptions', *Philosophical Review* 75, pp. 281–304.

Donnellan, K. 1978: 'Speaker Reference, Descriptions, and Anaphora', in P. Cole (ed.), *Syntax and Semantics*, 9: *Pragmatics*. New York: Academic Press, pp. 47–68.

Kripke, S. 1977: 'Speaker's Reference and Semantic Reference', in P. French, T. Uehling and H. Wettstein (eds), *Contemporary Perspectives in the Philosophy of Language*, Minneapolis: University of Minnesota Press, pp. 255–76.

Larson, R., and G. Segal 1995: *Knowledge of Meaning*, Cambridge, MA: MIT Press.

Ludlow, P. 2008: 'Descriptions', in Edward N. Zalta (ed.), *The Stanford Encyclopedia of Philosophy* (Fall 2008 edn), http://plato.stanford.edu/archives/fall2008/entries/descriptions/

Neale, S. 1990: *Descriptions*, Cambridge, MA: MIT Press.

Oliver, A. 2003: 'A Few more Remarks on Logical Form', *Proceedings of the Aristotelian Society* 99, pp. 247–72.

Ramachandran, M. 1993: 'A Strawsonian Objection to Russell's Theory of Descriptions', *Analysis* 53, pp. 209–12.

Recanati, F. 1986: 'Contextual Dependence and Definite Descriptions', *Proceedings of the Aristotelian Society* 87, pp. 57–73.

Russell, B. 1905: 'On Denoting', *Mind* 14, pp. 479–93.

Sainsbury, M. 1995: 'Philosophical Logic', in A. C. Grayling (ed.), *Philosophy: A Guide through the Subject*, Oxford: Oxford University Press, pp. 61–122.

Stanley, J. 1997: 'Names and Rigid Designation', in B. Hale and C. Wright (eds), *A Companion to the Philosophy of Language*. Oxford: Blackwell, pp. 555–85.

Stanley, J., and Z. Szabó. 2000: 'On Quantifier Domain Restriction', *Mind & Language* 15, pp. 219–61.

Wettstein, H. 1981: 'Demonstrative Reference and Definite Descriptions', *Philosophical Studies* 40, pp. 241–57.

Chapter 6

Bertrand Russell

DESCRIPTIONS

[. . .]

A "description" may be of two sorts, definite and indefinite (or ambiguous). An indefinite description is a phrase of the form "a so-and-so," and a definite description is a phrase of the form "the so-and-so" (in the singular). Let us begin with the former.

"Who did you meet?" "I met a man." "That is a very indefinite description." We are therefore not departing from usage in our terminology. Our question is: What do I really assert when I assert "I met a man"? Let us assume, for the moment, that my assertion is true, and that in fact I met Jones. It is clear that what I assert is not "I met Jones." I may say "I met a man, but it was not Jones"; in that case, though I lie, I do not contradict myself, as I should do if when I say I met a man I really mean that I met Jones. It is clear also that the person to whom I am speaking can understand what I say, even if he is a foreigner and has never heard of Jones.

But we may go further: not only Jones, but no actual man, enters into my statement. This becomes obvious when the statement is false, since then there is no more reason why Jones should be supposed to enter into the proposition than why anyone else should. Indeed the statement would remain significant, though it could not possibly be true, even if there were no man at all. "I met a unicorn" or "I met a sea-serpent" is a perfectly significant assertion, if we know what

it would be to be a unicorn or a sea-serpent, i.e. what is the definition of these fabulous monsters. Thus it is only what we may call the *concept* that enters into the proposition. In the case of "unicorn," for example, there is only the concept: there is not also, somewhere among the shades, something unreal which may be called "a unicorn." Therefore, since it is significant (though false) to say "I met a unicorn," it is clear that this proposition, rightly analysed, does not contain a constituent "a unicorn," though it does contain the concept "unicorn."

The question of "unreality," which confronts us at this point, is a very important one. Misled by grammar, the great majority of those logicians who have dealt with this question have dealt with it on mistaken lines. They have regarded grammatical form as a surer guide in analysis than, in fact, it is. And they have not known what differences in grammatical form are important. "I met Jones" and "I met a man" would count traditionally as propositions of the same form, but in actual fact they are of quite different forms: the first names an actual person, Jones; while the second involves a propositional function, and becomes, when made explicit: "The function 'I met x and x is human' is sometimes true." (It will be remembered that we adopted the convention of using "sometimes" as not implying more than once.) This proposition is obviously not of the form "I met x," which accounts for the existence of the proposition "I met a unicorn" in spite of the fact that there is no such thing as "a unicorn."

For want of the apparatus of propositional functions, many logicians have been driven to the conclusion that there are unreal objects. It is argued, *e.g.* by Meinong,[1] that we can speak about "the golden mountain," "the round square," and so on; we can make true propositions of which these are the subjects; hence they must have some kind of logical being, since otherwise the propositions in which they occur would be meaningless. In such theories, it seems to me, there is a failure of that feeling for reality which ought to be preserved even in the most abstract studies. Logic, I should maintain, must no more admit a unicorn than zoology can; for logic is concerned with the real world just as truly as zoology, though with its more abstract and general features. To say that unicorns have an existence in heraldry, or in literature, or in imagination, is a most pitiful and paltry evasion. What exists in heraldry is not an animal, made of flesh and blood, moving and breathing of its own initiative. What exists is a picture, or a description in words. Similarly, to maintain that Hamlet, for example, exists in his own world, namely, in the world of Shakespeare's imagination, just as truly as (say) Napoleon existed in the ordinary world, is to say something deliberately confusing, or else confused to a degree which is scarcely credible. There is only one world, the "real" world: Shakespeare's imagination is part of it, and the thoughts that he had in writing Hamlet are real. So are the thoughts that we have in reading the play. But it is of the very essence of fiction that only the thoughts, feelings, etc., in Shakespeare and his readers are real, and that there is not, in addition to them, an objective Hamlet. When you have taken account of all the feelings roused by Napoleon in writers and readers of history, you have not touched the actual man; but in the case of Hamlet you have come to the end of him. If no one thought about Hamlet, there would be nothing left of him; if no one had thought about Napoleon, he would have

soon seen to it that some one did. The sense of reality is vital in logic, and whoever juggles with it by pretending that Hamlet has another kind of reality is doing a disservice to thought. A robust sense of reality is very necessary in framing a correct analysis of propositions about unicorns, golden mountains, round squares, and other such pseudo-objects.

In obedience to the feeling of reality, we shall insist that, in the analysis of propositions, nothing "unreal" is to be admitted. But, after all, if there is nothing unreal, how, it may be asked, *could* we admit anything unreal? The reply is that, in dealing with propositions, we are dealing in the first instance with symbols, and if we attribute significance to groups of symbols which have no significance, we shall fall into the error of admitting unrealities, in the only sense in which this is possible, namely, as objects described. In the proposition "I met a unicorn," the whole four words together make a significant proposition, and the word "unicorn" by itself is significant, in just the same sense as the word "man." But the two words "a unicorn" do not form a subordinate group having a meaning of its own. Thus if we falsely attribute meaning to these two words, we find ourselves saddled with "a unicorn," and with the problem how there can be such a thing in a world where there are no unicorns. "A unicorn" is an indefinite description which describes nothing. It is not an indefinite description which describes something unreal. Such a proposition as "x is unreal" only has meaning when "x" is a description, definite or indefinite; in that case the proposition will be true if "x" is a description which describes nothing. But whether the description "x" describes something or describes nothing, it is in any case not a constituent of the proposition in which it occurs; like "a unicorn" just now, it is not a subordinate group having a meaning of its own. All this results from the fact that, when "x" is a description, "x is unreal" or "x does not exist" is not nonsense, but is always significant and sometimes true.

We may now proceed to define generally the meaning of propositions which contain ambiguous descriptions. Suppose we wish to make some statement about "a so-and-so," where "so-and-so's" are those objects that have a certain property ϕ, i.e. those objects x for which the propositional function ϕx is true. (E.g. if we take "a man" as our instance of "a so-and-so," ϕx will be "x is human.") Let us now wish to assert the property ψ of "a so-and-so," i.e. we wish to assert that "a so-and-so" has that property which x has when ψx is true. (E.g. in the case of "I met a man," ψx will be "I met x.") Now the proposition that "a so-and-so" has the property ψ is not a proposition of the form "ψx." If it were, "a so-and-so" would have to be identical with x for a suitable x; and although (in a sense) this may be true in some cases, it is certainly not true in such a case as "a unicorn." It is just this fact, that the statement that a so-and-so has the property ψ is not of the form ψx, which makes it possible for "a so-and-so" to be, in a certain clearly definable sense, "unreal." The definition is as follows:

The statement that "an object having the property ϕ has the property ψ"

means:

"The joint assertion of ϕx and ψx is not always false."

So far as logic goes, this is the same proposition as might be expressed by "some ϕ's are ψ's"; but rhetorically there is a difference, because in the one case there is a suggestion of singularity, and in the other case of plurality. This, however, is not the important point. The important point is that, when rightly analysed, propositions verbally about "a so-and-so" are found to contain no constituent represented by this phrase. And that is why such propositions can be significant even when there is no such thing as a so-and-so.

The definition of *existence*, as applied to ambiguous descriptions, results from what was said at the end of the preceding chapter [see original reading]. We say that "men exist" or "a man exists" if the propositional function "x is human" is sometimes true; and generally "a so-and-so" exists if "x is so-and-so" is sometimes true. We may put this in other language. The proposition "Socrates is a man" is no doubt *equivalent* to "Socrates is human," but it is not the very same proposition. The *is* of "Socrates is human" expresses the relation of subject and predicate; the *is* of "Socrates is a man" expresses identity. It is a disgrace to the human race that it has chosen to employ the same word "is" for these two entirely different ideas—a disgrace which a symbolic logical language of course remedies. The identity in "Socrates is a man" is identity between an object named (accepting "Socrates" as a name, subject to qualifications explained later) and an object ambiguously described. An object ambiguously described will "exist" when at least one such proposition is true, i.e. when there is at least one true proposition of the form "x is a so-and-so," where "x" is a name. It is characteristic of ambiguous (as opposed to definite) descriptions that there may be any number of true propositions of the above form—Socrates is a man, Plato is a man, etc. Thus "a man exists" follows from Socrates, or Plato, or anyone else. With definite descriptions, on the other hand, the corresponding form of proposition, namely, "x is the so-and-so" (where "x" is a name), can only be true for one value of x at most. This brings us to the subject of definite descriptions, which are to be defined in a way analogous to that employed for ambiguous descriptions, but rather more complicated.

We come now to the main subject of the present chapter, namely, the definition of the word *the* (in the singular). One very important point about the definition of "a so-and-so" applies equally to "the so-and-so"; the definition to be sought is a definition of propositions in which this phrase occurs, not a definition of the phrase itself in isolation. In the case of "a so-and-so," this is fairly obvious: no one could suppose that "a man" was a definite object, which could be defined by itself. Socrates is a man, Plato is a man, Aristotle is a man, but we cannot infer that "a man" means the same as "Socrates" means and also the same as "Plato" means and also the same as "Aristotle" means, since these three names have different meanings. Nevertheless, when we have enumerated all the men in the world, there is nothing left of which we can say, "This is a man, and not only so, but it is the 'a man,' the quintessential entity that is just an indefinite man without being anybody in particular." It is of course quite clear that whatever there is in the world is definite: if it is a man it is one definite man and not any other. Thus there cannot be such an entity as "a man" to be found in the world, as opposed to specific men. And accordingly it is natural that we do not define "a man" itself, but only the propositions in which it occurs.

In the case of "the so-and-so" this is equally true, though at first sight less obvious. We may demonstrate that this must be the case, by a consideration of the difference between a *name* and a *definite description*. Take the proposition, "Scott is the author of *Waverley*." We have here a name, "Scott," and a description, "the author of *Waverley*," which are asserted to apply to the same person. The distinction between a name and all other symbols may be explained as follows:

A name is a simple symbol whose meaning is something that can only occur as subject, i.e. something of the kind that, in Chapter XIII [see original reading], we defined as an "individual" or a "particular." And a "simple" symbol is one which has no parts that are symbols. Thus "Scott" is a simple symbol, because, though it has parts (namely, separate letters), these parts are not symbols. On the other hand, "the author of *Waverley*" is not a simple symbol, because the separate words that compose the phrase are parts which are symbols. If, as may be the case, whatever *seems* to be an "individual" is really capable of further analysis, we shall have to content

ourselves with what may be called "relative individuals," which will be terms that, throughout the context in question, are never analysed and never occur otherwise than as subjects. And in that case we shall have correspondingly to content ourselves with "relative names." From the standpoint of our present problem, namely, the definition of descriptions, this problem, whether these are absolute names or only relative names, may be ignored, since it concerns different stages in the hierarchy of "types," whereas we have to compare such couples as "Scott" and "the author of *Waverley*," which both apply to the same object, and do not raise the problem of types. We may, therefore, for the moment, treat names as capable of being absolute; nothing that we shall have to say will depend upon this assumption, but the wording may be a little shortened by it.

We have, then, two things to compare: (1) a *name*, which is a simple symbol, directly designating an individual which is its meaning, and having this meaning in its own right, independently of the meanings of all other words; (2) a *description*, which consists of several words, whose meanings are already fixed, and from which results whatever is to be taken as the "meaning" of the description.

A proposition containing a description is not identical with what that proposition becomes when a name is substituted, even if the name names the same object as the description describes. "Scott is the author of *Waverley*" is obviously a different proposition from "Scott is Scott": the first is a fact in literary history, the second a trivial truism. And if we put anyone other than Scott in place of "the author of *Waverley*," our proposition would become false, and would therefore certainly no longer be the same proposition. But, it may be said, our proposition is essentially of the same from as (say) "Scott is Sir Walter," in which two names are said to apply to the same person. The reply is that, if "Scott is Sir Walter" really means "the person named 'Scott' is the person named 'Sir Walter,' " then the names are being used as descriptions: i.e. the individual, instead of being named, is being described as the person having that name. This is a way in which names are frequently used in practice, and there will, as a rule, be nothing in the phraseology to show whether they are being used in this way or *as* names. When a name is used directly, merely to indicate what we are speaking about, it is no part of the *fact* asserted, or of the falsehood if our assertion happens to be false: it is merely part of the symbolism by which we express our thought. What we want to express is something which might (for example) be translated into a foreign language; it is something for which the actual words are a vehicle, but of which they are no part. On the other hand, when we make a proposition about "the person called 'Scott,' " the actual name "Scott" enters into what we are asserting, and not merely into the language used in making the assertion. Our proposition will now be a different one if we substitute "the person called 'Sir Walter.' " But so long as we are using names *as* names, whether we say "Scott" or whether we say "Sir Walter" is as irrelevant to what we are asserting as whether we speak English or French. Thus so long as names are used *as* names, "Scott is Sir Walter" is the same trivial proposition as "Scott is Scott." This completes the proof that "Scott is the author of *Waverley*" is not the same proposition as results from substituting a name for "the author of *Waverley*," no matter what name may be substituted.

When we use a variable, and speak of a propositional function, ϕx say, the process of applying general statements about x to particular cases will consist in substituting a name for the letter "x," assuming that ϕ is a function which has individuals for its arguments. Suppose, for example, that ϕx is "always true"; let it be, say, the "law of identity," $x = x$. Then we may substitute for "x" any name we choose, and we shall obtain a true proposition. Assuming for the moment that "Socrates," "Plato," and "Aristotle" are names (a very rash assumption), we can infer from the law of identity that Socrates is Socrates,

Plato is Plato, and Aristotle is Aristotle. But we shall commit a fallacy if we attempt to infer, without further premisses, that the author of *Waverley* is the author of *Waverley*. This results from what we have just proved, that, if we substitute a name for "the author of *Waverley*" in a proposition, the proposition we obtain is a different one. That is to say, applying the result to our present case: If "x" is a name, "$x = x$" is not the same proposition as "the author of *Waverley* is the author of *Waverley*," no matter what name "x" may be. Thus from the fact that all propositions of the form "$x = x$" are true we cannot infer, without more ado, that the author of *Waverley* is the author of *Waverley*. In fact, propositions of the form "the so-and-so is the so-and-so" are not always true: it is necessary that the so-and-so should *exist* (a term which will be explained shortly). It is false that the present King of France is the present King of France, or that the round square is the round square. When we substitute a description for a name, propositional functions which are "always true" may become false, if the description describes nothing. There is no mystery in this as soon as we realise (what was proved in the preceding paragraph) that when we substitute a description the result is not a value of the propositional function in question.

We are now in a position to define propositions in which a definite description occurs. The only thing that distinguishes "the so-and-so" from "a so-and-so" is the implication of uniqueness. We cannot speak of "*the* inhabitant of London," because inhabiting London is an attribute which is not unique. We cannot speak about "the present King of France," because there is none; but we can speak about "the present King of England." Thus propositions about "the so-and-so" always imply the corresponding propositions about "a so-and-so," with the addendum that there is not more than one so-and-so. Such a proposition as "Scott is the author of *Waverley*" could not be true if *Waverley* had never been written, or if several people had written it; and no more could any other proposition resulting from a propositional function x by the substitution of "the author of *Waverley*" for "x." We may say that "the author of *Waverley*" means "the value of x for which 'x wrote *Waverley*' is true." Thus the proposition "the author of *Waverley* was Scotch," for example, involves:

(1)   "x wrote *Waverley*" is not always false;
(2)   "if x and y wrote *Waverley*, x and y are identical" is always true;
(3)   "if x wrote *Waverley*, x was Scotch" is always true.

These three propositions, translated into ordinary language, state:

(1)   at least one person wrote *Waverley*;
(2)   at most one person wrote *Waverley*;
(3)   whoever wrote *Waverley* was Scotch.

All these three are implied by "the author of *Waverley* was Scotch." Conversely, the three together (but no two of them) imply that the author of *Waverley* was Scotch. Hence the three together may be taken as defining what is meant by the proposition "the author of *Waverley* was Scotch."

We may somewhat simplify these three propositions. The first and second together are equivalent to: "There is a term c such that 'x wrote *Waverley*' is true when x is c and is false when x is not c." In other words, "There is a term c such that 'x wrote *Waverley*' is always equivalent to 'x is c.' " (Two propositions are "equivalent" when both are true or both are false.) We have here, to begin with, two functions of x, "x wrote *Waverley*" and "x is c," and we form a function of c by considering the equivalence of these two functions of x for all values of x; we then proceed to assert that the resulting function of c is "sometimes true," i.e. that it is true for at least one value of c. (It obviously cannot be true for more than one value of c.) These two conditions together are defined as giving the meaning of "the author of *Waverley* exists."

We may now define "the term satisfying the function ϕx exists." This is the general form of which the above is a particular case. "The author of *Waverley*" is "the term satisfying the function 'x wrote *Waverley*.' " And "the so-and-so" will always involve reference to some propositional function, namely, that which defines the property that makes a thing a so-and-so. Our definition is as follows:—

"The term satisfying the function ϕx exists" means:

"There is a term c such that ϕx is always equivalent to 'x is c.' "

In order to define "the author of *Waverley* was Scotch," we have still to take account of the third of our three propositions, namely, "Whoever wrote *Waverley* was Scotch." This will be satisfied by merely adding that the c in question is to be Scotch. Thus "the author of *Waverley* was Scotch" is:

"There is a term c such that (1) 'x wrote *Waverley*' is always equivalent to 'x is c,' (2) c is Scotch."

And generally: "the term satisfying ϕx satisfies ψx" is defined as meaning:

"There is a term c such that (1) ϕx is always equivalent to 'x is c,' (2) ψc is true."

This is the definition of propositions in which descriptions occur.

It is possible to have much knowledge concerning a term described, i.e. to know many propositions concerning "the so-and-so," without actually knowing what the so-and-so is, i.e. without knowing any proposition of the form "x is the so-and-so," where "x" is a name. In a detective story propositions about "the man who did the deed" are accumulated, in the hope that ultimately they will suffice to demonstrate that it was A who did the deed. We may even go so far as to say that, in all such knowledge as can be expressed in words—with the exception of "this" and "that" and a few other words of which the meaning varies on different occasions—no names, in the strict sense, occur, but what seem like names are really descriptions. We may inquire significantly whether Homer existed, which we could not do if "Homer" were a name. The proposition "the so-and-so exists" is significant, whether true or false; but if *a* is the so-and-so (where "*a*" is a name), the words "*a* exists" are meaningless. It is only of descriptions—definite or indefinite—that existence can be significantly asserted; for, if "*a*" is a name, it *must* name something: what does not name anything is not a name, and therefore, if intended to be a name, is a symbol devoid of meaning, whereas a description, like "the present King of France," does not become incapable of occurring significantly merely on the ground that it describes nothing, the reason being that it is a *complex* symbol, of which the meaning is derived from that of its constituent symbols. And so, when we ask whether Homer existed, we are using the word "Homer" as an abbreviated description: we may replace it by (say) "the author of the *Iliad* and the *Odyssey*." The same considerations apply to almost all uses of what look like proper names.

When descriptions occur in propositions, it is necessary to distinguish what may be called "primary" and "secondary" occurrences. The abstract distinction is as follows. A description has a "primary" occurrence when the proposition in which it occurs results from substituting the description for "*x*" in some propositional function ϕx; a description has a "secondary" occurrence when the result of substituting the description for *x* in ϕx gives only *part* of the proposition concerned. An instance will make

this clearer. Consider "the present King of France is bald." Here "the present King of France" has a primary occurrence, and the proposition is false. Every proposition in which a description which describes nothing has a primary occurrence is false. But now consider "the present King of France is not bald." This is ambiguous. If we are first to take "*x* is bald," then substitute "the present King of France" for "*x*," and then deny the result, the occurrence of "the present King of France" is secondary and our proposition is true; but if we are to take "*x* is not bald" and substitute "the present King of France" for "*x*," then "the present King of France" has a primary occurrence and the proposition is false. Confusion of primary and secondary occurrences is a ready source of fallacies where descriptions are concerned.

Descriptions occur in mathematics chiefly in the form of *descriptive functions*, i.e. "the term having the relation R to *y*," or "the R of *y*" as we may say, on the analogy of "the father of *y*" and similar phrases. To say "the father of *y* is rich," for example, is to say that the following propositional function of *c*: "*c* is rich, and '*x* begat *y*' is always equivalent to '*x* is *c*,'" is "sometimes true," i.e. is true for at least one value of *c*. It obviously cannot be true for more than one value.

The theory of descriptions, briefly outlined in the present chapter, is of the utmost importance both in logic and in theory of knowledge. But for purposes of mathematics, the more philosophical parts of the theory are not essential, and have therefore been omitted in the above account, which has confined itself to the barest mathematical requisites.

Note

1   *Untersuchungen zur Gegenstandstheorie und Psychologie*, 1904.

Chapter 7

P. F. Strawson

ON REFERRING

I

We very commonly use expressions of certain kinds to mention or refer to some individual person or single object or particular event or place or process, in the course of doing what we should normally describe as making a statement about that person, object, place, event, or process. I shall call this way of using expressions the "uniquely referring use". The classes of expressions which are most commonly used in this way are: singular demonstrative pronouns ("this" and "that"); proper names (*e.g.* "Venice", "Napoleon", "John"); singular personal and impersonal pronouns ("he", "she", "I", "you", "it"); and phrases beginning with the definite article followed by a noun, qualified or unqualified, in the singular (*e.g.* "the table", "the old man", "the king of France"). Any expression of any of these classes can occur as the subject of what would traditionally be regarded as a singular subject-predicate sentence; and would, so occurring, exemplify the use I wish to discuss.

I do not want to say that expressions belonging to these classes never have any other use than the one I want to discuss. On the contrary, it is obvious that they do. It is obvious that anyone who uttered the sentence, "The whale is a mammal", would be using the expression "the whale" in a way quite different from the way it would be used by anyone who had occasion seriously to utter the sentence, "The whale

struck the ship". In the first sentence one is obviously *not* mentioning, and in the second sentence one obviously is mentioning, a particular whale. Again if I said, "Napoleon was the greatest French soldier", I should be using the word "Napoleon" to mention a certain individual, but I should not be using the phrase, "the greatest French soldier", to mention an individual, but to say something about an individual I had already mentioned. It would be natural to say that in using this sentence I was talking *about* Napoleon and that what I was *saying* about him was that he was the greatest French soldier. But of course I *could* use the expression, "the greatest French soldier", to mention an individual; for example, by saying: "The greatest French soldier died in exile". So it is obvious that at least some expressions belonging to the classes I mentioned *can* have uses other than the use I am anxious to discuss. Another thing I do not want to say is that in any given sentence there is never more than one expression used in the way I propose to discuss. On the contrary, it is obvious that there may be more than one. For example, it would be natural to say that, in seriously using the sentence, "The whale struck the ship", I was saying something about both a certain whale and a certain ship, that I was using each of the expressions "the whale" and "the ship" to mention a particular object; or, in other words, that I was using each of these expressions in the uniquely referring way. In general, however, I shall confine my attention to cases where an expression used in this way occurs as the grammatical subject of a sentence.

I think it is true to say that Russell's Theory of Descriptions, which is concerned with the last of the four classes of expressions I mentioned above (i.e. with expressions of the form "the so-and-so") is still widely accepted among logicians as giving a correct account of the use of such expressions in ordinary language. I want to show, in the first place, that this theory, so regarded, embodies some fundamental mistakes.

What question or questions about phrases of the form "the so-and-so" was the Theory of Descriptions designed to answer? I think that at least one of the questions may be illustrated as follows. Suppose some one were now to utter the sentence, "The king of France is wise". No one would say that the sentence which had been uttered was meaningless. Everyone would agree that it was significant. But everyone knows that there is not at present a king of France. One of the questions the Theory of Descriptions was designed to answer was the question: how can such a sentence as "The king of France is wise" be significant even when there is nothing which answers to the description it contains, i.e., in this case, nothing which answers to the description "The king of France"? And one of the reasons why Russell thought it important to give a correct answer to this question was that he thought it important to show that another answer which might be given was wrong. The answer that he thought was wrong, and to which he was anxious to supply an alternative, might be exhibited as the conclusion of either of the following two fallacious arguments. Let us call the sentence "The king of France is wise" the sentence S. Then the first argument is as follows:

(1) The phrase, "the king of France", is the subject of the sentence S. Therefore

(2) if S is a significant sentence, S is a sentence *about* the king of France. But

(3) if there in no sense exists a king of France, the sentence is not about anything, and hence not about the king of France. Therefore

(4) since S is significant, there must in some sense (in some world) exist (or subsist) the king of France.

And the second argument is as follows:

(1) If S is significant, it is either true or false.

(2) S is true if the king of France is wise and false if the king of France is not wise.

(3) But the statement that the king of France is wise and the statement that the king of France is not wise are alike true only if there is (in some sense, in some world) something which is the king of France.

Hence

(4) Since S is significant, there follows the same conclusion as before.

These are fairly obviously bad arguments, and, as we should expect, Russell rejects them. The postulation of a world of strange entities, to which the king of France belongs, offends, he says, against "that feeling for reality which ought to be preserved even in the most abstract studies". The fact that Russell rejects these arguments is, however, less interesting than the extent to which, in rejecting their conclusion, he concedes the more important of their principles. Let me refer to the phrase, "the king of France", as the phrase D. Then I think Russell's reasons for rejecting these two arguments can be summarised as follows. The mistake arises, he says, from thinking that D, which is certainly the *grammatical* subject of S, is also the *logical* subject of S. But D is not the logical subject of S. In fact S, although grammatically it has a singular subject and a predicate, is not logically a subject-predicate sentence at all. The proposition it expresses is a complex kind of *existential* proposition, part of which might be described as a "uniquely existential" proposition. To exhibit the logical form of the proposition, we should re-write the sentence in a logically appropriate grammatical form; in such a way that the deceptive similarity of S to a sentence expressing a subject-predicate proposition would disappear, and we should be safeguarded against arguments such as the bad ones I outlined above. Before recalling the details of Russell's analysis of S, let us notice what his answer, as I have so far given it, seems to imply. His answer seems to imply that in the case of a sentence which is similar to S in that (1) it is grammatically of the subject-predicate form and (2) its grammatical subject does not refer to anything, then the only alternative to its being meaningless is that it should not really (i.e. logically) be of the subject-predicate form at all, but of some quite different form. And this in its turn seems to imply that if there are any sentences which are genuinely of the subject-predicate form, then the very fact of their being significant, having a meaning, guarantees that there is something referred to by the logical (and grammatical) subject. Moreover, Russell's answer seems to imply that there are such sentences. For if it is true that one may be misled by the grammatical similarity of S to other sentences into thinking that it is logically of the subject-predicate form, then surely there must be other sentences grammatically similar to S, which *are* of the subject-predicate form. To show not only that Russell's answer seems to imply these conclusions, but that he accepted at least the first two of them, it is enough to consider what he says about a class of expressions which he calls "logically proper names" and contrasts with expressions, like D, which he calls "definite descriptions". Of logically proper names Russell says or implies the following things:

(1)   That they and they alone can occur as subjects of sentences which are genuinely of the subject-predicate form;
(2)   that an expression intended to be a logically proper name is *meaningless* unless there is some single object for which it stands:

for the *meaning* of such an expression just is the individual object which the expression designates. To be a name at all, therefore, it *must* designate something.

It is easy to see that if anyone believes these two propositions, then the only way for him to save the significance of the sentence S is to deny that it is a logically subject-predicate sentence. Generally, we may say that Russell recognises only two ways in which sentences which seem, from their grammatical structure, to be about some particular person or individual object or event, can be significant:

(1)   The first is that their grammatical form should be misleading as to their logical form, and that they should be analysable, like S, as a special kind of existential sentence;
(2)   The second is that their grammatical subject should be a logically proper name, of which the meaning is the individual thing it designates.

I think that Russell is unquestionably wrong in this, and that sentences which are significant, and which begin with an expression used in the uniquely referring way fall into neither of these two classes. Expressions used in the uniquely referring way are never either logically proper names or descriptions, if what is meant by calling them "descriptions" is that they are to be analysed in accordance with the model provided by Russell's Theory of Descriptions.

There are no logically proper names and there are no descriptions (in this sense).

Let us now consider the details of Russell's analysis. According to Russell, anyone who asserted S would be asserting that:

(1)   There is a king of France.
(2)   There is not more than one king of France.
(3)   There is nothing which is king of France and is not wise.

It is easy to see both how Russell arrived at this analysis, and how it enables him to answer the question with which we began, *viz.* the question: How can the sentence S be significant when there is no king of France? The way in which he arrived at the analysis was clearly by asking himself what would be the circumstances in which we would say that anyone who uttered the sentence S had made a true assertion. And it does seem pretty clear, and I have no wish to dispute, that the sentences (1)–(3) above do describe circumstances which are at least necessary conditions of anyone making a true assertion by uttering the sentence S. But, as I hope to show, to say this is not at all the same thing as to say that Russell has given a correct account of the use of the sentence S or even that he has given an account which, though incomplete, is correct as far as it goes; and is certainly not at all the same thing as to say that the model translation provided is a correct model for all (or for any) singular sentences beginning with a phrase of the form "the so-and-so".

It is also easy to see how this analysis enables Russell to answer the question of how the sentence S can be significant, even when there is no king of France. For, if this analysis is correct, anyone who utters the sentence S to-day would be jointly asserting three propositions, one of which (*viz.* that there is a king of France) would be false; and since the conjunction of three propositions, of which one is false, is itself false, the assertion as a whole would be significant, but false. So neither of the bad arguments for subsistent entities would apply to such an assertion.

II

As a step towards showing that Russell's solution of his problem is mistaken, and towards providing the correct solution, I want now to draw certain distinctions. For this purpose I shall, for the remainder of this section, refer to an expression which has a uniquely referring use as "an expression" for short; and to a sentence beginning with such an expression as "a sentence" for short. The distinctions I shall draw are rather rough and ready, and, no doubt, difficult cases could be produced which would call for their refinement. But I think they will serve my purpose. The distinctions are between:

(A1) a sentence,
(A2) a use of a sentence,
(A3) an utterance of a sentence,

and, correspondingly, between:

(B1) an expression,
(B2) a use of an expression,
(B3) an utterance of an expression.

Consider again the sentence, "The king of France is wise". It is easy to imagine that this sentence was uttered at various times from, say, the beginning of the seventeenth century onwards, during the reigns of each successive French monarch; and easy to imagine that it was also uttered during the subsequent periods in which France was not a monarchy. Notice that it was natural for me to speak of "the sentence" or "this sentence" being uttered at various times during this period; or, in other words, that it would be natural and correct to speak of *one and the same* sentence being uttered on all these various occasions. It is in the sense in which it would be correct to speak of one and the same sentence being uttered on all these various occasions that I want to use the expression (A1) "a sentence". There are, however, obvious differences between different *occasions of the use* of this sentence. For instance, if one man uttered it in the reign of Louis XIV and another man uttered it in the reign of Louis XV, it would be natural to say (to assume) that they were respectively talking about different people; and it might be held that the first man, in using the sentence, made a true assertion, while the second man, in using the same sentence, made a false assertion. If on the other hand two different men simultaneously uttered the sentence (*e.g.* if one wrote it and the other spoke it) during the reign of Louis XIV, it would be natural to say (assume) that they were both talking about the same person, and, in that case, in using the sentence, they *must* either both have made a true assertion or both have made a false assertion. And this illustrates what I mean by *a use* of a sentence. The two men who uttered the sentence, one in the reign of Louis XV and one in the reign of Louis XIV, each made a different use of the same sentence; whereas the two men who uttered the sentence simultaneously in the reign of Louis XIV, made the same use[1] of the same sentence. Obviously in the case of this sentence, and equally obviously in the case of many others, we cannot talk of *the sentence* being true or false, but only of its being used to make a true or false assertion, or (if this is preferred) to express a true or a false proposition. And equally obviously we cannot talk of *the sentence* being *about* a particular person, for the same sentence may be used at different times to talk about quite different particular persons, but only of *a use* of the sentence to talk about a particular person. Finally it will make sufficiently clear what I mean by an utterance of a sentence if I say that the two men who simultaneously uttered the sentence in the reign of Louis XIV made two different utterances of the same sentence, though they made the same *use* of the sentence.

If we now consider not the whole sentence, "The king of France is wise", but that part of it which is the expression, "the king of France", it is obvious that we can make analogous, though not identical distinctions between (1) the expression, (2) a use of the expression and (3) an utterance of the expression. The distinctions will not be identical; we obviously cannot correctly talk of the expression "the king of France" being used to express a true or false proposition, since in general only sentences can be used truly or falsely; and similarly it is only by using a sentence and not by using an expression alone, that you can talk about a particular person. Instead, we shall say in this case that you *use* the

expression to *mention* or *refer to* a particular person in the course of using the sentence to talk about him. But obviously in this case, and a great many others, the *expression* (B1) cannot be said to mention, or refer to, anything, any more than the *sentence* can be said to be true or false. The same expression can have different mentioning-uses, as the same sentence can be used to make statements with different truth-values. "Mentioning", or "referring", is not something an expression does; it is something that some one can use an expression to do. Mentioning, or referring to, something is a characteristic of *a use* of an expression, just as "being about" something, and truth-or-falsity, are characteristics of *a use* of a sentence.

A very different example may help to make these distinctions clearer. Consider another case of an expression which has a uniquely referring use, *viz.* the expression "I"; and consider the sentence, "I am hot". Countless people may use this same sentence; but it is logically impossible for two different people to make *the same use* of this sentence: or, if this is preferred, to use it to express the same proposition. The expression "I" may correctly be used by (and only by) any one of innumerable people to refer to himself. To say this is to say something about the expression "I": it is, in a sense, to give its meaning. This is the sort of thing that can be said about *expressions*. But it makes no sense to say of the *expression* "I" that it refers to a particular person. This is the sort of thing that can be said only of a particular use of the expression.

Let me use "type" as an abbreviation for "sentence or expression". Then I am not saying that there are sentences and expression (types), *and* uses of them, *and* utterances of them, as there are ships *and* shoes *and* sealing-wax. I am saying that we cannot say *the same things* about types, uses of types, and utterances of types. And the fact is that we do talk about types; and that confusion is apt to result from the failure to notice the differences between what we can say about these and what we can say only about the *uses* of types. We are apt to fancy we are talking about sentences and expressions when we are talking about the uses of sentences and expressions.

This is what Russell does. Generally, as against Russell, I shall say this. Meaning (in at least one important sense) is a function of the sentence or expression; mentioning and referring and truth or falsity, are functions of the use of the sentence or expression. To give the meaning of an expression (in the sense in which I am using the word) is to give *general directions* for its use to refer to or mention particular objects or persons; to give the meaning of a sentence is to give *general directions* for its use in making true or false assertions. It is not to talk about any particular occasion of the use of the sentence or expression. The meaning of an expression cannot be identified with the object it is used, on a particular occasion, to refer to. The meaning of a sentence cannot be identified with the assertion it is used, on a particular occasion, to make. For to talk about the meaning of an expression or sentence is not to talk about its use on a particular occasion, but about the rules, habits, conventions governing its correct use, on all occasions, to refer or to assert. So the question of whether a sentence or expression *is significant or not* has nothing whatever to do with the question of whether the sentence, **uttered on a particular occasion**, is, on that occasion, being used to make a true-or-false assertion or not, or of whether the expression is, on that occasion, being used to refer to, or mention, anything at all.

The source of Russell's mistake was that he thought that referring or mentioning, if it occurred at all, must be meaning. He did not distinguish B1 from B2; he confused expressions with their use in a particular context; and so confused meaning with mentioning, with referring. If I talk about my handkerchief, I can, perhaps, produce the object I am referring to out of my pocket. I can't produce the meaning of the expression, "my handkerchief", out of my pocket. Because Russell confused meaning with mentioning, he thought that if there were any

expressions having a uniquely referring use, which were what they seemed (*i.e.* logical subjects) and not something else in disguise, their meaning must be the particular object which they were used to refer to. Hence the troublesome mythology of the logically proper name. But if some one asks me the meaning of the expression "this"—once Russell's favourite candidate for this status—I do not hand him the object I have just used the expression to refer to, adding at the same time that the meaning of the word changes every time it is used. Nor do I hand him all the objects it ever has been, or might be, used to refer to. I explain and illustrate the conventions governing the use of the expression. This is giving the meaning of the expression. It is quite different from giving (in any sense of giving) the object to which it refers; for the expression itself does not refer to anything; though it can be used, on different occasions, to refer to innumerable things. Now as a matter of fact there is, in English, a sense of the word "mean" in which this word does approximate to "indicate, mention or refer to"; *e.g.* when somebody (unpleasantly) says, "I mean you"; or when I point and say, "That's the one I mean". But *the one I meant* is quite different from *the meaning of the expression* I used to talk of it. In this special sense of "mean", it is people who mean, not expressions. People use expressions to refer to particular things. But the meaning of an expression is not the set of things or the single thing it may correctly be used to refer to: the meaning is the set of rules, habits, conventions for its use in referring.

It is the same with sentences: even more obviously so. Every one knows that the sentence, "The table is covered with books", is significant, and every one knows what it means. But if I ask, "What object is that sentence about?" I am asking an absurd question—a question which cannot be asked about the sentence, but only about some use of the sentence: and in this case the sentence hasn't been used, it has only been taken as an example. In knowing what it means, you are knowing how it could correctly be used to talk about things: so knowing the meaning hasn't anything to do with knowing about any particular use of the sentence to talk about anything. Similarly, if I ask: "Is the sentence true or false?" I am asking an absurd question, which becomes no less absurd if I add, "It must be one or the other since it's significant". The question is absurd, because the *sentence* is neither true nor false any more than it's *about* some object. Of course the fact that it's significant is the same as the fact that it *can* correctly be used to talk about something and that, in so using it, some one will be making a true or false assertion. And I will add that it will be used to make a true or false assertion *only* if the person using it is talking about something. If, when he utters it, he is not talking about anything, then his use is not a genuine one, but a spurious or pseudo-use: he is not making either a true or a false assertion, though he may think he is. And this points the way to the correct answer to the puzzle to which the Theory of Descriptions gives a fatally incorrect answer. The important point is that the question of whether the sentence is significant or not is quite independent of the question that can be raised about a particular use of it, *viz.* the question whether it is a genuine or a spurious use, whether it is being used to talk about something, or in make-believe, or as an example in philosophy. The question whether the sentence is significant or not is the question whether there exist such language habits, conventions or rules that the sentence logically could be used to talk about something; and is hence quite independent of the question whether it is being so used on a particular occasion.

III

Consider again the sentence, "The king of France is wise", and the true and false things Russell says about it.

There are at least two true things which Russell would say about the sentence:

(1)   The first is that it is significant; that if anyone were now to utter it, he would be uttering a significant sentence.
(2)   The second is that anyone now uttering the sentence would be making a true assertion only if there in fact at present existed one and only one king of France, and if he were wise.

What are the false things which Russell would say about the sentence? They are:

(1)   That anyone now uttering it would be making a true assertion or a false assertion;
(2)   That part of what he would be asserting would be that there at present existed one and only one king of France.

I have already given some reasons for thinking that these two statements are incorrect. Now suppose some one were in fact to say to you with a perfectly serious air: "The king of France is wise". Would you say, "That's untrue"? I think it's quite certain that you wouldn't. But suppose he went on to *ask* you whether you thought that what he had just said was true, or was false; whether you agreed or disagreed with what he had just said. I think you would be inclined, with some hesitation, to say that you didn't do either; that the question of whether his statement was true or false simply *didn't arise*, because there was no such person as the king of France.[2] You might, if he were obviously serious (had a dazed astray-in-the-centuries look), say something like: "I'm afraid you must be under a misapprehension. France is not a monarchy. There is no king of France". And this brings out the point that if a man seriously uttered the sentence, his uttering it would in some sense be *evidence* that he *believed* that there was a king of France. It would not be evidence for his believing this simply in the way in which a man's reaching for his raincoat is evidence for his believing that it is raining. But nor would it be evidence for his believing this in the way in which a man's saying, "It's raining" is evidence for his believing that it is raining. We might put it as follows. To say, "The king of France is wise" is, in some sense of "imply", to imply that there is a king of France. But this is a very special and odd sense of "imply". "Implies" in this sense is certainly not equivalent to "entails" (or "logically implies"). And this comes out from the fact that when, in response to his statement, we say (as we should) "There is no king of France", we should certainly not say we were contradicting the statement that the king of France is wise. We are certainly not saying that it's false. We are, rather, giving a reason for saying that the question of whether it's true or false simply doesn't arise.

And this is where the distinction I drew earlier can help us. The sentence, "The king of France is wise", is certainly significant; but this does not mean that any particular use of it is true or false. We use it truly or falsely when we use it to talk about some one; when, in using the expression, "The king of France", we are in fact mentioning some one. The fact that the sentence and the expression, respectively, are significant just is the fact that the sentence *could* be used, in certain circumstances, to say something true or false, that the expression *could* be used, in certain circumstances to mention a particular person; and to know their meaning is to know what sort of circumstances these are. So when we utter the sentence without in fact mentioning anybody by the use of the phrase, "The king of France", the sentence doesn't cease to be significant: we simply *fail* to say anything true or false because we simply fail to mention anybody by this particular use of that perfectly significant phrase. It is, if you like, a spurious use of the sentence, and a spurious use of the expression; though we may (or may not) mistakenly think it a genuine use.

And such spurious uses are very familiar. Sophisticated romancing, sophisticated fiction,[3] depend upon them. If I began, "The king of France is wise", and went on, "and he lives in a golden castle and has a hundred wives", and so on, a hearer would understand me perfectly well,

without supposing *either* that I was talking about a particular person, *or* that I was making a false statement to the effect that there existed such a person as my words described. (It is worth adding that where the use of sentences and expressions is overtly fictional, the sense of the word "about" may change. As Moore said, it is perfectly natural and correct to say that some of the statements in *Pickwick Papers* are *about* Mr. Pickwick. But where the use of sentences and expressions is not overtly fictional, this use of "about" seems less correct; *i.e.* it would not *in general* be correct to say that a statement was about Mr. X or the so-and-so, unless there were such a person or thing. So it is where the romancing is in danger of being taken seriously that we might answer the question. "Who is he talking about?" with "He's not talking about anybody"; but, in saying this, we are not saying that what he is saying is either false or nonsense.)

Overtly fictional uses apart, however, I said just now that to use such an expression as "The king of France" at the beginning of a sentence was, in some sense of "imply", to imply that there was a king of France. When a man uses such an expression, he does not *assert*, nor does what he says *entail*, a uniquely existential proposition. But one of the conventional functions of the definite article is to act as a *signal* that a unique reference is being made—a signal, not a disguised assertion. When we begin a sentence with "the such-and-such" the use of "the" shows, but does not state, that we are, or intend to be, referring to one particular individual of the species "such-and-such". *Which* particular individual is a matter to be determined from context, time, place and any other features of the situation of utterance. Now, whenever a man uses any expression, the presumption is that he thinks he is using it correctly: so when he uses the expression, "the such-and-such", in a uniquely referring way, the presumption is that he thinks both that there is *some* individual of that species, and that the context of use will sufficiently determine which one he has in mind. To use the word "the" in this way is then to imply (in the relevant sense of "imply") that the existential conditions described by Russell are fulfilled. But to use "the" in this way is not to *state* that those conditions are fulfilled. If I begin a sentence with an expression of the form, "the so-and-so", and then am prevented from saying more, I have made no statement of any kind; but I may have succeeded in mentioning some one or something.

The uniquely existential assertion supposed by Russell to be part of any assertion in which a uniquely referring use is made of an expression of the form "the so-and-so" is, he observes, a compound of two assertions. To say that there is a ϕ is to say something compatible with there being several ϕs; to say there is not more than one ϕ is to say something compatible with there being none. To say there is one ϕ and one only is to compound these two assertions. I have so far been concerned mostly with the alleged assertion of existence and less with the alleged assertion of uniqueness. An example which throws the emphasis on to the latter will serve to bring out more clearly the sense of "implied" in which a uniquely existential assertion is implied, but not entailed, by the use of expressions in the uniquely referring way. Consider the sentence, "The table is covered with books". It is quite certain that in any normal use of this sentence, the expression "the table" would be used to make a unique reference, i.e. to refer to some one table. It is a quite strict use of the definite article, in the sense in which Russell talks on p. 30 of *Principia Mathematica*, of using the article "strictly, so as to imply uniqueness". On the same page Russell says that a phrase of the form "the so-and-so", used strictly, "will only have an application in the event of there being one so-and-so and no more". Now it is obviously quite false that the phrase "the table" in the sentence "the table is covered with books", used normally, will "only have an application in the event of there being one table and no more". It is indeed tautologically true that, in such a use, the phrase will have an application only in the event of there being

one table and no more *which is being referred to*, and that it will be understood to have an application only in the event of there being one table and no more which it is understood as being used to refer to. To use the sentence is not to assert, but it is (in the special sense discussed) to imply, that there is only one thing which is *both* of the kind specified (i.e. a table) *and is being referred to* by the speaker. It is obviously not to assert this. To refer is not to say you are referring. To say there is *some table or other* to which you are referring is not the same as referring to a particular table. We should have no use for such phrases as "the individual I referred to" unless there were something which counted as referring. (It would make no sense to say you had pointed if there were nothing which counted as pointing.) So once more I draw the conclusion that referring to or mentioning a particular thing cannot be dissolved into any kind of assertion. To refer is not to assert, though you refer in order to go on to assert.

Let me now take an example of the uniquely referring use of an expression not of the form, "the so-and-so". Suppose I advance my hands, cautiously cupped, towards someone, saying, as I do so, "This is a fine red one". He, looking into my hands and seeing nothing there, may say: "What is? What are you talking about?" Or perhaps, "But there's nothing in your hands". Of course it would be absurd to say that in saying "But you've got nothing in your hands", he was *denying* or *contradicting* what I said. So "this" is not a disguised description in Russell's sense. Nor is it a logically proper name. For one must know what the sentence means in order to react in that way to the utterance of it. It is precisely because the significance of the word "this" is independent of any particular reference it may be used to make, though not independent of the way it may be used to refer, that I can, as in this example, use it to *pretend* to be referring to something.

The general moral of all this is that communication is much less a matter of explicit or disguised assertion than logicians used to suppose. The particular application of this general moral in which I am interested is its application to the case of making a unique reference. It is a part of the significance of expressions of the kind I am discussing that they can be used, in an immense variety of contexts, to make unique references. It is no part of their significance to assert that they are being so used or that the conditions of their being so used are fulfilled. So the wholly important distinction we are required to draw is between:

(1) using an expression to make a unique reference; and
(2) asserting that there is one and only one individual which has certain characteristics (*e.g.* is of a certain kind, or stands in a certain relation to the speaker, or both).

This is, in other words, the distinction between

(1) sentences containing an expression used to indicate or mention or refer to a particular person or thing; and
(2) uniquely existential sentences.

What Russell does is progressively to assimilate more and more sentences of class (1) to sentences of class (2), and consequently to involve himself in insuperable difficulties about logical subjects, and about values for individual variables generally: difficulties which have led him finally to the logically disastrous theory of names developed in the *Enquiry* and in *Human Knowledge*. That view of the meaning of logical-subject-expressions which provides the whole incentive to the Theory of Descriptions at the same time precludes the possibility of Russell's ever finding any satisfactory substitutes for those expressions which, beginning with substantival phrases, he progressively degrades from the status of logical subjects.[4] It is not simply, as is sometimes said, the fascination of the relation between a name and its bearer, that is the root of the trouble. Not even names come up to the impossible standard set. It is rather the combination of two more

radical misconceptions: first, the failure to grasp the importance of the distinction (section II above) between what may be said of an expression and what may be said of a particular use of it; second, a failure to recognise the uniquely referring use of expressions for the harmless, necessary thing it is, distinct from, but complementary to, the predicative or ascriptive use of expressions. The expressions which can in fact occur as singular logical subjects are expressions of the class I listed at the outset (demonstratives, substantival phrases, proper names, pronouns): to say this is to say that these expressions, together with context (in the widest sense) are what one uses to make unique references. The point of the conventions governing the uses of such expressions is, along with the situation of utterance, to secure uniqueness of reference. But to do this, enough is enough. We do not, and we cannot, while referring, attain the point of complete explicitness at which the referring function is no longer performed. The actual unique reference made, if any, is a matter of the particular use in the particular context; the significance of the expression used is the set of rules or conventions which permit such references to be made. Hence we can, using significant expressions, pretend to refer, in make-believe or in fiction, or mistakenly think we are referring when we are not referring to anything.

This shows the need for distinguishing two kinds (among many others) of linguistic conventions or rules: rules for referring, and rules for attributing and ascribing; and for an investigation of the former. If we recognise this distinction of use for what it is, we are on the way to solving a number of ancient logical and metaphysical puzzles.

My last two sections are concerned, but only in the barest outline, with these questions.

IV

One of the main purposes for which we use language is the purpose of stating facts about things and persons and events. If we want to fulfil this purpose, we must have some way of forestalling the question, "What (who, which one) are you talking about?" as well as the question, "What are you saying about it (him, her)?" The task of forestalling the first question is the referring (or identifying) task. The task of forestalling the second is the attributive (or descriptive or classificatory or ascriptive) task. In the conventional English sentence which is used to state, or to claim to state, a fact about an individual thing or person or event, the performance of these two tasks can be roughly and approximately assigned to separable expressions.[5] And in such a sentence, this assigning of expressions to their separate roles corresponds to the conventional grammatical classification of subject and predicate. There is nothing sacrosanct about the employment of separable expressions for these two tasks. Other methods could be, and are, employed. There is, for instance, the method of uttering a single word or attributive phrase in the conspicuous presence of the object referred to; or that analogous method exemplified by, e.g. the painting of the words "unsafe for lorries" on a bridge, or the tying of a label reading "first prize" on a vegetable marrow. Or one can imagine an elaborate game in which one never used an expression in the uniquely referring way at all, but uttered only uniquely existential sentences, trying to enable the hearer to identify what was being talked of by means of an accumulation of relative clauses. (This description of the purposes of the game shows in what sense it would be a game: this is not the normal use we make of existential sentences.) Two points require emphasis. The first is that the necessity of performing these two tasks in order to state particular facts requires no transcendental explanation: to call attention to it is partly to elucidate the meaning of the phrase, "stating a fact". The second is that even this elucidation is made in terms derivative from the grammar of the conventional singular sentence; that even the overtly functional, linguistic distinction between the identifying and attributive roles that words may play in language is prompted by the fact that ordinary speech offers us separable expressions to which the different functions may be plausibly and approximately assigned. And this functional distinction has cast long philosophical shadows. The distinctions between particular and universal, between substance and quality, are such pseudo-material shadows, cast by the grammar of the conventional sentence, in which separable expressions play distinguishable roles.

To use a separate expression to perform the first of these tasks is to use an expression in the uniquely referring way. I want now to say something in general about the conventions of use for expressions used in this way, and to contrast them with conventions of ascriptive use. I then proceed to the brief illustration of these general remarks and to some further applications of them.

What in general is required for making a unique reference is, obviously, some device, or devices, for showing both *that* a unique reference is intended and *what* unique reference it is; some device requiring and enabling the hearer or reader to identify what is being talked about. In securing this result, the context of utterance is of an importance which it is almost impossible to exaggerate; and by "context" I mean, at least, the time, the place, the situation, the identity of the speaker, the subjects which form the immediate focus of interest, and the personal histories of both the speaker and those he is addressing. Besides context, there is, of course, convention;—linguistic convention. But, except in the case of genuine proper names, of which I shall have more to say later, the fulfilment of more or less precisely stateable contextual conditions is *conventionally* (or, in a wide sense of the word, *logically*) required for the correct referring use of expressions in a sense in which this is not true of correct ascriptive uses. The requirement for the correct application of an expression in its ascriptive use to a certain thing is simply that the thing should be of a certain kind, have certain characteristics. The requirement for the correct application of an expression in its referring use to a certain thing is something over and above any requirement derived from such ascriptive meaning as the expression may have; it is, namely, the requirement that the thing should be in a certain relation to the speaker and to the context of utterance. Let me call this the contextual requirement. Thus, for example, in the limiting case of the word "I" the contextual requirement is that the thing should be identical with the speaker; but in the case of most expressions which have a referring use this requirement cannot be so precisely specified. A further, and perfectly general, difference between conventions for referring and conventions for describing is one we have already encountered, *viz.* that the fulfilment of the conditions for a correct ascriptive use of an expression is a part of what is stated by such a use; but the fulfilment of the conditions for a correct referring use of an expression is never part of what is stated, though it is (in the relevant sense of "implied") implied by such a use.

Conventions for referring have been neglected or misinterpreted by logicians. The reasons for this neglect are not hard to see, though they are hard to state briefly. Two of them are, roughly: (1) the preoccupation of most logicians with definitions; (2) the preoccupation of some logicians with formal systems. (1) A definition, in the most familiar sense, is a specification of the conditions of the correct ascriptive or classificatory use of an expression. Definitions take no account of contextual requirements. So that in so far as the search for the meaning or the search for the analysis of an expression is conceived as the search for a definition, the neglect or misinterpretation of conventions other than ascriptive is inevitable. Perhaps it would be better to say (for I do not wish to legislate about "meaning" or "analysis") that logicians have failed to notice that problems of use are wider than problems of analysis and meaning. (2) The influence of the preoccupation with mathematics and formal

logic is most clearly seen (to take no more recent examples) in the cases of Leibniz and Russell. The constructor of calculuses, not concerned or required to make factual statements, approaches applied logic with a prejudice. It is natural that he should assume that the types of convention with whose adequacy in one field he is familiar should be really adequate, if only one could see how, in a quite different field—that of statements of fact. Thus we have Leibniz striving desperately to make the uniqueness of unique references a matter of logic in the narrow sense, and Russell striving desperately to do the same thing, in a different way, both for the implication of uniqueness and for that of existence.

It should be clear that the distinction I am trying to draw is primarily one between different rôles or parts that expressions may play in language, and not primarily one between different groups of expressions; for some expressions may appear in either rôle. Some of the kinds of words I shall speak of have predominantly, if not exclusively, a referring rôle. This is most obviously true of pronouns and ordinary proper names. Some can occur as wholes or parts of expressions which have a predominantly referring use, and as wholes or parts of expressions which have a predominantly ascriptive or classificatory use. The obvious cases are common nouns; or common nouns preceded by adjectives, including participial adjectives; or, less obviously, adjectives or participial adjectives alone. Expressions capable of having a referring use also differ from one another in at least the three following, not mutually independent, ways:

(1)   They differ in the extent to which the reference they are used to make is dependent on the context of their utterance. Words like "I" and "it" stand at one end of this scale—the end of maximum dependence—and phrases like "the author of *Waverley*" and "the eighteenth king of France" at the other.

(2)   They differ in the degree of "descriptive meaning" they possess: by "descriptive meaning" I intend "conventional limitation, in application, to things of a certain general kind, or possessing certain general characteristics". At one end of this scale stand the proper names we most commonly use in ordinary discourse; men, dogs and motor-bicycles may be called "Horace". The pure name has no descriptive meaning (except such as it may acquire *as a result of* some one of its uses as a name). A word like "he" has minimal descriptive meaning, but has some. Substantival phrases like "the round table" have the maximum descriptive meaning. An interesting intermediate position is occupied by 'impure' proper names like "The Round Table"—substantival phrases which have grown capital letters.

(3)   Finally, they may be divided into the following two classes: (i) those of which the correct referring use is regulated by some *general* referring-cum-ascriptive conventions. To this class belong both pronouns, which have the least descriptive meaning, and substantival phrases which have the most; (ii) those of which the correct referring use is regulated by no general conventions, either of the contextual or the ascriptive kind, but by conventions which are *ad hoc* for each particular use (though not for each particular utterance). Roughly speaking, the most familiar kind of proper names belong to this class. Ignorance of a man's name is not ignorance of the language. This is why we do not speak of the meaning of proper names. (But it won't do to say they are meaningless.) Again an intermediate position is occupied by such phrases as "The Old Pretender". Only an old pretender may be so referred to; but to know which old pretender is not to know a general, but an *ad hoc*, convention.

In the case of phrases of the form "the so-and-so" used referringly, the use of "the" together with the position of the phrase in the sentence (i.e. at the beginning, or following a transitive verb or preposition) acts as a signal *that* a unique reference is being made; and the following noun, or noun and adjective, together with the context of utterance, shows *what* unique reference is being made. In general the functional difference between common nouns and adjectives is that the former are naturally and commonly used referringly, while the latter are not commonly, or so naturally, used in this way, except as qualifying nouns; though they can be and are, so used alone. And of course this functional difference is not independent of the descriptive force peculiar to each word. In general we should expect the descriptive force of nouns to be such that they are more efficient tools for the job of showing what unique reference is intended when such a reference is signalised; and we should also expect the descriptive force of the words we naturally and commonly use to make unique reference to mirror our interest in the salient, relatively permanent and behavioural characteristics of things. These two expectations are not independent of one another; and, if we look at the differences between the commoner sort of common nouns and the commoner sort of adjectives, we find them both fulfilled. These are differences of the kind that Locke quaintly reports, when he speaks of our ideas of substances being *collections* of simple ideas; when he says that "powers make up a great part of our ideas of substances"; and when he goes on to contrast the identity of real and nominal essence in the case of simple ideas with their lack of identity and the shiftingness of the nominal essence in the case of substances. "Substance" itself is the troublesome tribute Locke pays to his dim awareness of the difference in predominant linguistic function that lingered even when the noun had been expanded into a more or less indefinite string of adjectives. Russell repeats Locke's mistake with a difference when, admitting the inference from syntax to reality to the extent of feeling that he can get rid of this metaphysical unknown only if he can purify language of the referring function altogether, he draws up his programme for "abolishing particulars"; a programme, in fact, for abolishing the distinction of logical use which I am here at pains to emphasise.

The contextual requirement for the referring use of pronouns may be stated with the greatest precision in some cases (*e.g.* "I" and "you") and only with the greatest vagueness in others ("it" and "this"). I propose to say nothing further about pronouns, except to point to an additional symptom of the failure to recognise the uniquely referring use for what it is; the fact, namely, that certain logicians have actually sought to elucidate the nature of a variable by offering such *sentences* as "he is sick", "it is green", as examples of something in ordinary speech like a *sentential function*. Now of course it is true that the word "he" may be used on different occasions to refer to different people or different animals: so may the word "John" and the phrase "the cat". What deters such logicians from treating these two expressions as quasi-variables is, in the first case, the lingering superstition that a name is logically tied to a single individual, and, in the second case, the descriptive meaning of the word "cat". But "he", which has a wide range of applications and minimal descriptive force, only acquires a use as a referring word. It is this fact, together with the failure to accord to expressions used referringly, the place in logic which belongs to them (the place held open for the mythical logically proper name), that accounts for the misleading attempt to elucidate the nature of the variable by reference to such words as "he", "she", "it".

Of ordinary proper names it is sometimes said that they are essentially words each of which is used to refer to just one individual. This is obviously false. Many ordinary personal names—names par excellence—are correctly used to refer to numbers of people. An ordinary

personal name, is, roughly, a word, used referringly, of which the use is *not* dictated by any descriptive meaning the word may have, and is *not* prescribed by any such general rule for use as a referring expression (or a part of a referring expression) as we find in the case of such words as "I", "this" and "the", but is governed by *ad hoc* conventions for each particular set of applications of the word to a given person. The important point is that the correctness of such applications does not follow from any *general* rule or convention for the use of the word as such. (The limit of absurdity and obvious circularity is reached in the attempt to treat names as disguised description in Russell's sense; for what is in the special sense implied, but not entailed, by my now referring to some one by name is simply the existence of some one, *now being referred to*, who is *conventionally referred to* by that name.) Even this feature of names, however, is only a symptom of the purpose for which they are employed. At present our choice of names is partly arbitrary, partly dependent on legal and social observances. It would be perfectly possible to have a thorough-going *system* of names, based *e.g.* on dates of birth, or on a minute classification of physiological and anatomical differences. But the success of any such system would depend entirely on the convenience of the resulting name-allotments for the purpose of making unique references; and this would depend on the multiplicity of the classifications used and the degree to which they cut haphazard across normal social groupings. Given a sufficient degree of both, the selectivity supplied by context would do the rest; just as is the case with our present naming habits. Had we such a system, we could use name-words descriptively (as we do at present, to a limited extent and in a different way, with some famous names) as well as referringly. But it is by criteria derived from consideration of the requirements of the referring task that we should assess the adequacy of any system of naming. From the naming point of view, no kind of classification would be better or worse than any other simply because of the kind of classification—natal or anatomical—that it was.

I have already mentioned the class of quasi-names, of substantival phrases which grow capital letters, and of which such phrases as "the Glorious Revolution", "the Great War", "the Annunciation", "the Round Table" are examples. While the descriptive meaning of the words which follow the definite article is still relevant to their referring role, the capital letters are a sign of that extra-logical selectivity in their referring use, which is characteristic of pure names. Such phrases are found in print or in writing when one member of some class of events or things is of quite outstanding interest in a certain society. These phrases are embryonic names. A phrase may, for obvious reasons, pass into, and out of, this class (*e.g.* "the Great War").

V

I want to conclude by considering, all too briefly, three further problems about referring uses.

(*a*) *Indefinite references.* Not all referring uses of singular expressions forestall the question "What (who, which one) are you talking about?" There are some which either invite this question, or disclaim the intention or ability to answer it. Examples are such sentence-beginnings as "A man told me that . . .", "Some one told me that . . ." The orthodox (Russellian) doctrine is that such sentences are existential, but not uniquely existential. This seems wrong in several ways. It is ludicrous to suggest that part of what is asserted is that the class of men or persons is not empty. Certainly this is *implied* in the by now familiar sense of implication; but the implication is also as much an implication of the *uniqueness* of the particular object of reference as when I begin a sentence with such a phrase as "the table". The difference between the use of the definite and indefinite articles is, very roughly, as follows. We use "the" either when a previous reference has been made, and when "the" signalises that the same reference is being

made; or when, in the absence of a previous indefinite reference, the context (including the hear's assumed knowledge) is expected to enable the hearer to tell *what* reference is being made. We use "a" either when these conditions are not fulfilled, or when, although a definite reference *could* be made, we wish to keep dark the identity of the individual to whom, or to which, we are referring. This is the *arch* use of such a phrase as "a certain person" or "some one"; where it could be expanded, not into "some one, but you wouldn't (or I don't) know who" but into "some one, but I'm not telling you who".

(*b*) *Identification statements.* By this label I intend statements like the following:

(i*a*) That is the man who swam the channel twice on one day.
(ii*a*) Napoleon was the man who ordered the execution of the Duc D'Enghien.

The puzzle about these statements is that their grammatical predicates do not seem to be used in a straightforwardly ascriptive way as are the grammatical predicates of the statements:

(i*b*) That man swam the channel twice in one day.
(ii*b*) Napoleon ordered the execution of the Duc D'Enghien.

But if, in order to avoid blurring the difference between (i*a*) and (i*b*) and (ii*a*) and (ii*b*), one says that the phrases which form the grammatical complements of (i*a*) and (ii*a*) are being used referringly, one becomes puzzled about what is being said in these sentences. We seem then to be referring to the same person twice over and either saying nothing about him and thus making no statement, or identifying him with himself and thus producing a trivial identity.

The bogey of triviality can be dismissed. This only arises for those who think of the object referred to by the use of an expression as its meaning, and thus think of the subject and complement of these sentences as meaning the same because they could be used to refer to the same person.

I think the differences between sentences in the (*a*) group and sentences in the (*b*) group can best be understood by considering the differences between the circumstances in which you would say (i*a*) and the circumstances in which you would say (i*b*). You would say (i*a*) instead of (i*b*) if you knew or believed that your hearer knew or believed that *some one* had swum the channel twice in one day. You say (i*a*) when you take your hearer to be in the position of one who can ask: "Who swam the channel twice in one day?" (And in asking this, he is not saying that anyone did, though his asking it implies—in the relevant sense—that some one did.) Such sentences are like answers to such questions. They are better called "identification-statements" than "identities". Sentence (i*a*) does not assert more or less than sentence (i*b*). It is just that you say (i*a*) to a man whom you take to know certain things that you take to be unknown to the man to whom you say (i*b*).

This is, in the barest essentials, the solution to Russell's puzzle about "denoting phrases" joining by "is"; one of the puzzles which he claims for the Theory of Descriptions the merit of solving.

(*c*) *The logic of subjects and predicates*. Much of what I have said of the uniquely referring use of expressions can be extended, with suitable modifications, to the non-uniquely referring use of expressions; i.e. to some uses of expressions consisting of "the" "all the", "all", "some", "some of the", etc. followed by a noun, qualified or unqualified, in the plural; to some uses of "they", "them", "those", "these"; and to conjunctions of names. Expressions of the first kind have a special interest. Roughly speaking, orthodox modern criticism, inspired by mathematical logic, of such traditional doctrines as that of the Square of Opposition and of some of the forms of the syllogism traditionally recognised as valid,

rests on the familiar failure to recognise the special sense in which existential assertions may be implied by the referring use of expressions. The universal propositions of the fourfold schedule, it is said, must *either* be given a negatively existential interpretation (*e.g.*, for A, "there are no Xs which are not Ys") or they must be interpreted as conjunctions of negatively and positively existential statements of, *e.g.*, the form (for A) "there are no Xs which are not Ys, and there are Xs". The I and O forms are normally given a positively existential interpretation. It is then seen that, whichever of the above alternatives is selected, some of the traditional laws have to be abandoned. The dilemma, however, is a bogus one. If we interpret the propositions of the schedule as neither positively, nor negatively, nor positively *and* negatively, existential, but as sentences such that *the question of whether they are being used to make true or false assertions does not arise except when the existential condition is fulfilled for the subject term*, then all the traditional laws hold good together. And this interpretation is far closer to the most common uses of expressions beginning with "all" and "some" that is any Russellian alternative. For these expressions are most commonly used in the referring way. A literal-minded and childless man asked whether all his children are asleep will certainly not answer "Yes" on the ground that he has none; but nor will he answer "No" on this ground. Since he has no children, the question does not arise. To say this is not to say that I may not use the sentence, "All my children are asleep", with the intention of letting some one know that I have children, or of deceiving him into thinking that I have. Nor is it any weakening of my thesis to concede that singular phrases of the form "the so-and-so" may sometimes be used with a similar purpose. Neither Aristotelian nor Russellian rules give the exact logic of any expression of ordinary language; for ordinary language has no exact logic.

Notes

1   This usage of 'use' is, of course, different from (a) the current usage in which 'use' (of a particular word, phrase, sentence) = (roughly) 'rules for using' = (roughly) 'meaning'; and from (b) my own usage in the phrase "uniquely referring use of expressions" in which 'use' = (roughly) 'way of using'.

2   Since this article was written, there has appeared a clear statement of this point by Mr Geach in *Analysis* Vol. 10, No. 4, March, 1950.

3   The unsophisticated kind begins: "Once upon time there was . . .".

4   And this in spite of the danger-signal of that phrase, "*misleading* grammatical form".

5   I neglect relational sentences; for these require, not a modification in the principle of what I say, but a complication of the detail.

Chapter 8

Bertrand Russell

MR. STRAWSON ON REFERRING

Mr. P. F. Strawson published in *Mind* of 1950 an article called "On Referring" [this volume, Chapter 7]. This article is reprinted in *Essays in Conceptual Analysis*, selected and edited by Professor Antony Flew. The references that follow are to this reprint. The main purpose of the article is to refute my theory of descriptions. As I find that some philosophers whom I respect consider that it has achieved its purpose successfully, I have come to the conclusion that a polemical reply is called for. I may say, to begin with, that I am totally unable to see any validity whatever in any of Mr. Strawson's arguments. Whether this inability is due to senility on my part or to some other cause, I must leave readers to judge.

The gist of Mr. Strawson's argument consists in identifying two problems which I have regarded as quite distinct—namely, the problem of descriptions and the problem of egocentricity. I have dealth with both these problems at considerable length, but as I have considered them to be different problems, I have not dealt with the one when I was considering the other. This enables Mr. Strawson to pretend that I have overlooked the problem of egocentricity.

He is helped in this pretence by a careful selection of material. In the article in which I first set forth the theory of descriptions, I dealt specially with two examples: "The present King of France is bald" and "Scott is the author of *Waverley*". The latter example does not suit Mr.

Strawson, and he therefore entirely ignores it except for one quite perfunctory reference. As regards "the present King of France", he fastens upon the egocentric word "present" and does not seem able to grasp that, if for the word "present" I had substituted the words "in 1905", the whole of his argument would have collapsed.

Or perhaps not quite the whole for reasons which I had set forth before Mr. Strawson wrote. It is, however, not difficult to give other examples of the use of descriptive phrases from which egocentricity is wholly absent. I should like to see him apply his doctrine to such sentences as the following: "the square-root of minus one is half the square-root of minus four", or "the cube of three is the integer immediately preceding the second perfect number". There are no egocentric words in either of these two sentences, but the problem of interpreting the descriptive phrases is exactly the same as if there were.

There is not a word in Mr. Strawson's article to suggest that I ever considered egocentric words, still less, that the theory which he advocates in regard to them is the very one which I had set forth at great length and in considerable detail.[1] The gist of what he has to say about such words is the entirely correct statement that what they refer to depends upon when and where they are used. As to this, I need only quote one paragraph from *Human Knowledge* (p. 107):

'This' denotes whatever, at the moment when the word is used, occupies the centre of attention. With words which are not egocentric what is constant is something about the object indicated, but 'this' denotes a different object on each occasion of its use: what is constant is not the object denoted, but its relation to the particular use of the word. Whenever the word is used, the person using it is attending to something, and the word indicates this something. When a word is not egocentric, there is no need to distinguish between different occasions when it is used, but we must make this distinction with egocentric words, since what they indicate is something having a given relation to the particular use of the word.

I must refer also to the case that I discuss (pp. 101 ff.) in which I am walking with a friend on a dark night. We lose touch with each other and he calls, "Where are you?" and I reply "Here I am!" It is of the essence of a scientific account of the world to reduce to a minimum the egocentric element in an assertion, but success in this attempt is a matter of degree, and is never complete where empirical material is concerned. This is due to the fact that the meanings of all empirical words depend ultimately upon ostensive definitions, that ostensive definitions depend upon experience, and that experience is egocentric. We can, however, by means of egocentric words, *describe* something which is not egocentric; it is this that enables us to use a common language.

All this may be right or wrong, but, whichever it is, Mr. Strawson should not expound it as if it were a theory that he had invented, whereas, in fact, I had set it forth before he wrote, though perhaps he did not grasp the purport of what I said. I shall say no more about egocentricity since, for the reasons I have already given, I think Mr. Strawson completely mistaken in connecting it with the problem of descriptions.

I am at a loss to understand Mr. Strawson's position on the subject of names. When he is writing about me, he says: "There are no logically proper names and there are no descriptions (in this sense)" (p. 26) [p. 90 above]. But when he is writing about Quine, in *Mind*, October, 1956, he takes a quite different line. Quine has a theory that names are unnecessary and can always be replaced by descriptions. This theory shocks Mr. Strawson for reasons which, to me, remain obscure. However, I will leave the defence of Quine to Quine, who is quite capable of looking after himself. What is important for my purpose is to elucidate the meaning of the words, "in this sense" which Mr. Strawson puts in brackets. So far as I can discover from the context, what he objects to is the belief that there are words which are only significant because there is something that they mean, and if there were not this something, they would be empty noises, not words. For my part, I think that there must be such words if language is to have any relation to fact. The necessity for such words is made obvious by the process of ostensive definition. How do we know what is meant by such words as "red" and "blue"? We cannot know what these words mean unless we have seen red and seen blue. If there were no red and no blue in our experience, we might, perhaps, invent some elaborate description which we could substitute for the word "red" or for the word "blue". For example, if you were dealing with a blind man, you could hold a red-hot poker near enough for him to feel the heat, and you could tell him that red is what he would see if he could see—but of course for the word "see" you would have to substitute another elaborate description. Any description which the blind man could understand would have to be in terms of words expressing experiences which he had had. Unless fundamental words in the individual's vocabulary had this kind of direct relation to fact, language in general would have no such relation. I defy Mr. Strawson to give the usual meaning to the word "red" unless there is something which the word designates.

This brings me to a further point. "Red" is usually regarded as a predicate and as designating a universal. I prefer for purposes of philosophical analysis a language in which "red" is a subject, and, while I should not say that it is a positive error to call it a universal, I should say that calling it so invites confusion. This is connected with what Mr. Strawson calls my "logically disastrous theory of names" (p. 39) [p. 90 above]. He does not deign to mention why he considers this theory "logically disastrous". I hope that on some future occasion he will enlighten me on this point.

This brings me to a fundamental divergence between myself and many philosophers with whom Mr. Strawson appears to be in general agreement. They are persuaded that common speech is good enough not only for daily life, but also for philosophy. I, on the contrary, am persuaded that common speech is full of vagueness and inaccuracy, and that any attempt to be precise and accurate requires modification of common speech both as regards vocabulary and as regards syntax. Everybody admits that physics and chemistry and medicine each require a language which is not that of everyday life. I fail to see why philosophy, alone, should be forbidden to make a similar approach towards precision and accuracy. Let us take, in illustration, one of the commonest words of everyday speech: namely, the word "day". The most august use of this word is in the first chapter of *Genesis* and in the Ten Commandments. The desire to keep holy the Sabbath "day" has led orthodox Jews to give a precision to the word "day" which it does not have in common speech: they have defined it as the period from one sunset to the next. Astronomers, with other reasons for seeking precision, have three sorts of day: the true solar day; the mean solar day; and the sidereal day. These have different uses: the true solar day is relevant if you are considering lighting-up time; the mean solar day is relevant if you are sentenced to fourteen days without the option; and the sidereal day is relevant if you are trying to estimate the influence of the tides in retarding the earth's rotation. All these four kinds of day—decalogical, true, mean, and sidereal—are more precise than the common use of the word "day". If astronomers were subject to the prohibition of precision which some recent philosophers apparently favour, the whole science of astronomy would be impossible.

For technical purposes, technical languages differing from those of daily life are indispensable. I feel that those who object to linguistic novelties, if they had lived a hundred and fifty years ago, would have stuck to feet and ounces, and would have maintained that centimetres and grams savour of the guillotine.

In philosophy, it is syntax, even more than vocabulary, that needs to be corrected. The subject-predicate logic to which we are accustomed depends for its convenience upon the fact that at the usual temperature of the earth there are approximately permanent "things". This would not be true at the temperature of the sun, and is only roughly true at the temperatures to which we are accustomed.

My theory of descriptions was never intended as an analysis of the state of mind of those who utter sentences containing descriptions. Mr. Strawson gives the name "S" to the sentence, "The King of France is wise", and he says of me "The way in which he arrived at the analysis was clearly by asking himself what would be the circumstances in which we would say that anyone who uttered the sentence S had made a true assertion". This does not seem to me a correct account of what I was doing. Suppose (which God forbid) Mr. Strawson were so rash as to accuse his char-lady of thieving: she would reply indignantly, "I ain't never done no harm to no one". Assuming her a pattern of virtue, I should say that she was making a true assertion, although, according to the rules of syntax which Mr. Strawson would adopt in his own speech, what she said should have meant: "there was at least one moment when I was injuring the whole human race". Mr. Strawson would not have supposed that this was what she meant to assert, although he would not have used her words to express the same sentiment. Similarly, I was concerned to find a more accurate and analysed thought to replace the somewhat confused thoughts which most people at most times have in their heads.

Mr. Strawson objects to my saying that "the King of France is wise" is false if there is no King of France. He admits that the sentence is significant and not true, but not that it is false. This is a mere question of verbal convenience. He considers that the word "false" has an unalterable meaning which it would be sinful to regard as adjustable, though he prudently avoids telling us what this meaning is. For my part, I find it more convenient to define the word "false" so that every significant sentence is either true or false. This is a purely verbal question; and although I have no wish to claim the support of common usage, I do not think that he can claim it either. Suppose, for example, that in some country there was a law that no person could hold public office if he considered it false that the Ruler of the Universe is wise. I think an avowed atheist who took advantage of Mr. Strawson's doctrine to say that he did not hold this proposition false, would be regarded as a somewhat shifty character.

It is not only as to names and as to falsehood that Mr. Strawson shows his conviction that there is an unalterably right way of using words and that no change is to be tolerated however convenient it may be. He shows the same feeling as regards universal affirmatives—i.e. sentences of the form "All A is B". Traditionally, such sentences are supposed to imply that there are A's, but it is much more convenient in mathematical logic to drop this implication and to consider

that "All A is B" is true if there are no A's. This is wholly and solely a question of convenience. For some purposes the one convention is more convenient, and for others, the other. We shall prefer the one convention or the other according to the purpose we have in view. I agree, however, with Mr. Strawson's statement (p. 52 [p. 103 above]) that ordinary language has no exact logic.

Mr. Strawson, in spite of his very real logical competence, has a curious prejudice against logic. On page 43 [p. 99 above], he has a sudden dithyrambic outburst, to the effect that life is greater than logic, which he uses to give a quite false interpretation of my doctrines.

Leaving detail aside, I think we may sum up Mr. Strawson's argument and my reply to it as follows:

There are two problems, that of descriptions and that of egocentricity. Mr. Strawson thinks they are one and the same problem, but it is obvious from his discussion that he has not considered as many kinds of descriptive phrases as are relevant to the argument. Having confused the two problems, he asserts dogmatically that it is only the egocentric problem that needs to be solved, and he offers a solution of this problem which he seems to believe to be new, but which in fact was familiar before he wrote. He then thinks that he has offered an adequate theory of descriptions, and announces his supposed achievement with astonishing dogmatic certainty. Perhaps I am doing him an injustice, but I am unable to see in what respect this is the case.

Note

1 Cf. *Inquiry into Meaning and Truth*, chap. vii, and *Human Knowledge*, Part II, chap. iv.

PART FOUR

Rigidity vs descriptivism

INTRODUCTION TO PART FOUR

IN PART THREE we considered singular *definite descriptions* – complex expressions such as 'the capital city of France', which pick out individual objects by specifying properties they exhibit uniquely. Before the appearance in 1905 of Russell's 'On Denoting', it was widely assumed that definite descriptions are singular terms – expressions whose contributions to the meanings of sentences in which they feature might be isolated as a single 'unit of significance' – whether that unit is thought to be the term's *referent*, or on Frege's theory, its *sense*. Our principal focus in Part Three was Russell's contention that on the contrary, definite descriptions are devices of *quantification:* phrases which do not mean anything on their own, but which, in sentential contexts, deliver information about *how many* objects exhibit given features or properties.

The *description theory* is a theory about the meanings of proper names and other noun phrases, which, in its most basic version, contends simply that these are synonymous with certain definite descriptions. Thus, e.g. an advocate might suggest that the meaning of 'Paris' is given by the description, 'the capital city of France', and that 'Bertrand Russell' is synonymous with, 'the author of "On Denoting" '.[1] (Part of the appeal of the idea is then that we can deploy Russell's analysis of definite descriptions to explain the semantics of names.) More sophisticated versions of the theory refine this basic picture in two ways which are worth mentioning right at the outset. First, many advocates propose that meanings are captured not by single descriptions, but by 'clusters' of them. Thus, e.g. the suggestion might be that the meaning a speaker associates with a name is given by a *set* of descriptive beliefs she associates with it – and the elements of this set might be 'weighted' to reflect the idea that some of them are more relevant to meaning than others. Second, descriptivists assume that understanding the terms in question is a matter of associating them with the

---

[1] The view is commonly attributed to both Frege and Russell, and although both attributions are contested, it is fairly easy to see why. Frege's notion of a mode of presentation is somewhat imprecise, and one way in which we can try to pin it down is by way of the proposal that grasping the sense of a name is a matter of thinking of its referent as the satisfier of a definite description. (Indeed, Frege himself seems to suggest as much in Chapter 4 above (note 11, p. 55).) In Chapter 6 above, Russell suggests that when we ask whether Homer existed, we use the word 'Homer' as an 'abbreviated description – we may replace it by (say) "the author of the *Iliad* and the *Odyssey*" ' – and he suggests that 'The same considerations apply to almost all uses of what look like proper names' (p. 87 above). As we saw in Part Three, Russell's theory of descriptions was motivated – inter alia – by the need to explain two apparent data: that definite descriptions which lack satisfying objects can be meaningful, and that pairs of sentences which differ only in respect of co-referring definite descriptions can exhibit different cognitive values. But as is familiar from Part Two, ordinary proper names ('Ulysses'; 'Bob Dylan' and 'Robert Zimmerman', etc.) give rise to analogous problems.

properties specified by such (clusters of) descriptions – not with the descriptions themselves qua linguistic entities. Thus (as Jackson emphasizes in the second reading below) descriptivists need not suppose that speakers can always articulate the relevant descriptions, nor even that their language affords the resources to do so.

During the 1960s and 1970s the description theory was subjected to a variety of attacks, mainly from advocates of the direct reference view of names. The most thoroughly developed and sustained of these came from Saul Kripke, in influential lectures first published in 1972, and from which the first reading below is an excerpt. Kripke begins the Lecture by listing six theses which he takes to be characteristic of the description theory. This provides a much more precise formulation than we attempted above, and readers are encouraged to work through these six carefully, to assess for themselves whether they are all essential to the descriptivist view, and whether some are more fundamentally so than others. The critical remarks that make up the remainder of the lecture are somewhat disjointed, but it has become customary to think of his and his allies' anti-descriptivist campaign as roughly divisible into three arguments, commonly labelled 'epistemic', 'semantic' and 'modal'.

Advocates of the description theory maintain that understanding a name is a matter of associating it with a certain property or set of properties. This seems to entail that someone who understands a name can know *a priori* – just by reflection on the name's meaning – that the name's referent exhibits these properties. The 'epistemic argument' (which does not feature prominently in the extract below) exploits this consequence. Speakers do not generally know *a priori* that Paris is the capital of France, that Russell wrote 'On Denoting', etc., so if those are the descriptions claimed by the descriptivist to be synonymous with the names, then what the descriptivist says has implausible epistemic consequences.

The 'semantic argument' focuses on two apparent features of the clusters of properties which ordinary speakers associate with names. First, they are often too coarsely grained to determine a unique object as the name's referent. E.g. many people do not know any more about Bertrand Russell than that he was a British twentieth-century philosopher, but even so, they succeed in referring to a *particular* British twentieth-century philosopher when they use his name. Second, some of the properties speakers associate with names are not in fact exhibited by the names' referents. Kripke's example is the nineteenth-century mathematician, Peano, whom most people believe to have discovered a certain set of arithmetical axioms (known as the 'Peano axioms'), and about whom most people have practically no other beliefs. In fact, the theorems are misattributed: they were discovered by Dedekind, a distinct mathematician. Even so, Kripke argues, ordinary (misinformed) users of the name 'Peano' refer with it to Peano, not to Dedekind.

The 'modal argument' focuses on an apparent contrast between the behaviour of names and descriptions in the contexts of sentences involving necessity and possibility. Consider, e.g.:

(1)   Necessarily, the capital city of France is the capital city of France;
(2)   Necessarily, Paris is the capital city of France.

Sentence (1) is true, while sentence (2) is false: hence the name 'Paris' is not synonymous with the description, 'the capital city of France'. And it seems unlikely that we can protect the description theory against this kind of objection by replacing that simple description with a *cluster* of properties that people associate with the name, because the majority (if not all) of these are at best contingent properties of the city.

Wholehearted though he is in his rejection of descriptivism, Kripke is somewhat reluctant to declare an affiliation with an alternative theory. Notwithstanding this modesty, his sympathies clearly lie with the direct reference view, and his positive remarks on this have also proven influential. According to him, the relation between a contemporary speaker's use of a name like 'Bertrand Russell' and the referent of the name is direct in the sense that it is not mediated by properties the speaker associates with the name; however, in another, *causal* sense the relation is indirect. If a contemporary speaker can use a name like 'Bertrand Russell' to refer to its referent, this will typically be because she learned the name from someone else, who learned it from someone else, and so on. This chain of acquisitions (each a causal relation) began with a *baptism:* an event at which (whether explicitly or implicitly) the object was given the name.

Kripke is less modest in respect of necessity and possibility. Consider the following sentence:

(3)   If John McCain had won the 2008 presidential election, the 44th president of the US would be (or would have been) a Republican.

In (3), the definite description 'the 44th president of the US' denotes John McCain rather than Barack Obama. Kripke recommends formulating this kind of consideration in terms of 'possible worlds'. There is a possible world in which McCain, and not Obama, won the 2008 election; and the description, 'the 44th president of the US' denotes McCain in this possible world, while it denotes Obama in the 'actual' world. Kripke observes that names do not seem to behave in this way. Consider, e.g., the following:

(4)   If John McCain had won the 2008 presidential election, Barack Obama would have had more free time in 2009;
(5)   If Bertrand Russell had not written 'On Denoting', someone else would have formulated the theory of descriptions.

It is plausible that in contrast to the description in (3), the names 'Barack Obama' in (4) and 'Bertrand Russell' in (5) denote the very same objects as they do in sentences which do not envisage non-actual situations: i.e. they denote the same objects in the possible worlds invoked by those sentences as they do in the actual world. Kripke's celebrated doctrine that proper names are '*rigid designators*' generalizes this result. According to this doctrine, a proper name has the same referent in every possible world in which the object exists.

An arresting consequence of the view that proper names are rigid designators is that the propositions expressed by sentences which use co-referring names to attribute the relation of identity, e.g.,

(6)   Bob Dylan is Robert Zimmerman,

are, if true, *necessarily* true, and this is so notwithstanding the fact that they cannot typically be known a priori.

As we suggested above, the description theory can be applied to types of noun phrase other than proper names. Although Kripke accepts some of these applications, he is critical of others, for reasons analogous to those he brings to bear on the proper-name case. Prominent amongst these are 'natural kind terms' – expressions such as 'water', 'H_2O', 'tiger', etc. which are commonly assumed to designate objective kinds or properties (i.e. to 'cut nature at its joints'). According to Kripke, these are, like proper names, rigid designators; and in consequence, propositions such as the one expressed by

(7)   Water is H_2O

are, like (6), necessarily true if they are true; even though as empirical, scientific discoveries, they are paradigm examples of propositions our knowledge of which is a posteriori.[2]

To defend their view against Kripke's attack, advocates of the description theory usually argue that he fails properly to consider the best candidates for the roles of meaning-codifying descriptions (or better: the best candidates for the roles of proper-ties whose association by speakers with terms constitutes their understanding). They concede that Kripke is right (in his positive remarks) to emphasize the causal chains through which such terms are passed from one speaker to another, but respond to the semantic arguments by proposing that such causal-historical properties number amongst those that typical speakers associate with the expressions. Thus, e.g., even people who do not have many true beliefs about Bertrand Russell's distinctive work and deeds associate with the name 'Bertrand Russell' the property of *being the causal source* of the information they associate with the name. In most ordinary cases, however indiscriminating or even inaccurate that information may be, this property of being its causal source is uniquely exhibited by the referent of the name. Kripke anticipates and criticizes this kind of response explicitly in the first reading below, and in the final section of the second, Jackson responds to this (and other) criticisms: we leave it to the reader to adjudicate this important debate.

Jackson's response to Kripke's modal argument comes earlier in his paper. The key move is his observation that descriptions which make essential reference to the *actual*

---

[2] Some prominent sympathetic commentators, e.g. Salmon 2004, maintain that in sentences like (7), natural kind terms operate as proper names (of kinds). Others, e.g. Soames 2002, contend that some of them (e.g. 'H_2O') operate as predicate expressions. Salmon and Soames agree that the terms are rigid, but as you would expect, there are important differences between their characterizations of rigidity as it applies to such terms.

world are rigid designators – he calls these 'rigidified descriptions'. The description, 'the capital city of France' designates different objects in different possible worlds, but it is plausible that the description, 'the *actual* capital city of France' designates the same object in every possible world. Thus, if a descriptivist wishes to concede to Kripke that proper names such as 'Paris' are rigid designators, she can accommodate this by characterizing the descriptions she claims to codify the meaning of names as descriptions of this latter, rigidified kind.[3]

[3] Most descriptivists do concede that ordinary proper names are rigid. A prominent exception is Dummett. See his 1981, ch. 5, appendix.

Questions and tasks

1   Do you think the cluster version of the description theory is better equipped to evade Kripke's objections than the simple version that identifies the meaning of a name or natural kind term with that of a single description?

2   In your own words and using your own examples, explain Kripke's theory that proper names are 'rigid designators'. Can you think of any rigid designators that are not names?

3   For which kinds of expressions (if any) does Kripke accept the description theory?

4   How plausible are Kripke's assessments of the beliefs ordinary speakers have about Feynman, Cicero, Peano, etc.? Are there any beliefs which ordinary speakers associate with such names, and in terms of which a description theorist might formulate a version of her theory that evades Kripke's semantic argument(s)?

5   How plausible is Kripke's claim that natural kind terms such as 'water' and 'H_2O' are rigid designators? Do you think these terms are names? If not, what does it mean to describe them as rigid designators?

6   Is there a difference in meaning between the descriptions, 'the capital city of France' and 'the actual capital city of France'? If you think there is, try to articulate what it consists of in your own words.

7   On the basis of the various responses he makes to different objections to the description theory, precisely how do you think Jackson would characterize the meanings of the terms, 'Bertrand Russell', 'Paris' and 'water'? Does this account evade Kripke's objections?

References and further reading

Braun, D. 2006: 'Names and Natural Kind Terms', in E. Lepore and B. Smith (eds), *The Oxford Handbook of Philosophy of Language*, Oxford: Oxford University Press, pp. 490–515.

Chalmers, D. 2006: 'Two-Dimensional Semantics', in E. Lepore and B. Smith (eds), *The Oxford Handbook of Philosophy of Language*, Oxford: Oxford University Press, pp. 574–606.

Davies, M., and Humberstone, L. 1980: 'Two Notions of Necessity', *Philosophical Studies* 38, pp. 1–30.

Devitt, M. 1981: *Designation*, New York: Columbia University Press.

Donnellan, K. 1966: 'Reference and Definite Descriptions', *Philosophical Review* 77, pp. 281–304.

Donnellan, K. 1972: 'Proper Names and Identifying Descriptions', in D. Davidson and G. Harman, (eds), *Semantics of Natural Language*, Dordrecht: D. Reidel, pp. 356–79.

Dummett, M. 1981: *Frege. Philosophy of Language*, 2nd edn, London: Duckworth.

Evans, G. 1973: 'The Causal Theory of Names', *Proceedings of the Aristotelian Society Supplementary Volume* 47, pp. 187–208; reprinted in G. Evans, *Collected Papers*, Oxford: Oxford University Press (1985).

Evans, G. 1979: 'Reference and Contingency,' *Monist* 62, pp. 160–89.

Kaplan, D. 1989: 'Demonstratives', in J. Almog, H. Wettstein, and J. Perry (eds), *Themes from Kaplan*, Oxford: Oxford University Press, pp. 481–563.

Kripke, S. 1980: *Naming and Necessity*, Oxford: Blackwell.

LaPorte, J. 2008: 'Rigid Designators', in Edward N. Zalta (ed.), *The Stanford Encyclopedia of Philosophy* (Fall 2008 edn), http://plato.stanford.edu/archives/fall2008/entries/rigid-designators/

Noonan, H. 2001: Ch. 5 of *Frege: A Critical Introduction*, Cambridge, UK: Polity Press.

Salmon, N. 2004: *Reference and Essence* (Revised edn), Amherst, MA: Prometheus Books; 1st edn, Oxford: Oxford University Press (1982).

Salmon, N. 2005: 'Are General Terms Rigid?', *Linguistics and Philosophy* 28, pp. 117–34.

Searle, J. 1958: 'Proper Names', *Mind* 67, pp. 166–73.

Soames, S. 2002: *Beyond Rigidity: The Unfinished Semantic Agenda of Naming and Necessity*, Oxford: Oxford University Press.

Soames, S. 2005: *Reference and Description: The Case against Two-Dimensionalism*, Princeton, NJ: Princeton University Press.

Sainsbury, M. 1993: 'Russell on Names and Communication', in A. D. Irvine and G. A. Wedeking (eds), *Russell and Analytic Philosophy*, Toronto: University of Toronto Press; reprinted in M. Sainsbury, *Departing from Frege*, London: Routledge (2002).

Stanley, J. 1997: 'Names and Rigid Designation', in B. Hale and C. Wright (eds), *A Companion to the Philosophy of Language*, Oxford: Blackwell, pp. 555–85.

Chapter 9

Saul Kripke

NAMING AND NECESSITY (LECTURE II)

Last time we ended up talking about a theory of naming [see original reading for references to previous and planned lectures] which is given by a number of these here on the board.

(1) To every name or designating expression 'X', there corresponds a cluster of properties, namely the family of those properties φ such that A believes 'φX'.

(2) One of the properties, or some conjointly, are believed by A to pick out some individual uniquely.

(3) If most, or a weighted most, of the φ's are satisfied by one unique object y, then y is the referent of 'X'.

(4) If the vote yields no unique object, 'X' does not refer.

(5) The statement, 'If X exists, then X has most of the φ's' is known *a priori* by the speaker.

(6) The statement, 'If X exists, then X has most of the φ's' expresses a necessary truth (in the idiolect of the speaker).

(C) For any successful theory, the account must not be circular. The properties which are used in the vote must not themselves involve the notion of reference in such a way that it is ultimately impossible to eliminate.

(C) is not a thesis but a condition on the satisfaction of the other theses. In other words, Theses (1)–(6) cannot be satisfied in a way which leads to a circle, in a way which does not lead to any independent determination of reference. The example I gave last time of a blatantly circular attempt to satisfy these conditions was a theory of names mentioned by William Kneale. I was a little surprised at the statement of the theory when I was reading what I had copied down, so I looked it up again. I looked it up in the book to see if I'd copied it down accurately. Kneale *did* use the past tense. He said that though it is not trifling to be told that Socrates was the greatest philosopher of ancient Greece, it is trifling to be told that Socrates was called 'Socrates'. Therefore, he concludes, the name 'Socrates' must simply mean 'the individual called "Socrates" '. Russell, as I've said, in some places gives a similar analysis. Anyway, as stated using the past tense, the condition wouldn't be circular, because one certainly could decide to use the term 'Socrates' to refer to whoever was called 'Socrates' by the Greeks. But, of course, in that sense it's not at all trifling to be told that Socrates was called 'Socrates'. If this is any kind of fact, it might be false. Perhaps we know that *we* call him 'Socrates'; that hardly shows that the Greeks did so. In fact, of course, they may have pronounced the name differently. It may be, in the case of this particular name, that transliteration from the Greek is so good that the English version is not pronounced *very* differently from the Greek. But that won't be so in the general case. Certainly it is not trifling to be told that Isaiah was called 'Isaiah'. In fact, it is false to be told that Isaiah was called 'Isaiah'; the prophet wouldn't have recognized this name at all. And of course the Greeks didn't call their country anything like 'Greece'. Suppose we amend the thesis so that it reads: it's trifling to be told that Socrates is called 'Socrates' by us, or at least, by me, the speaker. Then in some sense this is fairly trifling. I don't think it is necessary or analytic. In the same way, it is trifling to be told that horses are called 'horses', without this leading to the conclusion that the word 'horse' simply *means* 'the animal called a "horse" '. As a theory of the reference of the name 'Socrates' it will lead immediately to a vicious circle. If one was determining the referent of a name like 'Glunk' to himself and made the following decision, 'I shall use the term "Glunk" to refer to the man that I call "Glunk" ', this would get one nowhere. One had better have some independent determination of the referent of 'Glunk'. This is a good example of a blatantly circular determination. Actually sentences like 'Socrates is called "Socrates" ' are very interesting and one can spend, strange as it may seem, hours talking about their analysis. I actually did, once, do that. I won't do that, however, on this occasion. (See how high the seas of language can rise. And at the lowest points too.) Anyway this is a useful example of a violation of the noncircularity condition. The theory will satisfy all of these statements, perhaps, but it satisfies them only because there is some independent way of determining the reference independently of the particular condition: being the man called 'Socrates'.

I have already talked about, in the last lecture, Thesis (6). Theses (5) and (6), by the way, have converses. What I said for Thesis (5) is that the statement that if X exists, X has most of the φ's, is *a priori* true for the speaker. It will also be true under the given theory that certain converses of this statement hold true also *a priori* for the speaker, namely: if any unique thing has most of the properties φ in the properly weighted sense, it is X. Similarly a certain converse to this will be *necessarily* true, namely: if

anything has most of the properties φ in the properly weighted sense, it is X. So really one can say that it is both *a priori* and necessary that something is X if and only if it uniquely has most of the properties φ. This really comes from the previous Theses (1)–(4), I suppose. And (5) and (6) really just say that a sufficiently reflective speaker grasps this theory of proper names. Knowing this, he therefore sees that (5) and (6) are true. The objections to Theses (5) and (6) will *not* be that some speakers are unaware of this theory and therefore don't know these things.

What I talked about in the last lecture is Thesis (6). It's been observed by many philosophers that, if the cluster of properties associated with a proper name is taken in a very narrow sense, so that only one property is given any weight at all, let's say one definite description to pick out the referent—for example, Aristotle was the philosopher who taught Alexander the Great—then certain things will seem to turn out to be necessary truths which are not necessary truths—in this case, for example, that Aristotle taught Alexander the Great. But as Searle said, it is not a necessary truth but a contingent one that Aristotle ever went into pedagogy. Therefore, he concludes that one must drop the original paradigm of a single description and turn to that of a cluster of descriptions.

To summarize some things that I argued last time, this is not the correct answer (whatever it may be) to this problem about necessity. For Searle goes on to say,

> Suppose we agree to drop 'Aristotle' and use, say, 'the teacher of Alexander', then it is a necessary truth that the man referred to is Alexander's teacher—but it is a contingent fact that Aristotle ever went into pedagogy, though I am suggesting that it is a necessary fact that Aristotle has the logical sum, inclusive disjunction, of properties commonly attributed to him. . . .[1]

This is what is not so. It just is not, in any

intuitive sense of necessity, a necessary truth that Aristotle had the properties commonly attributed to him. There is a certain theory, perhaps popular in some views of the philosophy of history, which might both be deterministic and yet at the same time assign a great role to the individual in history. Perhaps Carlyle would associate with the meaning of the name of a great man his achievements. According to such a view it will be necessary, once a certain individual is born, that he is destined to perform various great tasks and so it will be part of the very nature of Aristotle that he should have produced ideas which had a great influence on the western world. Whatever the merits of such a view may be as a view of history or the nature of great men, it does not seem that it should be trivially true on the basis of a theory of proper names. It would seem that it's a contingent fact that Aristotle ever did *any* of the things commonly attributed to him today, *any* of these great achievements that we so much admire. I must say that there is *something* to this feeling of Searle's. When I hear the name 'Hitler', I do get an illusory 'gut feeling' that it's sort of analytic that that man was evil. But really, probably not. Hitler might have spent all his days in quiet in Linz. In that case we would not say that then this man would not have been Hitler, for we use the name 'Hitler' just as the name of that man, even in describing other possible worlds. (This is the notion which I called a *rigid designator* in the previous talk.) Suppose we do decide to pick out the reference of 'Hitler', as the man who succeeded in having more Jews killed than anyone else managed to do in history. That is the way we pick out the reference of the name; but in another counterfactual situation where some one else would have gained this discredit, we wouldn't say that in that case that other man would have been Hitler. If Hitler had never come to power, Hitler would not have had the property which I am supposing we use to fix the reference of his name. Similarly, even if we define what a meter is by reference to the standard meter stick,

it will be a contingent truth and not a necessary one that that particular stick is one meter long. If it had been stretched, it would have been longer than one meter. And that is because we use the term 'one meter' rigidly to designate a certain length. Even though we fix what length we are designating by an accidental property of that length, just as in the case of the name of the man we may pick the man out by an accidental property of the man, still we use the name to designate that man or that length in all possible worlds. The property we use need not be one which is regarded in any way as necessary or essential. In the case of a yard, the original way this length was picked out was, I think, the distance when the arm of King Henry I of England was outstretched from the tip of his finger to his nose. If this was the length of a yard, it nevertheless will not be a necessary truth that the distance between the tip of his finger and his nose should be a yard. Maybe an accident might have happened to foreshorten his arm; that would be possible. And the reason that it's not a necessary truth is not that there might be other criteria in a 'cluster concept' of yardhood. Even a man who strictly uses King Henry's arm as his one standard of length can say, counterfactually, that if certain things had happened to the King, the exact distance between the end of one of his fingers and his nose would not have been exactly a yard. He need not be using a cluster as long as he uses the term 'yard' to pick out a certain fixed reference to be that length in all possible worlds.

These remarks show, I think, the intuitive bizarreness of a good deal of the literature on 'transworld identification' and 'counterpart theory'. For many theorists of these sorts, believing, as they do, that a 'possible world' is given to us only qualitatively, argue that Aristotle is to be 'identified in other possible worlds', or alternatively that his counterparts are to be identified, with those things in other possible worlds who most closely resemble Aristotle in his most important properties. (Lewis, for example, says: 'Your counterparts . . . resemble you . . . in important respects . . . more closely than do the other things in their worlds . . . weighted by the importance of the various respects and by the degrees of the similarities.'') Some may equate the important properties with those properties used to identify the object in the actual world.

Surely these notions are incorrect. To me Aristotle's most important properties consist in his philosophical work and Hitler's in his murderous political role; both, as I have said, might have lacked these properties altogether. Surely there was no logical fate hanging over either Aristotle or Hitler which made it in any sense inevitable that they should have possessed the properties we regard as important to them; they could have had careers completely different from their actual ones. *Important* properties of an object need not be essential, unless 'importance' is used as a synonym for essence; and an object could have had properties very different from its most striking actual properties, or from the properties we use to identify it.

To clear up one thing which some people have asked me: When I say that a designator is rigid, and designates the same thing in all possible worlds, I mean that, as used in *our* language, it stands for that thing, when *we* talk about counterfactual situations. I don't mean, of course, that there mightn't be counterfactual situations in which in the other possible worlds people actually spoke a different language. One doesn't say that 'two plus two equals four' is contingent because people might have spoken a language in which 'two plus two equals four' meant that seven is even. Similarly, when we speak of a counterfactual situation, we speak of it in English, even if it is part of the description of that counterfactual situation that we were all speaking German in that counterfactual situation. We say, 'suppose we had all been speaking German' or 'suppose we had been using English in a nonstandard way'. Then we are describing a possible world or counterfactual situation in which people including ourselves, did speak in a certain way different from the way we speak. But

still, in describing that world, we use English with *our* meanings and *our* references. It is in this sense that I speak of a rigid designator as having the same reference in all possible worlds. I also don't mean to imply that the thing designated exists in all possible worlds, just that the name refers rigidly to that thing. If you say 'suppose Hitler had never been born' then 'Hitler' refers here, still rigidly, to something that would not exist in the counterfactual situation described.

Given these remarks, this means we must cross off Thesis (6) as incorrect. The other theses have nothing to do with necessity and can survive. In particular Thesis (5) has nothing to do with necessity and it can survive. If I use the name 'Hesperus' to refer to a certain planetary body when seen in a certain celestial position in the evening, it will not therefore be a necessary truth that Hesperus is ever seen in the evening. That depends on various contingent facts about people being there to see and things like that. So even if I should say to myself that I will use 'Hesperus' to name the heavenly body I see in the evening in yonder position of the sky, it will not be necessary that Hesperus was ever seen in the evening. But it may be *a priori* in that this is how I have determined the referent. If I have determined that Hesperus is the thing that I saw in the evening over there, then I will know, just from making that determination of the referent, that if there is any Hesperus at all it's the thing I saw in the evening. This at least survives as far as the arguments we have given up to now go.

How about a theory where Thesis (6) is eliminated? Theses (2), (3), and (4) turn out to have a large class of counterinstances. Even when Theses (2)–(4) are true, Thesis (5) is usually false; the truth of Theses (3) and (4) is an empirical 'accident', which the speaker hardly knows *a priori*. That is to say, other principles really determine the speaker's reference, and the fact that the referent coincides with that determined by (2)–(4) is an 'accident', which we were in no position to know *a priori*. Only in a rare class of cases, usually initial baptisms, are all of (2)–(5) true.

What picture of naming do these Theses ((1)–(5)) give you? The picture is this. I want to name an object. I think of some way of describing it uniquely and then I go through, so to speak, a sort of mental ceremony: By 'Cicero' I shall mean the man who denounced Catiline; and that's what the reference of 'Cicero' will be. I will use 'Cicero' to designate rigidly the man who (in fact) denounced Catiline, so I can speak of possible worlds in which he did not. But still my intentions are given by first, giving some condition which uniquely determines an object, then using a certain word as a name for the object determined by this condition. Now there may be some cases in which we actually do this. Maybe, if you want to stretch and call it description, when you say: I shall call that heavenly body over there 'Hesperus'.[3] That is really a case where the theses not only are true but really even give a correct picture of how the reference is determined. Another case, if you want to call this a name, might be when the police in London use the name 'Jack' or 'Jack the Ripper' to refer to the man, whoever he is, who committed all these murders, or most of them. Then they are giving the reference of the name by a description.[4] But in many or most cases, I think the theses are false. So let's look at them.[5]

Thesis (1), as I say, is a definition. Thesis (2) says that one of the properties believed by A of the object, or some conjointly, are believed to pick out some individual uniquely. A sort of example people have in mind is just what I said: I shall use the term 'Cicero' to denote the man who denounced Catiline (or first denounced him in public, to make it unique). This picks out an object uniquely in this particular reference. Even some writers such as Ziff in *Semantic Analysis*, who don't believe that names have meaning in any sense, think that this is a good picture of the way reference can be determined.

Let's see if Thesis (2) is true. It seems, in some *a priori* way, that it's got to be true, because if you don't think that the properties you have in mind pick out anyone uniquely—let's say they're all

satisfied by two people—then how can you say which one of them you're talking about? There seem to be no grounds for saying you're talking about the one rather than about the other. Usually the properties in question are supposed to be some famous deeds of the person in question. For example, Cicero was the man who denounced Catiline. The average person, according to this, when he refers to Cicero, is saying something like 'the man who denounced Catiline' and thus has picked out a certain man uniquely. It is a tribute to the education of philosophers that they have held this thesis for such a long time. In fact, most people, when they think of Cicero, just think of *a famous Roman orator*, without any pretension to think either that there was only one famous Roman orator or that one must know something else about Cicero to have a referent for the name. Consider Richard Feynman, to whom many of us are able to refer. He is a leading contemporary theoretical physicist. Everyone *here* (I'm sure!) can state the contents of one of Feynman's theories so as to differentiate him from Gell-Mann. However, the man in the street, not possessing these abilities, may still use the name 'Feynman'. When asked he will say: well he's a physicist or something. He may not think that this picks out anyone uniquely. I still think he uses the name 'Feynman' as a name for Feynman.

But let's look at some of the cases where we do have a description to pick out someone uniquely. Let's say, for example, that we know that Cicero was the man who first denounced Catiline. Well, that's good. That really picks someone out uniquely. However, there is a problem, because this description contains another name, namely 'Catiline'. We must be sure that we satisfy the conditions in such a way as to avoid violating the noncircularity condition here. In particular, we must not say that Catiline was the man denounced by Cicero. If we do this, we will really not be picking out anything uniquely, we will simply be picking out a pair of objects A and B, such that A denounced B. We do not think that this was the only pair where such denunciations ever occurred; so we had better add some other conditions in order to satisfy the uniqueness condition.

If we say Einstein was the man who discovered the theory of relativity, that certainly picks out someone uniquely. One can be sure, as I said, that everyone *here* can make a compact and independent statement of this theory and so pick out Einstein uniquely; but many people actually don't know enough about this stuff, so when asked what the theory of relativity is, they will say: 'Einstein's theory', and thus be led into the most straightforward sort of vicious circle.

So Thesis (2), in a straightforward way, fails to be satisfied when we say Feynman is a famous physicist without attributing anything else to Feynman. In another way it may not be satisfied in the proper way even when it is satisfied: If we say Einstein was 'the man who discovered relativity theory', that does pick someone out uniquely; but it may not pick him out in such a way as to satisfy the noncircularity condition, because the theory of relativity may in turn be picked out as 'Einstein's theory'. So Thesis (2) seems to be false.

By changing the conditions φ from those usually associated with names by philosophers, one could try to improve the theory. There have been various ways I've heard; maybe I'll discuss these later on. Usually they think of famous achievements of the man named. Certainly in the case of famous achievements, the theory doesn't work. Some student of mine once said, 'Well, Einstein discovered the theory of relativity'; and he determined the reference of 'the theory of relativity' independently by referring to an encyclopedia which would give the details of the theory. (This is what is called a transcendental deduction of the existence of encyclopedias.) But it seems to me that, even if someone has heard of encyclopedias, it really is not essential for his reference that he should know whether this theory is given in detail in any encyclopedia. The reference might

work even if there had been no encyclopedias at all.

Let's go on to Thesis (3): If most of the φ's, suitably weighted, are satisfied by a unique object y, then y is the referent of the name for the speaker. Now, since we have already established that Thesis (2) is wrong, why should any of the rest work? The whole theory depended on always being able to specify unique conditions which are satisfied. But still we can look at the other theses. The picture associated with the theory is that only by giving some unique properties can you know who someone is and thus know what the reference of your name is. Well, I won't go into the question of knowing who someone is. It's really very puzzling. I think you *do* know who Cicero is if you just can answer that he's a famous Roman orator. Strangely enough, if you know that Einstein discovered the theory of relativity and nothing about that theory, you can both know who Einstein is, namely the discoverer of the theory of relativity, and who discovered the theory of relativity, namely Einstein, on the basis of this knowledge. This seems to be a blatant violation of some sort of noncircularity condition; but it is the way we talk. It therefore would seem that a picture which suggests this condition must be the wrong picture.

Suppose most of the φ's are in fact satisfied by a unique object. Is that object necessarily the referent of 'X' for A? Let's suppose someone says that Gödel is the man who proved the incompleteness of arithmetic, and this man is suitably well educated and is even able to give an independent account of the incompleteness theorem. He doesn't just say, 'Well, that's Gödel's theorem', or whatever. He actually states a certain theorem, which he attributes to Gödel as the discoverer. Is it the case, then, that if most of the φ's are satisfied by a unique object y, then y is the referent of the name 'X' for A? Let's take a simple case. In the case of Gödel that's practically the only thing many people have heard about him—that he discovered the incompleteness of arithmetic. Does it follow that whoever discovered the incompleteness of arithmetic is the referent of 'Gödel'?

Imagine the following blatantly fictional situation. (I hope Professor Gödel is not present.) Suppose that Gödel was not in fact the author of this theorem. A man named 'Schmidt', whose body was found in Vienna under mysterious circumstances many years ago, actually did the work in question. His friend Gödel somehow got hold of the manuscript and it was thereafter attributed to Gödel. On the view in question, then, when our ordinary man uses the name 'Gödel', he really means to refer to Schmidt, because Schmidt is the unique person satisfying the description, 'the man who discovered the incompleteness of arithmetic'. Of course you might try changing it to 'the man who *published* the discovery of the incompleteness of arithmetic'. By changing the story a little further one can make even this formulation false. Anyway, most people might not even know whether the thing was published or got around by word of mouth. Let's stick to 'the man who discovered the incompleteness of arithmetic'. So, since the man who discovered the incompleteness of arithmetic is in fact Schmidt, we, when we talk about 'Gödel', are in fact always referring to Schmidt. But it seems to me that we are not. We simply are not. One reply, which I will discuss later, might be: You should say instead, 'the man to whom the incompleteness of arithmetic is commonly attributed', or something like that. Let's see what we can do with that later.

But it may seem to many of you that this is a very odd example, or that such a situation occurs rarely. This also is a tribute to the education of philosophers. Very often we use a name on the basis of considerable misinformation. The case of mathematics used in the fictive example is a good case in point. What do we know about Peano? What many people in this room may 'know' about Peano is that he was the discoverer of certain axioms which characterize the sequence of natural numbers, the so-called 'Peano axioms'. Probably some people can even state them. I have been told that these axioms were not first discovered by Peano but by Dedekind. Peano was of course not a dishonest man. I am told that his footnotes include a credit to Dedekind. Somehow the footnote has been ignored. So on the theory in question the term 'Peano', as we use it, really refers to—now that you've heard it you see that you were really all the time talking about—Dedekind. But you were not. Such illustrations could be multiplied indefinitely.

Even worse misconceptions, of course, occur to the layman. In a previous example I supposed people to identify Einstein by reference to his work on relativity. Actually, I often used to hear that Einstein's most famous achievement was the invention of the atomic bomb. So when we refer to Einstein, we refer to the inventor of the atomic bomb. But this is not so. Columbus was the first man to realize that the earth was round. He was also the first European to land in the western hemisphere. Probably none of these things are true, and therefore, when people use the term 'Columbus' they really refer to some Greek if they use the roundness of the earth, or to some Norseman, perhaps, if they use the 'discovery of America'. But they don't. So it does not seem that if most of the φ's are satisfied by a unique object y, then y is the referent of the name. This seems simply to be false.[6]

Thesis (4): If the vote yields no unique object the name does not refer. Really this case has been covered before—has been covered in my previous examples. First, the vote may not yield a *unique* object, as in the case of Cicero or Feynman. Secondly, suppose it yields *no* object, that nothing satisfies most, or even any, substantial number, of the φ's. Does that mean the name doesn't refer? No: in the same way that you may have false beliefs about a person which may actually be true of someone else, so you may have false beliefs which are true of absolutely no one. And these may constitute the totality of your beliefs. Suppose, to vary the example about

Gödel, no one had discovered the incompleteness of arithmetic—perhaps the proof simply materialized by a random scattering of atoms on a piece of paper—the man Gödel being lucky enough to have been present when this improbable event occurred. Further, suppose arithmetic is in fact complete. One wouldn't really expect a random scattering of atoms to produce a correct proof. A subtle error, unknown through the decades, has still been unnoticed—or perhaps not actually unnoticed, but the friends of Gödel. . . . So even if the conditions are not satisfied by a unique object the name may still refer. I gave you the case of Jonah last week. Biblical scholars, as I said, think that Jonah really existed. It isn't because they think that someone ever was swallowed by a big fish or even went to Nineveh to preach. These conditions may be true of no one whatsoever and yet the name 'Jonah' really has a referent. In the case above of Einstein's invention of the bomb, possibly no one really deserves to be called the 'inventor' of the device.

Thesis (5) says that the statement 'If X exists, then X has most of the φ's', is *a priori* true for *A*. Notice that even in a case where (3) and (4) *happen* to be true, a typical speaker hardly knows *a priori* that they are, as required by the theory. I *think* that my belief about Gödel is in fact correct and that the 'Schmidt' story is just a fantasy. But the belief hardly constitutes *a priori* knowledge.

What's going on here? Can we rescue the theory?[7] First, one may try and vary these descriptions—not think of the famous achievements of a man but, let's say, of something else, and try and use that as our description. Maybe by enough furzing around someone might eventually get something out of this;[8] however, most of the attempts that one tries are open to counter-examples or other objections. Let me give an example of this. In the case of Gödel one may say, 'Well, "Gödel" doesn't mean "the man who proved the incompleteness of arithmetic" '. Look, all we really know is that most people *think* that Gödel proved the incompleteness of arithmetic, that Gödel is the man to whom

the incompleteness of arithmetic is commonly attributed. So when I determine the referent of the name 'Gödel', I don't say to myself, 'by "Gödel" I shall mean "the man who proved the incompleteness of arithmetic, whoever he is" '. That might turn out to be Schmidt or Post. But instead I shall mean 'the man who most people *think* proved the incompleteness of arithmetic'.

Is this right? First, it seems to me that it's open to counter-examples of the same type as I gave before, though the counter-examples may be more recherché. Suppose, in the case of Peano mentioned previously, unbeknownst to the speaker, most people (at least by now) thoroughly realize that the number-theoretic axioms should not be attributed to him. Most people don't credit them to Peano but now correctly ascribe them to Dedekind. So then even the man to whom this thing is commonly attributed will still be Dedekind and not Peano. Still, the speaker, having picked up the old outmoded belief, may still be referring to Peano, and hold a false belief about Peano, not a true belief about Dedekind.

But second, and perhaps more significantly, such a criterion violates the noncircularity condition. How is this? It is true that most of us think that Gödel proved the incompleteness of arithmetic. Why is this so? We certainly say, and sincerely, 'Gödel proved the incompleteness of arithmetic'. Does it follow from that that we believe that Gödel proved the incompleteness of arithmetic—that we attribute the incompleteness of arithmetic to this man? No. Not just from that. We have to be *referring to Gödel* when we say 'Gödel proved the incompleteness of arithmetic'. If, in fact, we were always referring to Schmidt, then we would be attributing the incompleteness of arithmetic to Schmidt and not to Gödel—if we used the sound 'Gödel' as the name of the man whom I am calling 'Schmidt'.

But we do in fact refer to Gödel. How do we do this? Well, not by saying to ourselves, 'By "Gödel" I shall mean the man to whom incompleteness of arithmetic is commonly attributed'. If we did that we would run into a circle. Here we are all in this room. Actually in this institution[9] some people have met the man, but in many institutions this is not so. All of us in the community are trying to determine the reference by saying 'Gödel is to be the man to whom the incompleteness of arithmetic is commonly attributed'. None of us will get started with any attribution unless there is some independent criterion for the reference of the name other than 'the man to whom the incompleteness of arithmetic is commonly attributed'. Otherwise all we will be saying is, 'We attribute this achievement to the man to whom we attribute it', without saying who that man is, without giving any independent criterion of the reference, and so the determination will be circular. This then is a violation of the condition I have marked 'C', and cannot be used in any theory of reference.

Of course you might try to avoid circularity by passing the buck. This is mentioned by Strawson, who says in his footnote on these matters that one man's reference may derive from another's.

The identifying description, though it must not include a reference to the speaker's own reference to the particular in question, may include a reference to another's reference to that particular. If a putatively identifying description is of this latter kind, then, indeed, the question, whether it is a genuinely identifying description, turns on the question, whether the reference it refers to is itself a genuinely identifying reference. So one reference may borrow its credentials, as a genuinely identifying reference, from another; and that from another. But this regress is not infinite.[10]

I may then say, 'Look, by "Gödel" I shall mean the man Joe thinks proved the incompleteness of arithmetic'. Joe may then pass the thing over to Harry. One has to be very careful that this doesn't come round in a circle. Is one really sure that this won't happen? If you could be sure yourself of knowing such a chain, and that everyone else in the chain is using the proper conditions and so is not getting out of it, then maybe you could get back to the man by referring to such a chain in that way, borrowing the references one by one. However, although in general such chains do exist for a living man, you won't know what the chain is. You won't be sure what descriptions the other man is using, so the thing won't go into a circle, or whether by appealing to Joe you won't get back to the right man at all. So you cannot use this as your identifying description with any confidence. You may not even remember from whom you heard of Gödel.

What is the true picture of what's going on? Maybe reference doesn't really take place at all! After all, we don't really know that any of the properties we use to identify the man are right. We don't know that they pick out a unique object. So what *does* make my use of 'Cicero' into a name of *him*? The picture which leads to the cluster-of-descriptions theory is something like this: One is isolated in a room; the entire community of other speakers, everything else, could disappear; and one determines the reference for himself by saying—'By "Gödel" I shall mean the man, whoever he is, who proved the incompleteness of arithmetic'. Now you can do this if you want to. There's nothing really preventing it. You can just stick to that determination. If that's what you do, then if Schmidt discovered the incompleteness of arithmetic you *do* refer to him when you say 'Gödel did such and such'.

But that's not what most of us do. Someone, let's say, a baby, is born; his parents call him by a certain name. They talk about him to their friends. Other people meet him. Through various sorts of talk the name is spread from link to link as if by a chain. A speaker who is on the far end of this chain, who has heard about, say Richard Feynman, in the market place or elsewhere, may be referring to Richard Feynman even though he can't remember from whom he first heard of Feynman or from whom he ever heard of Feynman. He knows that Feynman is a famous physicist. A certain passage of communication reaching ultimately to the man himself does reach the speaker. He then is referring to Feynman even though he can't identify him uniquely. He doesn't know what a Feynman diagram is, he doesn't know what the Feynman theory of pair production and annihilation is. Not only that: he'd have trouble distinguishing between Gell-Mann and Feynman. So he doesn't have to know these things, but, instead, a chain of communication going back to Feynman himself has been established, by virtue of his membership in a community which passed the name on from link to link, not by a ceremony that he makes in private in his study: 'By "Feynman" I shall mean the man who did such and such and such and such'.

How does this view differ from Strawson's suggestion, mentioned before, that one identifying reference may borrow its credentials from another? Certainly Strawson had a good insight in the passage quoted; on the other hand, he certainly shows a difference at least in emphasis from the picture I advocate, since he confines the remark to a footnote. The main text advocates the cluster-of-descriptions theory. Just because Strawson makes his remark in the context of a description theory, his view therefore differs from mine in one important respect. Strawson apparently requires that the speaker must *know* from whom he got his reference, so that he can say: 'By "Gödel" I mean the man *Jones* calls "Gödel" '. If he does not remember how he picked up the reference, he cannot give such a description. The present theory sets no such requirement. As I said, I may well not remember from whom I heard of Gödel, and I may think I remember from which people I heard the name, but wrongly.

These considerations show that the view advocated here can lead to consequences which actually *diverge* from those of Strawson's footnote. Suppose that the speaker has heard the name 'Cicero' from Smith and others, who use the name to refer to a famous Roman orator. He later thinks, however, that he picked up the name from Jones, who (unknown to the speaker) uses 'Cicero' as the name of a notorious German spy and has never heard of any orators of the ancient world. Then, according to Strawson's paradigm, the speaker must determine his reference by the resolution, 'I shall use "Cicero" to refer to the man whom Jones calls by that name', while on the present view, the referent will be the orator in spite of the speaker's false impression about where he picked up the name. The point is that Strawson, trying to fit the chain of communication view into the description theory, relies on what the speaker *thinks* was the source of his reference. If the speaker has forgotten his source, the description Strawson uses is unavailable to him; if he misremembers it, Strawson's paradigm can give the wrong results. On our view, it is not how the speaker thinks he got the reference, but the actual chain of communication, which is relevant.

I think I said the other time that philosophical theories are in danger of being false, and so I wasn't going to present an alternative theory. Have I just done so? Well, in a way; but my characterization has been far less specific than a real set of necessary and sufficient conditions for reference would be. Obviously the name is passed on from link to link. But of course not every sort of causal chain reaching from me to a certain man will do for me to make a reference. There may be a causal chain from our use of the term 'Santa Claus' to a certain historical saint, but still the children, when they use this, by this time probably do not refer to that saint. So other conditions must be satisfied in order to make this into a really rigorous theory of reference. I don't know that I'm going to do this because, first, I'm sort of too lazy at the moment; secondly, rather than giving a set of necessary and sufficient conditions which will work for a term like reference,

I want to present just a *better picture* than the picture presented by the received views.

Haven't I been very unfair to the description theory? Here I have stated it very precisely—more precisely, perhaps, than it has been stated by any of its advocates. So then it's easy to refute. Maybe if I tried to state mine with sufficient precision in the form of six or seven or eight theses, it would also turn out that when you examine the theses one by one, they will all be false. That might even be so, but the difference is this. What I think the examples I've given show is not simply that there's some technical error here or some mistake there, but that the whole picture given by this theory of how reference is determined seems to be wrong from the fundamentals. It seems to be wrong to think that we give ourselves some properties which somehow qualitatively uniquely pick out an object and determine our reference in that manner. What I am trying to present is a better picture—a picture which, if more details were to be filled in, might be refined so as to give more exact conditions for reference to take place.

One might never reach a set of necessary and sufficient conditions. I don't know, I'm always sympathetic to Bishop Butler's 'Everything is what it is and not another thing'—in the non-trivial sense that philosophical analyses of some concept like reference, in completely different terms which make no mention of reference, are very apt to fail. Of course in any particular case when one is given an analysis one has to look at it and see whether it is true or false. One can't just cite this maxim to oneself and then turn the page. But more cautiously, I want to present a better picture without giving a set of necessary and sufficient conditions for reference. Such conditions would be very complicated, but what is true is that it's in virtue of our connection with other speakers in the community, going back to the referent himself, that we refer to a certain man.

There may be some cases where the description picture is true, where some man really gives a name by going into the privacy of his room and saying that the referent is to be the unique thing with certain identifying properties. 'Jack the Ripper' was a possible example which I gave. Another was 'Hesperus'. Yet another case which can be forced into this description is that of meeting someone and being told his name. Except for a belief in the description theory, in its importance in other cases, one probably wouldn't think that that was a case of giving oneself a description, i.e., 'the guy I'm just meeting now'. But one can put it in these terms if one wishes, and if one has never heard the name in any other way. Of course, if you're introduced to a man and told, 'That's Einstein', you've heard of him before, it may be wrong, and so on. But maybe in some cases such a paradigm works—especially for the man who first gives someone or something a name. Or he points to a star and says, 'That is to be Alpha Centauri'. So he can really make himself this ceremony: 'By "Alpha Centauri" I shall mean the star right over there with such and such coordinates'. But in general this picture fails. In general our reference depends not just on what we think ourselves, but on other people in the community, the history of how the name reached one, and things like that. It is by following such a history that one gets to the reference.

More exact conditions are very complicated to give. They seem in a way somehow different in the case of a famous man and one who isn't so famous. For example, a teacher tells his class that Newton was famous for being the first man to think there's a force pulling things to the earth; I think that's what little kids think Newton's greatest achievement was. I won't say what the merits of such an achievement would be, but, anyway, we may suppose that just being told that this was the sole content of Newton's discovery gives the students a false belief *about Newton*, even though they have never heard of him before. If, on the other hand,[11] the teacher uses the name 'George Smith'—a man by that name is actually his next door neighbor—and says that George

Smith first squared the circle, does it follow from this that the students have a false belief about the teacher's neighbor? The teacher doesn't tell them that Smith is his neighbor, nor does he believe Smith first squared the circle. He isn't particularly trying to get any belief *about the neighbor* into the students' heads. He tries to inculcate the belief that there was a man who squared the circle, but not a belief about any particular man—he just pulls out the first name that occurs to him—as it happens, he uses his neighbor's name. It doesn't seem clear in that case that the students have a false belief about the neighbor, even though there is a causal chain going back to the neighbor. I am not sure about this. At any rate more refinements need to be added to make this even begin to be a set of necessary and sufficient conditions. In that sense it's not a theory, but is supposed to give a better picture of what is actually going on.

A rough statement of a theory might be the following: An initial 'baptism' takes place. Here the object may be named by ostension, or the reference of the name may be fixed by a description.[12] When the name is 'passed from link to link', the receiver of the name must, I think, intend when he learns it to use it with the same reference as the man from whom he heard it. If I hear the name 'Napoleon' and decide it would be a nice name for my pet aardvark, I do not satisfy this condition.[13] (Perhaps it is some such failure to keep the reference fixed which accounts for the divergence of present uses of 'Santa Claus' from the alleged original use.)

Notice that the preceding outline hardly *eliminates* the notion of reference; on the contrary, it takes the notion of intending to use the same reference as a given. There is also an appeal to an initial baptism which is explained in terms either of fixing a reference by a description, or ostension (if ostension is not to be subsumed under the other category).[14] (Perhaps there are other possibilities for initial baptisms.) Further, the George Smith case casts some doubt as to the sufficiency of the conditions. Even if the teacher

does refer to his neighbor, is it clear that he has passed on his reference to the pupils? Why shouldn't their belief be about any other man named 'George Smith'? If he says that Newton was hit by an apple, somehow his task of transmitting a reference is easier, since he has communicated a common misconception about Newton.

To repeat, I may not have presented a theory, but I do think that I have presented a better picture than that given by description theorists.

I think the next topic I shall want to talk about is that of statements of identity. Are these necessary or contingent? The matter has been in some dispute in recent philosophy. First, everyone agrees that descriptions can be used to make contingent identity statements. If it is true that the man who invented bifocals was the first Postmaster General of the United States—that these were one and the same—it's contingently true. That is, it might have been the case that one man invented bifocals and another was the first Postmaster General of the United States. So certainly when you make identity statements using descriptions—when you say 'the x such that φx and the x such that ψx are one and the same'—that can be a contingent fact. But philosophers have been interested also in the question of identity statements between names. When we say 'Hesperus is Phosphorus' or 'Cicero is Tully', is what we are saying necessary or contingent? Further, they've been interested in another type of identity statement, which comes from scientific theory. We identify, for example, light with electromagnetic radiation between certain limits of wavelengths, or with a stream of photons. We identify heat with the motion of molecules; sound with a certain sort of wave disturbance in the air; and so on. Concerning such statements the following thesis is commonly held. First, that these are obviously contingent identities: we've found out that light is a stream of photons, but of course it might not have been a stream of photons. Heat is in fact the motion of molecules;

we found that out, but heat might not have been the motion of molecules. Secondly, many philosophers feel damned lucky that these examples are around. Now, why? These philosophers, whose views are expounded in a vast literature, hold to a thesis called 'the identity thesis' with respect to some psychological concepts. They think, say, that pain is just a certain material state of the brain or of the body, or what have you—say the stimulation of C-fibers. (It doesn't matter what.) Some people have then objected, 'Well, look, there's perhaps a *correlation* between pain and these states of the body; but this must just be a contingent correlation between two different things, because it was an empirical discovery that this correlation ever held. Therefore, by "pain" we must mean something different from this state of the body or brain; and, therefore, they must be two different things.'

Then it's said, 'Ah, but you see, this is wrong! Everyone knows that there can be contingent identities.' First, as in the bifocals and Postmaster General case, which I have mentioned before. Second, in the case, believed closer to the present paradigm, of theoretical identifications, such as light and a stream of photons, or water and a certain compound of hydrogen and oxygen. These are all contingent identities. They might have been false. It's no surprise, therefore, that it can be true as a matter of contingent fact and not of any necessity that feeling pain, or seeing red, is just a certain state of the human body. Such psychophysical identifications can be contingent facts just as the other identities are contingent facts. And of course there are widespread motivations—ideological, or just not wanting to have the 'nomological dangler' of mysterious connections not accounted for by the laws of physics, one to one correlations between two different kinds of thing, material states, and things of an entirely different kind, which lead people to want to believe this thesis.

I guess the main thing I'll talk about first is identity statements between names. But I hold

the following about the general case. First, that characteristic theoretical identifications like 'Heat is the motion of molecules', are not contingent truths but necessary truths, and here of course I don't mean just physically necessary, but necessary in the highest degree—whatever that means. (Physical necessity, *might* turn out to be necessity in the highest degree. But that's a question which I don't wish to prejudge. At least for this sort of example, it might be that when something's physically necessary, it always is necessary *tout court*.) Second, that the way in which these have turned out to be necessary truths does not seem to me to be a way in which the mind-brain identities could turn out to be either necessary or contingently true. So this analogy has to go. It's hard to see what to put in its place. It's hard to see therefore how to avoid concluding that the two are actually different.

Let me go back to the more mundane case about proper names. This is already mysterious enough. There's a dispute about this between Quine and Ruth Barcan Marcus.[15] Marcus says that identities between names are necessary. If someone thinks that Cicero is Tully, and really uses 'Cicero' and 'Tully' as names, he is thereby committed to holding that his belief is a necessary truth. She uses the term 'mere tag'. Quine replies as follows, 'We may tag the planet Venus, some fine evening, with the proper name "Hesperus". We may tag the same planet again, some day before sunrise, with the proper name "Phosphorus". When we discover that we have tagged the same planet twice our discovery is empirical. And not because the proper names were descriptions.'[16] First, as Quine says when we discovered that we tagged the same planet twice, our discovery was empirical. Another example I think Quine gives in another book is that the same mountain seen from Nepal and from Tibet, or something like that, is from one angle called 'Mt. Everest' (you've heard of that); from another it's supposed to be called 'Gaurisanker'. It can actually be an empirical discovery that Gaurisanker is Everest. (Quine says that the example is actually false. He got the example from Erwin Schrödinger. You wouldn't think the inventor of wave mechanics got things that wrong. I don't know where the mistake is supposed to come from. One could certainly imagine this situation as having been the case; and it's another good illustration of the sort of thing that Quine has in mind.)

What about it? I wanted to find a good quote on the other side from Marcus in this book but I am having trouble locating one. Being present at that discussion, I remember[17] that she advocated the view that if you really have names, a good dictionary should be able to tell you whether they have the same reference. So someone should be able, by looking in the dictionary, to say that Hesperus and Phosphorus are the same. Now this does not seem to be true. It does seem, to many people, to be a consequence of the view that identities between names are necessary. Therefore the view that identity statements between names are necessary has usually been rejected. Russell's conclusion was somewhat different. He did think there should never be any empirical question whether two names have the same reference. This isn't satisfied for ordinary names, but it is satisfied when you're naming your own sense datum, or something like that. You say, 'Here, this, and that (designating the same sense datum by both demonstratives).' So you can tell without empirical investigation that you're naming the same thing twice; the conditions are satisfied. Since this won't apply to ordinary cases of naming, ordinary 'names' cannot be genuine names.

What should we think about this? First, it's true that someone can use the name 'Cicero' to refer to Cicero and the name 'Tully' to refer to Cicero also, and not know that Cicero is Tully. So it seems that we do not necessarily know a priori that an identity statement between names is true. It doesn't follow from this that the statement so expressed is a contingent one if true. This is what I've emphasized in my first lecture. There is a very strong feeling that leads one to think that, if you can't know something by a priori ratiocination, then it's got to be contingent: it might have turned out otherwise; but nevertheless I think this feeling is wrong.

Let's suppose we refer to the same heavenly body twice, as 'Hesperus' and 'Phosphorus'. We say: Hesperus is that star over there in the evening; Phosphorus is that star over there in the morning. Actually, Hesperus is Phosphorus. Are there really circumstances under which Hesperus wouldn't have been Phosphorus? Supposing that Hesperus is Phosphorus, let's try to describe a possible situation in which it would not have been. Well, it's easy. Someone goes by and he calls two *different* stars 'Hesperus' and 'Phosphorus'. It may even be under the same conditions as prevailed when we introduced the names 'Hesperus' and 'Phosphorus'. But are those circumstances in which Hesperus is not Phosphorus or would not have been Phosphorus? It seems to me that they are not.

Now, of course I'm committed to saying that they're not, by saying that such terms as 'Hesperus' and 'Phosphorus', when used as names, are rigid designators. They refer in every possible world to the planet Venus. Therefore, in that possible world too, the planet Venus is the planet Venus and it doesn't matter what any other person has said in this other possible world. How should *we* describe this situation? He can't have pointed to Venus twice, and in the one case called it 'Hesperus' and in the other 'Phosphorus', as we did. If he did so, then 'Hesperus is Phosphorus' would have been true in that situation too. He pointed maybe neither time to the planet Venus—at least one time he didn't point to the planet Venus, let's say when he pointed to the body he called 'Phosphorus'. Then in that case we can certainly say that the name 'Phosphorus' might not have referred to Phosphorus. We can even say that in the very position when viewed in the morning that we found Phosphorus, it might have been the case that Phosphorus was not there—that something else was there, and that even, under certain circumstances it would have been *called* 'Phosphorus'. But that still is not a case in which Phosphorus was not Hesperus. There might be a possible world in which, a possible counterfactual situation in which, 'Hesperus' and 'Phosphorus' weren't names of the things they in fact are names of. Someone, if he did determine their reference by identifying descriptions, might even have used the very identifying descriptions we used. But still that's not a case in which Hesperus wasn't Phosphorus. For there couldn't have been such a case, given that Hesperus is Phosphorus.

Now this seems very strange because in advance, we are inclined to say, the answer to the question whether Hesperus is Phosphorus might have turned out either way. So aren't there really two possible worlds—one in which Hesperus was Phosphorus, the other in which Hesperus wasn't Phosphorus—in advance of our discovering that these were the same? First, there's one sense in which things might turn out either way, in which it's clear that that doesn't imply that the way it finally turns out isn't necessary. For example, the four color theorem might turn out to be true and might turn out to be false. It might turn out either way. It still doesn't mean that the way it turns out is not necessary. Obviously, the 'might' here is purely 'epistemic'—it merely expresses our present state of ignorance, or uncertainty.

But it seems that in the Hesperus-Phosphorus case, something even stronger is true. The evidence I have before I know that Hesperus is Phosphorus is that I see a certain star or a certain heavenly body in the evening and call it 'Hesperus', and in the morning and call it 'Phosphorus'. I know these things. There certainly is a possible world in which a man should have seen a certain star at a certain position in the evening and called it 'Hesperus' and a certain star in the morning and called it 'Phosphorus'; and should have concluded—should have found out by empirical investigation—that he names two different stars, or two different heavenly bodies.

At least one of these stars or heavenly bodies was not Phosphorus, otherwise it couldn't have come out that way. But that's true. And so it's true that given the evidence that someone has antecedent to his empirical investigation, he can be placed in a sense in exactly the same situation, that is a qualitatively identical epistemic situation, and call two heavenly bodies 'Hesperus' and 'Phosphorus', without their being identical. So in that sense we can say that it might have turned out either way. Not that it might have turned out either way as to Hesperus's being Phosphorus. Though for all we knew in advance, Hesperus wasn't Phosphorus, that couldn't have turned out any other way, in a sense. But being put in a situation where we have exactly the same evidence, qualitatively speaking, it could have turned out that Hesperus was not Phosphorus; that is, in a counterfactual world in which 'Hesperus' and 'Phosphorus' were not used in the way that we use them, as names of this planet, but as names of some other objects, one could have had qualitatively identical evidence and concluded that 'Hesperus' and 'Phosphorus' named two different objects.[18] But we, using the names as we do right now, can say in advance, that if Hesperus and Phosphorus are one and the same, then in no other possible world can they be different. We use 'Hesperus' as the name of a certain body and 'Phosphorus' as the name of a certain body. We use them as names of those bodies in all possible worlds. If, in fact, they are the *same* body, then in any other possible world we have to use them as a name of that object. And so in any other possible world it will be true that Hesperus is Phosphorus. So two things are true: first, that we do not know *a priori* that Hesperus is Phosphorus, and are in no position to find out the answer except empirically. Second, this is so because we could have evidence qualitatively indistinguishable from the evidence we have and determine the reference of the two names by the positions of two planets in the sky, without the planets being the same.

Of course, it is only a contingent truth (not

true in every other possible world) that the star seen over there in the evening is the star seen over there in the morning, because there are possible worlds in which Phosphorus was not visible in the morning. But that contingent truth shouldn't be identified with the statement that Hesperus is Phosphorus. It could only be so identified if you thought that it was a necessary truth that Hesperus is visible over there in the evening or that Phosphorus is visible over there in the morning. But neither of those are necessary truths even if that's the way we pick out the planet. These are the contingent marks by which we identify a certain planet and give it a name.

Notes

1 J. Searle, 'Proper Names', in Caton, C. (ed.), *Philosophy and Ordinary Language*, University of Illinois Press (1963), p. 160

2 D. Lewis, 'Counterpart theory and Quantified Modal Logic', *Journal of Philosophy* 65 (1968), pp. 114–15.

3 An even better case of determining the reference of a name by description, as opposed to ostension, is the discovery of the planet Neptune. Neptune was hypothesized as the planet which caused such and such discrepancies in the orbits of certain other planets. If Leverrier indeed gave the name 'Neptune' to the planet before it was ever seen, then he fixed the reference of 'Neptune' by means of the description just mentioned. At that time he was unable to see the planet even through a telescope. At this stage, an *a priori* material equivalence held between the statements 'Neptune exists' and 'some one planet perturbing the orbit of such and such other planets exists in such and such a position', and also such statements as 'if such and such perturbations are caused by a planet, they are caused by Neptune' had the status of *a priori* truths. Nevertheless, they were not *necessary* truths, since 'Neptune' was introduced as a name rigidly designating a certain planet. Leverrier could well have believed that if Neptune had been knocked off its course one million years earlier, it would have caused no such perturbations and even that some other object might have caused the perturbations in its place.

4 Following Donnellan's remarks on definite descriptions [see Donnellan, K. 1966: 'Reference and Definite Descriptions', *Philosophical Review 77*, pp. 281–304], we should add that in some cases, an object may be identified, and the reference of a name fixed, using a description which may turn out to be false of its object. The case where the reference of 'Phosphorus' is determined as the 'morning star', which later turns out not to be a star, is an obvious example. In such cases, the description which fixes the reference clearly is in no sense known *a priori* to hold of the object, though a more cautious substitute may be. If such a more cautious substitute is available, it is really the substitute which fixes the reference in the sense intended in the text.

5 Some of the theses are sloppily stated in respect of fussy matters like use of quotation marks and related details. (For example, Theses (5) and (6), as stated, presuppose that the speaker's language is English.) Since the purport of the theses is clear, and they are false anyway, I have not bothered to set these things straight.

6 The cluster-of-descriptions theory of naming would make 'Peano discovered the axioms for number theory' express a trivial truth, not a misconception, and similarly for other misconceptions about the history of science. Some who have conceded such cases to me have argued that there are *other* uses of the same proper names satisfying the cluster theory. For example, it is argued, if we say, 'Gödel proved the incompleteness of arithmetic', we are, of course, referring to Gödel, not to Schmidt. But, if we say, 'Gödel relied on a diagonal argument in this step of the proof', don't we here, perhaps, refer to *whoever proved the theorem*? Similarly, if someone asks, 'What did Aristotle (or Shakespeare) have in mind here?', isn't he talking about the author of the passage in question, whoever he is? By analogy to Donnellan's usage for descriptions, this might be called an 'attributive' use of proper names. If this is so, then assuming the Gödel-Schmidt story, the sentence 'Gödel proved the incompleteness theorem' is false, but 'Gödel used a diagonal argument in the proof' is (at least in some contexts) true, and the reference of the name 'Gödel' is ambiguous. Since some counter-examples remain, the

cluster-of-descriptions theory would still, in general, be false, which was my main point in the text; but it would be applicable in a wider class of cases than I thought. I think, however, that no such ambiguity need be postulated. It is, perhaps, true that sometimes when someone uses the name 'Gödel', his main interest is in whoever proved the theorem, and *perhaps*, in some sense, he 'refers' to him. I do not think that this case is different from the case of Smith and Jones in n. 3, p. 25 [see original reading]. If I mistake Jones for Smith, I may *refer* (in an appropriate sense) to Jones when I say that Smith is raking the leaves; nevertheless I do not use 'Smith' ambiguously, as a name sometimes of Smith and sometimes of Jones, but univocally as a name of Smith. Similarly, if I erroneously think that Aristotle wrote such-and-such passage, I may perhaps sometimes use 'Aristotle' to *refer* to the actual author of the passage, even though there is no ambiguity in my use of the name. In both cases, I will withdraw my original statement, and my original use of the name, if apprised of the facts. Recall that, in these lectures 'referent' is used in the technical sense of the thing named by a name (or uniquely satisfying a description), and there should be no confusion.

7   It has been suggested to me that someone might argue that a name is associated with a 'referential' use of a description in Donnellan's sense. For example, although we identify Gödel as the author of the incompleteness theorem, we are talking about him even if he turns out not to have proved the theorem. Theses (2)–(6) could then fail; but nevertheless each name would abbreviate a description, though the role of description in naming would differ radically from that imagined by Frege and Russell. As I have said above, I am inclined to reject Donnellan's formulation of the notion of referential definite description. Even if Donnellan's analysis is accepted, however, it is clear that the present proposal should not be. For a referential definite description, such as 'the man drinking champagne', is typically withdrawn when the speaker realizes that it does not apply to its object. If a Gödelian fraud were exposed, Gödel would no longer be called 'the author of the incompleteness theorem' but he would still be called 'Gödel'. The name, therefore, does not abbreviate the description.

8   As Robert Nozick pointed out to me, there is a sense in which a description theory must be trivially true if any theory of the reference of names, spelled out in terms independent of the notion of reference, is available. For if such a theory gives conditions under which an object is to be the referent of a name, then it of course uniquely satisfies these conditions. Since I am not pretending to give any theory which eliminates the notion of reference in this sense, I am not aware of any such trivial fulfillment of the description theory and doubt that one exists. (A description using the notion of the reference of a name is easily available but circular, as we saw in our discussion of Kneale.) If any such trivial fulfillment were available, however, the arguments I have given show that the description must be one of a completely different sort from that supposed by Frege, Russell, Searle, Strawson and other advocates of the description theory.

9   Princeton University.

10   P. F. Strawson, *Individuals*, London: Methuen (1959), p. 282n.

11   The essential points of this example were suggested by Richard Miller.

12   A good example of a baptism whose reference was fixed by means of a description was that of naming Neptune in n. 33, p. 79 [see note 3, above]. The case of a baptism by ostension can perhaps be subsumed under the description concept also. Thus the primary applicability of the description theory is to cases of initial baptism. Descriptions are also used to fix a reference in cases of designation which are similar to naming except that the terms introduced are not usually called 'names'. The terms 'one meter', '100 degrees Centigrade', have already been given as examples, and other examples will be given later in these lectures. Two things should be emphasized concerning the case of introducing a name via a description in an initial baptism. First, the description used is not synonymous with the name it introduces but rather fixes its reference. Here we differ from the usual description theorists. Second, most cases of initial baptism are far from those which originally inspired the description theory. Usually a baptizer

is acquainted in some sense with the object he names and is able to name it ostensively. Now the inspiration of the description theory lay in the fact that we can often use names of famous figures of the past who are long dead and with whom no living person is acquainted; and it is precisely these cases which, on our view, cannot be correctly explained by a description theory.

13   I can transmit the name of the aardvark to other people. For each of these people, as for me, there will be a certain sort of causal or historical connection between my use of the name and the Emperor of the French, but not one of the required type.

14   Once we realize that the description used to fix the reference of a name is not synonymous with it, then the description theory can be regarded as presupposing the notion of naming or reference. The requirement I made that the description used not itself involve the notion of reference in a circular way is something else and is crucial if the description theory is to have any value at all. The reason is that the description theorist supposes that each speaker essentially uses the description he gives in an initial act of naming to determine his reference. Clearly, if he introduces the name 'Cicero' by the determination, 'By "Cicero" I shall refer to the man I call "Cicero" ', he has by this ceremony determined no reference at all.

Not all description theorists thought that they were eliminating the notion of reference altogether. Perhaps some realized that some notion of ostension, or primitive reference, is required to back it up. Certainly Russell did.

15   Ruth Barcan Marcus, 'Modalities and Intensional Languages' (comments by W. V. Quine, plus discussion) *Boston Studies in the Philosophy of Science*, volume I, Reidel, Dordrecht, Holland, 1963, pp. 77–116.

16   p. 101.

17   p. 115.

18   There is a more elaborate discussion of this point in the third lecture, where its relation to a certain sort of counterpart theory is also mentioned.

Chapter 10

Frank Jackson

REFERENCE AND DESCRIPTION REVISITED[1]

Many today speak of the description theory of reference in terms suitable for the grand old, refuted theories of the past: it belongs with behaviourism, phenomenalism, libertarianism, verificationism, and cartesian dualism. I have never understood why. The objections brought against the theory all seem to me either to misunderstand the theory in one way or another, or to overlook obvious candidates to be the descriptions or properties that secure reference according to the theory. To argue this in detail is the work of a book, not an article. I will outline how to defend a description theory of reference for spoken and written language, giving, I hope, enough detail to show what the book might look like. The paper has a rather negative cast; there is a good deal of listing of well-known objections followed by rebuttal. But that is how it has to be when you are taking on conventional wisdom, and some positive points are made in developing the rebuttals. I should also note that although I am in a substantial minority, there have always been defenders of the description theory, and many of the things I say have been said in one form or another, somewhere or other, by someone or other.[2]

I start with some necessary background about language before proceeding to look critically at some of the some of the most influential objections to the description theory.

Language and communication

I often want to communicate my view about how things are to someone else. Perhaps I think that some course of action is dangerous and want to tell you so, or perhaps I have a view about who will best govern the country and hope to sway you to my view by telling you, or perhaps. . . . There are a number of ways I might seek to achieve my end: by pointing, by holding up pictures, by engaging in charades, or, most simply, if you and I share a language, by uttering words and sentences in the language we share (and know that we share, and know that we know that we share, . . .). Language—or much of language, and in any case that aspect of language we will be concerned with—is a convention generated set of physical structures that has as a principal function making it easy to articulate, and in consequence easy to record, transmit in communication, debate the correctness of, and so on, how someone—you, me, the enemy, the ideal observer, . . .—takes things to be.

I am going to presume this Lockean picture of language. To avoid misunderstanding, though, I should note an unfortunate ambiguity in talk of language having the capacity and principal function of capturing and thereby facilitating the communication of how we take things to be. It might be read as saying, implausibly, that language is principally about states of belief, or it might be read as saying, plausibly, that language is about what states of belief are about, namely, how things are.³ On the first reading, the sentence 'There are electrons' makes a claim about what someone believes; on the second, sentences and beliefs alike represent how things are, including that there are electrons, and if you want to make a claim about what someone believes, you instead use a sentence like 'She believes that there are electrons'.

With this as background, we can see the attraction of the description theory of reference. If we are to use physical structures to give information on how we take things to be, we need associations in the minds of transmitters and receivers of the putative information between the various structures and the various ways things might be. We use flags to give information about deaths of the famous, roadworks, the nationalities of visiting dignitaries, and so on. The system depends on known associations. Flying a flag at half-mast flag would not be much use for telling about the death of someone famous if the association between flying the flag at half-mast and death were a dark secret. In the same way, if we are to use the physical structures known as words to tell about how we take things to be, we must associate various words with various ways things might be; or, as we will put it, we must associate words with properties. Here the term 'property' does not signify a universal in the sense that figures in debates over the one and the many, but is simply a short word for a way things might be in the wide sense that includes relational and dispositional ways things might be. This way-things-might-be need not be a particularly unified way things might be. If I tell you that something is a fish or a fowl, I tell you something about how it is. Hence, being a fish or a fowl is, in our relaxed sense, a property —possessed by all the fish and all the fowl, and by nothing that is not one or the other—despite its evidently disjunctive nature. Also, there need not be only one property associated with a word. There may instead be a number of properties. The word may be one to use when we want to

say that there is something with a goodly number of certain list of properties; the word may be, that is, a cluster term. Finally, I should emphasise that in some cases the associated property will be that of being thought about, that is, being what a thought refers to. I might stipulate that the word 'Fred' in my mouth stands simply for the object I am thinking about at the time of uttering the word—this stipulation might be useful in playing charades, for example. In this case, the associated property for the word 'Fred' would be the property of being the thing thought about at the time of utterance. This highlights a point we will return to: the description theory of reference I am defending is not a theory of reference in thought. It is a theory of reference for terms in a public language (in the sense that the language tokens are publicly available—they are written or spoken or engraved or . . .) that presupposes that we can refer in thought. This means that I will be taking no position on whether or not thoughts about objects are nothing other than thoughts that there are things that are thus and so—a matter often linked to the description theory. We can grant that 'Fred' in my mouth at t refers to whatever has the property of being thought about by me at t without committing ourselves to the further view that my thought will be that something is thus and so and the object thought about is simply whatever is thus and so. The description theory of reference for terms in a public language is distinct from the description theory of what it is to be an object of thought.⁴

If lots of words are associated with properties—something that follows from the way we use words to give and receive information—it is useful to have a name for the relation between these words and the things that have the properties associated with them. The description theory of reference says, first, that a good name for this relation is 'reference', and, second, that the words we use to give and receive information via their association with properties include those known as proper and common nouns. As we might say it, using the pre-analytic or folk term 'about': terms like 'London', 'Pluto', 'water', and 'inert gas' are used by speakers to talk *about* whatever has the properties they associate with the term in question; or, as philosophers of language might say it, a name T used by S *refers* to whatever has the properties that S associates with T.[5] This quick statement will be refined and explained as we undertake our sceptical tour of the various objections to the description theory of reference, but will remain our guiding thought.

We now start the sceptical tour.

The passing the buck objection

This objection has been put by Michael Devitt in a number of places. Here is a recent statement of it.

> Description theories are *essentially incomplete*. A description theory explains the reference of a word by appealing to the application of descriptions associated with the word. So the theory explains the reference of the word by appealing to the reference of other words. How then is the reference of those other words to be explained? Perhaps we can use description theories to explain their reference too. This process cannot, however, go on forever: There must be some words whose referential properties are not parasitic on those of others. . . . Description theories pass the buck. But the buck must stop somewhere.[6]

This objection misunderstands the theory, or at least misunderstands the theory in the Locke-inspired form that I accept. The description theory explains the reference of a word as that which possesses the *property* or *properties* associated with the word. Just as we said above. It is not an essential part of the theory that we should have words, or 'other words', for these properties. Indeed, as far as the theory is concerned, there might be a one word language and the reference of that one word might be to whatever has the

property or properties associated with that single word. Perhaps one word languages are impossible, but if they are, this is an additional thesis in the philosophy of language—not a very plausible one, in my view; it is not part of the description theory of reference. In any case, the important point is that the talk of descriptions applying is to be understood in terms of the possession of properties, not in terms of the application of (other) words in the language in question.

Defenders of the language of thought sometimes say that the problem of reference for public words is essentially the same as the problem of reference for words in mentalese, and it might be suggested that we should rephrase the buck passing objection in terms of the language of thought. The rephrased version might run somewhat as follows. According to the description theory, the reference of T in the mouth of S is to the thing that has the properties S associates with T; but for S to associate properties with T is for S to have words in mentalese that refer to those properties. This, the objection might conclude, makes it clear that the problem of reference for words in a public language is simply being handed across to words in the language of thought. The buck is being passed from words in public language to words in mentalese.

For the sake of the argument, I will accept that there is a language of thought. The real problem with the rephrased objection is that the problem of reference for words in a public language is very different from the problem of reference for words in mentalese. The difference derives from the point that Locke put by saying that words are *voluntary signs*.[7] A word like 'water' might have referred to gold, and would have done so if we had agreed to use the word 'gold' in the circumstances we in fact use the word 'water' in: which words in a public language refer to which things is in part a matter of the largely implicit conventions of usage we enter into.[8] This is crucial to the plausibility of the description theory of reference. It is plausible that we follow the convention of using 'water' when confronted with stuff we take to be thus and so, and this is why it is plausible that we use the word for stuff that is thus and so. But this picture only makes sense for words in a public language; it would be a nonsense to suppose that we entered into a convention to use the words of mentalese in certain circumstances. Because we do not know what they are, we cannot make agreements concerning them. Moreover, even if we did know what they are, we could not choose when to use them in accord with a convention of usage; changing when we 'use' some word of mentalese calls for brain surgery, not a mere change in the conventions of usage. There is of course an important problem of reference for the words of mentalese (if such there be), and more generally for how we refer in thought, but, as signalled earlier, this is not the problem of reference that the Lockean description theory we are defending is concerned with.

The objection that reference is in part a matter of how things are outside the head

Immediately after the passage quoted above, Devitt goes on to say

> This deep failing of description theories is brought out by Hilary Putnam's slogan- . . . "Meanings just ain't in the *head*". . . . The association of descriptions with a word is an inner state of the speaker. No such inner state can make the word refer to a particular referent. For that we must look for some relation that language and mind have to things outside themselves—we must look for an external relation.[9]

We can say straight off that there must be something wrong with this objection. It is *too* good. The description theory is correct for some words. We do use some words simply as abbreviations for definite descriptions, and the question

as to what they refer to is nothing other than the question as to what has the property associated with the abbreviated description.[10] This is granted by critics of the description theory. As Saul Kripke notes, you might say to yourself 'By "Gödel" I shall mean the man, whoever he is, who proved the incompleteness of arithmetic', and grants that in this case 'Gödel' in your mouth would refer to Schmidt if it was indeed Schmidt who proved the theorem. Kripke is explicit that his claim is that, as a matter of fact, this is not what most of us do; not that we could not have done it, and not that we never do it.[11] Indeed, it would be extraordinary if the description theory were not true for some words. As noted earlier, we use flags to give information about how things are, and this depends on there being a conventional association between flag configurations and properties in the minds of those who use and see the flags. It would be extraordinary if we never did with words what we do do with flags.

Moreover, the description theory *does* give a major role to the world in settling what refers to what. According to it, what settles the reference of words like 'London' and 'cow' is the combination of the properties associated with the words and a fact about the world, namely, what in the world has the properties. It is, therefore, false that the theory deprives the world of a role in settling what a term refers to.

It might be objected that I have misunderstood the sense in which Devitt is insisting that the world must play a major role in settling reference. Of course, what a word refers to *at* a world on the description theory depends on the nature of that world. The trouble is, rather, that the world does not play a role in settling the reference *conditions* of a word on the description theory in the sense of what the word refers to at w for any w. But in fact description theorists *per se* are not committed to denying the actual world a role in settling reference conditions. Description theorists should (and do) allow that some words function like rigidified definite descriptions, and the reference conditions of rigidified descriptions depend on the nature of the actual world.

The core idea behind the description theory is that a term refers to that which has the property or properties the speaker associates with the term. One way to spell this out is by saying that, at any world w, T refers to x just if x has the associated property or properties in w. Another way, equally faithful to the core idea, is by saying that, at any world w, T refers to x just if x is the thing with the associated property or properties *in the actual world*. The second way of spelling matters out is the right way if T is a rigidified definite description, a description like 'the actually tallest person in 1991'. For the actually tallest person at any world is whoever is the tallest at the actual world. But if description theorists should (and do) count rigidified definite descriptions as referring expressions, then it is transparent that they should (and do) allow that reference conditions may depend on how things actually are. The reference of a rigidified definite description at any world w is precisely something that depends on how things actually are.

The objection that the description theory is a species of eliminativism about reference

If the language we are concerned with has predicates for the various properties the description theory holds serve to secure the reference of the names in that language, the description theory becomes in effect the view that names, be they of things or kinds, are really a style of abbreviated definite description: if the language has F as the predicate for the property that settles the reference of N, the description theory amounts to the view that N is an abbreviation of 'the F'. The objection is that Russell teaches us that definite descriptions are not referring expressions, that they do not refer, and so the description theory eliminates the very phenomenon it is supposed to be analysing.

I accept Russell's account (when due account is taken of various niceties to do with conversational context) but I think that it is misleading to say that it means that definite descriptions are not referring expressions. Russell famously shows us how to give the truth conditions for certain sentences containing definite descriptions in terms that do not contain the definite descriptions themselves and do not contain anything equivalent to them as semantically significant units. According to his account,

(1)   The F is G

iff

(2)   There is an F which is G and every F is identical with it.

But to think that this shows that definite descriptions are not referring expressions, that they do not refer, misunderstands the sense of 'reference' in which the description theory is a theory of reference. Nothing in Russell's theory goes against the fact that the words 'the tallest person alive in 1990' are quite distinct from the person who is the tallest person alive in 1990, and that there is some important relation between the words and the person which warrants a name. It is this relation that the description theorist calls 'reference', and it is this relation that the description theorist sees as holding also between names and the things they name. It is, of course, open to anyone to withold the word 'reference' for this relation on the ground that we can give a contextual analysis of definite descriptions—or perhaps for some other reason—but then they will need a new term for the relation between the words 'the tallest man alive in 1990' and the tallest man in 1990. But now the objection has come down to a claim about how best to label theories; it is no longer an objection to the description theory as such.

Moreover, an equally 'contextual' account in the spirit of Russell can be offered of rigidified definite descriptions, as follows.

(3)   The actual F is G

is true at w iff

(4)   w is the actual world and there is an F in w
       which is G in w and every F in w is identical
       with it, or w is not the actual world and
       there is something in w which is F in the
       actual world and every F in the actual
       world is identical with it, which is G in w.

So one who says that definite descriptions are not
referring expressions on the basis of a Russell
style story about them is committed to saying
that rigidified definite descriptions are not referring expressions either. This is hard to believe. It
means for starters that we cannot explain what a
rigidified definite description is by saying that it
is one which *refers* at every world to what it *refers*
to at the actual world—it never refers at all, on
the view in question.

It might be responded that *of course* there is *some*
relation between the words 'the tallest man' and
the tallest man, and that we are free to call this
relation 'reference'. But it differs markedly from
the relation between, on the one hand, the
rigidified definite description 'the actual tallest
man' or some other descriptive name, or a
proper name of the man, and, on the other hand,
the man himself.[12] More generally, there are
many differences between definite descriptions,
on the one hand, and rigidified definite descriptions and names, on the other—a familiar
example is their behaviour in counterfactual and
modal contexts. The issue, then, the response
might run, is whether there is enough in common between the cases to justify describing
them alike; whether there is, as Gareth Evans puts
it, 'any natural semantic kind' here.[13]

One reply to this response is that, whatever
their differences, definite descriptions, descriptive names, and proper names are united in
being markedly different from words like 'and',
'is', and 'to'. But the really important point is
that we do not have in this response a *free standing*

objection to regarding definite descriptions as
referring terms: it is a good objection to treating
definite descriptions as referring terms only if
there is *independent* good reason to reject the
description theory of reference. For if the
description theory of reference is correct, there
is an obvious natural semantic kind in common
between definite descriptions, descriptive names
and proper names: they are all associated with
properties in the minds of their users, and hence
they have a special relation to whatever possesses
the associated properties. In consequence, we
cannot have in the 'there are many differences'
point an objection to the description theory of
reference. For only if the theory is false, is it at all
plausible that the differences are enough to stop
us acknowledging that there is an important
semantic kind in common to definite descriptions, descriptive names, and names—a semantic kind that we might as well describe as their all
being referring expressions.

It is often said that the description theory of
reference holds that names are synonymous with
definite descriptions. But in fact the key claim in
the theory is that the fundamental mechanism
whereby names and definite descriptions secure
reference is the same, namely, via possession
of associated properties—it is only in this sense
that names (in rich enough languages) can be
thought of as abbreviated definite descriptions.
This is consistent with the referential behaviour
of names and definite descriptions differing in
various contexts in ways that would warrant
saying that they differ in meaning. Take, for
example, the widely observed differences
between the behaviour of names and definite
descriptions under counterfactual assumptions:
the reference of a name does not change under
counterfactual assumptions, the reference of a
definite description may change.[14] But this does
not affect the basic claim that reference is via
associated properties in both cases; it simply
means that in the case of names, the reference
under counterfactual assumptions is to what
has the associated property *in fact*, whereas the

reference of a definite description may be to what has the property under the counterfactual assumption. Once we see that the essential claim of the description theory of reference is not a synonymy one, but instead about the sharing of a fundamental mechanism, it is clear that the manifest variety among referential devices concerning their behaviour in various contexts is no reason to deny the underlying semantic unity postulated by the description theory.

The objection from ignorance and error [15]

Surely, runs this objection, there are cases where it is intuitively clear that speakers refer to something O by their use of T, where one or both of the following applies: (a) a speaker knows nothing, and maybe knows that they know nothing, that individuates O from many other things, and (b) most of what a speaker believes about O is wrong. But if reference is by possession of associated properties, then (a) these properties must be sufficient to individuate O—the user of T must not be ignorant of what individuates O, and (b) O must have these properties—the user of T cannot be in error about O having them.

The cases offered to support the claim about ignorance of individuating properties all seem to me to overlook obvious candidates to be the needed individuating properties. Hilary Putnam claims that he does not know what separates beeches from elms but insists that he succeeds in referring to beeches when he says, say, that he does not know how beeches differ from elms. [16] I agree that he does refer to beeches, but point out that he does know how they differ from elms: only they are called 'beeches' by the experts in his language community. Putnam responds that, because the word in French for beech is different from our word, this reply would commit description theorists to holding that a not very knowledgeable, monolingual English speaker's concept of a beech will be different from that of a not very knowledgeable, monolingual French

speaker. But how is this a problem? Peoples' concepts of one and the same thing can and do differ, and it is hard to see why this should not count as a case.

There are though cases where appeal to knowledge that certain words are used by experts does not turn the trick for the description theory. Perhaps I read in the paper about someone called 'Smith' who was robbed last night in Washington. Can't I refer to him even though there may well be more than one person called 'Smith' robbed in Washington last night? And there are examples of meeting someone late on at a party. It seems that I can refer to him next morning—perhaps in some such sentence as 'I wonder if I insulted that man I only vaguely remember who I met as I was finishing the bottle'—despite his having no obvious individuating marks that I can recall. But in fact I do know something that individuates what I refer to in cases of these kinds. They are the causal source of the information-carrying trace that I am presented with. Out of the possibly many Smiths robbed in Washington last night, there will be one that is the causal origin of the story in the paper, in the sense that it is his being robbed that led to the passage of prose in the paper in front of me. Or, rather, there had better be if the case is to be a test case for theories of reference: if it turns out that the reporter muddled up a number of robbed Smiths, and the passage of prose can equally be thought of as sourced in any, or none, of them, we lose the intuition that there is one particular Smith that I refer to. Similarly, there will be only one person who is the right kind of causal origin of my vague, somewhat disturbing memory of the party that is prompting my morning after reflections (and who will, most likely, also be the only person I would recognise as such were I to meet him). Hence, the description theorist can explain how I manage to refer in this kind of case by appealing to an association with the property of being a certain kind of causal origin (and maybe the property of being apt to be recognised as such by me).

Suggestions of these kinds in support of a description theory of reference are not new.[17] Their impact has, however, been lessened by the belief that they face serious problems. I will consider three of the problems most often brought up.

First, the appeal to language use by experts suggests an implicit circularity. It looks circular to say that 'beech' in the mouths of the ignorant refers to whatever 'beech' in the mouths of the experts *refers* to, and isn't that what the 'reference borrowing' suggestion really amounts to?[18] However, the circularity is not vicious. We can spell the suggestion out without explicit mention of reference. The suggestion is simply that the property the ignorant associate with the word 'beech' is having the property, whatever it is, that the experts associate with the word 'beech'. Hence, on the description theory, 'beech' in their mouths refers to whatever has the property the experts associate with the word 'beech'—which ensures, as it should, that 'beech' in the mouths of the ignorant has the same reference as it has in the mouths of the experts.

Secondly, it is observed that it may be unclear who the experts are in the sense that it is unknown to the ignorant users, and yet reference still occurs.[19] Many folk refer to quarks when they use the word 'quark', despite the fact that they do not know whether it is a term from physics or from biology, and so do not know which department contains the experts. For when such a person asks, 'Should I go to the physics or biology department to find out about quarks?', it is plausible that they are asking a question about *quarks*. However, these folk do know that there are some experts somewhere or other, and that these experts lie at one end of a reference borrowing chain that has whoever they themselves borrowed the term from at the other—or at least this had better be the case, for otherwise the example is no longer one where it is plausible to say that these folk refer to quarks. But now we can specify the property these folk associate with the word 'quark'. It is having the

property the group of users of the word 'quark' that they are borrowing from associate with the word 'quark'. And what property does this second group of users associate with the term 'quark'? Either they are the experts, in which case it is property Q (whatever that is, I am not one of the experts) or they are not the experts, in which case it is having the property some third group of users associates with 'quark'. And what property does this third group of users associate with the word 'quark'? Either they are the experts, in which case it is property Q, or they are not the experts, in which case it is having the property some fourth group of users associate with the word 'quark'. . . . We have, that is, a recursive story akin to the familiar recursive account of a wff in logic.

The third problem raised turns on the point that the key issue is not whether there is some individuating property of the thing referred to. It is whether there is some individuating property of the thing referred to which is associated with the word in question by the speakers (and maybe hearers) in question. The objection is that the kinds of properties we have mentioned are fancy ones that philosophers of language and unusually alert members of the folk might think of; they are not properties ordinary, folk speakers associate with words like 'beech' and 'quark'. A quick reply to this objection is that the folk often say things which make it clear that they are well aware of these properties and which strongly suggest that they are relying on them to secure reference. People who do not know much physics, and know that they do not know much physics, often ask questions like, Is it established for sure that quarks exist? When asked precisely what question they are asking, they answer that they are asking about the things physicists use the word 'quark' for. Or think of what has happened with the spread of computer speak. It is a commonplace that people say things like 'I haven't a clue what RAM is, but I know that the new PC I am buying has 32 of whatever it is that computer people use the term for'.

However, we need to say more by way of reply. Although the folk are aware of the relevant individuating properties and say things that suggest they are relying on them to secure reference, they are not much good at articulating them in detail (nor, if it comes to that, are defenders of the description theory of reference—we do a fair bit of hand-waving). The longer reply is that this failure to articulate the relevant property or properties in detail is no objection to the description theory *provided* that what is meant by the expression 'properties associated with a word or phrase' in statements of the description theory is understood in the right way.

Sometimes it is obvious which properties are associated with a word. Perhaps the speaker tells us loud and clear. But typically the association is implicit or tacit rather than explicit. It is something we can extract in principle from speakers' patterns of word usage, not something actually explicitly before their mind when they use the words. I know this way of putting things—familiar though it is—will ring some alarm bells. Some will want to say that if the association is in the mind, as the description theory says, it must be explicit. They think of appeal to the implicit or tacit in this context as a kind of cheat—a way of saying something and then taking it back.

However, there is a way of being implicit and yet before the mind in the relevant sense that is no great mystery. Consider the situation good logic students find themselves in before they are given the recursive definition of a wff. They cannot specify what it is to be a wff, but they can reliably classify formulae into wffs and non-wffs. But it would be a mistake to see their ability as like that of chicken sexers. Chicken sexers have no idea which property trigers their reliable classifications (although they know, of course, that the property is correlated with the sex of the chicken). By contrast, logic students can say for any ill-formed formula what triggers their judgement that it is ill-formed. When presented with '(p v q', they do not say that they can see

that it is ill-formed but cannot say where the problem is. They know exactly where the problem is and how to fix it—add a RH bracket after the 'q'. Similarly, they know what changes to a particular wff would make it ill-formed. They are in the following position: for each particular example, they can say whether or not it is a wff, and why; but they cannot give in words a story that covers all cases. The same is true for all of us in our judgements of grammaticality. We can say, for particular examples, whether and why they are or are not grammatical, but cannot give the general story in words. In the case of wffs, many of us know what the general story is, and tell students when we give the recursive definition of wff-ness; in the case of grammar, we (with the possible exception of Quirk and Greenbaum) don't know the general story.

Description theorists can and should say essentially the same about the sense in which speakers associate properties with words. If you say enough about any particular possible world, speakers can say what, if anything, words like 'water', 'London', 'quark', and so on refer to in that possible world. (This does not mean that there is always a definite answer: sometimes saying what 'London' refers to in a certain possible world will amount to saying that it is indeterminate what if anything it refers to in this world.) Our ability to answer questions about what various words refer to in various possible worlds, it should be emphasised, is common ground with critics of the description theory. The critics' writings are full of descriptions (*descriptions*) of possible worlds and claims about what refers, or fails to refer, to what in these possible worlds. Indeed, their impact has derived precisely from the intuitive plausibility of many of their claims about what refers, or fails to refer, to what in various possible worlds. But if speakers can say what refers to what when various possible worlds are described to them, description theorists can identify the property associated in their minds with, for example, the word 'water': it is the disjunction of the properties that guide the speakers in each particular possible world when they say which stuff, if any, in each world counts as water. This disjunction is in their minds in the sense that they can deliver the answer for each possible world when it is described in sufficient detail, but is implicit in the sense that the pattern that brings the various disjuncts together as part of the, possibly highly complex, disjunction may be one they cannot state. This is not to say that, after reflection on their classifications in the various possible cases, perhaps aided by doing a course in the philosophy of language, they won't be able to make a good stab at stating the pattern; something like: belonging to the kind which most of the clear, potable samples, acquaintance with which led to the introduction of the word 'water' in our language, is roughly right—and if you describe a case that this formula fails to cover, you do not show that there is no pattern, but that my stab at it was not good enough.[20]

We can now deal quickly with the error side of the objection. The claim is that speakers may have most of the properties of O wrong and yet still refer to O by their use of T. But what matters for successful reference is that O has the properties speakers *associate* with T, and this is consistent with O's lacking most of the properties speakers think it has. There may be only one property speakers associate with T, in which case they refer to O when they use T provided just that O has that property; it will not matter if everything else they believe about O is mistaken.

[. . .]

Notes

1 I am much indebted to Sam Guttenplan, Richard Holton, and especially David Braddon-Mitchell and David Lewis.

2 See, e.g., Locke (1690), book III, Kroon (1978), Linsky (1977), Searle (1983), Lewis (1984), Strawson (1971), Braddon-Mitchell and Jackson (1996), Neale (1990).

3 Locke (1690), book III, ch. 2 sometimes puts matters in a way that invites the first reading.

4 I am indebted here to Jakob Hohwy.

5 Some description theorists hold that adjectives like 'square' refer to the property associated with them; some that they refer to the things that have the property; some that they refer to the set of things that have the property; and some that there is no substantive issue here: we will confine our attention to nouns and noun phrases.

6 Devitt (1996), p. 159. See also Devitt and Sterelny (1987).

7 Locke (1690), book III, ch. 2, § 2. I am indebted here to discussions with Monima Chadha.

8 For how a convention might be implicit, see Lewis (1969).

9 Devitt (1996), p. 160. Incidentally, I am not sure why Devitt says that the 'association of descriptions with a word is an inner state of the speaker'—I happen to agree but am surprised that the point should be taken as obvious given the popularity of externalist accounts of psychological states.

10 If you hold that definite descriptions do not refer, the point could be made with descriptive names or rigidified definite descriptions. I argue against the view that definite descriptions do not refer below.

11 Kripke (1980), p. 91 [Chapter 9 above, p. 125].

12 I take descriptive names to be abbreviated rigidified definite descriptions, and so will, from now on, treat them together. As far as I can see, nothing important for what follows turns on this.

13 Evans (1982), p. 57.

14 Evans (1982), p. 57.

15 This is perhaps the most common objection to the description theory. I take the name of the objection from Devitt and Sterelny (1987).

16 Putnam (1975), p. 226.

17 The earliest stressing of the importance of causal links I know is Strawson (1959), ch. 1.

18 This issue is discussed at length by Kripke (1980), lecture II [Chapter 9 above]. See also Devitt and Sterelny (1987), p. 50.

19 See, e.g., Devitt and Sterelny (1987), p. 50.

20 Or, maybe, that the way you introduced the story 'disturbed' the pattern. Description theorists can and should allow that the associations between words and properties are not set in stone.

References

Braddon-Mitchell, David and Frank Jackson (1996), *The Philosophy of Mind and Cognition*, Oxford, Basil Blackwell.

Devitt, Michael (1996), *Coming to Our Senses*, Cambridge, Cambridge University Press.

Devitt, Michael and Kim Sterelny (1987), *Language and Reality*, Oxford, Basil Blackwell.

Evans, Gareth (1982), *The Varieties of Reference*, Oxford, Clarendon Press.

Kripke, Saul (1980), *Naming and Necessity*, Oxford, Basil Blackwell.

Kroon, Fred (1978), 'Causal Descriptivism', *Australasian Journal of Philosophy*, 65: 1–17.

Lewis, David (1969), *Convention*, Cambridge, Mass., Harvard University Press.

Lewis, David (1984), 'Putnam's Paradox', *Australasian Journal of Philosophy*, 62: 221–36.

Linsky, Leonard (1977), *Name and Descriptions*, Chicago, Chicago University Press.

Locke, John (1690), *An Essay Concerning Human Understanding*.

Neale, Stephen (1990), *Descriptions*, Cambridge, Mass., MIT Press.

Putnam, Hilary (1975), 'The Meaning of "Meaning" ', in *Mind, Language and Reality*. Cambridge, Cambridge University Press.

Searle, John (1983), *Intentionality*. Cambridge, Cambridge University Press.

Strawson, P.F. (1959), *Individuals*, London, Methuen.

Strawson, P.F. (1971), *Logico-Linguistic Papers*, London, Methuen.

PART FIVE

Analyticity

INTRODUCTION TO PART FIVE

HITHERTO, MOST OF THE QUESTIONS we have considered have been reasonably fine-grained and concerned with specific linguistic phenomena (reference, compositionality, the logical form of sentences containing definite descriptions, etc.). In contrast, although the readings below contain plenty of fine-grained argumentation, the most important issues on which they bear are extremely broad, and belong to metaphysics and epistemology as much as to the philosophy of language.

European analytic philosophy during the early decades of the twentieth century was dominated by a family of views known as 'logical positivism' or 'logical empiricism'. A principal general aspiration of this movement was to bring what its advocates regarded as a *scientific* methodology and rigour to bear on philosophical problems. Like earlier empiricists (especially Hume) they were preoccupied by the nature of the relation(s) between, on the one hand, perceptual evidence, and on the other, the beliefs and theories it confirms and disconfirms. The logical empiricists' approach involved codifying these perceptual data, beliefs and theories in highly regimented, 'logical' language (a language exploiting innovations that Frege and Russell had recently developed in philosophical logic and the philosophy of language) so that classic epistemological issues could be transposed into questions about *sentences*. The most ambitious advocates of this approach – the philosophers Quine labels 'radical reductionists' – attempted to demonstrate that any meaningful sentence could, through a series of deductive inferences, be 'reduced' to a set of sentences about 'sense data' – i.e. (roughly) components of perceptual experiences. The reductionists articulated this as the proposal that the *meaning* of a sentence consists in a certain pattern of sense data – the pattern whose obtaining would *verify* the sentence. This is one, rather extreme, version of the semantic theory known as 'verificationism'. More moderate versions maintain that to specify the meaning of a sentence one must identify the *conditions* in which it would be verified, or the 'method' by which it would be verified, but without the reductionist supposition that such conditions or methods are wholly a matter of perceptual experiences.

At the beginning of 'Two Dogmas of Empiricism' Quine identifies *reductionism* as one of the 'dogmas' he aims to discredit. The other is the contention that a coherent distinction can be drawn between *analytic* and *synthetic* truths. Why is this distinction significant here? To answer this, we can consider what a logical empiricist should say about necessary truths, and truths which can be known a priori, e.g. theorems of mathematics and logic, and the propositions expressed by English sentences such as,

(1) Rabbits are animals
(2) No unmarried man is married
(3) No bachelor is married.

The logical empiricists accepted that truths like these are typically known a priori, and in light of this, they did not seek to 'reduce' sentences like (1)–(3) to sense data or empirical verification conditions. Such sentences were deemed to be exceptions, then, to the verificationist theory of meaning. Hume described these truths as 'relations of ideas' and in a similar spirit, Kant characterized (some of) them as *analytic*. The latter notion was taken up by the logical empiricists. For Kant, analyticity was a characteristic of *propositions*: a Kantian would say that (1) has to be true because the very *concept* of animalhood is in some sense 'contained' in that of rabbithood. The logical empiricists transposed this into a claim about language: (1) is true because the *meanings* of the terms 'rabbits' and 'animals' are related in such a way as to ensure that anything in the extension of the former expression is also in that of the latter. The analyticity of sentences like (1)–(3) consists in their being true *in virtue of the meanings of the expressions they contain*, and this explains why the truths they express are necessarily true and why they can be known a priori.

As Grice and Strawson observe in their response to Quine – the second reading below – it is not quite clear whether Quine's complaint about analyticity is that there aren't any analytic sentences or that the very notion of analyticity (or that of a distinction between analytic and synthetic sentences) is confused, incoherent, or unprincipled. His complaint seems to be that the notion cannot be – or at any rate, has never been – satisfactorily *analysed:* no sufficiently rigorous formulation is available of general necessary and sufficient conditions for a sentence's being analytic. Over the first four sections of the paper, Quine considers several attempts to provide such an analysis, but he rejects each one, usually on the ground that the candidate exploits notions belonging to the same 'family' as that of analyticity, and standing as badly in need of rigorous analysis. Thus e.g. Quine concedes that sentence (2) above is a 'logical truth' and he considers the suggestion that the analyticity of (3) might consist in the fact that it can be 'turned into' that logical truth by replacing 'bachelor' with its synonym, 'unmarried man'. The problem with this, according to Quine, is that the relevant notion of *synonymy* is problematic in the very same way as that of analyticity. He raises similar complaints, e.g. against the suggestion that synonyms are expressions which can be substituted for one another in sentences in which they fall within the scope of 'intensional' operators such as 'necessarily' without changing the truth value of the sentences, and against the suggestion that certain analytic sentences are made true by the 'semantical rules' supposed to characterize certain sorts of formal languages.

As Grice and Strawson point out, Quine's overall argument seems to depend on a dubious premise: that the notion of analyticity is coherent, clear, principled or whatever only if it can be *analysed* by necessary and sufficient conditions which do not invoke any member of the populous family of concepts to which it belongs. But many *prima facie* respectable concepts seem likely to fail this test: e.g. few would maintain that we can give necessary and sufficient conditions for an action's qualifying as 'morally wrong' which did not make use of some of the family of terms of which that term is a member, e.g., 'blameworthy', 'breach of moral rules', etc. Moreover, they argue, the facts (i) that philosophers tend without hesitation to apply the terms, 'analytic' and 'synthetic' to the very same sentences as one another (including sentences they have not considered before), and (ii) that non-philosophers converge similarly in respect of the non-technical notion of one sentence's meaning the same as another, provide strong *prima facie* evidence for the existence of a coherent distinction. Furthermore, they suggest, some members of the family (e.g. the notion of logical impossibility) can be explicated perfectly satisfactorily – albeit perhaps not in a way that meets Quine's distinctive standards.

Quine's argument against the 'dogma' of reductionism comes in §5 of his paper, and seems more compelling. Like most forms of verificationism, reductionism rests on a conception of the relation between evidence and theory which has come to be known as *confirmation atomism*. This is the view that corresponding to each synthetic (i.e. non-analytic) sentence is a unique and particular set of conditions or sense data whose obtaining would verify it. The problem with atomism which, following Pierre Duhem, Quine brings to light is that a particular datum (or set of data) confirms a hypothesis only in the context of many additional 'auxiliary' hypotheses. Thus, e.g., suppose you want to confirm the hypothesis that a given liquid is an acid, and to this end you observe that it appears to turn a piece of blue litmus paper red. This datum confirms the hypothesis only in the context of various further assumptions, e.g. that blue litmus paper turns red on contact with acid, that the liquid does not contain a red pigment which causes paper immersed in it to turn red independently of the acid-litmus chemical reaction, that the ambient lighting is not abnormal in any way that distorts colour perception, etc. In the context of different auxiliary assumptions, different data would be required to confirm the hypothesis in question. Moreover, if one had good reason to doubt the hypothesis that the liquid is an acid, one would thereby have good reason to take the datum of its appearing to turn the paper red not to confirm that hypothesis, but instead to disconfirm one of the auxiliary hypotheses.

The moral here is that verification and falsification are not relations between hypotheses and determinate units of experiential data; rather, at best, they are relations between hypotheses and large disjunctive *sets* of different data and auxiliary hypotheses. In the final section of the paper, Quine articulates a particularly radical (and infamous) version of confirmation holism, based, in effect, on the assumption that there is no principled way in which to restrict membership of these confirming sets: given appropriate auxiliary assumptions, any datum can confirm or disconfirm any hypothesis. Furthermore, as the auxiliary assumptions relevant to the verification or falsification of scientific hypotheses often include theorems of mathematics and logic, such theorems number amongst the beliefs which a scientist could, in principle, choose rationally to repudiate, in order to protect a cherished empirical hypothesis in the face of an appropriately 'recalcitrant' perceptual experience.[1] 'The unit of empirical significance is the whole of science'.

---

[1] The idea that mathematical or logical beliefs might be repudiated or revised to accommodate empirical data has been defended in real scientific cases. E.g. it is commonly supposed that theorems of Euclidean geometry have been discredited by astronomical observations; and logical systems in which the classical theorem of *distributivity* does not hold have been defended on the basis of results in quantum mechanics. (For sympathetic discussion, see Putnam 1968.)

Now, a natural reaction to this is to wonder whether we could accept the basic holist contention – that empirical hypotheses are confirmed not by unique individual data, but by complex sets containing data and auxiliary assumptions – but resist the unpalatably radical version of this picture championed by Quine. Many philosophers are attracted by this kind of merely moderate confirmation holism, but there is no consensus on the key question of how to delineate the set of beliefs and data which are in the required sense relevant to confirmation/disconfirmation in any given case. Here, we restrict our remarks to the observation that even a moderate version of confirmation holism seems to threaten most versions of verificationism, including reductionism, for those theories proceed on the assumption that to each synthetic sentence corresponds a unique, determinate, condition (or set of conditions) whose obtaining would verify the sentence.

The controversial doctrine of radical confirmation holism, then, may be more than Quine needs for his argument against the 'dogma' of reductionism. However, radical holism is also relevant to his rejection of the first 'dogma': the distinction between analytic and synthetic sentences. As he observes several times in the paper, it is natural to think of the truth value of a typical sentence as being determined by two factors: its meaning, and the state of the world it describes. However, with sentences that appear to express *necessary* truths or falsehoods, the second factor seems redundant, and so it is tempting to suggest that the truth values of these sentences are determined wholly by the first factor, their meanings. As long as we conceive of meaning in broadly epistemic terms – i.e. as a matter of conditions or methods of verification – radical confirmation holism threatens to undermine this picture, because it threatens the coherence of the distinction between the two factors envisaged to determine a sentence's truth value. Thus, even if the argument which Quine deploys against the analytic/synthetic distinction over the first four sections of 'Two Dogmas' is not compelling, the position which emerges over the final two sections may suffice to embarrass at least the empiricist advocates of the distinction whom Quine had in mind.[2]

---

[2] Confirmation holism is not the only holist doctrine relevant to the philosophy of language. Meaning holism is, roughly, the view that the meanings of expressions in a given language are determined together, and interdependently. For discussion, see Part Nine below.

Questions and tasks

1   Do you think Quine's thesis is that the distinction between analytic and synthetic sentences is confused/incoherent/vague/unprincipled, or is it more simply that the class of analytic sentences (or analytic sentences which are not logical truths) is *empty*?

2   Over the first four sections of 'Two Dogmas', Quine considers several notions in terms of which that of analyticity might be analysed. Do you think any member of this 'family' of notions can be explicated without invoking one or more of the others?

3   How plausible is the radical holist's claim that a logical or mathematical belief might be disconfirmed by empirical data?

4   Towards the end of their paper, Grice and Strawson suggest that a verificationist might accommodate confirmation holism by proposing that two statements are synonymous 'if and only if any experiences which, *on certain assumptions about the truth values of other statements*, confirm or disconfirm one of the pair, also *on the same assumptions*, confirm or disconfirm the other to the same degree' (p. 179). Is this a cogent rejoinder to Quine's anti-verificationist argument?

References and further reading

Barrett, R., and R. Gibson (eds) 1990: *Perspectives on Quine*, Oxford: Blackwell.

Boghossian, P. 1997: 'Analyticity', in B. Hale and C. Wright (eds) *A Companion to the Philosophy of Language*, Oxford: Blackwell, pp. 331–68.

Boghossian, P., and Peacocke, C. (eds) 2000: *New Essays on the A Priori*, Oxford: Oxford University Press.

Bonjour, L. 1998: *In Defense of Pure Reason*, Cambridge: Cambridge University Press.

Coffa, J. 1991: *The Semantic Tradition from Kant to Carnap: To the Vienna Station*, Cambridge: Cambridge University Press.

Davidson, D. 1982: 'Empirical Content', *Grazer Philosophische Studien* 16–17, pp. 471–89; reprinted in D. Davidson, *Subjective, Intersubjective, Objective*, Oxford: Oxford University Press (2001).

Davidson, D. 1990: 'Meaning, Truth and Evidence', in R. Barrett and R. Gibson (eds), *Perspectives on Quine*, Oxford: Blackwell, 68–79; reprinted in D. Davidson, *Truth, Language and History*, Oxford: Oxford University Press (2005).

Follesdal, D. (ed.) 2000: *Philosophy of Quine*, vol 1: *General Reviews and Analytic/Synthetic*, London: Routledge.

Hahn, L., and P. Schilpp (eds) 1986: *The Philosophy of W.V. Quine*, Chicago: Open Court.

Harman, G. 1967: 'Quine on Meaning and Existence I: The Death of Meaning', *Review of Metaphysics* 21, pp. 124–51; reprinted as 'The Death of Meaning' in G. Harman, *Reasoning, Meaning and Mind*, Oxford: Oxford University Press (1999).

Harman, G. 1996: 'Analyticity Regained', *Noûs* 30, no. 3, pp. 392–400; reprinted in G. Harman, *Reasoning, Meaning and Mind*, Oxford: Oxford University Press (1999).

Kripke, S. 1980: *Naming and Necessity*, Cambridge, MA: Harvard University Press.

Putnam, H. 1962: 'The Analytic and the Synthetic', in H. Feigl and G. Maxwell (eds), *Minnesota Studies in the Philosophy of Science*, vol. 3. Minneapolis: University of Minnesota Press, pp. 358–97; reprinted in H. Putnam, *Mind, Language, and Reality: Philosophical Papers*, vol. 2, Cambridge: Cambridge University Press (1975).

Putnam, H. 1968: 'Is Logic Empirical?', in R. Cohen and M. Wartofsky (eds), *Boston Studies in the Philosophy of Science*, vol. 5, Dordrecht: D. Reidel, 216–41;

reprinted as 'The Logic of Quantum Mechanics', in H. Putnam, *Mathematics, Matter and Method*, Cambridge: Cambridge University Press (1975).

Quine, W. V. 1960: *Word and Object*, Cambridge, MA: MIT Press.

Quine, W. V. 1992: *Pursuit of Truth* (Revised edn), Cambridge, MA: Harvard University Press.

Williamson, T. 2006: 'Conceptual Truth', *Proceedings of the Aristotelian Society Supplementary Volume* 80, pp. 1–41.

Wright, C. 1986: 'Inventing Logical Necessity', in J. Butterfield (ed.), *Language, Mind and Logic*, Cambridge: Cambridge University Press, pp. 187–209.

Chapter 11

W. V. Quine

TWO DOGMAS OF EMPIRICISM

Modern empiricism has been conditioned in large part by two dogmas. One is a belief in some fundamental cleavage between truths which are *analytic*, or grounded in meanings independently of matters of fact, and truths which are *synthetic*, or grounded in fact. The other dogma is *reductionism*: the belief that each meaningful statement is equivalent to some logical construct upon terms which refer to immediate experience. Both dogmas, I shall argue, are ill-founded. One effect of abandoning them is, as we shall see, a blurring of the supposed boundary between speculative metaphysics and natural science. Another effect is a shift toward pragmatism.

1 Background for analyticity

Kant's cleavage between analytic and synthetic truths was foreshadowed in Hume's distinction between relations of ideas and matters of fact, and in Leibniz's distinction between truths of reason and truths of fact. Leibniz spoke of the truths of reason as true in all possible worlds. Picturesqueness aside, this is to say that the truths of reason are those which could not possibly be false. In the same vein we hear analytic statements defined as statements whose denials are self-contradictory. But this definition has small explanatory value; for the notion of self-contradictoriness, in the quite broad sense needed for this definition of analyticity, stands in exactly the same need of clarification as does the notion of analyticity itself. The two notions are the two sides of a single dubious coin.

Kant conceived of an analytic statement as one that attributes to its subject no more than is already conceptually contained in the subject. This formulation has two shortcomings: it limits itself to statements of subject-predicate form, and it appeals to a notion of containment which is left at a metaphorical level. But Kant's intent, evident more from the use he makes of the notion of analyticity than from his definition of it, can be restated thus: a statement is analytic when it is true by virtue of meanings and independently of fact. Pursuing this line, let us examine the concept of *meaning* which is presupposed.

Meaning, let us remember, is not to be identified with naming.[1] Frege's example of 'Evening Star' and 'Morning Star', and Russell's of 'Scott' and 'the author of *Waverley*', illustrate that terms can name the same thing but differ in meaning. The distinction between meaning and naming is no less important at the level of abstract terms. The terms '9' and 'the number of the planets' name one and the same abstract entity but presumably must be regarded as unlike in meaning; for astronomical observation was needed, and not mere reflection on meanings, to determine the sameness of the entity in question.

The above examples consist of singular terms, concrete and abstract. With general terms, or

156 W. V. Quine

predicates, the situation is somewhat different but parallel. Whereas a singular term purports to name an entity, abstract or concrete, a general term does not; but a general term is *true of* an entity, or of each of many, or of none.[2] The class of all entities of which a general term is true is called the *extension* of the term. Now paralleling the contrast between the meaning of a singular term and the entity named, we must distinguish equally between the meaning of a general term and its extension. The general terms 'creature with a heart' and 'creature with kidneys', for example, are perhaps alike in extension but unlike in meaning.

Confusion of meaning with extension, in the case of general terms, is less common than confusion of meaning with naming in the case of singular terms. It is indeed a commonplace in philosophy to oppose intension (or meaning) to extension, or, in a variant vocabulary, connotation to denotation.

The Aristotelian notion of essence was the forerunner, no doubt, of the modern notion of intension or meaning. For Aristotle it was essential in men to be rational, accidental to be two-legged. But there is an important difference between this attitude and the doctrine of meaning. From the latter point of view it may indeed be conceded (if only for the sake of argument) that rationality is involved in the meaning of the word 'man' while two-leggedness is not; but two-leggedness may at the same time be viewed as involved in the meaning of 'biped' while rationality is not. Thus from the point of view of the doctrine of meaning it makes no sense to say of the actual individual, who is at once a man and a biped, that his rationality is essential and his two-leggedness accidental or vice versa. Things had essences, for Aristotle, but only linguistic forms have meanings. Meaning is what essence becomes when it is divorced from the object of reference and wedded to the word.

For the theory of meaning a conspicuous question is the nature of its objects: what sort of things are meanings? A felt need for meant entities may derive from an earlier failure to appreciate that meaning and reference are distinct. Once the theory of meaning is sharply separated from the theory of reference, it is a short step to recognizing as the primary business of the theory of meaning simply the synonymy of linguistic forms and the analyticity of statements; meanings themselves, as obscure intermediary entities, may well be abandoned.[3]

The problem of analyticity then confronts us anew. Statements which are analytic by general philosophical acclaim are not, indeed, far to seek. They fall into two classes. Those of the first class, which may be called *logically true*, are typified by:

(1)   No unmarried man is married.

The relevant feature of this example is that it not merely is true as it stands, but remains true under any and all reinterpretations of 'man' and 'married'. If we suppose a prior inventory of *logical* particles, comprising 'no', 'un-', 'not', 'if', 'then', 'and', etc., then in general a logical truth is a statement which is true and remains true under all reinterpretations of its components other than the logical particles.

But there is also a second class of analytic statements, typified by:

(2)   No bachelor is married.

The characteristic of such a statement is that it can be turned into a logical truth by putting synonyms for synonyms; thus (2) can be turned into (1) by putting 'unmarried man' for its synonym 'bachelor'. We still lack a proper characterization of this second class of analytic statements, and therewith of analyticity generally, inasmuch as we have had in the above description to lean on a notion of "synonymy" which is no less in need of clarification than analyticity itself.

In recent years Carnap has tended to explain

analyticity by appeal to what he calls state-descriptions.[4] A state-description is any exhaustive assignment of truth values to the atomic, or noncompound, statements of the language. All other statements of the language are, Carnap assumes, built up of their component clauses by means of the familiar logical devices, in such a way that the truth value of any complex statement is fixed for each state-description by specifiable logical laws. A statement is then explained as analytic when it comes out true under every state-description. This account is an adaptation of Leibniz's "true in all possible worlds." But note that this version of analyticity serves its purpose only if the atomic statements of the language are, unlike 'John is a bachelor' and 'John is married', mutually independent. Otherwise there would be a state-description which assigned truth to 'John is a bachelor' and to 'John is married', and consequently 'No bachelors are married' would turn out synthetic rather than analytic under the proposed criterion. Thus the criterion of analyticity in terms of state-descriptions serves only for languages devoid of extra-logical synonym-pairs, such as 'bachelor' and 'unmarried man'—synonym-pairs of the type which give rise to the "second class" of analytic statements. The criterion in terms of state-descriptions is a reconstruction at best of logical truth, not of analyticity.

I do not mean to suggest that Carnap is under any illusions on this point. His simplified model language with its state-descriptions is aimed primarily not at the general problem of analyticity but at another purpose, the clarification of probability and induction. Our problem, however, is analyticity; and here the major difficulty lies not in the first class of analytic statements, the logical truths, but rather in the second class, which depends on the notion of synonymy.

2 Definition

There are those who find it soothing to say that the analytic statements of the second class reduce to those of the first class, the logical truths, by *definition*; 'bachelor', for example, is *defined* as 'unmarried man'. But how do we find that 'bachelor' is defined as 'unmarried man'? Who defined it thus, and when? Are we to appeal to the nearest dictionary, and accept the lexicographer's formulation as law? Clearly this would be to put the cart before the horse. The lexicographer is an empirical scientist, whose business is the recording of antecedent facts; and if he glosses 'bachelor' as 'unmarried man' it is because of his belief that there is a relation of synonymy between those forms, implicit in general or preferred usage prior to his own work. The notion of synonymy presupposed here has still to be clarified, presumably in terms relating to linguistic behavior. Certainly the "definition" which is the lexicographer's report of an observed synonymy cannot be taken as the ground of the synonymy.

Definition is not, indeed, an activity exclusively of philologists. Philosophers and scientists frequently have occasion to "define" a recondite term by paraphrasing it into terms of a more familiar vocabulary. But ordinarily such a definition, like the philologist's, is pure lexicography, affirming a relation of synonymy antecedent to the exposition in hand.

Just what it means to affirm synonymy, just what the inter-connections may be which are necessary and sufficient in order that two linguistic forms be properly describable as synonymous, is far from clear; but, whatever these inter-connections may be, ordinarily they are grounded in usage. Definitions reporting selected instances of synonymy come then as reports upon usage.

There is also, however, a variant type of definitional activity which does not limit itself to the reporting of preëxisting synonymies. I have in mind what Carnap calls *explication*—an activity to which philosophers are given, and scientists also in their more philosophical moments. In explication the purpose is not merely to paraphrase the definiendum into an outright synonym, but actually to improve upon the definiendum by refining or supplementing its meaning. But even explication, though not merely reporting a preëxisting synonymy between definiendum and definiens, does rest nevertheless on *other* preëxisting synonymies. The matter may be viewed as follows. Any word worth explicating has some contexts which, as wholes, are clear and precise enough to be useful; and the purpose of explication is to preserve the usage of these favored contexts while sharpening the usage of other contexts. In order that a given definition be suitable for purposes of explication, therefore, what is required is not that the definiendum in its antecedent usage be synonymous with the definiens, but just that each of these favored contexts of the definiendum, taken as a whole in its antecedent usage, be synonymous with the corresponding context of the definiens.

Two alternative definientia may be equally appropriate for the purposes of a given task of explication and yet not be synonymous with each other; for they may serve interchangeably within the favored contexts but diverge elsewhere. By cleaving to one of these definientia rather than the other, a definition of explicative kind generates, by fiat, a relation of synonymy between definiendum and definiens which did not hold before. But such a definition still owes its explicative function, as seen, to preëxisting synonymies.

There does, however, remain still an extreme sort of definition which does not hark back to prior synonymies at all: namely, the explicitly conventional introduction of novel notations for purposes of sheer abbreviation. Here the definiendum becomes synonymous with the definiens simply because it has been created expressly for the purpose of being synonymous with the definiens. Here we have a really transparent case of synonymy created by definition; would that all species of synonymy were as intelligible. For the rest, definition rests on synonymy rather than explaining it.

The word 'definition' has come to have a dangerously reassuring sound, owing no doubt to its frequent occurrence in logical and mathematical writings. We shall do well to digress now into a brief appraisal of the role of definition in formal work.

In logical and mathematical systems either of two mutually antagonistic types of economy may be striven for, and each has its peculiar practical utility. On the one hand we may seek economy of practical expression—ease and brevity in the statement of multifarious relations. This sort of economy calls usually for distinctive concise notations for a wealth of concepts. Second, however, and oppositely, we may seek economy in grammar and vocabulary; we may try to find a minimum of basic concepts such that, once a distinctive notation has been appropriated to each of them, it becomes possible to express any desired further concept by mere combination and iteration of our basic notations. This second sort of economy is impractical in one way, since a poverty in basic idioms tends to a necessary lengthening of discourse. But it is practical in another way: it greatly simplifies theoretical discourse *about* the language, through minimizing the terms and the forms of construction wherein the language consists.

Both sorts of economy, though prima facie incompatible, are valuable in their separate ways. The custom has consequently arisen of combining both sorts of economy by forging in effect two languages, the one a part of the other. The inclusive language, though redundant in grammar and vocabulary, is economical in message lengths, while the part, called primitive notation, is economical in grammar and vocabulary. Whole and part are correlated by rules of translation whereby each idiom not in primitive notation is equated to some complex built up of primitive notation. These rules of translation are the so-called *definitions* which appear in formalized systems. They are best viewed not as adjuncts to one language but as correlations between two languages, the one a part of the other.

But these correlations are not arbitrary. They are supposed to show how the primitive notations can accomplish all purposes, save brevity and convenience, of the redundant language. Hence the definiendum and its definiens may be expected, in each case, to be related in one or another of the three ways lately noted. The definiens may be a faithful paraphrase of the definiendum into the narrower notation, preserving a direct synonymy[5] as of antecedent usage; or the definiens may, in the spirit of explication, improve upon the antecedent usage of the definiendum; or finally, the definiendum may be a newly created notation, newly endowed with meaning here and now.

In formal and informal work alike, thus, we find that definition—except in the extreme case of the explicitly conventional introduction of new notations—hinges on prior relations of synonymy. Recognizing then that the notion of definition does not hold the key to synonymy and analyticity, let us look further into synonymy and say no more of definition.

3 Interchangeability

A natural suggestion, deserving close examination, is that the synonymy of two linguistic forms consists simply in their interchangeability in all contexts without change of truth value—interchangeability, in Leibniz's phrase, *salva veritate*.[6] Note that synonyms so conceived need not even be free from vagueness, as long as the vaguenesses match.

But it is not quite true that the synonyms 'bachelor' and 'unmarried man' are everywhere interchangeable *salva veritate*. Truths which become false under substitution of 'unmarried man' for 'bachelor' are easily constructed with the help of 'bachelor of arts' or 'bachelor's buttons'; also with the help of quotation, thus:

'Bachelor' has less than ten letters.

Such counterinstances can, however, perhaps be set aside by treating the phrases 'bachelor of arts' and 'bachelor's buttons' and the quotation "bachelor" each as a single indivisible word and then stipulating that the interchangeability *salva veritate* which is to be the touchstone of synonymy is not supposed to apply to fragmentary occurrences inside of a word. This account of synonymy, supposing it acceptable on other counts, has indeed the drawback of appealing to a prior conception of "word" which can be counted on to present difficulties of formulation in its turn. Nevertheless some progress might be claimed in having reduced the problem of synonymy to a problem of word-hood. Let us pursue this line a bit, taking "word" for granted.

The question remains whether interchangeability *salva veritate* (apart from occurrences within words) is a strong enough condition for synonymy, or whether, on the contrary, some heteronymous expressions might be thus interchangeable. Now let us be clear that we are not concerned here with synonymy in the sense of complete identity in psychological associations or poetic quality; indeed no two expressions are synonymous in such a sense. We are concerned only with what may be called *cognitive* synonymy. Just what this is cannot be said without successfully finishing the present study; but we know something about it from the need which arose for it in connection with analyticity in §1. The sort of synonymy needed there was merely such that any analytic statement could be turned into a logical truth by putting synonyms for synonyms. Turning the tables and assuming analyticity, indeed, we could explain cognitive synonymy of terms as follows (keeping to the familiar example): to say that 'bachelor' and 'unmarried man' are cognitively synonymous is to say no more nor less than that the statement:

(3)   All and only bachelors are unmarried men

is analytic.[7] What we need is an account of cognitive synonymy not presupposing analyticity— if we are to explain analyticity conversely with help of cognitive synonymy as undertaken in §1. And indeed such an independent account of cognitive synonymy is at present up for consideration, namely, interchangeability *salva veritate* everywhere except within words. The question before us, to resume the thread at last, is whether such interchangeability is a sufficient condition for cognitive synonymy. We can quickly assure ourselves that it is, by examples of the following sort. The statement:

(4)   Necessarily all and only bachelors are bachelors

is evidently true, even supposing 'necessarily' so narrowly construed as to be truly applicable only to analytic statements. Then, if 'bachelor' and 'unmarried man' are interchangeable *salva veritate*, the result:

(5)   Necessarily all and only bachelors are unmarried men

of putting 'unmarried man' for an occurrence of 'bachelor' in (4) must, like (4), be true. But to say that (5) is true is to say that (3) is analytic, and hence that 'bachelor' and 'unmarried man' are cognitively synonymous. Let us see what there is about the above argument that gives it its air of hocus-pocus. The condition of interchangeability *salva veritate* varies in its force with variations in the richness of the language at hand. The above argument supposes we are working with a language rich enough to contain the adverb 'necessarily', this adverb being so construed as to yield truth when and only when applied to an analytic statement. But can we condone a language which contains such an adverb? Does the adverb really make sense? To suppose that it does is to suppose that we have already made satisfactory sense of 'analytic'. Then what are we so hard at work on right now?

Our argument is not flatly circular, but something like it. It has the form, figuratively speaking, of a closed curve in space.

Interchangeability *salva veritate* is meaningless until relativized to a language whose extent is specified in relevant respects. Suppose now we consider a language containing just the following materials. There is an indefinitely large stock of one-place predicates (for example, 'F' where 'Fx' means that x is a man) and many-place predicates (for example, 'G' where 'Gxy' means that x loves y), mostly having to do with extralogical subject matter. The rest of the language is logical. The atomic sentences consist each of a predicate followed by one or more variables 'x', 'y', etc.; and the complex sentences are built up of the atomic ones by truth functions ('not', 'and', 'or', etc.) and quantification.[8] In effect such a language enjoys the benefits also of descriptions and indeed singular terms generally, these being contextually definable in known ways.[9] Even abstract singular terms naming classes, classes of classes, etc., are contextually definable in case the assumed stock of predicates includes the two-place predicate of class membership.[10] Such a language can be adequate to classical mathematics and indeed to scientific discourse generally, except in so far as the latter involves debatable devices such as contrary-to-fact conditionals or modal adverbs like 'necessarily'.[11] Now a language of this type is extensional, in this sense: any two predicates which agree extensionally (that is, are true of the same objects) are interchangeable *salva veritate*.[12]

In an extensional language, therefore, interchangeability *salva veritate* is no assurance of cognitive synonymy of the desired type. That 'bachelor' and 'unmarried man' are interchangeable *salva veritate* in an extensional language assures us of no more than that (3) is true. There is no assurance here that the extensional agreement of 'bachelor' and 'unmarried man' rests on meaning rather than merely on accidental matters of fact, as does the extensional agreement of 'creature with a heart' and 'creature with kidneys'.

For most purposes extensional agreement is the nearest approximation to synonymy we need care about. But the fact remains that extensional agreement falls far short of cognitive synonymy of the type required for explaining analyticity in the manner of §1. The type of cognitive synonymy required there is such as to equate the synonymy of 'bachelor' and 'unmarried man' with the analyticity of (3), not merely with the truth of (3).

So we must recognize that interchangeability *salva veritate*, if construed in relation to an extensional language, is not a sufficient condition of cognitive synonymy in the sense needed for deriving analyticity in the manner of §1. If a language contains an intensional adverb 'necessarily' in the sense lately noted, or other particles to the same effect, then interchangeability *salva veritate* in such a language does afford a sufficient condition of cognitive synonymy; but such a language is intelligible only in so far as the notion of analyticity is already understood in advance.

The effort to explain cognitive synonymy first, for the sake of deriving analyticity from it afterward as in §1, is perhaps the wrong approach. Instead we might try explaining analyticity somehow without appeal to cognitive synonymy. Afterward we could doubtless derive cognitive synonymy from analyticity satisfactorily enough if desired. We have seen that cognitive synonymy of 'bachelor' and 'unmarried man' can be explained as analyticity of (3). The same explanation works for any pair of one-place predicates, of course, and it can be extended in obvious fashion to many-place predicates. Other syntactical categories can also be accommodated in fairly parallel fashion. Singular terms may be said to be cognitively synonymous when the statement of identity formed by putting '=' between them is analytic. Statements may be said simply to be cognitively synonymous when their biconditional (the result of joining them by 'if and only if') is analytic.[13] If we care to lump all categories into a single formulation, at the expense of assuming again the notion of "word" which was appealed to early in this section, we

can describe any two linguistic forms as cognitively synonymous when the two forms are interchangeable (apart from occurrences within "words") *salva* (no longer *veritate* but) *analyticitate*. Certain technical questions arise, indeed, over cases of ambiguity or homonymy; let us not pause for them, however, for we are already digressing. Let us rather turn our backs on the problem of synonymy and address ourselves anew to that of analyticity.

4 Semantical rules

Analyticity at first seemed most naturally definable by appeal to a realm of meanings. On refinement, the appeal to meanings gave way to an appeal to synonymy or definition. But definition turned out to be a will-o'-the-wisp, and synonymy turned out to be best understood only by dint of a prior appeal to analyticity itself. So we are back at the problem of analyticity.

I do not know whether the statement 'Everything green is extended' is analytic. Now does my indecision over this example really betray an incomplete understanding, an incomplete grasp of the "meanings", of 'green' and 'extended'? I think not. The trouble is not with 'green' or 'extended', but with 'analytic'.

It is often hinted that the difficulty in separating analytic statements from synthetic ones in ordinary language is due to the vagueness of ordinary language and that the distinction is clear when we have a precise artificial language with explicit "semantical rules." This, however, as I shall now attempt to show, is a confusion.

The notion of analyticity about which we are worrying is a purported relation between statements and languages: a statement S is said to be *analytic for* a language L, and the problem is to make sense of this relation generally, that is, for variable 'S' and 'L'. The gravity of this problem is not perceptibly less for artificial languages than for natural ones. The problem of making sense of the idiom 'S is analytic for L', with variable 'S' and 'L', retains its stubbornness even if we limit the range of the variable 'L' to artificial languages. Let me now try to make this point evident.

For artificial languages and semantical rules we look naturally to the writings of Carnap. His semantical rules take various forms, and to make my point I shall have to distinguish certain of the forms. Let us suppose, to begin with, an artificial language L_0 whose semantical rules have the form explicitly of a specification, by recursion or otherwise, of all the analytic statements of L_0. The rules tell us that such and such statements, and only those, are the analytic statements of L_0. Now here the difficulty is simply that the rules contain the word 'analytic', which we do not understand! We understand what expressions the rules attribute analyticity to, but we do not understand what the rules attribute to those expressions. In short, before we can understand a rule which begins 'A statement S is analytic for language L_0 if and only if . . .', we must understand the general relative term 'analytic for'; we must understand 'S is analytic for L' where 'S' and 'L' are variables.

Alternatively we may, indeed, view the so-called rule as a conventional definition of a new simple symbol 'analytic-for-L_0', which might better be written untendentiously as 'K' so as not to seem to throw light on the interesting word 'analytic'. Obviously any number of classes K, M, N, etc. of statements of L_0 can be specified for various purposes or for no purpose; what does it mean to say that K, as against M, N, etc., is the class of the "analytic" statements of L_0?

By saying what statements are analytic for L_0 we explain 'analytic-for-L_0' but not 'analytic', not 'analytic for'. We do not begin to explain the idiom 'S is analytic for L' with variable 'S' and 'L', even if we are content to limit the range of 'L' to the realm of artificial languages.

Actually we do know enough about the intended significance of 'analytic' to know that analytic statements are supposed to be true. Let us then turn to a second form of semantical rule,

which says not that such and such statements are analytic but simply that such and such statements are included among the truths. Such a rule is not subject to the criticism of containing the un-understood word 'analytic'; and we may grant for the sake of argument that there is no difficulty over the broader term 'true'. A semantical rule of this second type, a rule of truth, is not supposed to specify all the truths of the language; it merely stipulates, recursively or otherwise, a certain multitude of statements which, along with others unspecified, are to count as true. Such a rule may be conceded to be quite clear. Derivatively, afterward, analyticity can be demarcated thus: a statement is analytic if it is (not merely true but) true according to the semantical rule.

Still there is really no progress. Instead of appealing to an unexplained word 'analytic', we are now appealing to an unexplained phrase 'semantical rule'. Not every true statement which says that the statements of some class are true can count as a semantical rule—otherwise *all* truths would be "analytic" in the sense of being true according to semantical rules. Semantical rules are distinguishable, apparently, only by the fact of appearing on a page under the heading 'Semantical Rules'; and this heading is itself then meaningless.

We can say indeed that a statement is *analytic-for-L_0* if and only if it is true according to such and such specifically appended "semantical rules," but then we find ourselves back at essentially the same case which was originally discussed: 'S is analytic-for-L_0 if and only if. . . .' Once we seek to explain 'S is analytic for L' generally for variable 'L' (even allowing limitation of 'L' to artificial languages), the explanation 'true according to the semantical rules of L' is unavailing; for the relative term 'semantical rule of' is as much in need of clarification, at least, as 'analytic for'.

It may be instructive to compare the notion of semantical rule with that of postulate. Relative to a given set of postulates, it is easy to say what a postulate is: it is a member of the set. Relative to a given set of semantical rules, it is equally easy to say what a semantical rule is. But given simply a notation, mathematical or otherwise, and indeed as throughly understood a notation as you please in point of the translations or truth conditions of its statements, who can say which of its true statements rank as postulates? Obviously the question is meaningless—as meaningless as asking which points in Ohio are starting points. Any finite (or effectively specifiable infinite) selection of statements (perferably true ones, perhaps) is as much *a* set of postulates as any other. The word 'postulate' is significant only relative to an act of inquiry; we apply the word to a set of statements just in so far as we happen, for the year or the moment, to be thinking of those statements in relation to the statements which can be reached from them by some set of transformations to which we have seen fit to direct our attention. Now the notion of semantical rule is as sensible and meaningful as that of postulate, if conceived in a similarly relative spirit—relative, this time, to one or another particular enterprise of schooling unconversant persons in sufficient conditions for truth of statements of some natural or artificial language L. But from this point of view no one signalization of a subclass of the truths of L is intrinsically more a semantical rule than another; and, if 'analytic' means 'true by semantical rules', no one truth of L is analytic to the exclusion of another.[14]

It might conceivably be protested that an artificial language L (unlike a natural one) is a language in the ordinary sense *plus* a set of explicit semantical rules—the whole constituting, let us say, an ordered pair; and that the semantical rules of L then are specifiable simply as the second component of the pair L. But, by the same token and more simply, we might construe an artificial language L outright as an ordered pair whose second component is the class of its analytic statements; and then the analytic statements of L become specifiable simply as the statements in the second component of L. Or better still,

we might just stop tugging at our bootstraps altogether.

Not all the explanations of analyticity known to Carnap and his readers have been covered explicitly in the above considerations, but the extension to other forms is not hard to see. Just one additional factor should be mentioned which sometimes enters: sometimes the semantical rules are in effect rules of translation into ordinary language, in which case the analytic statements of the artificial language are in effect recognized as such from the analyticity of their specified translations in ordinary language. Here certainly there can be no thought of an illumination of the problem of analyticity from the side of the artificial language.

From the point of view of the problem of analyticity the notion of an artificial language with semantical rules is a *feu follet par excellence*. Semantical rules determining the analytic statements of an artificial language are of interest only in so far as we already understand the notion of analyticity; they are of no help in gaining this understanding.

Appeal to hypothetical languages of an artificially simple kind could conceivably be useful in clarifying analyticity, if the mental or behavioral or cultural factors relevant to analyticity—whatever they may be—were somehow sketched into the simplified model. But a model which takes analyticity merely as an irreducible character is unlikely to throw light on the problem of explicating analyticity.

It is obvious that truth in general depends on both language and extralinguistic fact. The statement 'Brutus killed Caesar' would be false if the world had been different in certain ways, but it would also be false if the word 'killed' happened rather to have the sense of 'begat'. Thus one is tempted to suppose in general that the truth of a statement is somehow analyzable into a linguistic component and a factual component. Given this supposition, it next seems reasonable that in some statements the factual component should be null; and these are the analytic statements. But, for all its a priori reasonableness, a boundary between analytic and synthetic statements simply has not been drawn. That there is such a distinction to be drawn at all is an unempirical dogma of empiricists, a metaphysical article of faith.

5 The verification theory and reductionism

In the course of these somber reflections we have taken a dim view first of the notion of meaning, then of the notion of cognitive synonymy, and finally of the notion of analyticity. But what, it may be asked, of the verification theory of meaning? This phrase has established itself so firmly as a catchword of empiricism that we should be very unscientific indeed not to look beneath it for a possible key to the problem of meaning and the associated problems.

The verification theory of meaning, which has been conspicuous in the literature from Peirce onward, is that the meaning of a statement is the method of empirically confirming or infirming it. An analytic statement is that limiting case which is confirmed no matter what.

As urged in §1, we can as well pass over the question of meanings as entities and move straight to sameness of meaning, or synonymy. Then what the verification theory says is that statements are synonymous if and only if they are alike in point of method of empirical confirmation or infirmation.

This is an account of cognitive synonymy not of linguistic forms generally, but of statements.[15] However, from the concept of synonymy of statements we could derive the concept of synonymy for other linguistic forms, by considerations somewhat similar to those at the end of §3. Assuming the notion of "word," indeed, we could explain any two forms as synonymous when the putting of the one form for an occurrence of the other in any statement (apart from occurrences within "words") yields a synonymous statement. Finally, given the concept of synonymy thus for linguistic forms generally, we could define analyticity in terms of synonymy and logical truth as in §1. For that matter, we could define analyticity more simply in terms of just synonymy of statements together with logical truth; it is not necessary to appeal to synonymy of linguistic forms other than statements. For a statement may be described as analytic simply when it is synonymous with a logically true statement.

So, if the verification theory can be accepted as an adequate account of statement synonymy, the notion of analyticity is saved after all. However, let us reflect. Statement synonymy is said to be likeness of method of empirical confirmation or infirmation. Just what are these methods which are to be compared for likeness? What, in other words, is the nature of the relation between a statement and the experiences which contribute to or detract from its confirmation?

The most naïve view of the relation is that it is one of direct report. This is *radical reductionism*. Every meaningful statement is held to be translatable into a statement (true or false) about immediate experience. Radical reductionism, in one form or another, well antedates the verification theory of meaning explicitly so called. Thus Locke and Hume held that every idea must either originate directly in sense experience or else be compounded of ideas thus originating; and taking a hint from Tooke we might rephrase this doctrine in semantical jargon by saying that a term, to be significant at all, must be either a name of a sense datum or a compound of such names or an abbreviation of such a compound. So stated, the doctrine remains ambiguous as between sense data as sensory events and sense data as sensory qualities; and it remains vague as to the admissible ways of compounding. Moreover, the doctrine is unnecessarily and intolerably restrictive in the term-by-term critique which it imposes. More reasonably, and without yet exceeding the limits of what I have called radical reductionism, we may take full statements as our significant units—thus demanding that our statements as wholes be translatable into sense-datum language, but not that they be translatable term by term.

This emendation would unquestionably have been welcome to Locke and Hume and Tooke, but historically it had to await an important reorientation in semantics—the reorientation whereby the primary vehicle of meaning came to be seen no longer in the term but in the statement. This reorientation, explicit in Frege ([1], §60), underlies Russell's concept of incomplete symbols defined in use;[16] also it is implicit in the verification theory of meaning, since the objects of verification are statements.

Radical reductionism, conceived now with statements as units, set itself the task of specifying a sense-datum language and showing how to translate the rest of significant discourse, statement by statement, into it. Carnap embarked on this project in the *Aufbau*.

The language which Carnap adopted as his starting point was not a sense-datum language in the narrowest conceivable sense, for it included also the notations of logic, up through higher set theory. In effect it included the whole language of pure mathematics. The ontology implicit in it (that is, the range of values of its variables) embraced not only sensory events but classes, classes of classes, and so on. Empiricists there are who would boggle at such prodigality. Carnap's starting point is very parsimonious, however, in its extralogical or sensory part. In a series of constructions in which he exploits the resources of modern logic with much ingenuity, Carnap succeeds in defining a wide array of important additional sensory concepts which, but for his constructions, one would not have dreamed were definable on so slender a basis. He was the first empiricist who, not content with asserting the reducibility of science to terms of immediate experience, took serious steps toward carrying out the reduction.

If Carnap's starting point is satisfactory, still his constructions were, as he himself stressed, only a fragment of the full program. The construction of even the simplest statements about the physical world was left in a sketchy state. Carnap's suggestions on this subject were, despite their sketchiness, very suggestive. He explained spatio-temporal point-instants as quadruples of real numbers and envisaged assignment of sense qualities to point-instants according to certain canons. Roughly summarized, the plan was that qualities should be assigned to point-instants in such a way as to achieve the laziest world compatible with our experience. The principle of least action was to be our guide in constructing a world from experience.

Carnap did not seem to recognize, however, that his treatment of physical objects fell short of reduction not merely through sketchiness, but in principle. Statements of the form 'Quality q is at point-instant $x;y;z;t$' were, according to his canons, to be apportioned truth values in such a way as to maximize and minimize certain overall features, and with growth of experience the truth values were to be progressively revised in the same spirit. I think this is a good schematization (deliberately oversimplified, to be sure) of what science really does; but it provides no indication, not even the sketchiest, of how a statement of the form 'Quality q is at $x;y;z;t$' could ever be translated into Carnap's initial language of sense data and logic. The connective 'is at' remains an added undefined connective; the canons counsel us in its use but not in its elimination.

Carnap seems to have appreciated this point afterward; for in his later writings he abandoned all notion of the translatability of statements about the physical world into statements about immediate experience. Reductionism in its radical form has long since ceased to figure in Carnap's philosophy.

But the dogma of reductionism has, in a subtler and more tenuous form, continued to influence the thought of empiricists. The notion lingers that to each statement, or each synthetic statement, there is associated a unique range of possible sensory events such that the occurrence of any of them would add to the likelihood of truth of the statement, and that there is associated also another unique range of possible sensory events whose occurrence would detract from that likelihood. This notion is of course implicit in the verification theory of meaning.

The dogma of reductionism survives in the supposition that each statement, taken in isolation from its fellows, can admit of confirmation or infirmation at all. My countersuggestion, issuing essentially from Carnap's doctrine of the physical world in the *Aufbau*, is that our statements about the external world face the tribunal of sense experience not individually but only as a corporate body.[17]

The dogma of reductionism, even in its attenuated form, is intimately connected with the other dogma—that there is a cleavage between the analytic and the synthetic. We have found ourselves led, indeed, from the latter problem to the former through the verification theory of meaning. More directly, the one dogma clearly supports the other in this way: as long as it is taken to be significant in general to speak of the confirmation and infirmation of a statement, it seems significant to speak also of a limiting kind of statement which is vacuously confirmed, *ipso facto*, come what may; and such a statement is analytic.

The two dogmas are, indeed, at root identical. We lately reflected that in general the truth of statements does obviously depend both upon language and upon extralinguistic fact; and we noted that this obvious circumstance carries in its train, not logically but all too naturally, a feeling that the truth of a statement is somehow analyzable into a linguistic component and a factual component. The factual component must, if we are empiricists, boil down to a range of confirmatory experiences. In the extreme case where the linguistic component is all that matters, a true statement is analytic. But I hope we are now impressed with how stubbornly the distinction between analytic and synthetic has resisted any

straightforward drawing. I am impressed also, apart from prefabricated examples of black and white balls in an urn, with how baffling the problem has always been of arriving at any explicit theory of the empirical confirmation of a synthetic statement. My present suggestion is that it is nonsense, and the root of much nonsense, to speak of a linguistic component and a factual component in the truth of any individual statement. Taken collectively, science has its double dependence upon language and experience; but this duality is not significantly traceable into the statements of science taken one by one.

The idea of defining a symbol in use was, as remarked, an advance over the impossible term-by-term empiricism of Locke and Hume. The statement, rather than the term, came with Frege to be recognized as the unit accountable to an empiricist critique. But what I am now urging is that even in taking the statement as unit we have drawn our grid too finely. The unit of empirical significance is the whole of science.

6 Empiricism without the dogmas

The totality of our so-called knowledge or beliefs, from the most casual matters of geography and history to the profoundest laws of atomic physics or even of pure mathematics and logic, is a man-made fabric which impinges on experience only along the edges. Or, to change the figure, total science is like a field of force whose boundary conditions are experience. A conflict with experience at the periphery occasions readjustments in the interior of the field. Truth values have to be redistributed over some of our statements. Reëvaluation of some statements entails reëvaluation of others, because of their logical interconnections—the logical laws being in turn simply certain further statements of the system, certain further elements of the field. Having reëvaluated one statement we must reëvaluate some others, which may be statements logically connected with the first or may be the statements of logical connections themselves. But the total field is so underdetermined by its boundary conditions, experience, that there is much latitude of choice as to what statements to reëvaluate in the light of any single contrary experience. No particular experiences are linked with any particular statements in the interior of the field, except indirectly through considerations of equilibrium affecting the field as a whole.

If this view is right, it is misleading to speak of the empirical content of an individual statement—especially if it is a statement at all remote from the experiential periphery of the field. Furthermore it becomes folly to seek a boundary between synthetic statements, which hold contingently on experience, and analytic statements, which hold come what may. Any statement can be held true come what may, if we make drastic enough adjustments elsewhere in the system. Even a statement very close to the periphery can be held true in the face of recalcitrant experience by pleading hallucination or by amending certain statements of the kind called logical laws. Conversely, by the same token, no statement is immune to revision. Revision even of the logical law of the excluded middle has been proposed as a means of simplifying quantum mechanics; and what difference is there in principle between such a shift and the shift whereby Kepler superseded Ptolemy, or Einstein Newton, or Darwin Aristotle?

For vividness I have been speaking in terms of varying distances from a sensory periphery. Let me try now to clarify this notion without metaphor. Certain statements, though *about* physical objects and not sense experience, seem peculiarly germane to sense experience—and in a selective way: some statements to some experiences, others to others. Such statements, especially germane to particular experiences, I picture as near the periphery. But in this relation of "germaneness" I envisage nothing more than a loose association reflecting the relative likelihood, in practice, of our choosing one statement rather than another for revision in the event of recalcitrant experience. For example, we can imagine recalcitrant experiences to which we would surely be inclined to accommodate our system by reëvaluating just the statement that there are brick houses on Elm Street, together with related statements on the same topic. We can imagine other recalcitrant experiences to which we would be inclined to accommodate our system by reëvaluating just the statement that there are no centaurs, along with kindred statements. A recalcitrant experience can, I have urged, be accommodated by any of various alternative reëvaluations in various alternative quarters of the total system; but, in the cases which we are now imagining, our natural tendency to disturb the total system as little as possible would lead us to focus our revisions upon these specific statements concerning brick houses or centaurs. These statements are felt, therefore, to have a sharper empirical reference than highly theoretical statements of physics or logic or ontology. The latter statements may be thought of as relatively centrally located within the total network, meaning merely that little preferential connection with any particular sense data obtrudes itself.

As an empiricist I continue to think of the conceptual scheme of science as a tool, ultimately, for predicting future experience in the light of past experience. Physical objects are conceptually imported into the situation as convenient intermediaries—not by definition in terms of experience, but simply as irreducible posits[18] comparable, epistemologically, to the gods of Homer. For my part I do, qua lay physicist, believe in physical objects and not in Homer's gods; and I consider it a scientific error to believe otherwise. But in point of epistemological footing the physical objects and the gods differ only in degree and not in kind. Both sorts of entities enter our conception only as cultural posits. The myth of physical objects is epistemologically superior to most in that it has proved more efficacious than other myths as a device for working a manageable structure into the flux of experience.

Positing does not stop with macroscopic physical objects. Objects at the atomic level are posited to make the laws of macroscopic objects, and ultimately the laws of experience, simpler and more manageable; and we need not expect or demand full definition of atomic and sub-atomic entities in terms of macroscopic ones, any more than definition of macroscopic things in terms of sense data. Science is a continuation of common sense, and it continues the common-sense expedient of swelling ontology to simplify theory.

Physical objects, small and large, are not the only posits. Forces are another example; and indeed we are told nowadays that the boundary between energy and matter is obsolete. More-over, the abstract entities which are the substance of mathematics—ultimately classes and classes of classes and so on up—are another posit in the same spirit. Epistemologically these are myths on the same footing with physical objects and gods, neither better nor worse except for differences in the degree to which they expedite our dealings with sense experiences.

The over-all algebra of rational and irrational numbers is underdetermined by the algebra of rational numbers, but is smoother and more convenient; and it includes the algebra of rational numbers as a jagged or gerrymandered part.[19] Total science, mathematical and natural and human, is similarly but more extremely underdetermined by experience. The edge of the system must be kept squared with experience; the rest, with all its elaborate myths or fictions, has as its objective the simplicity of laws.

Ontological questions, under this view, are on a par with questions of natural science.[20] Consider the question whether to countenance classes as entities. This, as I have argued elsewhere,[21] is the question whether to quantify with respect to variables which take classes as values. Now Carnap [6] has maintained that this is a question not of matters of fact but of choosing a convenient language form, a convenient conceptual scheme or framework for science.

With this I agree, but only on the proviso that the same be conceded regarding scientific hypotheses generally. Carnap ([6], p. 32n) has recognized that he is able to preserve a double standard for ontological questions and scientific hypotheses only by assuming an absolute distinction between the analytic and the synthetic; and I need not say again that this is a distinction which I reject.[22]

The issue over there being classes seems more a question of convenient conceptual scheme; the issue over there being centaurs, or brick houses on Elm Street, seems more a question of fact. But I have been urging that this difference is only one of degree, and that it turns upon our vaguely pragmatic inclination to adjust one strand of the fabric of science rather than another in accommodating some particular recalcitrant experience. Conservatism figures in such choices, and so does the quest for simplicity.

Carnap, Lewis, and others take a pragmatic stand on the question of choosing between language forms, scientific frameworks; but their pragmatism leaves off at the imagined boundary between the analytic and the synthetic. In repudiating such a boundary I espouse a more thorough pragmatism. Each man is given a scientific heritage plus a continuing barrage of sensory stimulation; and the considerations which guide him in warping his scientific heritage to fit his continuing sensory promptings are, where rational, pragmatic.

Notes

1 See Quine [2], p. 9.
2 See Quine [2], p. 10 and pp. 107–15.
3 See Quine [2], pp. 11f. and pp. 48f.
4 Carnap [3], pp. 9ff; [4], pp. 70ff.
5 According to an important variant sense of 'definition', the relation preserved may be the weaker relation of mere agreement in reference; see below, p. 132. But definition in this sense is better ignored in the present connection, being irrelevant to the question of synonymy.
6 Cf. Lewis [1], p. 373.

7 This is cognitive synonymy in a primary, broad sense. Carnap ([3], pp. 56ff) and Lewis ([2], pp. 83ff) have suggested how, once this notion is at hand, a narrower sense of cognitive synonymy which is preferable for some purposes can in turn be derived. But this special ramification of concept-building lies aside from the present purposes and must not be confused with the broad sort of cognitive synonymy here concerned.

8 Pp. 81ff, Quine [2], contain a description of just such a language, except that there happens there to be just one predicate, the two-place predicate '∈'.

9 See Quine [2], pp. 5–8; also pp. 85f, 166f.

10 See Quine [2], p. 87.

11 On such devices see also Quine [2], pp. 139–60.

12 This is the substance of Quine [1], *121.

13 The 'if and only if' itself is intended in the truth functional sense. See Carnap [3], p. 14.

14 The foregoing paragraph was not part of the present essay as originally published. It was prompted by Martin (see Bibliography [see "References," below]), as was the end of Quine [2], pp. 130–9.

15 The doctrine can indeed the formulated with terms rather than statements as the units. Thus Lewis describes the meaning of a term as "*a criterion in mind, by reference to which one is able to apply or refuse to apply the expression in question in the case of presented, or imagined, things or situations*" ([2], p. 133).—For an instructive account of the vicissitudes of the verification theory of meaning, centered however on the question of meaning *fulness* rather than synonymy and analyticity, see Hempel.

16 See Quine [2], p. 6.

17 This doctrine was well argued by Duhem, pp. 303–328. Or see Lowinger, pp. 132–140.

18 Cf. Quine [2] pp. 17f.

19 Cf. Quine [2] p. 18.

20 "L'ontologie fait corps avec la science elle-même et ne peut en être separée." Meyerson, p. 439.

21 Quine [2] pp. 12f; pp. 102ff.

22 For an effective expression of further misgivings over this distinction, see White [2].

References

Carnap, Rudolf, [3], *Meaning and Necessity* (Chicago: University of Chicago Press, 1947).

—— [4], *Logical Foundations of Probability* (Chicago: University of Chicago Press, 1950).

—— [6], "Empiricism, semantics, and ontology," *Revue internationale de philosophie* 4 (1950), 20–40. Reprinted in Linsky.

Duhem, Pierre, *La Théorie physique: son objet et sa structure* (Paris, 1906).

Frege, Gottlob [1], *Foundations of Arithmetic* (New York: Philosophical Library, 1950). Reprint of *Grundlagen der Arithmetik* (Breslau, 1884) with English translation in parallel.

Hempel, C. G. [1], "Problems and changes in the empiricist criterion of meaning," *Revue internationale de philosophie* 4 (1950), 41–63. Reprinted in Linsky.

Lewis, C. I. [1], *A Survey of Symbolic Logic* (Berkeley, 1918).

—— [2], *An Analysis of Knowledge and Valuation* (LaSalle, Ill.: Open Court, 1946).

Linsky, Leonard (ed.), *Semantics and the Philosophy of Language* (Urbana: University of Illinois Press, 1952).

Lowinger, Armand, *The Methodology of Pierre Duhem* (New York: Columbia University Press, 1941).

Martin, R. M., "On 'analytic'," *Philosophical Studies* 3 (1952), 42–47.

Meyerson, Émile, *Identité et réalité.* (Paris, 1908; 4th ed., 1932).

Quine, W. V. [1], *Mathematical Logic* (New York: Norton, 1940; Cambridge: Harvard University Press, 1947; rev. ed., Cambridge: Harvard University Press, 1951).

Quine, W. V. [2], *From a Logical Point of View*, Cambridge, MA: Harvard University Press (1953).

White, Morton [2], "The analytic and the synthetic: an untenable dualism," in Sidney Hook (ed.), *John Dewey: Philosopher of Science and Freedom* (New York: Dial Press, 1950), pp. 316–330. Reprinted in Linsky.

Chapter 12

H. Paul Grice and P. F. Strawson

IN DEFENSE OF A DOGMA

In his article "Two Dogmas of Empiricism,"[1] Professor Quine advances a number of criticisms of the supposed distinction between analytic and synthetic statements, and of other associated notions. It is, he says, a distinction which he rejects.[2] We wish to show that his criticisms of the distinction do not justify his rejection of it.

There are many ways in which a distinction can be criticized, and more than one in which it can be rejected. It can be criticized for not being a sharp distinction (for admitting of cases which do not fall clearly on either side of it); or on the ground that the terms in which it is customarily drawn are ambiguous (have more than one meaning); or on the ground that it is confused (the different meanings being habitually conflated). Such criticisms alone would scarcely amount to a rejection of the distinction. They would, rather, be a prelude to clarification. It is not this sort of criticism which Quine makes.

Again, a distinction can be criticized on the ground that it is not useful. It can be said to be useless for certain purposes, or useless altogether, and, perhaps, pedantic. One who criticizes in this way may indeed be said to reject a distinction, but in a sense which also requires him to acknowledge its existence. He simply declares he can get on without it. But Quine's rejection of the analytic-synthetic distinction appears to be more radical than this. He would certainly say he could get on without the distinction, but not in a sense which would commit him to acknowledging its existence.

Or again, one could criticize the way or ways in which a distinction is customarily expounded or explained on the ground that these explanations did not make it really clear. And Quine certainly makes such criticisms in the case of the analytic-synthetic distinction.

But he does, or seems to do, a great deal more. He declares, or seems to declare, not merely that the distinction is useless or inadequately clarified, but also that it is altogether illusory, that the belief in its existence is a philosophical mistake. "That there is such a distinction to be drawn at all," he says, "is an unempirical dogma of empiricists, a metaphysical article of faith."[3] It is the existence of the distinction that he here calls in question; so his rejection of it would seem to amount to a denial of its existence.

Evidently such a position of extreme skepticism about a distinction is not in general justified merely by criticisms, however just in themselves, of philosophical attempts to clarify it. There are doubtless plenty of distinctions, drawn in philosophy and outside it, which still await adequate philosophical elucidation, but which few would want on this account to declare illusory. Quine's article, however, does not consist wholly, though it does consist largely, in criticizing attempts at elucidation. He does try also to diagnose the causes of the belief in the distinction, and he offers some positive doctrine, acceptance of which he represents as incompatible with this belief. If there is any general prior presumption in favor of the existence of the distinction, it seems that Quine's radical rejection of it must rest quite heavily on this part of his article, since the force of any such presumption is not even impaired by philosophical failures to clarify a distinction so supported.

Is there such a presumption in favor of the distinction's existence? Prima facie, it must be admitted that there is. An appeal to philosophical tradition is perhaps unimpressive and is certainly unnecessary. But it is worth pointing out that Quine's objection is not simply to the words "analytic" and "synthetic," but to a distinction which they are supposed to express, and which at different times philosophers have supposed themselves to be expressing by means of such pairs of words or phrases as "necessary" and "contingent," "a priori" and "empirical," "truth of reason" and "truth of fact"; so Quine is certainly at odds with a philosophical tradition which is long and not wholly disreputable. But there is no need to appeal only to tradition; for there is also present practice. We can appeal, that is, to the fact that those who use the terms "analytic" and "synthetic" do to a very considerable extent agree in the applications they make of them. They apply the term "analytic" to more or less the same cases, withhold it from more or less the same cases, and hesitate over more or less the same cases. This agreement extends not only to cases which they have been *taught* so to characterize, but to new cases. In short, "analytic" and "synthetic" have a more or less established philosophical *use*; and this seems to suggest that it is absurd, even senseless, to say that there is no such distinction. For, in general, if a pair of contrasting expressions are habitually and generally used in application to the same cases, *where these cases do not form a closed list*, this is a sufficient condition for saying that there are *kinds* of cases to which the expressions apply; and nothing more is needed for them to mark a distinction.

In view of the possibility of this kind of argument, one may begin to doubt whether Quine really holds the extreme thesis which his words encourage one to attribute to him. It is for this reason that we made the attribution tentative. For on at least one natural interpretation of this extreme thesis, when we say of something true that it is analytic and of another true thing that it is synthetic, it simply never is the case that we thereby mark a distinction between them. And this view seems terribly difficult to reconcile with the fact of an established philosophical usage (i.e., of general agreement in application in an open class). For this reason, Quine's thesis might be better represented not as the thesis that there is *no difference at all* marked by the use of these expressions, but as the thesis that the nature of, and reasons for, the difference or differences are totally misunderstood by those who use the expressions, that the stories they tell themselves *about* the difference are full of illusion.

We think Quine might be prepared to accept this amendment. If so, it could, in the following way, be made the basis of something like an answer to the argument which prompted it. Philosophers are notoriously subject to illusion, and to mistaken theories. Suppose there were a particular mistaken theory about language or knowledge, such that, seen in the light of this theory, some statements (or propositions or sentences) appeared to have a characteristic which no statements really have, or even, perhaps, which it does not make sense to suppose that any statement has, and which no one who was not consciously or subconsciously influenced by this theory would ascribe to any statement. And suppose that there were other statements which, seen in this light, did not appear to have this characteristic, and others again which presented an uncertain appearance. Then philosophers who were under the influence of this theory would tend to mark the supposed presence or absence of this characteristic by a pair of contrasting expressions, say "analytic" and "synthetic." Now in these circumstances it still could not be said that there was no distinction at all being marked by the use of these expressions, for there would be at least the distinction we have just described (the distinction, namely, between those statements which appeared to have and those which appeared to lack a certain characteristic), and there might well be other assignable differences too, which would account for the difference in appearance; but it certainly could be said that *the* difference these philosophers supposed themselves to be marking by the use of the expressions simply did not exist, and perhaps also (supposing the characteristic in question to be one which it was absurd to ascribe to any statement) that these expressions, as so used, were senseless or without meaning. We should only have to suppose that such a mistaken theory was very plausible and attractive, in order to reconcile the fact of an established philosophical usage for a pair of contrasting terms with the claim that *the* distinction which the terms purported to mark did not exist at all, though not with the claim that there simply did not exist a difference of any kind between the classes of statements so characterized. We think that the former claim would probably be sufficient for Quine's purposes. But to establish such a claim on the sort of grounds we have indicated evidently requires a great deal more argument than is involved in showing that certain explanations of a term do not measure up to certain requirements of adequacy in philosophical clarification—and not only more argument, but argument of a very different kind. For it would surely be too harsh to maintain that the *general* presumption is that philosophical distinctions embody the kind of illusion we have described. On the whole, it seems that philosophers are prone to make too few distinctions rather than too many. It is their assimilations, rather than their distinctions, which tend to be spurious.

So far we have argued as if the prior presumption in favor of the existence of the distinction which Quine questions rested solely on the fact of an agreed *philosophical* usage for the terms "analytic" and "synthetic." A presumption with only

this basis could no doubt be countered by a strategy such as we have just outlined. But, in fact, if we are to accept Quine's account of the matter, the presumption in question is not only so based. For among the notions which belong to the analyticity-group is one which Quine calls "cognitive synonymy," and in terms of which he allows that the notion of analyticity could at any rate be formally explained. Unfortunately, he adds, the notion of cognitive synonymy is just as unclarified as that of analyticity. To say that two expressions x and y are cognitively synonymous seems to correspond, at any rate roughly, to what we should ordinarily express by saying that x and y have the same meaning or that x means the same as y. If Quine is to be consistent in his adherence to the extreme thesis, then it appears that he must maintain not only that the distinction we suppose ourselves to be marking by the use of the terms "analytic" and "synthetic" does not exist, but also that the distinction we suppose ourselves to be marking by the use of the expressions "means the same as," "does not mean the same as" does not exist either. At least, he must maintain this insofar as the notion of *meaning the same as*, in its application to predicate-expressions, is supposed to differ from and go beyond the notion of *being true of just the same objects as*. (This latter notion—which we might call that of "coextensionality"—he is prepared to allow to be intelligible, though, as he rightly says, it is not sufficient for the explanation of analyticity.) Now since he cannot claim this time that the pair of expressions in question (viz., "means the same," "does not mean the same") is the special property of philosophers, the strategy outlined above of countering the presumption in favor of their marking a genuine distinction is not available here (or is at least enormously less plausible). Yet the denial that the distinction (taken as different from the distinction between the coextensional and the non-coextensional) really exists, is extremely paradoxical. It involves saying, for example, that anyone who seriously remarks that "bachelor" means the same as "unmarried man" but that "creature with kidneys" does not mean the same as "creature with a heart"—supposing the last two expressions to be coextensional—*either* is not in fact drawing attention to any distinction at all between the relations between the members of each pair of expressions *or* is making a philosophical mistake about the nature of the distinction between them. In either case, what he says, taken as he intends it to be taken, is senseless or absurd. More generally, it involves saying that it is always senseless or absurd to make a statement of the form "Predicates x and y in fact apply to the same objects, but do not have the same meaning." But the paradox is more violent than this. For we frequently talk of the presence or absence of relations of synonymy between kinds of expressions—e.g., conjunctions, particles of many kinds, whole sentences—where there does not appear to be any obvious substitute for the ordinary notion of synonymy, in the way in which coextensionality is said to be a substitute for synonymy of predicates. Is all such talk meaningless? Is all talk of correct or incorrect *translation* of sentences of one language into sentences of another meaningless? It is hard to believe that it is. But if we do successfully make the effort to believe it, we have still harder renunciations before us. If talk of sentence-synonymy is meaningless, then it seems that talk of sentences having a meaning at all must be meaningless too. For if it made sense to talk of a sentence having a meaning, or meaning something, then presumably it would make sense to ask "What does it mean?" And if it made sense to ask "What does it mean?" of a sentence, then sentence-synonymy could be roughly defined as follows: Two sentences are synonymous if and only if any true answer to the question "What does it mean?" asked of one of them, is a true answer to the same question, asked of the other. We do not, of course, claim any clarifying power for this definition. We want only to point out that if we are to give up the notion of sentence-synonymy as senseless, we must give up the notion of

sentence-significance (of a sentence having meaning) as senseless too. But then perhaps we might as well give up the notion of sense.—It seems clear that we have here a typical example of a philosopher's paradox. Instead of examining the actual use that we make of the notion of *meaning the same*, the philosopher measures it by some perhaps inappropriate standard (in this case some standard of clarifiability), and because it falls short of this standard, or seems to do so, denies its reality, declares it illusory.

We have argued so far that there is a strong presumption in favor of the existence of the distinction, or distinctions, which Quine challenges—a presumption resting both on philosophical and on ordinary usage—and that this presumption is not in the least shaken by the fact, if it is a fact, that the distinctions in question have not been, in some sense, adequately clarified. It is perhaps time to look at what Quine's notion of adequate clarification is.

The main theme of his article can be roughly summarized as follows. There is a certain circle or family of expressions, of which "analytic" is one, such that if any one member of the circle could be taken to be satisfactorily understood or explained, then other members of the circle could be verbally, and hence satisfactorily, explained in terms of it. Other members of the family are: "self-contradictory" (in a broad sense), "necessary," "synonymous," "semantical rule," and perhaps (but again in a broad sense) "definition." The list could be added to. Unfortunately each member of the family is in as great need of explanation as any other. We give some sample quotations: "The notion of self-contradictoriness (in the required broad sense of inconsistency) stands in exactly the same need of clarification as does the notion of analyticity itself."[4] Again, Quine speaks of "a notion of synonymy which is in no less need of clarification than analyticity itself."[5] Again, of the adverb "necessarily," as a candidate for use in the explanation of synonymy, he says, "Does the adverb *really make sense?* To suppose that it does is to suppose that we have already *made satisfactory sense* of 'analytic.' "[6] To make "satisfactory sense" of one of these expressions would seem to involve two things. (1) It would seem to involve providing an explanation which does not incorporate any expression belonging to the family-circle. (2) It would seem that the explanation provided must be of the same general character as those rejected explanations which do incorporate members of the family-circle (i.e., it must specify some feature common and peculiar to all cases to which, for example, the word "analytic" is to be applied; it must have the same general form as an explanation beginning, "a statement is analytic if and only if . . ."). It is true that Quine does not explicitly state the second requirement; but since he does not even consider the question whether any other kind of explanation would be relevant, it seems reasonable to attribute it to him. If we take these two conditions together, and generalize the result, it would seem that Quine requires of a satisfactory explanation of an expression that it should take the form of a pretty strict definition but should not make use of any member of a group of inter-definable terms to which the expression belongs. We may well begin to feel that a satisfactory explanation is hard to come by. The other element in Quine's position is one we have already commented on in general, before enquiring what (according to him) is to count as a satisfactory explanation. It is the step from "We have not made satisfactory sense (provided a satisfactory explanation) of x" to "x does not make sense."

It would seem fairly clearly unreasonable to insist *in general* that the availability of a satisfactory explanation in the sense sketched above is a necessary condition of an expression's making sense. It is perhaps dubious whether *any* such explanations can *ever* be given. (The hope that they can be is, or was, the hope of reductive analysis in general.) Even if such explanations can be given in some cases, it would be pretty generally agreed that there other cases in which they cannot. One might think, for example, of the group of expressions which includes "morally wrong," "blameworthy," "breach of moral rules," etc.; or of the group which includes the propositional connectives and the words "true" and "false," "statement," "fact," "denial," "assertion." Few people would want to say that the expressions belonging to either of these groups were senseless on the ground that they have not been formally defined (or even on the ground that it was impossible formally to define them) except in terms of members of the same group. It might, however, be said that while the unavailability of a satisfactory explanation in the special sense described was not a *generally* sufficient reason for declaring that a given expression was senseless, it was a sufficient reason in the case of the expressions of the analytic-ity group. But anyone who said this would have to advance a reason for discriminating in this way against the expressions of this group. The only plausible reason for being harder on these expressions than on others is a refinement on a consideration which we have already had before us. It starts from the point that "analytic" and "synthetic" themselves are technical philo-sophical expressions. To the rejoinder that other expressions of the family concerned, such as "means the same as" or "is inconsistent with," or "self-contradictory," are not at all technical expressions, but are common property, the reply would doubtless be that, to qualify for inclusion in the family-circle, these expressions have to be used in specially adjusted and precise senses (or pseudo-senses) which they do not ordinarily possess. It is the fact, then, that all the terms belonging to the circle are *either* technical terms or ordinary terms used in specially adjusted senses, that might be held to justify us in being particularly suspicious of the claims of members of the circle to have any sense at all, and hence to justify us in requiring them to pass a test for significance which would admit-tedly be too stringent if generally applied. This point has some force, though we doubt if the special adjustments spoken of are in every case as considerable as it suggests. (This seems particularly doubtful in the case of the word "inconsistent"—a perfectly good member of the nontechnician's meta-logical vocabulary.) But though the point has some force, it does not have whatever force would be required to justify us in insisting that the expressions concerned should pass exactly that test for significance which is in question. The fact, if it is a fact, that the expressions cannot be explained in precisely the way which Quine seems to require, does not mean that they cannot be explained at all. There is no need to try to pass them off as expressing innate ideas. They can be and are explained, though in other and less formal ways than that which Quine considers. (And the fact that they are so explained fits with the facts, first, that there is a generally agreed philosophical use for them, and second, that this use is technical or specially adjusted.) To illustrate the point briefly for one member of the analyticity family. Let us suppose we are trying to explain to someone the notion of *logical impossibility* (a member of the family which Quine presumably regards as no clearer than any of the others) and we decide to do it by bringing out the contrast between logical and natural (or causal) impossibility. We might take as our examples the logical impossibility of a child of three's being an adult, and the natural impossibility of a child of three's understanding Russell's Theory of Types. We might instruct our pupil to imagine two conversations one of which begins by someone (X) making the claim:

(1) "My neighbor's three-year-old child understands Russell's Theory of Types,"

and the other of which begins by someone (Y) making the claim:

(1′) "My neighbor's three-year-old child is an adult."

It would not be inappropriate to reply to X, taking the remark as a hyperbole:

(2) "You mean the child is a particularly bright lad."

If X were to say:

(3) "No, I mean what I say—he really does understand it,"

one might be inclined to reply:

(4) "I don't believe you—the thing's impossible."

But if the child were then produced, and did (as one knows he would not) expound the theory correctly, answer questions on it, criticize it, and so on, one would in the end be forced to acknowledge that the claim was literally true and that the child was a prodigy. Now consider one's reaction to Y's claim. To begin with, it might be somewhat similar to the previous case. One might say:

(2′) "You mean he's uncommonly sensible or very advanced for his age."

If Y replies:

(3′) "No, I mean what I say,"

we might reply:

(4′) "Perhaps you mean that he won't grow any more, or that he's a sort of freak, that he's already fully developed."

Y replies:

(5′) "No, he's not a freak, he's just an adult."

At this stage—or possibly if we are patient, a little later—we shall be inclined to say that we just don't understand what Y is saying, and to suspect that he just does not know the meaning of some of the words he is using. For unless he is prepared to admit that he is using words in a figurative or unusual sense, we shall say, not that we don't believe him, but that his words have *no* sense. And whatever kind of creature is ultimately produced for our inspection, it will not lead us to say that what Y said was literally true, but at most to say that we now see what he meant. As a summary of the difference between the two imaginary conversations, we might say that in both cases we would tend to begin by supposing that the other speaker was using words in a figurative or unusual or restricted way; but in the face of his repeated claim to be speaking literally, it would be appropriate in the first case to say that we did not believe him and in the second case to say that we did not understand him. If, like Pascal, we thought it prudent to prepare against very long chances, we should in the first case know what to prepare for; in the second, we should have no idea.

We give this as an example of just one type of informal explanation which we might have recourse to in the case of one notion of the analyticity group. (We do not wish to suggest it is the only type.) Further examples, with different though connected types of treatment, might be necessary to teach our pupil the use of the notion of logical impossibility in its application to more complicated cases—if indeed he did not pick it up from the one case. Now of course this type of explanation does not yield a formal statement of necessary and sufficient conditions for the application of the notion concerned. So it does not fulfill one of the conditions which Quine seems to require of a satisfactory explanation. On the other hand, it does appear to fulfill the other. It breaks out of the family-circle. The distinction in which we ultimately come to rest is that between not believing something and not understanding something; or between incredulity yielding to conviction, and incomprehension yielding to comprehension. It would be rash to maintain that this distinction does not need clarification; but it would be absurd to maintain that it does not exist. In the face of the availability of this

informal type of explanation for the notions of the analyticity group, the fact that they have not received another type of explanation (which it is dubious whether *any* expressions *ever* receive) seems a wholly inadequate ground for the conclusion that the notions are pseudo-notions, that the expressions which purport to express them have no sense. To say this is not to deny that it would be philosophically desirable, and a proper object of philosophical endeavor, to find a more illuminating general characterization of the notions of this group than any that has been so far given. But the question of how, if at all, this can be done is quite irrelevant to the question of whether or not the expressions which belong to the circle have an intelligible use and mark genuine distinctions.

So far we have tried to show that sections 1 to 4 of Quine's article—the burden of which is that the notions of the analyticity group have not been satisfactorily explained—do not establish the extreme thesis for which he appears to be arguing. It remains to be seen whether sections 5 and 6, in which diagnosis and positive theory are offered, are any more successful. But before we turn to them, there are two further points worth making which arise out of the first two sections.

(1) One concerns what Quine says about *definition* and *synonymy*. He remarks that definition does not, as some have supposed, "hold the key to synonymy and analyticity," since "definition—except in the extreme case of the explicitly conventional introduction of new notations—hinges on prior relations of synonymy."[7] But now consider what he says of these extreme cases. He says: "Here the definiendum becomes synonymous with the definiens simply because it has been expressly created for the purpose of being synonymous with the definiens. Here we have a really transparent case of synonymy created by definition; would that all species of synonymy were as intelligible." Now if we are to take these words of Quine seriously, then his position *as a whole* is incoherent. It is like the position of a man to whom we are trying to

explain, say, the idea of one thing fitting into another thing, or two things fitting together, and who says: "I can understand what it means to say that one thing fits into another, or that two things fit together, in the case where one was specially made to fit the other; but I cannot understand what it means to say this in any other case." Perhaps we should not take Quine's words here too seriously. But if not, then we have the right to ask him exactly what state of affairs he thinks is brought about by explicit definition, what relation between expressions is established by this procedure, and why he thinks it unintelligible to suggest that the same (or a closely analogous) state of affairs, or relation, should exist in the absence of this procedure. For our part, we should be inclined to take Quine's words (or some of them) seriously, and reverse his conclusions; and maintain that the notion of synonymy by explicit convention would be unintelligible if the notion of synonymy by usage were not presupposed. There cannot be law where there is no custom, or rules where there are not practices (though perhaps we can understand better what a practice is by looking at a rule).

(2) The second point arises out of a paragraph on page 32 of Quine's book [p. 161 above]. We quote:

> I do not know whether the statement "Everything green is extended" is analytic. Now does my indecision over this example really betray an incomplete understanding, an incomplete grasp, of the "meanings" of "green" and "extended"? I think not. The trouble is not with "green" or "extended," but with "analytic."

If, as Quine says, the trouble is with "analytic," then the trouble should doubtless disappear when "analytic" is removed. So let us remove it, and replace it with a word which Quine himself has contrasted favorably with "analytic" in respect of perspicuity—the word "true." Does

the indecision at once disappear? We think not. The indecision over "analytic" (and equally, in this case, the indecision over "true") arises, of course, from a further indecision: viz., that which we feel when confronted with such questions as "Should we count a *point* of green light as *extended* or not?" As is frequent enough in such cases, the hesitation arises from the fact that the boundaries of application of words are not determined by usage in all possible directions. But the example Quine has chosen is particularly unfortunate for his thesis, in that it is only too evident that our hesitations are not *here* attributable to obscurities in "analytic." It would be possible to choose other examples in which we should hesitate between "analytic" and "synthetic" and have few qualms about "true." But no more in these cases than in the sample case does the hesitation necessarily imply any obscurity in the notion of analyticity; since the hesitation would be sufficiently accounted for by the same or a similar kind of indeterminacy in the relations between the words occurring within the statement about which the question, whether it is analytic or synthetic, is raised.

Let us now consider briefly Quine's positive theory of the relations between the statements we accept as true or reject as false on the one hand and the "experiences" in the light of which we do this accepting and rejecting on the other. This theory is boldly sketched rather than precisely stated.[8] We shall merely extract from it two assertions, one of which Quine clearly takes to be incompatible with acceptance of the distinction between analytic and synthetic statements, and the other of which he regards as barring one way to an explanation of that distinction. We shall seek to show that the first assertion is not incompatible with acceptance of the distinction, but is, on the contrary, most intelligibly interpreted in a way quite consistent with it, and that the second assertion leaves the way open to just the kind of explanation which Quine thinks it precludes. The two assertions are the following:

(1)   It is an illusion to suppose that there is any class of accepted statements the members of which are in principle "immune from revision" in the light of experience, i.e., any that we accept as true and must continue to accept as true whatever happens.

(2)   It is an illusion to suppose that an individual statement, taken in isolation from its fellows, can admit of confirmation or disconfirmation at all. There is no particular statement such that a particular experience or set of experiences decides once for all whether that statement is true or false, independently of our attitudes to all other statements.

The apparent connection between these two doctrines may be summed up as follows. Whatever our experience may be, it is in principle possible to hold on to, or reject, any particular statement we like, so long as we are prepared to make extensive enough revisions elsewhere in our system of beliefs. In practice our choices are governed largely by considerations of convenience: we wish our system to be as simple as possible, but we also wish disturbances to it, as it exists, to be as small as possible.

The apparent relevance of these doctrines to the analytic-synthetic distinction is obvious in the first case, less so in the second.

(1) Since it is an illusion to suppose that the characteristic of immunity in principle from revision, come what may, belongs, or could belong, to any statement, it is an illusion to suppose that there is a distinction to be drawn between statements which possess this characteristic and statements which lack it. Yet, Quine suggests, this is precisely the distinction which those who use the terms "analytic" and "synthetic" suppose themselves to be drawing. Quine's view would perhaps also be (though he does not explicitly say this in the article under consideration) that those who believe in the distinction are inclined at least sometimes to mistake the characteristic of strongly resisting

revision (which belongs to beliefs very centrally situated in the system) for the mythical characteristic of total immunity from revision.

(2)   The connection between the second doctrine and the analytic-synthetic distinction runs, according to Quine, through the verification theory of meaning. He says: "If the verification theory can be accepted as an adequate account of statement synonymy, the notion of analyticity is saved after all."[9] For, in the first place, two statements might be said to be synonymous if and only if any experiences which contribute to, or detract from, the confirmation of one contribute to, or detract from, the confirmation of the other, to the same degree; and, in the second place, synonymy could be used to explain analyticity. But, Quine seems to argue, acceptance of any such account of synonymy can only rest on the mistaken belief that individual statements, taken in isolation from their fellows, can admit of confirmation or disconfirmation at all. As soon as we give up the idea of a set of experiential truth-conditions for each statement taken separately, we must give up the idea of explaining synonymy in terms of identity of such sets.

Now to show that the relations between these doctrines and the analytic-synthetic distinction are not as Quine supposes. Let us take the second doctrine first. It is easy to see that acceptance of the second doctrine would not compel one to abandon, but only to revise, the suggested explanation of synonymy. Quine does not deny that individual statements are regarded as confirmed or disconfirmed, are in fact rejected or accepted, in the light of experience. He denies only that these relations between single statements and experience hold independently of our attitudes to *other* statements. He means that experience can confirm or disconfirm an individual statement, only given certain assumptions about the truth or falsity of other statements. When we are faced with a "recalcitrant experience," he says, we always have a choice of what statements to amend. What we have to renounce is determined by what we are anxious to keep. This view, however, requires only a slight modification of the definition of statement-synonymy in terms of confirmation and disconfirmation. All we have to say now is that two statements are synonymous if and only if any experiences which, *on certain assumptions about the truth-values of other statements*, confirm or disconfirm one of the pair, also, *on the same assumptions*, confirm or disconfirm the other to the same degree. More generally, Quine wishes to substitute for what he conceives to be an oversimple picture of the confirmation-relations between particular statements and particular experiences, the idea of a looser relation which he calls "germaneness" (p. 43) [p. 167 above]. But however loosely "germaneness" is to be understood, it would apparently continue to make sense to speak of two statements as standing in the same germaneness-relation to the same particular experiences. So Quine's views are not only consistent with, but even suggest, an amended account of statement-synonymy along these lines. We are not, of course, concerned to defend such an account, or even to state it with any precision. We are only concerned to show that acceptance of Quine's doctrine of empirical confirmation does not, as he says it does, entail giving up the attempt to define statement-synonymy in terms of confirmation.

Now for the doctrine that there is no statement which is in principle immune from revision, no statement which might not be given up in the face of experience. Acceptance of this doctrine is quite consistent with adherence to the distinction between analytic and synthetic statements. Only, the adherent of *this* distinction must also insist on another; on the distinction between that kind of giving up which consists in merely admitting falsity, and that kind of giving up which involves changing or dropping a concept or set of concepts. Any form of words at one time held to express something true may, no doubt, at another time, come to be held to express something false. But it is not only philosophers who would distinguish between the case

where this happens as the result of a change of opinion solely as to matters of fact, and the case where this happens at least partly as a result of a shift in the sense of the words. Where such a shift in the sense of the words is a necessary condition of the change in truth-value, then the adherent of the distinction will say that the form of words in question changes from expressing an analytic statement to expressing a synthetic statement. We are not now concerned, or called upon, to elaborate an adequate theory of conceptual revision, any more than we were called upon, just now, to elaborate an adequate theory of synonymy. If we can make sense of the idea that the same form of words, taken in one way (or bearing one sense), may express something true, and taken in another way (or bearing another sense), may express something false, then we can make sense of the idea of conceptual revision. And if we can make sense of this idea, then we can perfectly well preserve the distinction between the analytic and the synthetic, while conceding to Quine the revisability-in-principle of everything we say. As for the idea that the same form of words, taken in different ways, may bear different senses and perhaps be used to say things with different truth-values, the onus of showing that this is somehow a mistaken or confused idea rests squarely on Quine. The point of substance (or one of them) that Quine is making, by this emphasis on revisability, is that there is no absolute necessity about the adoption or use of any conceptual scheme whatever, or, more narrowly and in terms that he would reject, that there is no analytic proposition such that we *must* have linguistic forms bearing just the sense required to express that proposition. But it is one thing to admit this, and quite another thing to say that there are no necessities within any conceptual scheme we adopt or use, or, more narrowly again, that there are no linguistic forms which do express analytic propositions.

The adherent of the analytic-synthetic distinction may go further and admit that there may be cases (particularly perhaps in the field of science) where it would be pointless to press the question whether a change in the attributed truth-value of a statement represented a conceptual revision or not, and correspondingly pointless to press the analytic-synthetic distinction. We cannot quote such cases, but this inability may well be the result of ignorance of the sciences. In any case, the existence, if they do exist, of statements about which it is pointless to press the question whether they are analytic or synthetic, does not entail the nonexistence of statements which are clearly classifiable in one or other of these ways and of statements our hesitation over which has different sources, such as the possibility of alternative interpretations of the linguistic forms in which they are expressed.

This concludes our examination of Quine's article. It will be evident that our purpose has been wholly negative. We have aimed to show merely that Quine's case against the existence of the analytic-synthetic distinction is not made out. His article has two parts. In one of them, the notions of the analyticity group are criticized on the ground that they have not been adequately explained. In the other, a positive theory of truth is outlined, purporting to be incompatible with views to which believers in the analytic-synthetic distinction either must be, or are likely to be, committed. In fact, we have contended, no single point is established which those who accept the notions of the analyticity group would feel any strain in accommodating in their own system of beliefs. This is not to deny that many of the points raised are of the first importance in connection with the problem of giving a satisfactory general account of analyticity and related concepts. We are here only criticizing the contention that these points justify the rejection, as illusory, of the analytic-synthetic distinction and the notions which belong to the same family.

Notes

1 W. V. O. Quine, *From a Logical Point of View* (Cambridge, Mass., 1953), pp. 20–46. All references are to page numbers in this book [Chapter 11 above].
2 Page 46 [p. 168].
3 Page 37 [p. 164].
4 Page 20 [p. 155].
5 Page 23 [p. 156].
6 Page 30, our italics [p. 160].
7 Page 27 [p. 159].
8 Cf. pages 37–46 [p. 164–9].
9 Page 38 [p. 164].

PART SIX

Truth and meaning

INTRODUCTION TO PART SIX

THE DISPUTE BETWEEN Davidson and Foster concerns the following question: 'Can a theory of truth for a language serve as a theory of meaning for that language?' Davidson's thesis is that it can (at least given a number of provisos) while Foster thinks that it cannot. To the uninitiated, the question is bound to seem unmotivated, perhaps incomprehensible. So it will be useful to guide the reader through the considerations that Davidson uses to lead up to his thesis.

The first sentence of Davidson's article helps understand the overall project to which Davidson hopes to contribute: 'a satisfactory theory of meaning must give an account of how the meanings of sentences depend upon the meanings of words'. Davidson immediately goes on to say why this is a desideratum: we are manifestly able to learn a language, and this seems to involve understanding, i.e. knowing the meaning of, a 'potential infinitude of sentences'. How could we do this unless we knew the meanings of a set of basic expressions and also how the meaning of complex expressions made up from those basic expressions depends on the meanings of the basic expressions?[1]

It is Davidson's project to describe this kind of knowledge, i.e. knowledge that would allow one to understand all the sentences of some natural language. A theory of meaning for a natural language is just meant to be a theory knowledge of which would put one in a position to understand the sentences of the language. Davidson's paper falls roughly into two parts: in the first part, he raises objections to a series of ways in which one might think that such a theory could be constructed. These objections introduce constraints on the form a successful theory of meaning should take. In the second, positive part, he proposes his own way in which he thinks such a theory can be constructed, and deals with difficulties for that approach.

So the project is to describe the general form of a theory knowledge of which would suffice for competence with a particular natural language. The point of this is to help explain our manifest ability to acquire such competence, which includes knowing the meaning of sentences that one has never come across before. In some sense, therefore, the project is to provide a theoretical model of the information that language users rely on in their use of language, and which explains their abilities. The explanatory point suggests that Davidson wants to give a general description of the psychological states and processes in language users that underlie their linguistic abilities. It is worth considering whether, and if so, in what sense, Davidson's thesis is meant to be a psychological proposal, and whether it would be plausible as such.[2]

---

[1] Davidson discusses this desideratum in more detail in Davidson 1965.

[2] This point is debated explicitly by Evans and Wright in Part Eight below. See also Larson and Segal 1995, ch. 2. The debate in Part Seven of this book between Lewis, Hawthorne and Laurence is also relevant.

But for the moment it is enough to observe that officially, Davidson is merely looking for the form of a theory knowledge of which would *suffice* for understanding the sentences of some language.[3]

The first part begins by discussing the proposal to assign some entity to each word or significant syntactical feature of sentences. For example to assign the man Theaetetus to the term 'Theaetetus' and the property of flying to the expression 'flies'. Davidson says that a regress results if we try to say how the meaning of the sentence 'Theaetetus flies' results from these assignments of meanings to the two constituents of the sentence. As an exercise, the reader should try to articulate the regress involved.

Davidson next considers Frege's solution to this regress, namely to assign *functions* as meanings to some expressions, and objects to others. A function is a mapping, i.e. something that for each entity from a certain domain yields another entity as a value, just like the functions familiar from mathematics, where the function $f(x) = x^2$ is the function that maps each number x onto the square of x as a value. This works quite well for complex singular terms, such as 'The father of Annette', which can be seen as involving a concatenation (= chaining up) of two expressions: 'The father of' and 'Annette'. We can view the former as standing for the function that maps people onto their fathers. If we now say that the complex refers to the value of this function when taking the referent of 'Annette' as argument, then we have said how the reference of the complex depends on the referents of its constituents. Davidson says that we can easily state for each complex singular term constructed by prefixing 'the father of' one or more times to some singular term what that complex singular term refers to, and that in order to do this, we do not need to mention Frege's entity, i.e. the function that maps people onto their fathers.[4]

Davidson regards this mini-theory as a paradigm for the kind of theory of meaning he is looking for: there is an infinite number of complex singular terms that can be constructed by prefixing 'the father of' to some singular term, and the mini-theory specifies the reference of all these terms by stating a simple recursive[5] rule that tells us how the referent of the complex term depends on the referents of the constituents.

Frege himself expanded this strategy from complex singular terms to sentences by treating sentences in effect as complex singular terms (see Part Two of this book). Now, Frege argued that if we treat sentences in this way, i.e. as singular terms referring to entities, then we shall have to treat them as referring to truth values. In other words, all true sentences will refer to the same entity (truth), and all false sentences

---

[3] This leaves open the possibility that some theory of meaning is successful in providing knowledge that would suffice for understanding the sentences of some language, but that having this knowledge is not necessary for understanding. For there might be some other, distinct theory, knowledge of which also suffices for understanding that same language. And even if only one theory suffices for understanding, normal language understanding might not in fact involve knowledge of some theory.

[4] Task for the reader: State this.

[5] The rule is recursive, in the sense that it can be re-applied to the outcomes of its applications: once the rule tells us that 'the father of Annette' refers to the father of Annette, it can be re-applied to tell us what 'the father of the father of Annette' refers to. And so on.

will refer to the same entity (falsehood). If what a sentence refers to is its meaning, then this is unacceptable, for it would mean that all true sentences mean the same, and so do all false sentences, which is obviously false.[6] Davidson launches his own version of Frege's argument (which is often called the 'slingshot'). The reader ought to work through this argument by his or her self step by step.[7]

Getting back to the main thread: Davidson regards the mini-theory of reference for complex singular terms as an attractively simple model for a theory of meaning. However, the slingshot argument proves that we cannot think of the meaning of a sentence as an entity it refers to. It seems therefore that a theory of meaning, instead of telling us for each sentence what it refers to, should tell us the meaning of each sentence. Or, in other words, a theory of meaning for a language should be 'a theory that has as consequences all sentences of the form "s means m" where "s" is replaced by a structural description of a sentence and "m" is replaced by a singular term that refers to the meaning of that sentence'. A structural description of a sentence is one that describes the sentence in terms of its relevant syntactic structure – after all, the theory is supposed to generate these consequences by specifying how the meanings of complex sentences depend on the meanings of their syntactic parts. The crucial point, however, is that this theory must specify the meanings of sentences in a non-trivial way, i.e. in a way which would yield understanding. It is easy to specify the meanings of all sentences of a language in a trivial way, for example by saying about each sentence s that s means the meaning of s. Davidson's objection to a theory of meaning that generates theorems of the form 's means m' is simply that meanings 'have no demonstrated use'.[8]

Davidson next discusses a minimally different approach that does not involve the postulation of meanings. The idea is that instead of generating theorems of the form 's means m', for each sentence, a theory of meaning might generate theorems of the form 's means that p'. The advantage would be that we would not need to construe

---

[6] Question to the reader: How could Frege then maintain the theory that sentences are singular terms referring to truth values?

[7] To help with this, here is some useful background information: Davidson uses a certain set-theoretic notation that may not be familiar. In his notation, the expression '$\hat{x}\,(x > 4)$' is a complex singular term which abbreviates 'the set of all x such that x is greater that 4'. In general, any expression of the form '$\hat{x}\,(\ldots x\text{—})$' refers to a set, and the material in the brackets articulates a necessary and sufficient condition for membership in that set: for any x, if '$\ldots x\text{—}$' is true, then x is a member of the set, otherwise it is not. Another example would be '$\hat{x}\,(x$ is a philosopher)', which would be an abbreviation for 'The set of all x such that x is a philosopher'. Socrates is a member of that set, because he fulfils the condition for membership. Johnny Cash is not, because he doesn't. Now, $\hat{x}\,(x = x)$ would be the set of all and only things x such that $x = x$—in other words, the set of all things that are identical to themselves (question: Which things are not members of this set?). Similarly, but slightly confusingly, $\hat{x}\,(x = x$ and Davidson is a philosopher) is the set of all and only the things x such that $x = x$ and Davidson is a philosopher. Since Davidson is indeed a philosopher, adding the extra condition 'and Davidson is a philosopher' doesn't really make it any harder to be a member of this set than being a member of the previous set.

With this information, it should be possible to work through the slingshot argument on p. 194. One more hint: the reader should pay attention to the 'two reasonable assumptions' Davidson is making, and consider carefully how he is making use of them in the argument.

[8] Question for the reader: What use might postulating meanings have?

such theorems as making reference to meanings. For we are not obliged to view either '*p*' or 'that *p*' as *referring* to a meaning. Davidson does not find this approach promising either, on the following ground, expressed with extreme conciseness: 'in wrestling with the logic of the apparently non-extensional "means that" we will encounter problems as hard as, or perhaps identical with, the problems our theory is out to solve'. What Davidson means is that if we want to have a theory that has theorems of the form '*s* means that *p*' as logical consequences then we need to know the logical properties of contexts created by 'means that'. He regards this as difficult because 'means that' creates non-extensional contexts, i.e. contexts in which substituting one expression for another expression with the same extension (= reference) can affect the truth value. If the truth value of some sentence depends not only on the extension/reference of the expressions it contains, then the suspicion is that it depends on their meaning in some more fine-grained sense. So it seems that working out under what conditions we can validly infer one of the theorems of the form '*s* means that *p*' from some axioms, already requires some account of meaning.[9]

At this point, Davidson makes what he calls a 'radical' move: in our theorems of the form '*s* means that *p*', it is the words 'means that' that caused trouble. In a way, however, the important information that permits interpretation seems to consist in providing for each sentence *s* a sentence *p* that in some sense gives *s*'s meaning. So Davidson proposes to look for a different 'filling' between the description of a sentence, '*s*' and the interpreting sentence '*p*'. Seemingly without motivation, Davidson proposes to concoct the following filling: prefix '*p*' with a material biconditional, 'if and only if'. '*s*' cannot be directly concatenated with 'if and only if *p*', because it is a singular term, and the left-hand side of 'if and only if', just as the right-hand side, must be occupied by a sentence, not a singular term. So Davidson turns '*s*' into a sentence by combining it with a predicate, 'is T', which he leaves schematic for the time being. Thus, Davidson's proposal is that a theory of meaning for a language should entail for each of its sentences a theorem of the form

(T)   *s* is T if and only if *p*,

where '*s*' is replaced by a structural description of the sentence, and '*p*' is replaced by a translation of the sentence into the language of the theory (or by that sentence itself, in case the language of the theory is the same as the language whose sentences we are describing).

This is the point at which the arcane-looking proposal with which we began emerges, for Davidson argues that if a theory of this kind is a theory of meaning, then its role can be played by a *definition of truth* of the kind described in the 1930s by the logician Alfred Tarski: First, any meaning theory of this sort would determine the extension of the predicate 'is T' uniquely. Secondly, as Tarski has argued, a definition of truth needs to meet exactly the same desideratum as the one just spelled out by Davidson for meaning theories: it needs to 'entail all sentences got from schema

---

[9] Foster spells this out in more detail than Davidson on p. 6 of his original article (not reproduced here).

T when "*s*" is replaced by a structural description of a sentence of *L* and "*p*" by that sentence'. Tarski (1936) has shown how such a definition can be achieved, thus Tarski's work in effect shows how a theory of meaning can be constructed that shows how the meanings of sentences depend on the meanings of their parts.

The reader could be forgiven for thinking that there is an air of alchemy about the way in which Davidson arrives at the form (T) which the theorems of a meaning theory should take. Similarly, portraying it as a 'discovery' that a Tarskian definition of truth for the sentences of a language is in effect a theory of meaning for that language, will seem a device of exposition rather than a representation of the way in which Davidson himself arrived at his thesis. However, there is nothing arbitrary about the connection between truth and meaning, as Davidson points out on p. 197: 'the definition works by giving necessary and sufficient conditions for the truth of every sentence, and to give truth conditions is a way of giving the meaning of a sentence'. To know what it is for any sentence of a language to be true, he says, is to understand the language. Thus it is no coincidence that a theory defining truth should also serve as a theory of meaning.

Davidson also provides a clear view of how a theory of meaning of this kind can be empirically tested, namely in the way any theory can be tested, by testing the predictions it makes. In this case, the theory will make predictions of the form '*s* is true if and only if *p*', for example a theory of meaning for Spanish might predict that the sentence 'la nieve es blanca' is true if and only if snow is white. Anyone competent with Spanish can confirm that this is a correct prediction.

What if we aren't competent with the language whose theory of meaning we are testing? Davidson believes that there are empirical data that we could use to confirm or disconfirm a meaning theory even for a completely alien natural language. A so-called 'radical interpreter', i.e. someone who is trying to find a correct meaning theory for a completely unknown natural language, can at least observe the behaviour of the users of the language, which includes, according to Davidson, observing which sentences competent speakers 'accede' to. If the radical interpreter makes certain assumptions, such as the assumption that the language users accede to sentences only if they believe them to be true, and that most of what they believe is true, then she has a basis for testing a candidate meaning theory for the language, and for comparing it to rival candidates. In a simple case, one candidate meaning theory might predict that a certain sentence is true just if *p*, and another candidate meaning theory might predict that the same sentence is true just if *q*. Now suppose that users of the language accede to the sentence, and the radical interpreter knows that *p* is true, while *q* is false. Then this would constitute some evidence (*ceteris paribus*), that the first theory is better than the second, given the assumptions we made.[10]

The remainder of the paper is taken up with discussing a number of difficulties for the approach, some of which we ought to mention. One point is that Tarski explicitly writes about defining truth for *formal* languages, so there is an issue as to whether *natural* languages can be made amenable to the same treatment. Davidson himself

[10] Davidson 1973 and 1990, for example, contain a more detailed discussion of radical interpretation.

has contributed extensively to the work of making various natural language constructions amenable to Tarskian treatment, for example in his work on events and on
intensional contexts (the last paragraph of the essay contains a long list of difficult
natural language constructions). A second problem may arise with moral or evaluative sentences. Many people (evaluative non-cognitivists) will deny that moral or
evaluative sentences are capable of being true or false. But Davidson responds that
this should not prevent us from treating these sentences in the same way as others,
exhibiting how their meaning depends on their constituents, e.g. by saying that
'Bardot is good' is true if and only if Bardot is good.

A serious problem ('a large fly in the ointment') is posed by the fact that many
natural language sentences contain what Davidson calls 'demonstratives', i.e.
context-sensitive expressions, such as the sentence 'I am tired'. The truth of sentences
of this sort will depend on the context in which they are uttered, in this case on who
utters them and when. In response, Davidson proposes to alter the form of the theorems
in such a way as to reflect this dependence on context. Thus, the theorem for 'I am
tired' will not be ' "I am tired" is true if and only if I am tired', but rather '[for all p,
t:] "I am tired" is true as (potentially) spoken by p at t if and only if p is tired at t'.[11]

Foster, in his article, is primarily concerned with a central problem one aspect of
which Davidson himself mentions. There is no getting away from the fact that a mere
truth theory, or definition of truth, for a language L will merely generate theorems
of form (T). However, what kind of information do theorems of this form really give
us? They merely state certain conditions that are materially necessary and sufficient
for a sentence's truth. But all it takes for such material biconditionals to be
true is that both sides of the biconditional have the same truth value. Thus, just as it is
true that

(S1) 'La nieve es blanca' is true in Spanish if
    and only if snow is white

it is also true that

(S2) 'La nieve es blanca' is true in Spanish if
    and only if grass is green.

Thus, merely knowing (S1) is not sufficient for knowing the meaning of the sentence
mentioned in it. (S1) does not tell us what it is for the sentence 'La nieve es blanca' to
be true (at least not in any sense in which knowing what it is to be true amounts to
understanding). It does not tell us the 'truth-conditions' of that sentence in any sense
in which knowledge of truth-conditions amounts to understanding. For if it did, then
(S2) would do so also, and (S2) manifestly doesn't.

Foster answers this worry by reminding us that Davidson's proposal is *not* that
knowledge of any theorem of form (T) gives us knowledge of the meaning of the

---

[11] Davidson does not elaborate how exactly a theory can deliver these theorems. See Weinstein
1974 or Sainsbury 2008 for a more detailed discussion.

sentence mentioned in it, but rather that knowledge of the entire theory of truth is sufficient for understanding the entire language. Of course the entire truth theory will contain more information about each sentence than just the theorem of form (T). In particular, it will contain a clause for each constituent of a sentence as well as many theorems concerning sentences containing just some of its components. 'The meaning of each sentence is given not by that unique theorem which refers to it, but by that infinite set of theorems which refer to all sentences that contain any *S*-component' (p. 208).

However, as Foster argues, this does not yet remove the problem. For a Tarskian truth theory will not distinguish between predicates that have the same extension but differ in meaning. Foster's example is the two-place predicate '. . . is a part of . . .'. If a truth-theory for English contains the right clauses concerning which ordered pairs of objects satisfy this predicate, then these clauses will remain true if we replace in them any reference to the predicate '. . . is a part of . . .' with a reference to the predicate 'the earth moves and . . . is a part of . . .' (and the same for 'the earth is still or . . . is a part of . . .'). Thus knowledge of a truth-theory for a language does not suffice for understanding the language.

In section III of his paper, Foster considers a revised version of Davidson's thesis, namely the thesis that knowledge of a truth theory for a language *plus* knowledge that it is a truth theory will jointly suffice for understanding the language. Thus, if what a truth-theory for a language *L* states is that *p*, then while

(K1) knowledge that *p*

is not sufficient for understanding *L*,

(K2) knowledge that some true truth-theory
 states that *p*

will be sufficient.

Foster argues that this revision does not serve Davidson's purposes, because 'it brings back the kind of intensionality which conflicts with our philosophical aims: it takes for granted the concept of stating and the non-extensional syntax that goes with it' (p. 214). And indeed, it was the non-extensionality of 'means that' which Davidson cited against a meaning theory that delivers theorems of the form '*s* means that *p*'. At the end of the section, Foster considers whether Davidson could rescue the revised proposal by applying his so-called 'paratactic' analysis of intensional contexts. However, Foster's verdict is that this would again presuppose an account of meaning, and he concludes that 'Davidson's grand design is in ruins' (p. 216). We shall leave it to the interested reader to find out for herself what Davidson's reply was to Foster's final verdict (in Davidson 1976).

Questions and tasks

1   With reference to pp. 193–4: Consider the set of complex singular terms that can be generated by prefixing the expression 'the father of' to any singular term referring to a person. Why are there infinitely many such complex singular terms, even if we only allow two base expressions: 'the father of' and 'Annette'? State a theory that determines the referent for each such term, and do so without mentioning any functions.

2   Spell out Davidson's proof that if sentences refer to something, then all true sentences refer to the same thing. Can this argument be challenged?

3   Why do the theorems of a Davidsonian truth theory contain 'structural descriptions' of sentences? What are structural descriptions?

4   Why does a theory that entails all instances of (T) determine the extension of the predicate 'is T'?

5   Describe how one would compare two competing truth-theories for an unknown language, i.e. how one would proceed as a radical interpreter.

References and further reading

Davidson, Donald 1965: 'Theories of Meaning and Learnable Languages', in Y. Bar-Hillel (ed.), *Logic, Methodology and Philosophy of Science*, Amsterdam: North-Holland Publishing Co., pp. 383–94; reprinted in D. Davidson (1984), pp. 3–15.

Davidson, Donald 1968: 'On Saying That', *Synthese* 19, pp. 130–46; reprinted in D. Davidson (1984), pp. 93–108.

Davidson, Donald 1973: 'Radical Interpretation', *Dialectica* 27, pp. 313–23; reprinted in D. Davidson (1984), pp. 125–39.

Davidson, Donald 1976: 'Reply to Foster', in G Evans and J. McDowell (eds), *Truth and Meaning: Essays in Semantics*, Oxford: Oxford University Press; reprinted in D. Davidson (1984), pp. 171–9.

Davidson, Donald 1984: *Inquiries into Truth and Interpretation*, Oxford: Clarendon Press.

Davidson, Donald 1990: 'The Structure and Content of Truth', *Journal of Philosophy* 87, pp. 279–328.

Gross, Steven 2005: 'The Biconditional Doctrine: Contra Kölbel on a "Dogma" of Davidsonian Semantics', *Erkenntnis* 62, pp. 189–210.

Higginbotham, James 1992: 'Truth and Understanding', *Philosophical Studies* 65, pp. 3–16.

Kölbel, Max 2001: 'Two Dogmas of Davidsonian Semantics', *Journal of Philosophy* 98, 613–35.

Larson, Richard, and Gabriel Segal 1995: *Knowledge of Meaning*, Cambridge, MA: MIT Press.

Lepore, Ernest, and Kirk Ludwig: *Donald Davidson's Truth-theoretic Semantics*, Oxford: Oxford University Press 2007.

Ludwig, Kirk 2002: 'What Is the Role of a Truth Theory in a Meaning Theory?', in

J. K. Campbell, M. O'Rourke, and David Shier (eds), *Meaning and Truth*, New York: Seven Bridges, pp. 142–63.

McDowell, John 1976: §1 of 'Truth Conditions, Bivalence and Verificationism', in G. Evans and J. McDowell (ed.), *Truth and Meaning*, Oxford: Oxford University Press, pp. 42–66.

Miller, Alex 1998: Ch. 8 of *Philosophy of Language*, London: Routledge.

Platts, Mark 1997: *Ways of Meaning*, 2nd edn, Cambridge, MA: MIT Press.

Sainsbury, Mark 1979: 'Understanding and Theories of Meaning', *Proceedings of the Aristotelian Society* 80, pp. 127–44.

Sainsbury, Mark 2008: 'Fly Swatting: Davidsonian Truth Theories and Context', in M. C. Amoretti and N. Vassallo (eds), *Knowledge, Language, and Interpretation: On the Philosophy of Donald Davidson*. Frankfurt: Ontos, pp. 33–48.

Segal, Gabriel 1999: 'How a Truth Theory Can Do Duty as a Theory of Meaning', in Ursula M. Zeglen (ed.) *Donald Davidson*, London: Routledge, pp. 45–53.

Soames, Scott 1992: 'Truth, Meaning and Understanding', *Philosophical Studies* 65, no. 1–2, pp. 17–35.

Soames, Scott 2008: 'Truth and Meaning: In Perspective', *Midwest Studies in Philosophy* 32, pp. 1–19.

Taylor, Kenneth 1998: *Truth and Meaning: An Introduction to the Philosophy of Language*, Oxford: Blackwell.

Weinstein, Scott 1974: 'Truth and Demonstratives', *Noûs* 8, pp. 179–84.

Chapter 13

Donald Davidson

TRUTH AND MEANING

It is conceded by most philosophers of language, and recently by some linguists, that a satisfactory theory of meaning must give an account of how the meanings of sentences depend upon the meanings of words. Unless such an account could be supplied for a particular language, it is argued, there would be no explaining the fact that we can learn the language: no explaining the fact that, on mastering a finite vocabulary and a finitely stated set of rules, we are prepared to produce and to understand any of a potential infinitude of sentences. I do not dispute these vague claims, in which I sense more than a kernel of truth.[1] Instead I want to ask what it is for a theory to give an account of the kind adumbrated.

One proposal is to begin by assigning some entity as meaning to each word (or other significant syntactical feature) of the sentence; thus we might assign Theaetetus to 'Theaetetus' and the property of flying to 'flies' in the sentence 'Theaetetus flies'. The problem then arises how the meaning of the sentence is generated from these meanings. Viewing concatenation as a significant piece of syntax, we may assign to it the relation of participating in or instantiating; however, it is obvious that we have here the start of an infinite regress. Frege sought to avoid the regress by saying that the entities corresponding to predicates (for example) are 'unsaturated' or 'incomplete' in contrast to the entities that correspond to names, but this doctrine seems to label a difficulty rather than solve it.

The point will emerge if we think for a moment of complex singular terms, to which Frege's theory applies along with sentences. Consider the expression 'the father of Annette'; how does the meaning of the whole depend on the meaning of the parts? The answer would seem to be that the meaning of 'the father of' is such that when this expression is prefixed to a singular term the result refers to the father of the person to whom the singular term refers. What part is played, in this account, by the unsaturated or incomplete entity for which 'the father of' stands? All we can think to say is that this entity 'yields' or 'gives' the father of x as value when the argument is x, or perhaps that this entity maps people on to their fathers. It may not be clear whether the entity for which 'the father of' is said to stand performs any genuine explanatory function as long as we stick to individual expressions; so think instead of the infinite class of expressions formed by writing 'the father of' zero or more times in front of 'Annette'. It is easy to supply a theory that tells, for an arbitrary one of these singular terms, what it refers to: if the term is 'Annette' it refers to Annette, while if the term is complex, consisting of 'the father of' prefixed to a singular term t, then it refers to the father of the person to whom t refers. It is obvious that no entity corresponding to 'the father of' is, or needs to be, mentioned in stating this theory.

It would be inappropriate to complain that this little theory *uses* the words 'the father of' in giving the reference of expressions containing those words. For the task was to give the meaning of all expressions in a certain infinite set on the basis of the meaning of the parts; it was not in the bargain also to give the meanings of the atomic parts. On the other hand, it is now evident that a satisfactory theory of the meanings of complex expressions may not require entities as meanings of all the parts. It behoves us then to rephrase our demand on a satisfactory theory of meaning so as not to suggest that individual words must have meanings at all, in any sense that transcends the fact that they have a systematic effect on the meanings of the sentences in which they occur. Actually, for the case at hand we can do better still in stating the criterion of success: what we wanted, and what we got, is a theory that entails every sentence of the form 't refers to *x*' where 't' is replaced by a structural description[2] of a singular term, and '*x*' is replaced by that term itself. Further, our theory accomplishes this without appeal to any semantical concepts beyond the basic 'refers to'. Finally, the theory clearly suggests an effective procedure for determining, for any singular term in its universe, what that term refers to.

A theory with such evident merits deserves wider application. The device proposed by Frege to this end has a brilliant simplicity: count predicates as a special case of functional expressions, and sentences as a special case of complex singular terms. Now, however, a difficulty looms if we want to continue in our present (implicit) course of identifying the meaning of a singular term with its reference. The difficulty follows upon making two reasonable assumptions: that logically equivalent singular terms have the same reference, and that a singular term does not change its reference if a contained singular term is replaced by another with the same reference. But now suppose that 'R' and 'S' abbreviate any

two sentences alike in truth value. Then the following four sentences have the same reference:

(1) R
(2) $\hat{x} \ (x = x, R) = \hat{x} \ (x = x)$
(3) $\hat{x} \ (x = x, S) = \hat{x} \ (x = x)$
(4) S

For (1) and (2) are logically equivalent, as are (3) and (4), while (3) differs from (2) only in containing the singular term '$\hat{x} \ (x = x, S)$' where (2) contains '$\hat{x} \ (x = x, R)$' and these refer to the same thing if S and R are alike in truth value. Hence any two sentences have the same reference if they have the same truth value.[3] And if the meaning of a sentence is what it refers to, all sentences alike in truth value must be synonymous—an intolerable result.

Apparently we must abandon the present approach as leading to a theory of meaning. This is the natural point at which to turn for help to the distinction between meaning and reference. The trouble, we are told, is that questions of reference are, in general, settled by extralinguistic facts, questions of meaning not, and the facts can conflate the references of expressions that are not synonymous. If we want a theory that gives the meaning (as distinct from reference) of each sentence, we must start with the meaning (as distinct from reference) of the parts.

Up to here we have been following in Frege's footsteps; thanks to him, the path is well known and even well worn. But now, I would like to suggest, we have reached an impasse: the switch from reference to meaning leads to no useful account of how the meanings of sentences depend upon the meanings of the words (or other structural features) that compose them. Ask, for example, for the meaning of 'Theaetetus flies'. A Fregean answer might go something like this: given the meaning of 'Theaetetus' as argument, the meaning of 'flies' yields the meaning of 'Theaetetus flies' as value. The vacuity of this answer is obvious. We wanted to know what the meaning of 'Theaetetus flies' is; it is no progress to be told that it is the meaning of 'Theaetetus flies'. This much we knew before any theory was in sight. In the bogus account just given, talk of the structure of the sentence and of the meanings of words was idle, for it played no role in producing the given description of the meaning of the sentence.

The contrast here between a real and pretended account will be plainer still if we ask for a theory, analogous to the miniature theory of reference of singular terms just sketched, but different in dealing with meanings in place of references. What analogy demands is a theory that has as consequences all sentences of the form 's means m' where 's' is replaced by a structural description of a sentence and 'm' is replaced by a singular term that refers to the meaning of that sentence; a theory, moreover, that provides an effective method for arriving at the meaning of an arbitrary sentence structurally described. Clearly some more articulate way of referring to meanings than any we have seen is essential if these criteria are to be met.[4] Meanings as entities, or the related concept of synonymy, allow us to formulate the following rule relating sentences and their parts: sentences are synonymous whose corresponding parts are synonymous ('corresponding' here needs spelling out of course). And meanings as entities may, in theories such as Frege's, do duty, on occasion, as references, thus losing their status as entities distinct from references. Paradoxically, the one thing meanings do not seem to do is oil the wheels of a theory of meaning—at least as long as we require of such a theory that it non-trivially give the meaning of every sentence in the language. My objection to meanings in the theory of meaning is not that they are abstract or that their identity conditions are obscure, but that they have no demonstrated use.

This is the place to scotch another hopeful thought. Suppose we have a satisfactory theory of syntax for our language, consisting of an effective method of telling, for an arbitrary expression, whether or not it is independently meaningful (i.e. a sentence), and assume as usual that this involves viewing each sentence as composed, in allowable ways, out of elements drawn from a fixed finite stock of atomic syntactical elements (roughly, words). The hopeful thought is that syntax, so conceived, will yield semantics when a dictionary giving the meaning of each syntactic atom is added. Hopes will be dashed, however, if semantics is to comprise a theory of meaning in our sense, for knowledge of the structural characteristics that make for meaningfulness in a sentence, plus knowledge of the meanings of the ultimate parts, does not add up to knowledge of what a sentence means. The point is easily illustrated by belief sentences. Their syntax is relatively unproblematic. Yet, adding a dictionary does not touch the standard semantic problem, which is that we cannot account for even as much as the truth conditions of such sentences on the basis of what we know of the meanings of the words in them. The situation is not radically altered by refining the dictionary to indicate which meaning or meanings an ambiguous expression bears in each of its possible contexts; the problem of belief sentences persists after ambiguities are resolved.

The fact that recursive syntax with dictionary added is not necessarily recursive semantics has been obscured in some recent writing on linguistics by the intrusion of semantic criteria into the discussion of purportedly syntactic theories. The matter would boil down to a harmless difference over terminology if the semantic criteria were clear; but they are not. While there is agreement that it is the central task of semantics to give the semantic interpretation (the meaning) of every sentence in the language, nowhere in the linguistic literature will one find, so far as I know, a straightforward account of how a theory performs this task, or how to tell when it has been accomplished. The contrast with syntax is striking. The main job of a modest syntax is to characterize *meaningfulness* (or sentencehood). We may have as much confidence in the correctness of such a characterization as we have in the representativeness of our sample and our ability to say when particular expressions are meaningful (sentences). What clear and analogous task and test exist for semantics?[5]

We decided a while back not to assume that parts of sentences have meanings except in the ontologically neutral sense of making a systematic contribution to the meaning of the sentences in which they occur. Since postulating meanings has netted nothing, let us return to that insight. One direction in which it points is a certain holistic view of meaning. If sentences depend for their meaning on their structure, and we understand the meaning of each item in the structure only as an abstraction from the totality of sentences in which it features, then we can give the meaning of any sentence (or word) only by giving the meaning of every sentence (and word) in the language. Frege said that only in the context of a sentence does a word have meaning; in the same vein he might have added that only in the context of the language does a sentence (and therefore a word) have meaning.

This degree of holism was already implicit in the suggestion that an adequate theory of meaning must entail *all* sentences of the form 's means m'. But now, having found no more help in meanings of sentences than in meanings of words, let us ask whether we can get rid of the troublesome singular terms supposed to replace 'm' and to refer to meanings. In a way, nothing could be easier: just write 's means that p', and imagine 'p' replaced by a sentence. Sentences, as we have seen, cannot name meanings, and sentences with 'that' prefixed are not names at all, unless we decide so. It looks as though we are in trouble on another count, however, for it is reasonable to expect that in wrestling with the logic of the apparently non-extensional 'means that' we will encounter problems as hard as, or perhaps identical with, the problems our theory is out to solve.

The only way I know to deal with this difficulty is simple, and radical. Anxiety that we are enmeshed in the intensional springs from using the words 'means that' as filling between description of sentence and sentence, but it may be that the success of our venture depends not on the filling but on what it fills. The theory will have done its work if it provides, for every sentence s in the language under study, a matching sentence (to replace 'p') that, in some way yet to be made clear, 'gives the meaning' of s. One obvious candidate for matching sentence is just s itself, if the object language is contained in the metalanguage; otherwise a translation of s in the metalanguage. As a final bold step, let us try treating the position occupied by 'p' extensionally: to implement this, sweep away the obscure 'means that', provide the sentence that replaces 'p' with a proper sentential connective, and supply the description that replaces 's' with its own predicate. The plausible result is

(T)   s is T if and only if p.

What we require of a theory of meaning for a language L is that without appeal to any (further) semantical notions it place enough restrictions on the predicate 'is T' to entail all sentences got from schema T when 's' is replaced by a structural description of a sentence of L and 'p' by that sentence.

Any two predicates satisfying this condition have the same extension,[6] so if the metalanguage is rich enough, nothing stands in the way of putting what I am calling a theory of meaning into the form of an explicit definition of a predicate 'is T'. But whether explicitly defined or recursively characterized, it is clear that the sentences to which the predicate 'is T' applies will be just the true sentences of L, for the condition we have placed on satisfactory theories of meaning is in essence Tarski's Convention T that tests the adequacy of a formal semantical definition of truth.[7]

The path to this point has been tortuous, but the conclusion may be stated simply: a theory of meaning for a language L shows 'how the meanings of sentences depend upon the meanings of words' if it contains a (recursive) definition of truth-in-L. And, so far at least, we have no other idea how to turn the trick. It is worth emphasizing that the concept of truth played no ostensible role in stating our original problem. That problem, upon refinement, led to the view that an adequate theory of meaning must characterize a predicate meeting certain conditions. It was in the nature of a discovery that such a predicate would apply exactly to the true sentences. I hope that what I am saying may be described in part as defending the philosophical importance of Tarski's semantical concept of truth. But my defence is only distantly related, if at all, to the question whether the concept Tarski has shown how to define is the (or a) philosophically interesting conception of truth, or the question whether Tarski has cast any light on the ordinary use of such words as 'true' and 'truth'. It is a misfortune that dust from futile and confused battles over these questions has prevented those with a theoretical interest in language—philosophers, logicians, psychologists, and linguists alike—from seeing in the semantical concept of truth (under whatever name) the sophisticated and powerful foundation of a competent theory of meaning.

There is no need to suppress, of course, the obvious connection between a definition of truth of the kind Tarski has shown how to construct, and the concept of meaning. It is this: the definition works by giving necessary and sufficient conditions for the truth of every sentence, and to give truth conditions is a way of giving the meaning of a sentence. To know the semantic concept of truth for a language is to know what it is for a sentence—any sentence—to be true, and this amounts, in one good sense we can give to the phrase, to understanding the language. This at any rate is my excuse for a feature of the present discussion that is apt to shock old hands; my freewheeling use of the word 'meaning', for what I call a theory of meaning has after all turned out to make no use of meanings, whether of sentences or of words. Indeed, since a Tarski-type truth definition supplies all we have asked so far of a theory of meaning, it is clear that such a theory falls comfortably within what Quine terms the 'theory of reference' as distinguished from what he terms the 'theory of meaning'. So much to the good for what I call a theory of meaning, and so much, perhaps, against my so calling it.[8]

A theory of meaning (in my mildly perverse sense) is an empirical theory, and its ambition is to account for the workings of a natural language. Like any theory, it may be tested by comparing some of its consequences with the facts. In the present case this is easy, for the theory has been characterized as issuing in an infinite flood of sentences each giving the truth conditions of a sentence; we only need to ask, in sample cases, whether what the theory avers to be the truth conditions for a sentence really are. A typical test case might involve deciding whether the sentence 'Snow is white' is true if and only if snow is white. Not all cases will be so simple (for reasons to be sketched), but it is evident that this sort of test does not invite counting noses. A sharp conception of what constitutes a theory in this domain furnishes an exciting context for raising deep questions about when a theory of language is correct and how it is to be tried. But the difficulties are theoretical, not practical. In application, the trouble is to get a theory that comes close to working; anyone can tell whether it is right.[9] One can see why this is so. The theory reveals nothing new about the conditions under which an individual sentence is true; it does not make those conditions any clearer than the sentence itself does. The work of the theory is in relating the known truth conditions of each sentence to those aspects ('words') of the sentence that recur in other sentences and can be assigned identical roles in other sentences. Empirical power in such a theory depends on success in recovering the structure of a very complicated ability—the ability to speak and understand a language. We can tell easily enough when particular pronouncements of the theory comport with our understanding of the language; this is consistent with a feeble insight into the design of the machinery of our linguistic accomplishments.

The remarks of the last paragraph apply directly only to the special case where it is assumed that the language for which truth is being characterized is part of the language used and understood by the characterizer. Under these circumstances, the framer of a theory will as a matter of course avail himself when he can of the built-in convenience of a metalanguage with a sentence guaranteed equivalent to each sentence in the object language. Still, this fact ought not to con us into thinking a theory any more correct that entails ' "Snow is white" is true if and only if snow is white' than one that entails instead:

(S) 'Snow is white' is true if and only if grass is green,

provided, of course, we are as sure of the truth of (S) as we are of that of its more celebrated predecessor. Yet (S) may not encourage the same confidence that a theory that entails it deserves to be called a theory of meaning.

The threatened failure of nerve may be counteracted as follows. The grotesqueness of (S) is in itself nothing against a theory of which it is a consequence, provided the theory gives the correct results for every sentence (on the basis of its structure, there being no other way). It is not easy to see how (S) could be party to such an enterprise, but if it were—if, that is, (S) followed from a characterization of the predicate 'is true' that led to the invariable pairing of truths with truths and falsehoods with falsehoods—then there would not, I think, be anything essential to the idea of meaning that remained to be captured.[10]

What appears to the right of the biconditional in sentences of the form 's is true if and only if p' when such sentences are consequences of a theory of truth plays its role in determining the meaning of s not by pretending synonymy but by adding one more brush-stroke to the picture which, taken as a whole, tells what there is to know of the meaning of s; this stroke is added by virtue of the fact that the sentence that replaces 'p' is true if and only if s is.

It may help to reflect that (S) is acceptable, if it is, because we are independently sure of the truth of 'Snow is white' and 'Grass is green'; but in cases where we are unsure of the truth of a sentence, we can have confidence in a characterization of the truth predicate only if it pairs that sentence with one we have good reason to believe equivalent. It would be ill advised for someone who had any doubts about the colour of snow or grass to accept a theory that yielded (S), even if his doubts were of equal degree, unless he thought the colour of the one was tied to the colour of the other.[11] Omniscience can obviously afford more bizzare theories of meaning than ignorance; but then, omniscience has less need of communication.

It must be possible, of course, for the speaker of one language to construct a theory of meaning for the speaker of another, though in this case the empirical test of the correctness of the theory will no longer be trivial. As before, the aim of theory will be an infinite correlation of sentences alike in truth. But this time the theory-builder must not be assumed to have direct insight into likely equivalences between his own tongue and the alien. What he must do is find out, however he can, what sentences the alien holds true in his own tongue (or better, to what degree he holds them true). The linguist then will attempt to construct a characterization of truth-for-the-alien which yields, so far as possible, a mapping of sentences held true (or false) by the alien on to sentences held true (or false) by the linguist. Supposing no perfect fit is found, the residue of sentences held true translated by sentences held false (and vice versa) is the margin for error (foreign or domestic). Charity in interpreting the words and thoughts of others is unavoidable in another direction as well: just as we must maximize agreement, or risk not making sense of what the alien is talking about, so we must maximize the self-consistency we attribute to him, on pain of not understanding him. No single principle of optimum charity emerges; the constraints therefore determine no single theory. In a theory of radical translation (as Quine calls it) there is no completely disentangling questions of what the alien means from questions of what he believes. We do not know what someone means unless we know what he believes; we do not know what someone believes unless we know what he means. In radical interpretation we are able to break into this circle, if only incompletely, because we can sometimes tell that a person accedes to a sentence we do not understand.[12]

In the past few pages I have been asking how a theory of meaning that takes the form of a truth definition can be empirically tested, and have blithely ignored the prior question whether there is any serious chance such a theory can be given for a natural language. What are the prospects for a formal semantical theory of a natural language? Very poor, according to Tarski; and I believe most logicians, philosophers of language, and linguists agree.[13] Let me do what I can to dispel the pessimism. What I can in a general and programmatic way, of course, for here the proof of the pudding will certainly be in the proof of the right theorems.

Tarski concludes the first section of his classic essay on the concept of truth in formalized languages with the following remarks, which he italicizes:

> . . . *The very possibility of a consistent use of the expression 'true sentence' which is in harmony with the laws of logic and the spirit of everyday language seems to be very questionable, and consequently the same doubt attaches to the possibility of constructing a correct definition of this expression.* (165)

Late in the same essay, he returns to the subject:

> . . . the concept of truth (as well as other semantical concepts) when applied to colloquial language in conjunction with the normal laws of logic leads inevitably to confusions and contradictions. Whoever wishes, in spite of all difficulties, to pursue the semantics of colloquial language with the help of exact methods will be driven first to undertake the thankless task of a reform of this language. He will find it necessary to define its structure, to overcome the ambiguity of the terms which occur in it, and finally to split the language into a series of languages of greater and greater extent, each of which stands in the same relation to the next in which a formalized language stands to its metalanguage. It may, however be doubted whether the language of everyday life, after being 'rationalized' in this way, would still preserve its naturalness and whether it would not rather take on the characteristic features of the formalized languages. (267)

Two themes emerge: that the universal character of natural languages leads to contradiction (the semantic paradoxes), and that natural languages are too confused and amorphous to permit the direct application of formal methods. The first point deserves a serious answer, and I wish I had one. As it is, I will say only why I think we are justified in carrying on without having disinfected this particular source of conceptual anxiety. The semantic paradoxes arise when the range of the quantifiers in the object language is too generous in certain ways. But it is not really clear how unfair to Urdu or to Wendish it would be to view the range of their quantifiers as insufficient to yield an explicit definition of 'true-in-Urdu' or 'true-in-Wendish'. Or, to put the matter in another, if not more serious way, there may in the nature of the case always be something we grasp in understanding the language of another (the concept of truth) that we cannot communicate to him. In any case, most of the problems of general philosophical interest arise within a fragment of the relevant natural language that may be conceived as containing very little set theory. Of course these comments do not meet the claim that natural languages are universal. But it seems to me that this claim, now that we know such universality leads to paradox, is suspect.

Tarski's second point is that we would have to reform a natural language out of all recognition before we could apply formal semantical methods. If this is true, it is fatal to my project, for the task of a theory of meaning as I conceive it is not to change, improve, or reform a language, but to describe and understand it. Let us look at the positive side. Tarski has shown the way to giving a theory for interpreted formal languages of various kinds; pick one as much like English as possible. Since this new language has been explained in English and contains much English we not only may, but I think must, view it as part of English for those who understand it. For this fragment of English we have, *ex hypothesi*, a theory of the required sort. Not only that, but in interpreting this adjunct of English in old English we necessarily gave hints connecting old and new. Wherever there are sentences of old English with the same truth conditions as sentences in the adjunct we may extend the theory to cover them. Much of what is called for is to mechanize as far as possible what we now do by art when we put ordinary English into one or another canonical notation. The point is not that canonical notation is better than the rough original idiom, but rather that if we know what idiom the canonical notation is canonical for, we have as good a theory for the idiom as for its kept companion.

Philosophers have long been at the hard work of applying theory to ordinary language by the device of matching sentences in the vernacular with sentences for which they have a theory. Frege's massive contribution was to show how 'all', 'some', 'every', 'each', 'none', and associated pronouns, in some of their uses, could be tamed; for the first time, it was possible to dream

of a formal semantics for a significant part of a natural language. This dream came true in a sharp way with the work of Tarski. It would be a shame to miss the fact that as a result of these two magnificent achievements, Frege's and Tarski's, we have gained a deep insight into the structure of our mother tongues. Philosophers of a logical bent have tended to start where the theory was and work out towards the complications of natural language. Contemporary linguists, with an aim that cannot easily be seen to be different, start with the ordinary and work toward a general theory. If either party is successful, there must be a meeting. Recent work by Chomsky and others is doing much to bring the complexities of natural languages within the scope of serious theory. To give an example: suppose success in giving the truth conditions for some significant range of sentences in the active voice. Then with a formal procedure for transforming each such sentence into a corresponding sentence in the passive voice, the theory of truth could be extended in an obvious way to this new set of sentences.[14]

One problem touched on in passing by Tarski does not, at least in all its manifestations, have to be solved to get ahead with theory: the existence in natural languages of 'ambiguous terms'. As long as ambiguity does not affect grammatical form, and can be translated, ambiguity for ambiguity, into the metalanguage, a truth definition will not tell us any lies. The chief trouble, for systematic semantics, with the phrase 'believes that' in English lies not in its vagueness, ambiguity, or unsuitability for incorporation in a serious science: let our metalanguage be English, and all these problems will be carried without loss or gain into the metalanguage. But the central problem of the logical grammar of 'believes that' will remain to haunt us.

The example is suited to illustrating another, and related, point, for the discussion of belief sentences has been plagued by failure to observe a fundamental distinction between tasks: uncovering the logical grammar or form of sentences (which is in the province of a theory of meaning as I construe it), and the analysis of individual words or expressions (which are treated as primitive by the theory). Thus Carnap, in the first edition of *Meaning and Necessity*, suggested we render 'John believes that the earth is round' as 'John responds affirmatively to "the earth is round" as an English sentence'. He gave this up when Mates pointed out that John might respond affirmatively to one sentence and not to another no matter how close in meaning.[15] But there is a confusion here from the start. The semantic structure of a belief sentence, according to this idea of Carnap's, is given by a three-place predicate with places reserved for expressions referring to a person, a sentence, and a language. It is a different sort of problem entirely to attempt an analysis of this predicate, perhaps along behaviouristic lines. Not least among the merits of Tarski's conception of a theory of truth is that the purity of method it demands of us follows from the formulation of the problem itself, not from the self-imposed restraint of some adventitious philosophical puritanism.

I think it is hard to exaggerate the advantages to philosophy of language of bearing in mind this distinction between questions of logical form or grammar, and the analysis of individual concepts. Another example may help advertise the point.

If we suppose questions of logical grammar settled, sentences like 'Bardot is good' raise no special problems for a truth definition. The deep differences between descriptive and evaluative (emotive, expressive, etc.) terms do not show here. Even if we hold there is some important sense in which moral or evaluative sentences do not have a truth value (for example, because they cannot be verified), we ought not to boggle at ' "Bardot is good" is true if and only if Bardot is good'; in a theory of truth, this consequence should follow with the rest, keeping track, as must be done, of the semantic location of such sentences in the language as a whole—of their

relation to generalizations, their role in such compound sentences as 'Bardot is good and Bardot is foolish', and so on. What is special to evaluative words is simply not touched: the mystery is transferred from the word 'good' in the object language to its translation in the metalanguage.

But 'good' as it features in 'Bardot is a good actress' is another matter. The problem is not that the translation of this sentence is not in the metalanguage—let us suppose it is. The problem is to frame a truth definition such that ' "Bardot is a good actress" is true if and only if Bardot is a good actress'—and all other sentences like it— are consequences. Obviously 'good actress' does not mean 'good and an actress'. We might think of taking 'is a good actress' as an unanalysed predicate. This would obliterate all connection between 'is a good actress' and 'is a good mother', and it would give us no excuse to think of 'good', in these uses, as a word or semantic element. But worse, it would bar us from framing a truth definition at all, for there is no end to the predicates we would have to treat as logically simple (and hence accommodate in separate clauses in the definition of satisfaction): 'is a good companion to dogs', 'is a good 28-years old conversationalist', and so forth. The problem is not peculiar to the case: it is the problem of attributive adjectives generally.

It is consistent with the attitude taken here to deem it usually a strategic error to undertake philosophical analysis of words or expressions which is not preceded by or at any rate accompanied by the attempt to get the logical grammar straight. For how can we have any confidence in our analyses of words like 'right', 'ought', 'can', and 'obliged', or the phrases we use to talk of actions, events, and causes, when we do not know what (logical, semantical) parts of speech we have to deal with? I would say much the same about studies of the 'logic' of these and other words, and the sentences containing them. Whether the effort and ingenuity that have gone into the study of deontic logics, modal logics, imperative and erotetic logics have been largely futile or not cannot be known until we have acceptable semantic analyses of the sentences such systems purport to treat. Philosophers and logicians sometimes talk or work as if they were free to choose between, say, the truth-functional conditional and others, or free to introduce non-truth-functional sentential operators like 'Let it be the case that' or 'It ought to be the case that'. But in fact the decision is crucial. When we depart from idioms we can accommodate in a truth definition, we lapse into (or create) language for which we have no coherent semantical account—that is, no account at all of how such talk can be integrated into the language as a whole.

To return to our main theme: we have recognized that a theory of the kind proposed leaves the whole matter of what individual words mean exactly where it was. Even when the metalanguage is different from the object language, the theory exerts no pressure for improvement, clarification, or analysis of individual words, except when, by accident of vocabulary, straightforward translation fails. Just as synonymy, as between expressions, goes generally untreated, so also synonymy of sentences, and analyticity. Even such sentences as 'A vixen is a female fox' bear no special tag unless it is our pleasure to provide it. A truth definition does not distinguish between analytic sentences and others, except for sentences that owe their truth to the presence alone of the constants that give the theory its grip on structure: the theory entails not only that these sentences are true but that they will remain true under all significant rewritings of their non-logical parts. A notion of logical truth thus given limited application, related notions of logical equivalence and entailment will tag along. It is hard to imagine how a theory of meaning could fail to read a logic into its object language to this degree; and to the extent that it does, our intuitions of logical truth, equivalence, and entailment may be called upon in constructing and testing the theory.

I turn now to one more, and very large, fly in the ointment: the fact that the same sentence may at one time or in one mouth be true and at another time or in another mouth be false. Both logicians and those critical of formal methods here seem largely (though by no means universally) agreed that formal semantics and logic are incompetent to deal with the disturbances caused by demonstratives. Logicians have often reacted by downgrading natural language and trying to show how to get along without demonstratives; their critics react by downgrading logic and formal semantics. None of this can make me happy: clearly demonstratives cannot be eliminated from a natural language without loss or radical change, so there is no choice but to accommodate theory to them.

No logical errors result if we simply treat demonstratives as constants;[16] neither do any problems arise for giving a semantic truth definition. ' "I am wise" is true if and only if I am wise', with its bland ignoring of the demonstrative element in 'I', comes off the assembly line along with ' "Socrates is wise" is true if and only if Socrates is wise', with its bland indifference to the demonstrative element in 'is wise' (the tense).

What suffers in this treatment of demonstratives is not the definition of a truth predicate, but the plausibility of the claim that what has been defined is truth. For this claim is acceptable only if the speaker and circumstances of utterance of each sentence mentioned in the definition is matched by the speaker and circumstances of utterance of the truth definition itself. It could also be fairly pointed out that part of understanding demonstratives is knowing the rules by which they adjust their reference to circumstance; assimilating demonstratives to constant terms obliterates this feature. These complaints can be met, I think, though only by a fairly far-reaching revision in the theory of truth. I shall barely suggest how this could be done, but bare suggestion is all that is needed: the idea is technically trivial, and in line with work being done on the logic of the tenses.[17]

We could take truth to be a property, not of sentences, but of utterances, or speech acts, or ordered triples of sentences, times, and persons; but it is simplest just to view truth as a relation between a sentence, a person, and a time. Under such treatment, ordinary logic as now read applies as usual, but only to sets of sentences relativized to the same speaker and time; further logical relations between sentences spoken at different times and by different speakers may be articulated by new axioms. Such is not my concern. The theory of meaning undergoes a systematic but not puzzling change; corresponding to each expression with a demonstrative element there must in the theory be a phrase that relates the truth conditions of sentences in which the expression occurs to changing times and speakers. Thus the theory will entail sentences like the following:

'I am tired' is true as (potentially) spoken by p at t if and only if p is tired at t.

'That book was stolen' is true as (potentially) spoken by p at t if and only if the book demonstrated by p at t is stolen prior to t.[18]

Plainly, this course does not show how to eliminate demonstratives; for example, there is no suggestion that 'the book demonstrated by the speaker' can be substituted ubiquitously for 'that book' *salva veritate*. The fact that demonstratives are amenable to formal treatment ought greatly to improve hopes for a serious semantics of natural language, for it is likely that many outstanding puzzles, such as the analysis of quotations or sentences about propositional attitudes, can be solved if we recognize a concealed demonstrative construction.

Now that we have relativized truth to times and speakers, it is appropriate to glance back at the problem of empirically testing a theory of meaning for an alien tongue. The essence of the method was, it will be remembered, to correlate held-true sentences with held-true sentences by way of a truth definition, and within the bounds of intelligible error. Now the picture must be elaborated to allow for the fact that sentences are true, and held true, only relative to a speaker and a time. Sentences with demonstratives obviously yield a very sensitive test of the correctness of a theory of meaning, and constitute the most direct link between language and the recurrent macroscopic objects of human interest and attention.[19]

In this paper I have assumed that the speakers of a language can effectively determine the meaning or meanings of an arbitrary expression (if it has a meaning), and that it is the central task of a theory of meaning to show how this is possible. I have argued that a characterization of a truth predicate describes the required kind of structure, and provides a clear and testable criterion of an adequate semantics for a natural language. No doubt there are other reasonable demands that may be put on a theory of meaning. But a theory that does no more than define truth for a language comes far closer to constituting a complete theory of meaning than superficial analysis might suggest; so, at least, I have urged.

Since I think there is no alternative, I have taken an optimistic and programmatic view of the possibilities for a formal characterization of a truth predicate for a natural language. But it must be allowed that a staggering list of difficulties and conundrums remains. To name a few: we do not know the logical form of counterfactual or subjunctive sentences: nor of sentences about probabilities and about causal relations; we have no good idea what the logical role of adverbs is, nor the role of attributive adjectives; we have no theory for mass terms like 'fire', 'water', and 'snow', nor for sentences about belief, perception, and intention, nor for verbs of action that imply purpose. And finally, there are all the sentences that seem not to have truth values at all: the imperatives, optatives, interrogatives, and a host more. A comprehensive theory of meaning for a natural language must cope successfully with each of these problems.[20]

Notes

1 See Essay 1 [= Davidson 1965, see p. 191 above].

2 A 'structural description' of an expression describes the expression as a concatenation of elements drawn from a fixed finite list (for example of words or letters).

3 The argument derives from Frege. See A. Church, *Introduction to Mathematical Logic*, 24–5. It is perhaps worth mentioning that the argument does not depend on any particular identification of the entities to which sentences are supposed to refer.

4 It may be thought that Church, in 'A Formulation of the Logic of Sense and Denotation', has given a theory of meaning that makes essential use of meanings as entities. But this is not the case: Church's logics of sense and denotation are interpreted as being about meanings, but they do not mention expressions and so cannot of course be theories of meaning in the sense now under discussion.

5 For a recent statement of the role of semantics in linguistics, see Noam Chomsky, 'Topics in the Theory of Generative Grammar'. In this article, Chomsky (1) emphasizes the central importance of semantics in linguistic theory, (2) argues for the superiority of transformational grammars over phrase-structure grammars largely on the grounds that, although phrase-structure grammars may be adequate to define sentencehood for (at least) some natural languages, they are inadequate as a foundation for semantics, and (3) comments repeatedly on the 'rather primitive state' of the concepts of semantics and remarks that the notion of semantic interpretation 'still resists any deep analysis'.

6 Assuming, of course, that the extension of these predicates is limited to the sentences of L.

7 A. Tarski, 'The Concept of Truth in Formalized Languages'.

8 But Quine may be quoted in support of my usage: '. . . in point of *meaning* . . . a word may be said to be determined to whatever extent the truth or falsehood of its contexts is determined.' ('Truth by Convention', 82.) Since a truth definition determines the truth value of every sentence in the object language (relative to a sentence in the metalanguage), it determines the meaning of every word and sentence. This would seem to justify the title Theory of Meaning.

9 To give a single example: it is clearly a count in favour of a theory that it entails ' "Snow is white" is true if and only if snow is white'. But to contrive a theory that entails this (and works for all related sentences) is not trivial. I do not know a wholly satisfactory theory that succeeds with this very case (the problem of 'mass terms').

10 Critics have often failed to notice the essential proviso mentioned in this paragraph. The point is that (S) could not belong to any reasonably simple theory that also gave the right truth conditions for 'That is snow' and 'This is white'. (See the discussion of indexical expressions below.) [Footnote added in 1982.]

11 This paragraph is confused. What it should say is that sentences of the theory are empirical generalizations about speakers, and so must not only be true but also lawlike. (S) presumably is not a law, since it does not support appropriate counterfactuals. It's also important that the evidence for accepting the (time- and speaker-relativized) truth conditions for 'That is snow' is based on the causal connection between a speaker's assent to the sentence and the demonstrative presentation of snow. For further discussion see Essay 12. [= Davidson 1965, see p. 191 above.]

12 This sketch of how a theory of meaning for an alien tongue can be tested obviously owes it inspiration to Quine's account of radical translation in Chapter II of *Word and Object*. In suggesting that an acceptable theory of radical translation take the form of a recursive characterization of truth, I go beyond Quine. Toward the end of this paper, in the discussion of demonstratives, another strong point of agreement will turn up.

13 So far as I am aware, there has been very little discussion of whether a formal truth definition can be given for a natural language. But in a more general vein, several people have urged that the concepts of formal semantics be applied to natural language. See, for example, the contributions of Yehoshua Bar-Hillel and Evert Beth to *The Philosophy of Rudolph Carnap*, and Bar-Hillel's 'Logical Syntax and Semantics'.

14 The *rapprochement* I prospectively imagine between

transformational grammar and a sound theory of meaning has been much advanced by a recent change in the conception of transformational grammar described by Chomsky in the article referred to above (note 5). The structures generated by the phrase-structure part of the grammar, it has been realized for some time, are those suited to semantic interpretation; but this view is inconsistent with the idea, held by Chomsky until recently, that recursive operations are introduced only by the transformation rules. Chomsky now believes the phrase-structure rules are recursive. Since languages to which formal semantic methods directly and naturally apply are ones for which a (recursive) phrase-structure grammar is appropriate, it is clear that Chomsky's present picture of the relation between the structures generated by the phrase-structure part of the grammar, and the sentences of the language, is very much like the picture many logicians and philosophers have had of the relation between the richer formalized languages and

ordinary language. (In these remarks I am indebted to Bruce Vermazen.)

15 B. Mates, 'Synonymity'.

16 See W. V. Quine, *Methods of Logic*, 8.

17 This claim has turned out to be naïvely optimistic. For some serious work on the subject, see S. Weinstein, 'Truth and Demonstratives'. [Note added in 1982.]

18 There is more than an intimation of this approach to demonstratives and truth in J. L. Austin, 'Truth'.

19 These remarks derive from Quine's idea that 'occasion sentences' (those with a demonstrative element) must play a central role in constructing a translation manual.

20 For attempted solutions to some of these problems see Essays 6–10 of *Essays on Actions and Events*, and Essays 6–8 of *Inquiries into Truth and Interpretation*, Oxford: Oxford University Press, 1980 and 1984 respectively. There is further discussion in Essays 3, 4, 9, and 10, and reference to some progress in section 1 of Essay 9.

Chapter 14

John Foster

MEANING AND TRUTH THEORY

[...]

II Davidson's initial thesis

To summarize the discussion so far, we are
seeking a method of constructing theories of meaning for particular languages which
will yield the greatest philosophical insight into
the nature of meaning and language in general.
To yield this insight the theories must be genuinely interpretative: the facts they state must
suffice for the mastery of the languages they
characterize. In addition, their syntax should be
extensional, their logic sound and their essential
vocabulary free from the concept of meaning
and other concepts of an intensional kind. For a
theory to be interpretative, its designations of
expressions in the object language and its characterization of their meaning must be relevantly
scrutable, and, given the primacy of sentences as
vehicles of meaning, this suggests, as a general
format, the presence of a finite set of axioms
which, for each sentence of the language, entail a
theorem in which that sentence is structurally
designated and its English translation used. So
our task could be construed as that of devising
formulations of such suitably interpretative theorems that we can get a finite theory, meeting
our other constraints, to generate. As far as I
know, there is, in the literature, only one concrete
proposal as to how this can be done. It is the
proposal put forward by Donald Davidson in his
celebrated paper 'Truth and Meaning'.[1] In that
paper Davidson argues that what we are looking
for as a theory of meaning we find in a theory of
truth conforming, in effect, to Tarski's Convention T, a theory which, for each sentence S of
the object language, entails what is got from
the schema 'x is true if and only if p' by substituting the structural description of S for 'x' and our
English translation of S for 'p'.[2] I say 'in *effect*
conforming to Convention T' for two reasons.
In the first place, as formulated by Tarski, the
convention states the conditions for an explicit
definition of truth for a language, without the
use, in the methodological sector, of primitive
semantic terms; and granted we are meeting
the formal requirements of a definition, the
entailing of the relevant biconditionals, in which
on the right-hand side all references to L-expressions disappear, is the criterion of when
an adequate definition has been achieved. In
the hands of Davidson the convention tests the
adequacy not of a definition, but of a theory of
truth, of a set of axioms which entail the
biconditionals by employing truth and certain
related semantic properties as formally primitive. Secondly, as formulated by Tarski the
convention applies only to object languages
which are context-free, languages in which what
each sentence can be used to state does not
vary with the circumstances of utterance. In the
hands of Davidson this restriction is lifted: truth
becomes a three-place relation between a

sentence, a person (potentially uttering it) and a time (when he potentially utters it), and the biconditionals are reformulated as universally quantified sentences of the form '(P)(t)(S is true for P at t if and only if . . .)' where what fills the blank translates not S itself, but S relative to P at t. This second disparity between Tarski and Davidson is one which, for simplicity of discussion, I shall ignore. I shall assume the object language to be context-free so that the references to speakers and times are unnecessary. On the first point, however, I shall follow Davidson quite strictly, for the difference is of crucial importance—an importance which is not sufficiently emphasized in his paper. If the characterization of the truth predicate for L serves to explicate its sense, to say exactly what is meant by 'is true in L', it cannot also serve to interpret the expressions of L. The characterization can only serve as a theory of meaning if the truth predicate, thus employed, is already understood; for although the characterization tells us how in L truth applies, it is only by knowing that it is *truth* which thus applies that we can hope to gain an understanding of L. Thus the difference in the form of the characterization between Tarski and Davidson reflects a difference in their aims. Tarski is seeking to explain the concept of truth for a particular language, and to this end nothing could be better than the explicit definition of a previously uninterpreted predicate. Davidson is seeking to construct an interpretative theory of meaning, and this requires using the concept of truth as formally primitive. Of course, in saying that truth must be formally primitive, I mean primitive relative to the T-style truth theory. There is nothing to prevent this theory forming part of a larger theory in which the truth predicate is defined. What we cannot have is its definition by those very clauses which, by generating the Tarski biconditionals, form the theory of interpretation.

Given the task we have set ourselves, the merits of Davidson's proposal are obvious. A theory of truth meeting the modified version of

Convention T, a T-theory as I shall call it, exemplifies the general format we envisaged: for each sentence of the object language, it entails a theorem in which that sentence is structurally designated and its English translation used. But the method of linking the designated and the used has changed for the better: the intensional concept of meaning has given place to the extensional concept of truth, and the intensional idiom of oratio obliqua to the extensional idiom of material equivalence. Moreover, the prospects for constructing T-theories are favourable. Tarski's own method, suitably reconstrued, suffices for elementary quantificational languages, while Davidson and others have shown, and continue to show, how to adapt this method to languages of a richer grammatical structure.[3] So far, so good. But the crucial question is whether a T-theory is fully interpretative. And here, even before a detailed investigation, one has the suspicion that in relinquishing the intensional idiom we have relaxed our grip on meaning. Can we really hope that a characterization of truth for a language will also constitute a full characterization of meaning?

The suspicion of inadequacy may be due in part to a misunderstanding of how a T-theory is supposed to do its interpretative work. In shifting from the intensional to the extensional idiom, we diminish the interpretative force of each individual theorem. An extensional theorem of the form 'S is true if and only if p' says less than an intensional theorem of the form 'S means that p'. But it is not intended that a T-theory should interpret each sentence of the language by that unique theorem which states its truth conditions. It is not intended that our understanding of each sentence be based wholly on the truth-conditional for it which the theory entails. Rather, the theory purports to interpret each sentence by locating its position on the lines of truth determination for the language as a whole, by stating its truth conditions in the framework of the general principles by which the truth conditions of *any* sentence are determined by its structure. The meaning of each sentence S is given not by that unique theorem which refers to it, but by that infinite set of theorems which refer to all sentences that contain any S-component. In effect, the interpretation of S is the interpretation of the whole language in the perspective of that sentence. This gives an interesting slant to the dictum that the meaning of a sentence depends on the meanings of its elements, a slant in which the lines of dependence run in both directions. The meaning of a sentence does depend on the meanings of its elements, but, on a T-theoretical view, the meaning of each element consists in what it contributes to the truth conditions of the sentences which contain it. On such a view, the meaning of each expression, whether simple or complex, consists in the particular form in which its structure channels the contributions to truth conditions.

Once we have grasped how the work of interpreting each sentence is diffused throughout the whole theory, the weakness of the individual theorems is less alarming. But here there is room for a second misunderstanding, this time one which puts Davidson's thesis in a more favourable light than it deserves. Just as we might wrongly demand that the individual theorems accomplish more than they are supposed to, so we might mistakenly suppose that they accomplish more than they do. I have said that these theorems, T-sentences as Davidson calls them, state the truth conditions of the sentences they refer to. But this is so only in a special sense. As ordinarily understood, the truth conditions of a sentence are those conditions necessary and sufficient for its truth: two sentences are said to have the same truth conditions just in case they would, with their meaning held constant, have the same truth value in all possible circumstances—just in case there could not be circumstances of a kind which accords with what is stated by the one which were not also circumstances of a kind which accords with what is stated by the other. Similarly, as ordinarily

understood, to state the truth conditions of a sentence is to say what (indirect question) is necessary and sufficient for its truth, to demarcate, within the total range of possible circumstances, that subset with which the sentence accords. But this is not the sense in which a *T-sentence* states truth conditions. A T-sentence does not say that such and such a structural type *would be* true (meaning held constant) in all and only those circumstances in which it *was* the case that . . ., but merely that, things being as they are, this structural type is true if and only if . . . It suffices for the truth of a T-sentence that what fills the blank has the same truth value as what it structurally designates, and the only sense in which a T-sentence states truth conditions is a sense whereby two sentences have the same truth *conditions* if and only if they have the same truth *value*. This point may be obscured by the fact that to qualify as a T-sentence it is not enough that what is designated on the left have the same truth value as what is used on the right: it is necessary, in addition, that the latter be a *translation* of the former. Replacing either sentence by one that is materially equivalent preserves the truth value of the biconditional, but such replacements do not guarantee that what emerges is qualified to go in a T-theory. This may foster the illusion that T-sentences are stronger than they are: it may persuade us that the constraints on their formulation are reflected in the force of what they state, that a T-sentence states truth conditions in the ordinary, strong sense, because the English translation expresses just that range of circumstances with which the designated sentence accords. I would hesitate to ascribe this illusion to Professor Davidson. But on the other hand, once it has been dispelled, it becomes all too apparent, as I shall now show, that his thesis (as he *then* stated it) is mistaken.

To keep things simple, let us examine the form of a T-theory for an elementary quantificational language of the kind for which Tarski's own method, minus its definitional aspect, suffices. Let L be a language which consists, or can be represented as consisting, of a two-place predicate P, the truth-functional connective stroke with its normal meaning, the universal quantifier '∧' with its normal meaning, a denumerable stock of individual variables ordered as $v_1, v_2, v_3, \ldots$, the brackets '(' and ')', and all sentences, open and closed, formed from these elementary symbols by the standard formation rules of the predicate calculus. Assuming these formation rules have already been stated, the first step in constructing a T-theory for L is to introduce, either by explicit set-theoretical definition or as a primitive characterized by appropriate axioms, the concept of an infinite sequence of objects drawn from the universe of things over which the variables of L range. These sequences we shall call *assignments*, for, by its role in the theory, each sequence in effect assigns a unique value to each L-variable, the value of v_n for the sequence Σ being simply the nth element in Σ. (For the range of sequences to constitute the full range of assignments it is, of course, necessary that the same object *can* occur many times in the same sequence.) The next step is to find an English translation of the L-predicate P, and this, we will suppose, is provided by the predicate 'part of'. This brings us to the meat of the theory, which consists in the recursive characterization of the relation of satisfaction between assignments and sentences. We begin by saying that an assignment Σ satisfies an atomic L-sentence—a formula consisting of P followed by a pair of variables—if and only if the object which Σ assigns to the first of these variables is a part of the object which Σ assigns to the second. By similarly exploiting our translations of stroke and '∧' we can then characterize satisfaction for sentences of higher complexity. Thus Σ satisfies a sentence of the form $A ⌢ \text{stroke} ⌢ B$ if and only if Σ fails to satisfy either A or B; and Σ satisfies a sentence of the form '∧' $⌢ v_n ⌢ A$ if and only if A is satisfied by every assignment which differs from Σ, if at all, in at most its nth place. With satisfaction fully characterized, the final step is to say that an L-sentence is true if and only if it is

satisfied by all assignments. Suitably formalized, and enriched with the appropriate axioms of structural description and sequence theory, these clauses collectively constitute a T-theory for L: for each closed L-sentence S, they entail what is got from the schema 'x is true if and only if p' by substituting the structural description of S for 'x' and the translation of S for 'p'.

This theory—we will call it θ—gives an adequate characterization of truth in L. But it does not, however obliquely, give an adequate characterization of meaning. For, for every L-sentence, there are infinitely many and importantly different interpretations with which θ is consistent. Knowing the facts which θ states does not suffice for so much as an approximate understanding of a single sentence. This is most clearly seen by considering what θ says of the simple elements of which L-sentences are composed. For P, the crucial clause (we will call it the P-*clause*) is that which states that, for any integers i and j, an assignment satisfies $P ⌢ v_i ⌢ v_1$ if and only if its ith element is a part of its jth element. The other clauses are not crucial, since they are obviously consistent with any interpretation of P which is consistent with its grammatical parsing as a two-place predicate. But just what does the P-clause tell us? Only, in the context of the other clauses, that P applies to all and only those ordered pairs of objects that are related as part to whole. But this, while not compatible with *every* interpretation of P, is compatible with every interpretation which accords with its extension. If P′ is any predicate with the same extension as P, we can substitute in the P-clause the designation of P′ for the designation of P without altering its truth. Hence if there is or could be a predicate P′ with the same extension as P, but with a different sense, nothing in the P-clause or in any other clauses of θ precludes our falsely interpreting P to mean whatever it is that P′ means. All that remains is to show that there could be such a predicate. This is easy. Take any contingently true sentence of English, (say) 'the earth moves', and envisage P′ as what would be correctly translated by the English expression 'the earth moves and . . . is a part of . . .'. Since it is true that the earth moves, P and P' are coextensive: there is no pair of objects to which one applies and the other does not. But they differ in meaning; P' is, to put it technically, a proper determinate of P: it implies all that P implies and in addition the contingent proposition that the earth moves. There are obviously infinitely many examples of this type, as many as there are distinct truths of English. And there are also examples, again infinitely many, of other types. One type, closely related, would be to take any contingently false English sentence, (say) 'the earth is still', and envisage P' as what would be correctly translated by 'either the earth is still or . . . is a part of . . .'. Again P and P' would be coextensive, but this time P' would be a proper determinable of P, implied by anything that implies P, and in addition by the contingent proposition that the earth is still. Types of example and instances of each type could be multiplied indefinitely. But it is the principle they illustrate which matters, namely that θ, while it fixes the extension of P, comes nowhere near fixing its sense. For for each such P', θ says nothing to exclude a false interpretation of P along the lines of the correct interpretation envisaged for P'.

There is an exactly parallel argument to show that θ fails to interpret the connective and quantifier. We can envisage a connective stroke$^+$ translatable in English as 'the earth moves and either it is not the case that . . . or it is not the case that . . .', and we can envisage a quantifier '$\wedge^+$' translatable as 'for every object . . ., the earth moves and . . .'. These new operators have the same truth-relevant force as their counterparts in L, and θ says nothing to exclude a false interpretation of stroke along the lines of stroke$^+$, or a false interpretation of '$\wedge$' along the lines of '$\wedge^+$'. θ is obviously in a bad way. To ram the point home, consider any analytically true sentence of L, (say) '$\wedge \frown v_1 \frown P \frown v_1 \frown v_1$'. This sentence states the trivial truth that everything is a part of itself.

But θ says so little about '$\wedge$' and P that there is absolutely no contingent truth which we could not, compatibly with θ, construe this sentence to be stating. And if this is so, then whatever its merits as a theory of truth, θ is a very bad theory of meaning indeed.

The failure of θ to capture the meanings of the elements of L reflects the attenuated sense in which, quite generally, a T-theory for a language states the truth conditions of its sentences. Whatever these sentences mean, each T-sentence is true simply because the English sentence used on the right has the same truth value as the sentence designated on the left. Given a language X and its T-theory Y, a false interpretation of X is compatible with Y if revising the meanings of the X-sentences to accord with this interpretation preserves, in all cases, their grammar and truth values; and grammar and truth values are systematically preserved if the revision preserves all that the elements contribute to the truth values of the sentences which contain them. Because on such a revision Y would remain true (though no longer a T-theory), an interpretation which ascribes the revised meanings is both false of X as it actually is, and compatible with all that Y states. It is just this which the case of L and θ exemplifies. And from this case we can now draw the general conclusion which demolishes Davidson's thesis, namely that T-theorizing fails to be genuinely interpretative for all languages where the full significance of the elements, gauged by their contributions to what is stated by the sentences which contain them, exceeds their truth-relevant significance, gauged by what they contribute to the truth or falsity of these sentences. These languages will include, at the very least, all languages of an extensional kind, of which the elementary quantificational languages, exemplified by L, are the paradigm case.

There are four ways in which this conclusion, or the importance I attach to it, might be attacked. First, there is the argument, possibly ascribable to Hintikka, that I am reading more meaning into an extensional language than the austerity of its syntax allows, that in such a language the full significance of the elements does not exceed their truth-relevant significance, and that the extra meaning I thought I discerned has been, so to speak, misappropriated from the richer resources possessed by an extensional fragment of a larger non-extensional language.[4] Secondly, it might be argued that, while the case of extensional languages is as I have represented it, no natural, autonomous language could be purely extensional, since to speak a language requires having propositional attitudes, and to have such attitudes requires the ability to ascribe them to oneself and others by means of non-extensional idiom. So granted that Davidson's concern is with theories of meaning for natural language, my arguments do not touch him. Thirdly, and more weakly, it might be argued that, while there *could be* an extensional natural language, all known natural languages *are*, as a matter of fact, nonextensional, so that my conclusions are of little consequence. Fourthly, and finally, it could be argued that if the method of T-theorizing suffices for certain kinds of nonextensional language, we can readily adapt it to an extensional language by merely constructing the theory for some hypothetical nonextensional language of which that language would be a fragment. These four objections, while different and in certain cases inconsistent with each other, are variations on a common theme, namely that the defects I have ascribed to Davidson's thesis stem not from this thesis, but from my failure to grasp the peculiarity of those languages by which I have tested it. In their different ways they claim that I have misrepresented either the character or the importance of those extensional languages I have chosen as my battleground.

It would be nice to examine these objections in detail and expose all their misconceptions and mistakes. But I can afford to be brief, for I think that neither Davidson, nor anyone familiar with his work, would wish to press them. To begin with, someone who, along the lines of the last

two objections, regards intensional idiom as something to draw out the true strength of T-theorizing is simply ignorant of the kind of problems such idiom creates, problems which might make one despair of providing a T-theory at all. Nonextensionality in the object language is not an invigorating tonic which ensures that the lines of truth determination encompass richer fields of meaning, but a disease which threatens to prevent the truth theory ever developing. Davidson's own solution, and I can see no other, is, before applying the T-theory, to reconstrue the seemingly nonextensional idiom in extensional terms, an example of this being the paratactic analysis of oratio obliqua, as presented in his paper 'On Saying That'.[5] This paratactic analysis also disposes of the second objection; for even if we thought the analysis unsatisfactory for (say) English as it is, there obviously could be a language in which the ascription of propositional attitudes worked in the paratactic way. Finally, once we have accepted that an extensional language can, by such devices, do all the descriptive work of a natural language, the first objection loses even that modicum of plausibility which it had. The objection, if coherent at all, must amount to the claim that, given a community with an extensional language, there could be no grounds, in the observable features of linguistic usage, for deciding between the different interpretations compatible with its T-theory. But to claim such a degree of indeterminacy is absurd; for if extensionality does not as such restrict descriptive resources, it does not as such restrict the kind of empirical evidence relevant to interpretation.

III Davidson's revised thesis

Professor Davidson will, I think, accept the essentials of my argument so far. There may be dispute over detail, but I think he will concede that the thesis he put forward in 'Truth and Meaning', and endorsed, with only minor adjustments, in certain subsequent papers,[6] is wrong for the reasons I have given. But recently his position has undergone an important change, a change which appears to protect him from the particular criticisms I have made. So I want next to state this new position, if I have understood it correctly, and assess its merits.[7]

The right starting point is to note again something which has already come up, namely the disparity between the weakness of what T-sentences state and the constraints on their construction. Any sentence of the form 'x is true if and only if p' is true just in case the sentence designated by what we substitute for 'x' has the same truth value as the sentence we substitute for 'p'. But for this biconditional to qualify as a T-sentence, as a theorem of a theory meeting Convention T, it is necessary in addition that the sentence substituted for 'p' be a translation of the sentence designated by what we substitute for 'x'. But if so, it seems that a T-theory can, in some sense, serve as a theory of meaning. For although a T-theory is not itself a theory of meaning—since the facts it states do not suffice for mastery—if one knows a T-theory and knows that it is a T-theory, one knows enough to interpret the language. Let us develop this for the case of L and θ. θ fails as a theory of meaning because, while it captures what the elements of L contribute to the truth or falsity of the sentences which contain them, it fails to capture all that they contribute to what these sentences state. But suppose we add the knowledge that θ is a T-theory. Then for each L-sentence S, we know that θ's theorem for S is a T-sentence, in which the sentence on the right translates S. But this sentence on the right is one which we understand, indeed *have* to understand to understand θ; and if we both understand this sentence and know that it translates S, then we know what S states. In effect, equipped with a grasp of θ and the knowledge of its T-theoreticity, we can systematically reread each T-sentence as of the form 'x states that p'. With these rereadings in mind, we only have to work back from the T-sentences to their axioms to net all that the elements

contribute to what L-sentences state. And to have netted this is to know how to interpret any L-sentence on the basis of its structure.

This thesis, that within the framework of the knowledge that we are T-theorizing a T-theory serves as a theory of interpretation, is the first layer of Davidson's new account. Behind it is a second and older layer, which now takes on a new importance. This older layer consists, in effect, of an empirical account of the notion of translation.[8] So far, in formulating the conditions for being a T-theory, we have, like Tarski, taken this notion for granted: we have assumed that we understand what it is for a sentence on the right of a truth-conditional to translate what is designated on the left. If we were ever to use the character of T-theories to give leverage on the concept of meaning, there obviously had to come a time when this assumption was abandoned. And abandon it is just what Davidson does. In its place he holds that to be a T-theory is to be a theory which meets certain formal and empirical constraints. The formal constraints ensure the form of a fully developed theory of truth: they require the entailment of the characteristic truth-conditionals with structural designators on the left and no structural designators on the right. The empirical constraints ensure, or are intended to ensure, that the theory is accurate and, within the limits of indeterminacy, exemplifies, in its truth-conditional theorems, an accurate manual of translation: here, the main requirement is the maximizing of agreement between the truth-claims of the native speakers and the truth-claims of the theory—the better the theory, the more it represents the speakers as correct in what they hold true. This, the Principle of Charity as it is sometimes (mis)called, is the main empirical constraint, but once it has allowed the theory to take off, it is to be tempered by other considerations, such as the likelihood, in given circumstances, of native error, and the degree to which the beliefs ascribable to speakers on the basis of the theory are supported by independent behavioural evidence.

Davidson's new thesis is, then, that a theory of truth meeting certain formal and empirical constraints serves as a theory of meaning for one who knows that it meets these constraints. It may be possible to question whether Davidson's constraints are strong enough, whether they ensure the closest fit that indeterminacy allows between sentences of the object language and sentences of English. But such questions are, from my point of view, a matter of detail. The crucial point is that, given the right constraints, the new thesis appears to escape my earlier objections. My only achievement, it seems, is to have shown, perhaps more decisively than Davidson himself, *why* this new thesis should be adopted. However, matters are not so simple. Look again at the case of θ and L. The claim is that, given the knowledge that it is a T-theory (as defined by the relevant constraints), θ serves as a theory of meaning for L. This claim does not, of course, mean that, given the relevant knowledge, θ *becomes* a theory of meaning for L, that θ comes to state facts which suffice for a mastery of L. For obviously, however useful this extra knowledge, it cannot make any difference to what θ states. The claim is, rather, that knowing the facts which θ states and knowing that θ is a T-theory between them suffice for a mastery of L. But is this so? Suppose that θ' is an exact reformulation in French of all that θ states, and suppose that Pierre, a Frenchman with no understanding of English, accepts θ' on the authority of a compatriot François, who is an expert linguist. François, however, omits to mention that θ' is a T-theory. So Pierre, while he knows the facts which θ' states and, since they are the same, the facts which θ states, cannot yet use this knowledge to interpret L. Now suppose that next François, overrating his friend's linguistic capacities, writes out θ, specifies its rules of inference, informs Pierre that these English sentences, in the framework of these rules, constitute a T-theory for L, and supplies a formal criterion by which Pierre can recognize its T-sentences. Thus informed, Pierre knows that θ

is a T-theory for L and can, by deriving the T-sentences, work out the English translation of any selected L-sentence. So Pierre has both items of knowledge whose conjunction, it was claimed, suffices for mastery. He knows the facts stated by θ and he knows that θ is a T-theory. But, not knowing English, and not knowing that θ and θ' state the same facts, he cannot convert this knowledge into an understanding of L. Indeed, in his circumstances, the information that θ is a T-theory is wholly gratuitous.

This point, of course, harks back to the objections to a translation theory discussed much earlier. If formulated in English, a theory of translation from L to English can pose as a theory of meaning; for anyone who, in virtue of understanding English, understands the theory can interpret the sentences of L on the basis of their translation. But such a theory is not genuinely interpretative, since the understanding of L is not derived wholly from what the theory states. Davidson's new thesis is defective in the same way. What in effect he is offering, as a theory of meaning, is the combination of a T-theory and, by adding a clause which claims its T-theoreticity, a translation theory dressed up in empirically respectable terms. Given that we understand θ, claiming its T-theoreticity provides a translation manual from L to a language we understand, and we only have to inspect the manner in which the T-sentences, exhibiting the translations, are derived, to gain a full understanding of any expression of L. But the conjunction of θ and a clause which states that it is a T-theory is not, as the case of Pierre demonstrates, an adequate theory of meaning. What it *states* does not suffice for a mastery of L. Indeed, it is no more interpretative than θ on its own, since the additional clause states nothing which bears on the interpretation of L unless supplemented by an interpretation of English.

Thus if I have correctly represented it, Davidson's new thesis is no better than the original. Indeed, if anything it is worse, since it increases the complexity of the supposed theories of meaning without any gain in their interpretative power. There is, however, a closely related thesis which is seemingly more effective and perhaps what Davidson is trying to convey. The trouble with the present version is that the claim of T-theoreticity and the content of the T-theory do not interlock: our knowledge that θ is a T-theory has no direct contact with our knowledge of the facts which θ states. But the idea behind this thesis may be sound. For in effect what we need to know, for the mastery of L, are both the facts which θ states and that these facts, as known by us, are T-theoretical; we need to know both the θ-facts and that, in knowing these facts, we are T-theorizing. How then are we to put this, granted that the predicate 'T-theory' applies not to facts or knowledge, but to sets of sentences? The answer must surely be this: the facts which suffice for a mastery of L are those stated by the single sentence (θ^*): 'Some T-theory for L states that. . . .' where we fill the blank with the conjunction of all the clauses of θ. θ^* employs the predicate 'T-theory' in its established sense, but in it the claim of T-theoreticity encompasses the content of the truth theory—it tells us what we need to know, for an understanding of L, about the facts which θ states. Generalizing, we obtain the following revised thesis: for any language X, the theory of meaning for X is what is got from the schema 'Some T-theory for y states that p' by substituting a designator of X for 'y' and a T-theory for X for 'p'.

This revision takes care of the problem of interpretativeness. For consider again the trivial L-sentence '$\wedge$' v_1 P v_1 v_1, whose structural description, just used, we will abbreviate to 'D'. In θ this sentence has as its T-sentence: 'D is true if and only if $(x)(x$ is a part of $x)$'. Since this T-sentence is a logical consequence of θ, we can deduce from θ^* (not, of course, by means of standard extensional logic) that (1) some T-theory for L has as a logical consequence a sentence which states that D is true if and only if $(x)(x$ is a part of $x)$. And since any sentence which states this must be a T-sentence of any T-theory which logically entails it, we can deduce from (1) (again not by means of standard extensional logic) that (2) some T-theory for L has a T-sentence whose left half contains a designation of D and whose right half states that $(x)(x$ is a part of $x)$. But knowing the significance of the T-constraints, we can deduce from (2) that (3) a sentence which states that $(x)(x$ is a part of $x)$ is a translation of D. From which we can immediately deduce that (4) D states that $(x)(x$ is a part of $x)$. Since this same procedure is available for every L-sentence, by knowing the facts which θ^* states we can, with our wits about us, work out what any selected sentence states. And this general capacity, encompassing the totality of L-sentences, implies the capacity to interpret each sentence on the basis of its structure, since it implies the capacity to discern, not only what this sentence states, but what each of its elements contributes to what it states.

Interpretativeness, however, is θ^*'s only merit. In all other respects it falls short of our requirements. For it brings back the kind of intensionality which conflicts with our philosophical aims: it takes for granted the concept of stating and the nonextensional syntax which goes with it. There is not much to be gained in letting the claim of T-theoreticity and the content of the T-theory make contact, if the only means of connecting them are by the intensional idiom of 'stating that'. Why, after all, take the trouble to give an empirical account of translation, if such idiom can be assumed to be unproblematic? This idiom, moreover, is all the worse because the only genuinely semantic clauses, laying semantic conditions on structural types, fall on its opaque side. We have lost the explicit identification of L-expressions and the explicit description of their semantic significance. All that θ^* says of L is that some T-theory for it states that such and such, and we are left, as it were, to work out the semantics by discerning the concealed implications.

At this point Davidson may be tempted to

press his paratactic analysis of oratio obliqua, reformulating $O*$ as:

—.Some T-theory for L states that

where O fills the left hand blank and the demonstrative 'that' refers back to that particular O-utterance. For this not only extensionalizes the syntax, but leaves *stating* as a relation which, like translation before it, may yield to analysis. But thus construed, $O*$ ceases, as I shall now show, to be interpretative. To avoid terminological confusion, I shall use the word 'states' in its normal, non-Davidsonian sense and use the expression 'stands in the stating relation to' for that special relation, expressed in the reformulation, which holds between a theory and an utterance. Let us call that particular O-utterance 'U'. Now obviously someone may be able to identify U, (say) as the utterance made by so and so at such and such a time, without knowing what it is that U states. And consequently, someone who does not know what it is that U states may know, on good authority, that some T-theory for L stands in the stating relation to it. But if he does not know what it is that U states, knowing that some T-theory for L stands in the stating relation to it does not help him to interpret L. Moreover, someone who does not know what it is that U states may nonetheless know all the facts which U does state. So someone may know all that is stated by both components of the reformulated $O*$ without being able to interpret L: he may know both the facts stated by O and that some T-theory for L stands in the stating relation to U, without having any more interpretative knowledge of L than what is provided by O alone. In effect, by formulating $O*$ paratactically we sever that direct link between the claim of T-theoreticity and the content of O which the intensional idiom secured.

It may be objected that it is I who have severed the link by failing to discern the subtle way in which the two components of the paratactic whole interact. If Smith says to a French audience: 'The earth moves. Galileo said that', his interpreter (*interpreter* in the ordinary, not my special sense), who, we may think, is trying to stand in the same-saying relation to him, says: 'La terre tourne. Galilée a dit cela', in which the demonstrative 'cela' refers not to Smith's utterance of the English sentence 'The earth moves' but to his own utterance of the French sentence 'La terre tourne'. So it may be argued that to know the facts stated by the paratactic $O*$, to stand in the same-knowing relation to its utterer, is to know, not that some T-theory stands in the stating relation to U, but that some T-theory stands in the stating relation to one's own last utterance—where one's own last utterance is of a sentence stating the same facts as O. Well, this may be so. But if it is so, it can only be because the paratactic version of oratio obliqua is not what it purports to be. For the Davidsonian analysis of 'Galileo said that', as uttered by Smith, is 'some utterance of Galileo and my last utterance make Galileo and me same-sayers', and a strict French rendering of what Smith thereby *states* must preserve the reference to Smith's previous utterance. To insist, contrariwise, that rendering the *whole* of what Smith states requires changing the reference in the suggested way, is, in effect, to construe the paratactic version of oratio obliqua as a notational variant of the intensional version, to construe the apparent demonstrative as an intensional operator on the previous sentence. There is no denying, of course, that a good interpreter, in the ordinary sense, would change the reference from Smith's utterance to his own. But that is because a good interpreter would convey the information which Smith wants conveyed, not restate the facts or propositions which Smith states. Our concern, it must be emphasized, is with the stating of facts, not the conveying of information; otherwise we could have settled for a translation theory long ago.

That, I think, is the *coup de grâce* for Davidson's new approach. I, at any rate, cannot see any way of harnessing the claim of T-theoreticity that both secures interpretativeness and avoids intensionality. And if there is no way, and if a T-theory on its own is inadequate, Davidson's grand design is in ruins. The only remaining question is what we should put in its place.

[. . .]

Notes

1 *Synthese*, xvii (1967), 304.

2 A. Tarski, 'The Concept of Truth in Formalized Languages' in *Logic, Semantics, Metamathematics* (Clarendon Press, Oxford, 1956), p. 152.

3 E.g. Davidson, 'The Logical Form of Action Sentences', in *The Logic of Decision and Action*, ed. N. Rescher (Pittsburgh University Press, 1967), 81, 'Causal Relations', *Journal of Philosophy*, lxiv (1967), 691, and 'On Saying That', *Synthese*, xix (1968), 130.

4 Thus see J. Hintikka, 'Semantics for Propositional Attitudes', in *Philosophical Logic*, ed. J. W. Davis *et al.* (Reidel, Dordrecht, 1969), p. 21.

5 *Synthese*, xix (1968), 130.

6 See especially his 'Semantics for Natural Languages', in *Linguaggi nella Società e nella Tecnica* (Edizioni di Comunità, Milan, 1970), p. 177.

7 My representation of Davidson's new position is based on certain unpublished papers he delivered in Oxford in Trinity Term 1974.

8 The origins of the account date back to 'Truth and Meaning'.

PART SEVEN

Meaning, intention and convention

INTRODUCTION TO PART SEVEN

WHEN WE COMMUNICATE by using sentences of some natural language, such as English, we clearly rely on the linguistic meaning of the sentences we use. For example, when I let you know that I have made some coffee by uttering the words 'I have made some coffee', I am exploiting the fact that these words, i.e. these repeatable types of sound, have a certain linguistic meaning. But what is it for a natural language expression to have meaning? Many theorists agree that the linguistic meaning of an expression type in a language in some way depends on, and is constituted by, the way users of that language use that expression. The fact that, in English, the words 'I have made some coffee', mean something seems to be an empirical fact about English speakers. But which fact?

One influential proposal in this area stems from Grice. Grice thinks, roughly, that a sentence type *s* means that *p* in a community of language users, just if members of the community have the habit of speaker-meaning that *p* by uttering *s*, and they retain the habit conditionally upon other members doing likewise (Grice 1989, pp. 124–8). This account makes use of Grice's notion of *speaker-meaning* (or 'meaning$_{NN}$'), which he first developed in 'Meaning', the first essay in this book. To speaker-mean something when uttering some words is to utter the words with a certain kind of intention. More precisely, a speaker speaker-means that *p* by uttering *s* just if in uttering *s* the speaker intends his or her audience to think that *p* (or to think that the speaker believes that *p*) on the basis of the audience's recognition of that very intention. Thus ultimately, according to Grice, for a sentence-type to mean something in a language is a matter of the users of the language having a habit of uttering that sentence with certain intentions.

David Lewis, in the article here reproduced, takes up Grice's project. He too believes that for a sentence to mean something in a language is for the users of that language to exhibit certain regularities in their use of the sentence. He thinks that the regularity involved is actually a very specific kind of regularity, namely what he calls a 'convention'. Despite the basic similarity, however, Lewis approaches the issue from quite a different angle than Grice. This is because at the same time as specifying what precisely these habits of language users amount to, he also addresses a different question, namely the question of what it could be for a language *as described by a formal semantic theory* to be the language used by a population. It will be useful to provide a little background to this aspect of Lewis's paper.

Formal semantics is a discipline that studies artificial languages, i.e. languages that have exactly the properties we stipulate or define them to have. Broadly, stipulating the properties of an artificial language will involve first stipulating which expressions belong to the language (syntax), and then stipulating what the meanings of these expressions are to be (semantics). Very often, the syntax will introduce a limited set of atomic expressions, and then state how the expressions of the language can be combined to form complex expressions. Sometimes, the ways in which expressions can be combined to form new expressions are recursive, i.e. the rules for forming new expressions can be re-applied over and over again to complex expressions, thus creating the possibility of an infinity of expressions. In that case, the semantics, if it is to stipulate the meanings of all the expressions of the language will also have to be recursive, i.e. specify rules that tell us how the meanings of complex expressions result from the meanings of their component expressions.[1]

The languages studied in formal semantics can therefore be seen as functions that assign meanings to each expression in a certain domain of expressions. Let us call the values assigned by the function to the expressions of the language the 'semantic values' of the expressions. Now, the role of semantic values could in principle be played by any sort of entity or property. However, formal semanticists are usually interested in languages that assign semantic values of a certain kind. These languages contain a certain subset of expressions of the language, namely the *sentences* or *well-formed formulae* of the language, and assign semantic values to these expressions that are in some way evaluable as true or false. Sometimes the semantic values of sentences are *propositions*, i.e. abstract entities that can be seen as representing the world as being a certain way. Propositions, in turn, are sometimes conceived of as structured entities that have individual objects, properties and relations as constituents; and sometimes propositions are conceived of as sets of 'possible worlds', i.e. ways the world could be – this is the conception Lewis follows here. As we saw in Part Six above, other semanticists are opposed to propositions and instead assign semantic values by specifying for each sentence a condition that is necessary and sufficient for its truth. For current purposes, we can ignore these differences.

Formal semanticists examine various properties that artificial languages have in virtue of the stipulated syntax and semantics. Formal semantics is therefore an a priori discipline: the formal semanticist uses definitions or stipulations and examines their logical consequences. No empirical considerations need be brought to bear. The formal semanticist can therefore conduct her investigations in the comfort of her armchair. Natural language semanticists, by contrast, are interested in the languages actually used by human populations. Clearly, empirical methods will be relevant here, for the description of natural languages requires observation of empirical facts of language use. Thus, the natural language semanticist will have to get out of the metaphorical armchair. It is therefore initially puzzling how the methods and findings of formal semantics can be of use to the natural language semanticist. Nevertheless, natural language semanticists have for the most part tried just this: to describe natural languages with the means of formal semantics. How is formal semantics relevant to the study of natural languages?

---

[1] This desideratum of compositionality is already familiar from Part Two, where Frege introduced a principle of compositionality for sense as well as for reference, and from Part Six, where Davidson required a theory of meaning for a natural language to be compositional in order that it may explain the ability of language users to understand all of a potential infinity of sentences. The issue will make further appearances below, in Parts Eight and Eleven.

An obvious answer is that natural language semanticists hope to use the well-understood languages described in formal semantics as *models* of natural languages. Artificial languages might be in some respects similar to natural languages and thus provide a simplified, regimented model of natural languages. For example, if we can describe a tiny fragment of English, consisting merely of a list of simple names and simple predicates, by providing a formal syntax and an assignment of semantic values to all the sentences that are part of that fragment, then we have semantically described at least that tiny fragment of English. That answer no doubt captures something of what natural language semanticists are doing. However, it does not say anything about the most puzzling problem: How are we to know whether the semantics we have provided for a fragment of English is correct? Once we have defined a language by providing a syntax and assigning semantic values to each of its sentences, what does it mean to say that that language is used by some population? What predictions about a population's behaviour can be generated from the hypothesis that that population uses a language specified in the way done in formal semantics, i.e. defined as a function from a domain of sentences to a range of semantic values?

Lewis's answer relies on the fact that semantic values for sentences are standardly something capable of evaluation as true or false. He says that a population uses a language just if that population exhibits a convention of truthfulness and trust in that language. Truthfulness in a language involves trying to utter sentences of that language only if the sentence is true in that language. Trust in a language involves responding to the utterance by others of sentences of that language by coming to believe that the sentence is true in that language. The first task for the reader will be to find out from Lewis's article what in detail this means.

In his short article, John Hawthorne offers a very specific objection to Lewis's account (Schiffer 1993 makes a related point). On Lewis's account, a population's using a language requires that its members conform to certain regularities: the regularity of trying to utter a sentence of that language only if it is true in that language, and the regularity of responding to utterances of sentences of that language by coming to believe that the sentence is true in that language. Now, one way of conforming to such regularities with respect to a given sentence is never to utter the sentence, or never to witness the utterance of that sentence. For example, there are certain very long and awkward sentences of English that are never used by anyone, simply because they are too long. So, the population of English speakers exhibits a – vacuous – regularity of truthfulness and trust with respect to the long and awkward sentences of English. However, Lewis's account requires not just any kind of regularity, it requires a conventional regularity. Now, for a regularity to be conventional, it must be one of several regularities that would equally have served the communicative interests of the population, and *which are incompatible with one another* in the sense that one couldn't conform to several of them at once. Hawthorne's point concerns the fragment of English that contains only the long and awkward sentences: he says that 'the population couldn't fail to be truthful' (p. 247) in that language, so that there is no alternative regularity and *a fortiori* the vacuous regularity of truthfulness and trust in that fragment of English is not conventional. It might seem that this is not a problem for Lewis, for why should we say that we use that fragment of English which contains all the unuseably long sentences? We will leave it to the reader to work out why Hawthorne thinks this is a problem (hint: the answer is contained in the paragraph from which I have just quoted).

Stephen Laurence, in his paper, articulates more fundamental opposition to Lewis's account, which he takes to be exemplary of convention-based accounts. Laurence not only presents a number of objections to Lewis, he also sketches an alternative, 'Chomskyan' view. Lewis's account of linguistic conventions (which is nicely summarized in section 2 of Laurence's paper), requires that the users of a natural language have complex mental states – knowledge, beliefs and preferences – regarding the speech behaviour of all users (readers are encouraged to re-examine Lewis's account to establish the exact nature of the mental states required by Lewis). This, Laurence argues, suggests a strong correlation of linguistic abilities with general reasoning abilities and intelligence. But psychological data do not bear out this correlation, for there are humans who have impressive linguistic abilities, yet lack general reasoning abilities, and there are also humans with good general reasoning abilities but who lack linguistic abilities. Moreover, Laurence claims, any account of the conventions of language must allow for the conventionality not just of the semantic properties of utterances, but also of the conventionality of, for example, their syntactic properties. According to Laurence, Lewis's account does not make room for the latter.

On Laurence's alternative, 'Chomskyan' account, the linguistic properties of utterances are the result of the representations a dedicated human language-processing faculty associates with these utterances. This, he claims, explains the lack of correlation between general intelligence and linguistic competence. He also claims that this account extends naturally to the conventionality of syntax.

Questions and tasks

1   Consider Lewis's definition of convention in detail. Why does Lewis require that a conventional regularity be one of several regularities conformity to which would be preferred by participants if they believed others conform to it (condition [5])?

2   Suppose a member of a population witnesses an utterance of 'I am glad you could come', yet does not come to believe that the speaker is glad that she could come. Would this show that that population does not use English? Suppose that not just one member of the population once responds in this way, but that a substantial number of members do so frequently. Would *this* show that the population does not use English?

3   Is it plausible to say that language users have complex mutual knowledge of the sort spelled out in Lewis's definition of convention? What exactly does Lewis say about the psychological reality of linguistic conventions?

4   Does Lewis have a good answer to Hawthorne (Lewis 1992)?

5   Is Laurence right to claim that Lewis's account is inapplicable to the conventionality of syntax?

6   Does Lewis's account predict a correlation between linguistic ability and general intelligence?

7   Spell out Laurence's own proposal. Is this a viable alternative?

References and further reading

Avramides, Anita 1997: 'Intention and Convention', in B. Hale and C. Wright (eds), *A Companion to the Philosophy of Language*, Oxford: Blackwell, pp. 60–86.

Barber, Alex 2009: 'Idiolects', in Edward N. Zalta (ed.), *The Stanford Encyclopedia of Philosophy* (Spring 2009 edn), http://plato.stanford.edu/archives/spr2009/entries/idiolects

Bennett, Jonathan 1976: *Linguistic Behaviour*, Cambridge: Cambridge University Press.

Burge, Tyler 1975: 'On Knowledge and Convention', *Philosophical Review* 84, pp. 249–55.

Davidson, Donald 1973: 'Radical Interpretation', *Dialectica* 27, pp. 313–23; reprinted in D. Davidson, *Inquiries into Truth and Interpretation*, Oxford: Oxford University Press (1984), pp. 125–39.

Davidson, Donald 1982: 'Communication and Convention', in *Inquiries into Truth and Interpretation*, Oxford: Oxford University Press 1984, pp. 265–80.

Davidson, Donald 1986: 'A Nice Derangement of Epitaphs', in E. Lepore (ed.), *Truth and Interpretation: Perspectives on the Philosophy of Donald Davidson*, Oxford: Blackwell.

Gilbert, Margaret 1981: 'Game Theory and Convention', *Synthese* 46, pp. 41–93.

Grice, H. Paul 1968: 'Utterer's Meaning, Sentence–Meaning and Word–Meaning', *Foundations of Language* 4, pp. 1–18; reprinted in H. P. Grice, *Studies in the Way of Words*, Cambridge, MA: Harvard University Press (1989), pp. 117–37.

Higginbotham, James 1991: 'Remarks on the Metaphysics of Linguistics', *Linguistics and Philosophy* 14, pp. 555–66.

Kölbel, Max 1998: 'Lewis, Language, Lust and Lies', *Inquiry* 41, pp. 301–15.

Lewis, David 1969: *Convention*, Oxford: Blackwell.

Lewis, David 1992: 'Meaning without Use: Reply to Hawthorne', *Australasian Journal of Philosophy* 70, pp. 106–110.

McDowell, John 1980: 'Meaning, Communication and Knowledge', in Z. van Straaten (ed.), *Philosophical Subjects: Essays Presented to P.F. Strawson*, Oxford: Oxford University Press, pp. 117–35; reprinted in J. McDowell, *Meaning, Knowledge and Reality*, Cambridge, MA: Harvard University Press (1998).

Millikan, Ruth G. 2005: *Language: a Biological Model*, Oxford: Oxford University Press.

O'Leary-Hawthorne, John 1993: 'Meaning and Evidence: A Reply to Lewis', *Australasian Journal of Philosophy* 71, pp. 206–11.

Pietroski, Paul 2003: 'The Character of Natural Language Semantics', in A. Barber (ed.), *Epistemology of Language*, Oxford: Oxford University Press, pp. 217–56.

Rumfitt, Ian 1995: 'Truth Conditions and Communication', *Mind* 104, pp. 827–62.

Schiffer, Stephen 1993: 'Actual Language Relations', *Philosophical Perspectives* 7: *Language and Logic*, pp. 231–58.

Wilson, Deirdre, and Dan Sperber 2002: 'Truthfulness and Relevance', *Mind* 111, pp. 583–633.

Chapter 15

David K. Lewis

LANGUAGES AND LANGUAGE

I Thesis

What is a language? Something which assigns meanings to certain strings of types of sounds or of marks. It could therefore be a function, a set of ordered pairs of strings and meanings. The entities in the domain of the function are certain finite sequences of types of vocal sounds, or of types of inscribable marks; if σ is in the domain of a language L, let us call σ a *sentence* of L. The entities in the range of the function are meanings: if σ is a sentence of L, let us call $L(\sigma)$ the *meaning* of σ in L. What could a meaning of a sentence be? Something which, when combined with factual information about the world—or factual information about *any* possible world—yields a truth-value. It could therefore be a function from worlds to truth-values—or more simply, a set of worlds. We can say that a sentence σ is *true* in a language L at a world w if and only if w belongs to the set of worlds $L(\sigma)$. We can say that σ is *true* in L (without mentioning a world) if and only if our actual world belongs to $L(\sigma)$. We can say that σ is *analytic in* L if and only if every possible world belongs to $L(\sigma)$. And so on, in the obvious way.

II Antithesis

What is a language? A social phenomenon which is part of the natural history of human beings; a sphere of human action, wherein people utter strings of vocal sounds, or inscribe strings of marks, and wherein people respond by thought or action to the sounds or marks which they observe to have been so produced.

This verbal activity is, for the most part, rational. He who produces certain sounds or marks does so for a reason. He knows that someone else, upon hearing his sounds or seeing his marks, is apt to form a certain belief or act in a certain way. He wants, for some reason, to bring about that belief or action. Thus his beliefs and desires give him a reason to produce the sounds or marks, and he does. He who responds to the sounds or marks in a certain way also does so for a reason. He knows how the production of sounds or marks depends upon the producer's state of mind. When he observes the sounds or marks, he is therefore in a position to infer something about the producer's state of mind. He can probably also infer something about the conditions which caused that state of mind. He may merely come to believe these conclusions, or he may act upon them in accordance with his other beliefs and his desires.

Not only do both have reasons for thinking and acting as they do; they know something about each other, so each is in a position to replicate the other's reasons. Each one's replication of the other's reasons forms part of his own reason for thinking and acting as he does; and each is in a position to replicate the other's replication of his own reasons. Therefore the Gricean mechanism[1] operates: X intends to bring about a response on the part of Y by getting Y to recognize that X intends to bring about that response; Y does recognize X's intention, and is thereby given some sort of reason to respond just as X intended him to.

Within any suitable population, various regularities can be found in this rational verbal activity. There are regularities whereby the production of sounds or marks depends upon various aspects of the state of mind of the producer. There are regularities whereby various aspects of responses to sounds or marks depend upon the sounds or marks to which one is responding. Some of these regularities are accidental. Others can be explained, and different ones can be explained in very different ways.

Some of them can be explained as conventions of the population in which they prevail. Conventions are regularities in action, or in action and belief, which are arbitrary but perpetuate themselves because they serve some sort of common interest. Past conformity breeds future conformity because it gives one a reason to go on conforming; but there is some alternative regularity which could have served instead, and would have perpetuated itself in the same way if only it had got started.

More precisely: a regularity R, in action or in action and belief, is a *convention* in a population P if and only if, within P, the following six conditions hold. (Or at least they almost hold. A few exceptions to the "everyone"s can be tolerated.)

(1) Everyone conforms to R.
(2) Everyone believes that the others conform to R.
(3) This belief that the others conform to R gives everyone a good and decisive reason to conform to R himself. His reason may be that, in particular, those of the others he is now dealing with conform to R; or his reason may be that there is general or widespread conformity, or that there has been, or that there will be. His reason may

be a practical reason, if conforming to R is a matter of acting in a certain way; or it may be an epistemic reason, if conforming to R is a matter of believing in a certain way. First case: according to his beliefs, some desired end may be reached by means of some sort of action in conformity to R, provided that the others (all or some of them) also conform to R; therefore he wants to conform to R if they do. Second case: his beliefs, together with the premise that others conform to R, deductively imply or inductively support some conclusions; and in believing this conclusion, he would thereby conform to R. Thus reasons for conforming to a convention by believing something—like reasons for belief in general—are believed premises tending to confirm the truth of the belief in question. Note that I am *not* speaking here of practical reasons for acting so as to somehow produce in oneself a certain desired belief.

(4) There is a general preference for general conformity to R rather than slightly-less-than-general conformity—in particular, rather than conformity by all but any one. (This is not to deny that some state of *widespread* nonconformity to R might be even more preferred.) Thus everyone who believes that at least almost everyone conforms to R will want the others, as well as himself, to conform. This condition serves to distinguish cases of convention, in which there is a predominant coincidence of interest, from cases of deadlocked conflict. In the latter cases, it may be that each is doing the best he can by conforming to R, given that the others do so; but each wishes the others did not conform to R, since he could then gain at their expense.

(5) R is not the only possible regularity meeting the last two conditions. There is at least one alternative R′ such that the belief that the others conformed to R′ would give

everyone a good and decisive practical or epistemic reason to conform to R′ likewise; such that there is a general preference for general conformity to R′ rather than slightly-less-than-general conformity to R′; and such that there is normally no way of conforming to R and R′ both. Thus the alternative R′ could have perpetuated itself as a convention instead of R; this condition provides for the characteristic arbitrariness of conventions.

(6) Finally, the various facts listed in conditions (1) to (5) are matters of *common* (or *mutual*) *knowledge*: they are known to everyone, it is known to everyone that they are known to everyone, and so on. The knowledge mentioned here may be merely potential: knowledge that would be available if one bothered to think hard enough. Everyone must potentially know that (1) to (5) hold; potentially know that the others potentially know it; and so on. This condition ensures stability. If anyone tries to replicate another's reasoning, perhaps including the other's replication of his own reasoning, ..., the result will reinforce rather than subvert his expectation of conformity to R. Perhaps a negative version of (6) would do the job: no one disbelieves that (1) to (5) hold, no one believes that others disbelieve this, and so on.

This definition can be tried out on all manner of regularities which we would be inclined to call conventions. It is a convention to drive on the right. It is a convention to mark poisons with skull and crossbones. It is a convention to dress as we do. It is a convention to train beasts to turn right on "gee" and left on "haw." It is a convention to give goods and services in return for certain pieces of paper or metal. And so on.

The common interests which sustain conventions are as varied as the conventions themselves.

Our convention to drive on the right is sustained by our interest in not colliding. Our convention for marking poisons is sustained by our interest in making it easy for everyone to recognize poisons. Our conventions of dress might be sustained by a common aesthetic preference for somewhat uniform dress, or by the low cost of mass-produced clothes, or by a fear on everyone's part that peculiar dress might be thought to manifest a peculiar character, or by a desire on everyone's part not to be too conspicuous, or—most likely—by a mixture of these and many other interests.

It is a platitude—something only a philosopher would dream of denying—that there are conventions of language, although we do not find it easy to say what those conventions are. If we look for the fundamental difference in verbal behavior between members of two linguistic communities, we can be sure of finding something which is arbitrary but perpetuates itself because of a common interest in coordination. In the case of conventions of language, that common interest derives from our common interest in taking advantage of, and in preserving, our ability to control others' beliefs and actions to some extent by means of sounds and marks. That interest in turn derives from many miscellaneous desires we have; to list them, list the ways you would be worse off in Babel.

III Synthesis

What have languages to do with language? What is the connection between what I have called *languages*, functions from strings of sounds or of marks to sets of possible worlds, semantic systems discussed in complete abstraction from human affairs, and what I have called *language*, a form of rational, convention-governed human social activity? We know what to *call* this connection we are after: we can say that a given language L is *used by*, or is a (or the) language *of*, a given population P. We know also that this connection holds by virtue of the conventions of language prevailing in P. Under suitably different conventions, a different language would be used by P. There is some sort of convention whereby P uses L—but what is it? It is worthless to call it a convention to use L, even if it can correctly be so described, for we want to know what it is to use L.

My proposal[2] is that the convention whereby a population P uses a language L is a convention of *truthfulness* and *trust* in L. To be truthful in L is to act in a certain way: to try never to utter any sentences of L that are not true in L. Thus it is to avoid uttering any sentence of L unless one believes it to be true in L. To be trusting in L is to form beliefs in a certain way: to impute truthfulness in L to others, and thus to tend to respond to another's utterance of any sentence of L by coming to believe that the uttered sentence is true in L.

Suppose that a certain language L is used by a certain population P. Let this be a perfect case of normal language use. Imagine what would go on; and review the definition of a convention to verify that there does prevail in P a convention of truthfulness and trust in L.

(1) There prevails in P at least a regularity of truthfulness and trust in L. The members of P frequently speak (or write) sentences of L to one another. When they do, ordinarily the speaker (or writer) utters one of the sentences he believes to be true in L; and the hearer (or reader) responds by coming to share that belief of the speaker's (unless he already had it), and adjusting his other beliefs accordingly.

(2) The members of P believe that this regularity of truthfulness and trust in L prevails among them. Each believes this because of his experience of others' past truthfulness and trust in L.

(3) The expectation of conformity ordinarily gives everyone a good reason why he himself should conform. If he is a speaker, he expects his hearer to be trusting in L; wherefore he has reason to expect that by uttering certain sentences that are true in L according to his beliefs—by

being truthful in L in a certain way—he can impart certain beliefs that he takes to be correct. Commonly, a speaker has some reason or other for wanting to impart some or other correct beliefs. Therefore his beliefs and desires constitute a practical reason for acting in the way he does: for uttering some sentence truthfully in L.

As for the hearer: he expects the speaker to be truthful in L, wherefore he has good reason to infer that the speaker's sentence is true in L according to the speaker's beliefs. Commonly, a hearer also has some or other reason to believe that the speaker's beliefs are correct (by and large, and perhaps with exceptions for certain topics); so it is reasonable for him to infer that the sentence he has heard is probably true in L. Thus his beliefs about the speaker give him an epistemic reason to respond trustingly in L.

We have coordination between truthful speaker and trusting hearer. Each conforms as he does to the prevailing regularity of truthfulness and trust in L because he expects complementary conformity on the part of the other.

But there is also a more diffuse and indirect sort of coordination. In coordinating with his present partner, a speaker or hearer also is coordinating with all those whose past truthfulness and trust in L have contributed to his partner's present expectations. This indirect coordination is a four-way affair: between present speakers and past speakers, present speakers and past hearers, present hearers and past speakers, and present hearers and past hearers. And whereas the direct coordination between a speaker and his hearer is a coordination of truthfulness with trust for a single sentence of L, the indirect coordination with one's partner's previous partners (and with *their* previous partners, etc.) may involve various sentences of L. It may happen that a hearer, say, has never before encountered the sentence now addressed to him; but he forms the appropriate belief on hearing it—one such that he has responded trustingly in L—because his past experience with truthfulness in L has involved many sentences grammatically related to this one.

(4) There is in P a general preference for general conformity to the regularity of truthfulness and trust in L. Given that most conform, the members of P want all to conform. They desire truthfulness and trust in L from each other, as well as from themselves. This general preference is sustained by a common interest in communication. Everyone wants occasionally to impart correct beliefs and bring about appropriate actions in others by means of sounds and marks. Everyone wants to preserve his ability to do so at will. Everyone wants to be able to learn about the parts of the world that he cannot observe for himself by observing instead the sounds and marks of his fellows who have been there.

(5) The regularity of truthfulness and trust in L has alternatives. Let L′ be any language that does not overlap L in such a way that is is possible to be truthful and trusting simultaneously in L and in L′, and that is rich and convenient enough to meet the needs of P for communication. Then the regularity of truthfulness and trust in L′ is an alternative to the prevailing regularity of truthfulness and trust in L. For the alternative regularity, as for the actual one, general conformity by the others would give one a reason to conform; and general conformity would be generally preferred over slightly-less-than-general conformity.

(6) Finally, all these facts are common knowledge in P. Everyone knows them, everyone knows that everyone knows them, and so on. Or at any rate none believes that another doubts them, none believes that another believes that another doubts them, and so on.

In any case in which a language L clearly is used by a population P, then, it seems that there prevails in P a convention of truthfulness and trust in L, sustained by an interest in communication. The converse is supported by an unsuccessful search for counterexamples: I have not been able to think of any case in which there is

such a convention and yet the language L is clearly not used in the population P. Therefore I adopt this definition, claiming that it agrees with ordinary usage in the cases in which ordinary usage is fully determinate:

a language L is *used by* a population P if and only if there prevails in P a convention of truthfulness and trust in L, sustained by an interest in communication.

Such conventions, I claim, provide the desired connection between languages and language-using populations.

Once we understand how languages are connected to populations, whether by conventions of truthfulness and trust for the sake of communication or in some other way, we can proceed to redefine relative to a population all those semantic concepts that we previously defined relative to a language. A string of sounds or of marks is a *sentence of* P if and only if it is a sentence of some language L which is used in P. It has a certain *meaning in* P if and only if it has that meaning in some language L which is used in P. It is *true in* P at a world w if and only if it is true at w in some language L which is used in P. It is *true in P* if and only if it is true in some language L which is used in P.

The account just given of conventions in general, and of conventions of language in particular, differs in one important respect from the account given in my book *Convention*.[3]

Formerly, the crucial clause in the definition of convention was stated in terms of a conditional preference for conformity: each prefers to conform if the others do, and it would be the same for the alternatives to the actual convention. (In some versions of the definition, this condition was subsumed under a broader requirement of general preference for general conformity.) The point of this was to explain why the belief that others conform would give everyone a reason for conforming likewise, and so to explain the rational self-perpetuation of conventions. But a reason involving preference in this way must be a practical reason for acting, not an epistemic reason for believing. Therefore I said that conventions were regularities in action alone. It made no sense to speak of believing something in conformity to convention. (Except in the peculiar case that others' conformity to the convention gives one a practical reason to conform by acting to somehow produce a belief in oneself; but I knew that this case was irrelevant to ordinary language use.) Thus I was cut off from what I now take to be the primary sort of conventional coordination in language use: that between the action of the truthful speaker and the responsive believing of his trusting hearer. I resorted to two different substitutes.

Sometimes it is common knowledge how the hearer will want to act if he forms various beliefs, and we can think of the speaker not only as trying to impart beliefs but also as trying thereby to get the hearer to act in a way that speaker and hearer alike deem appropriate under the circumstances that the speaker believes to obtain. Then we have speaker-hearer coordination of action. Both conform to a convention of truthfulness for the speaker plus appropriate responsive action by the hearer. The hearer's trustful believing need not be part of the content of the convention, though it must be mentioned to explain why the hearer acts in conformity. In this way we reach the account of "signaling" in *Convention*, chapter IV.

But signaling was all-too-obviously a special case. There may be no appropriate responsive action for the hearer to perform when the speaker imparts a belief to him. Or the speaker and hearer may disagree about how the hearer ought to act under the supposed circumstances. Or the speaker may not know how the hearer will decide to act; or the hearer may not know that he knows; and so on. The proper hearer's response to consider is *believing*, but that is not ordinarily an action. So in considering language use in general, in *Convention*, chapter V, I was forced to give up on speaker-hearer coordin-

ation. I took instead the diffuse coordination between the present speaker and the past speakers who trained the present hearer. Accordingly, I proposed that the convention whereby a population P used a language L was simply a convention of truthfulness in L. Speakers conform; hearers do not, until they become speakers in their turn, if they ever do.

I think now that I went wrong when I went beyond the special case of signaling. I should have kept my original emphasis on speaker-hearer coordination, broadening the definition of convention to fit. It was Jonathan Bennett[4] who showed me how that could be done: by restating the crucial defining clause not in terms of preference for conformity but rather in terms of reasons for conformity—practical *or epistemic* reasons. The original conditional preference requirement gives way now to clause (3): the belief that others conform gives everyone a reason to conform likewise, and it would be the same for the alternatives to the actual convention. Once this change is made, there is no longer any obstacle to including the hearer's trust as part of the content of a convention.

(The old conditional preference requirement is retained, however, in consequence of the less important clause (4). Clause (3) as applied to practical reasons, but not as applied to epistemic reasons, may be subsumed under (4).)

Bennett pointed out one advantage of the change: suppose there is only one speaker of an idiolect, but several hearers who can understand him. Shouldn't he and his hearers comprise a population that uses his idiolect? More generally, what is the difference between (a) someone who does not utter sentences of a language because he does not belong to any population that uses it, and (b) someone who does not utter sentences of the language although he does belong to such a population because at present—or always, perhaps—he has nothing to say? Both are alike, so far as action in conformity to a convention of truthfulness goes. Both are vacuously truthful. In *Convention* I made it a condition of truthfulness in

L that one sometimes does utter sentences of L, though not that one speaks up on any particular occasion. But that is unsatisfactory: what degree of truthful talkativeness does it take to keep up one's active membership in a language-using population? What if someone just never thought of anything worth saying?

(There is a less important difference between my former account and the present one. Then and now, I wanted to insist that cases of convention are cases of predominant coincidence of interest. I formerly provided for this by a defining clause that seems now unduly restrictive; in any instance of the situation to which the convention applies, everyone has approximately the same preferences regarding all possible combinations of actions. Why *all*? It may be enough that they agree in preferences to the extent specified in my present clause (4). Thus I have left out the further agreement-in-preference clause.)

IV Objections and replies

Objection: Many things which meet the definition of a language given in the thesis—many functions from strings of sounds or of marks to sets of possible worlds—are not really possible languages. They could not possibly be adopted by any human population. There may be too few sentences, or too few meanings, to make as many discriminations as language-users need to communicate. The meanings may not be anything language-users would wish to communicate about. The sentences may be very long, impossible to pronounce, or otherwise clumsy. The language may be humanly unlearnable because it has no grammar, or a grammar of the wrong kind.

Reply: Granted. The so-called languages of the thesis are merely an easily specified superset of the languages we are really interested in. A language in a narrower and more natural sense is any one of these entities that could possibly—possibly in some appropriately strict sense—be used by a human population.

Objection: The so-called languages discussed in the thesis are excessively simplified. There is no provision for indexical sentences, dependent on features of the context of their utterance: for instance, tensed sentences, sentences with personal pronouns or demonstratives, or anaphoric sentences. There is no provision for ambiguous sentences. There is no provision for non-indicative sentences: imperatives, questions, promises and threats, permissions, and so on.

Reply: Granted. I have this excuse: the phenomenon of language would be not too different if these complications did not exist, so we cannot go too far wrong by ignoring them. Nevertheless, let us sketch what could be done to provide for indexicality, ambiguity, or non-indicatives. In order not to pile complication on complication we shall take only one at a time.

We may define an *indexical language* L as a function that assigns sets of possible worlds not to its sentences themselves, but rather to sentences paired with possible occasions of their utterance. We can say that σ is true in L at a world w on a possible occasion o of the utterance of σ if and only if w belongs to $L(\sigma, o)$. We can say that σ is true in L on o (without mentioning a world) if and only if the world in which o is located—our actual world if o is an actual occasion of utterance of σ, or some other world if not—belongs to $L(\sigma, o)$. We can say that a speaker is truthful in L if he tries not to utter any sentence σ of L unless σ would be true in L on the occasion of his utterance of σ. We can say that a hearer is trusting in L if he believes an uttered sentence of L to be true in L on its occasion of utterance.

We may define an *ambiguous language* L as a function that assigns to its sentences not single meanings, but finite sets of alternative meanings. (We might or might not want to stipulate that these sets are non-empty.) We can say that a sentence σ is true in L at w under some meaning if and only if w belongs to some member of $L(\sigma)$. We can say that σ is true in L under some meaning if and only if our actual world belongs to some member of $L(\sigma)$. We can say that someone is (minimally) truthful in L if he tries not to utter any sentence σ of L unless σ is true in L under some meaning. He is trusting if he believes an uttered sentence of L to be true in L under some meaning.

We may define a *polymodal language* L as a function which assigns to its sentences meanings containing two components: a set of worlds, as before; and something we can call a *mood*: indicative, imperative, etc. (It makes no difference what things these are—they might, for instance, be taken as code numbers.) We can say that a sentence σ is indicative, imperative, etc., in L according as the mood-component of the meaning L(σ) is indicative, imperative, etc. We can say that a sentence σ is true in L, regardless of its mood in L, if and only if our actual world belongs to the set-of-worlds-component of the meaning L(σ). We can say that someone is truthful in L with respect to indicatives if he tries not to utter any indicative sentence of L which is not true in L; truthful in L with respect to imperatives if he tries to act in such a way as to make true in L any imperative sentence of L that is addressed to him by someone in a relation of authority to him; and so on for other moods. He is trusting in L with respect to indicatives if he believes uttered indicative sentences of L to be true in L; trusting in L with respect to imperatives if he expects his utterance of an imperative sentence of L to result in the addressee's acting in such a way as to make that sentence true in L, provided he is in a relation of authority to the addressee; and so on. We can say simply that he is truthful and trusting in L if he is so with respect to all moods that occur in L. It is by virtue of the various ways in which the various moods enter into the definition of truthfulness and of trust that they deserve the familiar names we have given them. (I am deliberately stretching the ordinary usage of "true," "truthfulness," and "trust" in extending them to non-indicatives. For instance, truthfulness with respect to imperatives is roughly what we might call *obedience* in L.)

Any natural language is simultaneously index-ical, ambiguous, and polymodal; I leave the combination of complications as an exercise. Henceforth, for the most part, I shall lapse into ignoring indexicality, ambiguity, and non-indicatives.

Objection: We cannot always discover the meaning of a sentence in a population just by looking into the minds of the members of the population, no matter what we look for there. We may also need some information about the causal origin of what we find in their minds. So, in particular, we cannot always discover the meaning of a sentence in a population just by looking at the conventions prevailing therein. Consider an example: What is the meaning of the sentence "Mik Karthee was wise" in the language of our 137th-century descendants, if all we can find in any of their minds is the inadequate dictionary entry: "Mik Karthee: controversial American politician of the early atomic age"? It depends, we might think, partly on which man stands at the beginning of the long causal chain ending in that inadequate dictionary entry.

Reply: If this doctrine is correct, I can treat it as a subtle sort of indexicality. The set of worlds in which a sentence σ is true in a language L may depend on features of possible occasions of utterance of σ. One feature of a possible occasion of utterance—admittedly a more recondite feature than the time, place, or speaker—is the causal history of a dictionary entry in a speaker's mind.

As with other kinds of indexicality, we face a problem of nomenclature. Let a *meaning₁* be that which an indexical language L assigns to a sentence σ on a possible occasion o of its utterance: L(σ, o), a set of worlds on our account. Let a *meaning₂* be that fixed function whereby the meaning₁ in L of a sentence σ varies with its occasions of utterance. Which one is a meaning? That is unclear—and it is no clearer which one is a sense, intension, interpretation, truth-condition, or proposition.

The objection says that we sometimes cannot find the meaning₁ of σ on o in P by looking into the minds of members of P Granted. But what prevents it is that the minds do not contain enough information about *o*: in particular, not enough information about its causal history. We have been given no reason to doubt that we can find the meaning$_2$ of σ in P by looking into minds; and that is all we need do to identify the indexical language used by P.

An exactly similar situation arises with more familiar kinds of indexicality. We may be unable to discover the time of an utterance of a tensed sentence by looking into minds, so we may know the meaning$_2$ of the sentence uttered in the speaker's indexical language without knowing its meaning$_1$ on the occasion in question.

Objection: It makes no sense to say that a mere string of sounds or of marks can bear a meaning or a truth-value. The proper bearers of meanings and truth-values are particular speech acts.

Reply: I do not say that a string of types of sounds or of marks, by itself, can bear a meaning or truth-value. I say it bears a meaning and truth-value relative to a language, or relative to a population. A particular speech act by itself, on the other hand, can bear a meaning and truth-value, since in most cases it uniquely determines the language that was in use on the occasion of its performance. So can a particular uttered string of vocal sounds, or a particular inscribed string of marks, since in most cases that uniquely determines the particular speech act in which it was produced, which in turn uniquely determines the language.

Objection: It is circular to give an account of meanings in terms of possible worlds. The notion of a possible world must itself be explained in semantic terms. Possible worlds are models of the analytic sentences of some language, or they are the diagrams or theories of such models.[5]

Reply: I do not agree that the notion of a possible world ought to be explained in semantic terms, or that possible worlds ought to be eliminated from our ontology and replaced by their linguistic representatives—models or whatever.

For one thing, the replacement does not work properly. Two worlds indistinguishable in the representing language will receive one and the same representative.

But more important, the replacement is gratuitous. The notion of a possible world is familiar in its own right, philosophically fruitful, and tolerably clear. Possible worlds are deemed mysterious and objectionable because they raise questions we may never know how to answer: are any possible worlds five-dimensional? We seem to think that we do not understand possible worlds at all unless we are capable of omniscience about them—but why should we think that? Sets also raise unanswerable questions, yet most of us do not repudiate sets.

But if you insist on repudiating possible worlds, much of my theory can be adapted to meet your needs. We must suppose that you have already defined truth and analyticity in some base language—that is the price you pay for repudiating possible worlds—and you want to define them in general, for the language of an arbitrary population P. Pick your favorite base language with any convenient special properties you like: Latin, Esperanto, Begriffsschrift, Semantic Markerese, or what have you. Let's say you pick Latin. Then you may redefine a language as any function from certain strings of sound or of marks to sentences of Latin. A sentence σ of a language L (in your sense) is true, analytic, etc., if and only if $L(\sigma)$ is true, analytic, etc., in Latin.

You cannot believe in languages in my sense, since they involve possible worlds. But I can believe in languages in your sense. And I can map your languages onto mine by means of a fixed function from sentences of Latin to sets of worlds. This function is just the language Latin, in my sense. My language L is the composition of two functions: your language L, and my language Latin. Thus I can accept your approach as part of mine.

Objection: Why all this needless and outmoded hypostasis of meanings? Our ordinary talk about meaning does not commit us to believing in any such entities as meanings, any more than our ordinary talk about actions for the sake of ends commits us to believing in any such entities as sakes.

Reply: Perhaps there are some who hypostatize meanings compulsively, imagining that they could not possibly make sense of our ordinary talk about meaning if they did not. Not I. I hypostatize meanings because I find it convenient to do so, and I have no good reason not to. There is no point in being a part-time nominalist. I am persuaded on independent grounds that I ought to believe in possible worlds and possible beings therein, and that I ought to believe in sets of things I believe in. Once I have these, I have all the entities I could ever want.

Objection: A language consists not only of sentences with their meanings, but also of constituents of sentences—things sentences are made of—with their meanings. And if any language is to be learnable without being finite, it must somehow be determined by finitely many of its constituents and finitely many operations on constituents.

Reply: We may define a class of objects called *grammars*. A grammar Γ is a triple comprising (1) a large finite *lexicon* of *elementary constituents* paired with meanings; (2) a finite set of *combining operations* which build larger constituents by combining smaller constituents, and derive a meaning for the new constituent out of the meanings of the old ones; and (3) a *representing operation* which effectively maps certain constituents onto strings of sounds or of marks. A grammar Γ generates a function which assigns meanings to certain constituents, called *constituents in* Γ. It generates another function which assigns meanings to certain strings of sounds or of marks. Part of this latter function is what we have hitherto called a language. A grammar uniquely determines the language it generates. But a language does not uniquely determine the grammar that generates it, not even when we disregard superficial differences between grammars.

I have spoken of meanings for constituents in a grammar, but what sort of things are these? Referential semantics tried to answer that question. It was a near miss, failing because contingent facts got mixed up with the meanings. The cure, discovered by Carnap,[6] is to do referential semantics not just in our actual world but in every possible world. A meaning for a name can be a function from worlds to possible individuals; for a common noun, a function from worlds to sets; for a sentence, a function from worlds to truth-values (or more simply, the set of worlds where that function takes the value truth). Other derived categories may be defined by their characteristic modes of combination. For instance, an adjective combines with a common noun to make a compound common noun; so its meaning may be a function from common-noun meanings to common-noun meanings, such that the meaning of an adjective-plus-common-noun compound is the value of this function when given as argument the meaning of the common noun being modified. Likewise a verb phrase takes a name to make a sentence; so its meaning may be a function that takes the meaning of the name as argument to give the meaning of the sentence as value. An adverb (of one sort) takes a verb phrase to make a verb phrase, so its meaning may be a function from verb-phrase meanings to verb-phrase meanings. And so on, as far as need be, to more and more complicated derived categories.[7]

If you repudiate possible worlds, an alternative course is open to you: let the meanings for constituents in a grammar be phrases of Latin, or whatever your favorite base language may be.

A grammar, for us, is a semantically interpreted grammar—just as a language is a semantically interpreted language. We shall not be concerned with what are called grammars or languages in a purely syntactic sense. My definition of a grammar is meant to be general enough to encompass transformational or phrase-structure grammars for natural language[8] (when provided with semantic interpretations) as well as systems of formation and valuation rules for formalized languages. Like my previous definition of a language, my definition of a grammar is too general: it gives a large superset of the interesting grammars.

A grammar, like a language, is a set-theoretical entity which can be discussed in complete abstraction from human affairs. Since a grammar generates a unique language, all the semantic concepts we earlier defined relative to a language L—sentencehood, truth, analyticity, etc.—could just as well have been defined relative to a grammar Γ. We can also handle other semantic concepts pertaining to constituents, or to the constituent structure of sentences.

We can define the meaning in Γ, denotation in Γ, etc., of a subsentential constituent in Γ. We can define the meaning in Γ, denotation in Γ, etc., of a *phrase*: a string of sounds or of marks representing a subsentential constituent in Γ via the representing operation of Γ. We can define something we may call the *fine structure of meaning* in Γ of a sentence or phrase: the manner in which the meaning of the sentence or phrase is derived from the meanings of its constituents and the way it is built out of them. Thus we can take account of the sense in which, for instance, different analytic sentences are said to differ in meaning.

Now the objection can be restated: what ought to be called a language is what I have hitherto called a grammar, not what I have hitherto called a language. Different grammar, different language—at least if we ignore superficial differences between grammars. Verbal disagreement aside, the place I gave to my so-called languages ought to have been given instead to my so-called grammars. Why not begin by saying what it is for a grammar Γ to be used by a population P? Then we could go on to define sentencehood, truth, analyticity, etc., in P as sentencehood, truth, analyticity, etc., in whatever grammar is used by P. This approach would have the advantage that we could handle the semantics of constituents in a population in an

exactly similar way. We could say that a constituent or phrase has a certain meaning, denotation, etc., in P if it has that meaning, denotation, etc., in whatever grammar is used by P. We could say that a sentence or phrase has a certain fine structure of meaning in P if it has it in whatever grammar is used by P.

Unfortunately, I know of no promising way to make objective sense of the assertion that a grammar Γ is used by a population P whereas another grammar Γ' which generates the same language as Γ, is not. I have tried to say how there are facts about P which objectively select the languages used by P. I am not sure there are facts about P which objectively select privileged grammars for those languages. It is easy enough to define truthfulness and trust in a grammar, but that will not help: a convention of truthfulness and trust in Γ will also be a convention of truthfulness and trust in Γ' whenever Γ and Γ' generate the same language.

I do not propose to discard the notion of the meaning in P of a constituent or phrase, or the fine structure of meaning in P of a sentence. To propose that would be absurd. But I hold that these notions depend on our methods of evaluating grammars, and therefore are no clearer and no more objective than our notion of a *best* grammar for a given language. For I would say that a grammar Γ is used by P if and only if Γ is a best grammar for a language L that is used by P in virtue of a convention of P of truthfulness and trust in L; and I would define the meaning in P of a constituent or phrase, and the fine structure of meaning in P of a sentence, accordingly.

The notions of a language used by P, of a meaning of a sentence in P, and so on, are independent of our evaluation of grammars. Therefore I take these as primary. The point is not to refrain from ever saying anything that depends on the evaluation of grammars. The point is to do so only when we must, and that is why I have concentrated on languages rather than grammars.

We may meet little practical difficulty with

the semantics of constituents in populations, even if its foundations are as infirm as I fear. It may often happen that all the grammars anyone might call best for a given language will agree on the meaning of a given constituent. Yet there is trouble to be found: Quine's examples of indeterminacy of reference[9] seem to be disagreements in constituent semantics between alternative good grammars for one language. We should regard with suspicion any method that purports to settle objectively whether, in some tribe, "gavagai" is true of temporally continuant rabbits or time-slices thereof. You can give their language a good grammar of either kind—and that's that.

It is useful to divide the claimed indeterminacy of constituent semantics into three separate indeterminacies. We begin with undoubted objective fact: the dependence of the subject's behavioral output on his input of sensory stimulation (both as it actually is and as it might have been) together with all the physical laws and anatomical facts that explain it. (a) This information either determines or under-determines the subject's system of propositional attitudes: in particular, his beliefs and desires. (b) These propositional attitudes either determine or underdetermine the truth conditions of full sentences—what I have here called his language. (c) The truth conditions of full sentences either determine or underdetermine the meanings of sub-sentential constituents—what I have here called his grammar.

My present discussion has been directed at the middle step, from beliefs and desires to truth conditions for full sentences. I have said that the former determine the latter—provided (what need not be the case) that the beliefs and desires of the subject and his fellows are such as to comprise a fully determinate convention of truthfulness and trust in some definite language. I have said nothing here about the determinacy of the first step; and I am inclined to share in Quine's doubts about the determinacy of the third step.

Objection: Suppose that whenever anyone is party to a convention of truthfulness and trust in any language L, his competence to be party to that convention—to conform, to expect conformity, etc.—is due to his possession of some sort of unconscious internal representation of a grammar for L. That is a likely hypothesis, since it best explains what we know about linguistic competence. In particular, it explains why experience with some sentences leads spontaneously to expectations involving others. But on that hypothesis, we might as well bypass the conventions of language and say that L is used by P if and only if everyone in P possesses an internal representation of a grammar for L.

Reply: In the first place, the hypothesis of internally represented grammars is not an explanation—best or otherwise—of anything. Perhaps it is *part* of some theory that best explains what we know about linguistic competence; we can't judge until we hear something about what the rest of the theory is like.

Nonetheless, I am ready enough to believe in internally represented grammars. But I am much less certain that there are internally represented grammars than I am that languages are used by populations; and I think it makes sense to say that languages might be used by populations even if there were no internally represented grammars. I can tentatively agree that L is used by P if and only if everyone in P possesses an internal representation of a grammar for L, if that is offered as a scientific hypothesis. But I cannot accept it as any sort of analysis of "L is used by P", since the analysandum clearly could be true although the analysans was false.

Objection: The notion of a convention of truthfulness and trust in L is a needless complication. Why not say, straightforwardly, that L is used by P if and only if there prevails in P a convention to bestow upon each sentence of L the meaning that L assigns to it? Or, indeed, that a grammar Γ of L is used by P if and only if there prevails in P a convention to bestow upon each constituent in Γ the meaning that Γ assigns to it?

Reply: A convention, as I have defined it, is a

regularity in action, or in action and belief. If that feature of the definition were given up, I do not see how to salvage any part of my theory of conventions. It is essential that a convention is a regularity such that conformity by others gives one a reason to conform; and such a reason must either be a practical reason for acting or an epistemic reason for believing. What other kind of reason is there?

Yet there is no such thing as an action of bestowing a meaning (except for an irrelevant sort of action that is performed not by language-users but by creators of language) so we cannot suppose that language-using populations have conventions to perform such actions. Neither does bestowal of meaning consist in forming some belief. Granted, bestowal of meaning is conventional in the sense that it depends on convention: the meanings would have been different if the conventions of truthfulness and trust had been different. But bestowal of meaning is not an action done in conformity to a convention, since it is not an action, and it is not a belief-formation in conformity to a convention, since it is not a belief-formation.

Objection: The beliefs and desires that constitute a convention are inaccessible mental entities, just as much as hypothetical internal representations of grammars are. It would be best if we could say in purely behavioristic terms what it is for a language L to be used by a population P. We might be able to do this by referring to the way in which members of P would answer counterfactual questionnnaires; or by referring to the way in which they would or would not assent to sentences under deceptive sensory stimulation; or by referring to the way in which they would intuitively group sentences into similarity-classes; or in some other way.

Reply: Suppose we succeeded in giving a behavioristic operational definition of the relation "L is used by P." This would not help us to understand what it is for L to be used by P; for we would have to understand that already, and also know a good deal of common-sense

psychology, in order to check that the operational definition was a definition of what it is supposed to be a definition of. If we did not know what it meant for L to be used by P, we would not know what sort of behavior on the part of members of P would indicate that L was used by P.

Objection: The conventions of language are nothing more nor less than our famously obscure old friends, the rules of language, renamed.

Reply: A convention of truthfulness and trust in L might well be called a rule, though it lacks many features that have sometimes been thought to belong to the essence of rules. It is not promulgated by any authority. It is not enforced by means of sanctions except to the extent that, because one has some sort of reason to conform, something bad may happen if one does not. It is nowhere codified and therefore is not "laid down in the course of teaching the language" or "appealed to in the course of criticizing a person's linguistic performance."[10] Yet it is more than a mere regularity holding "as a rule"; it is a regularity accompanied and sustained by a special kind of system of beliefs and desires.

A convention of truthfulness and trust in L might have as consequences other regularities which were conventions of language in their own right: specializations of the convention to certain special situations. (For instance, a convention of truthfulness in L on weekdays.) Such derivative conventions of language might also be called rules; some of them might stand a better chance of being codified than the overall convention which subsumes them.

However, there are other so-called rules of language which are not conventions of language and are not in the least like conventions of language: for instance, "rules" of syntax and semantics. They are not even regularities and cannot be formulated as imperatives. They might better be described not as rules, but as clauses in the definitions of entities which are to be mentioned in rules: clauses in the definition of a language L, of the act of being truthful in L, of the act of stating that the moon is blue, etc.

Thus the conventions of language might properly be called rules, but it is more informative and less confusing to call them conventions.

Objection: Language is not conventional. We have found that human capacities for language acquisition are highly specific and dictate the form of any language that humans can learn and use.

Reply: It may be that there is less conventionality than we used to think: fewer features of language which depend on convention, more which are determined by our innate capacities and therefore are common to all languages which are genuine alternatives to our actual language. But there are still conventions of language; and there are still convention-dependent features of language, differing from one alternative possible convention of language to another. That is established by the diversity of actual languages. There are conventions of language so long as the regularity of truthfulness in a given language has even a single alternative.

Objection: Unless a language-user is also a set-theorist, he cannot expect his fellows to conform to a regularity of truthfulness and trust in a certain language L. For to conform to this regularity is to bear a relation to a certain esoteric entity: a set of ordered pairs of sequences of sound-types or of mark-types and sets of possible worlds (or something more complicated still, if L is a natural language with indexicality, ambiguity, and non-indicatives). The common man has no concept of any such entity. Hence he can have no expectations regarding such an entity.

Reply: The common man need not have any concept of L in order to expect his fellows to be truthful and trusting in L. He need only have suitable particular expectations about how they might act, and how they might form beliefs, in various situations. He can tell whether any actual or hypothetical particular action or belief-formation on their part is compatible with his expectations. He expects them to conform to a regularity of truthfulness and trust in L if any particular activity or belief-formation that would fit his expectations would fall under what *we*— but not *he*—could describe as conformity to that regularity.

It may well be that his elaborate, infinite system of potential particular expectations can only be explained on the hypothesis that he has some unconscious mental entity somehow analogous to a general concept of L—say, an internally represented grammar. But it does not matter whether this is so or not. We are concerned only to say what system of expectations a normal member of a language-using population must have. We need not engage in psychological speculation about how those expectations are generated.

Objection: If there are conventions of language, those who are party to them should know what they are. Yet no one can fully describe the conventions of language to which he is supposedly a party.

Reply: He may nevertheless know what they are. It is enough to be able to recognize conformity and non-conformity to his convention, and to be able to try to conform to it. We know ever so many things we cannot put into words.

Objection: Use of language is almost never a rational activity. We produce and respond to utterances by habit, not as the result of any sort of reasoning or deliberation.

Reply: An action may be rational, and may be explained by the agent's beliefs and desires, even though that action was done by habit, and the agent gave no thought to the beliefs or desires which were his reason for acting. A habit may be under the agent's rational control in this sense: if that habit ever ceased to serve the agent's desires according to his beliefs, it would at once be overridden and corrected by conscious reasoning. Action done by a habit of this sort is both habitual and rational. Likewise for habits of believing. Our normal use of language is rational, since it is under rational control.

Perhaps use of language by young children is

not a rational activity. Perhaps it results from habits which would not be overridden if they ceased to serve the agent's desires according to his beliefs. If that is so, I would deny that these children have yet become party to conventions of language, and I would deny that they have yet become normal members of a language-using population. Perhaps language is first acquired and afterward becomes conventional. That would not conflict with anything I have said. I am not concerned with the way in which language is acquired, only with the condition of a normal member of a language-using population when he is done acquiring language.

Objection: Language could not have originated by convention. There could not have been an agreement to begin being truthful and trusting in a certain chosen language, unless some previous language had already been available for use in making the agreement.

Reply: The first language could not have originated by an agreement, for the reason given. But that is not to say that language cannot be conventional. A convention is so-called because of the way it persists, not because of the way it originated. A convention need not originate by convention—that is, by agreement—though many conventions do originate by agreement, and others could originate by agreement even if they actually do not. In saying that language is convention-governed, I say nothing whatever about the origins of language.

Objection: A man isolated all his life from others might begin—through genius or a miracle—to use language, say to keep a diary. (This would be an accidentally private language, not the necessarily private language Wittgenstein is said to have proved to be impossible.) In this case, at least, there would be no convention involved.

Reply: Taking the definition literally, there would be no convention. But there would be something very similar. The isolated man conforms to a certain regularity at many different times. He knows at each of these times that he has conformed to that regularity in the past, and

he has an interest in uniformity over time, so he continues to conform to that regularity instead of to any of various alternative regularities that would have done about as well if he had started out using them. He knows at all times that this is so, knows that he knows at all times that this is so, and so on. We might think of the situation as one in which a convention prevails in the population of different time-slices of the same man.

Objection: It is circular to define the meaning in P of sentences in terms of the beliefs held by members of P. For presumably the members of P think in their language. For instance, they hold beliefs by accepting suitable sentences of their language. If we do not already know the meaning in P of a sentence, we do not know what belief a member of P would hold by accepting that sentence.

Reply: It may be true that men think in language, and that to hold a belief is to accept a sentence of one's language. But it does not follow that belief should be analyzed as acceptance of sentences. It should not be. Even if men do in fact think in language, they might not. It is at least possible that men—like beasts—might hold beliefs otherwise than by accepting sentences. (I shall not say here how I think belief should be analyzed.) No circle arises from the contingent truth that a member of P holds beliefs by accepting sentences, so long as we can specify his beliefs without mentioning the sentences he accepts. We can do this for men, as we can for beasts.

Objection: Suppose a language L is used by a population of inveterate liars, who are untruthful in L more often than not. There would not be even a regularity—still less a convention, which implies a regularity—of truthfulness and trust in L.

Reply: I deny that L is used by the population of liars. I have undertaken to follow ordinary usage only where it is determinate; and, once it is appreciated just how extraordinary the situation would have to be, I do not believe that ordinary usage is determinate in this case. There are many similarities to clear cases in which a language is used by a population, and it is understandable that we should feel some inclination to classify this case along with them. But there are many important differences as well.

Although I deny that the population of liars *collectively* uses L, I am willing to say that each liar *individually* may use L, provided that he falsely believes that he is a member—albeit an exceptional, untruthful member—of a population wherein there prevails a convention of truthfulness and trust in L. He is in a position like that of a madman who thinks he belongs to a population which uses L, and behaves accordingly, and so can be said to use L, although in reality all the other members of this L-using population are figments of his imagination.

Objection: Suppose the members of a population are untruthful in their language L more often than not, not because they lie, but because they go in heavily for irony, metaphor, hyperbole, and such. It is hard to deny that the language L is used by such a population.

Reply: I claim that these people are truthful in their language L, though they are not *literally truthful* in L. To be literally truthful in L is to be truthful in another language related to L, a language we can call literal-L. The relation between L and literal-L is as follows: a good way to describe L is to start by specifying literal-L and then to describe L as obtained by certain systematic departures from literal-L. This two-stage specification of L by way of literal-L may turn out to be much simpler than any direct specification of L.

Objection: Suppose they are often untruthful in L because they are not communicating at all. They are joking, or telling tall tales, or telling white lies as a matter of social ritual. In these situations, there is neither truthfulness nor trust in L. Indeed, it is common knowledge that there is not.

Reply: Perhaps I can say the same sort of thing about this non-serious language use as I did about non-literal language use. That is: their seeming untruthfulness in non-serious situations is untruthfulness not in the language L that they actually use, but only in a simplified approximation to L. We may specify L by first specifying the approximation language, then listing the signs and features of context by which non-serious language use can be recognized, then specifying that when these signs or features are present, what would count as untruths in the approximation language do not count as such in L itself. Perhaps they are automatically true in L, regardless of the facts; perhaps they cease to count as indicative.

Example: what would otherwise be an untruth may not be one if said by a child with crossed fingers. Unfortunately, the signs and features of context by which we recognize non-serious language use are seldom as simple, standardized, and conventional as that. While they must find a place somewhere in a full account of the phenomenon of language, it may be inexpedient to burden the specification of L with them.

Perhaps it may be enough to note that these situations of non-serious language use must be at least somewhat exceptional if we are to have anything like a clear case of use of L; and to recall that the definition of a convention was loose enough to tolerate some exceptions. We could take the non-serious cases simply as violations— explicable and harmless ones—of the conventions of language.

There is a third alternative, requiring a modification in my theory. We may say that a *serious communication situation* exists with respect to a sentence σ of L whenever it is true, and common knowledge between a speaker and a hearer, that (a) the speaker does, and the hearer does not, know whether σ is true in L; (b) the hearer wants to know; (c) the speaker wants the hearer to know; and (d) neither the speaker nor the hearer has other (comparably strong) desires as to whether or not the speaker utters σ. (Note that when there is a serious communication situation with respect to σ, there is one also with respect to synonyms or contradictories in L of σ, and probably also with respect to other logical relatives in L of σ.) Then we may say that the convention whereby P uses L is a convention of truthfulness and trust in L in serious communication situations. That is: when a serious communication situation exists with respect to σ, then the speaker tries not to utter σ unless it is true in L, and the hearer responds, if σ is uttered, by coming to believe that σ is true in L. If that much is a convention in P, it does not matter what goes on in other situations: they use L.

The definition here given of a serious communication resembles that of a signaling problem in *Convention*, chapter IV, the difference being that the hearer may respond by belief-formation only, rather than by what speaker and hearer alike take to be appropriate action. If this modification were adopted, it would bring my general account of language even closer to my account in *Convention* of the special case of signaling.

Objection: Truthfulness and trust cannot be a convention. What could be the alternative to uniform truthfulness—uniform untruthfulness, perhaps? But it seems that if such untruthfulness were not intended to deceive, and did not deceive, then it too would be truthfulness.

Reply: The convention is not the regularity of truthfulness and trust *simpliciter*. It is the regularity of truthfulness and trust in some particular language L. Its alternatives are possible regularities of truthfulness and trust in other languages. A regularity of uniform untruthfulness and non-trust in a language L can be redescribed as a regularity of truthfulness and trust in a different language anti-L complementary to L. Anti-L has exactly the same sentences as L, but with opposite truth conditions. Hence the true sentences of anti-L are all and only the untrue sentences of L.

There is a different regularity that we may call a regularity of truthfulness and trust *simpliciter*. That is the regularity of being truthful and trusting in whichever language is used by one's fellows. This regularity neither is a convention nor depends on convention. If any language whatever is used by a population P, then a regularity

(perhaps with exceptions) of truthfulness and trust *simpliciter* prevails in P.

Objection: Even truthfulness and trust in L cannot be a convention. One conforms to a convention, on my account, because doing so answers to some sort of interest. But a decent man is truthful in L if his fellows are, whether or not it is in his interest. For he recognizes that he is under a moral obligation to be truthful in L; an obligation to reciprocate the benefits he has derived from others' truthfulness in L, or something of that sort. Truthfulness in L may bind the decent man against his own interest. It is more like a social contract than a convention.

Reply: The objection plays on a narrow sense of "interest" in which only selfish interests count. We commonly adopt a wider sense. We count also altruistic interests and interests springing from one's recognition of obligations. It is this wider sense that should be understood in the definition of convention. In this wider sense, it is nonsense to think of an obligation as outweighing one's interests. Rather, the obligation provides one interest which may outweigh the other interests.

A convention of truthfulness and trust in L is sustained by a mixture of selfish interests, altruistic interests, and interests derived from obligation. Usually all are present in strength; perhaps any one would be enough to sustain the convention. But occasionally truthfulness in L answers only to interests derived from obligation and goes against one's selfish or even altruistic interests. In such a case, only a decent man will have an interest in remaining truthful in L. But I dare say such cases are not as common as moralists might imagine. A convention of truthfulness and trust among scoundrels might well be sustained—with occasional lapses—by selfish interests alone.

A convention persists because everyone has reason to conform if others do. If the convention is a regularity in action, this is to say that it persists because everyone prefers general conformity rather than almost-general conformity with himself as the exception. A (demythologized) social contract may also be described as a regularity sustained by a general preference for general conformity, but the second term of the preference is different. Everyone prefers general conformity over a certain state of general non-conformity called the state of nature. This general preference sets up an obligation to reciprocate the benefits derived from others' conformity, and that obligation creates an interest in conforming which sustains the social contract. The objection suggests that, among decent men, truthfulness in L is a social contract. I agree; but there is no reason why it cannot be a social contract and a convention as well, and I think it is.

Objection: Communication cannot be explained by conventions of truthfulness alone. If I utter a sentence σ of our language L, you—expecting me to be truthful in L—will conclude that I take σ to be true in L. If you think I am well informed, you will also conclude that probably σ is true in L. But you will draw other conclusions as well, based on your legitimate assumption that it is for some good reason that I chose to utter σ rather than remain silent, and rather than utter any of the other sentences of L that I also take to be true in L. I can communicate all sorts of misinformation by exploiting your beliefs about my conversational purposes, without ever being untruthful in L. Communication depends on principles of helpfulness and relevance as well as truthfulness.

Reply: All this does not conflict with anything I have said. We do conform to conversational regularities of helpfulness and relevance. But these regularities are not independent conventions of language; they result from our convention of truthfulness and trust in L together with certain general facts—not dependent on any convention—about our conversational purposes and our beliefs about one another. Since they are by-products of a convention of truthfulness and trust, it is unnecessary to mention them separately in specifying the conditions under which a language is used by a population.

Objection: Let L be the language used in P, and let L^- be some fairly rich fragment of L. That is, the sentences of L^- are many but not all of the sentences of L (in an appropriate special sense if L is infinite); and any sentence of both has the same meaning in both. Then L^- also turns out to be a language used by P; for by my definition there prevails in P a convention of truthfulness and trust in L^-, sustained by an interest in communication. Not one but many—perhaps infinitely many—languages are used by P.

Reply: That is so, but it is no problem. Why not say that any rich fragment of a language used by P is itself a used language?

Indeed, we will need to say such things when P is linguistically inhomogeneous. Suppose, for instance, that P divides into two classes: the learned and the vulgar. Among the learned there prevails a convention of truthfulness and trust in a language L; among P as a whole there does not, but there does prevail a convention of truthfulness and trust in a rich fragment L^- of L. We wish to say that the learned have a common language with the vulgar, but that is so only if L^-, as well as L, counts as a language used by the learned.

Another case: the learned use L_1, the vulgar use L_2, neither is included in the other, but there is extensive overlap. Here L_1 and L_2 are to be the most inclusive languages used by the respective classes. Again we wish to say that the learned and the vulgar have a common language: in particular, the largest fragment common to L_1 and L_2. That can be so only if this largest common fragment counts as a language used by the vulgar, by the learned, and by the whole population.

I agree that we often do not count the fragments; we can speak of *the* language of P, meaning by this not the one and only thing that is a language used by P, but rather the most inclusive language used by P. Or we could mean something else: the union of all the languages used by substantial sub-populations of P, provided that some quite large fragment of this union is used by (more or less) all of P. Note that the union as a whole need not be used at all, in my primary sense, either by P or by any sub-population of P. Thus in my example of the last paragraph, the language of P might be taken either as the largest common fragment of L_1 and L_2 or as the union of L_1 and L_2.

Further complications arise. Suppose that half of the population of a certain town uses English, and also uses basic Welsh; while the other half uses Welsh, and also uses basic English. The most inclusive language used by the entire population is the union of basic Welsh and basic English. The union of languages used by substantial sub-populations is the union of English and Welsh, and the proviso is satisfied that some quite large fragment of this union is used by the whole population. Yet we would be reluctant to say that either of these unions is the language of the population of the town. We might say that Welsh and English are the two languages of the town, or that basic English and basic Welsh are. It is odd to call either of the two language-unions a language; though once they *are* called that, it is no further oddity to say that one or other of them is the language of the town. There are two considerations. First: English, or Welsh, or basic English, or basic Welsh, can be given a satisfactory unified grammar; whereas the language-unions cannot. Second: English, or Welsh, or basic Welsh, or basic English, is (in either of the senses I have explained) the language of a large population outside the town; whereas the language-unions are not. I am not sure which of the two considerations should be emphasized in saying when a language is the language of a population.

Objection: Let L be the language of P; that is, the language that ought to count as the most inclusive language used by P. (Assume that P is linguistically homogeneous.) Let L^+ be obtained by adding garbage to L; some extra sentences, very long and difficult to pronounce, and hence never uttered in P, with arbitrarily chosen meanings in L^+. Then it seems that L^+ is a language used by P, which is absurd.

A sentence never uttered at all is *a fortiori* never uttered untruthfully. So truthfulness-as-usual in L plus truthfulness-by-silence on the garbage sentences constitutes a kind of truthfulness in L^+; and the expectation thereof constitutes trust in L^+. Therefore we have a prevailing regularity of truthfulness and trust in L^+. This regularity qualifies as a convention in P sustained by an interest in communication.

Reply: Truthfulness-by-silence is truthfulness, and expectation thereof is expectation of truthfulness; but expectation of truthfulness-by-silence is not yet trust. Expectation of (successful) truthfulness—expectation that a given sentence will not be uttered falsely—is a necessary but not sufficient condition for trust. There is no regularity of trust in L^+, so far as the garbage sentences are concerned. Hence there is no convention of truthfulness and trust in L^+, and L^+ is not used by P.

For trust, one must be able to take an utterance of a sentence as evidence that the sentence is true. That is so only if one's degree of belief that the sentence will be uttered falsely is low, not only absolutely, but as a fraction of one's degree of belief—perhaps already very low—that the sentence will be uttered at all. Further, this must be so not merely because one believes in advance that the sentence is probably true: one's degree of belief that the sentence will be uttered falsely must be substantially lower than the product of one's degree of belief that the sentence will be uttered times one's prior degree of belief that it is false. A garbage sentence of L^+ will not meet this last requirement, not even if one believes to high degrees both that it is true in L^+ and that it never will be uttered.

This objection was originally made, by Stephen Schiffer, against my former view that conventions of language are conventions of truthfulness. I am inclined to think that it succeeds as a counter-example to that view. I agree that L^+ is not used by P, in any reasonable sense, but I have not seen any way to avoid conceding that L^+ is a possible language—it might *really* be used—and that there does prevail in P a convention of truthfulness in L^+, sustained by an interest in communication. Here we have another advantage of the present account over my original one.

Objection: A sentence either is or isn't analytic in a given language, and a language either is or isn't conventionally adopted by a given population. Hence there is no way for the analytic-synthetic distinction to be unsharp. But not only can it be unsharp; it usually is, at least in cases of interest to philosophers. A sharp analytic-synthetic distinction is available only relative to particular rational reconstructions of ordinary language.

Reply: One might try to explain unsharp analyticity by a theory of degrees of convention. Conventions do admit of degree in a great many ways: by the strengths of the beliefs and desires involved, and by the fraction of exceptions to the many almost-universal quantifications in the definition of convention. But this will not help much. It is easy to imagine unsharp analyticity even in a population whose conventions of language are conventions to the highest degree in every way.

One might try to explain unsharp analyticity by recalling that we may not know whether some worlds are really possible. If a sentence is true in our language in all worlds except some worlds of doubtful possibility, then that sentence will be of doubtful analyticity. But this will not help much either. Unsharp analyticity usually seems to arise because we cannot decide whether a sentence would be true in some bizarre but clearly possible world.

A better explanation would be that our convention of language is not exactly a convention of truthfulness and trust in a single language, as I have said so far. Rather it is a convention of truthfulness and trust in whichever we please of some cluster of similar languages: languages with more or less the same sentences, and more or less the same truth-values for the sentences in worlds close to our actual world, but with increasing divergence in truth-values as we go to increasingly remote, bizarre worlds. The convention

confines us to the cluster, but leaves us with indeterminacies whenever the languages of the cluster disagree. We are free to settle these indeterminacies however we like. Thus an ordinary, open-textured, imprecise language is a sort of blur of precise languages—a region, not a point, in the space of languages. Analyticity is sharp in each language of our cluster. But when different languages of our cluster disagree on the analyticity of a sentence, then that sentence is unsharply analytic among us.

Rational reconstructions have been said to be irrelevant to philosophical problems arising in ordinary, unreconstructed language. My hypothesis of conventions of truthfulness and trust in language-clusters provides a defense against this accusation. Reconstruction is not—or not always—departure from ordinary language. Rather it is selection from ordinary language: isolation of one precise language, or of a sub-cluster, out of the language-cluster wherein we have a convention of truthfulness and trust.

Objection: The thesis and the antithesis pertain to different subjects. The thesis, in which languages are regarded as semantic systems, belongs to the philosophy of artificial languages. The antithesis, in which language is regarded as part of human natural history, belongs to the philosophy of natural language.

Reply: Not so. *Both* accounts—just like almost any account of almost anything—can most easily be applied to simple, artificial, imaginary examples. Language-games are just as artificial as formalized calculi.

According to the theory I have presented, philosophy of language is a single subject. The thesis and antithesis have been the property of rival schools; but in fact they are complementary essential ingredients in any adequate account either of languages or of language.

Notes

1 H. P. Grice, "Meaning," *Philosophical Review* 66 (1957): 377–88.

2 This proposal is adapted from the theory given in Erik Stenius, "Mood and Language-Game," *Synthese* 17 (1967): 254–74.

3 Cambridge, Mass.: Harvard University Press, 1969. A similar account was given in the original version of this paper, written in 1968.

4 Personal communication, 1971. Bennett himself uses the broadened concept of convention differently, wishing to exhibit conventional meaning as a special case of Gricean meaning. See his "The Meaning-Nominalist Strategy," *Foundations of Language* 10 (1973): 141–68.

5 Possible worlds are taken as models in S. Kripke, "A Completeness Theorem in Modal Logic," *Journal of Symbolic Logic* 24 (1959): 1–15; in Carnap's recent work on semantics and inductive logic, discussed briefly in secs. 9, 10, and 25 of "Replies and Systematic Expositions," *The Philosophy of Rudolf Carnap*, ed. by P. Schilpp (La Salle, Ill.: Open Court., 1963) and elsewhere. Worlds are taken as state-descriptions—diagrams of models—in Carnap's earlier work: for instance, sec. 18 of *Introduction to Semantics* (Cambridge, Mass.: Harvard Univ. Press, 1942). Worlds are taken as complete, consistent novels—theories of models—in R. Jeffrey, *The Logic of Decision* (New York: McGraw-Hill, 1965), sec. 12.8.

6 "Replies and Systematic Expositions," sec. 9.v. A better-known presentation of essentially the same idea is in S. Kripke, "Semantical Considerations on Modal Logic," *Acta Philosophica Fennica* 16 (1963): 83–94.

7 See my "General Semantics," in this volume [in Davidson and Harman (eds.), Semantics of Natural Language, Dordrecht: Reidel 1972. Reprinted in Lewis, *Philosophical Papers*, Vol. 1, Oxford: OUP, 1983].

8 For a description of the sort of grammars I have in mind (minus the semantic interpretation) see N. Chomsky. *Aspects of the Theory of Syntax* (Cambridge, Mass.: M.I.T. Press, 1965), and G. Harman, "Generative Grammars without Transformation Rules," *Language* 37 (1963): 597–616. My "constituents" correspond to semantically interpreted deep phrase-markers, or sub-trees thereof, in a transformational grammar. My "representing operation" may work in several steps and thus subsumes both the transformational and the phonological components of a transformational grammar.

9 W. V. Quine, "Ontological Relativity," *Journal of Philosophy* 65 (1968): 185–212; *Word and Object*, pp. 68–79.

10 P. Ziff, *Semantic Analysis*, pp. 34–35.

Chapter 16

John Hawthorne

A NOTE ON 'LANGUAGES AND LANGUAGE'

Under what conditions does a given population use some particular language? In 'Languages and Language', David Lewis claims that a population uses some language by virtue of certain conventions prevailing in that population.[1] In this paper, I shall raise a difficulty for Lewis's proposal which suggests that *no* purely convention-based account of language use is possible.

A convention, Lewis explains, is any regularity R in the actions or the actions and beliefs of a population satisfying the following six conditions:

[1] Everyone conforms to R.
[2] Everyone believes that the others conform to R.
[3] The belief that others conform to R gives each person a decisive reason to conform himself.
[4] There is a preference for conformity rather than slightly-less-than-general conformity.
[5] There is at least one other possible regularity R′ such that: [a] R and R′ are not compossible and [b] if there were general conformity to R′ [3] and [4] would be true of R′.
[6] That conditions [1] to [5] obtain is common knowledge.

With respect to language use, Lewis suggests that the conventions which operate are those of truthfulness and trust in some language L and that, moreover, a necessary and sufficient condition for language use can be given in terms of those conventions: 'a language L *is used by* a population P if and only if there prevails in P a convention of truthfulness and trust in L, sustained by an interest in communication' (169 [p. 229 above]). 'Truthfulness' and 'trust' are to be understood in the following way: 'To be truthful in L is to act in a certain way: to try never to utter any sentences of L that are not true in L. Thus it is to avoid uttering any sentence of L unless one believes it to be true in L' (167 [p. 228]); 'To be trusting in L is to form beliefs in a certain way: to impute truthfulness in L to others, and thus tend to respond to another's utterance of any sentence of L by coming to believe that the uttered sentence is true in L' (167 [p. 228]).

A language is here taken to be a function from strings to meanings. While Lewis construes meanings as sets of possible worlds, his account of language use as convention-based does not rely on construing meanings in that way.

There are clearly a great many English sentences that are extremely long. As any linguist will tell you, the class of English sentences which are so long that a person could not possibly utter one of them in her lifetime is much larger than the remaining class. Since it is uncontroversial that our language contains such sentences, it would be a grave problem for Lewis's account if it had as a consequence the exclusion of such sentences from our language. Unfortunately, his account has that very consequence.

Let us consider the fragment L* of English containing the lengthy sentences under consideration. There is certainly a *regularity* of truthfulness in that fragment. It is vacuously true that we never utter sentences of L* unless we believe them to be true. This is a case of what Lewis calls "truthfulness-by-silence" (187 [p. 243]). However, the regularity would not here be a *conventional* one. If the regularity of truthfulness in L* is to be conventional, there must be available some alternative regularity R′ such that it would be impossible to follow R and R′ simultaneously. No such alternative exists in the present case, since the population *couldn't fail* to be truthful in the relevant function from strings to meanings. Lewis recognises that we have a convention of truthfulness and trust in a language if and only if we have a convention of truthfulness and trust in every fragment of that language. Since English contains L*, it follows that we do not have a convention of truthfulness in English.

What about trust? As a preliminary, let us look at a passage where Lewis develops his account of trust in order to answer a different objection. The objection is formulated as follows:

Let L be the language of P; that is, the language that ought to count as the most inclusive language used by P. (Assume that P is linguistically homogenous.) Let L+ be obtained by adding garbage to L; some extra sentences, very long and difficult to pronounce, and hence never uttered in P, with arbitrarily chosen meanings in L+. Then it seems that L+ is a language used by P, which is absurd. (187 [p. 243])

He offers the following solution:

. . . expectation of truthfulness-by-silence is not yet trust . . . For trust, one must be able

to take an utterance of a sentence as evidence that the sentence is true. That is so only if one's degree of belief that the sentence will be uttered falsely is low, not only absolutely, but as a fraction of one's degree of belief— perhaps already very low—that the sentence will be uttered at all. Further, this must be so not merely because one believes in advance that the sentence is probably true: one's degree of belief that the sentence will be uttered falsely must be substantially lower than the product of one's degree of belief that the sentence will be uttered times one's prior degree of belief that it is false. (187 [p. 243])

Let us apply this machinery to the long sentences under consideration. Since we are considering that class of English sentences which no one will or could possibly utter, our prior degree of belief that those sentences will be uttered is zero. Therefore, the left half of Lewis's formula will not yield a lower value than the right in the case of these sentences, and so the conditions for a trust convention are not met here. Hence, while Lewis's formula successfully rules out garbage sentences from membership in our language, it rules out lengthy sentences of English at the same time.

Thus Lewis's criterion entails that we do not use the English language. Can it be rectified in order to avoid this troublesome consequence? The following consideration persuades me that it cannot. Let us suppose that you and I speak two different languages, A and B. A and B assign the same meanings to sentences of a length that at least one of us could possibly utter, but different meanings to sentences that are too long for either of us to utter. Would the fact that we spoke two different languages impede communication between us? Clearly not. Discourse between us would proceed very smoothly. From this I infer that we couldn't *as a matter of convention* speak language A rather than language B. For the conformity of others to language A wouldn't give me good reason to conform to A rather than B.

My interest in communication would be equally well served by A or B, even given that the rest of the population spoke language A. The third of the conditions deemed necessary for a convention to operate, namely that the conformity of others gives one a decisive reason to conform, will not be satisfied in the case of any human language containing very long sentences. One could tamper with Lewis's account of what constitutes a convention. However, I am inclined to think that the problem lies elsewhere.

Does this mean that the platitude that language is conventional turns out to be false? This does not follow. We operate with a convention of truthfulness and trust, but it is not a convention of truthfulness and trust in English; it is rather a convention of truthfulness and trust in some fragment of English. I don't wish to claim that there are no conventions of language, but only that a criterion of language use cannot be given in terms of convention alone. What account could we give, then, of the conditions under which a population uses a language containing some very long strings of words? The following solution might be proposed. Look at that fragment of English in which there is a convention of trust and truthfulness. There will be rules implicit in the fragment determining which other sentences belong to the English language. This proposal fails, since the fragment will not determine a unique set of rules. For example, the fragment will not determine whether the rules for each logical constant are recursive or not. More generally, for each subsentential expression, there will be alternative interpretations of the plus/quus variety. The problem is similar to the one presented by Kripke's Wittgenstein.[2] It is not surprising that there is no obvious solution to it.

Notes

1 Lewis, David, 'Languages and Language' in *Philosophical Papers Vol. 1*, Oxford University Press [1983]. All page references in text are to this paper [page references in square brackets are to the reprinted version in this volume].
2 In Saul Kripke, *Wittgenstein on Rules and Private Language*, Harvard University Press (1982).

Chapter 17

Stephen Laurence

A CHOMSKIAN ALTERNATIVE TO CONVENTION-BASED SEMANTICS

In virtue of what do the utterances we make mean what they do? What facts about these signs, about us, and about our environment make it the case that they have the meanings they do? According to a tradition stemming from H.P. Grice through David Lewis and Stephen Schiffer it is in virtue of facts about conventions that we participate in as language users that our utterances mean what they do (see Grice 1957, Lewis 1969, 1983, Schiffer 1972, 1982). This view currently enjoys widespread acceptance among philosophers of mind and language. Though most are not particularly interested in the details of such programs, the dominant view seems to be that something of the sort proposed by Grice, Lewis and Schiffer is basically right. Thus, Jerry Fodor, reflecting what I take to be prevalent attitudes in the field, writes,

> [C]onsider the fact that tokens of "talcum powder tastes nasty" are true iff talcum powder tastes nasty. It may well be that the best story we can tell about that fact adverts essentially to certain communicative intentions of speaker/hearers of English. I don't offer anything like a detailed account of how this story might go. . . . Perhaps it would implicate the speaker's intention that the token he produces should be *taken* to be true iff talcum powder tastes nasty; or perhaps what's crucial is the speaker's intention to adhere to a system of conventions, shared by members of his lan-

guage community . . . Though the details are disputed, some such account can be pieced together from the insights of philosophers like Grice, Schiffer, Lewis and Harnish, among others. (1990, p. 314)

I believe that convention-based accounts of the meaning of natural language utterances are fundamentally mistaken. They are accepted largely on the basis of the truism that language is in some sense conventional and because they are seen as "the only game in town". I do not dispute the fact that language is in *some* sense conventional; I do, however, dispute the claim that language is conventional in the sense that Lewis and other convention-based theorists have claimed. My discussion of convention-based accounts will focus on Lewis's version of the theory but I intend my argument to be general. I shall argue that convention-based accounts lack the generality we should want a theory of natural language semantic properties to have, and more importantly, that there is a simpler, more general alternative to such accounts. My alternative is based on the standard, Chomskian interpretation of linguistics (see for example Chomsky 1965, 1975). This latter theory is not usually taken to be in competition with convention-based accounts of semantic properties. Indeed a central claim of my paper is that, contrary to popular opinion, the Chomskian account, suitably extended, should be thought of as being in direct competition with convention-based accounts. Once we see the Chomskian account as a rival to the convention-based account, the latter is no longer "the only game in town". And, I will argue, relative to the Chomskian account, convention-based accounts are unmotivated, lacking in generality and empirically unsupported.

The general structure of my argument is as follows. In the first section, I will argue that Lewis's technical notion of "conventionality" is not the sense in which it is truistic that language is conventional; thus Lewis's account is similarly not truistic. It is open to challenge. In § 2, I argue that if the concern is to account for the conventionality of language, Lewis's account should generalize, since syntactic and other linguistic properties of utterances are exactly as conventional (in the ordinary pretheoretic sense of "conventional") as are semantic properties. In § 3, I present my alternative to convention-based semantics and show that this account generalizes to other linguistic properties, in particular, that it provides parallel accounts of syntactic (and other linguistic) properties. I also present a number of empirical considerations in this section which favour the Chomskian account over the convention-based account. In § 4, I argue that looking beyond literal expression meaning does not help the case for convention-based semantics.

Before I start, though, I should note two disclaimers. First, though I call my alternative a "Chomskian" alternative to convention-based semantics, it is not necessarily one which Chomsky himself would approve of, not least because Chomsky himself is highly sceptical about the project of truth conditional semantics. I call it "Chomskian" because I take it to be broadly in the spirit of Chomsky's views about the nature of linguistics. I also want to be agnostic about the relation between the language processor and the grammar, so far as this is consistent with central assumptions of recent work in linguistics and psycholinguistics. For expository purposes, however, I adopt a relatively strong thesis that Chomsky himself would probably not accept, even for syntactic properties.

The second disclaimer is that in arguing against convention-based accounts of (expression) meaning I am arguing against a popular view that has its roots in Grice's work. I am not thereby arguing against all Gricean views about language. My account in effect rejects the primacy of speaker meaning and the particular connection between contents of mental states and contents of utterances implicit in convention-based accounts. It does not (necessarily) thereby reject speaker meaning or communicative intentions, or beliefs regarding presuppositions of utterances, or beliefs arrived at by conversational implicature. As far as I can tell, my account leaves Grice's important work on conversational implicature in place, along with most other work in pragmatics. At the same time, I am not claiming that work on convention-based semantics stemming from Grice's 1957 paper "Meaning" should be interpreted as part of a theory of pragmatics. As we shall see, what I think is really at stake is how we construe semantics. In particular, the issue will be whether semantic properties should somehow or other be underwritten by our "general communicative abilities" or whether they should be taken to be more directly tied to features of the language processor, a special purpose cognitive mechanism for processing language.[1]

1 Two senses of "convention"

Lewis sees himself as defending the platitude that language is governed by convention. He uses the conventionality of language to pump our intuitions in favour of a convention-based account of the nature of semantic properties. His convention-based account, however, is based on a technical notion of "conventionality". In this section I present Lewis's account of "conventions" and the specific "conventions" which he takes to underwrite the semantic properties of natural language utterances. I argue that Lewis's account has powerful empirical consequences that are far from trivial or platitudinous—and that his account goes well beyond the intuitive pretheoretic sense in which language is thought to be conventional.

It may seem just *obvious* that language is conventional. After all, the semantic properties of natural language utterances are not *intrinsic* properties of the marks and sounds which have them. The noise "chocolate", for example, might not have meant *chocolate*. It might have meant *planet* or *train* or nothing at all. It might seem that this obvious conventionality lends a strong prima facie plausibility to the convention-based account. David Lewis suggests as much in his motivational remarks at the beginning of his book *Convention*.[2] There Lewis says:

> It is a platitude that language is ruled by convention. Words might be used to mean almost anything; and we who use them have made them mean what they do because somehow, gradually and informally, we have come to an understanding that this is what we shall use them to mean. We could perfectly well use these words otherwise—or use different words, as men in foreign countries do. We might change our conventions if we like. (1969, p. 1)

> The platitude that there are conventions of language . . . commands the immediate assent of any thoughtful person. (1969, p. 2)

We need *an account* of convention, though, in order to meet Quine's scepticism concerning the existence of such conventions of language. Lewis's project is to give an analysis of

> our common, established concept of convention, so that you will recognize that it explains what you must have had in mind when you said that language—like many other activities—is governed by conventions (1969, p. 3)

and thereby "rehabilitate analyticity" (1969, p. ix).

I completely agree that language is conventional in the trivial sense: it isn't an *intrinsic* property of the noise "chocolate" that it means *chocolate*. It might have meant *planet*, or whatever. I want to emphasize, however, just how big a step it is from this platitudinous sense of conventionality to the sorts of conventions Lewis ends up with and that convention-based accounts typically employ. It will make things easier if we introduce a small bit of terminology. I will refer to the intuitive pretheoretic sense in which language is thought to be conventional as "P-conventionality" (for Platitude-conventionality) and I will refer to the sense in which language is conventional on Lewis's account as "L-conventionality" (for Lewis-conventionality).

Lewis motivates his account of the conventions of language by noting several features we intuitively take to be part of the conventionality of language. The main one is that linguistic properties are not *intrinsic* properties of the signs which have them: it is in a certain sense arbitrary which linguistic properties are associated with a given utterance type.[3] As Lewis says:

> Words might be used to mean almost anything . . . We could perfectly well use [our] words otherwise—or use different words, as men in foreign countries do. (1969, p. 1)

Since linguistic properties are only contingently associated with the signs which have these properties, they cannot be intrinsic properties of the signs.

Lewis also notes that though we might speak any of a large number of possible languages, we have a common interest in communicating, and therefore we have a common interest in speaking the same language (1969, p. 177). I agree with Lewis that these are platitudes. And I will take these two features together to characterize "P-conventionality".[4]

1. *The P-conventionality of language*

1. Linguistic properties are not intrinsic properties of the utterances which have them. The marks and sounds we use could have (or could have had) linguistic properties other than those they in fact have.

2. Though we might speak any of a large number of possible languages, the members of a given linguistic community have a common interest in linguistic coordination (i.e., in speaking the same language), because they have a common interest in communication.

Lewis believes that his account unpacks the platitude that language is conventional and therefore provides a defence of the P-conventionality of language. He also intends his account to provide an explication of the nature of the semantic properties of natural language utterances (that is, an account of what makes it the case that natural language utterances mean what they do). In evaluating his account, then, we will have to keep both of these goals in mind. This section, however, is concerned only with the first of these goals.

Lewis's account consists of a general account of conventions together with a specific convention governing language.

2. *Lewis's General Account of Conventions*

A regularity R, in action or in action and belief, is a *convention* in a population P if and only if, within P, the following six conditions hold. . . .

1. Everyone conforms to R.

2. Everyone believes that the others conform to R.

3. This belief that the others conform to R gives everyone a good and decisive reason to conform to R himself. . . .

4. There is a general preference for general conformity to R rather than slightly-less-than-general conformity—in particular, rather than conformity by all but any one. . . .

5. R is not the only possible regularity meeting the last two conditions. . . .

6. Finally the various facts listed in conditions 1 to 5 are matters of *common* (or *mutual*) *knowledge*: They are known to everyone, it is known to everyone that they are known to everyone, and so on. (1983, p. 164–6, numbering slightly altered from original.)

The specific convention involved in language use is a convention of truthfulness and trust in a given language. Truthfulness and trust are explained as follows.

3. *Truthfulness and Trust*

To be truthful in L is to act in a certain way: to try never to utter any sentences of L that are not true in L. Thus it is to avoid uttering any sentence of L unless one believes it to be true in L. To be trusting in L is to form beliefs in a certain way: to impute truthfulness in L to others, and thus to tend to respond to another's utterance of any sentence of L by coming to believe that the uttered sentence is true in L. (1983, p. 167)

Here a language L is a function (in the mathematical sense) from utterance types to sets of possible worlds, where an utterance of type p is true in L just in case the set of worlds which is the value of the function L for the argument p contains the actual world (1983, p. 163).[5]

The version of Lewis's general account of L-conventionality that we end up with for natural language, then, is the following (here I am just taking his account of "truthfulness and trust" and plugging it into his general account of conventions).

4. *The L-conventionality of language*

1. There is a regularity of truthfulness and

trust in L among the population P. This means that,

(i) for any given utterance, everyone tries to avoid producing that utterance, unless they believe it to be true in L,

(ii) everyone believes that the others do the same and

(iii) everyone responds to utterances by others by coming to believe that the uttered sentence is true in L because they believe the others try to avoid producing utterances unless they believe them to be true in L.

2. Everyone in P believes that the other members of P conform to the regularity of truthfulness and trust in L. This means that everyone believes that the others are doing the same as them regarding 1:

(i) for any given utterance they are trying to avoid producing it, unless they believe it to be true in L,

(ii) they are believing that the others are doing the same and

(iii) they are responding to utterances by others by coming to believe that the utterances are true in L because they believe that the others are trying to avoid producing utterances unless they believe them to be true in L.

3. The belief that the others conform to the regularity of truthfulness and trust in L gives everyone in P a good and decisive reason to conform to the regularity of truthfulness and trust in L. That is, believing that 2 holds provides us with good and decisive reason for doing 1.

4. There is a general preference for general conformity to the regularity of truthfulness and trust in L, rather than slightly-less-than-general conformity— in particular, rather than conformity by all but any one. Thus there is a general preference that everyone, rather than everyone but one,

(i) avoid producing any given utterance, unless they believe it to be true in L,

(ii) believe that the others do the same

(iii) respond to utterances by others by coming to believe that the uttered sentence is true in L because they believe the others try to avoid producing utterances unless they believe them to be true in L,

(iv) believe that the others believe others avoid producing any given utterance, unless they believe it to be true in L, and

(v) believe that the others respond by coming to believe that the uttered sentence is true in L because they believe the others avoid producing any given L utterance, unless they believe it to be true in L.

5. The regularity of truthfulness and trust in L is not the only possible regularity meeting the conditions 3 and 4. (So, for example, a regularity of truthfulness and trust in L' would meet the conditions 3 and 4 as well.)

6. "Finally the various facts listed in conditions 1 to 5 are matters of *common* (or *mutual*) *knowledge*: They are known to everyone, it is known to everyone that they are known to everyone, and so on." (1983, p. 166 [p. 227 above])

Certainly there is quite a difference between the claim that language is P-conventional and Lewis's claim that language is L-conventional. I particularly want to emphasize that Lewis's account has some powerful empirical consequences. I think this can be brought out in a variety of ways.

One way to see this is to notice that the account is committed to the existence of a wide range of propositional attitudes distributed amongst the population of speakers, in some cases propositional attitudes with quite complex and esoteric contents. So, for example, from 4.1 we all believe of our own utterances (i.e., of the marks, sounds or whatever) that they are true in L. For Lewis this means that we all believe that these utterances are in the domain of a function L mapping these utterances to sets of possible worlds which include the actual world. Actually this is a considerably simplified version of what we must believe since the meaning of the technical term "true in L" must be considerably complicated to deal with indexicality, tense, ambiguity, mood and nonliteral uses of meaning (metaphor, irony, jokes, "white lies", etc.)— all of these being commonplace in natural language use. Of course, we needn't believe that-our-utterances-are-mapped-by-the-function-L-to-sets-of-possible-worlds-which-include-the-actual-world, *under that very description*. But we do need to believe it under *some* description.[6] What's more, from 4.2 we must believe that others avoid making utterances unless they similarly believe this of their utterances. It is because we believe that they avoid making utterances unless they similarly believe that we ourselves respond to their utterances by coming to believe that p when they produce some utterance of $\ulcorner p \urcorner$ (that is, when they produce some utterance of the type x where $L(x) = p$). These beliefs explain why we ourselves conform to the regularity, according to 4.3. From 4.4, we must have a preference that everyone, rather than everyone but one,

(i)   avoid producing any given utterance, unless they believe it to be true in L,
(ii) believe that the others do the same
(iii) respond to utterances by others by coming to believe that the uttered sentence is true in L because they believe the others try to avoid producing utterances unless they believe them to be true in L,
(iv) believe that the others believe others avoid producing any given utterance, unless they believe it to be true in L, and

(v)   believe that the others respond by coming to believe that the uttered sentence is true in L because they believe the others avoid producing any given utterance, unless they believe it to be true in L.

This is not to mention the fact that 1–5 are matters of common or mutual knowledge.[7]

A second way to see that the account is not simply platitudinous, but rather has strong empirical consequences, is to notice that it seems quite possible for the account to fail and yet for speakers to get on just fine. Imagine, for example, the following possible community. The community is small, unified and isolated and the members of the community are entirely unaware of the fact that natural languages vary. As far as they are concerned, there is only one language which everyone speaks. The speakers in this hypothetical community might well treat their linguistic symbols as if they had their linguistic properties *intrinsically*. It may never have occurred to them that the signs they use might not have meant what they do. When a speaker produces an utterance these speakers simply recognize that it has such and such linguistic properties. They needn't believe that the speaker believes the content. They needn't believe that the speaker believes that *the hearer* believes the speaker believes it. They needn't believe that everyone comes to believe that the utterance is true because they all know they all know that speakers try to avoid producing utterances unless they believe them true in L. And these beliefs certainly needn't provide them with any reason to conform to the regularity, or prefer that others do, since they needn't even recognize that alternative correlations of linguistic properties and sound types are possible. I see no reason why such a community should not be possible— indeed may well have been actual!

Finally, we can also see the empirical commitments of the account by noting some of the traditional objections which have been raised against it. For example, it is quite possible to produce utterances which you do not believe to be true in L (perhaps simply for fun) or which you do not believe your audience will believe to be true in L (either because you have no audience or because your audience is extremely unlikely to be receptive to the message you have to convey).[8]

These points are only meant to establish that it is not a platitude that language is L-conventional. So while L-conventionality may provide an adequate explication of *conventions* (such as the convention of driving on the left side of the road in England)—as I am perfectly willing to grant for the purposes of this paper—it need not underwrite the nature of linguistic meaning. Once we see that it is not a platitude that language is conventional in the convention-based theorist's sense, we are free to consider challenges to the account seriously, and to explore alternatives to it. In § 2, I will develop a reason for thinking that the account should be challenged in this way.

2 Conventions and other linguistic properties

Lewis uses the P-conventionality of semantic properties to motivate his L-convention based theory of the nature of semantic properties, suggesting that his theory would defend the (P-)conventionality of language against philosophical attack. If Lewis's account were the correct account of the nature of natural language semantic properties then we could see how the semantic properties of natural language utterances would not be intrinsic properties of them. This follows pretty much directly from 4.5 above, which says, in effect, that other conventions (e.g., a convention of truthfulness and trust in some language other than L, say L′), might just as easily have obtained among the speakers of L. To explain the second feature of P-conventionality we don't really need to appeal to Lewis's account at all. Since this feature of the conventionality of language follows simply from

the fact that if we didn't attribute more or less the same linguistic features to utterances we wouldn't be able to communicate using language. Since linguistic communication is in our interest, so is coordination.

So Lewis's account at least provides an account of the (P-)conventionality of the semantic properties of natural language utterances. The trouble is that semantic properties are not the only linguistic properties that are P-conventional. So are the syntactic, morphological and phonological features of language; and in just the same way. We can see this by considering some examples.

Consider the sound type corresponding to some utterance of (5)[9]

(5) Sue ate the chocolate.

The point about the semantic features of (5) being P-conventional is just that we might use (or might have used) the words in (5) to mean quite different things (or nothing at all). So, for example, we might have used (the sound type) "chocolate"[10] to mean *planet*, in which case (5) would mean something rather different from what it in fact means. It is in our common interest that all the speakers in our linguistic community mean the same thing by "chocolate", if we are to communicate using language. It would hamper communication if, by "chocolate" some meant *planet* and others meant *chocolate*, and communication would be impossible if this sort of variation were the rule rather than the exception. So it is in our common interest to use words to mean the same things.

However, much the same point can be made regarding the syntactic properties of an utterance. Clearly it is arbitrary what syntactic structure is associated with a given utterance type in just the way it is arbitrary what meaning is associated with it. Consider again sentence (5). Though it is the case that as we use (5) it has roughly the syntactic structure given in (6), we might use (or might have used) (5) in such a way that it had the syntactic structure given in (7) instead.

(6)

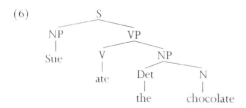

(7)

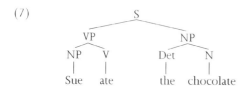

(6) has "Sue" as the subject, and "the chocolate" as the direct object, while (7) has "the chocolate" as subject and "Sue" as the direct object.

Clearly, it is also in our common interest that all the speakers in our linguistic community assign the same syntactic structures to expressions, if we are to communicate using language. It would hamper communication if some assigned the structure (6) to (5) while others assigned the structure (7) to (5). Communication would be impossible if this sort of variation were the rule rather than the exception. So it is in our common interest to all use expressions so as to assign the same syntactic structures to them.

Similar points can be made regarding the conventionality of word boundaries of phonetic typing. We might use (or might have used) the noises that make up a spoken utterance so that word boundaries occurred at different places, and we might use (or might have used) the noises that make up a spoken utterance so that they were phonetically typed with different sets of noise types. So, for example (to illustrate the latter claim), the t sound in the word "tasty" (as it is used) in (some spoken utterance of) (8) might be typed together with all the p sounds, rather than the t sounds.

(8) Chocolate is tasty and nutritious.

Clearly, it would be in our common interest for all the speakers in our linguistic community to assign the same word boundaries to utterances and to type sounds the same way phonetically, if we are to communicate using language. It would hamper communication if, for example, some assigned to (8) the phonetic structure I would associate with (9) while others assigned to (8) the structure I would associate with (10).[11]

(9) Chocolate is tasty and nutritious
(10) Chocolate is pasty and nutritious.

Communication would be impossible if this sort of variation were the rule rather than the exception. So it is in our common interest all to use expressions so as to assign the same word boundaries and phonetic structure to them.

Many (if not all) of the linguistic features of utterances are P-conventional. But how plausible is it that they are also L-conventional? How plausible is it that there are conventions (in Lewis's sense) which we participate in which make it the case that utterances have the phonological, morphological or syntactic features they do? If Lewis is trying to defend the conventionality of language, the default position would be for his theory to generalize to cover these other linguistic properties. However, a convention-based account similar to that offered for the semantic properties of natural language utterances does not look at all promising as an account of these other sorts of linguistic properties. I don't believe that anyone has ever suggested such an account of them.[12] This is most likely because no one seriously believes that speakers and hearers have the requisite attitudes or pattern of reasoning concerning the phonological, morphological or syntactic properties of utterances as is supposed in the case of semantic properties.

I think the moral is that the obvious conventionality of language gives us no reason at all to adopt a convention-based account of natural language semantic properties. Since syntactic, morphological and phonological properties are every bit as conventional in the trivial sense of conventionality (= non-instrinsic), but we are not in the least tempted to account for them in terms of the convention-based theorist's conventions, the fact that language is *obviously conventional* lends no credence to the convention-based account of semantic properties either. In fact, it gives us some reason doubt the convention-based account, since it fails to generalize to cover other properties which are equally obviously conventional. Fortunately, I think there is an alternative account which does not require us to make any use at all of Lewis's conventions to account for the various linguistic features (including semantic features) of utterances. I turn to that account now.

3 An alternative account

I noted at the outset that the convention-based account was the dominant view in philosophy concerning the nature of semantic properties of natural language utterances. Interestingly, the dominant view of the nature of the various other linguistic properties we have been discussing—syntactic, morphological and phonological properties—is a very different view, derived from the work of Noam Chomsky. Since it seems to me desirable, if possible, to have a unified treatment of natural language linguistic properties (on general grounds of simplicity and theoretical elegance), and since we have already seen that the convention-based account does not seem promising in this regard, it seems worthwhile to explore the possibility of "expanding" the Chomskian account to cover semantic properties in addition to the various other sorts of linguistic properties. I think that this is possible, and in this section I argue that the Chomskian alternative provides a satisfying account of the P-conventionality of language and provides a simpler and more general account of the nature of the linguistic properties of utterances than the convention-based account. I also note that the empirical evidence supports the empirical basis

for the Chomskian view, but provides no equivalent support for the convention-based view.

Chomsky claimed that linguistics is a branch of cognitive psychology, that linguistic claims are claims about (a significant subcomponent of) our capacity to produce and understand our native language. According to Chomsky, our capacity to process language is not simply a reflection of our general cognitive capacity to reason. Rather, there is a special purpose cognitive mechanism responsible for this capacity (Chomsky 1965, 1975). The claim that there is a special purpose cognitive mechanism responsible for our ability to process language is now usually interpreted as the claim that there is a language processing module in the sense articulated by Jerry Fodor (1983): principally, a system that is domain specific and informationally encapsulated, whose operations are fast and mandatory. I take the claim that our linguistic abilities are in this sense modular to be empirically well supported. But I do not think that the Chomskian view I am considering necessarily requires this particular sense of modularity.[13]

Similarly, I take there to be a range of broadly "Chomskian" accounts of the nature of linguistic properties. I count a view as Chomskian if it treats the linguistic properties of utterances as inherited from features of the language processor. Chomsky himself explicitly says that he does not think that linguistics directly provides a theory of language processing, and he has had a somewhat sceptical outlook on developments in psycholinguistics. Still, Chomsky insisted that linguistic competence—what he takes linguistic theory to be a theory of directly—is a central and essential component of our language processor. I therefore take accounts of the nature of linguistic properties which link them essentially to features of the language processor to be broadly Chomskian in spirit.[14]

We may illustrate the view further by considering a specific "Chomskian" view in more detail.[15] According to this view utterances have the linguistic properties they do in virtue of being associated, in the course of language processing, with mental representations having those properties.[16] To see how this account might work, we can adopt the following general picture of language processing. A sentence, (8) for example, is uttered.

(8) Chocolate is tasty and nutritious.

Processing is accomplished by successive computation of representations of this sentence at the phonological, syntactic, and semantic levels. The processing proceeds according to general principles and on the basis of information about the linguistic properties of words stored in the mental lexicon and the input representations from the prior level of processing (see Forster 1979, Garrett 1990, Frazier 1988). Such a model is an idealization. It is not really true, for example, that the processor computes the complete syntactic representation of a sentence before passing that representation on to the semantic level. Still, the majority of linguists and psycholinguists working within Chomsky's broad theoretical framework would accept this picture in rough outline.[17]

According to this picture though, the processor constructs representations corresponding to the linguistically significant levels of description, including a semantic level of processing, corresponding perhaps to the linguistic level of "logical form", which, following Robert May, we may think of as

that level of representation which interfaces the theories of linguistic form and interpretation. . . . it represents whatever properties of syntactic form are relevant to semantic interpretation—those aspects of semantic structure which are expressed syntactically. (1985, p. 2)

On this version of the Chomskian view, the semantic properties of utterances would be thought of as being "inherited" from the semantic properties of the representations at this level, and, in general, the linguistic properties of utterances would be inherited from the associated representations at each of the various levels of processing. The model I have in mind here is actually very straightforward. Given the empirical claim that language processing consists in recovering a series of representations at various linguistic levels, the view is simply that *it is in virtue of being associated, in language processing, with these representations that an utterance has the linguistic properties it has.* So, just as an utterance has a certain syntactic structure in virtue of being associated with a representation which has that structure, so it has a certain content or meaning in virtue of being associated with a representation which has that content or meaning.[18]

This leaves unexplained in virtue of what an internal representation could have semantic properties in the first place. But this is not an explanatory debt peculiar to the Chomskian theory. Lewis's account also appealed to internal states with unanalysed semantic content (e.g., beliefs). In both cases the project is simply to reduce the problem of providing an account of natural language semantic properties to the problem of providing an account of the semantic properties of mental states. Both accounts simply assume internal states with semantic content. The difference is simply a matter of which sorts of internal states with content are supposed to underwrite the natural language semantic properties.

That, in rough outline, is the Chomskian alternative. Like Lewis's account, it is compatible with and can account for the fact that semantic properties of utterances are P-conventional. The first and main feature of the P-conventionality of language (1.1 above) is that linguistic properties are not intrinsic properties of the utterances that have them. That means that the marks and sounds we use could have (or could have had) linguistic properties other than those they in fact have. On the Chomskian account under consideration, linguistic properties are not intrinsic in that the mechanisms responsible for processing might have been constructed during language acquisition so as to respond to different utterances the way they now respond to English utterances, and they might have been constructed so as to respond differently (or not at all) to English utterances. Similarly, these mechanisms might be altered in such a way as to respond differently to English utterances, or to respond to different utterances as they now respond to English utterances. Limits are set on what sorts of variation are possible in attaching linguistic properties to utterances by our capacity for language acquisition and the malleability of the existing processing mechanisms.

The other feature of P-conventionality is that it is mutually in our best interest to coordinate our language use. As was noted above, no theory-specific considerations are required to explain this feature of P-conventionality. The account of this feature is just the same as that given above: if we did not attribute more or less the same linguistic features to utterances we would not be able to communicate using language, and given that linguistic communication is in our interest, so is coordination.

Unlike Lewis's account, the Chomskian account I have presented also generalizes to other linguistic properties. Moreover, it also provides an account of the nature of linguistic properties generally—providing equally good accounts of the *nature* of the phonological and syntactic properties of utterances as it provides of the nature of their semantic properties. The Chomskian account is also simpler, or more direct. No complicated set of beliefs or intentions is required: we just look to the mental representations directly associated with the utterance by the language processor.

The crucial point, however, is a more directly empirical point: the language processing mechanism does not need to make any use of the mental states Lewis's theory posits. If language

processing is accomplished by a special purpose cognitive mechanism, there is no need to reason along Lewisian lines in order to process language or recover the semantic properties of utterances. The language processor can be thought of as treating utterances *as if* they had their linguistic properties *intrinsically*, in the sense that *the processor does not take the arbitrariness of linguistic properties into account at all in processing utterances*. In assigning syntactic structure to strings, for example, the processor seems to take into account only information stored in the mental lexicon about the words in the utterance such as their syntactic category (noun, verb, . . .) and subcategorization information (e.g., that "gave" takes a direct object and an indirect object), and general principles of assigning structure such as Minimal Attachment or respect for the Theta Criterion. The language processor does not need to reason along Lewisian lines because it has access to special linguistic "knowledge" and processing principles that do all the work. It is easier to see now how the hypothetical community considered in § 1 above is possible. Indeed, in many respects, we are such a community, since though it is possible for us to recognize the conventionality of language, by and large this recognition plays no role in our linguistic dealings with one another.

In addition to the automaticity of language processing, a variety of empirical considerations can be marshalled both in favour of the Chomskian account and against the convention-based account. I want to focus my attention here on the latter sort of considerations.[19] I take the real *core* of the convention-based theory to be that linguistic communication is to be assimilated to communication in general. Lewis, like other convention-based theorists, completely embeds his discussion of linguistic communication into a larger discussion of communication generally, and clearly emphasizes the affinities between the linguistic and nonlinguistic cases. In linguistic communication, as in communication generally, we engage in a process of reasoning to determine what the other person is trying to communicate. I point to me and then to a distant spot and point to you, and then the same spot, and you infer by some process of reasoning that I want to meet you over there. Linguistic communication is much the same, according to this view. It is this core, and not the details of any specific account, that I want to look at now.

Since language, on this view, is a rather direct reflection of general abilities to reason about one's own mental states and the mental states of one's conspecifics, we should expect the ability to use language to correlate strongly with these general capacities. In particular, given the obvious advantages of having a language, we should expect any agent with these basic capacities to develop linguistic abilities. Given that linguistic communication is simply one facet of a more general communicative capacity, and essentially involves some sort of reasoning about communicative intentions, we should expect that linguistic ability would strongly correlate with both communicative ability and general intelligence and reasoning ability. A number of considerations, however, suggest that this correlation does not in fact hold. I will break the argument down into several stages, each of which presents independent considerations, but considerations which I think are mutually reinforcing.

First, general intelligence does not correlate with linguistic ability. The correlation breaks down in both directions. There are severely intellectually challenged agents with normal linguistic abilities and there are intelligent agents who do not possess anything approaching normal linguistic abilities. The former sort of case is illustrated by subjects with Williams syndrome. Steven Pinker comments on a number of such cases in *The Language Instinct* (1994). To illustrate the linguistic abilities of such subjects, consider the following passage taken from a transcript of a woman named Crystal who has Williams syndrome.

This is a story about chocolates. Once upon a time, in Chocolate World there used to be a Chocolate Princess. She was such a yummy princess. She was on her chocolate throne and then some chocolate man came to see her. And the man bowed to her and he said these words to her. The man said to her, "Please, Princess Chocolate. I want you to see how I do my work. And it's hot outside in Chocolate World, and you might melt to the ground like melted butter. And if the sun changes to a different colour, then the Chocolate World— and you—won't melt. You can be saved if the sun changes to a different colour. And if it doesn't change to a different colour, you and Chocolate World are doomed". (Pinker 1994, p. 53)

Clearly this woman has intact linguistic abilities. But, according to Pinker, Crystal and other people with Williams syndrome have an IQ of about 50 and are not able to do such simple things as find their way home, add, or retrieve things from the cupboard (Pinker 1994, p. 52).

The same point can be made even more dramatically by considering the case of a subject, Christopher, studied by Neil Smith and Ianthi-Maria Tsimpli (1991 and 1995). According to Smith and Tsimpli, Christopher has a nonverbal IQ between 60 and 70 and finds ordinary tasks like "doing up a button, cutting his fingernails or vacuuming the carpet" to be "tasks of major difficulty" (Smith and Tsimpli 1991, p. 117). In spite of this his English is "entirely comparable to that of normal speakers" (1995, p. 44) and, amazingly, "when given a passage written in any of some 15 or 16 languages—[he] simply translates it into English at about the speed one would normally read aloud a piece written in English" (1991, p. 317). Though his competence is rather varied in the different languages, his overall abilities are impressive on any scale. Here are two examples from Smith and Tsimpli (1991, pp. 319–20):

Greek (the passage was in Greek script)

Otan perase t'amaksi, epsakse ja tis pantufles tis, ala ena paljopedho ihe pari ti mja ki efevje jelontas.

translation: When the car passed, she looked for her slippers, but a naughty (lit: old) child had taken one and was leaving laughing.

C's translation: "When she passed the car . . . when the car passed, she was looking for her slippers, but an old child had taken one away and left . . . and was laughing."

Polish

Musiałem go wrzucić do wozu siłą. Położył się na pldłodze i zamknął oczy, nie chcąc widzieć, co go jeszcze czeka.

translation: I had to throw him into the car with force. He lay down on the floor and closed his eyes, not wishing to see what awaited him.

C's translation: "I had to take him out of the car strongly and put—he put himself on the floor and opened his eyes—and shut his eyes, not wishing to see what was waiting for him."

Smith and Tsimpli (1991, pp. 318–22) also provide examples of his translations of passages from Danish, Dutch, Finnish, French, German, Hindi, Italian, Norwegian, Portuguese, Russian, Spanish, Swedish, Turkish and Welsh.

On the other hand, there are also cases of intelligent agents who do not possess anything approaching normal linguistic abilities. The classic cases are those involving persons exposed to language after the critical period for language acquisition. (We might also note that some apes have IQs as high as 80 (Wallman 1992, p. 20), but language skills not even approaching Crystal's much less Christopher's!) Perhaps the most famous case involves a woman named Genie who was the victim of severe abuse and neglect as a child. Until the age of 13 she grew up in isolation and was almost never spoken to. Needless to say, when she was discovered she had very little cognitive or linguistic abilities, and was severely emotionally damaged. It turned out that

though she was able to recover significantly, she was never able to acquire anything like normal linguistic abilities. Susan Curtiss, who was one of the main researchers to study Genie's development, describes her as a "powerfully effective nonlinguistic communicator" (1988, p. 98) but notes that her knowledge of the basic rules of English did not develop past that of a 2 year old in the 8 years in which she was studied. Here are some illustrative examples of Genie's speech:

> "applesauce buy store"
> "man motorcycle have"
> "Genie bad cold live father house" (Curtiss 1988, pp. 98)

Genie's case is difficult because of the severe abuse she suffered as a child. The deficits may be explainable in other ways. The case of another woman, Chelsea, is perhaps better in this respect. Chelsea is a severely hearing impaired person who was misdiagnosed as being mentally retarded as a child. Since people attributed her inability to learn a language as being due to her alleged mental retardation, rather than her inability to hear the language, no effort was made to expose her to a sign language. When it was discovered that she had a severe hearing impairment (unbelievably, in her 30's), she was fitted with hearing aids, and an attempt was made to teach her language. Like Genie, she has not been able to acquire normal linguistic abilities, despite being otherwise of normal intelligence. Here are some examples of Chelsea's speech:

> "The small a the hat"
> "Breakfast eating girl"
> "They are is car in the Tim" (Curtiss 1988, p. 99)

Unlike Genie, she makes free use of determiners, prepositions and such. But her use of language is often so ungrammatical that it is unintelligible.

Cases like those of Crystal, Christopher, Genie

and Chelsea are typically taken to show that linguistic ability is in some sense modular, since it can be dissociated in these ways from general intellectual ability. Possibly, however, general intelligence is not to the point in the case of convention-based semantics. The core of the convention-based account is an assimilation to general communicative abilities, not general intelligence. However it is worth noting just how severe this dissociation can be. Christopher and Crystal, we are told, find such tasks as buttoning a button or adding to be extremely difficult, and yet they are clearly rather proficient language users. Yet according to the convention-based account, language users must engage in some (notoriously) rather complex reasoning processes, at times involving quite complex and esoteric contents.[20]

The next stage in the argument is based on the fact that similar dissociations can be found concerning the possession of a so-called "theory of mind"—a general ability for reasoning about the mental states of others in terms of, for example, propositional attitudes. Evidence from recent studies of autistic individuals suggests that a central component of autism is the lack of a theory of mind (for a review of some of this literature, see Happe 1994). Although most autistic individuals have poor or nonexistent linguistic abilities and very low IQs, some "high functioning" individuals have normal IQs and, despite some rather serious communicative abnormalities (being withdrawn, or overly inquisitive, or otherwise socially inappropriate), they can also have nearly normal linguistic abilities. Genie and Chelsea illustrate the other side of the dissociation here as well, apparently possessing normal theory of mind abilities, but lacking linguistic abilities. This argument poses a more direct challenge to the convention-based theorist. It is extremely puzzling how someone lacking a theory of mind could use language according to the convention-based theorist, given that the account posits numerous attitudes concerning

the propositional attitudes of other members of the community. It is also extremely puzzling why someone possessing a theory of mind and normal intelligence should fail to acquire normal linguistic abilities, given the obvious advantages of being able effectively to communicate using language.

The next stage in the argument is based on evidence for the dissociation of general linguistic ability and the capacity for communication. One source of evidence comes from aphasiacs, where much of the ability to use language may be lost (though not through motor damage), but general communicative skills seem to remain intact. A particularly interesting case here involves aphasiac "speakers" of American Sign Language (ASL), since in this case linguistic and nonlinguistic communication is often in the same (gestural) modality. Poizner, Bellugi and Klima (1987) tested a number of such aphasiacs for their ability to imitate nonlinguistic representational gestures, to imitate nonlinguistic nonrepresentational gestures, and to interpret pantomime. All but one[21] performed normally on these tests, though each had severe linguistic deficits.

An even more striking case arguing much the same point is provided by the case of children learning ASL. When English speaking children first learn the pronouns "me" and "you" they often make errors, referring to themselves as "you" and to others as "me". In ASL, the signs for "me" and "you" are pointing gestures—pointing to me for "me" and you for "you". Deaf children, like hearing children regularly point to objects of interest in their environments in their prelinguistic phase. So one might expect that children learning ASL would not be prone to the sort of reversal errors that children learning English pronouns are, given that the ASL sign, and the prelinguistic sign, are physically identical, and the children seem to have mastered the sign in their prelinguistic phase. We would be especially likely to suppose this, of course, if we thought that natural language was basically just a reflection of a general communicative ability, as the convention-based account suggests.

It turns out, quite surprisingly, that children learning ASL make the same sorts of reversal errors as children learning English. Children learning ASL stop using pointing gestures to refer to people for a while around the age of two, and then shortly after, at about the same age as children learning English acquire pronouns, pointing gestures reappear—with the reversal errors (Petitto 1987).

If language were a direct reflection of general abilities to reason about one's own mental states and the mental states of others, we should expect the ability to use language to correlate strongly with these general communicative capacities. We would not expect radical discontinuities between linguistic and nonlinguistic use of what is physically *the same symbol*. The fact that it does not correlate and that such discontinuities exist suggests that the ability to speak a language is not simply a reflection of general communicative or intellectual ability.

The final sort of evidence I will consider shows how specific linguistic constraints (which appear to be due to Universal Grammar) can override what would otherwise seem to be decisive general communicative considerations —namely, fitting the language you "learn" to the model you are given. One striking sort of case involves children who actually *opt out* of the "linguistic" practices in their "linguistic" environment. Deaf isolates are deaf children born to hearing parents and not exposed to any natural sign language. These children construct for themselves a sign language with many of the marks of standard natural languages, despite the fact that the only "language" they are exposed to is the primitive signing of their parents, which does not constitute a natural language.[22] Amazingly, the linguistic developmental pattern of these children is much the same as normal children (through age 3 or 4) despite the fact that they effectively have *no model at all*, and therefore *no training* in the use of

this language (since they are making it up!). The children's language takes on a number of language-like features that go beyond the parental input. For example, the children use pointing gestures to indicate not just objects in the immediate environment, but also objects located in imaginary space, not present in the immediate environment, and at least some of these children develop their own inflectional system for verbs where action signs are displaced toward the position of the sign for the object in motion (a common device in standard sign languages).[23] Moreover, the parents' sign system never develops to the same degree as the children's, and when the parents' system does develop to some degree, it is in *response* to the spontaneous changes in the children's language and not the other way around. Also, the children's "vocabulary" overlap with their mothers' symbols is only an estimated 33% (Jackendoff 1994, p. 129).

Exactly the same sort of phenomenon seems to occur when children are exposed to a pidgin language: they seem to opt out of the "linguistic" practices of their "linguistic" community. A pidgin is a makeshift amalgam of several natural languages used for communication among a group of speakers with no single dominant language. Children exposed only to pidgins reject them in favour of new languages of their own creation (creoles). The creole which children create is far richer and more systematic than the pidgin on which it is "based" and is uniform across the community (see Pinker 1994, Ch. 2 and Jackendoff 1994, pp. 130–5). These children effectively turn the primitive signing of their parents into a natural language through expansion and regularization of various sorts. What is interesting from the current perspective is that in going beyond the "language" of their environment, they are ignoring the conventional assignments of linguistic properties to utterances which are found in their "linguistic" environment: thus they would be opting out of the conventions in their linguistic environment. On the standard convention-based account it is hard to see why they would do this.

These phenomena ranging from the cases of Williams syndrome, to autistic individuals, to individuals past the critical period, to the deaf isolates and children exposed to pidgins pose very serious empirical difficulties for the convention-based account (while lending considerable support to the Chomskian account). In my view, they leave no serious doubt that the convention-based account is fundamentally mistaken.

4 Looking beyond literal expression meaning

In § 3 we saw that standard accounts treat language processing as a more or less automatic and autonomous process. Such an account leaves no real role for the various propositional attitudes invoked by the convention-based account. Further empirical considerations suggested that, contrary to the picture of linguistic communication implicit in such accounts, linguistic communication is not continuous with nonlinguistic communication or a general capacity for reasoning and intelligence.

We are not, however, forced to accept the view that speakers have no propositional attitudes about themselves, their partners in communication, or their mode of communication, nor need we claim that such attitudes play no role at all in linguistic communication. The model of language processing in § 3 is compatible with the existence of a level of processing at which language users employ general cognitive faculties in attempting to infer speakers' beliefs, intentions and expectations, and we have powerful reasons to suppose that there is such a level of processing. If we did not monitor the flow of discourse in this way, how would we be able to infer the nonliteral meanings of utterances or know what sort of response was appropriate in a given circumstance? I will call the "level" at which we keep track of the beliefs and intentions of our conversational partners (as well as various other information pertaining to the immediate environment, and relevant general world knowledge) the "level" of discourse monitoring.[24]

Several possibilities for the convention-based theorist present themselves at this point.[25] Perhaps this is where the Lewisian reasoning that determines the literal semantic properties of utterances takes place. Or perhaps it is not literal semantic properties of utterances that we get an account of, but some other level of meaning which includes the nonliteral meaning of utterances, and perhaps the Lewisian reasoning which determines *these* properties of utterances takes place at the level of discourse monitoring.

However, even if we suppose that the relevant reasoning occurs at the level of discourse monitoring, the convention-based account would still only be plausible as an account of the (literal or nonliteral) *semantic* properties of utterances. The account would obviously still lack the generality we should expect. It is totally implausible that the beliefs and intentions regarding syntax and phonology required by a convention-based account of the syntactic and phonological properties of utterances should be present at the level of discourse monitoring or any other level. Therefore the Chomskian account should be our default hypothesis in each case, and we should abandon it only with great reluctance, given its theoretical virtues of simplicity and generality. This suggests that *even if the relevant Lewisian reasoning occurred* at, for example, the level of discourse monitoring, general considerations of simplicity and theoretical elegance dictate that we should not take this reasoning to *determine* the semantic properties of utterances, unless the Chomskian account is unavailable.

Furthermore, the level of analysis involved in computing nonliteral meaning or determining which utterance is conversationally appropriate (i.e., discourse monitoring) seems to require the prior analysis of literal meaning. This suggests that the relevant Lewisian reasoning plays no role in the processing of the literal meaning of utterances. The nonliteral meaning of an utterance is arrived at partly on the basis of the literal meaning of the utterance. And an appropriate response to an utterance is generated on the basis of beliefs about the environment and the person one is responding to (including her beliefs, intentions and expectations) in conjunction with the literal meaning of the utterance in question. Something like the literal meaning of an utterance is plausibly recovered from a representation of the syntactic structure of the utterance, together with recognition of the lexical items involved and retrieval of stored lexical representations. So the mental states posited by the convention-based theory do not seem to be involved in the processing of literal meaning. Thus if the relevant mental states do occur, they occur only after the literal semantic properties of an utterance have already been recovered.

Is it likely that the relevant Lewisian reasoning does in fact occur at the level of discourse monitoring? At this point some of the traditional problems for convention-based accounts that were briefly mentioned above seem relevant. Consider, for example, the case of a speaker addressing a hostile or unreceptive audience, or a cognitive agent producing utterances with no intended audience, perhaps talking to herself, or writing notes in a margin which she never intends to be read (see Chomsky 1975, Schiffer 1972, 1982, 1987). In both of these cases Lewis's account would seem to fail. Others do not respond to her utterances by coming to believe that they are true in L, and she does not believe that others are so coming to believe. Thus at least the first two clauses of Lewis's account are not satisfied.[26] To take a different sort of case, I might utter a sentence I believe to be false in metaphorical, sarcastic or hyperbolic uses of language. For example believing that Jones has done a really bad job, I might say in a sarcastic tone of voice:

(11) Nice job Jones!

Similarly, I might utter a sentence which I know to be false, as an example of such a sentence, or just to be silly, or as part of a story, or in an effort to deceive my audience, or just because I feel like it. I might produce (12), for example, knowing full well that it is not true:

(12) Ronald Reagan was born with no nose.

Despite the fact that Lewis's account is not satisfied with respect to my utterances in such cases (I don't believe them to be true for starters), they certainly have semantic properties; the utterances are not meaningless.[27]

I think it is clear that the Chomskian account being offered here most directly provides an account of the so-called "expression meaning" of an utterance. The basic idea is that an expression like (11), for example, is correlated in language processing with an LF representation, say, containing the mental words "nice", "job" and "Jones" in such a combination that the principles of compositional semantics governing these representations yield the truth condition, roughly, of a sincere utterance of (13):

(13) [You did a] nice job Jones.

The so-called "speaker/hearer meaning" is derived from this expression meaning.[28] The Chomskian has no need somehow to construct the expression meaning of an utterance out of possible speaker meanings. Rather the expression meaning is simply that meaning which is associated with the utterance in the course of language processing directly through principles of the compositional semantics embodied in the language processor. The speaker/hearer meaning is the intended/inferred ultimate meaning associated with the utterance, in this case through some further process of reasoning, presumably based on the utterance's expression meaning, and further facts. It seems that we might also think of this further meaning as being encapsulated in a mental representation with that content and inherited by the utterance in the Chomskian manner as well.

In the end, I think that it is unlikely that the conditions of any convention-based account are satisfied for any linguistic properties at any level at all. Even at the level of discourse monitoring, and even for semantic properties, there is substantial reason to doubt that the conditions of a convention-based account are satisfied. Certainly, speakers keep track of who their conversational partners are and attribute various speech acts to them. But this does not seem to require that the conditions of any convention-based account of meaning be satisfied. It seems more plausible that the language processor computes various linguistic properties of utternaces, while speakers are independently tracked at the level of discourse monitoring and assigned speech acts and other pragmatic aspects of the utterance are computed.

These considerations reinforce the suggestion that the Chomskian hypothesis should be the default hypothesis: it should be the default hypothesis in the case of the linguistic properties computed at the level of discourse analysis no less than in the case of linguistic properties computed at other levels of processing. Presumably the "output" of the discourse monitoring level of processing will be a representation of some (not necessarily literal) "meaning" of the utterance. Our default hypothesis should be that the utterance inherits this "meaning" in the Chomskian manner as well, regardless of what propositional attitudes play a role in the reasoning at the level of discourse monitoring which assigns such a representation to the utterance.

Considerations from reasoning at the level of discourse monitoring do not seem to provide any real help to the convention-based theorist. Such considerations offer no reason to believe that the empirical basis of the convention-based account is satisfied, for any linguistic properties at all. And the general theoretical considerations

which establish the Chomskian account as the default hypothesis remain in place.

5 Conclusion

Where does all this leave us? If the language processor is thought of along standard lines as a special purpose cognitive mechanism, we can see language processing as basically an automatic process. The language processor can be seen as treating utterances as if they had their linguistic properties *intrinsically* in the sense that the processor does not take the arbitrariness of linguistic properties into account in processing utterances. In light of this, the various mental states which the convention-based theorist takes to underlie the semantic properties of natural language utterances seem strangely unmotivated.

It might be objected that convention-based theorists do not really intend to give a theory of processing at all. I think that this is right. My point however, is that if we do not have reason to believe that the basis of their account is satisfied by considering the states required for processing language, what reason *do* we have for believing that this basis is satisfied? The question becomes especially pressing when we see that an alternative account is available, and that there is good reason to believe that *its* empirical basis is satisfied. If there is an alternative account of the nature of the semantic properties of natural language utterances, as I claim there is, the need for an account of these properties no longer provides us with good reason to believe that the empirical basis of the convention-based account is satisfied. And given that there is no independent motivation (from processing considerations) for believing that the empirical basis of the convention-based account is satisfied, why think that the convention-based account is true?[29]

Can independent motivation for the states underlying convention-based accounts be found elsewhere? Perhaps, for example, the convention-based account is more plausibly viewed as an account of how conventions get *established* rather than as an account of how they are *sustained*. Perhaps convention-based accounts might be required to explain language acquisition, or the evolution of language. More generally, there might be ways of making the Chomskian account and the convention-based account *compatible*. Perhaps the web of attitudes the convention-based account posits mediates the content relation for LFs. Perhaps it is necessary to account for the division of linguistic labour. Perhaps it is necessary to account for the establishing of sound meaning pairings (either developmentally or evolutionarily). If this were true, then we would not have to give up either account.

There are several points to make about these suggestions. First, and most importantly, I am perfectly willing to grant that the two accounts *may* be compatible. On the other hand, the bare possibility that the accounts can be made compatible shows very little. For all I know some theory incorporating phlogiston can be made compatible with current theories about oxidation. Maybe the phlogiston-based theory can be taken as a theory of some other vaguely related phenomena. On the face of it, though, we have two theories claiming to provide an account of the same thing—the nature of natural language semantic properties—and I claim to have argued for the conceptual and empirical superiority of one of these accounts. It hardly seems incumbent upon me to show that there is *no* way that the convention-based theory could be made compatible with this. Rather it would seem to be the burden of defenders of the convention-based account to find some interesting explanatory work for their theory to do. And in this I wish them luck. I claim only that it will not do as a theory of the nature of semantic properties of natural language utterances, since there is a better account of these.

Second, I am not claiming that propositional attitudes of various sorts concerning speakers and hearers or "the community" generally are irrelevant to semantics. It may be, for example,

that the content of my mental representations is in some cases partly determined by the fact that I am willing to defer to experts. I see no reason why this is necessarily incompatible with the proposals of this paper, and so I can remain neutral on this question.

Third, and finally, although it is possible that the convention-based account can be made compatible with the Chomskian account, the defender of the convention-based account has to face the empirical and conceptual considerations raised above, and analogous considerations that might be raised for other possible explananda. Unfortunately I do not have space for a full consideration of these issues. However, I do not find any of the suggestions mentioned above at all plausible. The states underlying convention-based accounts seem to be as irrelevant to the process of language acquisition, for example, as they were to the account of language processing. The dominant view of language acquisition sees acquisition proceeding by means of the triggering of specific settings in an innate universal system of parameters. The acquisition of individual word meanings does not seem to require anything like the sorts of beliefs and intentions posited by the convention-based theorist either. Children's hypotheses concerning the possible meanings of words in their language are obviously highly constrained. While I am not really sure how the story would go for the convention-based theorist, the simplest formulations of such constraints do not seem to require the sorts of states that the convention-based theorist posits. (For some discussion of word learning see, for example, Markman 1989, Gleitman 1990, and Bloom 1993.) Regarding the evolution of language, very little, of course, is known. Though it is not really clear exactly what the convention-based theorist's account here is, an analogous position concerning, for example, the evolution of vision—that we must have entered into primitive vision conventions for vision to have evolved—just seems silly. And I do not see any reason to suppose that a convention-based account of the evolution of language should be taken any more seriously.

Much of the general theoretical and empirical support for the Chomskian view of language has come to light only fairly recently. So philosophers have not yet fully appreciated the implications of these results. In my view they provide powerful reason to believe that the convention-based approach is fundamentally mistaken and that the alternative Chomskian account is basically correct. Once we think in terms of a special purpose cognitive mechanism for language processing, we see that it is not necessary to reason in terms of agents' beliefs and intentions regarding utterances and other agents' mental states in order to recover the semantic (or other linguistic) properties of utterances. It is not necessary to reason in this way, and there is no reason to suppose we do. Communicating in language is fundamentally different from signalling that I want to meet you over there by pointing vigorously in that direction.

Notes

1 For some, this will in turn imply that the issue is whether semantics can be assimilated to the domain of the natural sciences. I think that if this assimilation is possible, then the enormously increased explanatory power it promises would provide a compelling reason for it. I further believe that it is possible to assimilate semantics to the domain of the natural sciences, and that the "Chomskian" account I advocate is the best strategy for accomplishing this.

2 And also in his later paper "Languages and Language": "It is a platitude—something only a philosopher would dream of denying that there are conventions of language, although we do not find it easy to say what those conventions are." (1983, p. 166 [p. 227])

3 Utterance types are nonlinguistic physical types corresponding to some token utterance of a linguistic expression. So they are types of sounds (in spoken language), marks (in written language) or gestures (in sign language).

4 In his motivational remarks, Lewis also suggests that it is part of the platitude that language is conventional that we

> have made [our words] mean what they do because somehow, gradually and informally, we have come to an understanding that this is what we shall use them to mean. (1969, p. 1)

It certainly seems true enough that we never all got together and formally decided at some point that we would use these words to mean what they do. And if this is all he means by this remark, I am willing enough to accept it. But Lewis seems to be making some stronger positive claim here, which he later spells out in his account of conventions (see below). I do not regard this further claim as a platitude about language, as I will argue below.

5 This account of "true in *L*" gets significantly complicated in response to various facets of natural language such as indexicality, tense, ambiguity, mood and nonliteral uses of language (metaphor, irony, jokes, "white lies", etc.). Lewis says that he is "deliberately stretching the ordinary usage of 'true', 'truthfulness' and 'trust' in extending them" in these ways (1983, p. 172 [p. 232]).

6 See Schiffer (1987, pp. 258–61), for discussion of this point.

7 Lewis qualifies this last point rather substantially in "Languages and Language", apparently in light of considerations of the plausibility of the "psychological reality" of the account:

> The knowledge mentioned here [in clause (6)] may be merely potential: knowledge that would be available if one bothered to think hard enough. . . . Perhaps a negative version of (6) would do the job: no one disbelieves that (1) to (5) hold, no one believes that others disbelieve this, and so on. (1983, p. 165–6 [p. 227])

8 For more on these traditional objections, see § 4 below.

9 I will be referring back to numbered sentences in what follows. Such references should be interpreted as referring to the sound type corresponding to some utterance of that sentence (the same sound type throughout the discussion of

that particular sentence) rather than to the sentence (type or token) itself.

10 Taking this sound type to be a proper part of the one we are associating with (5).

11 Differences of assignments of roughly this sort do exist among dialectical variants of a language; and, of course, these sometimes do lead to difficulties in communication!

12 I suppose that we could mimic the Lewisian conventions of truthfulness and trust, and attribute to speakers conventions of "grammaticality and trust", wherein speakers intended to utter phonologically, morphologically and syntactically well-formed utterances of their language, and people believed that others so intended and therefore interpreted the utterances of others as phonologically, morphologically and syntactically well-formed, and so on.

13 The issue of modularity in language processing is a focus of lively debate within psycholinguistics (see, for example, Marslen-Wilson and Tyler 1987, Frazier 1987, and other papers in Garfield 1987). Nonmodular parsers are not necessarily incompatible with the Chomskian account I present here since a parser could make use of contextual information and still successively compute the representations corresponding to the various linguistic levels of description. Furthermore, while nonmodular parsers would make use of contextual information, there is no reason to suppose that they would involve Lewisian reasoning.

14 For discussion of some alternatives see Stabler (1983) and Matthews (1991).

15 The particular account I offer is not the only possible Chomskian account. The general model of language processing and the suggestion I present as "the Chomskian alternative" are offered for the sake of concreteness and expository simplicity. As noted above, Chomsky's suggestion points us towards a certain range of accounts about the nature of linguistic properties, each compatible with a range of general processing models. A different and perhaps more plausible model might posit a less direct relation between the utterance and the linguistic properties, perhaps in terms of a modal relation of some sort (say, constructability given the nature of items stored in a mental lexicon

and combinatorial rules represented in a stored mental grammar). Which sort of model is best will depend on various empirical and theoretical considerations (about which not enough is now known to make any clear choice). I take the detailed nature of the relationship between linguistic theory (semantics included) and the psychological mechanisms underlying our capacity to process our native language to be a matter for empirical psycholinguistic research. This does not mean that the view is vacuous or impossible to refute. It may well turn out that none of the claims in this general range can be sustained.

16 See J.A. Fodor (1975) and Matthews (1991).

17 Not all psycholinguists would accept this model, even in rough outline. Not all psycholinguists, for example, would even accept that there are distinct levels of processing corresponding to the linguistically significant levels of description (see, e.g., Marslen-Wilson and Tyler 1987). If these theorists are correct, then the specific Chomskian theory I present cannot be right (though of course some other broadly Chomskian account might be—see note 15). Naturally I take it to be an open empirical question whether the empirical consequences of the actual Chomskian account I present obtain.

18 A different, related, account would have it that the representations constructed in language processing were representations to the effect that such-and-such an utterance had so-and-so linguistic properties. Since my aim here is not to decide which amongst various competing Chomskian accounts is best, I prefer the simpler account in the text for expository purposes. Again see note 15 above.

19 Among the forms of evidence of the former sort are various more direct types of psycholinguistic evidence for levels of processing from speech errors (Garrett 1988), from processing breakdown in normal and aphasiac subjects (Pritchett 1992, Zurif 1990), and from experiments involving cross modal priming (Swinney et al. 1988, cited in J.D. Fodor 1990), to cite just a few of many possible sources of evidence.

20 The Chomskian explanation for their linguistic abilities is that they are compatible with severe nonlinguistic deficits because linguistic ability has

little or nothing to do with "general intellectual abilities".

21 The one exception was to the test of imitating nonlinguistic representational gestures, and the deficit was predictable from the particular lesion involved, according to current theory: Poizner et al. 1987, pp. 170–2.

22 Though I take it to be a theoretical issue (to be settled by linguistic theory) just what counts as a natural language, we can note here briefly that the "language" which these children's parents use to communicate with them typically lacks many important features of natural languages (for example, they typically have no inflectional system). For discussion, see Jackendoff 1994, pp. 126–30 (on which my remarks are based), or the original research Jackendoff describes there (Goldin-Meadow and Mylander 1990 and Goldin-Meadow et. al. 1994).

23 Data is rather limited due to the huge effort required to interpret the children's language with strict controls to ensure maximally objective coding. For more detailed information, see Jackendoff 1994, pp. 126–30 and the papers he cites.

24 It is not clear to what extent these processes should be thought of as a single unified "level" of processing. Some aspects of our pragmatic processing may be relatively susceptible to such treatment, others not. Nothing I say turns on our being able to identify some particular "level" of processing, though I will continue to talk in terms of a "level" of discourse monitoring, for expository simplicity; I mean simply to refer to whatever aspects of our cognitive processing are involved in these processes.

25 Though many of the difficulties raised in the last section would remain difficulties on these suggestions.

26 It is not clear to me which, if any, of the others are satisfied in these cases either. Clause 3, for example, seems to require belief that clause 2 holds. Similar points would seem to hold for the remainder of the clauses of Lewis's account.

27 Lewis suggests three possible responses to the sorts of problems raised here (1983, pp. 183–4 [p. 240]). The first is that we might simply stipulate that such "non-serious" language is automatically true in L. The second is that we might

treat all such uses as exceptions. And the third is that we might define a certain set of core communication situations ("serious" ones) for which the conditions of the account must obtain. And this is all that would be required for a population to speak a language (it would not matter what would happen in the noncore cases). I am uncomfortable with the first sort of response because it further complicates the beliefs required by speakers to participate in Lewis's conventions. The other suggestions are possible moves Lewis could make. Of course we would still want the exceptions, or the noncore cases to *have semantic properties*. Presumably they must get them through their relation to core cases. The natural assumption would be that such utterances are relevantly of the same type as some core case. Perhaps they have the semantic properties that they would have if they were produced in some serious communication situation. There are at least two difficulties for this view. First, it may be that there are sound types corresponding to utterances which would *only* be produced in nonserious uses of language—sarcastic utterances of sentences, for example, often have different physical realisations than their non-sarcastic counterparts. And, second, we need some noncircular way of determining which situations are core/serious.

28 I am not sure how much theoretical weight the terms "speaker meaning" and "expression meaning" can bear. They seem to me to be used in a variety of senses, which may or may not cohere. I only use them here to make contact with the literature.

29 Language processing and acquisition are without question central explananda of a theory of language. Arguably, we should look to such central explanatory roles of a given kind (asking what best explains them) in determining the nature of that kind. Since the Chomskian account ties the nature of linguistic properties directly to these central explanatory roles of linguistic kinds, it thereby seems to have a strong claim to being an account of the nature of these kinds.

References

Bloom, Paul 1993: "Where Do Constraints on Word Meaning Come From?", in Clark 1993, pp. 23–34.

Chomsky, Noam 1965: *Aspects of the Theory of Syntax*. Cambridge, MA: MIT Press.

—— 1975: *Reflections on Language*. New York: Pantheon Books/Random House.

Clark, Eve (ed.) 1993: *The Proceedings of the Twenty-Fourth Annual Child Language Research Forum*. Stanford, CA: CSLI.

Cooper, William and Walker, Edward (eds.) 1979: *Sentence Processing*. Hillsdale, NJ: L. Erlbaum Associates.

Curtiss, Susan 1988: "Abnormal Language Acquisition and the Modularity of Language", in Newmeyer 1988, pp. 96–116.

Fodor, Janet D. 1991: "Sentence Processing and the Mental Grammar", in Sells, Sheiber, and Wasow 1991, pp. 83–113.

Fodor, Jerry A. 1975: *The Language of Thought*. Cambridge, MA: Harvard University Press.

—— 1983: *The Modularity of Mind*. Cambridge, MA: MIT Press

—— 1990: "Psychosemantics: or Where Do Truth Conditions Come From?", in Lycan 1990, pp. 312–37.

Forster, Kenneth 1979: "Levels of Processing and the Structure of the Language Processor", in Cooper and Walker 1979, pp. 27–85.

Frazier, Lyn 1987: "Theories of Sentence Processing", in Garfield 1987, pp. 291–307.

—— 1988: "Grammar and Language Processing", in Newmeyer 1988, pp. 15–34.

Garfield, Jay, ed. 1987: *Modularity in Knowledge Representation and Natural-Language Understanding*. Cambridge, MA: MIT Press.

Garrett, Merrill 1990: "Sentence Processing", in Osherson and Lasnik 1990, pp. 133–75.

Gleitman, Lila 1990: "The Structural Sources of Word Meaning". *Language Acquisition*, 1, pp. 3–55.

Goldin-Meadow, Susan and Mylander, Carolyn 1990: "Beyond the Input Given: The Child's Role in the Acquisition of Language". *Language*, 66, 323–55.

Goldin-Meadow, Susan, Butcher, Cynthia, Mylander, Carolyn and Dodge, Mark 1994: "Nouns and Verbs in a Self-Styled Gesture System: What's in a Name?". *Cognitive Psychology*, 27, 259–319.

Grice, H.P. 1989: "Meaning", in Grice 1989, pp. 213–23. Originally published in 1957 in *The Philosophical Review*, 66, pp. 377–88.

—— 1989: *Studies in the Way of Words*. Cambridge, MA: Harvard University Press.

Happe, Francesca 1994: *Autism*. London: UCL Press.

Jackendoff, Ray 1994: *Patterns in the Mind*. New York: Harper Press.

Kasher, Asa (ed.) 1991: *The Chomskyan Turn*. Oxford: Basil Blackwell.

Lewis, David 1969: *Convention*. Cambridge, MA: Harvard University Press.

—— 1983: "Languages and Language", in Lewis 1983a, pp. 163–88.

—— 1983a: *Philosophical Papers*, vol. 1. Oxford: Oxford University Press.

Lycan, William (ed.) 1990: *Mind and Cognition*. Oxford: Basil Blackwell.

Markman, Ellen 1989: *Categorization and Naming in Children: Problems of Induction*. Cambridge, MA: MIT Press.

Marslen-Wilson, William and Tyler, Lorraine Komisarjevsky 1987: "Against Modularity", in Garfield 1987, pp. 37–62.

Matthews, Robert 1991: "Psychological Reality of Grammars", in Kasher 1991, pp. 182–99.

May, Robert 1985: *Logical Form: Its Structure and Implications*. Cambridge, MA: MIT Press.

Newmeyer, Frederick (ed.) 1988: *Linguistics: The Cambridge Survey*, vol 2. Cambridge: Cambridge University Press.

Osherson, Daniel and Lasnik, Howard (eds). 1990: *Language*. Cambridge, MA: MIT Press.

Petitto, Laura 1987: "On the Autonomy of Language and Gesture". *Cognition*, 27, pp. 1–52.

Pinker, Steven 1994: *The Language Instinct*. London: Penguin Books.

Poizner, Howard, Klima, Edward and Bellugi, Ursula 1987: *What the Hands Reveal About the Brain*. Cambridge, MA: MIT Press.

Prichett, Bradley 1992: *Grammatical Competence and Parsing Performance*. Chicago: University of Chicago Press.

Schiffer, Stephen 1972: *Meaning*. Oxford: Clarendon Press.

—— 1982: "Intention-Based Semantics". *The Notre Dame Journal of Formal Logic*, 23, pp. 119–56.

—— 1987: *Remnants of Meaning*. Cambridge, MA: MIT Press.

Sells, Peter, Sheiber, Stuart and Wasow, Thomas (eds). 1991: *Foundational Issues in Natural Language Processing*. Cambridge, MA: MIT Press.

Smith, Neil and Tsimpli, Ianthi-Maria, 1991:

"Linguistic Modularity? A Case Study of a 'Savant' Linguist". *Lingua*, 84, pp. 15–51.

—— 1995: *The Mind of a Savant*. Oxford: Basil Blackwell.

Stabler, Edward 1983: "How Are Grammars Represented?". *Behavioral and Brain Sciences*, 6, pp. 391–421.

Swinney, D., Ford, M., Bresnan, J. and Frauenfelder, U. 1988: "Coreference Assignment During Sentence Processing". Unpublished Manuscript.

Wallman, Joel 1992: *Aping Language*. Cambridge: Cambridge University Press.

Zurif, Edgar 1990: "Language and the Brain", in Osherson and Lasnik 1990, pp. 177–98.

PART EIGHT

Knowledge of language

INTRODUCTION TO PART EIGHT

PROFICIENCY IN A LANGUAGE is – at least in part – an *epistemic* matter: it involves *knowing* which signs count as expressions of the language, and knowing what such expressions mean. This observation is apt to seem innocuous at first, but as we shall see in this part of the book, it raises a good number of highly contentious issues.

As we have seen, linguistic expressions come in a variety of types: singular terms, predicates, quantifiers, sentences, etc. The type of which practically all theorists agree that speakers have knowledge is the *sentence*. This is because it is sentences which speakers typically use to express thoughts, to communicate, to reason, etc., and when speakers use expressions of other types, it is usually in the context of whole sentences.[1] At least two kinds of knowledge are involved in understanding sentences. First, there is *syntactic* or *'grammatical'* knowledge: knowledge of which strings of symbols qualify as sentences of the language at issue, and of what kinds of sentences they are. Next there is *semantic* knowledge: knowledge of what these sentences mean. Cognitive linguists have tended to focus on the former kind of knowledge, while philosophers of language are usually more interested in the latter; however, the distinction should not be of much significance below.

But how do speakers *come* to know these things about sentences, and in particular, how do they do so – more or less spontaneously – when confronted with sentences they have not encountered before? Prima facie, a promising beginning to an answer is that they acquire this knowledge about sentences on the basis of prior knowledge about the sentences' constituent expressions: on the syntactic side, knowledge about which categories of expressions they belong to, and the kinds of positions members of those categories are allowed to occupy in sentences of the language in question; and on the semantic side, knowledge of what the expressions mean in that language. Theories of the syntax and semantics of natural languages are almost invariably *systematic:* syntactic theories codify general principles proposed to determine which strings of symbols qualify as sentences of which kinds; and as we have seen elsewhere in this book, semantic theories are usually formulated on the assumption that meanings are *compositional:* i.e. that the meaning of a sentence depends on the meanings of the sub-sentential expressions it contains, and on their manner of combination. The best reason for adopting these systematic approaches to the study of natural languages is the expectation that the theories yielded will help us to explain how speakers come to understand novel sentences.

Notice, however, that the expectation that these theories can help to explain how

---

[1] For a recent critique of the assumption that sentences are fundamental in some of these respects, see Stainton 2009.

speakers understand novel sentences seems to depend on the assumption that the information they encode corresponds in some sense or other to speakers' psychological, cognitive economies. The most straightforward proposal is that speakers in some sense *know* the information codified in the theories, and use it to *derive* syntactic and semantic knowledge about sentences. The problem is that, invariably, the systematic theories which linguists and philosophers develop are extremely complex, are formulated in highly technical vocabulary and in some (particularly syntactic) cases are developed on the basis of rather rarefied empirical scientific evidence. Typical speakers need not, it seems, be aware of this complexity, they would not understand the technical vocabulary, and they have little access to the scientific evidence: so the proposal that they *know* the contents of such theories is prima facie implausible. A standard response is that while speakers may not know the information encoded in the theories in the ordinary sense of 'knowledge', they nonetheless count in some sense or other as having *tacit* or *implicit* knowledge of them. The challenge, then, is to explicate a suitable notion of tacit knowledge: a notion which, on the one hand, sustains a plausible attribution of such knowledge of complex syntactic and semantic theories to ordinary speakers, and yet on the other, engenders genuine explanations of speakers' abilities to understand novel sentences.

In the first reading below, the influential linguist and philosopher Noam Chomsky defends his contention that speakers tacitly know complex systematic theories. During the first half of the twentieth century it was generally assumed that proficiency in a language was largely a matter of habitual, *practical* ability, which infants acquired 'from scratch' on the basis of practical training and 'generalized learning mechanisms'. According to Chomsky's 'cognitivist' alternative, what infants acquire is not so much a practical ability as a systematic representation of 'the form and meaning of expressions of [a] language' – what he calls a 'generative grammar' for that language. Moreover, he argues, infants' acquisition of this representation cannot be explained in terms only of training and environmental stimuli. Empirical linguistic research suggests that all (natural) human languages share a significant number of deep structural (roughly, syntactic) features which Chomsky calls 'universal grammar'. His hypothesis is that these features are encoded in 'an innate component of the human mind' – the 'language faculty' – and that infants' acquisition of generative grammars for their native languages owes as much to their innate possession of universal grammar as it does to their training and environmental conditions. The well-known argument for this which he rehearses over the second half of the reading involves several grammatically complex linguistic examples, but its basic form is very simple. According to Chomsky, infants acquire proficiency with strikingly little training. If infants learned native languages from scratch by practical habituation and inductive and analogical inference, we would expect them to make grammatical 'errors' of various kinds which – empirical evidence establishes – they do not make.[2]

Gareth Evans's interest, in the second reading, is not with generative grammars, but rather *meaning theories*, but his position is similar to Chomsky's in several

---

[2] For an accessible and entertaining introduction to this and other aspects of the Chomskian approach, see Pinker 1994. Cowie 1998 resists Chomsky's nativism.

important respects. A meaning theory is a kind of systematic calculus intended to codify the semantic properties exhibited by the various expressions of a language. As Evans says, meaning theories are normally expected to be 'structure reflecting': the semantic properties they encode should include the *relational* ones which advocates of the compositionality thesis expect to find. Meaning theories of this kind are typically formulated as sets of 'axioms', some encoding the semantic properties of the language's sub-sentential expressions, and others codifying the ways in which meanings of sentences in the language are determined by the semantic properties of the sub-sentential expressions they contain, and by their modes of combination. These axioms permit the derivation of 'theorems', each one of which specifies the meaning of a sentence of the language. To illustrate, Evans sketches a systematic meaning theory for a very simple hypothetical language which we shall call 'L'. L contains just 10 names, 10 one-place predicate expressions, and the 100 sentences which result from concatenating names with predicates. Evans assumes for argument's sake that the meanings of L-sentences are their *truth conditions* (the conditions in which they would be true) and so the axioms he envisages are tailored to generate truth-conditions-specifying theorems. He suggests a set of 21 such axioms: 10 assigning referents to the names, 10 assigning satisfaction conditions to predicates, and a final one encoding how the truth conditions of an L-sentence are determined by the referent of the name it contains and the satisfaction conditions of the predicate it contains.[3]

In a cognitivist, Chomskian spirit, Evans holds that for a meaning theory for a natural language such as English to be correct, it is not sufficient that its axioms systematically generate theorems correctly specifying the meanings of all of its sentences: it must also pass muster as 'a theory of the competence of speakers of the language'. And to do this, Evans suggests, its axioms must correspond in some sense to psychological states of speakers of the language – states of 'tacit knowledge' which (he seems to accept) involve the 'unconscious deployment of information' about semantic properties of sub-sentential expressions etc., and which might feature in explanations of the speakers' abilities to understand novel sentences.

Evans's article first appeared as a response to a paper by Crispin Wight, in which Wright argued that the assumption that speakers enjoy such states of tacit knowledge betrays an implausible conception of the metaphysics and epistemology of meaning: a conception upon which linguistic understanding is a matter of *tracking* independently configured, objective meanings.[4] Evans does not propose to answer this challenge directly, but he accepts that advocates of the requirement that meaning theories reflect speakers' psychologies in his way are obliged to provide an explication of their rather imprecise-looking notion of tacit knowledge.

To fix ideas, Evans considers a challenge to the thesis that speakers tacitly know axioms of meaning theories based on one which Quine (1970) made to Chomsky's thesis that they know generative grammars. Quineans assume that since linguistic behaviour involves only the use of whole sentences, attributions to speakers of tacit

---

[3] See Part Six above for discussion of meaning theories of this type.
[4] Wright's arguments against this conception are based on considerations about *rule-following* which he attributes to Wittgenstein. See the introduction to Part Twelve for a little more on this.

knowledge of particular grammars or sets of meaning-theoretic axioms must be based exclusively on evidence involving their uses of whole sentences. The problem is that while this kind of evidence might justify the attribution to a speaker of knowledge corresponding to the *theorems* of a meaning theory, it does not justify the attribution of knowledge of the *axioms* of any particular meaning theory, and this is because it is always possible to formulate distinct sets of axioms which are 'extensionally equivalent': i.e. which generate the same theorems. Evans illustrates this dramatically by considering an 'unstructured' theory for L which consists simply in 100 axioms, each one simply specifying the truth conditions of an L-sentence. This theory is extensionally equivalent to the 21-axiom 'structured' one, and the Quinean challenge is that no amount of behavioural evidence could justify attribution of tacit knowledge of the structured theory, since an attribution of knowledge of the unstructured one would be equally well supported by such evidence.

Many cognitivists respond to the Quinean challenge by rejecting the behaviourist conception of evidence on which it rests.[5] Evans's response is more subtle. He suggests that tacit knowledge states are 'dispositions' involving judgements that speakers make about the truth conditions of sentences, and he explains that by this term he does not intend the mere *patterns* of 'reactions' that speakers have to sentences, but rather the 'categorical' (psychological or neural) states that cause these reactions. Tacit knowledge of the unstructured, 100-axiom theory would consist in possession of 100 distinct such dispositions, each one a state which causes the speaker correctly to judge the truth conditions of a given L-sentence. Meanwhile tacit knowledge of the structured theory would consist in possession of 20 dispositions – one for each name and predicate of L. A complication arises here: although the states corresponding to axioms of the structured theory are assumed to cause judgements of the same kind as those corresponding to the unstructured one, the former never do their causing alone: if a speaker tacitly knows the structured theory, two such states are involved in the generation of each judgement of the relevant kind – one corresponding to a name, and one to a predicate. This makes it harder to *identify* states corresponding to axioms of the structured theory. However Evans argues that this difficulty can be surmounted: we can 'inter-define' the dispositions by formulating 20 specifications, each of which makes reference to some of the others.

After outlining these specifications of tacit knowledge states, Evans addresses the Quinean challenge by proposing that we consider evidence involving *patterns* exhibited by speakers' proficiencies: in particular, patterns involving *acquisition* and *loss* (e.g. in the event of brain damage) of abilities to make correct judgements about the meanings of sentences. E.g. (simplifying somewhat) if a speaker who acquired or lost the ability to understand one sentence of L tended simultaneously to acquire or lose the ability to understand other sentences which share one of its sub-sentential components, that would count in favour of an attribution to her of tacit knowledge of the structured theory over one of the unstructured ones. If on the other hand she tended to acquire or lose understanding of individual sentences without simultaneously

---

[5] See e.g. Chomsky's own 1969.

acquiring or losing understanding of any sentences that share components with them, that would point in the opposite direction.

In the final two sections of his paper, Evans qualifies his account in two important ways. First, he argues that tacit knowledge states are not *beliefs* – are not genuine *propositional attitudes*. An important characteristic of genuine beliefs concerns the holistic ways in which they relate inferentially to other propositional attitudes – most paradigmatically, to desires – and a consequence of this is that genuine beliefs can be manifested in a heterogeneous variety of different ways. Thus, e.g., consider a subject who believes that a certain substance is poisonous. If he also desires to have a long and healthy life, he might manifest the belief by avoiding the substance; if on the other hand his desire is to end his life, he might manifest the belief by eating it; if it is to harm an enemy, he might manifest the belief by feeding it to her, etc. There seems to be no limit to the number and diversity of ways in which a given belief may be manifested in a subject's behaviour. In contrast, tacit knowledge states, as Evans envisages them, are manifested by behaviour in only one way: through speakers' judgements about the meanings of sentences, and this is because, in contrast to beliefs, tacit knowledge states are not integrated inferentially with propositional attitudes in general.

Evans's second qualification concerns the question whether attributions to speakers of tacit knowledge of meaning-theoretic axioms can help to explain their abilities to understand novel sentences. He concedes that because the 'inter-definitions' with which he *identifies* tacit knowledge states are in effect formulated in terms of speakers' abilities to understand the sentences they can understand, attributions of such states cannot *in general* play this explanatory role. However, he suggests that they might, more modestly, feature in explanations involving *particular* sentences: we might explain how a speaker comes to understand a particular novel sentence by attributing tacit knowledge states involving its components, and which she came to enjoy through exposure to other sentences.

In the third reading, Crispin Wright presents a critical analysis of the thesis that speakers tacitly know the axioms of meaning theories, with a particular focus on Evans's version. He begins in sympathetic spirit, arguing that the facts that meaning theories are hugely complex and are articulated in terms which ordinary speakers would not understand do not by themselves suggest a compelling objection to the thesis. Wright's next point, however, is to endorse and reinforce the considerations raised by Evans about the dearth and homogeneity of the inferential connections supposed to be exhibited by such states. Finally – and this is probably the part of Wright's discussion of most immediate interest here – he presents three criticisms of Evans's own proposal.

The first of these concerns Evans's response to the Quinean challenge. Wright concedes that evidence involving patterns of acquisition and loss amongst a speaker's abilities to understand sentences could provide evidence for the claim that the causal mechanisms that underpin those abilities exhibit one structure rather than another, extensionally equivalent one. However, according to Wright, Evans has provided no reason to describe such causal mechanisms in *cognitive, semantic* terms: as states which – however unlike beliefs they might be in respect of inferential integration –

ought nonetheless to be regarded as bearing *informational contents*. For dramatic illustration, Wright suggests that the evidence which favours an attribution of tacit knowledge of the structured theory for L over the unstructured one might be explained equally well by an attribution of knowledge of the unstructured theory, 'supplemented with some appropriate hypothesis, of a non-semantic sort, about the presumed causal substructure of the dispositions which [the unstructured theory] describes'.[6]

Wright's second objection concerns an apparent lack of fit between the structured theory outlined by Evans and the dispositions in which tacit knowledge of its axioms are said to consist. As we saw, the theory has 21 axioms; however, a consequence of the way in which Evans specifies the dispositions in which he proposes tacit knowledge of the axioms to consist is that L-speakers are said to enjoy only 20 such states. Wright's third objection relates to the way in which the dispositions in which Evans holds tacit knowledge of the structured theory's axioms to consist are specified in terms of one another. Because the dispositions are 'inter-defined' in this way, it seems at least prima facie fair to complain that sets of such specifications are *circular*, and so fail to identify determinate sets of psychological states.[7]

[6] If our interpretation of Wright's concern is correct, the controversy here is related to some of those that surround the notion of *non-conceptual content* in the philosophy of mind. For some germane recent work, see Gunther 2003, and for a useful recent survey, Bermúdez and Cahen 2008.
[7] Davies 1987 responds to Wright's three objections. For further discussion, see Miller 1997 and Byrne 2004.

Questions and tasks

1   How convincing is Chomsky's argument against the claim that knowledge of language is 'a practical ability to speak and understand'?
2   Why does Evans insist (p. 294) that 'the structure-reflecting requirement has nothing whatever to do with *finiteness*'?
3   Explain in your own words the kind of explanatory role that – at the end of his paper – Evans holds attributions of tacit knowledge of meaning-theoretic axioms can play. Do you agree with him?
4   How should an advocate of Evans's account respond to Wright's worry that there seems to be a mismatch between the number of dispositional states in which tacit knowledge of the structured theory is proposed to consist, and the number of axioms in the structured theory?
5   Do you think Evans's disposition-specifications are problematically *circular*? Wright concedes that 'a more sophisticated account of the notion of a disposition' might enable a response to his third objection to Evans's proposal. Try to formulate such an account and evaluate the response it makes possible.

References and further reading

Barber, A. (ed.), 2003: *Epistemology of Language*, Oxford: Oxford University Press.
Bermúdez, J., and A. Cahen 2008: 'Nonconceptual Mental Content', in Edward

N. Zalta (ed.), *The Stanford Encyclopedia of Philosophy* (Winter 2008 edn) http://plato.stanford.edu/archives/win2008/entries/content-nonconceptual

Byrne, D. 2004: 'Three Notions of Tacit Knowledge', *Ágora: Papeles de Filosofía*, 23/2, pp. 61–85.

Chomsky, N. 1969: 'Quine's Empirical Assumptions', in D. Davidson and J. Hintikka (eds), *Words and Objections: Essays on the Work of W. V. Quine*, Dordrecht: Reidel, pp. 53–68.

Chomsky, N. 1976: *Reflections on Language*, London: Fontana.

Chomsky, N. 1986: *Knowledge of Language: Its Nature, Origin, and Use*, New York: Praeger.

Cowie, F. 1998: *What's within? Nativism Reconsidered*, Oxford: Oxford University Press.

Davies. M. 1981: Meaning, *Quantification, Necessity*, London: Routledge and Kegan Paul.

Davies, M. 1987: 'Tacit Knowledge and Semantic Theory: Can a Five Per Cent Difference Matter?', *Mind* 96, pp. 441–62.

Davies, M. 1989: 'Tacit Knowledge and Subdoxastic States', in A. George (ed.), *Reflections on Chomsky*, Oxford: Blackwell, pp. 131–52.

Dummett, M. 1993: 'What Do I Know When I Know a Language?', in M. Dummett, *The Seas of Language*, Oxford: Oxford University Press, pp. 94–105.

Fodor, J. 1981: 'Some Notes on What Linguistics Is About', in N. Block (ed.), *Readings in the Philosophy of Psychology*, vol. 2, Cambridge, MA: MIT Press, 197–207; reprinted in J. Katz (ed.), *The Philosophy of Linguistics*, Oxford: Oxford University Press (1985).

Fodor, J. 1983: *The Modularity of Mind*, Cambridge, MA: MIT Press.

Gunther, Y. (ed.) 2003: *Essays on Nonconceptual Content*, Cambridge, MA: MIT Press.

Higginbotham, J. 1983: 'Is Grammar Psychological?', in Leigh S. Cauman, Isaac Levi, Charles Parsons, and Robert Schwartz (eds), *How Many Questions? Essays in Honor of Sidney Morgenbesser*, Indianapolis: Hackett, pp. 276–300.

Larson, R., and G. Segal 1995: *Knowledge of Meaning: An Introduction to Semantic Theory*, Cambridge, MA: MIT Press.

Matthews, R. 2003: 'Does Linguistic Competence Require Knowledge of Language?', in A. Barber (ed.), *Epistemology of Language*, Oxford: Oxford University Press, pp. 187–213.

Matthews, R. 2006: 'Knowledge of Language and Linguistic Competence', in E. Sosa and E. Villanueva (eds), *Philosophy of Language* (Philosophical Issues, vol. 16), Oxford: Blackwell, pp. 200–20.

Miller, A. 1997: 'Tacit Knowledge', in B. Hale and C. Wright (eds.), *A Companion to the Philosophy of Language*, Oxford: Blackwell, pp. 146–74.

Pinker, S. 1994: *The Language Instinct*, London: Penguin.

Quine, W. V. 1970: 'Methodological Reflections on Current Linguistic Theory', *Synthese* 221, pp. 386–98.

Smith, B. 2006: 'What I Know When I Know a Language', in E. Lepore and B. Smith (eds), *The Oxford Handbook of Philosophy of Language*, Oxford: Oxford University Press, pp. 941–82.

Stainton, R. 2006: 'Meaning and Reference: Some Chomskian Themes', in E. Lepore and B. Smith (eds.), *The Oxford Handbook of Philosophy of Language*, Oxford: Oxford University Press, pp. 913–40.

Stainton, R. 2009: *Words and Thoughts: Subsentences, Ellipsis, and the Philosophy of Language*, Oxford: Oxford University Press.

Wright, C. 1981: Rule-Following, Objectivity and the Theory of Meaning', in S. H. Holtzman and C. M. Leich (eds) *Wittgenstein: To Follow a Rule*, London: Routledge and Kegan Paul, pp. 99–117.

Chapter 18

Noam Chomsky

KNOWLEDGE OF LANGUAGE AS A FOCUS OF INQUIRY

The study of language has a long and rich history, extending over thousands of years. This study has frequently been understood as an inquiry into the nature of mind and thought on the assumption that "languages are the best mirror of the human mind" (Leibniz). A common conception was that "with respect to its *substance* grammar is one and the same in all languages, though it does vary *accidentally*" (Roger Bacon). The invariant "substance" was often taken to be the mind and its acts; particular languages use various mechanisms—some rooted in human reason, others arbitrary and adventitious—for the expression of thought, which is a constant across languages. One leading eighteenth century rational grammarian defined "general grammar" as a deductive science concerned with "the immutable and general principles of spoken or written language" and their consequences; it is "prior to all languages," because its principles "are the same as those that direct human reason in its intellectual operations" (Beauzée). Thus, "the science of language does not differ at all from the science of thought." "Particular grammar" is not a true "science" in the sense of this rationalist tradition because it is not based solely on universal necessary laws; it is an "art" or technique that shows how given languages realize the general principles of human reason. As John Stuart Mill later expressed the same leading idea, "The principles and rules of grammar are the means by which the forms of language are made to correspond with the universal forms of thought. . . . The structure of every sentence is a lesson in logic." Others, particularly during the Romantic period, argued that the nature and content of thought are determined in part by the devices made available for its expression in particular languages. These devices may include contributions of individual genius that affect the "character" of a language, enriching its means of expression and the thoughts expressed without affecting its "form," its sound system and rules of word and sentence formation (Humboldt).

With regard to the acquisition of knowledge, it was widely held that the mind is not "so much to be filled therewith from without, like a vessel, as to be kindled and awaked" (Ralph Cudworth); "The growth of knowledge . . . [rather resembles] . . . the growth of Fruit; however external causes may in some degree cooperate, it is the internal vigour, and virtue of the tree, that must ripen the juices to their just maturity" (James Harris).[1] Applied to language, this essentially Platonistic conception would suggest that knowledge of a particular language grows and matures along a course that is in part intrinsically determined, with modifications reflecting observed usage, rather in the manner of the visual system or other bodily "organs" that develop along a course determined by genetic instructions under the triggering and shaping effects of environmental factors.

With the exception of the relativism of the

Romantics, such ideas were generally regarded with much disapproval in the mainstream of linguistic research by the late nineteenth century and on through the 1950s. In part, this attitude developed under the impact of a rather narrowly construed empiricism and later behaviorist and operationalist doctrine. In part, it resulted from the quite real and impressive successes of historical and descriptive studies conducted within a narrower compass, specifically, the discovery of "sound laws" that provided much understanding of the history of languages and their relationships. In part, it was a natural consequence of the investigation of a much richer variety of languages than were known to earlier scholars, languages that appeared to violate many of the allegedly *a priori* conceptions of the earlier rationalist tradition.[2] After a century of general neglect or obloquy, ideas resembling those of the earlier tradition re-emerged (initially, with virtually no awareness of historical antecedents) in the mid-1950s, with the development of what came to be called "generative grammar"—again, reviving a long-lapsed and largely forgotten tradition.[3]

The generative grammar of a particular language (where "generative" means nothing more than "explicit") is a theory that is concerned with the form and meaning of expressions of this language. One can imagine many different kinds of approach to such questions, many points of view that might be adopted in dealing with them. Generative grammar limits itself to certain elements of this larger picture. Its standpoint is that of individual psychology. It is concerned with those aspects of form and meaning that are determined by the "language faculty," which is understood to be a particular component of the human mind. The nature of this faculty is the subject matter of a general theory of linguistic structure that aims to discover the framework of principles and elements common to attainable human languages; this theory is now often called "universal grammar" (UG), adapting a traditional term to a new context of inquiry. UG may be regarded as a characteriza-

tion of the genetically determined language faculty. One may think of this faculty as a "language acquisition device," an innate component of the human mind that yields a particular language through interaction with presented experience, a device that converts experience into a system of knowledge attained: knowledge of one or another language.[4]

The study of generative grammar represented a significant shift of focus in the approach to problems of language. Put in the simplest terms, to be elaborated below, the shift of focus was from behavior or the products of behavior to states of the mind/brain that enter into behavior. If one chooses to focus attention on this latter topic, the central concern becomes knowledge of language: its nature, origins, and use.

The three basic questions that arise, then, are these:

(1)

   (i)   What constitutes knowledge of language?

   (ii) How is knowledge of language acquired?

   (iii) How is knowledge of language put to use?

The answer to the first question is given by a particular generative grammar, a theory concerned with the state of the mind/brain of the person who knows a particular language. The answer to the second is given by a specification of UG along with an account of the ways in which its principles interact with experience to yield a particular language; UG is a theory of the "initial state" of the language faculty, prior to any linguistic experience. The answer to the third question would be a theory of how the knowledge of language attained enters into the expression of thought and the understanding of presented specimens of language, and derivatively, into communication and other special uses of language.

So far, this is nothing more than the outline of

a research program that takes up classical questions that had been put aside for many years. As just described, it should not be particularly controversial, since it merely expresses an interest in certain problems and offers a preliminary analysis of how they might be confronted, although as is often the case, the initial formulation of a problem may prove to be far-reaching in its implications, and ultimately controversial as it is developed.

Some elements of this picture may appear to be more controversial than they really are. Consider, for example, the idea that there is a language faculty, a component of the mind/brain that yields knowledge of language given presented experience. It is not at issue that humans attain knowledge of English, Japanese, and so forth, while rocks, birds, or apes do not under the same (or indeed any) conditions. There is, then, some property of the mind/brain that differentiates humans from rocks, birds, or apes. Is this a distinct "language faculty" with specific structure and properties, or, as some believe, is it the case that humans acquire language merely by applying generalized learning mechanisms of some sort, perhaps with greater efficiency or scope than other organisms? These are not topics for speculation or *a priori* reasoning but for empirical inquiry, and it is clear enough how to proceed: namely, by facing the questions of (1). We try to determine what is the system of knowledge that has been attained and what properties must be attributed to the initial state of the mind/brain to account for its attainment. Insofar as these properties are language-specific, either individually or in the way they are organized and composed, there is a distinct language faculty.

Generative grammar is sometimes referred to as a theory, advocated by this or that person. In fact, it is not a theory any more than chemistry is a theory. Generative grammar is a topic, which one may or may not choose to study. Of course, one can adopt a point of view from which chemistry disappears as a discipline (perhaps it is all

done by angels with mirrors). In this sense, a decision to study chemistry does stake out a position on matters of fact. Similarly, one may argue that the topic of generative grammar does not exist, although it is hard to see how to make this position minimally plausible. Within the study of generative grammar there have been many changes and differences of opinion, often reversion to ideas that had been abandoned and were later reconstructed in a different light. Evidently, this is a healthy phenomenon indicating that the discipline is alive, although it is sometimes, oddly, regarded as a serious deficiency, a sign that something is wrong with the basic approach. I will review some of these changes as we proceed.

In the mid-1950s, certain proposals were advanced as to the form that answers to the questions of (1) might take, and a research program was inaugurated to investigate the adequacy of these proposals and to sharpen and apply them. This program was one of the strands that led to the development of the cognitive sciences in the contemporary sense, sharing with other approaches the belief that certain aspects of the mind/brain can be usefully construed on the model of computational systems of rules that form and modify representations, and that are put to use in interpretation and action. From its origins (or with a longer perspective, one might say "its reincarnation") about 30 years ago, the study of generative grammar was undertaken with an eye to gaining some insight into the nature and origins of systems of knowledge, belief, and understanding more broadly, in the hope that these general questions could be illuminated by a detailed investigation of the special case of human language.

This research program has since been running its course, along a number of different paths. I will be concerned here with only one of these, with the problems it faced and the steps that were taken in an effort to deal with them. During the past 5–6 years, these efforts have converged in a somewhat unexpected way, yielding a rather different conception of the nature of language and its mental representation, one that offers interesting answers to a range of empirical questions and opens a variety of new ones to inquiry while suggesting a rethinking of the character of others. This is what accounts for an unmistakable sense of energy and anticipation—and also uncertainty—which is reminiscent of the period when the study of generative grammar in the modern sense was initiated about 30 years ago. Some of the work now being done is quite different in character from what had previously been possible as well as considerably broader in empirical scope, and it may be that results of a rather new kind are within reach, or at least within sight. I would like to try to explain why this may be so, beginning with some remarks about goals, achievements, and failures of the past years.

To avoid misunderstanding, I am not speaking here about all of the study of language but rather of generative grammar, and even here I will not attempt anything like a real history of the course of research but rather will give a somewhat idealized picture that is in part clearer in retrospect than it was at the time. Furthermore, what I am describing has represented a minority position throughout, and probably still does, although in my view it is the correct one. A number of different current approaches share properties of the sort discussed here and may be intertranslatable to a considerable extent. I will not consider this important topic here and will also make no effort to survey the range of ideas, often conflicting, that fall within the particular tendency that I will discuss—what is now sometimes called "government-binding (GB) theory."

I want to consider, then, two major conceptual shifts, one that inaugurated the contemporary study of generative grammar, and a second, more theory-internal, that is now in process and that offers some new perspectives on traditional problems.[4]

Traditional and structuralist grammar did not deal with the questions of (1), the former because of its implicit reliance on the unanalyzed intelligence of the reader, the latter because of its narrowness of scope. The concerns of traditional and generative grammar are, in a certain sense, complementary: a good traditional or pedagogical grammar provides a full list of exceptions (irregular verbs, etc.), paradigms and examples of regular constructions, and observations at various levels of detail and generality about the form and meaning of expressions. But it does not examine the question of how the reader of the grammar uses such information to attain the knowledge that is used to form and interpret new expressions or the question of the nature and elements of this knowledge essentially the questions of the above. Without too much exaggeration, one could describe such a grammar as a structured and organized version of the data presented to a child learning a language, with some general commentary and often insightful observations. Generative grammar, in contrast, is concerned primarily with the intelligence of the reader, the principles and procedures brought to bear to attain full knowledge of a language. Structuralist theories, both in the European and American traditions, did concern themselves with analytic procedures for deriving aspects of grammar from data, as in the procedural theories of Nikolay Trubetzkoy, Zellig Hams, Bernard Bloch, and others, but primarily in the areas of phonology and morphology. The procedures suggested were seriously inadequate and in any event could not possibly be understood (and were not intended) to provide an answer to question (lii), even in the narrower domains where most work was concentrated. Nor was there an effort to determine what was involved in offering a comprehensive account of the knowledge of the speaker/hearer.

As soon as these questions were squarely faced, a wide range of new phenomena were discovered, including quite simple ones that had passed unnoticed, and severe problems arose that had previously been ignored or seriously misunderstood. A standard belief 30 years ago was that language acquisition is a case of "over-learning." Language was regarded as a habit system, one that was assumed to be much overdetermined by available evidence. Production and interpretation of new forms was taken to be a straightforward matter of analogy, posing no problems of principle.[5] Attention to the questions of (1) quickly reveals that exactly the opposite is the case: language poses in a sharp and clear form what has sometimes been called "Plato's problem," the problem of "poverty of stimulus," of accounting for the richness, complexity, and specificity of shared knowledge, given the limitations of the data available. This difference of perception concerning where the problem lies—overlearning or poverty of evidence—reflects very clearly the effect of the shift of focus that inaugurated the study of generative grammar.

A great many examples have been given over the years to illustrate what clearly is the fundamental problem: the problem of poverty of evidence. A familiar example is the structure-dependence of rules, the fact that without instruction or direct evidence, children unerringly use computationally complex structure-dependent rules rather than computationally simple rules that involve only the predicate "leftmost" in a linear sequence of words.[6] To take some other examples, to which we will return, consider sentences (2)–(7):

(2) I wonder who [the men expected to see them]

(3) [the men expected to see them]

(4) John ate an apple

(5) John ate

(6) John is too stubborn to talk to Bill

(7) John is too stubborn to talk to

Both (2) and (3) include the clause bounded by brackets, but only in (2) may the pronoun *them* be referentially dependent on the antecedent *the men*; in (3) the pronoun is understood as referring in some manner indicated in the situational or discourse context, but not to the men. Numerous facts of this sort, falling under what is now generally called "binding theory," are known without relevant experience to differentiate the cases. Such facts pose a serious problem that was not recognized in earlier work: How does every child know, unerringly, to interpret the clause differently in the two cases? And why does no pedagogic grammar have to draw the learner's attention to such facts (which were, in fact, noticed only quite recently, in the course of the study of explicit rule systems in generative grammar)?

Turning to examples (4)–(7), sentence (5) means that John ate something or other, a fact that one might explain on the basis of a simple inductive procedure: *ate* takes an object, as in (4), and if the object is missing, it is understood as arbitrary. Applying the same inductive procedure to (6) and (7), it should be that (7) means that John is so stubborn that he (John) will not talk to some arbitrary person, on the analogy of (6). But the meaning is, in fact, quite different: namely, that John is so stubborn that some arbitrary person won't talk to him (John). Again, this is known without training or relevant evidence.[7]

The situation is, in fact, more complex. Although plausible, the inductive procedure suggested for the relatively straightforward examples (4)–(5) does not seem correct. As noted by Howard Lasnik, the word *eat* has a somewhat different meaning in its intransitive usage, something like *dine*. One can say "John ate his shoe," but "John ate" cannot be understood to include this case. The observation is general for such cases. The intransitive forms differ from normal intransitives in other respects; for example, we can form "the dancing bear" (corresponding to "the bear that dances"), but not "the eating man" (corresponding to "the man who eats").[8] Such facts pose further problems of poverty of stimulus.

Children do not make errors about the interpretation of such sentences as (6)–(7) past a certain stage of development, and if they did, the errors would largely be uncorrectable. It is doubtful that even the most compendious traditional or teaching grammar notes such simple facts as those illustrated in (2)–(7), and such observations lie far beyond the domain of structural grammars. A wide variety of examples of this sort immediately come to attention when one faces the questions formulated in (1).

Knowledge of language is often characterized as a practical ability to speak and understand, so that questions (li) and (liii) are closely related, perhaps identified. Ordinary usage makes a much sharper distinction between the two questions, and is right to do so. Two people may share exactly the same knowledge of language but differ markedly in their ability to put this knowledge to use. Ability to use language may improve or decline without any change in knowledge. This ability may also be impaired, selectively or in general, with no loss of knowledge, a fact that would become clear if injury leading to impairment recedes and lost ability is recovered. Many such considerations support the commonsense assumption that knowledge cannot be properly described as a practical ability. Furthermore, even if this view could somehow be maintained, it would leave open all of the serious questions. Thus, what is the nature of the "practical ability" manifested in our interpretation of the sentences (2)–(7), how is it properly described, and how is it acquired?

Often it is not immediately obvious what our knowledge of language entails in particular cases, a fact illustrated even with short and simple sentences such as (8)–(10):

(8) His wife loves her husband
(9) John is too clever to expect us to catch Bill
(10) John is too clever to expect us to catch

In the case of (8), it takes some thought to determine whether *his* can be referentially dependent on *her husband* if *her* is dependent on *his*

wife—that is, if the reference of either *he* or *she* is not somehow contextually indicated.[9] Examples (9) and (10) are, in fact, analogous to (6) and (7), respectively, but again, it takes some thought to discover that (10) means that John is so clever that an arbitrary person cannot expect us to catch him (John), although it is clear at once that it does not mean that John is so clever that he (John) cannot catch some arbitrary person, on the analogy of (9) (and (4), (5)). Our abilities seem limited somehow in such cases (and there are far more complex ones), but it would make little sense to speak of our knowledge of language as "limited" in any comparable way.

Suppose we insist on speaking of knowledge of language as a practical ability to speak and understand. Then normal usage must be revised in numerous cases such as those just discussed. Suppose that Jones takes a public speaking course and improves his ability to speak and understand without any change in his knowledge of English, as we would describe the situation in normal usage. We must now revise this commonsense usage and say, rather, that Jones has improved his ability$_1$ to use his ability$_2$ to speak and understand; similar translations are required in the other cases. But the two occurrences of "ability" in this description are hardly more than homonyms. Ability$_1$ is ability in the normal sense of the word: it can improve or decline, can be inadequate to determine consequences of knowledge, and so on. Ability$_2$, however, remains stable while our ability to use it changes, and we have this kind of "ability" even when we are unable to detect what it entails in concrete cases. In short, the neologism "ability$_2$" is invested with all the properties of knowledge. Note that there are cases when we do speak of abilities that we cannot put to use: for example, the case of swimmers who cannot swim because their hands are tied, although they retain the ability to swim. The cases in question are not of this sort, however.

The purpose of the attempt to reduce knowledge to ability is, presumably, to avoid problematic features that seem to inhere in the concept of knowledge, to show that these can be explained in dispositional or other terms more closely related to actual behavior (whether this is possible even in the case of ability$_1$, the normal sense, is another question). But nothing of the sort is achieved by this departure from ordinary usage; the problems remain, exactly as before, now embedded in terminological confusion. The task of determining the nature of our knowledge (= ability$_2$), and accounting for its origins and use, remains exactly as challenging as before, despite the terminological innovations.

Other examples similar to (8)–(10) raise further questions. Consider the following sentences:

(11) John is too stubborn to expect anyone to talk to Bill
(12) John is too stubborn to visit anyone who talked to Bill

Suppose we delete Bill from (11) and (12), yielding (13) and (14), respectively:

(13) John is too stubborn to expect anyone to talk to
(14) John is too stubborn to visit anyone who talked to

Sentence (13) is structurally analogous to (10), and is understood in the same manner: it means that John is so stubborn that an arbitrary person would not expect anyone to talk to him (John). "By analogy," then, we would expect sentence (14) to mean that John is so stubborn that an arbitrary person would not visit anyone who talked to him (John). But it does not have that meaning; in fact, it is gibberish. Here we have a double failure of analogy. Sentence (14) is not understood "on the analogy" of (4), (5), (6), (9), and (12) (hence meaning that John is so stubborn that he (John) would not visit anyone who talked to some arbitrary person), nor is it understood "on the analogy" of (7), (10), and

(13); rather, it has no interpretation at all. And while the status of (11), (12), and (14) is immediately obvious, it takes some thought or preparation to see that (13) has the interpretation it does have, and thus to determine the consequences of our knowledge in this case.

Again, these are facts that we know, however difficult it may be to determine that our system of knowledge has these consequences. We know these facts without instruction or even direct evidence, surely without correction of error by the speech community. It would be absurd to try to teach such facts as these to people learning English as a second language, just as no one taught them to us or even presented us with evidence that could yield this knowledge by any generally reliable procedure. This is knowledge without grounds, without good reasons or support by reliable procedures in any general or otherwise useful sense of these notions. Were we to insist that knowledge is a kind of ability, we would have to claim that we lack the ability to understand "John is too stubborn to talk to" as meaning "John is too stubborn to talk to someone or other" (on the analogy of "John ate an apple"—"John ate"), and that we lack the ability to understand (14) on the analogy of "John ate an apple"—"John ate" (so that it means that John is too stubborn to visit anyone who talked to someone or other) or on the analogy of "John is too stubborn to talk to," with the "inversion strategy" that we somehow use in this case (so that (14) means that John is too stubborn for someone or other to visit anyone who talked to him, John). But these would be odd claims, to say the least. These are not failures of ability. It is not that we are too weak, or lack some special skill that could be acquired. We are perfectly capable of associating the sentence (14), for example, with either of the two meanings that would be provided "by analogy" (or others), but we know that these are not the associations that our knowledge of the language provides; ability is one thing, knowledge something quite different. The system of knowledge that has somehow developed in our minds has certain consequences, not others; it relates sound and meaning and assigns structural properties to physical events in certain ways, not others.

It seems that there is little hope in accounting for our knowledge in terms of such ideas as analogy, induction, association, reliable procedures, good reasons, and justification in any generally useful sense, or in terms of "generalized learning mechanisms" (if such exist). And it seems that we should follow normal usage in distinguishing clearly between knowledge and ability to use that knowledge. We should, so it appears, think of knowledge of language as a certain state of the mind/brain, a relatively stable element in transitory mental states once it is attained; furthermore, as a state of some distinguishable faculty of the mind—the language faculty—with its specific properties, structure, and organization, one "module" of the mind.[10]

Notes

1 On these and many other discussions, primarily in the seventeenth–nineteenth centuries, see Chomsky (1966). For discussion of some misinterpretation of this work, see Bracken (1984).

2 The alleged *a priorism* of work in this tradition has often been exaggerated. See Chomsky (1966) and more recent work for discussion of this point.

3 The tradition, in this case, is a different one, represented in its most advanced form in the early work of the Indian grammarians 2,500 years ago. See Kiparsky (1982). A modern counterpart is Bloomfield (1939), which was radically different in character from the work of the period and inconsistent with his own theories of language, and remained virtually without influence or even awareness despite Bloomfield's great prestige.

4 See Newmeyer (1980) for one view of the history of this period prior to the second major conceptual shift; and for some more personal comments, the introduction to Chomsky (1975a), a somewhat abbreviated version of a 1956 revision of a 1955 manuscript, both unpublished. See Lightfoot (1982) and Hornstein and Lightfoot (1981) for

discussion of the general backgrounds for much current work, and Radford (1981) for an introduction to the work that led to the second conceptual shift. See Chomsky (1981) for a more technical presentation of some of the ideas that entered into this conceptual shift and van Riemsdijk and Williams (1985) for an introductory study of this current work.

5 Although basically adopting this point of view W.V. Quine, however, argued that there is a very severe, in fact, insuperable problem of underdetermination affecting all aspects of language and grammar, and much of psychology more generally (Quine, 1960, 1972). I do not think that he succeeded in showing that some novel form of indeterminacy affects the study of language beyond the normal underdetermination of theory by evidence; his own formulations of the thesis furthermore involve internal inconsistency (see Chomsky, 1975b, 1980). There seems no reason on these grounds, then, to distinguish linguistics or psychology in principle from the natural sciences in accordance with what Hockney (1975) calls Quine's "bifurcation thesis." A similar conclusion is reached by Putnam (1981) in his abandonment of metaphysical realism on Quinean grounds. His step also abandons the bifurcation thesis, although in the opposite direction.

6 See Chomsky (1975a). See Crain and Nakayama (1984) for empirical study of this question with 3–5-year-old children.

7 The reaction to such phenomena, also unnoticed until recently, again illustrates the differene of outlook of structuralist-descriptive and generative grammar. For some practitioners of the former, the statement of the facts, which is straightforward enough once they are observed, is the answer—nothing else is necessary; for the latter, the statement of the facts poses the problem to be solved. Cf. Ney (1983), particularly, his puzzlement about the "peculiar view of grammar [that] unnecessarily complicates the whole matter" by seeking an explanation for the facts. Note that there is no question of right or wrong here, but rather of topic of inquiry.

8 In early work, such facts were used to motivate an analysis of intransitives such as *eat* as derived from corresponding transitives by a system of ordered

rules that excluded the unwanted cases; see Chomsky (1962).

9 On structures of this type, and problems of binding theory, more generally, see Higginbotham (1983), among much other work.

10 See Fodor (1983). But it is too narrow to regard the "language module" as an input system in Fodor's sense, if only because it is used in speaking and thought. We might consider supplementing this picture by adding an "output system," but plainly this must be linked to the input system; we do not expect a person to speak only English and understand only Japanese. That is, the input and output systems must each access a fixed system of knowledge. The latter, however, is a central system which has essential problems of modularity, a fact that brings the entire picture into question. Furthermore, even regarded as an input system, the language module does not appear to have the property of rapidity of access that Fodor discusses, as indicated by (8)–(14). Note also that even if Fodor is right in believing that there is a sharp distinction between modules in his sense and "the rest," which is holistic in several respects, it does not follow that the residue is unstructured. In fact, this seems highly unlikely, if only because of the "epistemic boundedness" that he notes. Many other questions arise concerning Fodor's very intriguing discussion of these issues, which I will not pursue here.

References

Bloomfield, L. (1939). "Menomini Morphophonemics." *Travaux du cercle linguistique de Prague.*

Bracken, H. (1984). *Mind and Language* (Dordrecht: Foris).

Chomsky, N. (1962). "A Transformational Approach to Syntax." In A.A. Hill (ed.), *Proceedings of the Third Texas Conference on Problems of Linguistic Analysis in English* (1958) (Austin: University of Texas Press).

—— . (1966). *Cartesian Linguistics* (New York: Harper & Row).

—— . (1975a). *Logical Structure of Linguistic Theory* (New York: Plenum); drawn from an unpublished 1955–56 manuscript.

—— . (1975b). *Reflections on Language* (New York, Pantheon).

—— . (1980). *Rules and Representations* (New York: Columbia University Press).

—— . (1981). *Lectures on Government and Binding* (Dordrecht: Foris).

Crain, S. & Nakayama, M. (1984). "Structure Dependence in Grammar Formation." ms., University of Connecticut.

Fodor, J. (1983). *The Modularity of Mind* (Cambridge: MIT Press).

Higginbotham, J. (1983). "Logical Form, Binding and Nominals." *Linguistic Inquiry* 14.3.

Hockney, D. (1975). "The Bifurcation of Scientific Theories and Indeterminacy of Translation." *Philosophy of Science*, 42.4.

Hornstein, N. & Lightfoot, D. (eds.). (1981). *Explanation in Linguistics* (London: Longman).

Kiparsky, P. (1982). *Some Theoretical Problems in Panim's Grammar* (Poona: Bhandarkar Oriental Research Institute).

Lightfoot, D.

—— . (1982). *The Language Lottery* (Cambridge: MIT Press).

Newmeyer, F.J. (1980). *Linguistic Theory in America* (New York: Academic Press).

Ney, J. (1983). "Review of Chomsky (1982)." *Language Sciences* 5.2.

Putnam, H. (1981). *Reason, Truth and History* (Cambridge: Cambridge University Press).

Quine, W.V. (1960). *Word and Object* (Cambridge: MIT Press).

—— . (1972). "Methodological Reflections on Current Linguistic Theory." In G. Harman & D. Davidson, (eds.). *Semantics of Natural Language* (New York: Humanities Press).

Radford, A. (1981). *Transformational Syntax* (Cambridge: Cambridge University Press).

Riemsdijk, H. van & Williams, E. (1985). *Introduction to the Theory of Grammar* (Cambridge: MIT Press).

Chapter 19

Gareth Evans

SEMANTIC THEORY AND TACIT KNOWLEDGE[1]

I

In his provocative paper, Prof. Wright threw down several challenges to philosophers like myself who have been attracted by, and supposed themselves to be participating in, the enterprise of constructing a systematic theory of meaning for a natural language. I shall have time this evening to take up only one of his challenges, which I hope is the most important.

Prof. Wright notes that those who are interested in constructing a theory of meaning for a natural language insist that it should be what he calls 'structure-reflecting'; as he says, all the interest of the theories or sub-theories which have been constructed lies in their capacity to exhibit the meanings of complex expressions as a function of the meanings of their parts. Prof. Wright then takes this 'structure-reflecting' requirement in one hand and examines various accounts of the nature of a theory of meaning which might justify its imposition. He considers three such accounts.

The first is this: the task of a theory of meaning is simply to enable one to state what each of the sentences of a language means. He argues, I think correctly, that if this is the task of a theory of meaning, the structure-reflecting requirement cannot be justified; indeed, and here again I agree with him, in the special case in which the language under study is included in the language in which the theory is being stated, a single axiom schema:

True $(\bar{\varphi}) \equiv \varphi$

will serve the purpose.

(Like Prof. Wright, I will concentrate upon theories of meaning which yield statements of sentences' truth-conditions, since, as he says, his scepticism about theories of meaning arises equally for theories whose central motion is not that of truth but, say, warranted assertibility, or falsifiability. In order to focus upon the question of structure, we can assume that no question is being raised about the empirical content of the *theorems* of the theory of meaning; the question is about the significance of their being derived from a finite set of principles (axioms) in a structure-revealing way.)

Prof. Wright argues that if the structure-reflecting requirement is to be justified, a theory of meaning must in some way or other be regarded as a theory of the competence of speakers of the language, but in what way? We can say that the theory states something which speakers of the language tacitly know, but what does this mean? Two interpretations provide the second and third account which Prof. Wright considers. One he finds relatively weak, and acceptable, but unable to justify the requirement; the other he finds inadequately explained and open to serious objection.

According to the weak sense of 'tacit knowledge', 'to attribute implicit knowledge of such a "theory" . . . is to do no more than obliquely to describe their behaviour; it is to say that they behave in just the way which someone would behave who successfully tried to suit his behaviour to . . . an explicit statement [of the theory]'[2]. Let us call two theories of meaning which attribute the same meanings to sentences of a language – which agree in their theorems – *extensionally equivalent* (by analogy with the notion of extensional equivalence applied to grammars). According to Prof. Wright, to suit one's behaviour to a theory of meaning is to suit one's behaviour to its theorems. Consequently, if the behaviour of native speakers is the same as one who suits his behaviour to the explicitly formulated theory T, it is the same as one who suits his behaviour to an explicit statement of any extensionally equivalent theory T′. Hence, native speakers tacitly know all extensionally equivalent theories, whether those theories discern different structures in native sentences or, in the case of a theory formulated with a single axiom schema, do not discern structure in their sentences at all. So, while this weak notion of tacit knowledge is perfectly clear, it does not provide one with the basis for preferring one extensionally equivalent theory to another.

We come then to the third account which Prof. Wright considered. It would be quite unfair to complain that Prof. Wright did not make this third option terribly clear, for it is one of his points that it is not very clear. But in the absence of an explicit statement, we must rest content with hints. The notion of tacit knowledge is richer, and allows for the idea of 'unconscious deployment of information'. It is also capable of figuring in an *explanation* of a speaker's capacity to understand new sentences. Though this indicates the kind of direction in which Prof. Wright thinks one who seeks to justify the structure-reflecting requirement must be pushed, he expressed doubt about whether a genuine explanation could be provided by the use of the notion of tacit knowledge; to invoke tacit knowledge of a theory of meaning to explain a speaker's capacity to understand new sentences is vacuous, in the way in which explanations invoking the notion of a universal are vacuous. Secondly, he suggests that any such rich notion of tacit knowledge of a theory of meaning is only dubiously consistent with Wittgenstein's rule-following considerations:

the thesis seems to involve thinking of mastery of the language as consisting in (unconscious) equipment with the information which systematically settles the content of so far unconstructed and unconsidered sentences. Such a conception is far from patently coherent with the repudiation of the objectivity of sameness of use involved in the scepticism about investigation-independence sketched above.[3]

Though it is not my intention to focus on this aspect of his paper, I am unsure how Wittgenstein's considerations, at least as interpreted by Prof. Wright, can threaten this, as yet unborn, third option. Prof. Wright says that Wittgenstein's rule-following considerations:

do not . . . impugn the legitimacy of at least the most basic purpose with which such a theory might be devised: that of securing a description of the use of . . . the object language of such a kind that to be apprised of that description would be to know how to participate in the use of . . . the language.[4]

Someone who knows a finite theory for an infinite language is in some sense in possession of information which *settles in advance* (allows him to predict) the meanings of as yet unconstructed sentences. It is unclear to me why those who wish to argue that speakers of an infinite language tacitly know a finite theory of meaning need suppose the theory to determine the meanings of unconstructed sentences in any stronger, or more objectionable, sense than the one Prof. Wright implicitly accepts in the passage I have just quoted.

However good or bad the reasons for Prof. Wright's pessimism might be, he certainly threw down a challenge, and I want to take it up. I want to try to explain how the structure-reflecting requirement might be justified. But I must immediately mention two limitations on my attempt. I do not pretend that it is the only possible way of replying to Prof. Wright's challenge, nor do I think that it would command universal assent among theorists of meaning. For example, I am fairly sure that Prof. Davidson would dissent from it, since, contrary to what Prof. Wright suggests, he has conspicuously avoided reference to the psychological states of language users in his explanation of the nature of a theory of meaning. Second, I propose to do merely what I say: to defend the enterprise on which the structure-reflecting requirement is a constraint. I do not propose to defend the claim that philosophical insights and benefits accrue from taking the enterprise seriously.

Those who have followed recent debates in grammatical theory will be aware that Prof. Wright's challenge to the theorist of meaning is very similar to Quine's challenge to the grammarian:

> Implicit guidance is a moot enough idea to demand some explicit methodology. If it is to make sense to say that a native was implicitly guided by one system of rules rather than another, extensionally equivalent one, this sense must link up somehow with the native's dispositions to behave in observable ways in observable circumstances.[5]

However, in a way Prof. Wright's challenge is more radical, because it is not possible to formulate even a merely extensionally adequate grammar by the use of a single axiom schema. But this idea, that all a semantic theorist needs to say about English in English can be encapsulated

in a single axiom schema, must surely lead us to begin upon our task of meeting Prof. Wright's challenge with a conviction that it can be met. Can it seriously be suggested that there is nothing to be said about the semantics of specific constructions – of adverbs, tense, modality, intensional contexts, pronouns, quantifiers, proper names, definite descriptions and the like? A good deal has already been said on these subjects by Frege, Russell, Davidson, Geach, Dummett and many others, and though I can detect deficiencies in this work, they do not lead me to think that there are simply no questions of the kind these theorists are attempting to answer. Prof. Wright has criticized semantic theorists for ignoring the ideas of 'the most original philosophical thinker of the twentieth century', but it is surely equally deplorable if students of those ideas act as intellectual Luddites, dismissing the entirety of a sophisticated and developing intellectual tradition without a detailed consideration of its findings, and an alternative account of the enterprise to which the obviously compelling distinctions and observations it contains do properly belong. I do not say that Prof. Wright would himself join, or even encourage, the fanatics wrecking the machines, and I am prepared to concede that his challenge has not been squarely faced, but I should have liked to see a little more evidence that the questions he posed were 'expecting the answer "Yes" ', rather than 'expecting the answer "No" '.

II

Let us begin by considering a little elementary and finite language which contains ten names, a, b, c, . . . and ten monadic predicates F, G, H, . . .; in all, the language has 100 possible sentences. I consider this case partly for simplicity, but also in order to stress that the structure-reflecting requirement has nothing whatever to do with *finiteness*. The fact that a language has an infinite number of possible sentences is a sufficient is a sufficient but not necessary condition of its having semantically significant structure, as our little language will illustrate. (It is unfortunate that Chomsky's writings have led people to equate the *creativity* of language use with the *unboundedness* natural languages display. Linguistic creativity is manifested in the capacity to understand new sentences, and the speaker of a finite language such as the one I have described can manifest it.) I want to consider two possible theories of meaning for this language. T_1 has 100 axioms; one for each sentence of the language. Examples would be:

> *Fa* is true iff John is bald
> *Fb* is true iff Harry is bald
> . . .
> *Ga* is true iff John is happy
> *Gb* is true iff Harry is happy.

T_1 treats each of the sentences as unstructured. T_2, on the other hand, has twenty-one axioms – one for each 'word' of the language, and a general, compositional one. Ten of the axioms are of the form:

> *a* denotes John
> *b* denotes Harry

and ten are of the form:

> An object satisfies F iff it is bald
> An object satisfies G iff it is happy.

The compositional axiom is:

> A sentence coupling a name with a predicate is true iff the object denoted by the name satisfies the predicate.

One can derive from these twenty-one axioms a statement of the truth-conditions of each of the 100 sentences of the language – the very statements which T_1 takes as axioms. T_2 treats a sentence like *Fa* as structured; it discerns two distinct elements in it; the name *a* and the

predicate F. Thus, T_1 and T_2 are extensionally equivalent in our sense, and our question is: what can be meant by saying that the practice of speakers of the language shows that one of these is to be preferred to the other, or equivalently, that they tacitly know one of these theories rather than the other?

It is tempting to answer this question by saying that T_1 is a theory tacitly known by someone who has had to receive training with, or exposure to the practice with, each one of the 100 sentences taken individually – someone who had not realized, or who could make no use of the fact, that the same expressions occur in different sentences – whereas T_2 is tacitly known by someone who has the capacity to understand *new* sentences of this simple subject-predicate form (e.g. *Kc*), provided that he has been exposed to the practice with a sufficiency of sentences containing the name *c* and the predicate K. However, though this contains the essence of the answer, it will not do as it stands, since it may reasonably be objected that T_1 also comprises a statement of what *Kc* means, so that someone who tacitly knew T_1 would be able to understand it.

I suggest that we construe the claim that someone tacitly knows a theory of meaning as ascribing to that person a set of dispositions – one corresponding to each of the expressions for which the theory provides a distinct axiom. In the case of T_1, it is easy to see what these dispositions are: one tacitly knows T_1 iff one has 100 distinct dispositions, each one being a disposition to judge utterances of the relevant sentence type as having such-and-such truth-conditions. It is more difficult to specify the dispositions which tacit knowledge of T_2 requires of a speaker, because they are interconnected. The only judgments which we are prepared to ascribe to speakers are judgments about the truth-conditions of whole sentences – this, of course, is why we must speak of the knowledge of the axioms being tacit. However, if the subject tacitly knows T_2, we shall regard any such judgment as the exercise of two distinct dispositions. Consequently, the dispositions which tacit knowledge of T_2 requires can never be manifested singly. The dispositions must be inter-defined, but though this makes the task of specifying the dispositions more difficult, it does not make it impossible.

For example, we might say that a speaker U tacitly knows that the denotation of a is John iff he has a disposition such that:

($\Pi\Phi$) ($\Pi\Psi$) if
(i)   U tacitly knows that an object satisfies Φ iff it is Ψ
(ii)   U hears an utterance having the form $\Phi\frown a$,

then U will judge the utterance is true iff John is Ψ.

Connectedly, we say that a speaker U tacitly knows that an object satisfies F iff it is bald iff he has a disposition such that:

(Πx) (Πa) if
(i)   U tacitly knows that the denotation of a is x.
(ii)   U hears an utterance having the form $F\frown a$,

then U will judge that the utterance is true iff x is bald.

In these formulations, 'Π' is a universal substitutional quantifier, with variables having the following substitution classes: Φ, names of predicate expressions of the (object) language; a, names of names of the (object) language; Ψ, predicate expressions of our language (the meta-language); and 'x', proper names of our language.

Now, it is essential that the notion of a disposition used in these formulations be understood in a full-blooded sense. These statements of tacit knowledge must not be regarded as simple statements of regularity, for if they were, anyone who correctly judged the meanings

of complete sentences would have a tacit knowledge of T_2. When we ascribe to something the disposition to V in circumstances C, we are claiming that there is a state S which, when taken together with C, provides a causal explanation of all the episodes of the subject's V-ing (in C). So we make the claim that there is a common explanation to all those episodes of V-ing. Understood in this way, the ascription of tacit knowledge of T_2 does not merely report upon the regularity in the way in which the subject reacts to sentences containing a given expression (for this regularity can be observed in the linguistic behaviour of someone for whom the sentence is unstructured). It involves the claim that there is a single state of the subject which figures in a causal explanation of why he reacts in this regular way to all the sentences containing the expression. Tacit knowledge of T_2 requires that there should be twenty such states of the subject — one corresponding to each expression of the language which the theory treats separately — such that the causal explanation of why the subject reacts in the way that he does to any sentence of the language involves two of these states, and any one of these states is involved in the explanation of the way he reacts to ten sentences containing a common element.

The difference between the ascription of tacit knowledge of T_1 and T_2 can be brought out diagrammatically, with the diagrams representing two extremely abstract and schematic psychological models of a subject's capacity to understand sentences. Tacit knowledge of T_1 and T_2 are incompletely represented in figures 19.1 and 19.2 respectively. Forget about the dotted lines for a moment. You will observe that in the first model, there are two *independent* links between the speech-analysing device and the subject's store of knowledge of John (and in a full representation there would be ten such independent links), whereas in the second model, there is just one link between the speech-analysing device and the subject's store

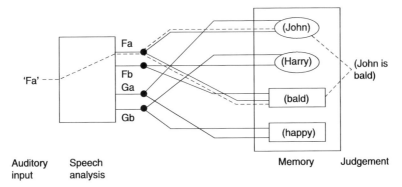

Figure 19.1

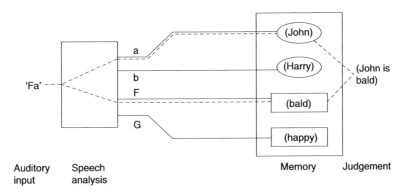

Figure 19.2

of knowledge of John. The dotted lines are intended to indicate what happens when the subject hears the sentence Fa. If you imagine dotted lines drawn to trace the consequences of the subject's hearing the sentence Ga, you will observe that in the former case they will not, and in the latter case they will, share a pathway with the dotted line already on the diagram. This is a representation of the fact that in the former case there is not, and in the latter case there is, a common factor which must be invoked in the explanation of the speaker's reaction to the two sentences.

It appears to me that there is a clear empirical difference between these two models of competence, and hence between tacit knowledge of T_1 and T_2 interpreted in the way I have suggested.

The decisive way to decide which model is correct is by providing a causal, presumably neurophysiologically based, explanation of comprehension. With such an explanation in hand, we can simply see whether or not there is an appeal to a common state or structure in the explanation of the subject's comprehension of each of the sentences containing the proper name a. However, even in the absence of such an explanation, we can have very good empirical reasons for preferring one model of competence to the other.

In the first place, we can examine the way in which the dispositions to react to sentences (the capacity to understand them) are acquired. We might find that the acquisition of the language progressed in quite definite ways, and involved a subject's acquiring the capacity to understand sentences he had never heard before. For example, suppose a subject had progressed in his mastery of the language to the point where he understood all of the sentences which could be constructed from the vocabulary *a*, *b*, *c*, *d*, *e*, and *F*, *G*, *H*, *I*, *J*. Suppose further that he is exposed to the sentences Ff and Gf in surroundings which, or with instructions which, made it clear what they mean. Whether this exposure leads to his acquiring the capacity to understand new sentences, and which new sentences he was able to understand, would cast very considerable light upon the structure of his competence with the language, both antecedent and subsequent to the introduction of new vocabulary.

If he acquired the capacity to understand the sentences Hf, If, Jf, never having heard them before (and no others), this would strongly confirm the second model of his competence, for this is exactly what it predicts. On the second model, the understanding of these sentences is consequential upon the subject's possession of dispositions specific to the expressions H, I, J, and f. Further, if the second model is correct, the subject's understanding of the fragment of the language without the new name f showed that he possessed the first three relevant dispositions, while the exposure to just two sentences containing the name f can suffice for the establishment of the fourth, provided the circumstances are such that it is clear what those sentences mean. So, according to the second model, all the ingredients of understanding of some sentences are present before any of them have been heard, and they are specifically the sentences Hf. If. Jf.

The first model generates no predictions as to the understanding of unheard sentences. According to it, the understanding of each sentence is a separate capacity, and there is absolutely no reason why the inculcation of competence in the two sentences Ff and Gf should induce competence with any others. If it does so, this can only be accommodated on the first model by additional postulates, but why light dawns upon the particular sentences Hf, If, Jf, rather than Li or Mj, must be left totally unexplained.

Thus, we can see more clearly what bearing the capacity to understand new sentences has upon the choice between T_1 and T_2. The fact that someone has the capacity to understand the unheard sentence Hf does not refute the ascription to him of tacit knowledge of T_1 *outright* – it just makes the ascription extremely implausible.

Evidence of a parallel kind can be derived from the way in which competence is lost. Suppose a subject is such that, if he loses his competence with any sentence of the form $\Phi^\frown a$ (while retaining his competence with some sentences of the form $\Phi^\frown \beta$), he simultaneously loses his competence with *every* sentence of that form. This would also favour the second model of the subject's competence, since this is, once again, what that model predicts. On the first model, however, it is *inexplicable* why the loss of the capacity to understand one sentence should drag the comprehension of other sentences with it. (Evidence of this kind would be equally valuable whether the loss of competence was simply due to the subject's forgetting the meanings of words, or to brain damage.)

There is evidence of a third kind which might be used to decide between the models, since they carry with them different accounts of sentence perception. The second model requires that the subject perceive the sentence Fa, for example, *as* structured, that is to say, as containing the expression *a*. There is a clear difference between perceiving a sentence which does in fact contain the expression *a*, and perceiving a sentence *as* containing the expression *a*. Consequently, we can regard as relevant to the decision between the two models the various psychological tests which have been devised for identifying perceived acoustic structure, for example, the click test originally devised by Ladefoged and Broadbent.[6]

Thus, it seems to me that Prof. Wright's challenge can be met. It is possible to link tacit knowledge of one theory (rather than one of its extensionally equivalent rivals) to 'the native's dispositions to behave in observable ways in observable situations'. But to do this, one must look further than just to the dispositions to respond to, or to use, whole sentences. It is possible that the scepticism which Prof. Wright expresses is due in a small way to the mistaken thought that facts of native usage which bear upon the content possessed by whole sentences are all the facts to which a theory of meaning can or need be sensitive.

Bearing in mind the interpretation of 'tacit knowledge' which I have proposed, let us briefly consider infinite languages. What would be involved in the tacit knowledge of the theory for such a language which is formulated with the use of a single axiom schema?

An axiom schema is not a theory; it is a compendious specification by their syntactic form of the sentences which do constitute the theory. In the case of an infinite language, there are an infinite number of such sentences. Someone would possess tacit knowledge of such a theory only if he possessed an infinite number of *distinct* linguistic dispositions: one corresponding to each of the sentences of the language. This we know no one can possess. I have concentrated upon the more challenging case of a finite language because it is important to stress the point that there can be compelling evidence that someone *does* not possess a battery of distinct dispositions other than the fact that no one *can* possess them, so that we may want to do for a speaker of a finite language what we are forced to do for a speaker of an infinite language.

Infinity in language results from recursiveness: syntactic and semantic rules which operate upon their own output. A standard clause for the recursive element 'and' runs like this:

A sentence of the form S ⁀ 'and' ⁀ S′ is true iff S is true and S′ is true

Generalizing the procedure used earlier, we can say that a speaker U tacitly knows this principle iff he has a disposition such that:

(ΠS) (ΠP) (ΠS′) (ΠP′) if:
(i)   U is disposed to judge that S is true iff P

(ii)   U is disposed to judge that S′ is true iff P′
(iii)   U hears an utterance having the form S ⁀ 'and' ⁀ S′, then U will judge that the utterance is true iff P and P′.

(The substitution classes for the variables S and S′, and P and P′, are names of sentences of the object language, and sentences of the meta-language, respectively.) More difficult is the clause for an existential quantifier. It might run:

A sentence of the form '(∃x)' ⁀ Φ is true iff there is something y such that, letting β be its name, the sentence Φ^{β}/x is true.

This is a simplified 'Fregean' clause for an objectual quantifier.[7] 'Φ^{β}/x' abbreviates 'the result of substituting β for all occurrences of x in Φ'. Then we can say that U tacitly knows this principle iff he has a disposition such that:

(ΠΦ) (ΠΨ), if:
(i)   (Πβ) (Πx) (If U tacitly knows the denotation of β is x, then Γ is disposed to judge that the sentence Φ^{β}/x is true iff x is Ψ)
(ii)   U hears an utterance of the form '(∃x)' ⁀ Φ then U is disposed to judge that the utterance is true iff something is Ψ.

(In this instance, the substitution class for Φ are structural-descriptive names of object-language propositional functions in the variable x.)

III

Prof. Wright and I are agreed that tacit knowledge of the semantic rules of a language is a 'logical construction' out of the use of whole sentences. I have suggested that the idea that we may tacitly know one rather than another of two extensionally equivalent theories which differ in the amount of structure they discern in sentences leads one to the thought of a correspondence between the separable principles of a theory and a series of internal states of the subject, dispositionally characterized. Nevertheless, I would agree with Prof. Wright that to regard these states as states of knowledge or belief, that is to say, states of the same kind as are identified by the ordinary use of those words, is wrong and capable of leading to confusions of the kind he gestures at. To establish this point would require another paper. However, I shall say a brief word about it now, since I believe it is to this point, rather than the very idea of a psychological underpinning to the theory of meaning, that Prof. Wright's criticisms are legitimately directed.

There is no doubt in what the similarity between the states of tacit knowledge and the ordinary states of knowledge and belief is taken to consist. At the level of output, one who possesses the tacit knowledge that p is disposed to do and think some of the things which one who had the ordinary belief that p would be inclined to do and think (given the same desires). At the level of input, one who possesses the state of tacit knowledge that p will very probably have acquired that state as the result of exposure to usage which supports or confirms (though far from conclusively) the proposition that p, and hence in circumstances which might well induce in a rational person the ordinary belief that p. But these analogies are very far from establishing tacit knowledge as a species of belief. After all, similar analogies at the level of input and output exist between the state of a rat who avoids a certain food which has upset it in the past ('bait-shyness') on the one hand, and the belief that a man might have that a certain food is poisonous, on the other.

It is true that many philosophers would be prepared to regard the dispositional state of the rat as a belief. But such a view requires blindness to the fundamental differences which exist between the state of the rat and the belief of the man – differences which suggest that fundamentally different mechanisms are at work. We might begin with this disanalogy: The rat manifests the 'belief' in only one way – by not eating – whereas there is no limit to the ways in which the ordinary belief that something is poisonous might be manifested. The subject might manifest it by, e.g., preventing someone else from eating the food, or by giving it to a hated enemy, or by committing suicide with it. These variations stem from the different projects with which the belief may interact, but similar variations arise from combining the belief with other beliefs. It might, for example, lead to a subject's consuming a small amount of the food every day, when combined with the belief that the consumption of small doses of a poison renders one immune to its effects. (The existence of other beliefs induces a similar variability in the ways in which the belief that something is poisonous might be established.) It is of the essence of a belief state that it be at the service of many distinct projects, and that its influence on any project be mediated by other beliefs. The rat simply has a disposition to avoid a certain food; the state underlying this disposition is not part of a system which would generate widely varying behaviour in a wide variety of situations according to the different projects and further 'beliefs' it may possess.

So, one who possesses a belief will typically be sensitive to a wide variety of ways in which it can be established (what it can be inferred from), and a wide variety of different ways in which it can be used (what can be inferred from it) – if we think of plans for intentional action as being generated from beliefs by the same kind of rational inferential process as yields further beliefs from beliefs. To have a belief requires one to appreciate its location in a network of beliefs; this is why Wittgenstein says. 'When we first begin to *believe* anything, what we believe is not a single proposition, it is a whole system of propositions. (Light dawns gradually over the whole.)' (OC, §141.) To think of beliefs in this way forces us to think of them as structured states; the subject's appreciation of the inferential potential of one belief (e.g. the belief that *a* is F) at least partly depending upon the same general capacity as his appreciation of the inferential potential of others (e.g. the belief that *b* is F). After all, the principle of an *inference*, of *reasoning*, can never be specific to the set of propositions involved.[8] Possession of this general capacity is often spoken of as mastery of a concept, and the point I am making is frequently made by saying that belief involves the possession of concepts (e.g. the concept of *poison*). Behind the idea of a system of beliefs lies that of a system of concepts, the structure in which determines the inferential properties which thoughts involving an exercise of the various component concepts of the system are treated as possessing. At the ground floor of the structure will be observational concepts whose possession requires the subject to be able to discriminate (in suitable favourable circumstances) instances of the concept. Inferential links connect these concepts with more theoretical concepts 'higher' in the structure, and they in their turn will be connected with concepts yet more remote from observation.

Concepts are exercised in the first instance in thoughts: beliefs may be regarded as dispositions to entertain thoughts in the 'believing mode' – i.e. to make judgements: if we think of belief in this way, we shall not be prepared to attribute to a subject the belief that *a* is F (for some particular object *a*, and property F) unless we can suppose the subject to be capable of entertaining the supposition (having the thought) that *b* is F, for every object *b* of which he has a conception. For example, we will not be inclined to explain a subject's actions by attributing to him the belief that *he* is F (e.g. he is in pain) unless we suppose him capable of entertaining the supposition with respect to individuals distinct from himself that they are F (e.g. that the person is in pain).[9] Now, it is true that the 'believing mode' of thought cannot be characterized without reference to its influence upon the subject's actions; the traditional accounts of belief which I am largely following went wrong in trying to identify the difference between judgment and mere thought

in terms of some introspectible feature of accompaniment of the thought. A judgment is (*ceteris paribus*) a thought one acts upon (if a suitable plan for action is derived from it). But we are now far away from the rat's disposition to avoid certain food. For one thing, there is an enormous gap between belief (a disposition to judge that p when the question whether p is raised) and action. Even though a subject believes a substance is posionous he may not slip it to an enemy he wants to kill and knows no other way to kill either because he 'didn't think of it' or because, having thought of it, he 'forgot' what to do when the time came.

Tacit knowledge of the syntactic and semantic rules of the language are not states of the same kind as the states we identify in our ordinary use of the terms 'belief' and 'knowledge'. Possession of tacit knowledge is exclusively manifested in speaking and understanding a language; the information is not even potentially at the service of any other project of the agent, nor can it interact with any other beliefs of the agent (whether genuine beliefs or other tacit 'beliefs') to yield further beliefs. Such concepts as we use in specifying it are not concepts we need to suppose the subject to possess, for the state is inferentially insulated from the rest of the subject's thoughts and beliefs. There is thus no question of regarding the information being brought by the subject to bear upon speech and interpretation in rational processes of thought, or of making sense of the subject's continued possession of the information despite incorrect performance, due to his 'not thinking' of the rule at the appropriate time, etc. Remarks which Prof. Wright makes ('unconscious deployment of information', etc.) suggest that he considers the proponent of his third option as holding that tacit knowledge is a real species of belief, but with all the relevant inferential processes made by the subject somehow taking place outside his ken. This is certainly a mysterious and confused position.

I disagree with Prof. Wright only in denying

that the proponent of a structure-reflecting theory of meaning need have anything to do with it.

IV

I come finally to the question of whether there
is any sense in which the theorist of meaning
provides an explanation of a speaker's capacity
to understand new sentences. Now it is implicit
in what has gone before that the notion of tacit
knowledge of a structure-reflecting theory of
meaning, explained as I have explained it,
cannot be used to explain the capacity to understand new sentences. I have given a purely
dispositional characterization of tacit knowledge, and though this does not just amount to a
re-description of the speaker's capacities to
understand sentences (including the new ones)
what it provides, in addition to a description of
those capacities, is not itself something that
could be involved in an explanation of them. The
surplus concerned the form which an explanation of the capacities would take, and to say that
a group of phenomena have a common explanation is obviously not yet to say what the
explanation is. So I agree with what Prof. Wright
writes:

> there is no reason to think that it is within the
> power of the sort of theory which we are
> considering to serve up anything which could
> rightly be considered an *explanation* of the
> infinitary character of competence with its
> object-language.[10]

But while I agree with this, I disagree with his
claim that a proponent of structure-reflecting
theories of meaning must somehow be committed to the view that they are providing an explanation of speakers' capacity to understand new
sentences.

Nevertheless, I believe that there is a way of
explaining a speaker's capacity to understand
new sentences to which provision of a
structure-reflecting theory of meaning is

indispensable. For we can provide a genuine
explanation of a speaker's capacity to understand a certain novel utterance by citing his
exposure, in the past, to the elements of that
sentence occurring in sentences whose meaning
was, or was made, manifest. I envisage an
explanatory chain like this:

Exposure to corpus of sentences containing parts of the given sentence being used in determinate ways	$\Rightarrow$	Complex set of dispositions = tacit knowledge of clauses in theory of meaning	$\Rightarrow$	Understanding of a given new sentence

This chain can be genuinely explanatory even
though the last link of the chain by itself is not.
The attribution to a subject of tacit knowledge of
T_1 is neither more nor less explanatory of the
capacity to understand the given new sentence
than the attribution of T_2, but tacit knowledge of
T_2 belongs in an explanation of the capacity to
understand a new sentence because we understand how those dispositions might have been
acquired as a result of exposure to the corpus of
utterances which the subject has heard. Now,
we can cite a subject's exposure to a corpus of
utterances in explanation of his capacity to
understand a new one only if we believe that the
use of expressions in the new sentence is in
conformity with their use in the previously heard
corpus. Only in this case will we be able to show
what set of dispositions the subject might
have acquired which meets the two conditions:
(1) exercising them yields the observed (and
correct) interpretation of the new sentence; (2)
it would have been exercised in, and hence could
have been acquired by exposure to, the previous
use. Consequently, when a capacity to understand novel sentences is observed, the theorist of
meaning has an indispensable role to play in its

explanation, since he must exhibit the regularity between the old and the new.

I have more or less deliberately spoken in terms which might well offend some of those present, for I believe that some of those present, though not, I think Prof. Wright, believe that Wittgenstein's arguments on rule-following show that the ambition to exhibit such regularity must be based upon some kind of mistake. Perhaps this is so, and if it is so, I hope that we shall hear tonight why it is so. Since I do not have time to discuss the arguments of such philosophers, let me end by addressing two connected questions to them.

1. Is it their opinion that all capacities to understand novel sentences (to *know*, I stress, what they mean) are equally inexplicable, or do they believe that scope is provided for one kind of explanation of how it is that a speaker knows what a new sentence means when and only when it can be shown to contain elements which also occur in sentences with whose use he is already familiar?

On the assumption that their answer to my first question is 'Yes', I come to my second:

2. Do they think that it is sufficient to provide an explanation of the kind which the occurrence of familiar expressions makes possible simply by showing that the new sentence does contain expressions which also occur in sentences with whose use he

is already familiar, or do they believe, in view of the evident possibility of ambiguity, that something else must be provided? If so, how does this further part of the explanation differ from a statement of the regularity between the old use and the new?

Notes

1   [Editors' note: this paper was written in reply to Crispin Wright's 'Rule-following, objectivity and the theory of meaning', in S. Holtzman and C. Leich (eds.), *Wittgenstein: To Follow a Rule*, London: Routledge and Kegan Paul, 1981.]
2   Wright, *op. cit.*, p. 110.
3   *Ibid.*, p. 112.
4   *Ibid.*, pp. 115–16.
5   W. V. Quine, 'Methodological reflections on current linguistic theory', in D. Davidson and G. Harman (eds), *Semantics of Natural Languages*, Reidel, Dordrecht, 1972, pp. 442–54.
6   P. Ladefoged and D. E. Broadbent, 'Perception of sequence in auditory events', *Quarterly Journal of Experimental Psychology* 13 (1960), pp. 162–70. See also J. A. Fodor and T. G. Bever, 'The psychological reality of linguistic segments', *Journal of Verbal Learning and Verbal Behaviour* 4 (1965), pp. 414–20.
7   For an account of the 'Fregean' approach to quantifiers, see my paper 'Pronouns, quantifiers and relative clauses (1)', *Canadian Journal of Philosophy* 7 (1977), pp. 467–536.
8   See T. Nagel, *The Possibility of Altruism*, Clarendon, Oxford, 1970, Chapter 7.
9   See P. F. Strawson, *Individuals*, Methuen, London, 1959, Chapter 3, Section 4.
10 Wright, *op. cit.*, p. 113.

Chapter 20

Crispin Wright

THEORIES OF MEANING AND SPEAKERS' KNOWLEDGE

[. . .]

III

In order for a theory of meaning to be explanatory of the linguistic capacities of actual speakers, there has to be, it seems, a sense in which its axioms are true of them; or, at least, there have to be properties of the speakers for whose description the axioms are needed. It would be an error to suppose that the notion that speakers *implicitly know* the content of such a set of axioms is the only way of meeting this condition. It is evidently a tempting and natural suggestion – witness the widespread use of such ideas in the writings of theoretical linguists. But it is exceedingly difficult to be clear whether it is ultimately coherent.

The most immediate objection is based on the thought that the axioms of a theory of meaning ought to correspond to semantic *rules*. To amplify: such an axiom is supposed to describe the semantically relevant features of an expression; how could it do that if it failed to embody a condition on the correct use of that expression? For the meaning of an expression is essentially something normative; it is, crudely, only because expressions have meaning that there is such a thing as correct, or incorrect, use of them. This normativity does not *per se* conflict with the capacity of the theory to contribute towards the explanation of speakers' linguistic

'creativity' – their capacity to understand novel utterances; the proposal will be that the feature of a speaker which such an axiom can reflect is precisely his knowledge of it. If we are given, for instance, a statement of the powers of the pieces in chess, there is no tension about supposing that it may serve both to articulate the norms determining what is and is not a legal move and to contribute towards the explanation of players' capacity to recognize the legality/illegality of moves which they have not previously encountered. The double function is secured by the bridging assumption that the players recognize exactly the rules which the statement describes. The salient point is therefore the need for a bridging assumption which hypothesizes practitioners' recognition of the set of norms which the axioms describe.

So what is the objection? Well, if something like a Davidsonian theory is indeed possible for English, it is a mighty iceberg about whose overall shape we have very little idea. We know that it would be a theory of great complexity which would impose a good deal of regimentation on the surface grammar of our language. The handling of tense, adverbs, predicate modifiers, modality, intentionality and even quantifiers are all controversial topics. The tendency, understandably, among researchers in the field has been to stay close to the Tarskian prototype and to the syntax of predicate calculus. But while interesting work has been done, even the most committed would have to allow that progress towards realization of the grand design has not been spectacular. Accordingly, someone who believes that English, or at least a good deal of it, does indeed admit of complete semantic description by means of a compositional formal theory would at present be hard pressed to justify a high degree of confidence that work has proceeded along the right sort of lines, or has been inspired by the most fruitful paradigms. In other words, apart from knowing that it will be difficult to design, will be complex of articulation and is likely to contain at present unforeseen devices, we have *very little* idea what a formal theory of meaning for a natural language of expressive power comparable to that of English would be like. Yet it is the axioms of such a theory which the implicit knowledge proposal would have us regard as *normative* with respect to our linguistic practice. Are there not manifest philosophical difficulties with the idea that our linguistic behaviour should be regarded as informed by our recognition of principles which we cannot state, which played no explicit part in our linguistic training, which will probably involve concepts of great sophistication and technicality, and which we might not recognize even if presented with a formulation? How can a principle function as a rule if those who engage in the practice which it is supposed to regulate have no consciousness of it?

Dummett writes:

What plays the role, within a theory of meaning of Davidson's kind, of a grasp of the meanings of the words is a knowledge of the axioms governing those words: in our example [that of 'the earth moves'] these may be stated as ' "the earth" denotes the earth' and 'it is true to say of something "it moves" if and only if that thing moves'. (This latter formulation of the axiom governing 'moves' is stated without appeal to the technical device of satisfaction by an infinite sequence, and is only an approximate indication of what

is wanted: but, if we are intending a serious representation of what is known by anyone able to speak English, we cannot literally credit him with an understanding of that technical device.)[1]

We can sympathize with Dummett's reservations: it is a plausible enough constraint upon the significant attribution of belief, *a fortiori* of knowledge, that a subject possesses the concepts which figure in the content of the belief attributed to him, and it is utterly implausible that ordinary speakers of English should be credited with an understanding, at any level, of concepts like satisfaction, infinite sequence and the star functor. But Dummett's thought here is vulnerable to a simple dilemma. If this sort of technical apparatus is necessary for the development of a theory of meaning for a typical natural language, then speakers may not, on his own admission, be credited with a full implicit knowledge of that theory but only, perhaps, of a part of it; and the claims of the theory to provide a model of how speakers actually achieve an understanding of novel utterances must therefore be severely qualified. If, on the other hand, the technical apparatus is merely a convenience, an explanation is owing of how it may be dispensed with and the axiomatic and recursive basis of the theory developed purely in terms of concepts whose attribution to speakers is altogether more plausible. The promise of a thory of meaning to illuminate actual speakers' linguistic 'creativity' will then depend entirely on the success of this explanation – an explanation which we have, so far, not the slightest idea how to construct.

It will be apparent that there are two special and separate difficulties here which vindication of the notion of implicit knowledge in general would not necessarily resolve. There is the problem of explaining how a *rule* can be implicitly known, how, that is, it can function as a rule – exert a regulative influence – if practitioners are unaware of it. And there is the problem of how contents, putatively implicitly known, may involve concepts for their possessing which there is no direct evidence in practitioners' performance and which may, indeed, be sufficiently abstruse to be beyond their powers – at least their *apparent* powers – of comprehension. However I do not think that either problem is immediately fatal. It is true, of course, that a rule as a possible object of consultation has to be a possible object of consciousness. But it is perfectly obvious that the axioms of a homophonic theory of meaning are not meant to be rules in this sense since – because they use the expressions which they mention – only someone who already understood those expressions, and hence had no need to consult such 'rules', would be capable of consulting them. It does not follow that the axioms cannot be regarded as statements of rule at all, however. It would indeed be fatal to their claim to contain a theory of *meaning* if they could not. But the simple fact is that the characterization of a convention does not have to proceed in terms which could be used to explain the convention to someone previously ignorant of it. It is a convention of English that 'red' in its most basic, literal sense, is correctly predicated only of things which are red. Speakers of English who are credited with an understanding of 'red' in its most basic and literal sense are thereby credited, inter alia, with the intention to uphold this pattern of predication as a matter of convention. There is no better statement of the convention than the one I have given. And it is, at the same time, perfectly useless as an explanation of what the convention is to someone who doesn't already know it. The dilemma is therefore a false one: the axioms of a theory of meaning do not have to be explanatory, or 'objects of consultation', on pain of failing to concern meaning. It suffices that they describe linguistic conventions. And the question of speakers' implicit knowledge of them is thus, in effect, the question whether speakers may be regarded as implicitly recognizing the conventions which they state.

The proper analysis of the notion of convention is a subtle business.[2] It may be that the idea of a convention which is merely implicitly recognized would turn out to put the notion under great strain. But prima facie there seems no reason to expect so.[3] Whatever the details of a correct analysis, convention is going to turn out to supervene upon peoples' intentions, fundamentally the intention to uphold the regularity which the convention prescribes. The crucial question is therefore whether – whether or not they are, or can be brought to be, aware of it – the axioms and recursions of a theory of meaning might succeed in describing a set of linguistic constraints which competent speakers of English may be regarded as intending to uphold. If the answer is negative, the attempt to interpret the relation between speakers and an appropriate theory of meaning for their language as that of implicit knowledge must fail; but if affirmative, that interpretation has a chance of success. In any event it is to assail a man of straw to insist that the implicit knowledge theorist should explain how a principle can be actively regulative of a practice when none of the participants can profess to know it.[4] The issue rather concerns constraints on the ascription of intention. Does it make sense to ascribe intentions to people which they cannot articulate? Or intentions a correct description of which they cannot recognize when given it?

It is important to recognize that what is at issue here is not the propriety of *extending* the notion of intention so as to accommodate the implicit knowledge theorist's needs. If ordinary practice is to be the guide, it is clear that we *already* use intention, and cognate notions, in ways that can make his position seem quite natural. The attribution of intention is entailed whenever we credit a subject with agency; and we implicitly credit a subject with agency – the capacity for action, in the proper sense of the word – whenever we deem it appropriate to offer *rationalistic* explanations of its performance, explanations which proceed by the ascription of a system of beliefs and desires. Now the fact is — philosophically suspect, or not, as the practice may be — that we go in for simple rationalistic explanations of the behaviour of more intelligent animals. If a dog sets off from his home at roughly the same time each day, no one would think it outrageous to be offered the explanation that he expects his master to be returning home at about that time and wants to see him. Some philosophers (ironically enough, Davidson)[5] would argue that any rationalistic explanation of the behaviour of a languageless creature is misconceived. My point is only the descriptive one that such explanations are *commonplace*: in the above example, the dog is implicitly credited with the intention to intercept his master — an intention of which it can neither give nor recognize an adequate description.

Consider this case. It does not happen, but might, that small children could learn to play chess long before they could learn to understand speech — or at least to attain the level of understanding necessary to give or follow explicit descriptions of the rules of chess, or of points in the theory of the game, etc. They learn the moves, let us suppose, by just the sort of patient mixture of drill, demonstration and (inadvertent) reward by which any ordinary child learns the names for colours, or farmyard animals. And then, remarkably, some of them acquire the ability to play not merely legally but well, responding with subtlety and inventiveness to board configurations which they have never encountered before. It would be overwhelmingly natural to credit such children not merely with knowledge of the rules of chess but with the sort of insight into the potentialities of a situation which any good chess player possesses. It is, however, difficult to understand how such insight should be supposed to function if it is not essentially a faculty of *inference*: inference which goes to work on premises including, inter alia, the rules determining the powers of movement and capture of the various types of piece. It seems to me undeniable that, pre-philosophically

as it were, we should be quite content to explain such childrens' performance by ascribing to them the knowledge and intentions constitutive of an understanding of, and the practice of playing by, the rules of chess; we would regard them as able to apprehend the implications of those rules for the potentialities of a particular state of play and thereby able to inform their selection of moves with the aim of winning, or at least avoiding defeat.

The parallel with the demands made by the implicit-knowledge interpretation of the theory of meaning, the speakers being credited with knowledge of the axioms and with the capacity to apprehend their more or less remote consequences, is obvious. Indeed the analogy may seem close enough to call the validity of what I have suggested would be our natural response to the hypothetical children into question. But to stress: my point is only that, whether or not the implicit-knowledge interpretation of the theory of meaning is ultimately coherent, the objection to it — for all we have so far seen, at least — ought not to be that it puts an impossible strain on our *ordinary* understanding of notions like knowledge, belief, intention, inference, etc. On the contrary, it is aspects of our ordinary understanding of those notions which make the implicit knowledge interpretation seem natural. If it is to be rejected, the prospect is thus not of excision of an unwarranted extension of our ordinary understanding but of revision of it.

The example of the dog is suggestive in a different way. Since Brentano, it has been the more or less received wisdom in the philosophy of mind that the truth-conditions of ascriptions of propositional attitude are indifferent to reference failure in the proposition in question, but sensitive to the inter-substitution of co-referential expressions. Whether or not these are genuinely semantic (contrast, pragmatic) phenomena, it is open to question whether either is a feature of the sorts of context in which we ascribe beliefs to, e.g. a dog. As far as indifference to existence is concerned, we go in for the ascription of propositional attitudes to animals only with a view to rationalizing, after a fashion, their modes of interaction with items which figure in their experience; since no non-existent items so figure, there is simply no explanatory role to be played by the ascription to them of attitudes to propositions which we can express only by recourse to empty singular terms.[6] Inter-substitutivity is less straightforward. It is natural to report that the dog expects to see his master in the road, unnatural to report that he expects to see Joe Smith, or the high street newsagent. But the latter descriptions strike us as unacceptable only because we are unwilling to impute to the dog any conception of a personal proper name or the institution of newspaper selling. And the fact is that matters stand no better with the relevant concept *master*. A dog's master is, inter alia, ultimately responsible for its welfare and ultimately liable for its good conduct. He has the right to move it around (within, e.g. restrictions imposed by quarantine laws), and even to dispose of it. Does the dog know all that? There is a temptation to reply the dog has, as it were, a *thinner* conception of his master – one shorn of institutional trappings and based entirely on the history of interaction between them. I advise anyone who feels this temptation to attempt to specify this alleged conception, bearing in mind that the terms used must no way exceed the concepts which may plausibly be attributed to the dog. I do not anticipate success. The truth, I suggest, is that we have no definite idea what concept we are attributing to a dog in describing its behaviour in this sort of way; and that the (unsurprising) explanation of this unclarity is that we are not seriously attributing a *concept* at all. 'His master' is a term which we use for the convenience of ourselves or our audience; there is no constraint of fidelity to a mode of conceiving employed by the dog. If the man in question was known to most of those present as the high street newsagent, whose arrival was keenly awaited, and if the relation of the dog to this man were of no importance in context, it

would not be unnatural to report that the dog had rushed off in the expectation of meeting the newsagent on the road.[7]

It is, of course, uncontentious that it is not *always* a paramount constraint on the satisfactory reportage of propositional attitudes that the content-specifying part involve only concepts attributable to the subject. So much has long been recognized. What I am now suggesting is something stronger: it is our practice, in certain cases, to ascribe propositional attitudes in such a way that not only do we not intend the form of words which we use to reflect the modes of conceiving pursued by the subject but, more, there is no form of words which, if it were important to us, would suit that purpose. One response would be that this, if true, displays a serious indeterminacy in the beliefs, etc., attributed and so calls into doubt the propriety of the attribution. But a different response is possible: that it may be perfectly proper to ascribe certain propositional attitudes to a subject even though there is no, as it were, *canonical* specification of the content of those attitudes, no specification of their content which exactly captures their content-for-the-subject. Despite the recent concentration of effort on 'folk psychology' and the intentional, I think we are some distance from the insights to motivate either response. But if the second is tenable, the likely abstruseness of the concepts necessary for the formulation of a full-blown theory of meaning need no longer constitute an objection to the implicit knowledge conception. Crudely: if a dog may have beliefs of which there is no formulation save by the use of concepts some of which should not be attributed to the dog, then perhaps speakers of a natural language may have intentions of which there is, again, no satisfactory account save by recourse to technicalities of which they have no concept. I do not know what it is right to think about this. I would urge only that those who would treat the objection from technicality as decisive against the implicit knowledge conception should recognize what they are doing: it is not so much a matter of siding with common sense as taking (to the best of my knowledge) an unargued stance on fundamental questions in the philosophy of mind concerning the proper limits of explanation by the postulation of intentional states and the proper constraints on the reportage of the content of such states.

There are, however, more subtle objections to the implicit knowledge conception. Let it be accepted that the prodigious children could properly be described as implicitly knowing the rules of chess and as possessing an appropriate range of intentions, and a measure of insight, which that knowledge served to inform. Still, the situation is not perfectly parallel to what is required in the case of a theory of meaning. The difference is that the axioms and recursions of a theory of meaning do not relate to correct linguistic practice as the 'axioms' of a theory of chess – i.e. the rules of the game – relate to correct play. Someone who intentionally and in good faith moves his Queen in the manner of a Knight shows that he doesn't know the rules prescribing the powers of movement of the Queen. There is no comparably simple and direct way of showing that you do not know the axiom governing the use, in English, of 'red' or 'elephant'. This is because only a use of a *sentence* makes, as Wittgenstein put it, a move in the language game. Thus an illicit move cannot violate a single axiom; rather, it has to violate a meaning-delivering theorem, and thereby all the axioms and recursive clauses involved in its derivation. Which among these you should then be deemed to be in ignorance of is a matter to be settled by reference to your use of other sentences in the derivation of whose meaning-delivering theorems those same clauses are involved, in the light of holistic constraints.

So much is obvious enough. Why does it constitute a problem? What it shows is that, even if the chess example is deemed to be entirely persuasive of the propriety in *general* of the ideas of implicit knowledge of rules, and of implicit inference, it cannot commit us to more, in the

case of the theory of meaning, than the propriety of the notion that speakers implicitly know the meaning-delivering *theorems*, and can carry out (implicit) inferences from them. Whereas, of course, what needs to be legitimated is implicit knowledge of the axioms; and implicit inferences to the theorems (which, in any case, speakers are likely to know explicitly). The attraction of attributing implicit knowledge of the rules of chess to the fictional children is based on two things: first, their behaviour has all the trappings of intelligence, insight and purpose which would make it virtually impossible for us to regard it as anything but intentional; second, since they behave exactly as if they knew the rules of chess, the kind of rationalistic explanation which viewing their behaviour as intentional demands can hardly do better than ascribe such knowledge to them. The strength of the analogy is that both points apply to linguistic competence too: it manifestly has the richness which invites rationalistic explanation, and – if a theory of meaning is possible at all – the behaviour which would display knowledge of it would be exactly the behaviour constitutive of linguistic competence. But the weakness of the analogy is that behaving, in all respects short of explicit statement, as if one knew a theory of meaning cannot be distinguished from behaving as if one knew its meaning-delivering theorems; whereas there is no proper subset of the theorems of the 'theory' of chess whose knowledge would constitute the ability to play. The suggestion that speakers implicitly know a full theory of meaning for their language thus makes demands on the notion of implicit knowledge which have no counterpart in the chess example.

The additional demands, of course, are precisely what have to be made if the implicit knowledge conception is to provide an explanation of speakers' capacity to understand novel utterances. But is it not a welcome and foreseen effect of the attribution of implicit knowledge of the rules of chess to the children that we thereby secure the means to explain their recognition of the legality, or otherwise, of moves that they have never considered before? Surely. The difference is that the case for attributing implicit knowledge of the rules of chess to the children does not entirely consist in this phenomenon, but can be stated independently of it. The rules of chess comprise the *smallest* theory – (of this particular subject matter; we shall, of course, need to attribute a lot of other information to them, of different sorts) – which we need in order to give the envisaged sort of rationalistic explanation of their behaviour. Moreover, each item of knowledge which we thereby attribute to them has its own distinctive kind of behavioural display. If we seek a theory of meaning with these same two features, in contrast, we shall wind up with the sort of infinitary axiom schema which figured in the discussion of Foster above. The explanation of the children's ability to judge novel moves in point of legality may thus be viewed as a welcome by-product of an *independently* motivated attribution of implicit knowledge to them. That is not at all the situation with the implicit knowledge conception of the theory of meaning; linguistic 'creativity' here provides the entire *raison d'être*.

The response will be that it cannot be satisfactory just to credit speakers with knowledge of what is stated by perhaps indefinitely many meaning-delivering theorems, some of which concern sentences which they have never encountered, and leave it at that. The question must arise: what is the basis of this knowledge? My point, however, is not that we should discount this question but that the kind of play made with implicit knowledge in the fictional chess case – which was meant to epitomize the strength of the intuitions that underlie the implicit knowledge conception – provides no precedent for the supposition that this question should have a *psychological* answer. There has to be a perfectly respectable scientific question about the sources of our possession of the knowledge which the meaning-delivering theorems of a satisfactory theory of meaning would describe.

But there is no a priori reason why the answer to this question should have to proceed via the postulation of further cognitive states. The sought-for finite basis may be better described in non-psychological terms.

There is an argument in Gareth Evans's discussion[8] which suggests that extending the notion of speakers' implicit knowledge to encompass the axioms and derivations within a theory of meaning would be a definite error. A rat may acquire the disposition to avoid a kind of foodstuff which is poisonous and has caused it sickness in the past. And we might casually ascribe its unwillingness to eat this material – or one that looked/smelt similar – to the belief that it was poisonous. But we should not, Evans urges, let casual language induce casual thought. Beliefs are essentially things which interact with desires and intentions in the production of behaviour. They are also essentially involved in the production of other beliefs. To ascribe a belief is significant only as part of the ascription of a *system* of beliefs. And what behaviour is expressive of a certain belief depends, in general, upon the other ingredients in this system and in the system of the subject's intentions and desires. Thus my belief that a certain substance is poisonous may manifest itself in a literally indefinite variety of ways. I may, like the rat, avoid the substance. But I may also take steps to ensure my family avoid it, or take steps to ensure they don't! I may take small but daily increasing quantities of the stuff in the belief that I can thereby inure myself against its effects and that background circumstances are such that it may stand to my advantage to have done so. I may take a large quantity if I wish to commit suicide; and a smaller one if I wish to malinger my way out of some obligation. My belief that the substance is poisonous is thus, as Evans puts it, at the service of indefinitely many potential projects corresponding to indefinitely many transformations in my other beliefs and desires. With the rat, in contrast, concepts like the desire for suicide, or malign intent, can get no grip. The 'desires' which we are prepared to attribute to it are restricted, in the present context, to avoidance of distress; and its 'belief' that the substance is poisonous has consequently no other expression than in shunning it.

Evans's point, well made by this example, is that rationalistic explanations of behaviour are so much idle patter unless we are willing to credit the subject with the sophistication of a manifold system of interacting and evolving beliefs and desires, of a degree of organization sufficient to obstruct straightforward dispositional reductions of any particular belief ascription. There is no such obstruction in the case of the rat. Describing it as believing that the substance is poisonous adds nothing to the claim that it has suffered from it in the past and is now disposed to avoid it. If the rat were, e.g. to shift some of the substance to the habitual feeding place of an aggressor, to prevent her children from taking it, and to introduce some of it into the tea cup of the experimenter, on the other hand, we might begin to feel an incentive for serious rationalistic theorizing.

The force of this train of thought becomes apparent as soon as we ask how a defender of the implicit knowledge conception can distinguish those putatively intentional states, whose content he specifies using the axioms of a theory of meaning which he wishes to attribute to speakers, from the sort of dispositions whose behavioural expression is so inflexibly related to them as to disqualify them from the role of components in serious rationalistic theorizing. One of the chess-playing children will standardly manifest his knowledge of the rule governing the powers of movement and capture of the Queen by conforming to it. But other manifestations are possible: he may attempt to correct an opponent who breaks the rule, refuse to play with someone who makes a habit of doing so, or even deliberately break the rule himself as a somewhat unconventional mode of resignation, or by way of a pretended incompetence in the hope of short-circuiting a game he would rather

not play. Likewise, someone who is credited with implicit knowledge of a meaning-delivering theorem may express his knowledge in an indefinite variety of ways, including, in appropriate contexts, lying, assent and silence. But the (implicit) knowledge of a meaning theoretic *axiom* would seem to be harnessed to the single project of forming beliefs about the content of sentences which contain the expression, or exemplify the mode of construction, which it concerns. Certainly, the precise beliefs which are formed will vary as a function of the content of the other relevant axioms of which a subject is also being supposed to have implicit knowledge. But what is supposed to be the role of *desire*? What is the (implicit?) desire which explains why the subject puts his semantic axiomatic beliefs to just this use, and what are the different uses to which they might be put if his desires were different?

The question draws a complete blank. The case is, in fact, worse than with the rat. We can begin to tell some sort of story – I did so above – of what sort of enrichment and complication of rodent behaviour might enable us to regard the belief that a substance was poisonous as manifested, via a particular kind of behaviour, along with something other than the desire to avoid discomfort. But what is the desire which, in conjunction with the knowledge represented by the meaning-theoretic axioms, is manifested in the formation of beliefs about the meanings of sentences? And what other manifestation might that knowledge have if this desire was different?[9] The truth is that the content of ascribing implicit knowledge of a meaning-theoretic axiom would appear to be no more than the ascription of a disposition to form beliefs about the meanings of sentences featuring the expression, or mode of construction, which it concerns: the disposition, precisely, to form beliefs which are appropriately constrained by the content of the axiom. Although Evans allows his discussion to proceed in terms of what he calls 'tacit knowledge', his own response to this train of thought is to abjure any form of intentionalistic construal of the relation between speakers and the axiomatic content of a theory of meaning. Rather, the axioms should indeed be seen precisely as describing certain dispositions which competent speakers have.[10]

The reader must form his own judgement about whether the point really is fatal to the prospects of any sort of intentionalistic construal of the relation between speakers and axioms. Let me, though, attempt to ensure that he does so in awareness of some limitations of Evans's own positive proposals. I shall pursue Evans's example of a simple language containing just ten singular terms, a,b,c . . ., and ten one-place predicates, F,G,H, . . ., together with the single sentence-forming operation of singular term-predicate concatenation. The language thus has 100 possible sentences, and allows of a finite but non-compositional truth-theoretic axiomatization consisting of 100 corresponding instances of the T-schema. Call this axiomatization T_1; and contrast it with the compositional axiomatization, T_2 which has 21 axioms: ten assigning denotations to the singular terms; ten stipulating satisfaction-conditions for the predicates; and a compositional axiom to the effect that a sentence coupling a name with a predicate is true if and only if the object denoted by the name satisfies the predicate. Evans's negative proposal is that T_2 should not be seen as describing the contents of any sort of intentional states of speakers of the object language. His positive proposal is that it should be seen as describing dispositions which they have; and, crucially, that even when so interpreted, it may be preferable to T_1.

The immediate question is: *what* dispositions, exactly, does T_2 describe? Evans's own account proceeds in terms of a notion of 'tacit knowledge' – (by way of deference, no doubt, to the free-wheeling use made of intentional terminology by so many psychologists and psycholinguists) – which, in contrast with what the considerations above might prompt us to regard as *genuinely* intentional states, does admit

of an apparently straightforward dispositional account. His suggestion is that a speaker U tacitly knows that, for instance, the denotation of a is John if and only if he has a disposition such that:

($\Pi\phi$) ($\Pi\psi$) [if U tacitly knows that an object satisfies ϕ if and only if it is ψ; and U hears an utterance having the form ϕa; then U will judge that: the utterance is true if and only if John is ψ].

Likewise a speaker U tacitly knows that, for instance, an object satisfies F if and only if it is bald, if and only if he has a disposition such that:

(Πx) (Πa) [if U tacitly knows that the denotation of a is x, and U hears an utterance having the form Fa, then U will judge that: the utterance is true if and only if x is bald].[11]

These proposals seem more or less inevitable. 'Tacit knowledge' ought to be a disposition which constitutes understanding; and what is it to understand a sub-sentential expression of Evans's simple language except to be disposed to make the right judgements about the truth-conditions of sentences containing it provided one understands the accompanying name or predicate? But there are a number of difficulties.

The first is, once again, that it is not clear how this interpretation of the relation between speakers and the axioms can provide a reason for preferring T_2 to T_1. The dispositions which T_2 assigns to speakers are dispositions of judgement concerning whole sentences; so why not simply describe them directly by using T_1? Evans's answer is that he intends the notion of disposition to which he is appealing to be understood in a 'full-blooded sense': the ascription of a disposition is to be interpreted as the ascription of an underlying state from which the relevant patterns of behaviour, described in the conditional which articulates what the disposition is a disposition to do, (causally) flow. Thus the difference between T_1 and T_2 is that the former ascribes 100 distinct such states to competent speakers of the object language whereas

> tacit knowledge of T_2 requires that there should be 20 such states of the subject – one corresponding to each expression of the language which the theory treats separately – such that the causal explanation of why the subject reacts in the way that he does to any sentence of the language involves two of these states, and any one of these states is involved in the explanation of the way he reacts to 10 sentences containing a common element.[12]

In Evans's view the claims of T_1 and T_2 to describe speakers' competence may thus, under favourable circumstances, be empirically adjudicated. A satisfactory neurophysiological account of competence would be decisive;[13] but even in advance of attaining that, strong evidence for the superiority of T_2 would be afforded by the empirical findings (a) that speakers acquire the capacity to understand so far unencountered specimens from among the 100 possible sentences on the basis of exposure to utterances which contain the relevant constituents; and (b) that when speakers *lose* competence with any of the sentences – owing to forgetfulness, or disease, or damage – they tend simultaneously to lose competence with all the sentences which feature one, or both of its constituents.

Now, although I think Evans's deference to neurophysiology is mistaken – since it is evidence of types (a) and (b) which would determine our conception of what kind of neurophysiological theory to settle for – and although it is not clear exactly what account of identity and distinctness among (neurophysiological) *states* should provide the backcloth to his suggestions, the kind of data which he envisages would obviously be highly significant. But the question, of course, is why such data would properly motivate the adoption of T_2, rather than T_1 supplemented with some appropriate hypotheses, of a non-semantical sort, about the

presumed causal substructure of the dispositions which T_1 describes. This is essentially the objection which featured in the discussion of the 'Mirror Constraint' earlier [Wright, C. *Realism, Meaning and Truth* (2nd Ed.), Oxford: Blackwell (1993), pp. 212–16], and Evans's discussion contains, so far as I can see, no answer to it. The requirement that a theory of meaning should both describe the dispositions which the competent display in their handling of whole sentences and reflect the underlying causal structure of those dispositions – as witnessed by the details of their acquisition and loss and, perhaps, by their neurophysiology – provides absolutely no basis for preferring a theory of meaning to a description, or list, of the meaning-delivering theorems, supplemented by claims like

> Some single neurophysiological state is involved in the causal explanation of a speaker's competence with any sentence which features the expression *a*.

Why adopt T_2, or any theory whose axioms have a *semantical* subject matter, if the task is to reflect the *causal* structure of the dispositions which correspond to the meaning-delivering theorems?

There is a connection between this point and a peculiarity in Evans's exposition which the alert reader will already have noticed. Why does Evans speak of tacit knowledge of T_2 as involving 20 states of the subject when the axioms of T_2 are 21? The answer is obvious enough. The account which Evans offers of the dispositions which constitute tacit knowledge of the denotations of singular terms and the satisfaction conditions of predicates have the effect that a speaker who possesses them is thereby disposed to attach the proper significance to name-predicate coupling – since he is thereby disposed to attach the proper significance to sentences formed by coupling names and predicates. But this leaves Evans's proposal open to a simple objection. T_2 would be crippled without the compositional axiom, but if the brief of its axioms were *merely* the description of the dispositions which, on Evans's account, constitute tacit knowledge of them, the compositional axiom ought to be redundant. However there is in view no plausible modification of Evans's proposals concerning the dispositions relevant to singular terms and predicates which would need to be supplemented by a separate dispositional account concerning the compositional axiom. So the conclusion has to be that Evans's proposals misdescribe the content of the axioms of T_2. The conclusion of the preceding argument is therefore reinforced. We can grant that Evans has provided reason why a theory which concerned itself with a description of the dispositions which constituted a speakers' competence might wish to construe some of these dispositions as concerned with subsentential expressions. But since any compositional theory of meaning for a typical natural language will incorporate something like T_2, and since T_2 will not sustain that interpretation of its brief, Evans has provided no reason why we should seek a compositional theory of meaning.

Evans's proposal is apt to seem dissatisfying in a further respect. His account of what tacit knowledge of the denotation of a singular term disposes a subject to do appeals to a prior understanding of what it is to have tacit knowledge of the satisfaction conditions of a predicate; and vice versa. The two sets of dispositions are thus, as Evans acknowledges, 'interdefined'. Why is that not a recipe for vicious circularity? No one can follow Evans's characterization of what it is for U tacitly to know that the denotation of *a* is John unless he already understands what it is for U to have tacit knowledge of the satisfaction conditions of predicates in the language in question. If he doesn't understand that, Evans's account will plainly be of no avail to him, since it demands a prior understanding of what it is for U tacitly to know – of some arbitrarily selected singular term, which might be *a* – that its denotation is so-and-so.

This circularity may seem harmless for two reasons. First, it reflects an undoubted feature of our intuitive conception of what it is to understand sub-sentential expressions: to understand a name is to have the capacity to understand utterances in which it figures, provided one understands the remaining constituents and the mode of construction; and to understand the remaining constituents and the mode of construction is to have the capacity to understand utterances in which they feature provided one understands the rest of the sentence, which, in the basic case, takes us back to proper names. Second, circularity of this sort need in any case be no objection if the task is not to provide an *introductory* explanation of the concepts in question but to offer some measure of characterization of them.

Both of these points are fair. But the worry is not that the 'interdefinability' of Evans's axiomatic dispositions reflects no feature of our intuitive conception of what it is to understand the constituents of a sentence, but that, naively perhaps, one wants something better in the characterization of a *disposition*. To characterize a disposition ought to be to characterize both what it is a disposition to do and the circumstances under which it will be manifest. Often we settle for very imperfectly precise characterizations of both. But the complaint here is not of imprecision. If, for instance, I characterize the ductility of a metal by reference to certain observable phenomena which occur under background circumstances *including* the possession by the substance of certain further dispositions; and if it then turns out that a characterization of the distinctive manifestations of some of these further dispositions is possible only by reference to background circumstances in which the substances are assumed to be ductile – if that is the best that can be done, the reproach does not seem foolish that I have so far simply *failed to say* what ductility is. Evans's proposals would seem to leave the dispositions which they aim to characterize in this uncomfortable-seeming position. However, I offer the point more as something which someone who wished to advance Evans's account should say something about than as an objection. Perhaps a more sophisticated account of the notion of a disposition would remove the worry; my own suggestion would be that Evans's proposal should have proceeded by reference to states of a different sort – his real interest, after all, is in the underlying 'categorical' bases. But I anticipate.

One final point about Evans's treatment is worth emphasis. He writes

> . . . it is implicit in what has gone before that the notion of tacit knowledge of a [compositional] theory of meaning, explained as I have explained it, cannot be used to explain the capacity to understand new sentences.[14]

This is because the dispositions which, on Evans's account, constitute tacit knowledge of the axioms of T_2, e.g., precisely *are* the dispositions to judge correctly the truth-conditions of novel sentences in the language in question. Evans's claim on behalf of a compositional theory of meaning is that it is likely to give the empirically best attested description of what these dispositions are. I think he is right that, even there is no force whatever in the foregoing objections, this is the most that, on his account of the matter, could be claimed. Accordingly, an *explanation* of speakers' 'creativity' would have to consist, for Evans, in an account of how it is that speakers are prone to acquire just these dispositions on the basis of the incomplete and imperfect sampling in which a typical training in the use of a natural language consists.

This still leaves a theorist of meaning with a contribution to make to the explanatory project. Before an account can be given of the aetiology of the relevant dispositions, we need to know what they are. The ability of a learner to understand a novel utterance can, presumably, be made to seem non-miraculous only if the sample of uses which induced in him the dispositions which he thereby exercises themselves involved

exercise of corresponding dispositions on the part of those whose speech he witnessed.

> Consequently, when a capacity to understand novel sentences is observed, the theorist of meaning has an indispensable role to play in its explanation, since he must exhibit the regularity between the old and the new.[15]

What is striking about this suggestion is the width of the gulf which it opens between what, on Evans's account, the theorist of meaning should be about and what in practice those philosophers who have taken an interest – none more than Evans – in the project of a theory of meaning have been content to do. One clear implication of Evans's account, for instance, is that the construction of a useful theory of meaning does demand elevation from the arm-chair. Data are needed about trainees' learning patterns – about just what 'projections' they tend to be able to make on the basis of exposure to just what sorts of sample – and about patterns of loss, before we can so much as form a best guess at the syntactic categories in terms of which Evans's basic dispositions should be described. This is not what has happened. The relevant syntactic categories have been persistently supposed to be, more or less, those which Frege invented; 'regimentation' of the surface grammar of natural language is acknowledged to be inevitable in the construction of a theory of the sought-for kind. I submit that if Evans's account of the project is the right one, this a priori indifference to the *overt form* of many of the utterances which the novice speaker is able 'creatively' to understand is rather strange methodology. Not that the surface/depth grammar distinction may not be amenable to excellent empirical motivation. My point is that philosophical theorists of meaning seem to have assumed its propriety without reliance on the kind of data which, if Evans's account of their project were correct, it ought to depend on.

I do not mean to suggest that those

philosophers who have set about the Davidsonian project with respect to (fragments of) English have relied on no data which could properly be viewed as empirical. They have relied, of course, on a rich set of intuitions about particular meanings, and the significance of particular constructions, which competent speakers of English tend to share. The point is rather that they have, by and large, relied on no data concerning language acquisition and loss. Admittedly, this may be taken as showing not that Evans's account of how we should conceive the relation between actual speakers and the target theory is altogether misconceived but only that the right account has not greatly impinged upon the consciousness of workers in the field. So it is worth noting, to conclude this section, that there is a proposal, similar in spirit to Evans's but different in detail, which harmonizes rather better with the relatively a prioristic approach that theorists have followed.

As is familiar, certain species of bird display what appears to be a remarkable ability to find their way home from distant and unfamiliar locations. The ability appears remarkable because unless we were allowed to rely on special equipment and knowledge – compasses, charts, the disposition of the stars and so on – we could not emulate it. How do they do it? There are, of course, a number of differences between this problem and that of linguistic creativity. For one thing, there is no analogue of compositionality; no platitudinous answer, like 'By understanding the words and the way in which they are put together', is in the offing to constrain a satisfactory answer. For another, part of what has to be resolved is the range of sensory cues to which the birds should be thought of as responding – whereas it is taken to be a *datum* that speakers respond to the overt visible or audible structure of a sentence. But what is importantly parallel is that we do not know how to approach the question about, in particular, pigeons unless we are allowed to construct a theory which, like a theory of meaning, serves to articulate possible

modes of information processing. We would seek, that is to say, a theory which, if conjoined with supplementary information about features of its novel location which would, according to our best account of a pigeon's sensory apparatus, be discernible by the bird, would serve to issue in theorems whose content would be an instruction about what (sensed object) to fly towards. Of course, the suggestion that actual birds might *know* the content of such a theory would be vulnerable to the principal objection raised above. But it is in any case a suggestion to which we are not tempted; we do not, in setting about devising such a theory, regard ourselves as committed to viewing pigeons as intentional agents. On the contrary: the idea is to make them intelligible as a sophisticated sort of *mechanism*.

In a way, it is incidental that there are any such creatures. Even if there were not, the question could be posed whether a device could be designed which would 'home' in the way that pigeons actually do. A positive answer to the question would require a demonstration how a mechanism sensitive to certain features of its environment could process the data thereby accumulated so as to be disposed to relocate itself in the appropriate way. At the first stage, this is *entirely* an information-processing problem: it calls, in effect, for the devising of an appropriate computer program. At the second state, the problem would be that of explaining how this program, plus the relevant capacities of sensitivity and movement, might be incorporated into a physically possible device. The sort of understanding of the actual capacities of pigeons which is called for would be achieved exactly when enough was known about them to enable us to understand how in detail they embody such a device. And, of course, there can be no such understanding before we have formed the appropriate theoretical conception of the powers which the device must have. Doing that requires writing the computer program.

Three points are notable. First, devising such a program is not an *empirical* problem. What is sought is an axiomatic theory which, fed with (successive) appropriately formulated descriptions of environments distinct from 'home', will generate (successive) theorems encoding a successful homing strategy. This is a kind of problem which, when sufficiently precisely formulated, can be cracked in the armchair. The corresponding armchair problem for the theorist of meaning is to devise a theory which will take us from a description of relevant features of an arbitrary utterance to a theorem which characterizes its meaning. Second, the theorist will not best serve the next stage of the explanatory project – that of making good the claim that actual human beings embody, as it were, the relevant program – if he produces a theory with an infinitary axiom base. We do not understand what it would be to build a computer which incorporated infinitely many logically independent items of information in its program but no finite axiomatization of them. Simply to postulate that biological evolution can do what we cannot would be to reformulate rather than solve the original problem. And it is in any case unclear what could constitute neurophysiological reason for thinking that a pigeon, or human being, was the living embodiment of such a theory. A finiteness constraint at least thus appears to flow naturally from consideration of the overall character of the explanation which we are seeking. Finally, the connection between the axioms of the theory and speakers' (or pigeons') dispositions is less direct than on Evans's account. A completed explanation along the lines envisaged will of course involve the identification of (presumably neurophysiological) states which embody the various items of information corresponding to the axioms of the program. But these states need not be individuated, so far as I can see, as (categorical bases for) distinct dispositions; nor, in general, does there appear to be any a priori reason why the correspondence between the axioms and their neurophysiological realizations should be one-to-one.

I claim for this approach only that it may indicate the shape of a better account of the relevance of a theory of meaning to explaining the capacities of actual speakers than can be provided by play with the notion of 'implicit' intentional states, or by Evans's dispositionalist account. No doubt it will encounter problems of its own. It is obvious, above all, that clarification is needed of what it is for a system to 'embody' information – clarification which only a philosopher who is unusually well-informed in computational, psychological and neurophysiological science is likely to be able to achieve – and that there has to be, at least initially, a legitimate doubt in any case about the extension of this sort of notion to natural systems. I have wanted to indicate only that the horizon is not empty of all prospect of satisfactorily yoking together the philosophical project of a theory of meaning and the explanation of actual speakers' linguistic 'creativity'.

Notes

1 'What is a Theory of Meaning?', pp. 109–10.

2 The *locus classicus* is David Lewis's *Convention: a Philosophical Study*.

3 I intend no judgement, by this remark, about whether the very strong epistemic conditions involved in Lewis's original account would permit meaning-theoretic axioms of which subjects were unaware to encode conventions. But the crucial question is in any case that about intention to which the text now moves.

4 One cause for complaint about Baker's and Hacker's *Language, Sense and Nonsense*, is their predilection for such opposition. There are other causes. See my review, 'Understanding Novel Utterances'.

5 See 'Thought and Talk', Essay 11 of his *Inquiries into Truth and Interpretation*.

6 Any apparent counter-example to this claim is going to be controversial and marginal at best. One possibility: if humans, who share a magic mushroom, e.g., can co-hallucinate – 'Look at that little green man sitting by the window' – there might be circumstances in which a dog would best be described as e.g. barking at such a 'common

object' of hallucination. But I can envisage no other circumstances in which we would have cause to use an empty singular term – rather than a quantifier – in ascribing an intentional state to an animal.

7 Indeed, why ascribe to a dog so much as a *sortal concept* of man, a conception of his master as a recurrent *particular*, rather than view it as operating a primitive feature-placing scheme of concepts? Note however that if the main claim of the text – that 'there is no constraint of fidelity to [the subject's] mode of conceiving' in such cases – is correct, it does not follow that co-extensive expressions will be unrestrictedly intersubstitutive in the relevant class of contexts. Whether that is so will depend on what *other* (audience- and reporter-related) constraints are in operation. Any purported counter-example to the main claim will therefore have to be shown not to be the effect of other such constraints.

8 Gareth Evans, 'Semantic Theory and Tacit Knowledge' [Chapter 19 above]. See especially section III. Compare Davies. *Meaning, Quantification, Necessity,* pp. 83–6.

9 Matters stand quite differently, of course, once the knowledge becomes *explicit*: lying, assent, silence, sarcastic denial, etc. all provide differing modes of expressing it, *modulo* variable contexts and desires. This, I think, is the correct form of reply to John Campbell's point in 'Knowledge and Understanding' about the relative paucity of projects which knowledge, e.g. of the plot structure of *Bleak House,* might be 'at the service of'. In the relevant sense – that of explaining covarying behaviour as other beliefs and desires are varied – such knowledge is indeed at the service of many projects.

10 It is notable that Evans's argument is explicitly directed only against the supposition that speakers *believe* what the axioms state. Earlier we had cause to take seriously the suggestion that *intention* might be the best candidate, from the point of view of the implicit knowledge conception, for the psychological bond between speakers and the contents of the axioms. The proposal was, roughly, that speakers should be credited with whatever (implicit) intentions would suffice to confer the status of conventions on the axioms. Might this make a difference? For there does not seem to be

the same kind of holistic flexibility in what counts as manifesting a particular intention which obtains in the case of belief. If the belief that a substance is poisonous may be manifested in any number of ways, among which avoiding eating it is only one – though a usual – case, the intention to avoid eating it, for instance, is manifested by doing just that.

The suggestion is difficult to appraise in the absence of a detailed proposal. But there is some cause for pessimism. It is, to begin with, an error to suppose that there is a simple analytic connection between the content of an intention and the behaviour which manifests it. There is such a connection, but it is with whatever behaviour *implements* the intention; whereas the intention may be manifested by unsuccessful efforts to implement it, and indeed by any behaviour which the subject believes may (help to) carry it through. Intention, properly so regarded, will accordingly sustain a similar variety of possible modes of expression to that which characterizes belief. Evans's challenge ought therefore still to be good: how is the attribution of implicit intentions to be distinguished from, and justified in preference to, the attribution of dispositions to speak, and interpret the speech of others, in accordance with the meaning-theoretic axioms? Intention is distinguished from a mere disposition by the possibility of misguided attempts at fulfilment and by the subject's adaptability: his capacity to envisage a variety of ways in which it might be fulfilled and to modify his path accordingly. How can these ideas be made to grip in the present case?

In any case, intention cannot be the *whole* story. To be party to a convention is to have both intentions of a certain sort *and* beliefs – beliefs about just what regularities upholding the convention will require to be sustained. In David Lewis's study, for instance, it is necessary, if a regularity is to be conventional, that each of the participants expects the others to sustain it and that everyone prefers to sustain it if the others do (since a solution to a 'co-ordination problem' is thereby achieved.) So the challenge is immediate: how is the putative *belief* that everyone else will conform to the axioms of a theory of meaning to be distinguished from the *disposition* to form beliefs, as one successfully encounters novel utterances, that their behaviour will, *ceteris paribus*, conform to the requirements of the meaning-delivering theorems for those utterances?

11   'Π' is here a universal substitutional quantifier; and the variables ϕ, a, ψ, and x, have, respectively, the substitution classes of names of predicate expressions of the object-language, names of names of the object-language, predicate expressions of the metalanguage (English) and proper names of the metalanguage (English). Cf. Evans, 'Semantic Theory and Tacit Knowledge', pp. 124–5 [p. 296 above].

12   'Semantic Theory and Tacit Knowledge', p. 125 [p. 296].

13   Ibid., p. 127.

14   Ibid., pp. 135–6 [p. 302].

15   Ibid., pp. 135–6 [p. 302].

References

Baker, G. P. and Hacker, P. M. S. *Language, Sense and Nonsense*, Oxford, Blackwell, 1984.

Campbell, J. 'Knowledge and Understanding', *Philosophical Quarterly*, 32 (1982), pp. 17–34.

Davidson, Donald, 'Thought and Talk' in S. Guttenplan (ed.), *Mind and Language*, pp. 7–23; reprinted in D. Davidson, *Inquiries into Truth and Interpretation*, pp. 155–70.

—— *Inquiries into Truth and Interpretation*, Oxford, Oxford University Press, 1984.

Davies, Martin. *Meaning, Quantification, Necessity*, London, Routledge and Kegan Paul, 1981.

Dummett Michael, 'What is a Theory of Meaning?' in S. Guttenplan (ed.), *Mind and Language*, pp. 97–138; reprinted in his *The Seas of Language*, OUP, 1993.

Evans, Gareth 'Reply: Semantic Theory and Tacit Knowledge' in S. H. Holtzman and C. M. Leich (eds), *Wittgenstein: to Follow a Rule*, pp. 118–37; reprinted in G. Evans, *Collected Papers*, pp. 322–42 [Chapter 19 above].

Guttenplan, S. (ed.), *Mind and Language*, Oxford, Oxford University Press, 1974.

Holtzman, S. H. and Leich, C. M. (eds), *Wittgenstein: to Follow a Rule*, London, Routledge and Kegan Paul, 1981.

Lewis, David. *Convention: A Philosophical Study*, Cambridge, Massachusetts, Harvard University Press, 1969.

Wright, Crispin 'Understanding Novel Utterances', *Times Literary Supplement*, 11 January, 1985.

PART NINE

Meaning, holism and conceptual role

INTRODUCTION TO PART NINE

SEVERAL TIMES ALREADY (most explicitly in Part One) we have encountered a fundamental *metaphysical* question about language: what *determines* a linguistic expression's meaning? Or as Fodor and Lepore put it in the first reading below, '*where do semantic properties come from?*' At the beginning of the paper they describe a pointed contrast between two kinds of view, both of which agree that semantic properties are determined by – *supervene on* – properties of some other sort: i.e. that semantic properties are not basic, irreducible 'properties that things *just* have'. According to the first kind of view, which they label 'Old Testament' semantics, the meaning of an expression is determined by its '*relation to things in the world*'. Contemporary versions include those more commonly known as 'information-theoretic' accounts, which characterize meanings in terms of causal, counterfactual or nomic relations between speakers and the objects, properties etc. which their expressions pick out. On the other hand, 'New Testament' theories hold that the meaning of an expression is determined by its '*role in a language*'. As they suggest, a standard way to explicate the idea of an expression's role in a language is in terms of *inferences* that speakers make to and from sentences containing the expression. Thus, a basic version of the idea might suggest that the meaning a speaker attaches to the word 'dog' is determined by such facts as that she accepts the inference from 'This is a dog' to 'This is an animal', and from 'This is a robot' to 'This is not a dog'; rather than by causal, counterfactual or nomic relations between the speaker and dogs.[1]

We shall use the label '*inferential role semantics*' (IRS) for theories that maintain that the meanings of expressions are determined by inferential roles. Such theories are versions of '*conceptual role semantics*' (CRS), and although the issues we'll discuss seem relevant to all versions of the latter, it's worth pointing out that the category is generally agreed to include a wider range of theories than are explicitly introduced here by Fodor and Lepore. In general, conceptual role theories hold that the meaning of an expression for a speaker is determined by its role in her *thinking*. And while most versions emphasize inferential relations between sentences – relations which are discharged, as it were, *within* individual speakers and within the languages at issue – other versions broaden the range of meaning-determinants to include relations between sentences and extra-linguistic items: on the one hand, *perceptual experiences*, or indeed, the *objects* of such experiences, and on the other, *actions*. This means that advocates of CRS can allow that the relations upon which meanings

---

[1] Fodor, Lepore and others sometimes write of patterns of 'inference' from one predicate to another predicate, e.g., 'dog → animal'. We are not sure whether this is intended simply as a convenient shorthand for inferences from one sentence to another, of the kind envisaged above. In the interests of clarity and brevity, in this introduction we shall consider only inferences involving sentences.

supervene include relations between speakers and objects such as dogs, and so there is reason to question the accuracy of Fodor and Lepore's characterization of the background topography. Moreover, they seem to use the terms 'inferential role' and 'conceptual role' interchangeably, and they seem not to consider theories of the less austere kind that we have labelled 'CRS'. Fortunately, nothing in what follows depends on the possibility of conceptual roles involving extra-linguistic items, so after making a couple of further preliminary remarks, we shall ignore this complication, and for argument's sake, think of the debate simply as one between advocates of IRS and their 'Old Testament' critics.[2]

We have characterized IRS/CRS as concerned with the meanings of linguistic expressions, but it is worth noting that the theories are often propounded as accounts of the contents of *propositional attitudes*. In some influential versions (e.g. Block 1986) the theory is advanced as part of a defence of naturalism or physicalism in the metaphysics of mind. Here it is assumed that the conceptual roles of mental states can be characterized in terms of causal functions. If so, then IRS/CRS helps to explain the representational characteristics of propositional attitudes, in causal, functional terms. A complication is that many advocates of this naturalizing project hold that typical cognitive processes such as inferences do not occur 'in' natural languages such as English – but occur instead in a 'language of thought': i.e. a system of symbols realized in the thinker's brain, whose semantic properties are determined by their syntactic and causal properties. (The idea came up briefly in Part One above.) Proponents of this conception who also endorse IRS/CRS sometimes speak of the meanings of 'expressions' being determined by their inferential/conceptual roles, but by 'expressions' they usually mean symbols in a language of thought. Theorists of this ilk may even deny that the meanings of natural language expressions are determined by their inferential/conceptual roles, preferring to hold that only the meanings of symbols in the language of thought are determined in this way, while those of natural language expressions are determined by their relations to symbols in the language of thought.

A final preliminary point emerges here. Not all advocates of IRS/CRS have such reductive naturalizing aspirations. (See e.g. Peacocke 1992, and Brandom 1994, 2000.) One reason for reticence on this score is that it is far from obvious that inferential/conceptual roles are just *causal* roles. Inferences and other conceptual roles are commonly taken to be *normative* relations, and so there are versions of IRS/CRS which characterize meanings not in terms of the inferences etc. that speakers are disposed to make, but rather in terms of those they *ought* to make. (For discussion of the idea that meanings are normative, see Part Twelve below.) Another reason to doubt whether inferential/conceptual roles can be straightforwardly explicated in causal terms is the thought that conceptual/inferential roles are relations not between sentences or other symbols, but between *propositions* or the *contents* of propositional attitudes.

---

[2] For a useful recent sympathetic survey of CRS which emphasizes the catholicity of the doctrine, see Greenberg and Harman 2006.

Fodor and Lepore characterize IRS as 'intractably holistic', and undertake to undermine the theory by demonstrating its incompatibility with the widely accepted thesis that meanings are *compositional*. As we have seen in other parts of this book, this is the thesis that the meaning of a complex expression such as a sentence is determined by the meanings of its constituent expressions and their mode of composition. Notice that like the theses introduced above, this is a contribution to the *metaphysics* of meaning: a claim about how meanings (of sentences) are *determined*. To explain why IRS might seem to conflict with compositionality, we need to clarify Fodor and Lepore's observation that it is *holistic*. The basic idea here is that there are significant relations between the various inferences that speakers are disposed to make. E.g. if a speaker is disposed to infer from 'This is a dog' to 'This is an animal', and from 'This is an animal' to, 'This is an organism', then she will be disposed also to infer from 'This is a dog' to 'This is an organism'. If patterns of inference are connected or interdependent in this way, and if meanings are determined by inference-patterns, then as Peter Pagin puts it in the second reading below, 'the meanings of expressions in a language L are determined *together*, by a *totality* of relations between expressions of L'.

This is enough to give rise to an intuitive concern about holistic IRS. Different speakers endorse different inferences, and so IRS seems to imply that that they associate different meanings with the expressions involved. If these contentious expressions are relatively few, this might not seem such an unpalatable result – until we consider holism. Holistic IRS seems to entail that if two people differ in respect of inferences which are meaning-determining for one expression, then they associate different meanings not only with that expression, but also with others – perhaps all others – which they share. The unpalatable upshot is that no speaker is ever likely to mean the same by an expression as any other – or indeed the same as he himself means at a different time.

Fodor and Lepore note this problem in passing, but their principal objection to holistic IRS concerns compositionality. The problem is that the inferences that speakers are disposed to endorse featuring complex expressions do not seem to be determined by the inferences they are disposed to make featuring the complex expressions' constituents; and this seems to conflict with the presumption that the meanings of the complexes are determined by those of the constituents. Thus e.g. someone who believes that brown cows are dangerous may be disposed to infer from 'This is a brown cow' to 'This is dangerous'; but it would be implausible to insist that this disposition is determined by the speaker's inferential dispositions in respect of the terms, 'brown' and 'cow'. A speaker's belief that brown cows are dangerous would typically be based on empirical information about brown cows, rather than on the inferential roles of the simpler expressions it contains.

In light of this, an advocate of IRS might be tempted to suggest that the meaning of an expression for a speaker is determined not by all of the inferences featuring it she is disposed to make, but by a certain sub-set of those inferences. But which ones? Fodor and Lepore consider a version of IRS according to which the meaning-determining inferences are the *analytic* ones. Thus e.g., it might be suggested, the inference from 'This is a dog' to 'This is an animal' bears on the meanings of the terms involved, but the inference from 'This is a brown cow' to 'This is dangerous' does not, because the sentence 'If this is a dog, then this is an animal' is analytically true, while the sentence, 'If this is a brown cow, then this is dangerous' is not. Fodor and Lepore object to the invocation of analyticity here on several grounds, one of them being that the proposal now seems circular. IRS is supposed to provide an explication of the meanings of linguistic expressions, but analytic inferential roles are just those that are warranted by the meanings of the expressions involved.

Pagin's aim in the second reading below is not to defend IRS *per se*, but to demonstrate the compatibility of holism with the thesis that meanings are compositional. He considers three arguments against the claim that the theses are compatible, and responds to each in turn. The first argument exploits an apparent conflict between the claims about *order of determination* made by the theses. The compositionality thesis says that the meanings of complex expressions are determined by those of their constituents, whereas holism seems to suggest that all meanings are determined together. In response to this worry, Pagin suggests that we construe holism as the thesis that the meanings of all *simple* expressions are interdependently co-determined. The meanings of simple expressions may then be presumed to determine those of complex expressions, as compositionality requires.

The second argument Pagin considers for the claim that holism and compositionality conflict with one another is the one we attributed to Fodor and Lepore above. As we saw, Fodor and Lepore characterize this as an argument against holistic IRS, but as Pagin suggests, it seems that an analogous argument can be made against any holistic theory of meaning. According to Pagin, the questionable assumption upon which Fodor and Lepore's argument depends is that the function from meaning-determining inferential roles to meanings is *one-one*: i.e. every distinct inferential role determines a distinct meaning. If the relation is one-one, then corresponding to the relations between meanings such as those which the compositionality thesis leads us to expect, there will be analogous relations between the inferential roles assumed to determine those meanings. And as Fodor and Lepore demonstrate with their example of the eccentric speaker who infers from 'This is a brown cow' to 'This is dangerous', the inferences that speakers accept do not always fit these patterns. On the other hand, according to Pagin, a version of IRS which allows the relation between roles and meanings to be *many-one* – i.e. allows that different inferential roles can determine the same meanings – does not have these unpalatable consequences. For in this case, while we can derive the meaning of an expression from a specification of its inferential role (and those of other expressions in the language) we cannot derive anything about a speaker's inferential roles from a specification of her meanings. Hence in particular, we cannot, from considerations about the compositional relations between meanings, derive consequences about the relations between meaning-determining inferential roles, such as those that seem to conflict with the inferential behaviour of the eccentric speaker.

As Pagin in effect observes, the many-one version of holistic IRS also evades the 'intuitive concern' we noted above, because it allows that speakers with suitably different inferential roles may nonetheless associate the same meanings with expressions as one another.

The third argument Pagin considers against the compatibility of holism and compositionality is the charge that holism conflicts with the widely held assumption that compositionality can help to explain how speakers come to know the meanings of sentences they have not previously encountered. (See Part Eight above for discussion of this assumption.) The problem, very roughly, is that compositionality can help to provide a satisfactory explanation of speakers' understanding of novel sentences only if the sub-sentential expressions at issue mean the same before and after the novel sentence is considered. But consideration of a new sentence can engender a *change* to the patterns of inferences a speaker accepts, and so, on some versions of holism at least (including some which consider the function from inferential roles to be *many-one* as Pagin recommends) they can effect just such a change in meaning. Pagin's response, again very roughly, is that while consideration of new sentences could effect such changes, this does not seem often to occur – i.e. it looks as though the version of holism which characterizes our language is not a version which delineates the kinds of reactions speakers typically have to new sentences as the kinds of reactions which would engender meaning changes. And according to Pagin, this response is not *ad hoc*, for compositionality helps to explain why this is so: 'I will decide to accept or reject a sentence on the basis of my understanding of it and of my already settled beliefs, and my understanding of it can usually be predicted according to compositional principles'.

Questions and tasks

1   Do you agree with Fodor and Lepore that 'the fact that a word . . . means what it does can't be a brute fact'?

2   Fodor and Lepore characterize their argument as involving a dilemma: either a speaker's meanings are determined by *all* inferences she is disposed to make in which it figures (in which case, they claim, there is a conflict with compositionality) or they are determined by the analytic inferences amongst these (in which case the account is circular, etc.). Do these two 'horns' exhaust the reasonable possibilities available to the advocate of IRS?

3   Explain the first response Pagin considers we might make to the first argument he considers against the compatibility of holism and compositionality. Why does he reject the response?

4   What does Pagin mean by 'Global Role'? Explain how he exploits this notion to demonstrate that if the function from inferential roles to meanings is *many-one*, then holistic IRS does not have the unpalatable consequences attributed to it by Fodor and Lepore.

5   How do you think Fodor and Lepore should respond to Pagin's argument?

6   Explain Pagin's distinction between 'holism as a principle of meaning determination, and holism as a principle of meaning individuation'. What is the significance of the distinction?

References and further reading

Block, N. 1986: 'Advertisement for a Semantics for Psychology', in P. French, T. Uehling, and H. Wettstein (eds), *Midwest Studies in Philosophy* 10, pp. 615–78.

Block, N. 1998: 'Semantics, Conceptual Role', in E. Craig (ed.), *The Routledge Encyclopedia of Philosophy*, London: Routledge, vol. 8, pp. 652–7. http://www.rep.routledge.com/article/W037 (accessed 27 May 2009).

Boghossian, P. 1993 'Does an Inferential Role Semantics Rest Upon a Mistake?', *Mind & Language* 8, pp. 27–40.

Boghossian, P. 1994: 'Inferential Role Semantics and the Analytic/Synthetic Distinction', *Philosophical Studies* 73, pp. 109–22.

Boghossian, P. 2003: 'Blind Reasoning', *Proceedings of the Aristotelian Society Supplementary Volume* 77, pp. 225–48.

Brandom, R. 1994: *Making It Explicit*, Cambridge, MA: Harvard University Press.

Brandom, R. 2000: *Articulating Reasons: An Introduction to Inferentialism*, Cambridge, MA: Harvard University Press.

Dummett, M. 1991: *The Logical Basis of Metaphysics*, Cambridge, MA: Harvard University Press, Ch. 10.

Field, H. 1977: 'Logic, Meaning and Conceptual Role', *Journal of Philosophy* 69, pp. 379–408.

Greenberg, M., and G. Harman 2006: 'Conceptual Role Semantics', in E. Lepore and B. Smith (eds), *The Oxford Handbook of Philosophy of Language*, Oxford: Oxford University Press.

Harman, G. 1987: '(Nonsolipsistic) Conceptual Role Semantics', in E. Lepore (ed.), *New Directions in Semantics*, London: Academic Press, pp. 55–81; reprinted in G. Harman, *Reasoning, Meaning, and Mind*, Oxford: Oxford University Press (1999).

Horwich, P. 1998: *Meaning*, Oxford: Oxford University Press.

Peacocke, C. 1992: *A Study of Concepts*, Cambridge, MA: MIT Press.

Peacocke, C. 1997: 'Holism', in B. Hale and C. Wright (eds), *A Companion to the Philosophy of Language*, Oxford: Blackwell, pp. 227–47.

Sellars, W. 1953: 'Inference and Meaning', *Mind* 62, pp. 313–38.

Williamson, T. 2003: 'Understanding and Inference', *Aristotelian Society Supplementary Volume* 77, pp. 249–93.

Chapter 21

Jerry A. Fodor and Ernest Lepore

WHY MEANING (PROBABLY) ISN'T CONCEPTUAL ROLE[1]

Introduction

It's an achievement of the last couple of decades that people who work in linguistic semantics and people who work in the philosophy of language have arrived at a friendly de facto agreement as to their respective job descriptions. The terms of this agreement are that the semanticists do the work and the philosophers do the worrying. The semanticists try to construct actual theories of meaning (or truth theories, or model theories, or whatever) for one or another kind of expression in one or another natural language; for example, they try to figure out how the temperature could be rising compatible with the substitutivity of identicals. The philosophers, by contrast, keep an eye on the large, foundational issues, such as: what's the relation between sense and denotation; what's the relation between thought and language; whether translation is determinate; and whether life is like a fountain. Every now and then the philosophers and the semanticists are supposed to get together and compare notes on their respective progress. Or lack thereof.

Accordingly, this paper is not about semantics but about the philosophy of language. Jerry and I have been poking around in the basement of meaning theory, and we seem to have discovered a large, nasty crack; as far as we can tell, one of the foundation stones is coming unstuck. We

thought we'd better tell you about it before things get worse.

We'll proceed as follows: First, we'll try to say where in the foundations the problem is located; then we'll try to say what the problem is; and then we'll make a suggestion or two about what to do about the problem. The first part of the discussion will be very broad; the second part will be rather more specific; the third part will be practically nonexistent.

Here goes.

1 Where the problem is

A traditional foundational problem in the theory of meaning is: *Where do semantic properties come from?* The presupposition of this question is that the fact that a word (or a sentence, or whatever) means what it does can't be a brute fact. It can't be a brute fact, for example, that 'dog' means *dog* and not *proton* and that 'proton' means *proton* and not *dog*. Rather, 'dog' must have some *non-*semantic property in virtue of which it means *dog* and not *proton*; and 'proton' must have some (different) non-semantic property in virtue of which it means *proton* and not *dog*. To put it in the standard philosophical jargon, semantic properties must *supervene* on non-semantic properties. There may be some properties that things *just* have; that they have for no reason at all. But if there are, they are the kinds of properties that basic physics talks about (like mass, charge, and charm). They certainly don't include the kinds of properties that semanticists talk about (like meaning *dog* or being a synonym of 'bachelor').

We remark in passing that none of this is to be construed as an attempt to legislate physicalism. For present purposes we are content that semantic properties should be, for example, irreducibly intentional, or irreducibly epistemological, or irreducibly teleological. But we take it to be not in the cards that they are irreducibly semantic. In short, we don't care whether semantic properties supervene on something that is *physical* just as long as they supervene on something other than themselves.

So the question arises: What *do* the semantic properties of symbols supervene on? Over the years, philosophers of language have been enthusiastic for two quite different (perhaps, indeed, incompatible) kinds of answers to this question. There's what we will call the 'Old Testament' story, according to which the meaning of an expression supervenes on *the expression's relation to things in the world*; and there's what we will call the 'New Testament' story, according to which the meaning of an expression supervenes on the expression's *role in a language*. The disagreement between these two sorts of story is venerable, and we don't propose to go into the details here. Just a paragraph or two by way of assembling reminders.

Old Testament semantics derives most directly from the British Empiricists and has, among its modern representatives, behaviorist psychologists like Watson and Skinner and a handful of philosophers in the 'naturalized semantics' movement (including Dretske, Stampe, Millikan, Papineau, Barwise and Perry in certain of their moods, and one or more of the Fodors). The basic idea is that 'dog' means *dog* because of some (non-semantic) relation that holds between the symbol and the animal. If you are a British Empiricist (or, at least, if you're Hume), you say that this relation comes down to some variant on resemblance; 'dog' means *dog*

rather than *proton* because 'dog' is associated with a certain mental image that means *dog* rather than *proton*. And the mental image means *dog* rather than *proton* because it resembles dogs quite a lot but resembles protons hardly at all. If you are a behaviorist psychologist, you say that the symbol-world relation that semantic properties supervene on is *causal* (typically associative); 'dog' means *dog* rather than *proton* because, in consequence of the speaker's history of conditioning (or something) dogs cause utterances of 'dog' and protons don't. Recent developments of Old Testament Semantics propose still other variations on this theme, including, for example, appeals to nomological and/or informational relations between symbols and the world.

Now, this Old Testament story about meaning has come under a lot of criticism, both in philosophy and in linguistics. Perhaps the basic objection is one that derives from Frege: Meaning *can't* be a symbol-world relation, according to this objection, because *identity* of symbol-world relations is compatible with *difference* of meaning. Thus, it's plausible that the expressions 'the Morning Star' and 'the Evening Star' are both attached to the same non-linguistic thing (viz. to Venus); but it's also plausible that they don't *mean* the same thing. If they did, you couldn't deny that the Morning Star is the Evening Star without self contradiction or assert that it is without tautology. Both of which, in fact, you can.

So, then, according to this argument, the meaning of an expression doesn't supervene on the way that it's attached to the world. So what does it supervene on?

The New Testament story is an elaboration of the following idea: the expressions 'the Morning Star' and 'the Evening Star' mean different things, despite their both being attached to Venus, because they have different *roles in the (English) language*. Frege says "only in the context of a sentence does a word have a meaning" and Wittgenstein adds that "to understand a sentence is to understand a language". The core idea is that it's the way they are connected *to one another* that determines what the expressions in a language mean. Very often (in fact, in all the semantic theories that we will discuss) this notion of 'role in the language' is given an epistemological twist: To master a linguistic expression is to recognize the validity of some core set of *inferences* that fix its semantic relation to other expressions in the language. To master the expression 'dog' is, inter alia, to recognize the validity of inferring 'Rover is an animal' from 'Rover is a dog'. To master the expression 'The Morning Star' is, inter alia, to recognize the validity of inferring from 'is the Morning Star' to 'rises in the Morning'. And so forth.

We want to emphasize that, at this stage, we're using notions like *infer* and *disposed to infer* as blank checks. For the moment we'll let any disposition to have one belief cause another count as a disposition to infer the second from the first. So deductive inferences, and inductive inferences, and plausible inferences, and prudential inferences, and mere associations, and Heaven knows what all else, are included pro tem. A lot of this discussion will be about the problems that arise when a New Testament Semanticist tries to say exactly which inferences are constitutive of the meanings of the terms that enter into them.

This New Testament picture is quite close to one that's familiar from Structuralist linguistics, according to which the meaning of an expression is its role in a 'system of differences'. To know what 'dog' means is to know that it excludes 'cat' and cohabits with 'animal'. To know what 'bachelor' means is to know that it excludes 'spinster' and cohabits with 'unmarried'. Notice that it follows from this view that if English didn't contain words that mean what 'cat' and 'animal' do, *it couldn't contain a word that means what 'dog' does*. This is a kind of conclusion that structuralists in semantics have, with varying degrees of enthusiasm, quite generally been prepared to embrace.

Although, as far as we can tell, one or other version of the New Testament view is held

practically as gospel not only in linguistics and philosophy, but throughout the Cognitive Sciences, it is nevertheless possessed of well known problems. For example, New Testament Semantics appears to be intractably holistic. This is because, once you start identifying the content of a belief with its inferential role in a system of beliefs (mutatis mutandis the meaning of an expression with its inferential role in a language), it's hard to avoid proceeding to identify the content of a belief with its *whole* inferential role in the systems of beliefs. And, having gone that far, it's hard to avoid the conclusion that if belief systems differ at all in respect of the propositions they endorse, then they differ entirely in respect of the propositions they can express.[2] This is a well-greased, and well travelled, slippery slope; having arrived at the bottom, one finds oneself accepting such prima facie outlandish doctrines as that there is no such relation as translation; that no two people ever mean the same thing by what they say; that no two time slices of *the same* person ever mean the same thing by what they say; that no one can ever change his mind; that no statements, or beliefs, can ever be contradicted (to say nothing of refuted); and so forth. It's a moot question how to get the goodness out of inferential role semantics without paying this extravagant price. Indeed, it's moot whether it is possible to do so.

Serious though these worries are, however, they are all, as it were, *external* to functional role semantics as such; they impugn its consequences for epistemology and ontology rather than its coherence. And a convinced New Testament Semanticist might be prepared to bite the bullet. If the doctrine that meaning supervenes on intra-linguistic relations has relativistic, idealistic or even solipsistic consequences, then perhaps we had better learn to live with relativism, idealism or even solipsism. There are many, especially on the West Coast, who clearly long to do so.

Well, so much for the background; now here's the problem. It looks as though there are serious *linguistic* problems for the conceptual role approach to meaning. We want to argue that, quite aside from ontology and epistemology, it looks like New Testament Semantics can't be squared with a pair of linguistic hypotheses that practically everybody thinks there are very good reasons to endorse; and which, de facto, most New Testament Semanticists actually *do* endorse. These are, first, that natural languages are compositional, and, second, that the a/s distinction is unprincipled. (This means not that the distinction is *vague*—what empirical distinction isn't?—but that there aren't any expressions that are true or false solely in virtue of what they mean.) The foundational problem to which we wish to call your attention is that these two principles (compositionality and the denial of the a/s distinction) together with New Testament Semantics form an inconsistent triad. At least one of the three will have to go.

The next section of this paper sketches our argument for this claim; the third asks what on earth to do about it.

2 Compositionality, analyticity and inferential role semantics

There is, we believe, an internal connection between analyticity and compositionality that hasn't previously been remarked upon and that has dire implications for the New Testament identification of meanings with inferential roles. First, a few remarks about compositionality.

A language is *compositional* iff (idioms aside) the meaning of its syntactically complex expressions is a function of their syntactic structures together with the meanings of their syntactic constituents. For present purposes, a language is compositional iff the meaning of its sentences is a function of their structural descriptions together with the meanings of their lexical constituents. We take the doctrine that natural languages are compositional to be, as one says in Britain, non-negotiable.

No doubt connectionist psychologists (and a handful of philosophers) have occasionally been moved to dispense with compositionality. But that just indicates the desperateness of their plight. For, compositionality is at the heart of some of the most striking properties that natural languages exhibit. The most obvious of these are *productivity* (roughly, the fact that every natural language can express an open ended set of propositions) and *systematicity* (roughly, the fact that any natural language that can express the proposition P will also be able to express many propositions that are semantically close to P. If, for example, a language can express the proposition that *aRb*, then it can express the proposition that *bRa*; if it can express the proposition that P → Q, then it can express the proposition that Q → P; and so forth.)

We digress to remark (since the issue often comes up) that pairs like 'John calculated the answer' and *'The answer calculated John' are not exceptions to the systematicity of English. Systematicity requires that if a language can express the proposition P and the proposition P is semantically close to the proposition Q, then the language can also express Q. If, however, there is *no* such proposition as Q, it is no objection to its systematicity that a language can't express it. We are inclined to assume that there is no such proposition as that the answer calculated John; hence, that the present examples do not constitute an objection to the systematicity of English. We do not, however, wish to dogmatize. If there is such a proposition as that the answer calculated John, then English *can* express it; indeed the form of words "the answer calculated John" does so. English is thus systematic on either assumption.

Connected to both productivity and systematicity is a further, apparently perfectly universal, feature of natural languages. The structure of sentences is, in the following sense, *isomorphic* to the structure of the propositions they express: *If a sentence S expresses the proposition that P, then syntactic constituents of S express the constituents of P.* If, for example, a sentence expresses the proposition that P and Q, then there will be one syntactic constituent of the sentence that expresses the proposition that P and another syntactic constituent that expresses the proposition that Q. If a sentence expresses the proposition that John loves Mary, then there will be a syntactic constituent of the sentence that refers to John, another syntactic constituent of the sentence that refers to Mary, and another syntactic constituent of the sentence that expresses a relation such that, necessarily, that relation holds between x and y iff x loves y. Notice that, though all of this is patent, none of it is truistic. Idioms and other 'holophrastic' constructions are all exceptions, albeit the sorts of exceptions that prove the rule.[3]

Our point is that these three generalizations about natural languages—productivity, systematicity and isomorphism—are connected and explained on the assumption of compositionality; they all depend upon the principle that the meaning of a sentence is composed from the meanings of its parts. And they appear to be completely baffling otherwise. So, we intend to insist on compositionality in what follows.

Now we get to the crack in the foundation. It turns out that compositionality is an *embarrassment* for the kind of New Testament Semantics that identifies the meaning of an expression with its inferential role. In particular, it invites the following kind of prima facie argument:

— Meanings are compositional.
— But inferential roles are *not* compositional.
— So, meanings can't be inferential roles.

The second step is, of course, the one that's doing the work. But it seems pretty obviously sound. Consider the meaning of the phrase 'brown cow'; it depends on the meanings of 'brown' and 'cow' together with its syntax, just as compositionality requires. To a first approximation, 'brown' means—if you like, it connotes the property—BROWN, 'cow' means COW, and the semantic interpretation of the syntactic structure (ADJECTIVE + NOUN)$_N$ is property conjunction. (We are aware that there are problems

about decoy ducks and the like; but the assumption that language is compositional is the assumption that such problems can be solved.) But now, prima facie, the inferential role of 'brown cow' depends not only on the inferential role of 'brown' and the inferential role of 'cow', *but also on what you happen to believe about brown cows.* So, unlike meaning, inferential role is, in the general case, not compositional.

Suppose, for example, you happen to think that brown cows are dangerous; then it's part of the inferential role of 'brown cow' in your dialect that it does (or can) figure in inferences like 'brown cow → dangerous'. But, first blush anyhow, this fact about the inferential role of 'brown cow' doesn't seem to derive from corresponding facts about the inferential roles of its constituents. You can see this by contrasting the present case with, for example, the validity of inferences like 'brown cow → brown animal' or 'brown cow → not-green cow'. 'Brown cow' entails 'brown animal' because 'cow' entails 'animal'; 'brown cow' entails 'not-green cow' because 'brown' entails 'not-green'. But it doesn't look like either 'brown' or 'cow' entails 'dangerous', so, to this extent, it doesn't look like the inference from 'brown cow' to 'dangerous' is compositional.

In short, it appears that some, but not all, of the inferential potential of 'brown cow' (some of its 'role in the language') is determined by the respective inferential potentials of 'brown' and 'cow', the rest being determined by one's "real world" beliefs about brown cows. This should not seem surprising or contentious; it's just a way of saying that 'brown cows are dangerous' (unlike 'brown cows are animals' and 'brown cows are not-green' and 'brown cows are brown') is clearly synthetic; i.e., 'brown cows are dangerous' is *contingently* true, true in virtue of the facts about brown cows, not in virtue of the facts about meanings (assuming that it's true at all).

But, to repeat, if meanings are compositional and inferential roles aren't, then it follows that meanings can't be inferential roles.

As far as we can tell, this line of argument is quite robust; in particular, it doesn't depend on detailed assumptions about how an inferential role semantics construes the notion of inferential role. There is, for example, an influential paper by Harry Field in which inferential role is analyzed in terms of subjective probabilities; in effect, the inferential role of your thought that P is identified with the subjective probability that you (would) assign to P contingent on each of the other thoughts that you (can) entertain (Field, 1977). So, for example, the inferential role of your thought that it's raining is determined in part by the subjective probability that you (would) assign to that thought on the assumption that the streets are wet; and in part by the subjective probability that you (would) assign to it on the assumption that the sun is out; and in part by the subjective probability that you (would) assign to it on the assumption that elephants have wings . . . and so forth. Like other species of New Testament Semantics, this treatment generalizes, in fairly obvious ways, from a theory according to which inferential roles are assigned to thoughts to one in which they are assigned to linguistic expressions, or to both.

Our point is that the construal of inferential roles in terms of subjective probabilities, whatever other virtues it may have, does nothing to help with the compositionality problem. This is because *subjective probabilities are not themselves compositional*. For example, the subjective probability one assigns to the thought that (*brown cows are dangerous*) is not a function of the subjective probability one assigns to the thought that (*cows are dangerous*), together with the subjective probability that one assigns to the thought that (*brown things are dangerous*). If this seems unobvious, consider a world (or rather a belief world, since the probabilities at issue are supposed to be subjective) where there are very many things that are cows, almost none of which is dangerous, and very many things that are brown, almost none of which is dangerous, and a very small number of brown cows, almost all of which are very, very

fierce. On these assumptions, the probability that something that is brown is dangerous is small, and the probability that something that is a cow is dangerous is small, but the probability that a brown cow is dangerous is as big as you please.

We intend the argument so far as one horn of a dilemma, and we anticipate the following reply: "OK, so if the compositionality of meaning is assumed, meanings can't be identified with inferential roles as such". But this doesn't *really* embarrass New Testament Semantics because meanings can still be identified with roles in *analytic* inferences. Thus, on the one hand, the inference 'brown cow → brown animal' is compositional (it's inherited from the inference 'cow → animal'); and, on the other hand, precisely because it is compositional, 'brown cow → brown animal' is analytic. Compositional inferences will always be analytic and analytic inferences will always be compositional; the compositionality of an inference and its the analyticity of an inference are the same thing.

Look at it this way: If 'brown cow → brown animal' is compositional, then it's warranted by the inferential roles of the expressions 'brown' and 'cow'. That's what it is for an inference to be compositional. But, according to New Testament Semantics, the inferential roles of 'brown' and 'cow' *are their meanings*. So, then, that 'brown cow → brown animal' is warranted follows from the *meanings* of 'brown' and 'cow': But for an inference to be analytic *just* is for it to be warranted by the meanings of its constituent expressions. So the compositionality of 'brown cow → brown animal'—or, mutatis mutandis of any other inference—*entails* its analyticity. The same argument also works the other way around: for an inference to be analytic is for it to be warranted by the meanings of its constituents. But, according to New Testament Semantics, meanings are inferential roles. So, for an inference to be analytic is for its warrant to be determined by the inferential roles of its constituents. But for the warrant of an inference to be determined by the inferential roles of its constituents is for the inference to be compositional. So compositionality entails analyticity and vice versa. So, then, meaning is compositional and inferential role isn't and role in analytic inference is. What all that shows is just that we need a revised version of New Testament Semantics; one which identifies meaning with role in analytic inference.

The first thing to say about this new suggestion is that the threat of circularity is now very close to the surface. It is proposed that we reconcile CRT with the compositionality of meaning by identifying the meaning of an expression with its role in analytic inferences. But the difference between analytic inferences and inferences *tout court* is just that the validity of the former is guaranteed *by the meanings* of their constituent expressions. So analyticity, meaning (and compositionality) scrape out a living by doing one another's wash, and Quine gets to say 'I told you so'.

Notice also that the naturalizability of inferential role semantics is jeopardized by the present proposal. A lot of the attraction of identifying meaning with inferential role lies in the thought that the inferential role of an expression might in turn be identified with *causal* role, thereby conceivably providing the basis for a naturalistic solution to Brentano's problem. That causal relations reconstruct inferential relations is a foundational assumption of computational theories of mental processes, so perhaps there is hope here of a unification of semantics with psychology. But, barring proposals for a causal theory of analyticity, this tactic in unavailable to the philosopher who identifies meaning with the role of an expression in *analytic* inference.[4] The idea that mental processes are computational may provide the basis for a naturalistic account of inference, but it offers no insight at all into the nature of analyticity. Nor, as far as we can see, does anything else.

We can now say pretty exactly what our problem is: You can't identify meanings with inferential roles *tout court*, since, unlike meanings, inferential roles *tout court* aren't compositional.

You *can* identify meanings with roles in *analytic* inferences, however, because analytic inferences *are* compositional. But, of course, the cost of identifying meanings with roles in analytic inferences is buying into the a/s distinction. So the cost of New Testament Semantics is buying into the a/s distinction. But, these days, practically everybody thinks that the a/s distinction is unprincipled. Indeed, it's widely thought that the discovery that the a/s distinction is unprincipled is one of the two most important achievements of modern philosophy of language; the other being precisely the theory that meaning supervenes on inferential role. If, then, we continue to assume that compositionality is non-negotiable, it follows that one of these foundational principles of the philosophy of language is going to have to go. Which one? And with what are we to replace it?

3 What now?

This is where we ought to tell you how to go about mending the cracked foundations; we would if we could. Since we can't, however, we'll restrict ourselves to a few more or less jaundiced remarks on what we take the visible options to be and on what we think that adopting one or other of them is likely to cost.

The first possibility one might consider is to try resuscitating the a/s distinction. There is a certain face plausibility to this suggestion. We've been seeing that compositionality and analyticity come to much the same thing so long as you accept the New Testament view that meaning supervenes on inferential role. But, in fact, it's plausible that compositionality entails analyticity *whether or not* you accept New Testament Semantics. So, for example, it's hard to see how anybody could claim that the meaning of 'brown cow' is *compositional* while denying that the inference from 'brown cow' to 'brown' is *analytically valid*. If it is undeniable the meaning of 'brown cow' is constructed from the meaning of 'brown' and 'cow', it seems equally undeniable, and for the same reasons, that the inference from 'brown cow' to 'brown' is guaranteed by the linguistic principles that effect this construction. But an inference that is guaranteed by linguistic principles *just is* an analytic inference. In short, the very structural relations among the constituents of a sentence that ground its compositionality would appear to engender the analyticity of some of the inferences in which its constituents are involved.

So, to repeat, it appears that compositionality underwrites certain analyticities all by itself, without further appeal to the principle that meaning supervenes on inferential roles. A New Testament Semanticist might thus reasonably argue that if compositionality is non-negotiable, so too is analyticity; hence that the rejection of Quine's anti-analyticity arguments is independently motivated.[5] But if the revival of the a/s distinction can be defended, it looks as though everything is all right. We've seen that you can't have New Testament Semantics and compositionality *and the rejection of the a/s*, but you certainly can have the first two if you drop the third.

We emphasize, however, that the kind of a/s distinction that compositionality underwrites holds only between expressions and their *syntactic constituents*. It thus serves to distinguish, say, 'brown cow → brown' from 'brown cow → dangerous'. But it does *not* underwrite a distinction between, say, 'brown cow → animal', and 'brown cow → dangerous'. That is, it doesn't underwrite an a/s distinction among inferences that turn on the lexical inventory of the premises as opposed to their linguistic structure. It is, however, precisely the lexically governed inferences that make trouble for New Testament Semantics.

If the meaning of 'brown cow' derives from the meanings of 'brown' and 'cow' (as it must if the meaning of 'brown cow' is compositional) and if the meaning of 'cow' is its inferential role (as it must be if New Testament Semantics is right), then it must somehow be arranged that 'brown cow' inherits the inference 'animal' *but not the inference 'dangerous'* from the meanings of its

constituents. But that requires that we must exclude from the semantic representation of 'cow' such information as, for example, 'cow → x kind of thing such that the brown ones are dangerous' (and analogously, we must exclude from the semantic representation of 'brown' such information as 'brown → x kind of thing such that the cow ones are dangerous').[6] But to say that we must treat these inferences as excluded from the semantic representations of 'cow' and 'brown' is just to say that they are both contingent; that they are *not* constitutive of the meanings of 'cow' and 'brown'. But to say that is to presuppose an a/s distinction that applies to lexically governed inferences. It is precisely an a/s distinction for lexically governed inferences that the familiar Quinean polemics are widely supposed to jeopardize.

We've been putting a lot of weight on the difference between analyticities that are engendered by the compositional structure of an expression and those that are generated by the meanings of items in its vocabulary. This distinction is, of course, undermined if you assume that there is a level of representation at which lexical items are semantically decomposed: to posit such a level is, in effect, to hold that lexical meaning is itself compositional. So, if there is lexical decomposition, then we can identify the meaning of an expression with its role in those inferences that are determined by its compositional structure *including the compositional structure of its lexical constituents*. The effect is to assimilate inferences like 'brown cow → animal' to inferences like 'brown cow → brown' since, at the level of semantic representation, both involve relations between expressions and their constituents. And both are distinguished from 'brown cow → dangerous' since, presumably 'dangerous' isn't a constituent of the representations of either 'brown cow' at *any* linguistic level.

But, of course, to resolve the present worries by taking lexical decomposition for granted simply begs the question against Quine. If lexical meanings were compositional, then lexical items would be definable; and it's part of Quine's story that there is no principled notion of definition. If Quine's arguments show anything, they show that there is no way to reconstruct the intuition that 'brown cow → animal' is definitional and 'brown cow → dangerous' isn't.

We conclude that, although there may be reasons for resuscitating the a/s distinction, the non-negotiability of compositionality isn't one of them. Compositionality licenses a distinction between 'brown cow → brown' and 'brown cow → cow' but not between 'brown cow → dangerous' and 'brown cow → animal'. So the original problem stands: If compositionality isn't negotiable, then either there is an a/s distinction for lexically governed inferences (contra Quine) or inferential roles aren't what meanings supervene on (contra New Testament Semantics).

Our second point is that the present situation is rife with ironies. We remarked above that once you say that the meaning of an expression supervenes on its inferential role, it's hard to stop short of saying that the meaning of an expression supervenes on its *whole* inferential role. That is, it's hard to stop short of relativizing the meaning of an expression to the whole language that contains it, with the consequences that expressions in different languages are semantically incommensurable. There is a sort of linguistic Idealist who delights in these holistic implications of New Testament Semantics; you see more than a trace of this sensibility among the 'cognitive linguistics' crowd, among connectionists, and, of course, among philosophers like Rorty, Putnam, Kuhn and Derrida. It now appears, however, that inferential role semantics *doesn't* have any holistic implications after all, so relativism loses however the argument turns out.

Here, roughly, is how the argument from inferential role semantics to semantic holism is supposed to go:

Premise 1. New Testament Semantics: The meaning of an expression is (at least partially) constituted by its inferential relations.

Premise 2. No A/S Distinction: There is no principled distinction between those of its inferential relations that constitute the meaning of an expression and those that don't.

Conclusion. Semantic Holism: The meaning of an expression is constituted by *all* of its inferential relations, hence by all of its role in a language.

There are, we think, lots of reasons to disapprove of this way of defending semantic holism; not least that it depends, apparently ineliminably, upon a form of slippery slope argument, and these are notorious for leading from true premises to false conclusions. (That is, it depends on arguing from 'There's no principled difference between the F's that are G and the F's that aren't' to 'Either none of the F's is G or all of them are'.) For present purposes, however, we're prepared to ignore all that. The point we want to emphasize is that the argument can't be better than its second premise; that is, the argument from inferential role semantics to semantic holism explicitly *depends on* denying the a/s distinction.

So, the situation is this: if the a/s distinction is principled, then the second premise is false and the argument is unsound. But if the a/s distinction is unprincipled, then the first premise is false. This is because, as we've been seeing, if compositionality is assumed, then meanings can be identified with inferential roles only insofar as the inferences that constitute a role are analytic; but the argument that there is no a/s distinction is the argument that there are no analytic inferences. We assume the law of excluded middle—either there is an a/s distinction or there isn't. Either way, then, the argument from inferential role semantics to semantic holism has to be unsound. We suppose that this demonstration should darken the skies of West Coast semantic holists. So be it; they need the rain.

The foundational problem, to recapitulate, is that you can't do all of the following: endorse inferential role semantics AND endorse compositionality AND abandon the a/s distinction. If compositionality is non-negotiable, that leaves you with only two options: endorse the a/s distinction or reject the idea that meaning supervenes on inferential role. We can't tell you which of these it would be best to do, but we do want to insist that wriggling isn't likely to get you off the hook. In particular, lots of cognitive scientists have hoped to reconcile themselves to the Quinean arguments by opting for a graded, or a contextualized, or otherwise denatured notion of analyticity. The idea is that, although Quine may have shown that the notion of *identity* of meaning is in trouble, it's still open that a notion of *similarity* of meaning might be evolved. It's supposed that grading the a/s distinction would allow us to have *both* compositionality *and* the supervenience of meaning on inferential role. New Testament Semantics would thus be vindicated, albeit in a sort of soft-edged version.

Nobody has shown that this can't be done; nor does anybody have the slightest idea of how to do it. It seems to us that the arguments against a principled notion of identity of meaning work just as well against a principled notion of similarity of meaning. But we won't try to make that case here.[7] Suffice it for present purposes to remark that the connections between analyticity and compositionality that we've been examining makes the search for a graded notion of analyticity look unpromising. Compositionality is, after all, a principle that governs relations *among meanings* (it governs the relation between the meaning of a complex expression and the meanings of its constituents). So, if your semantic theory reconstructs meaning in terms of analytic inference and if you have only a graded notion of analyticity, *then you will have to live with a graded notion of compositionality as well.* But what would a graded notion of compositionality be like? And, in particular, how would such a notion do what compositionality is required to do; viz. account for systematicity, isomorphism and productivity?

Wouldn't a graded notion of compositionality entail, at best, that a finite acquaintance with a language is adequate to *sort of understand* expressions not previously encountered? Or that if a language is capable of expressing the proposition that *aRb*, then it is sort of capable of expressing the proposition that *bRa*? Or that if the sentence S expresses the proposition P, then the constituents of S sort of express the constituents of P? But is there any sense to be made of such claims as, for example, that ('John loves Mary' sort of expresses the proposition that John loves Mary) only if 'John' sort of refers to John? These are muddy waters and we do not recommend that you wade in them.

It's worth mentioning that combining the denial of a/s with the espousal of CRT is perhaps the received position in cognitive science. The idea is that, on the one hand, concepts (meanings and the like) are prototypes; they're something like bundles of probable or typical traits. But, on the other hand, on one of the traits belonging to such a bundle is defining, so the a/s distinction fails. We take it that this option is closed when one notices the connection between compositionality and analytcity. If meaning is compositional, then either meaning isn't inferential role, or it is role in analytic inference. It's precisely because the bundles of inferences that constitute prototypes aren't analytic (and hence aren't compositional) that meanings belong to the brown prototype of the cow prototype. (Indeed, the prototypical brown cow can be dangerous even if the prototypical cow is a pussycat.) So, again; either the meanings of 'brown' and 'cow' are their roles in analytic inferences, or they aren't their roles in inferences at all. If, as we suspect, Quine is right about a/s, then only the second disjunct remains open.

Here's where we've gotten to: Compositionality is non-negotiable; inferential roles are compositional only if the a/s distinction is tenable for inferences that are governed by the lexical inventory. So, if Quine is right about the a/s distinction, the only remaining alternative is to give up on the New Testament idea that the meaning of lexical items is constituted by their inferential roles. Barring some proposal for an entirely new kind of semantics, this requires going back to the Old Testament view that what makes 'dog' mean *dog* is some sort of symbol-world connection; perhaps some sort of causal or informational or nomological connection between tokens of the expression and tokens of the animal. There are, as we remarked above, various accounts of this currently on offer and, who knows, maybe one of them can be made to work.

The spin-offs for epistemology would be of some interest since the plausible candidates for the semantically relevant symbol to world relations all look to be *atomistic*. If 'dog' means *dog* because dogs cause 'dog' tokenings, then it looks like your language could have a word that means what 'dog' means in English even if your language didn't have any other words that mean what English words do. Prima facie, in fact, it looks as though your language could have a word that means what 'dog' means in English even if it doesn't have any other words at *all*. All sorts of holistic arguments against the possibility of translation (and, more generally, against the 'commensurability' of languages and ideologies) would then appear to be likely to collapse. More darks skies on the West Coast.

We're not, to repeat the point one last time, actually urging you to follow any course. On the contrary, a lot of linguists will have good reason for not wanting to do so. For example, if Old Testament Semantics is essentially right, what becomes of such linguistic studies as 'lexical semantics'? You can't study the semantic relations among lexical items unless there are semantic relations among lexical items; and it's the burden of Old Testament Semantics that there aren't. Old Testament Semantics has it that semantic relations hold between lexical items *and the world* and *only* between lexical items and the world.[8] Old Testament Semantics has, therefore, no truck with semantic fields, lexical decompositions, conceptual networks and the like. If,

indeed, what you mean by 'the semantic level of linguistic description' is the level of description at which sentences that differ only in synonymous expressions are identically represented, the natural way to read the Old Testament is as denying that there is a semantic level of linguistic description. So generative semantics goes, and interpretive semantics *also* goes, and the highest level of linguistic description is, as it might be, syntax or logical form; viz. a level where the surface inventory of nonlogico-syntactic vocabulary is preserved. The God of the Old Testament is an austere God.

As previously remarked, our present purpose isn't to sell you any such chilly theology; just to point out that there seems to be this crack in the foundations of the structure in which semanticists and philosophers of language have recently been cohabiting. And to urge that somebody do something about it not later than sometime before the roof falls in.

Notes

1 The material in this paper is adapted from our forthcoming book *Holism: A Shopper's Guide*, Basil Blackwell, 1992.

2 The issues we'll be concerned with arise in precisely parallel ways for theories of the meanings of linguistic expressions and theories of contents of thoughts. In the rest of what follows, we will not bother to draw this distinction unless something turns on it.

3 Our statement of the isomorphism principles is intentionally left pretty vague; deep issues arise when more precision is attempted. Suppose, for example, that you hold that (in a null discourse) the sentence 'It's raining' expresses the proposition that it's raining here. Then either you must say that 'it's raining' has more constituents than appear on its surface or that the isomorphism principle can be violated by pragmatically carried information. For present purposes, we propose not to broach these sorts of issues.

4 There are causal theories of meaning around; see, for example, Skinner [1957], Dretske [1981], and

Fodor [1991], among many others. And, like any account of meaning, each of them imply a corresponding notion of analyticity. But all these theories are externalist and atomist and thus offer no comfort either to CRT or to holism. They don't legitimate a construal of meaning in terms of analytic inference because they reject CRT; they don't reconstruct meaning in terms of inference at all.

5   It's worth mentioning in this respect, that Quine says little or nothing about examples like 'brown cow → brown', where the analyticity of an inference depends on the *structure* of its premises rather than their lexical content.

6   Jim Higginbotham has pointed out to us that excluding *dangerous* from the semantic representations of 'brown' and 'cow' isn't sufficient to insure that 'brown cows are dangerous' comes out synthetic. This is because compositionality requires only that there be a function that determines the meaning of 'brown cow' given the syntax and lexical constituency of the expression. It doesn't, strictly speaking, also require that the semantic representation of 'brown cow' include the semantic representations of 'brown' and 'cow' (though many treatments of analyticity in the Kantian tradition have made this further assumption). This is alright with us; our point is that if 'brown cow' inherits *dangerous* from its compositional structure (in whatever way), then 'brown cows are dangerous' comes out analytic. Which is an unacceptable result.

7   See Chapters 1 and 7 of Fodor and Lepore (forthcoming).

8   More precisely, the Old Testament view holds that, if there are semantic relations among lexical items, they are derived not from relations between their roles in the language but from relations between their connections to the world; ceteris paribus, two expressions connected to the world in the same way will be synonyms. But it is, of course, precisely the inferential relations among lexical items, and not their symbol-world relations, that the semantic level of lexical description has always been supposed to represent.

References

Dretske, F., 1981: *Knowledge and the Flow of Information*, Cambridge, MA: MIT Press.

Field, H., 1977: 'Logic, Meaning and Conceptual Role', *Journal of Philosophy*: 74, pp. 379–409.

Fodor, J. 1991: *A Theory of Content and Other Essays*, Cambridge, MA: MIT Press.

Fodor J. and Lepore, E., 1992: *Holism: A Shopper's Guide*, Oxford: Blackwell.

Skinner, B.F., 1957, *Verbal Behaviour*, New York: Appleton Century Crofts Inc.

Chapter 22

Peter Pagin

IS COMPOSITIONALITY COMPATIBLE
WITH HOLISM?

Is the principle of semantic compositionality compatible with the principle of semantic holism? In this paper I consider three problems for compatibility. I argue that each has an acceptable solution. The first is a problem about the order and mode of determination of meaning of complex expressions. It is familiar, and so are the proposed solutions. The second is a problem about the individuation of meanings. This problem is also well known, thanks to the writings of Fodor and Lepore. The solution proposed here is not as well known, although in essence it has been suggested before. The third problem concerns the explanatory role of compositionality. To my knowledge, it has not been considered so far, but it is related to a problem raised by Michael Dummett, concerning learnability.

1 Preliminaries

On the face of it, the principle of semantic compositionality flatly contradicts the principle of semantic holism. The former implies that the meaning of a complex expression depends only on the meanings of its parts, while the latter implies that it also depends on the meanings of other expressions in the language. Is there a genuine inconsistency here, or just a tension or resolvable conflict, or perhaps not even that? In order to assess the situation you must of course be careful about what you mean by 'compositionality' and by 'holism'. Both these terms can

be defined in detail in many ways. In this paper I shall keep a fairly intuitive understanding of them, and add more precision only insofar as the discussion requires.

Before proceeding with these concepts I shall clear one point. When I talk about compatibility between compositionality and holism I mean compatibility as regards the same *meanings*, or the same *aspects* of meaning. Of course you can be a holist about, e.g. some version of *conceptual role* and a compositionalist about *truth conditions*, given that these are taken to be distinct aspects of meaning.[1] There will then be no problem whatsoever about compatibility, but may be a question whether there is any interesting relation between these aspects.[2]

1.1 *Compositionality*

By 'the principle of semantic compositionality' (Compositionality, for short) I shall, to begin with, understand just what is expressed in the standard formulation:

(C) The meaning of a complex expression is determined by the meanings of its parts together with its mode of composition.

(C) can be interpreted in several ways. When I say that Compositionality is compatible with (semantic) holism my claim is that this holds for at least one *reasonable* interpretation of (C).

1.2 Holism

As is more than well known, many different theories can be understood under the heading of 'semantic holism'. I shall not here intend this term as Fodor and Lepore do.[3] Rather I shall try to hold on to a more traditional and intuitive sense. As I understand it, the principle of semantic holism is a principle of *determination* of meaning. It is a principle concerning the general *pattern* of determination. In order to conform to the format of (C) we can state the principle of semantic holism (Holism, for short) as:

(H)   The meanings of expressions in a language L are determined *together*, by a *totality* of relations between expressions in L.

I intend (H) to be understood along the following lines. Let us think of a theory of meaning for a language L as a theory that accomplishes two things. First, it specifies non-semantic properties of, and relations between, expressions of L, and second, it specifies the principles according to which the meanings of expressions of L are determined by, or supervene on, those non-semantic properties and relations. Then, such a theory is *Holistic* if, and only if, two conditions are met.

First, if some particular non-semantic property *A*, or relation R, is relevant for determination of meaning, then the theory must specify the *whole* extension (as far as L is concerned), of *A*, or R. The whole extension, and not just some selected subset, is relevant for meaning determination.

Second, the meanings get determined *together*. They get determined together because assignments of meanings to different expressions are *interdependent*. What meaning expression *a* can have depends on what meaning expressions *β* and *γ* can have, and vice versa. Many combinations of meaning assignments are excluded. In the extreme case no two expressions of a language can have their meanings determined

independently of each other. And *at least* Holism requires that there will be *widespread* interdependence between expressions that do not share any constituent parts, e.g. between syntactically simple expressions. This will ensure that no single non-semantic fact about some expression by itself can determine any meaning, and that no single expression can get its meaning determined irrespective of the rest of the language.

It should be noted that when I speak of *determination* of meaning, in connection with holism, I intend this metaphysically: if the meanings of expressions are determined by factors F, G and H, then, those factors are what expressions' having the meanings they have really *depends* on. Thus 'determination', as here used is not an epistemic notion: it does not in itself involve any assumption about our capacities to arrive at knowledge of meaning. There is, however, another common ambiguity involved in the term 'determination', between the metaphysical understanding and an understanding according to which the mere existence of a function from the As to the Bs allows you to say that the Bs are determined by the As. This ambiguity is discussed again in Section 2.

Of course, this is still an extremely rough characterization of Holism. It will become a bit better, for in Section 3 I shall provide an example of a kind of Holistic theory.

As before, my claim is that there is a *reasonable* interpretation of (H), as elaborated above, which is compatible with Compositionality.

1.3 Expressions

By 'expression' and related terms ('sentence', etc.) I intend here not just syntactic objects of public languages. The discussion is concerned not only with holism about public languages but also with holism about the contents of attitudes (or other inner states that might be relevant). Thus if some type of inner state, like the occurrence of a mentalese sentence, does have content, and if it also holds that this state can be identified irrespective of content (e.g. as a neurophysio-logical state), then there can be a holistic theory about the determination of content of that type of state, and then I intend the present discussion to be relevant. That is, I would include that inner state in the extension of, what I here understand by, 'expression'.

2 First problem: locality and order of determination

The first problem, which is well known, is that there seems to be a conflict between Compositionality and Holism over the *mode and order of determination* of meaning.

Compositionality seems to imply that the meaning of a complex expression is determined *locally*, by nothing else than what is internal to it, i.e. the meaning of its parts and its mode of composition. So the parts must have a meaning *prior* to the complex expression itself.

But this is apparently inconsistent with Holism. Holism claims that the meanings of expressions, including complex expressions, are determined by relations to other expressions in the rest of the language, not only by what is internal to it. And Holism claims that expressions get their meanings determined together, by common factors, and so the parts of a complex expression apparently cannot have their meanings determined first.

Holism and Compositionality *can* be understood as incompatible on this count. However, there are at least two natural ways of resolving the conflict, the first one depending on how we understand Compositionality, the second on how we understand Holism as well as Compositionality.

The first way of resolving the conflict depends on how we understand 'determined by' in (C), our statement of Compositionality. The interpretation which generates a conflict is a metaphysical interpretation. Understood metaphysically, Compositionality involves a claim about *order* of determination, and about the

factors that metaphysically generate the meaning of complex expressions. So understood, the parts of a complex expression must have meaning prior to the determination of meaning of the complex expressions, because it is the meaning of those parts, together with mode of composition, which actually produces the meaning of the complex expression.

However, Compositionality need not be understood as a metaphysical principle of meaning determination. Holism, as I understand it, is such a principle, but Compositionality can be taken as a purely mathematical principle. We can interpret 'determined by' in (C) as expressing only a *functional relation*. On this interpretation we understand Compositionality as the requirement that there be a *function* that takes the meanings of the parts, and mode of composition, as arguments and yields the meaning of the whole as value. The function is just a mathematical entity, neutral as regards the metaphysics or the epistemology of meaning determination. The function need be nothing more than a set theoretic many-one relation. It is compatible with any order and pattern of meaning determination.

Indeed, in 'Universal Grammar' Richard Montague (1974) implements compositionality by introducing the notion of a *homomorphism* from a syntactic algebra to a semantic algebra. This homomorphism is a function h assigning semantic values to syntactic items. The requirement is that for each syntactic function f from expressions to (more complex) expressions, there shall be a corresponding semantic function g from semantic values to semantic values such that:

$$h(f(a_1, \ldots, a_n)) = g(h(a_1), \ldots, h(a_n)).$$

Any metaphysics or epistemology of priority of meaning is done away with. This way of resolving the apparent conflict with Holism is quite well known (e.g. Dummett, 1991, p. 225; Block, 1993, p. 6). It works just as well for resolving the conflict between Compositionality and various *molecular* theories of meaning, i.e. theories that take sentences to be the primary bearers of meaning. According to molecularity, individual words and other subsentential expressions get their meaning determined derivatively, according to the role they play in sentences. Again we have a possible conflict over the mode and order of determination of meaning, between Compositionality and Molecularity. That conflict, too, is resolved by way of understanding Compositionality as above, i.e. as a purely mathematical principle.

However, this is not the only way of resolving the conflict between Compositionality and Holism. We *can* take Compositionality as a metaphysical principle. And there is good reason to, because Compositionality is often invoked as an *explanatory* principle. It is not obvious that the explanatory purposes that Compositionality is to serve *can* be served by a mere mathematical principle. I shall return to the question of explanatory purpose in Section 4.

In the rest of the paper I shall, unless otherwise noted, understand Compositionality in this metaphysical sense: the meanings of complex expressions really depend on the meanings of their parts. And, unless otherwise noted, when I speak of the existence of a function from As to Bs, I don't mean just the existence of some abstract entity, but the existence of an entity that corresponds to the way the Bs really *depend* on the As.

The other reason, then, why Compositionality need not conflict with Holism, as regards mode and order of determination, is that Compositionality says nothing about how the meanings of the *simple parts* are determined. It is consistent with Compositionality that the meaning of simple expressions is determined in a holistic manner. It *may* be the case, as far as Compositionality goes, that the meaning of any simple expression depends on the meaning of every other simple expression. It does *not*, of course, square with Compositionality, as a principle of meaning determination, that the meaning of

simple expressions in general depend on the meaning of complex expressions of which they are constituent parts. In this case the dependency relation must be non-symmetric, but as between simple expressions it may be symmetric.

The second question, about this way of resolving conflict, is whether it is compatible with Holism. Our statement (H) requires that expressions in a language get their meanings determined 'together', and this does not appear to square well with assigning priority to simple expressions. And indeed, there are reasonable versions of Holism that are inconsistent with letting the meaning of any expression be independent of the meaning of any other. However, there are also reasonable versions for which this does not hold. As I see it, it is the very heart of holism, as a principle of meaning determination, that the meaning of expressions does depend on the meaning of other expressions with which they share no grammatically significant parts, and that this dependency is mutual and widespread in the language. And we can well have holism in this sense if there is mutual dependency only between simple expressions.

It will still hold that the expressions of the language do get their meanings determined together. For suppose that s and s' are two sentences that have no common parts, and that the meaning of s is determined. As it is determined by the meanings of its parts and its mode of composition, the meaning of its parts, and ultimately of its simple parts, must be determined as well. By assumption the meanings of simple expressions are totally interdependent, and so the meaning of the simple parts of s depends on the meaning of the simple parts of s'. Hence these are determined. But, again by Compositionality, the mode of composition of s', together with the meaning of its simple parts, determines the meaning of s'. Hence the compositional dependence of the meaning of complex expressions on the meaning of their proper parts, together with total interdependence of the meaning of simple expressions, ensures that no expression of the language can have a determinate meaning unless every other expression of the language also has a determinate meaning. This is a holistic feature, by any standard.

However, this result raises a question: if no expression can have a determinate meaning unless every expression has, in what does the difference between the *interdependence* of simple expressions and the *unilateral* dependence of complex expressions on simple expressions consist? One possible answer would be this: we can keep the simple expressions of the language, their meanings and the way they are semantically interdependent, but *change* the principles of semantic composition, to the effect that complex expressions get different meanings. This would make simple expressions independent of complex expressions.

I don't think that is an adequate answer, however. It is only in virtue of the way simple expressions interact, i.e. the way they *combine* to yield meanings of complex expressions, that they are semantically interdependent at all. So the *way* simple expressions are interdependent must depend, in part, on which principles of semantic composition the language has. We cannot keep the former and change the latter.

Rather, the right answer must be something like this: you can take away subsets of sentences from the language while retaining the old semantics for the remaining fragment. The idea is that what remains is semantically independent of what is taken away, while what is taken away does not retain any meaning in isolation. Thus take any complex expression a of language L. Form a new language L′ by removing from L every expression that has a as a constituent part. Then any expression in L′ has the same meaning as it has in L. And if you add to L′ the set of syntactic objects that were taken away, then the result is precisely L, since the principles of composition of L′ will assign *meanings*, to those syntactic objects, which coincide with the meanings they have in L. The result is that no simple

expression semantically depends on any complex expression and that every complex expression depends on its parts.[4]

From the point of view of Holism, then, compositional structure is seen as *part of* the general pattern of meaning determination. Meaning does supervene on non-semantic properties and relations, and it is a feature of the supervenience relation, i.e. the relation between supervenient semantic facts and subvenient non-semantic facts, that compositional relations hold.

Compositional structure can make simple expressions interdependent in different ways. For instance, it may be that all, or nearly all, members in some particular set of sentences must come out true, whatever they mean. Then, because truth conditions of a sentence are, or depend on, meaning, and because the meaning of a sentence depends on its structure and on the meanings of its parts, the meanings of the parts must fit together in order to yield truth conditions that are met. The supervenience relation determines meanings that do fit together. Then the simple parts do not get their meanings determined independently of their contributions to determining the meanings of complex expressions. It does hold, as Holism requires, that the expressions in the language get their meanings determined *together*, by the subvenient non-semantic properties and relations, and, as Compositionality requires, that the meanings of complex expressions are determined through their structure and the meanings of their parts.

In this way compositionality and holism can be seen as reconciled in Donald Davidson's (1984) theory of meaning.[5] First, the meaning, and the structure, of an expression a in language L is the meaning assigned to it by the best T-theory[6] for L. Second, T-theories are *required* to exhibit compositional structure (hence, the language must have compositional structure). And third, T-theories can be tested only as *whole theories* against the *totality* of evidence.[7] No part of a T-theory, concerning only a fragment of the language, can be verified or falsified in isolation. This confirmation holism of the T-theory corresponds to semantic holism of its subject matter.

The basic evidence, in Davidson's case, is a speaker's set of *holding true* attitudes. Some sentences are held true absolutely, some in particular types of situation, some, perhaps, on condition that others are also held true. The property of being held true by a speaker, or being held true in a certain range of situations, is a non-semantic property of a sentence. That a sentence is held true by a speaker is a *consequence* of semantic properties of the sentence, and of what the speaker believes, as Davidson has pointed out in many places, but it is itself a non-semantic fact. Therefore, facts of this kind can serve as facts which semantic facts supervene on.[8]

So I do think that in Davidson's philosophy of language we have an example of a combination of Compositionality and Holism that resolves the potential conflict. It is more of an open question whether Davidson would prefer the first or the second way of resolving it. His argument against the conventionality of language[9] is a reason, I believe, for attributing to him a preference for the first way.

Another theory which combines holistic and compositional ingredients is due to Gilbert Harman (1973). Harman writes both that the representational character of a sentence in the inner language 'depends on its potential role [. . .] in the functional system' (p. 60) and also that it 'depends on its truth conditional structure' (p. 82), but I am not clear about how Harman thought that the potential conflict between these two ingredients was avoided.

3 Second problem: the individuation of meanings

In Section 2 I presented two ways of solving the first problem of incompatibility between Compositionality and Holism. Both ways can be characterized by saying that Compositionality is made to serve the Interests of Holism. Compositional

structure becomes part of the Holistic pattern of meaning determination. However, this solution may itself lead to a new problem, concerning the individuation of meanings.

This second problem is well brought out by Fodor and Lepore (1992, 1994) in their discussion of Conceptual Role Semantics.[10] Fodor and Lepore consider what they call 'Inferential Role Semantics' (IR), a version of Conceptual Role Semantics. According to IR, the meaning of an expression consists in its *inferential role*. The inferential role can be identified with the set of accepted inferences crucially involving the expression. For instance, the inference:

$$p \,\&\, q \Rightarrow p$$

is clearly an inference crucially involving '&'. However, if Holism is added to IR, we get the result that *every* accepted inference belongs to meaning. Then, suppose that a speaker accepts the inference:

(1) brown cow $\Rightarrow$ dangerous

(Fodor and Lepore's example), because he thinks that brown cows are dangerous. According to holistic IR, this means that it is part of the *meaning* of 'brown cow' that this inference is valid.

However, the requirement of Compositionality now means that the meaning of 'brown cow' shall be a function from the meaning of 'brown' and the meaning of 'cow', according to the semantic significance of the modifier-head construction. But this seems absurd. The speaker need not accept either of:

(2) brown $\Rightarrow$ dangerous
(3) cow $\Rightarrow$ dangerous

and so there is no *natural* assignment of meanings to the constituent parts of 'brown cow', which yields the desired meaning of the complex expression. What we have here is apparently a *reductio ad absurdum* of Holistic IR.

And Holistic IR is just one example. The general problem is that if Compositionality shall be made to fit the requirements of some Holistic theory, then the result will be that we must assign either strange meanings to components of complex expressions, or strange semantic significance to syntactic constructions, or both. The result *seems* to be that Holism and Compositionality, although formally compatible, can't be combined in any reasonable way.

However, so far, the example suffers from a somewhat sketchy presentation. Further, Fodor and Lepore has assumed that meaning is to be *identified* with inferential role. Holistic inferential role would require only that meaning shall be *determined* by, or supervene on, inferential role. I shall therefore recast the example in terms of the present conception of Holism. This will provide us with an example, even if a crude example, of a kind of Holistic theory. The presentation is a little bit technical, but the technicalities allow us to get clearer about what does and what doesn't follow concerning the relation with compositionality.

3.1 Holistic inferential role

We are interested in the meaning of expressions in a language L (as) used by a speaker S. L in itself is just syntax. L is, or contains, an infinite number of sentences and other complex expressions. The complex expressions have syntactic structure: they have other expressions as constituent parts.

Now we have a (subvenient) relation I. This is a relation holding between expressions (or, more generally, between sets of expressions and expressions). The expressions are either sentences, or else predicates (property expressions).

I holds between a and β just in case S *accepts* the inference from a to β. This does not by itself imply that the inference is valid, i.e. truth preserving. It does not imply that S takes a to *entail* β. It only means that S is prepared to accept β, given acceptance of a. Thus in the extension of I we

find $\langle$'snow is white and grass is green', 'snow is white'$\rangle$ as well as $\langle$'brown cow', 'dangerous'$\rangle$.

Secondly, we have a (subvenient) relation C that holds between two expressions just in case the first is a constituent part of the second. Thus $\langle$'brown', 'brown cow'$\rangle$ belongs to the extension of C.

With the relation C we have basic facts about S's attitudes, which are to serve as meaning determining. However, in order to make finer discriminations, we need also consider how simpler expressions occur in those sentences and predicates that figure in inferences that S accepts.

To this purpose we define the relations L and R (intuitively the 'left' relation and the 'right' relation) as follows:

$$L(a, \beta, \gamma) \text{ iff } C(a, \beta) \text{ and } I(\beta, \gamma)$$

$$R(a, \beta, \gamma) \text{ iff } C(a, \gamma) \text{ and } I(\beta, \gamma).$$

So L holds between a, β and γ in case a is part of β and there is an inference which S accepts, from β to γ. (This is the 'left' relation, since β, which a is part of, being the premiss in the accepted inference, occurs to the left in the linear representation of the inference). Similarly, R holds between a, β and γ in case a is part of γ, and there is an inference, accepted by S, from β to γ. Note again that all that matters is the constituency relation and S's acceptance of inferences. (We could also capture simple holding true and simple holding false in this pattern, by saying that a sentence held true by S is a sentence S infers from every other sentence, and that a sentence held false by S is a sentence from which S infers the truth of every other sentence.)

This is extremely crude, since it ignores *how* an expression occurs as constituent of another, but it serves the purpose of illustration.

Now we can define what we can call the *Global Role*, $G(a)$, for a *simple* expression a:

$$G(a) = \langle \{\langle \beta, \gamma \rangle : L(a, \beta, \gamma)\}, \{\langle \beta, \gamma \rangle : R(a, \beta, \gamma)\} \rangle.$$

The Global Role of a, then, is a pair of sets, each set being a pair of sets of expressions. If S accepts the inference from β to γ, and a is part of γ, then the pair $\langle \beta, \gamma \rangle$ is an element of the set that is the right element in the Global Role of a. This makes Global Role for simple expressions sensitive to what inferences S accepts.

For complex expressions Holistic IR is also very crude: it assigns to a complex expression β the global role that is the tuple of the global roles of its immediate constituent parts, in the order they occur. Thus if β has $a_1, \ldots a_n$, in that order, as immediate constituent parts, then

$$G(\beta) = \langle G(a_1), \ldots G(a_n) \rangle.$$

Now we can easily see that if S, e.g. begins to accept a new inference $\beta \Rightarrow \gamma$, which S up to this point was agnostic about, or rejected, then for every expression a that occurs in β or in γ it holds that the Global Role of a, as well as the Global Role of every sentence in which a occurs, changes.

The example could be elaborated upon to the effect that if an expression a occurs in a sentence s such that the global role of s changes (at some point), then the global role of a changes as well. This would provide an intuitively more holistic theory.

We have now provided the subvenient properties and relations. The next step is to outline how meaning supervenes on these. Formally, meaning supervenes on the relevant non-semantic facts by being a function of Global Role. The meaning of an expression is directly determined by its Global Role. Nothing is lost by this expedient. Global Role is itself a kind of Holistic property: Global Roles are determined by the totality of subvenient facts, and Global Roles of expressions, including simple expressions, are largely interdependent. For instance $\langle$'brown cow', 'dangerous'$\rangle$ cannot be an element of the left part of the Global Role of 'brown' unless it is also an element of the left part of the Global Role of 'cow', and also an

element of the right part of the Global Role of 'dangerous'.

So what we need for the second step is a function from Global Roles to meanings. That is, we need a function that has as its domain the set of possible Global Roles of expressions in L, and as its range the total set of meanings that are possible for those expressions. Let h be such a function.[11] Here, h is supposed to be *one–one*, meaning that h does not assign the same meaning to any two distinct Global Roles. This is the crucial assumption, and I will return to it shortly. For the time being we are to see the consequences of that assumption.

Further, for each syntactic function g, mapping expressions $a_1, \ldots a_n$ on some complex expression β, there is a function f from meanings to meanings, such that the homomorphism requirement on h is fulfilled:

$$h(G(\beta)) = h(\langle G(a_1), \ldots, G(a_n) \rangle) = f\,(h(G(a_1)), \ldots, h(G(a_n))).$$

This ensures that Holistic IR is a compositional theory for L (as spoken by S).

Finally, we add to Holistic IR the stipulation:

INF   If $L(a, \beta, \gamma)$ or $R(a, \beta, \gamma)$, then $\beta \Rightarrow \gamma$ is a valid inference.

INF should be regarded, if accepted as valid, not as an extra stipulation, but as a restriction on admissible functions from Global Roles to meanings.

Now it is time to see whether what Fodor and Lepore say about holism and compositionality is true of Holistic IR. They say that for holistic Inferential Role Semantics it is part of the meaning of 'brown cow' that the inference:

(1)   brown cow $\Rightarrow$ dangerous

is valid. This can be confirmed. In the same breath we can confirm more: Fodor and Lepore also say that because of Compositionality the validity of the inference must be determined by the meaning of 'brown', the meaning of 'cow' and the modifier-head construction. This can also be confirmed. In fact, according to Holistic IR, it is part of the meaning of 'brown', and part of the meaning of 'cow', and also part of the meaning of 'dangerous', that (1) is valid. Why? The answer is that since h is *one–one* it has an inverse h^{-1}. Since h is *one–one* 'brown' would not have the meaning it does unless it had the global role that it does. And the value of h^{-1} for the meaning of 'brown', as argument, contains ⟨'brown cow', 'dangerous'⟩ in its left part, which immediately implies that L('brown', 'brown cow', 'dangerous'). According to INF this means that (1) is valid.

This may indeed seem counterintuitive. And not only this. We can go on to confirm more of what Fodor and Lepore (1992, pp. 13–14) say about holism. They say:

> For, consider the property T* which a belief has iff it expresses a proposition that is the content of a belief of mine. According to the present assumptions, if T* is anatomic, then it is holistic. And if T* is holistic, then (assuming that thoughts are individuated by their propositional contents) it might turn out that nobody has thoughts that are tokens of the same type as my thought about Auntie's pen unless he also has thoughts that are tokens of the same type as, as it might be, my thought that the cat is on the mat, my thought that black holes are odd kinds of objects, my thought that Salome will never sell in Omaha. This too might be considered an interesting, even counter-intuitive, result in the philosophy of mind.

Is this a consequence of Holistic IR? Well, not quite. We could have made it a consequence, had we elaborated a bit on our notion of Global Role. But things are bad enough as they are. Let's assume that thought content is determined in accordance with Holistic IR. Then, again because

the assignment h of meaning to Global Role is *one–one*, we have the result that if S changes her mind about the validity of some inference, say (1), this will bring about a change in the meaning of 'brown', the meaning of 'cow', and the meaning of 'dangerous'. It will also bring with it a change in the meaning of *every* complex expression, every sentence, that contains any of these three expressions.

Thus suppose that you and I speak L and are exactly alike as regards acceptance of inferences. Both of us accept (1). But suddenly I change my mind. I now reject the inference from 'brown cow' to 'dangerous'. Because of this the content which I express with:

(4)   mad dogs are dangerous

is now different from the content that you express by the same sentence. This is because my meaning of 'dangerous' is now different from yours. We used to agree that mad dogs are dangerous, but now we don't, for we don't think the same thought.

According to Holistic IR we can still agree, e.g. that:

(5)   black holes are odd kinds of objects

provided we are exactly alike as concerns our uses of 'black', 'hole', etc. Chances are, however, that we are not. So our intuitive picture of intersubjective understanding will not fare well if we accept something like Holistic IR as our preferred theory of meaning.

However, now it is time to object. Holistic IR is Holistic in virtue of two features: that the *totality* of accepted inferences (jointly) determine meaning, and that possible meanings are *interdependent*. This was captured by way of Global Role: the meaning of an expression is a function of its Global Role, and Global Roles themselves satisfy the Holistic principles: they depend on the totality of subvenient, non-semantic facts, and they are interdependent. It is not part of the

Holistic character of Holistic IR that the function from Global Roles to meanings be *one–one*. It can be *many–one*. And it is precisely because h was assumed to be *one–one* that Holistic IR has such absurd consequences.

Thus suppose we drop this part of Holistic IR. Our revised theory, HIR*, has the same Global Roles but a different function, h*, from Global Roles to meanings, and h* is assumed to be *many–one*. Then h* does not have an inverse. More than one Global Role for 'brown' yields the same meaning. Suppose 'brown' is assigned a meaning M('brown'). It does *not* follow from this that L('brown', 'brown cow', 'dangerous') is true. That is, it does not follow unless ⟨'brown cow', 'dangerous'⟩ is an element in *all* Global Roles which h* maps on M('brown'), and that is clearly no necessary feature of Holism.

Given this property of HIR*, the property that different, perhaps many different, Global Roles can yield the same meaning, we also have the result that the Global Role of an expression may *change* without bringing with it a change in meaning. In the example above you and I were exactly alike up to the point where I gave up my adherence to (1). This changed some of my Global Roles, and made them different from yours, but if difference in Global Role need not imply difference in meaning, then there *need* not be a difference in meaning between, say, 'brown cow' in your mouth and 'brown cow' in mine. So it is not an intrinsic feature of Holism, considered as a principle of meaning determination, that communication, or change of mind, turns out as impossible.

Why has it seemed otherwise? The immediate reason is that the distinction has not been clear between holism as a principle of meaning *determination*, and holism as a principle of meaning *individuation*. The general idea of holistic individuation is often expressed by saying that something is individuated, or identified, by its position in a 'space', 'system', or 'network'. This passage from Davidson's 'Thought and Talk' (1984, p. 157) is characteristic:

There are good reasons for not insisting on any particular list of beliefs that are needed if a creature is to wonder whether a gun is loaded. Nevertheless, it is necessary that that there be endless interlocked beliefs. The system of such beliefs identifies a thought by locating it in a logical and epistemic space.

This intuitive idea of an holistically individuated property is exemplified by Global Role. Think of a network simply as a set of objects together with a set of properties and relations over these objects. This can be represented as a netlike diagram. In our case we have expressions of the language L as objects, and as relations we have the constituency relation, and the relation between premise and conclusion of accepted inferences (above partly fused into the three place relations L and R). The *position* of an object is then primarily determined by what properties it has and what other objects it is related to, secondly by what properties these *other* objects have and what yet further objects *they* are related to, and so on as far as is relevant. A holistic, or holistically individuated, kind of property, is then a kind of property such that changes always occur when changes in position occur. It is maximally holistic, if *everything* in the network is relevant, i.e. if any change in the position of any object brings with it a change in the position of every other object. Global Role is a holistic kind of property in this sense (indeed identical with position), but not, as it was defined, a maximally holistic one.

Meanings would be holistically individuated as well if any change in position (Global Role) of an expression forced a change in its meaning. But, again, this is not part of Holism as a principle of meaning determination. It is one thing that an expression must *have* such a position in a network,[12] and that its meaning *depends* on its position, and another that its meaning be individuated along with that position. It is perfectly consistent to claim that meanings consist in referential relations and that what meaning an expression has is determined in a Holistic fashion. Holism will remain as long as assignment of meaning to an expression is sensitive to assignments of meaning to other expressions (beside its own parts).[13]

The point I have made here is essentially anticipated by Brian McLaughlin, although in a different conceptual framework, without making the general determination/individuation distinction.[14]

I shall also remark just briefly on the question of the analyticity of, for instance, (1). Above, by appeal to the principle INF of Holistic IR, we concluded that (1) is valid, given, e.g. the meaning of 'brown'. By an ordinary understanding of analyticity, this makes (1) analytically valid, since it is valid in virtue of meaning.[15] Similarly we can say that:

(6)   brown cows are dangerous

is analytically true. This conclusion depends on two features of Holistic IR. First it depends on the fact that the function h, from Global Roles to meanings, was assumed to be *one–one*. If h were not *one–one*, then 'brown' might have had the same meaning, M('brown'), and yet another Global Role, one that did not include ⟨'brown cow', 'dangerous'⟩ in its left part, and then (1) would not be valid.

Secondly, the analyticity of (1), in Holistic IR, also depends on the principle INF, the principle, roughly, that if the *acceptance* of an inference, like (1), takes part in determining the meanings of the expressions involved, then that inference shall come out as valid. This principle is not part of Holism as I have presented it. We can drop INF, and still have Holism, but without analyticity, at least without this kind of analytical inferences.

Something like INF can indeed *motivate* a Holistic theory, as Davidson's holism has been motivated by the principle that we should seek the interpretation which makes the interpretee as right as possible (maximizes truth; one

version of the principle of charity). But it is a mistake to think that it is a part of Holism as such. It is part of Holism that assignments of meanings to different expressions are largely *interdependent*, but that interdependence can be created in different ways. Taking INF as a valid, meaning-constitutive principle is just one way.[16]

It may, finally, be in order to point out that for all I have said about the two kinds of Holistic Inferential Role Semantics, there need not be any meaning-theoretically plausible theory of either kind. I am not an adherent of Inferential Role Semantics, and not committed to the claim that the correct, or the best, account of meaning, or even a workable account of meaning, can be given along this line. Such a project may fail for reasons not considered here. I have only been concerned with the very idea of Holistic Inferential Role Semantics, as the best understood kind of holistic semantics, and whether this idea is compatible with compositionality.

4 Third problem: the explanation of productivity

The first problem was a problem about direct inconsistency between Compositionality and Holism. The second problem was one about incoherence in a somewhat looser sense. It seemed that combining Compositionality and Holism was inconsistent with plausible views about the individuation of meanings. The third problem exhibits an incoherence in a yet wider sense. It seems that, if Holism is true we will have to give up some *explanations* that make appeal to Compositionality.

Perhaps most often, Compositionality has been invoked for explaining our ability to understand *new sentences*. I may read in my morning paper something like:

(7)   The inflation rate in Finland has dropped twice as much as that in Denmark.

No one has explained to me the meaning of this

sentence. I have never spoken, written, thought, heard or read it before. Yet I immediately understand it.[1] How is this possible? The answer is that I know the meanings of the components of (7), and the semantic significance of its mode of composition, and this is sufficient for me to understand it. The meaning of (7) is determined in accordance with Compositionality, and because of this my prior knowledge of English enables me to understand it.

I don't know how old this explanation is, but it has been part of analytic philosophy since early on, and it is good. It gives us a reason for believing that Compositionality is true. And if we had to give up this explanation, most of us would probably give up Compositionality with it. For short I shall call it *Novelty*. So Novelty is the thesis that Compositionality is the correct explanation of our ability to understand new sentences. If there is a direct conflict between Holism and Novelty, then there is an indirect conflict between Holism and Compositionality, since Novelty is one of our main reasons for believing in Compositionality.

Is there a conflict between Holism and Novelty? No doubt, some versions of Holism do conflict directly with Novelty. If I am to understand a new sentence in the compositional way, the meaning of its familiar parts must have been preserved over time, and so must the principles of semantic composition. If we have a version of Holism according to which the subvenient semantic facts change erratically, beyond my cognitive control, then clearly past semantic knowledge will be of no help for present understanding, whether of old or of new sentences. I would reject any such version of Holism.

A particularly interesting question is whether theories like our Holistic Inferential Role, for which the subvenient facts are speakers' acceptance of sentences and inferences, conflict with Novelty. It is interesting partly because of their prominence in recent analytic philosophy, but also because the understanding of new sentences,

according to such theories, is closely connected with changes in the subvenient facts, to the effect that we have reason to suspect a clash with Novelty.

Consider the following tenet:

(+) Assent to [dissent from] a new sentence does not change its meaning.

Clearly, (+) is hard to disagree with. But not only does a denial of (+) strike you as absurd in itself, it would also undercut the explanatory value of Compositionality. For what is the point of understanding a new sentence if it acquires a *different* meaning once you have decided to count it as true, or as false? However, this is the situation we seem to end up in with Holistic Inferential Role and similar Holistic theories.

Assume the following. HIR* is true, where HIR* is a theory which is like Holistic IR except that its function h^* from Global Roles to meanings is *many—one*. Then there is a set of Σ_i of all sentences and inferences that I accept at time t_i. Included in this set is:

(4) mad dogs are dangerous
(8) black holes are dense.

Further, the function h^* from Global Roles to meanings is such that given Σ_i it assigns the truth function of conjunction to '&' as I have used it, and the truth function of negation to '$\neg$'. Then, at time t_i, for the first time, I consider the sentence:

(9) mad dogs are dangerous & black holes are dense.

This sentence strikes me as implausible, not because I have forgotten or changed my attitudes to (4) and (8), or because I don't recognize them as occurring in (9), but just because this new sentence, composed as it is, strikes me as false. I reject it. I assent rather to

(10) ~ (mad dogs are dangerous & black holes are dense).

This produces a new set Σ_j of all sentences and inferences that I accept at time t_j. A great number of Global Roles will have changed. That happens every time I assent to, or dissent from, a new sentence. If *one–one* Holistic IR were true, with Holistic individuation of meanings, then there would be a great number of changes in meaning each time I took a stand on a new sentence (and each time I revised my attitude to an old one).

However, when I take the step of adding (10) to my totality of accepted sentences, alongside with (4) and (8), something will have to change even on the *many–one* HIR* model. In HIR* the INF principle is still assumed true. Remember that INF required the inferences (and hence sentences) a speaker *accepts* to come out valid (true) in his language. So, once I have accepted (4), (8) and (10), all of these must be true. But then it cannot be the case that, at time t_j, '&' still means conjunction and '~' still means negation. For then at least one out of (4), (8) and (10) is false. So the meaning of at least one of the constants must have changed.

Given our intuitive understanding of things, this sounds bad in itself. But take Compositionality into account, and it becomes worse. For before I decided to reject (9) and accept (10), '&' still meant conjunction and '~' still meant negation. And if understood (9) before my new decision I understand it as a conjunction of two sentences that I accepted. And if I understood (10), I understood it as the negation of (9). However, *after* my decision it was something else. And the principles of composition that determined the meaning of (10) before the decision was made, do not tell you what meaning (10) (along with every other sentence containing '~', or '&') has *after* the decision has been made. Holistic Inferential Role says what the meanings of expressions are, at each time, depending on what inferences (including sentences) you accept at that time, *regardless* of what meaning the

expressions had *before*. There is simply no requirement of continuity, of conservation of meaning across time, built into HIR*.

Our immediate problem with conjunction and negation in the example can be dispelled by rejecting INF: if it is not necessary that something *held* true by a speaker must be assigned meaning so that it also *comes out* true, then we can still say that (10) is false in my language, despite my acceptance of it, since that fits in with the best *overall* assignment of meanings to expressions in my language. It is possible to filter out as unhappy my decision to treat (10) as true.

However, this solution is only temporary. If I were to go on to make precisely the same kind of apparently inconsistent decisions in a number of other cases, then it would no longer be plausible that the best overall interpretation of me would be to filter out those decisions as unhappy. And if that is the case, there will always be *some* deviant decision which tips the balance in favour of assigning new meanings to my expressions rather than preserving the old ones.

And so it seems that the explanatory task of Compositionality cannot be achieved. Compositionality was meant to explain not just how we can simply *understand* new sentences, but also how we can acquire *new knowledge* by verbal information. There is hardly any value in understanding new sentences if you cannot assimilate what you understand as new knowledge, or at least new belief. And this is what we want Compositionality to explain.

To sum up. Given that Holistic Inferential Role and related theories determine the meaning of an expression regardless of its earlier meaning, and given that a decision concerning a new sentence can change the meaning of that sentence (and many others with it), can Compositionality really *explain* how we can get new beliefs through our understanding of new sentences? This is the question. And the answer is: For all that is said so far, yes!

Clearly, Compositionality could *not* fulfil the intended explanatory role if meanings often *did* change because of new decisions, as in the example. But is there any reason to believe that, if Holism is true, they also *do* clash, in ways similar to the example? After all, people don't do such things as asserting (10) while being fully aware of assenting to (4) and (8) (given the normal meaning of '&' and '~'). And speakers rarely say things that are so strange as to invite their interpreters to change their interpretational habits (like claiming to have a hippo in the refrigerator).

This normal course of affairs is theoretically significant if two conditions can be met. First, it should be compatible with Holism in general, and with HIR* in particular, that *when* people make normal decisions about new sentences, i.e. decisions that we would not *intuitively* count as conceptually deviant, then meaning *is preserved*. That is, it should be compatible with Holism that the meanings assigned to my expressions at time t_i, based on the set Σ_i of sentences and inferences that I accept then, are the *same* as the meanings assigned to my expressions at time Σ_k, based on the new set Σ_k of sentences and inferences I accept at t_k, *provided* my decisions between t_i and t_k are normal. And clearly this condition is fulfilled. It is consistent with the very idea of HIR*, and *a fortiori* with Holism, that the meanings of my expressions *will be* preserved as long as I do not make extremely non-standard decisions regarding sentences and inferences, new and old.

The second condition is that the normality of the normal course of affairs can be *explained* by Compositionality. Our question was whether the intended explanatory role of Compositionality was compatible with Holism. In order that they be compatible, it is not enough that the Holistic principles *in fact* preserve meaning across time, but it must also be possible to invoke Compositionality for explaining *why* meaning is preserved across time. And as far as I can see, this condition is also met. To return to our example: given that I am aware of assenting to (4) and (8), and know the customary meanings of '&' and '~', only temporary insanity can make me reject (9) and

accept (10). I am so guided and constrained by my understanding of these sentences that, unless because of some accident, my decision will be to accept (9) and reject (10). And this understanding is explained by Compositionality. I will decide to accept or reject a sentence on the basis of my understanding of it and of my already settled beliefs, and my understanding of it can usually be predicted according to compositional principles.

I *could* decide differently, and if I were to decide differently, often meaning *would* change. Compositionality explains why it does not.

This problem about preservation of meaning across time is related to a question that has been pressed against semantic holism by Michael Dummett: If holism is true, how can you learn an entire language? Dummett (1976, p. 79) says that:

[...] on a holistic view, it is impossible fully to understand any sentence without knowing the entire language [...]

[...] there can be nothing between not knowing the language at all and knowing it completely.

So, if Dummett's appreciation of semantic holism is correct, holism makes it impossible to learn a language incrementally, piece by piece, and thus virtually impossible to learn it at all.

Dummett's perspective on language is different from that of our previous examples. As Dummett sees it, a natural language is the common property of a speech community. Individual speakers have a cognitive relation to it: they know it, better or worse. What an expression means is determined by facts about the speech community as a whole, and for its members it is a question of knowing those meanings.

From this perspective it appears that Holism makes it impossible to know *a proper fragment* of a language, to know part of the language but not all. Suppose that the meaning determining facts about expressions are their respective *uses* in the speech community, and suppose that *use* is a Holistic kind of property in the sense of Section 3. Then we have the following situation. An expression *a* belongs to a fragment L′ of L. If we consider L′ in isolation, the Holistic principles assign a meaning to *a*, based on the use of *a* in L′. *a* has a wider use in the whole of L, and the Holistic principles assign a meaning to *a*, based on the use of *a* in L. These two meanings need not coincide. And so, to know what meaning *a* has in L, you must know the use of *a* in L. It is not sufficient to know the use of *a* in L′. If you belong to a community of L-speakers and you have only mastered L′ yourself, you do not really understand what they are saying, since you do not really know what their words mean.

This problem about learnability is related to the problem about new sentences. In both cases you have a situation where an addition to previous meaning determining facts may fail to preserve the old meanings. In our first case, where the speaker made a new decision about a sentence, there may be a genuine change of meaning. In our second case there is an epistemic problem: if I do not know the *further* meaning determining facts which are already at hand in the speech community, then I may get the meanings of familiar expressions wrong.

I think there are basically two replies you can make on behalf of Holism against Dummett's criticism. The first one has been delivered by Bilgrami (1986). According to this view Dummett's description is partly right. Before you know the whole language you do not have a complete knowledge of the meaning of any single expression. What you have is a *partial* knowledge of those meanings. As you learn new parts of the language your knowledge of the meanings of already familiar expressions increases, until finally you understand them fully. Dummett is wrong in arguing that because you cannot know just part of a language, there is nothing between knowing a language completely and not knowing it at all. There are stages

in between, since there is such a thing as partial knowledge of the meaning of an expression.

I think that this reply is adequate as regards some expressions. Some expressions are such that you can master their use in some types of contexts, and still fail to master their use in some other types of context, even though there is no ambiguity. To take an extravagant example, you may well master the use of 'at the same time', or 'simultaneously', in everyday situations, but fail to do so in the context of relativity theory. So in this case you clearly know only part of the meaning. What you don't know may not matter very much to your understanding of the expression in the everyday contexts where you use it.

So far Bilgrami's reply is all right, but I think it is quite inadequate for most ordinary expressions. For instance, it would be quite counterintuitive to claim that speakers may fail in their understanding of 'very', 'chair', 'but', 'if—then', 'walk' and so on for lack of knowledge in physics, history, geography, anatomy or other disciplines. If Holism requires us to say so, then surely there is a case against it.

However, Holism doesn't require this. Remember that on the *many–one* model of Holistic meaning determination it is quite possible that meanings are preserved when new meaning determining facts, such as uses, are introduced. The addition of relativity theory or ancient history to everyday English surely does not change the meaning of 'if-then', or 'walk', and this is perfectly compatible with, e.g. the HIR* kind of Holism.

So, assuming that the meaning of 'if-then' which is determined in the language fragment of some ten-year-old speaker, is the *same* as that determined in the language fragment of a fully competent speaker, what shall we say about the understanding of the ten-year-old? You *can* say that he does not really understand 'if-then', the reason being that he does not know all the meaning determining facts of the English language. However, this is implausible, or at least it does not yield the most relevant sense of 'understand'.

I think that we should say that he *does* understand the expression, because he does associate the *right* meaning with it (the meaning it has in English), and because he does so *on good grounds*. We should not say that he understands only in virtue of associating the right meaning with the expression, since that would turn any successful guesswork into understanding. We need also to say that understanding takes place only if the association is made on good grounds.

However, why *should* we say that our ten-year-old speaker does have good grounds for, tacitly, taking 'if-then' to have the same meaning in the entire language as it has in the fragment he knows (or rather, as it would have if that fragment were the whole language)? I think that, although those meanings might differ, the *default option* is that they will not. If this is the default option, then the ten-year-old speaker does have good grounds. Acting as if the meanings are the same will usually lead him right.

Again, the *explanation* of this, i.e. the explanation of why sameness of meaning is the default option in such a case, is Compositionality. That the meaning of a sentence is determined by the meanings of its parts and its mode of composition is, *inter alia*, the best explanation of how we easily can enlarge our linguistic knowledge by way of learning how to relate new expressions, in definitions and in use, to already familiar expressions. This explanation implies that normally, the familiar expressions retain their already familiar *meanings* in the new contexts. And that, in turn, is the reason for taking preservation of meaning to be the default option. Because Compositionality in general does provide part of a good explanation of language learning, in this context Compositionality can also explain why Holism, on the *many–one* model, is not incompatible with the traditional picture of language learning.

Notes

1 Hartry Field (1977) was perhaps the first, in 'Logic, Meaning and Conceptual Role', to suggest

this combination. Of course, compositionality is not one of the main concerns of that paper. A similar line is taken by Ned Block (1986, 1993), who combines holistic narrow content and truth conditions, but Block does not really claim that these are different parts or aspects of (the same) meaning.

2 This question is pressed by Jerry Fodor and Ernest Lepore (1992).

3 Fodor and Lepore (1992) define 'holistic property' to be a property such that, if one entity has it, then a lot of entities have it (p. 2). Semantic holism (meaning holism, content holism), as they understand it, is then the doctrine that generic semantic properties, like the property of having meaning, are holistic (p. 5).

  I do not follow their usage, since I am interested in the principles of determination of meaning, or content, of expressions of natural, or mentalese, languages (and they, the expressions, are a lot to begin with). I am not here concerned with the possibility, e.g. of having just a single, or just a few, beliefs.

4 It is presupposed that, in L, a simple expression $\in$ can combine with different other expressions according to the same principle of semantic composition, so that $\in$ still interacts with other simple expression if one combination, one complex expression, together with every other expression containing it, is removed. However, this need not, of course, hold for L′ because we can remove all complex expressions by repeating the process. Still, if you start out with L′, you can add a, and then remove some other complex expression, with the same result.

5 I base this on Davidson's (1984) early papers, such as 'Truth and Meaning' [Chapter 13 above] and 'Radical Interpretation'.

6 Or T-theories, but we can presently ignore indeterminacy.

7 These conditions correspond, in reversed order, to my two conditions on Holistic theories stated in the preliminary remarks.

8 It is, of course, odd to say that some non-semantic F fact is a consequence of a semantic fact F′ that supervenes on F. The simplest way of removing the oddity is to think of the consequence relation involved as a purely formal relation,

something that again is part of the pattern of meaning determination.

9 For instance in 'Communication and Convention', in Davidson, 1984.

10 See Fodor and Lepore (1992, ch. 6; 1994).

11 Of course, we can skip Global Role and define directly a function which takes a set of subvenient facts, and an expression, as arguments, and yields a meaning as value. What makes such a function Holistic? Beside involving the relevant totality of non-semantic facts, its Holistic character consists precisely in the interdependence of its outputs. For instance, given the acceptance of (1), some possible meanings of 'brown' do not combine with some possible meanings of 'cow'.

12 This is the feature underlying Fodor and Lepore's definition of holism.

13 As far as I can see, this model is fully compatible with Donald Davidson's semantic holism. It even strikes me as the more natural alternative. Thus, Davidson's semantic holism does not seem to suffer from the drawbacks noted by Fodor and Lepore.

14 At least so I have interpreted McLaughlin. On p. 656 McLaughlin writes: 'Moreover, the conceptual role semantics in question allows that there can be multiple distinct conceptual roles that are partly constitutive of the same meaning'. Which is to say, a many–one relation. Judging from their reply in the same issue, Fodor and Lepore have taken McLaughlin to make a different point.

To some extent I am also anticipated by Ned Block, who thinks there can be 'a many–one relation between thought contents and meanings, and a many–one relation between meanings and truth conditions' (1993, p. 16), but I am not completely clear about how Block's views fit in with the present ones.

The related general observation, that a supervenient kind need not inherit all the properties of its supervenience base, has been made against Fodor and Lepore by Ted Warfield (1993). (I thank Ernie Lepore for the reference.)

The present remarks were developed independently, and presented at the SILFS conference on holism in Rome, in December 1994.

15 Of course, given the classic conception of analyticity, we should add 'irrespective of the way the world is'. Here I shall ignore that, and hence ignore the fundamental issue of the analytic/synthetic distinction.

16 Both Block (1993, p. 20) and Boghossian (1993, pp. 35–6), argue against the need for Inferential Role Semantics to accept inferences as analytic. In my terminology, they argue against the need of accepting INF.

17 This is in fact a controversial statement, but the present paper is not the right place to go into that issue.

References

Bilgrami, A. 1986: Meaning, Holism and Use. In E. Lepore (ed.), *Truth and Interpretation: Perspectives on the Philosophy of Donald Davidson*. Oxford: Basil Blackwell.

Block, N. 1986: Advertisement for a Semantics for Psychology. *Midwest Studies in Philosophy*, 10, 1986, 615–78.

Block, N. 1993: Holism, Hyper-analyticity and Hyper-compositionality. *Mind and Language*, 8, 1–26.

Boghossian, P. 1993: Does Inferential Role Semantics Rest Upon a Mistake. *Mind and Language* 8, 27–48.

Davidson, D. 1984: *Inquiries into Truth and Interpretation*. Oxford: Clarendon Press.

Dummett, M. 1976: What Is a Theory of Meaning? (II). In G. Evans and J. McDowell (eds), *Truth and Meaning*. Oxford University Press.

Dummett, M. 1991: *The Logical Basis of Metaphysics*. London: Duckworth.

Field, H. 1974: Logic, Meaning and Conceptual Role. *Journal of Philosophy*, 74, 347–75.

Fodor, J. and Lepore, E. 1992: *Holism: A Shopper's Guide*. Oxford: Basil Blackwell.

Fodor, J. and Lepore, E. 1994: Why Meaning (Probably) Isn't Conceptual Role. In Stich and Warfield (eds), *Mental Representation*. Oxford: Basil Blackwell [Chapter 21 above].

Harman, G. 1974: *Thought*. Princeton University Press.

McLaughlin, B. 1993: On Punctate Content and Conceptual Role. *Philosophy and Phenomenological Research*, 53, 653–60.

Montague, R. 1974: Universal Grammar. In *Formal Philosophy*, ed. R. Thomason. New Haven, CT: Yale University Press.

Warfield, T. 1993: On a Semantic Argument Against Conceptual Role Semantics. *Analysis*, 53, 298–304.

PART TEN

Implicature

INTRODUCTION TO PART TEN

SUPPOSE A FUND MANAGER has invested all your savings on the stock market. One day, you ask her how your investments are doing. She answers

(1)   Some of your shares have gone down.

If it turns out later that in fact *all* of your shares have gone down, you could be forgiven for thinking that your fund manager has deceived you. There is a distinct impression that what she has told you implies

(2)   Not all of your shares have gone down.

Let us formalize the sentence the fund manager used in the way standardly used in logic classes (where 'YSx' stands for 'x is your share' and 'GDx' stands for 'x has gone down'):

(1F) $(\exists x)$ (YS$x \wedge$ GDx) [There is at least one x such that x is your share and x has gone down].

(1F) is perfectly compatible with '$(\forall x)$ (YS$x \supset$ GDx)', thus it does not entail

(2F) $\neg(\forall x)$ (YS$x \supset$ GDx) [It is not the case that for all x, if x is your share then x has gone down].

There are two different conclusions one might draw from the fact that (1) seems to entail (2), while (1F) does not entail (2F). One is the conclusion that (1F) and (2F) are not after all the correct formalizations of (1) and (2), because they differ in meaning. In particular, one might conclude that there must be a difference in meaning between 'Some' and '$(\exists x)$'. The other conclusion one might draw is that our impression that (1) entails (2) was after all mistaken. In that case, the fund manager can at least claim not to have lied.

   Grice's paper 'Logic and Conversation' offers a general framework that allows us to explain why we might have the *impression* that (1) is incorrect and implies (2), even though strictly speaking, (1) is true and does not logically entail (2). On his view, the impression stems from the fact that in a conversation, we assume that our interlocutors are *cooperative*, and what the fund manager said would only have been a cooperative contribution if she had also believed (2). This is so, because according to Grice being cooperative includes (everything else being equal) being as informative as is required, and (1) clearly is not as informative as required if the fund manager knows the much more informative (2).

From the very beginnings of modern logic, logicians have thought about the relationship between the truth-functional connectives and quantifiers of classical logic on the one hand, and certain expressions in natural language on the other. At first sight, what Grice calls the 'formal devices' seem roughly to correspond to certain natural language expressions: '∧' to 'and', '∨' to 'or', '¬' to 'it's not the case that', '⊃' to 'if . . ., then—', '(∃x)' to 'Some' and '(∀x)' to 'All'. Moreover, the formal devices were in fact invented roughly to mirror these natural language counterparts. However, logicians have assumed from the start that the correspondence between the formal devices and their natural counterparts is at best imperfect, i.e. that there are clear differences in meaning. For example, it is sufficient for the truth of a truth-functional conditional, that the antecedent (the clause preceding '⊃') be false or the consequent (the clause succeeding '⊃') be true. However, the fact that ice is less dense than water doesn't seem sufficient for the truth of 'If ice is denser than water, then ice floats on water'; and similarly, the truth of 'ice floats on water' does not seem sufficient for the truth of 'If ice does not float on water, then ice floats on water'.[1]

As Grice points out, some theorists, such as Frege, have maintained that this assumed divergence in meaning is due to an imperfection in natural languages (Frege is in Grice's terms a 'formalist'), while others, like Austin, have taken an 'informalist' stance, i.e. maintained that the formal languages are just inadequate as tools for describing the properties of natural languages. Grice himself believes that his own theory of conversation will allow us to deny that there is such a divergence in the first place, for it offers an alternative explanation of the data that motivate the thesis of divergence. For example, his theory of conversation offers an explanation of the datum that (1) *seems* to imply (2) which is compatible with (1) being correctly formalized as (1F). This explanation is not ad hoc – on the contrary, it is part of a general theory of conversation which unifies a whole range of related phenomena. This theory has been extremely influential and can be seen as marking the beginning of the discipline within linguistics and the philosophy of language which is known as 'pragmatics'.

In order to introduce his theory of conversation, Grice makes a distinction between two different types of content or message that can be conveyed by an utterance: what is *said* by an utterance, and what is *implicated* by it. The two verbs 'to say' and 'to implicate' are meant by Grice to be technical terms, and he explains them by giving a number of examples, as well as by specifying their role in his theory. It is clear that on Grice's view, what is said by an utterance and what it implicates are both *propositions*. Grice says that what is said is 'closely related to the conventional meaning of the words'. One further important idea Grice seems to have is that what is said by an utterance determines whether the utterance is *strictly speaking* true or false: if the proposition that is said is true, then the utterance is true, while if what it says is false, then the utterance is false. If an utterance merely implicates a false proposition, by contrast, it may still be true, if what is said is true. This happens in our example: what the fund manager's utterance of (1) says is true. However, it implicates something

---

[1] These examples are from Sainsbury 2001, p. 89.

false, namely (2). This shows that what an utterance merely implicates does not follow logically from what it says, for if it did, then this could not happen.

Grice distinguishes different types of implicatures. Amongst them, what he calls 'conversational' implicatures are the main topic of the essay. Grice believes that conversational implicatures are generated because conversations are a special case of co-operative intentional action and are as such subject to certain principles of conduct. When two agents are co-operating in carrying a sofa up a flight of stairs, they both have certain expectations about how the other will act, and these expectations are based on the assumption that the other shares the common aim and will act in ways that he or she believes will further that aim. Similarly, all parties to a conversation expect the others to act in a co-operative manner, i.e. in a manner that furthers the common aim, e.g. exchanging information. These mutual expectations allow hearers to make certain inferences about what the speaker intended to communicate, which in turn allows speakers reasonably to expect hearers to make such inferences. In general, Grice holds, participants of a conversation 'will be expected (ceteris paribus) to observe' what he calls the 'Cooperative Principle' (CP): 'Make your conversational contribution such as is required at the stage at which it occurs, by the accepted purpose or direction of the talk exchange in which you are engaged' (p. 369–70). Grice goes on to describe in more detail what observing the CP involves, by listing four 'maxims', the maxims of Quantity, Quality, Relation and Manner. Grice claims that the basis for expecting the CP to be observed is a general expectation that people will act in instrumentally rational ways: 'anyone who cares about the goals that are central to conversation/communication (such as giving and receiving information, influencing and being influenced by others) must be expected to have an interest, given suitable circumstances, in participation in talk exchanges that will be profitable only on the assumption that they are conducted in general accordance with the CP' (p. 372).

Grice characterizes conversational implicatures by recourse to the CP: a speaker S conversationally implicates that q in saying p, just if

(1) S is to be presumed to be observing the CP,
(2) S's saying that p is consistent with the presumption in (1) only if S is aware that or thinks that q, and
(3) S thinks (and would expect the audience to think that S thinks) that it is within the competence of the audience to work out (2). (pp. 372–3)

This gives rise to a general pattern of deriving implicatures from what a speaker has said. Grice spends much of the remainder of the article illustrating his thesis with a wide range of examples.

Robyn Carston's article was published 35 years after Grice's. It can't be denied that Carston, like many contemporary linguists and pragmaticists, builds on Grice's work. For example, she, like many others, accepts a distinction that roughly corresponds to Grice's distinction between what is said and what is implicated. However, she is also critical of several aspects of Grice's article. According to Carston, the theory of implicature should be viewed as part of cognitive science, i.e. as providing a model of the mental processes of communication. She thinks that taking this task seriously will lead us to reject some of Grice's views.

Grice is clearly committed to the view that the derivation of implicatures is a personal, rather than a sub-personal mental process. Carston and other relevance theorists deny this. According to them, implicature derivation is a sub-personal, i.e. unconscious and automatic, process.

According to Grice, what is said by an utterance (a) is a proposition, (b) is determined by the semantics (the conventional meaning) of the linguistic types used, and (c) figures as the input into a pragmatic process of deriving any implicatures the utterance may have. Carston, along with other contextualists, believes that there is nothing that fulfils (a), (b) and (c). Belief that nothing meets all three characteristics postulated for what is said has led to terminological uncertainty.[2] But whatever the terminology, merely 'decoding' the linguistic form (even after disambiguating and assigning referents to indexicals) does not, according to Carston, yield a complete proposition. A second step, taken by many contextualists, is to argue that what is said (in the sense of the input to the process of implicature derivation, or the semantic content) involves so-called 'unarticulated constituents'.[3]

Many contemporary pragmaticists preserve Grice's idea that utterances have an explicit semantic content, and that this explicit content serves as the input to a separate pragmatic system, which derives implicit contents (implicatures). There is a temporal succession: first, the explicit semantic content is worked out from the linguistic meaning of the words used, and possibly bringing to bear 'free enrichment' in order to work out any unarticulated constituents of the explicit semantic content. Implicature derivation takes place, in a separate and different process, *after* explicit semantic contents have already been derived. Carston denies this. According to her, there is a single system which 'takes decoded linguistic meaning as its input and delivers the propositions communicated (explicatures and implicatures)' (p. 389).

---

[2] Recanati (2001, 2004 – though no longer in his 2007) accepts (a) and (c) as definitive of what is said, while Bach (1994, 2001) regards (b) and (c) as essential.

[3] This is a debate on which it would have been worth including a part in this book in its own right. See for example Perry 1986, Recanati 2002, 2004 (in favour of unarticulated constituents) and Stanley 2000, 2002, and Stanley and Szabó 2000 (against). Minimalists like Borg 2004 and Cappelen and Lepore 2005 also deny the existence of unarticulated constituents.

Questions and tasks

1   If I utter 'My car looks like a Porsche', and in fact my car *is* a Porsche, then my utterance seems intuitively incorrect. Someone might argue that this shows that what I have said entails that my car is not a Porsche. Use Grice's theory to undermine this argument.

2   The last sentence of Grice's article claims that sometimes implicatures are disjunctions of several potentially implicated propositions, each of which would explain why the speaker said what he or she said. Go through Grice's examples and find two cases where this applies.

3   Examine how exactly Grice introduces his notion of 'what is said'. Do his remarks succeed in defining what is said?

4   What are 'generalized conversational implicatures' and how do they differ from conventional implicatures?

5   Consider how Grice's theory might be used to support Russell's theory of descriptions (Part Three above). (You can either rely on your own ingenuity or get some inspiration from, for example, ch. 17 of Grice 1989 or Neale 1990.)

6   Is Grice committed to the thesis that implicature derivation is a personal, rather than a sub-personal process?

7   How does Carston support her thesis that there is a single, sub-personal pragmatic processor which takes subpropositional meanings as input and explicit contents as well as implicatures as output? Does her view still allow for a distinction between explicit semantic contents and implicatures?

References and further reading

Bach, Kent 1994: 'Conversational Impliciture', *Mind & Language* 9, pp. 124–62.

Bach, Kent 2001: 'You Don't Say?', *Synthese* 128, pp. 15–44.

Borg, Emma 2004: *Minimal Semantics*. Oxford: Clarendon Press.

Cappelen, Herman, and Ernie Lepore 2005: *Insensitive Semantics: A Defense of Semantic Minimalism and Speech Act Pluralism*. Oxford: Blackwell.

Grice, H. P. 1989: *Studies in the Way of Words*, Cambridge, MA: Harvard University Press.

Jackson, F. 1987: *Conditionals*, Cambridge: Cambridge University Press.

Larson, Richard, and Segal, Gabriel 1995: *Knowledge of Meaning*, Cambridge, MA: MIT Press.

Neale, Stephen 1990: *Descriptions*, Cambridge, MA: MIT Press.

Perry, John 1986: 'Thought without Representation', *Proceedings of the Aristotelean Society Supplementary Volume* 60, pp. 137–52.

Recanati, François 2001: 'What Is Said', *Synthese* 128, pp. 75–91.

Recanati, François 2002: 'Unarticulated Constitutents', *Linguistics and Philosophy* 25, pp. 299–345.

Recanati, François 2004: *Literal Meaning*, Cambridge: Cambridge University Press.

Recanati, François 2007: *Moderate Relativism*, Oxford: Oxford University Press.

Sainsbury, Mark 2001: *Logical Forms* (especially ch. 2, §§5–8), Oxford: Blackwell.

Saul, Jenny 2002: What Is Said and Psychological Reality: Grice's Project and Relevance Theorists' Criticisms, *Linguistics and Philosophy* 25, pp. 347–72.

Sperber, Dan, and Deirdre Wilson 1995 [1986]: *Relevance: Communication and Cognition*, 2nd edn, Oxford: Blackwell.

Stanley, Jason 2000: 'Context and Logical Form', *Linguistics and Philosophy* 23, pp. 391–434.

Stanley, Jason 2002: 'Making It Articulated'. *Mind & Language* 17, pp. 149–68.

Stanley, Jason, and Zoltán Szabó 2000: 'On Quantifier Domain Restriction', *Mind & Language* 15, pp. 219–61.

Chapter 23

H. Paul Grice

LOGIC AND CONVERSATION

It is a commonplace of philosophical logic that there are, or appear to be, divergences in meaning between, on the one hand, at least some of what I shall call the formal devices— ~, ∧, ∨, ⊃, (∀x), (∃x), (ιx) (when these are given a standard two-valued interpretation)—and, on the other, what are taken to be their analogues or counterparts in natural language—such expressions as *not, and, or, if, all, some* (or *at least one*), *the*. Some logicians may at some time have wanted to claim that there are in fact no such divergences; but such claims, if made at all, have been somewhat rashly made, and those suspected of making them have been subjected to some pretty rough handling.

Those who concede that such divergences exist adhere, in the main, to one or the other of two rival groups, which I shall call the formalist and the informalist groups. An outline of a not uncharacteristic formalist position may be given as follows: Insofar as logicians are concerned with the formulation of very general patterns of valid inference, the formal devices possess a decisive advantage over their natural counterparts. For it will be possible to construct in terms of the formal devices a system of very general formulas, a considerable number of which can be regarded as, or are closely related to, patterns of inferences the expression of which involves some or all of the devices: Such a system may consist of a certain set of simple formulas that must be acceptable if the devices have the

meaning that has been assigned to them, and an indefinite number of further formulas, many of which are less obviously acceptable and each of which can be shown to be acceptable if the members of the original set are acceptable. We have, thus, a way of handling dubiously acceptable patterns of inference, and if, as is sometimes possible, we can apply a decision procedure, we have an even better way. Furthermore, from a philosophical point of view, the possession by the natural counterparts of those elements in their meaning, which they do not share with the corresponding formal devices, is to be regarded as an imperfection of natural languages; the elements in question are undesirable excrescences. For the presence of these elements has the result both that the concepts within which they appear cannot be precisely or clearly defined, and that at least some statements involving them cannot, in some circumstances, be assigned a definite truth value; and the indefiniteness of these concepts not only is objectionable in itself but also leaves open the way to metaphysics—we cannot be certain that none of these natural language expressions is metaphysically "loaded." For these reasons, the expressions, as used in natural speech, cannot be regarded as finally acceptable, and may turn out to be, finally, not fully intelligible. The proper course is to conceive and begin to construct an ideal language, incorporating the formal devices, the sentences of which will be clear, determinate in truth value, and certifiably free from meta-physical implications; the foundations of science will now be philosophically secure, since the statements of the scientist will be expressible (though not necessarily actually expressed) within this ideal language. (I do not wish to suggest that all formalists would accept the whole of this outline, but I think that all would accept at least some part of it.)

To this, an informalist might reply in the following vein. The philosophical demand for an ideal language rests on certain assumptions that should not be conceded; these are, that the primary yardstick by which to judge the adequacy of a language is its ability to serve the needs of science, that an expression cannot be guaranteed as fully intelligible unless an explication or analysis of its meaning has been provided, and that every explication or analysis must take the form of a precise definition that is the expression or assertion of a logical equivalence. Language serves many important purposes besides those of scientific inquiry; we can know perfectly well what an expression means (and so a fortiori that it is intelligible) without knowing its analysis, and the provision of an analysis may (and usually does) consist in the specification, as generalized as possible, of the conditions that count for or against the applicability of the expression being analyzed. Moreover, while it is no doubt true that the formal devices are especially amenable to sys-tematic treatment by the logician, it remains the case that there are very many inferences and arguments, expressed in natural language and not in terms of these devices, which are never-theless recognizably valid. So there must be a place for an unsimplified, and so more or less unsystematic, logic of the natural counterparts of these devices; this logic may be aided and guided by the simplified logic of the formal devices but cannot be supplanted by it. Indeed, not only do the two logics differ, but sometimes they come into conflict; rules that hold for a formal device may not hold for its natural counterpart.

On the general question of the place in phil-osophy of the reformation of natural language, I shall, in this essay, have nothing to say. I shall confine myself to the dispute in its relation to the alleged divergences. I have, moreover, no intention of entering the fray on behalf of either contestant. I wish, rather, to maintain that the common assumption of the contestants that the divergences do in fact exist is (broadly speaking) a common mistake, and that the mistake arises from inadequate attention to the nature and importance of the conditions governing conver-sation. I shall, therefore, inquire into the general conditions that, in one way or another, apply to conversation as such, irrespective of its subject matter. I begin with a characterization of the notion of "implicature."

Implicature

Suppose that A and B are talking about a mutual friend, C, who is now working in a bank. A asks B how C is getting on in his job, and B replies, *Oh quite well, I think; he likes his colleagues, and he hasn't been to prison yet*. At this point, A might well inquire what B was implying, what he was suggesting, or even what he meant by saying that C had not yet been to prison. The answer might be any one of such things as that C is the sort of person likely to yield to the temptation provided by his occupation, that C's colleagues are really very unpleasant and treacherous people, and so forth. It might, of course, be quite unnecessary for A to make such an inquiry of B, the answer to it being, in the context, clear in advance. It is clear that whatever B implied, suggested, meant in this example, is distinct from what B said, which was simply that C had not been to prison yet. I wish to introduce, as terms of art, the verb *implicate* and the related nouns *implicature* (cf. *implying*) and *implicatum* (cf. *what is implied*). The point of this maneuver is to avoid having, on each occasion, to choose between this or that member of the family of verbs for which *implicate* is to do general duty. I shall, for the time being at least, have to assume to a considerable extent an intuitive understanding of the meaning of *say* in such contexts, and an ability to recognize particular verbs as members of the family with which *implicate* is associated. I can, however, make one or two remarks that may help to clarify the more problematic of these assumptions, namely, that connected with the meaning of the word *say*.

In the sense in which I am using the word *say*, I intend what someone has said to be closely related to the conventional meaning of the words (the sentence) he has uttered. Suppose someone to have uttered the sentence *He is in the grip of a vice*. Given a knowledge of the English language, but no knowledge of the circumstances of the utterance, one would know something about what the speaker had said, on the assumption that he was speaking standard English, and speaking literally. One would know that he had said, about some particular male person or animal x, that at the time of the utterance (whatever that was), either (1) x was unable to rid himself of a certain kind of bad character trait or (2) some part of x's person was caught in a certain kind of tool or instrument (approximate account, of course). But for a full identification of what the speaker had said, one would need to know (a) the identity of x, (b) the time of utterance, and (c) the meaning, on the particular occasion of utterance, of the phrase *in the grip of a vice* [a decision between (1) and (2)]. This brief indication of my use of *say* leaves it open whether a man who says (today) *Harold Wilson is a great man* and another who says (also today) *The British Prime Minister is a great man* would, if each knew that the two singular terms had the same reference, have said the same thing. But whatever decision is made about this question, the apparatus that I am about to provide will be capable of accounting for any implicatures that might depend on the presence of one rather than another of these singular terms in the sentence uttered. Such implicatures would merely be related to different maxims.

In some cases the conventional meaning of the words used will determine what is implicated, besides helping to determine what is said. If I say (smugly), *He is an Englishman; he is, therefore, brave*, I have certainly committed myself, by virtue of the meaning of my words, to its being the case that his being brave is a consequence of (follows from) his being an Englishman. But while I have said that he is an Englishman, and said that he is brave, I do not want to say that I have *said* (in the favored sense) that it follows from his being an Englishman that he is brave, though I have certainly indicated, and so implicated, that this is so. I do not want to say that my utterance of this sentence would be, *strictly speaking*, false should the consequence in question fail to hold. So *some* implicatures are conventional, unlike the one with which I introduced this discussion of implicature.

I wish to represent a certain subclass of nonconventional implicatures, which I shall call *conversational* implicatures, as being essentially connected with certain general features of discourse; so my next step is to try to say what these features are. The following may provide a first approximation to a general principle. Our talk exchanges do not normally consist of a succession of disconnected remarks, and would not be rational if they did. They are characteristically, to some degree at least, cooperative efforts; and each participant recognizes in them, to some extent, a common purpose or set of purposes, or at least a mutually accepted direction. This purpose of direction may be fixed from the start (e.g., by an initial proposal of a question for discussion), or it may evolve during the exchange; it may be fairly definite, or it may be so indefinite as to leave very considerable latitude to the participants (as in a casual conversation). But at each stage, *some* possible conversational moves would be excluded as conversationally unsuitable. We might then formulate a rough general principle which participants will be expected (ceteris paribus) to observe, namely: Make your conversational contribution such as is required, at the stage at which it occurs, by the accepted purpose or direction of the talk exchange in which you are engaged. One might label this the Cooperative Principle.

On the assumption that some such general principle as this is acceptable, one may perhaps distinguish four categories under one or another of which will fall certain more specific maxims and submaxims, the following of which will, in general, yield results in accordance with the Cooperative Principle. Echoing Kant, I call these categories Quantity, Quality, Relation, and Manner. The category of Quantity relates to the quantity of information to be provided, and under it fall the following maxims:

1. Make your contribution as informative as is required (for the current purposes of the exchange).
2. Do not make your contribution more informative than is required.

(The second maxim is disputable; it might be said that to be over-informative is not a transgression of the Cooperative Principle but merely a waste of time. However, it might be answered that such overinformativeness may be confusing in that it is liable to raise side issues; and there may also be an indirect effect, in that the hearers may be misled as a result of thinking that there is some particular *point* in the provision of the excess of information. However this may be, there is perhaps a different reason for doubt about the admission of this second maxim, namely, that its effect will be secured by a later maxim, which concerns relevance.)

Under the category of Quality falls a supermaxim—"Try to make your contribution one that is true"—and two more specific maxims:

1. Do not say what you believe to be false.
2. Do not say that for which you lack adequate evidence.

Under the category of Relation I place a single maxim, namely, "Be relevant." Though the

maxim itself is terse, its formulation conceals a number of problems that exercise me a good deal: questions about what different kinds and focuses of relevance there may be, how these shift in the course of a talk exchange, how to allow for the fact that subjects of conversation are legitimately changed, and so on. I find the treatment of such questions exceedingly difficult, and I hope to revert to them in later work.

Finally, under the category of Manner, which I understand as relating not (like the previous categories) to what is said but, rather, to *how* what is said is to be said, I include the supermaxim—"Be perspicuous"—and various maxims such as:

1. Avoid obscurity of expression.
2. Avoid ambiguity.
3. Be brief (avoid unnecessary prolixity).
4. Be orderly.

And one might need others.

It is obvious that the observance of some of these maxims is a matter of less urgency than is the observance of others; a man who has expressed himself with undue prolixity would, in general, be open to milder comment than would a man who has said something he believes to be false. Indeed, it might be felt that the importance of at least the first maxim of Quality is such that it should not be included in a scheme of the kind I am constructing; other maxims come into operation only on the assumption that this maxim of Quality is satisfied. While this may be correct, so far as the generation of implicatures is concerned it seems to play a role not totally different from the other maxims, and it will be convenient, for the present at least, to treat it as a member of the list of maxims.

There are, of course, all sorts of other maxims (aesthetic, social, or moral in character), such as "Be polite," that are also normally observed by participants in talk exchanges, and these may also generate nonconventional implicatures. The conversational maxims, however, and the conversational implicatures connected with them, are specially connected (I hope) with the particular purposes that talk (and so, talk exchange) is adapted to serve and is primarily employed to serve. I have stated my maxims as if this purpose were a maximally effective exchange of information; this specification is, of course, too narrow, and the scheme needs to be generalized to allow for such general purposes as influencing or directing the actions of others.

As one of my avowed aims is to see talking as a special case or variety of purposive, indeed rational, behavior, it may be worth noting that the specific expectations or presumptions connected with at least some of the foregoing maxims have their analogues in the sphere of transactions that are not talk exchanges. I list briefly one such analogue for each conversational category.

1.   *Quantity.* If you are assisting me to mend a car, I expect your contribution to be neither more nor less than is required. If, for example, at a particular stage I need four screws, I expect you to hand me four, rather than two or six.

2.   *Quality.* I expect your contributions to be genuine and not spurious. If I need sugar as an ingredient in the cake you are assisting me to make, I do not expect you to hand me salt; if I need a spoon, I do not expect a trick spoon made of rubber.

3.   *Relation.* I expect a partner's contribution to be appropriate to the immediate needs at each stage of the transaction. If I am mixing ingredients for a cake, I do not expect to be handed a good book, or even an oven cloth (though this might be an appropriate contribution at a later stage).

4.   *Manner.* I expect a partner to make it clear what contribution he is making and to execute his performance with reasonable dispatch.

These analogies are relevant to what I regard as a fundamental question about the Cooperative Principle and its attendant maxims, namely, what the basis is for the assumption which we seem to make, and on which (I hope) it will appear that a great range of implicatures depends, that talkers will in general (ceteris paribus and in the absence of indications to the contrary) proceed in the manner that these principles prescribe. A dull but, no doubt at a certain level, adequate answer is that it is just a well-recognized empirical fact that people do behave in these ways; they learned to do so in childhood and have not lost the habit of doing so; and, indeed, it would involve a good deal of effort to make a radical departure from the habit. It is much easier, for example, to tell the truth than to invent lies.

I am, however, enough of a rationalist to want to find a basis that underlies these facts, undeniable though they may be; I would like to be able to think of the standard type of conversational practice not merely as something that all or most do in fact follow but as something that it is *reasonable* for us to follow, that we *should not* abandon. For a time, I was attracted by the idea that observance of the Cooperative Principle and the maxims, in a talk exchange, could be thought of as a quasi-contractual matter, with parallels outside the realm of discourse. If you pass by when I am struggling with my stranded car, I no doubt have some degree of expectation that you will offer help, but once you join me in tinkering under the hood, my expectations become stronger and take more specific forms (in the absence of indications that you are merely an incompetent meddler); and talk exchanges seemed to me to exhibit, characteristically, certain features that jointly distinguish cooperative transactions:

1.   The participants have some common immediate aim, like getting a car mended; their ultimate aims may, of course, be independent and even in conflict—each may want to get the car mended in order to

drive off, leaving the other stranded. In characteristic talk exchanges, there is a common aim even if, as in an over-the-wall chat, it is a second-order one, namely, that each party should, for the time being, identify himself with the transitory conversational interests of the other.

2.   The contributions of the participants should be dovetailed, mutually dependent.

3.   There is some sort of understanding (which may be explicit but which is often tacit) that, other things being equal, the transaction should continue in appropriate style unless both parties are agreeable that it should terminate. You do not just shove off or start doing something else.

But while some such quasi-contractual basis as this may apply to some cases, there are too many types of exchange, like quarreling and letter writing, that it fails to fit comfortably. In any case, one feels that the talker who is irrelevant or obscure has primarily let down not his audience but himself. So I would like to be able to show that observance of the Cooperative Principle and maxims is reasonable (rational) along the following lines: that anyone who cares about the goals that are central to conversation/communication (such as giving and receiving information, influencing and being influenced by others) must be expected to have an interest, given suitable circumstances, in participation in talk exchanges that will be profitable only on the assumption that they are conducted in general accordance with the Cooperative Principle and the maxims. Whether any such conclusion can be reached, I am uncertain; in any case, I am fairly sure that I cannot reach it until I am a good deal clearer about the nature of relevance and of the circumstances in which it is required.

It is now time to show the connection between the Cooperative Principle and maxims, on the one hand, and conversational implicature on the other.

A participant in a talk exchange may fail to fulfill a maxim in various ways, which include the following:

1.   He may quietly and unostentatiously *violate* a maxim; if so, in some cases he will be liable to mislead.

2.   He may *opt out* from the operation both of the maxim and of the Cooperative Principle; he may say, indicate, or allow it to become plain that he is unwilling to cooperate in the way the maxim requires. He may say, for example, *I cannot say more; my lips are sealed.*

3.   He may be faced by a *clash*: He may be unable, for example, to fulfill the first maxim of Quantity (Be as informative as is required) without violating the second maxim of Quality (Have adequate evidence for what you say).

4.   He may *flout* a maxim; that is, he may blatantly fail to fulfill it. On the assumption that the speaker is able to fulfill the maxim and to do so without violating another maxim (because of a clash), is not opting out, and is not, in view of the blatancy of his performance, trying to mislead, the hearer is faced with a minor problem: How can his saying what he did say be reconciled with the supposition that he is observing the overall Cooperative Principle? This situation is one that characteristically gives rise to a conversational implicature; and when a conversational implicature is generated in this way, I shall say that a maxim is being *exploited*.

I am now in a position to characterize the notion of conversational implicature. A man who, by (in, when) saying (or making as if to say) that p has implicated that q, may be said to have conversationally implicated that q, provided that (1) he is to be presumed to be observing the conversational maxims, or at least the Cooperative Principle; (2) the supposition that he is aware that, or thinks that, q is required in order to make his saying or making as if to say p (or doing so in *those* terms) consistent with this presumption; and (3) the speaker thinks (and would expect the hearer to think that the speaker thinks) that it is within the competence of the hearer to work out, or grasp intuitively, that the supposition mentioned in (2) is required. Apply this to my initial example, to B's remark that C has not yet been to prison. In a suitable setting A might reason as follows: "(1) B has apparently violated the maxim 'Be relevant' and so may be regarded as having flouted one of the maxims conjoining perspicuity, yet I have no reason to suppose that he is opting out from the operation of the Cooperative Principle; (2) given the circumstances, I can regard his irrelevance as only apparent if, and only if, I suppose him to think that C is potentially dishonest; (3) B knows that I am capable of working out step (2). So B implicates that C is potentially dishonest."

The presence of a conversational implicature must be capable of being worked out; for even if it can in fact be intuitively grasped, unless the intuition is replaceable by an argument, the implicature (if present at all) will not count as a conversational implicature; it will be a conventional implicature. To work out that a particular conversational implicature is present, the hearer will rely on the following data: (1) the conventional meaning of the words used, together with the identity of any references that may be involved; (2) the Cooperative Principle and its maxims; (3) the context, linguistic or otherwise, of the utterance; (4) other items of background knowledge; and (5) the fact (or supposed fact) that all relevant items falling under the previous headings are available to both participants and both participants know or assume this to be the case. A general pattern for the working out of a conversational implicature might be given as follows: "He has said that p; there is no reason to suppose that he is not observing the maxims, or at least the Cooperative Principle; he could not be doing this unless he thought that q; he knows (and knows that I know

that he knows) that I can see that the supposition that he thinks that q is required; he has done nothing to stop me thinking that q; he intends me to think, or is at least willing to allow me to think, that q; and so he has implicated that q."

Examples of conversational implicature

I shall now offer a number of examples, which I shall divide into three groups.

GROUP A: Examples in which no maxim is violated, or at least in which it is not clear that any maxim is violated

A is standing by an obviously immobilized car and is approached by B; the following exchange takes place:

(1) A: *I am out of petrol.*
     B: *There is a garage round the corner.*

(Gloss: B would be infringing the maxim "Be relevant" unless he thinks, or thinks it possible, that the garage is open, and has petrol to sell; so he implicates that the garage is, or at least may be open, etc.)

In this example, unlike the case of the remark *He hasn't been to prison yet*, the unstated connection between B's remark and A's remark is so obvious that, even if one interprets the supermaxim of Manner, "Be perspicuous," as applying not only to the expression of what is said but also to the connection of what is said with adjacent remarks, there seems to be no case for regarding that supermaxim as infringed in this example. The next example is perhaps a little less clear in this respect:

(2) A: *Smith doesn't seem to have a girlfriend these days.*
     B: *He has been paying a lot of visits to New York lately.*

B implicates that Smith has, or may have, a

girlfriend in New York. (A gloss is unnecessary in view of that given for the previous example.)

In both examples, the speaker implicates that which he must be assumed to believe in order to preserve the assumption that he is observing the maxim of Relation.

GROUP B: Examples in which a maxim is violated, but its violation is to be explained by the supposition of a clash with another maxim

A is planning with B an itinerary for a holiday in France. Both know that A wants to see his friend C, if to do so would not involve too great a prolongation of his journey:

(3)   A: *Where does C live?*
       B: *Somewhere in the South of France.*

(Gloss: There is no reason to suppose that B is opting out; his answer is, as he well knows, less informative than is required to meet A's needs. This infringement of the first maxim of Quantity can be explained only by the supposition that B is aware that to be more informative would be to say something that infringed the second maxim of Quality. "Don't say what you lack adequate evidence for," so B implicates that he does not know in which town C lives.)

GROUP C: Examples that involve exploitation, that is, a procedure by which a maxim is flouted for the purpose of getting in a conversational implicature by means of something of the nature of a figure of speech

In these examples, though some maxim is violated at the level of what is said, the hearer is entitled to assume that that maxim, or at least the overall Cooperative Principle, is observed at the level of what is implicated.

(1a) A flouting of the first maxim of Quantity

A is writing a testimonial about a pupil who is a candidate for a philosophy job, and his letter reads as follows: "Dear Sir, Mr. X's command of English is excellent, and his attendance at tutor-ials has been regular. Yours, etc." (Gloss: A cannot be opting out, since if he wished to be uncooperative, why write at all? He cannot be unable, through ignorance, to say more, since the man is his pupil; moreover, he knows that more information than this is wanted. He must, therefore, be wishing to impart information that he is reluctant to write down. This supposition is tenable only if he thinks Mr. X is no good at philosophy. This, then, is what he is implicating.)

Extreme examples of a flouting of the first maxim of Quantity are provided by utterances of patent tautologies like *Women are women* and *War is war*. I would wish to maintain that at the level of what is said, in my favored sense, such remarks are totally noninformative and so, at the level, cannot but infringe the first maxim of Quantity in any conversational context. They are, of course, informative at the level of what is implicated, and the hearer's identification of their informative content at this level is dependent on his ability to explain the speaker's selection of this particular patent tautology.

(1b) An infringement of the second maxim of Quantity. "Do not give more information than is required," on the assumption that the existence of such a maxim should be admitted

A wants to know whether p, and B volunteers not only the information that p, but information to the effect that it is certain that p, and that the evidence for its being the case that p is so-and-so and such-and-such.

B's volubility may be undesigned, and if it is so regarded by A it may raise in A's mind a doubt as to whether B is as certain as he says he is ("Methinks the lady doth protest too much"). But if it is thought of as designed, it would be an oblique way of conveying that it is to some degree controversial whether or not p. It is, how-ever, arguable that such an implicature could be explained by reference to the maxim of Relation without invoking an alleged second maxim of Quantity.

(2a) Examples in which the first maxim of Quality is flouted

Irony. X, with whom A has been on close terms until now, has betrayed a secret of A's to a business rival. A and his audience both know this. A says *X is a fine friend*. (Gloss: It is perfectly obvious to A and his audience that what A has said or has made as if to say is something he does not believe, and the audience knows that A knows that this is obvious to the audience. So, unless A's utterance is entirely pointless, A must be trying to get across some other proposition than the one he purports to be putting forward. This must be some obviously related proposition; the most obviously related proposition is the contradictory of the one he purports to be putting forward.)

Metaphor. Examples like *You are the cream in my coffee* characteristically involve categorial falsity, so the contradictory of what the speaker has made as if to say will, strictly speaking, be a truism; so it cannot be *that* that such a speaker is trying to get across. The most likely supposition is that the speaker is attributing to his audience some feature or features in respect of which the audience resembles (more or less fancifully) the mentioned substance.

It is possible to combine metaphor and irony by imposing on the hearer two stages of interpretation. I say *You are the cream in my coffee*, intending the hearer to reach first the metaphor interpretant "You are my pride and joy" and then the irony interpretant "You are my bane."

Meiosis. Of a man known to have broken up all the furniture, one says *He was a little intoxicated.*

Hyperbole. Every nice girl loves a sailor.

(2b) Examples in which the second maxim of Quality, "Do not say that for which you lack adequate evidence," is flouted are perhaps not easy to find, but the following seems to be a specimen. I say of X's wife, *She is probably deceiving him this evening*. In a suitable context, or with a suitable gesture or tone of voice, it may be clear that I have no adequate reason for supposing this to be the case. My partner, to preserve the assumption that the conversational game is still being played, assumes that I am getting at some related proposition for the acceptance of which I do have a reasonable basis. The related proposition might well be that she is given to deceiving her husband, or possibly that she is the sort of person who would not stop short of such conduct.

(3) Examples in which an implicature is achieved by real, as distinct from apparent, violation of the maxim of Relation are perhaps rare, but the following seems to be a good candidate. At a genteel tea party, A says Mrs. X is an old bag. There is a moment of appalled silence, and then B says The weather has been quite delightful this summer, hasn't it? B has blatantly refused to make what he says relevant to A's preceding remark. He thereby implicates that A's remark should not be discussed and, perhaps more specifically, that A has committed a social gaffe.

(4) Examples in which various maxims falling under the supermaxim "Be perspicuous" are flouted

Ambiguity. We must remember that we are concerned only with ambiguity that is deliberate, and that the speaker intends or expects to be recognized by his hearer. The problem the hearer has to solve is why a speaker should, when still playing the conversational game, go out of his way to choose an ambiguous utterance. There are two types of cases:

(a) Examples in which there is no difference, or no striking difference, between two interpretations of an utterance with respect to straightforwardness; neither interpretation is notably more sophisticated, less standard, more recondite or more far-fetched than the other. We might consider Blake's lines: "Never seek to tell thy love, Love that never told can be." To avoid the complications introduced by the presence of the imperative mood, I shall consider the related sentence, *I sought to tell my love, love that never told can be*. There may be a double ambiguity here. *My love* may refer to either a state of emotion or an object of emotion, and *love that never told can be* may mean either "Love that cannot be told" or "love that if told cannot continue to exist." Partly because of the sophistication of the poet and partly because of internal evidence (that the ambiguity is kept up), there seems to be no alternative to supposing that the ambiguities are deliberate and that the poet is conveying both what he would be saying if one interpretation were intended rather than the other, and vice versa; though no doubt the poet is not explicitly saying any one of these things but only conveying or suggesting them (cf. "Since she [nature] pricked thee out for women's pleasure, mine be thy love, and thy love's use their treasure").

(b) Examples in which one interpretation is notably less straightforward than another. Take the complex example of the British General who captured the province of Sind and sent back the message *Peccavi*. The ambiguity involved ("I have Sind"/"I have sinned") is phonemic, not morphemic; and the expression actually used is unambiguous, but since it is in a language foreign to speaker and hearer, translation is called for, and the ambiguity resides in the standard translation into native English.

Whether or not the straightforward interpretant ("I have sinned") is being conveyed, it seems that the nonstraightforward interpretant must be. There might be stylistic reasons for conveying by a sentence merely its nonstraightforward interpretant, but it would be pointless, and perhaps also stylistically objectionable, to go to the trouble of finding an expression that nonstraightforwardly conveys that *p*, thus imposing on an audience the effort involved in finding this interpretant, if this interpretant were otiose so far as communication was concerned. Whether the straightforward interpretant is also being conveyed seems to depend on whether such a supposition would conflict with other conversational requirements, for example, would it be relevant, would it be something the speaker could be supposed to accept, and so on. If such requirements are not satisfied, then the straight-

forward interpretant is not being conveyed. If they are, it is. If the author of *Peccavi* could naturally be supposed to think that he had committed some kind of transgression, for example, had disobeyed his orders in capturing Sind, and if reference to such a transgression would be relevant to the presumed interests of the audience, then he would have been conveying both interpretants: otherwise he would be conveying only the nonstraightforward one.

Obscurity. How do I exploit, for the purposes of communication, a deliberate and overt violation of the requirement that I should avoid obscurity? Obviously, if the Cooperative Principle is to operate, I must intend my partner to understand what I am saying despite the obscurity I import into my utterance. Suppose that A and B are having a conversation in the presence of a third party, for example, a child, then A might be deliberately obscure, though not too obscure, in the hope that B would understand and the third party not. Furthermore, if A expects B to see that A is being deliberately obscure, it seems reasonable to suppose that, in making his conversational contribution in this way, A is implicating that the contents of his communication should not be imparted to the third party.

Failure to be brief or succinct. Compare the remarks:

(a)   Miss X sang "Home Sweet Home."
(b)   Miss X produced a series of sounds that corresponded closely with the score of "Home Sweet Home."

Suppose that a reviewer has chosen to utter (b) rather than (a). (Gloss: Why has he selected that rigmarole in place of the concise and nearly synonymous *sang*? Presumably, to indicate some striking difference between Miss X's performance and those to which the word *singing* is usually applied. The most obvious supposition is that Miss X's performance suffered from some hideous defect. The reviewer knows that this supposition is what is likely to spring to mind, so that is what he is implicating.)

Generalized conversational implicature

I have so far considered only cases of what I might call "particularized conversational implicature"—that is to say, cases in which an implicature is carried by saying that p on a particular occasion in virtue of special features of the context, cases in which there is no room for the idea that an implicature of this sort is normally carried by saying that p. But there are cases of generalized conversational implicature. Sometimes one can say that the use of a certain form of words in an utterance would normally (in the absence of special circumstances) carry such-and-such an implicature or type of implicature. Noncontroversial examples are perhaps hard to find, since it is all too easy to treat a generalized conversational implicature as if it were a conventional implicature. I offer an example that I hope may be fairly noncontroversial.

Anyone who uses a sentence of the form *X is meeting a woman this evening* would normally implicate that the person to be met was someone other than X's wife, mother, sister, or perhaps even close platonic friend. Similarly, if I were to say *X went into a house yesterday and found a tortoise inside the front door*, my hearer would normally be surprised if some time later I revealed that the house was X's own. I could produce similar linguistic phenomena involving the expressions *a garden, a car, a college*, and so on. Sometimes, however, there would normally be no such implicature ("I have been sitting in a car all morning"), and sometimes a reverse implicature ("I broke a finger yesterday"). I am inclined to think that one would not lend a sympathetic ear to a philosopher who suggested that there are three senses of the form of expression *an X*: one in which it means roughly "something that satisfies the conditions defining the word X," another in which it means approximately "an X (in the first sense) that is only remotely related in a certain way to some person indicated by the context," and yet another in which it means "an X (in the

first sense) that is closely related in a certain way to some person indicated by the context." Would we not much prefer an account on the following lines (which, of course, may be incorrect in detail): When someone, by using the form of expression *an X*, implicates that the X does not belong to or is not otherwise closely connected with some identifiable person, the implicature is present because the speaker has failed to be specific in a way in which he might have been expected to be specific, with the consequence that it is likely to be assumed that he is not in a position to be specific. This is a familiar implicature situation and is classifiable as a failure, for one reason or another, to fulfill the first maxim of Quantity. The only difficult question is why it should, in certain cases, be presumed, independently of information about particular contexts of utterance, that specification of the closeness or remoteness of the connection between a particular person or object and a further person who is mentioned or indicated by the utterance should be likely to be of interest. The answer must lie in the following region: Transactions between a person and other persons or things closely connected with him are liable to be very different as regards their concomitants and results from the same sort of transactions involving only remotely connected persons or things; the concomitants and results, for instance, of my finding a hole in my roof are likely to be very different from the concomitants and results of my finding a hole in someone else's roof. Information, like money, is often given without the giver's knowing to just what use the recipient will want to put it. If someone to whom a transaction is mentioned gives it further consideration, he is likely to find himself wanting the answers to further questions that the speaker may not be able to identify in advance; if the appropriate specification will be likely to enable the hearer to answer a considerable variety of such questions for himself, then there is a presumption that the speaker should include it in his remark; if not, then there is no such presumption.

Finally, we can now show that, conversational implicature being what it is, it must possess certain features:

1. Since, to assume the presence of a conversational implicature, we have to assume that at least the Cooperative Principle is being observed, and since it is possible to opt out of the observation of this principle, it follows that a generalized conversational implicature can be canceled in a particular case. It may be explicitly canceled, by the addition of a clause that states or implies that the speaker has opted out, or it may be contextually canceled, if the form of utterance that usually carries it is used in a context that makes it clear that the speaker is opting out.

2. Insofar as the calculation that a particular conversational implicature is present requires, besides contextual and background information, only a knowledge of what has been said (or of the conventional commitment of the utterance), and insofar as the manner of expression plays no role in the calculation, it will not be possible to find another way of saying the same thing, which simply lacks the implicature in question, except where some special feature of the substituted version is itself relevant to the determination of an implicature (in virtue of one of the maxims of Manner). If we call this feature nondetachability, one may expect a generalized conversational implicature that is carried by a familiar, nonspecial locution to have a high degree of nondetachability.

3. To speak approximately, since the calculation of the presence of a conversational implicature presupposes an initial knowledge of the conventional force of the expression the utterance of which carries the implicature, a conversational implicatum will be a condition that is not included in the original specification of the expression's conventional force. Though it may not be impossible for what starts life, so to speak, as a conversational implicature to become conventionalized, to suppose that this is so in a given case would require special justification. So, initially at least, conversational implicata are not part of the meaning of the expressions to the employment of which they attach.

4. Since the truth of a conversational implicatum is not required by the truth of what is said (what is said may be true—what is implicated may be false), the implicature is not carried by what is said, but only by the saying of what is said, or by "putting it that way."

5. Since, to calculate a conversational implicature is to calculate what has to be supposed in order to preserve the supposition that the Cooperative Principle is being observed, and since there may be various possible specific explanations, a list of which may be open, the conversational implicatum in such cases will be disjunction of such specific explanations; and if the list of these is open, the implicatum will have just the kind of indeterminacy that many actual implicata do in fact seem to possess.

Chapter 24

Robyn Carston

LINGUISTIC MEANING, COMMUNICATED MEANING AND COGNITIVE PRAGMATICS

1 Pragmatics as a cognitive system

1.1 From philosophy of language to cognitive science

Broadly speaking, there are two perspectives on pragmatics: the 'philosophical' and the 'cognitive'. From the philosophical perspective, an interest in pragmatics has been largely motivated by problems and issues in semantics. A familiar instance of this was Grice's concern to maintain a close semantic parallel between logical operators and their natural language counterparts, such as 'not', 'and', 'or', 'if', 'every', 'a/some', and 'the', in the face of what look like quite major divergences in the meaning of the linguistic elements (see Grice 1975, 1981). The explanation he provided was pragmatic, i.e. in terms of what occurs when the logical semantics of these terms is put to rational communicative use.

Consider the case of 'and':

(1) a. Mary went to a movie and Sam read a novel.
     b. She gave him her key and he opened the door.
     c. She insulted him and he left the room.

While (a) seems to reflect the straightforward truth-functional symmetrical connection, (b) and (c) communicate a stronger asymmetric relation: temporal sequence in (b) and a cause-consequence relation in (c). The semantic options for accounting for this are unappealing: either a three-way ambiguity (hence three lexical items 'and', only one of which is semantically identical with the logical conjunction operator), or a single item whose semantics is considerably richer than the logical operator, in that it includes temporal and causal features. However, we don't have to accept either of these. The Gricean approach maintains that the natural language connective is unambiguously truth-functional and explains the richer connections as a function of maxims concerning proper conversational practice; what the words 'say' (the semantics of the utterance) and what the speaker means diverge. So, in the case of (1c), for instance, 'what is said', or the proposition expressed, is a truth-functional conjunction while, on the basis of considerations of communicative informativeness and/or relevance, we infer that 'what the speaker meant' is that there is a cause-consequence relation between the conjuncts:

(2) what is said: P & Q
     what is meant: Q IS A CONSEQUENCE OF P

The role of pragmatics is essentially to siphon off any elements of understood meaning that might complicate the semantics and interfere with the hoped-for parallels between logic and natural language. The proposition meant is a conversational *implicature* and implicatures, which are the result of such extra-linguistic considerations as communicative appropriateness, have no bearing at all on the truth conditions of the utterance. Each of the 'and' conjunction cases in (1) is true provided just that each of the conjunct clauses is true.

On this view, the role of the communicative norms (truthfulness, informativeness, relevance, etc) is confined to the inferential derivation of implicatures; the central truth-conditional core of the utterance is given semantically. This Gricean implicature gambit has been widely employed by semanticists in order to defend a favoured semantic analysis of some natural language expression. For instance, Neale (1990) has preserved a Russellian quantificational semantics for definite descriptions by treating their apparent referentiality on particular uses as a case of conversational implicature. Others have claimed that the two sentences in (3) (with different but co-referring names) express the same proposition and are truth-conditionally equivalent, with the obvious difference between them being captured at the level of implicature (for discussion, with dissociation, see Recanati 1993, section 17.2):

(3) a. Lois Lane believes Superman is valiant.
     b. Lois Lane believes Clark Kent is valiant.

The advent of cognitive pragmatics, specifically of the relevance-theoretic approach, has brought a rather different orientation: 'pragmatics' is a capacity of the mind, a kind of information-processing system, a system for interpreting a particular phenomenon in the world, namely human communicative behaviour (see Sperber and Wilson (1986/95) and this volume). It is a proper object of study in itself, no longer to be seen as simply an adjunct to natural language semantics. Set within a cognitive-scientific framework, this kind of pragmatic theorising is answerable to quite dif-

ferent sources of evidence and criteria of adequacy from that of any philosophical analytical investigation. For instance, evidence from children's communicative development, from people with specific communicative and interpretive difficulties or deficits and from certain psycholinguistic experiments on comprehension may well have a bearing on an account of how the pragmatic system works, as may facts about the functioning and architecture of other mental capacities which interact with the utterance comprehension system, such as the language faculty and the so-called 'theory of mind' mechanism for interpreting people's behaviour in terms of certain of their mental states (beliefs, desires, intentions). Many of the papers in this issue [*Mind and Language* 17 (2002), No. 1 and 2] reflect the way in which these sorts of considerations bear on pragmatics (see, in particular, Bloom, Happé and Loth, Langdon, Davies and Coltheart, and Papafragou [all 2002]).

There are (at least) three possible stances on the domain of pragmatics and so on what sort of a cognitive system it is. In order of increasing specificity, these positions are that: (a) It is a system for interpreting human actions/behaviour in terms of the mental states (beliefs, intentions) underlying them (i.e. it is identical to the general 'theory of mind' system); (b) It is a system for the understanding of *communicative* behaviour, that is, for figuring out what the producer of the ostensive behaviour is trying to communicate; (c) It is dedicated to the understanding of specifically *linguistic* communicative behaviour. Obviously, no matter which of these one takes as the domain of pragmatics, linguistic communication is included, so there must be an interface with natural language semantics, but on this cognitively-oriented approach to pragmatics, natural language semantics is not taken to be the point of investigative departure. The relevance-theoretic account advocates the second position: the domain of pragmatics is a natural class of environmental phenomena, that of ostensive (= communicative) stimuli; verbal utterances are the central case, but not the only one, and they themselves are frequently accompanied by other ostensive gestures of the face, hands, voice, etc, all of which have to be interpreted together if one is to correctly infer what is being communicated. For the most part in this paper, I will focus on linguistic ostensive stimuli (i.e. utterances).

The move from the 'semantic adjunct' view to the 'cognitive system' view of relevance theory brings a range of changes with it. The components of the theory are quite different from those of Gricean and other philosophical descriptions; they include on-line cognitive processes, input and output representations, processing effort and cognitive effects (see Sperber and Wilson, 2002). The phenomenon of conversational implicature is no longer thought of as a 'useful tool for philosophical analysis', but rather as a representational level, derived in a particular way and playing a particular role in the process of understanding. The semantics of the linguistic expression type employed in an utterance, while clearly crucial to comprehension, is seen as having just an evidential, rather than a fully determining, role in the identification of what a speaker has explicitly communicated ('what is said'). This is most obvious in the case of subsentential utterances, which abound in actual communication. These are generally blatantly subpropositional, so have no determinate truth conditions as a matter of their intrinsic linguistic meaning (or even linguistic meaning topped up by contextual disambiguation and reference determination).

Consider the following very ordinary situation: it's breakfast time and, coming into the kitchen, I see my companion searching around in the lower reaches of a cupboard; knowing his breakfast habits, I guess that he's looking for a jar of marmalade and I utter:

(4)   On the top shelf.

Although the proposition I have expressed here is something like *The marmalade is on the top shelf*, the linguistic semantic input to the pragmatic processor is, arguably, just whatever meaning the language confers on that prepositional phrase, that is, a far from fully propositional logical form, one which consists of just a location constituent (which denotes a property).

Given that, on the particular cognitive conception of pragmatics adopted here, the content of a communicative intention may be inferred in the complete absence of any coded material (say, on the basis of just an ostensive facial or hand movement), it is not surprising that when a code is involved it need do no more than provide whatever clues, whatever piece of evidence, the speaker judges necessary to channel the inferential process in the right direction. The linguistically encoded element of an utterance is not generally geared towards achieving as high a degree of explicitness as possible, but rather towards keeping processing effort down (no more than is necessary for the recovery of the intended cognitive effects), so information that is clearly already highly activated in the addressee's mind ('*The marmalade* is here somewhere', for instance) is often not given linguistic expression.

In the next subsection, I outline a distinction between two kinds of explanation of mental activity, with a view to considering the kind appropriate for an account of pragmatics construed as a cognitive system as opposed to that more characteristic of philosophical accounts in the Gricean tradition.

1.2 Levels of explanation: the personal and the sub-personal

The distinction between the 'personal' and the 'sub-personal' levels of explanation of human behaviour was first introduced by Daniel Dennett (1969). Persons are conscious thinking agents, who engage in actions (voluntary behaviours) which can be explained in terms of reasons, that is, in terms of commonsense psychological attributions of beliefs, desires and practical inferences that would normally lead to such actions. A mundane example of such personal-level explanation is the following: X picked up her umbrella before she went out of doors because she believed it was going to rain and she wanted to stay dry. This Intentional (belief/desire) explanation makes her action reasonable or justified, makes it an intelligible behaviour. The hallmark of this sort of explanation is that it is normative, it is given in terms of what *ought* to be the case; we find someone intelligible as a person by interpreting her behaviour as embedded in a wider pattern of rational activity (see Elton 2000, p. 2). For instance, we might explain what a speaker meant by her utterance in terms of what it would be rational for her to have meant given the words she used in the particular context.

Sub-personal explanation, on the other hand, deals in entities and properties that can be shown to play a *causal role* in the action or behaviour, without necessarily standing in rational or normative relations to it. A physiological account in terms of the neuronal activity in the brain which accompanies the production, or the understanding, of an utterance would have nothing to do with considerations of people as agents with reasons and would be an obvious instance of a sub-personal explanation. However, if the current cognitive-scientific case for an autonomous level of unconscious syntactically-driven mental computation holds, there would seem to be another level of subpersonal explanation, a psychological level of information-processing mechanisms, which is, arguably, not reducible to the neurological (see Davies, 2000). Talk of the sub-personal level of description and explanation in this paper is directed solely at this assumed level of psychological mechanisms.

On the assumption that this is a distinction which has useful application to all areas of mental theorising (something that might be questioned), let us consider how it stands for the case of pragmatics. At which level is an account of utterance interpretation (to be) conducted, the personal or the sub-personal (or both)? Discussion of pragmatics within the philosophy of language is most often conducted at the level of the person (the hearer/interpreter as person reasoning about the speaker/actor as person). For instance, Recanati (2002a, p. 106) presents the Gricean view of pragmatics, one which he largely endorses, as follows: 'It [pragmatic interpretation] is not concerned with language per se, but with human action. When someone acts, whether linguistically or otherwise, there is a reason why she does what she does. To provide an interpretation for that action is to find that reason, that is, to ascribe the agent a particular intention in terms of which we can make sense of the action. . . . Pragmatic interpretation is possible only if we presuppose that the agent is *rational*. . . .' On this view of pragmatics, understanding an utterance is one instance of a more general personal-level activity of interpreting other people's purposeful behaviour: the hearer's interpretation of the speaker's linguistic behaviour rests on the assumption that the speaker is a rational agent acting in accordance with certain norms (truthfulness, an appropriate degree of informativeness, etc) and he attributes to her beliefs and intentions that provide reasons for her to have spoken as she did. The Gricean schema for figuring out a speaker's conversational implicature(s) from what he or she has said is a clear case of such personal-level practical belief/desire reasoning; it is conscious, rational and normative: 'He has said that p; there is no reason to suppose that he is not observing the maxims, or at least the CP [Cooperative Principle]; he could not be doing this unless he thought that q; he knows (and knows that I know that he knows) that I can see that the supposition that he thinks that q is required; he has done nothing to stop me thinking that q; he intends me to think, or is at least willing to allow me to think, that q; and so he has implicated that q' (Grice, 1975, p. 50).

The relevance-theoretic approach, on the

other hand, embedded as it is within the assumptions and methods of current cognitive science, aims at a causal mechanistic account, an account in terms of the processes of interacting sub-personal systems. In recent years, this orientation has become particularly clearly established with the proposal that the comprehension system is a mental *module*: it is fast and automatic, and, more crucial to the position, it is domain-specific, in that it is activated exclusively by ostensive stimuli and employs its own proprietary concepts and processing strategies and routines (see Sperber, 1994b and Sperber and Wilson, this volume). This move constitutes a leap across the Fodorian modular/nonmodular divide (Fodor, 1983, 2000). Fodor's persistent claim is that while input and output systems are domain-specific, encapsulated systems, that is, modules, the central conceptual systems are architecturally unstructured and holistic, that is, nonmodular. Alan Leslie and others are currently making the modularity claim for another central interpretive system, the 'theory of mind' mechanism (ToMM) (see, for instance, Scholl and Leslie, 1999, Leslie, 2000a, 2000b). The two systems are closely related (if not one and the same, as some have claimed): the theory of mind system interprets the behaviour of others by attributing to them such Intentional (that is, world-representing) mental states as beliefs, desires and intentions, and the pragmatic comprehension system interprets communicative behaviour in terms of an intention on the part of the speaker to bring about a certain belief state in the addressee. Currently, the idea is being developed that the latter is a sub-system of the former, that is, that the relevance-based comprehension module may be a sub-module of the more general mental-state attributing module (see Sperber, 2000 and Sperber and Wilson, this volume).

The explanatory vocabulary in these (sub-personal-level) accounts of how we interpret each other's behaviour (whether it is communicative or noncommunicative) includes the propositional attitude terminology ('intention', 'belief', etc) which is typical of explanation at the level of the person. In effect, the 'theory of mind' mechanism is an information-processing system which, in a presumably limited, unconscious and automatic way, computes interpretations which are a counterpart to conscious, rational and reflective personal-level explanations of human actions. Some of the mental states which might be cited as *reasons* for a particular action by a personal-level thinker, intent on making a person's behaviour intelligible, are given a sub-personal *causal* status in the workings of the 'theory of mind' mechanism. So, for instance, an explanation along the lines of 'he *believes* the bus is about to arrive, and he *wants* to get on it and . . .' for someone's behaviour of running towards a bus-stop might occur as part of a rationalising personal-level explanation or as an interpretive output of the theory of mind mechanism. Much the same convergence of personal-level explanation and output of a sub-personal mechanism appears to hold for utterance interpretation; a personal-level explanation might have the form 'her reason for saying that it is late is that she wants her addressee to believe that it is time to leave' and this might be matched in the sub-personal comprehension mechanism by an input representation, 'she has said it is late', and an output representation, 'she intends me to believe that (she wants me to believe that) it is time to leave' (see Sperber, 1994a for discussion of the multi-level metarepresentation here). Of course, the unconscious inferential processes internal to the modular mental systems, which mediate input and output representations, are very likely to be quite distinct from the conscious, normative rationalisations of personal-level thinking.

I assume that a cognitive-scientific account of pragmatics is, or at least aims at, sub-personal description and explanation.[1] However, this assumption does not go unchallenged, as will be seen in section 4, where Francois Recanati's account of pragmatic processes is compared with the relevance-theoretic account. In the next section, I outline some of the pragmatic processes that, according to both accounts, mediate the transition from linguistic meaning to explicit utterance content.

2 Pragmatic processes of explicature derivation

2.1 Linguistic input and pragmatic output

A major development in pragmatics since Grice's work is the recognition that linguistically decoded information is usually very incomplete and that pragmatic inference plays an essential role in the derivation of the proposition explicitly communicated. This is especially clear in the case of subsentential utterances, such as that discussed above, but it holds also for the vast majority of fully sentential cases. Various terms for this are used in the literature; the linguistic expression employed is described as providing an incomplete logical form, a 'semantic' skeleton, 'semantic' scaffolding, a 'semantic' template, a proposition/assumption schema (see, for instance, Sperber and Wilson, 1986/95, Recanati, 1993, Bach, 1994, Taylor, 2001). What all of these different locutions entail is that the linguistic contribution is not propositional, it is not a complete semantic entity, not truth-evaluable.

On the other hand, what is communicated, that is, the output of the pragmatic processor, is usually a set of fully propositional thoughts or assumptions, which are either true or false of an external state of affairs in the world. There are two kinds of communicated propositions, those that are explicitly communicated and those that are implicitly communicated There is some debate about the precise nature of this explicit/implicit distinction, how it is to be drawn, and whether any such two-way distinction can do justice to the levels and kinds of meaning involved in utterance interpretation. However, it is generally agreed that while implicatures are

wholly external to, and distinct from, the linguistic meaning, the proposition explicitly communicated is, in some sense, built out of the semantic template contributed by the linguistic expression used. There are several different, and somewhat confusing, terms in currency for the propositions 'explicitly' communicated, including 'explicature' (in Sperber and Wilson's relevance theory), 'what is said' (in Recanati's reconstrual of the Gricean term) and 'implicature' (used by Kent Bach (1994), who takes this communicated proposition to be 'implicit' in what is actually said). Very much the same sort of entity is denoted by these three terms, though there are some major differences in the wider semantic/pragmatic frameworks they inhabit, one of which is discussed in section 4.

It is uncontentious that processes of disambiguation and indexical reference assignment play a crucial role in identifying the explicature of an utterance, but there is some disagreement about how they are effected, about what guides or drives them, specifically about whether or not the speaker's communicative intention plays a role (hence whether or not pragmatic maxims or principles are involved). I won't attempt to argue it here, but given the plainly highly context-sensitive nature of sense selection and reference assignment, I take it that they are matters of speaker meaning, not determinable by any linguistic rule or procedure for mapping a linguistic element to a contextual value, and so just as dependent on pragmatic principles as the processes of implicature derivation. For more detail and argument, see Carston (2000, forthcoming b) and Recanati (2001, 2002a).

Identifying the intended sense of an ambiguous word or structure and giving values to indexicals (also known as 'saturation') are mandatory processes, that is, they must be carried out in all contexts in which the ambiguous or indexical form is used. In the next two subsections, I consider two other kinds of contribution that, according to relevance theorists, and certain other cognitively-oriented theorists, pragmatics can make to the derivation of the explicature(s) of an utterance. These are optional or 'free' processes in the sense that they need not occur in every context in which the linguistic expression at issue is used.

2.2 Unarticulated constituents and ' 'free' pragmatic enrichment

There is a wide range of cases where it seems that pragmatics contributes a component to the explicitly communicated content of an utterance although there is no linguistic element indicating that such a component is required. That is, there is no overt indexical, nor is there any compelling reason to suppose there is a covert element in the logical form of the utterance, and yet a contextually supplied constituent appears in the explicature. Consider utterances of the following sentences, whose interpretation, in many contexts, would include the bracketed element which is provided on pragmatic grounds alone.

(5) a. Sally has a brain. [VERY GOOD BRAIN]
     b. Something has happened. [SOME-THING IMPORTANT/TERRIBLE]
     c. I've had a shower. [TODAY]
     d. It's snowing. [IN LOCATION X]
     e. Mary gave John a pen and he wrote down her address. [AND THEN] [WITH THE PEN MARY GAVE HIM]
     f. Sam left Jane and she became very depressed. [AND AS A RESULT]

Given disambiguation and saturation of indexicals, each of these would, arguably, express a proposition (hence be truth-evaluable) without the addition of the bracketed constituent, but in most contexts that minimal proposition would not be what is communicated (speaker meant). One class of cases, represented here by (5a) and (5b), would express a trivial truth (after all, every person has a brain, and, at any given moment, something or other has

happened), and it is easy to set up cases of obvious falsehoods (the negations of (5a) and (5b), for instance). Others, such as (5c) and (5d), are so vague and general as to be very seldom what a speaker would intend to communicate (they would not yield sufficient cognitive effects). Across most contexts in which these sentences might be uttered, obvious implicatures of the utterance would depend on the enriched proposition: in (5a), for instance, the implicated proposition that Sally will make an intelligent contribution to a debate; in (5c), the implicature that the speaker doesn't need to take a shower at the time of utterance. The relevance-theoretic position, then, is that, in the vast majority of contexts, it is the enriched propositions that are communicated as explicatures, with the uninformative, irrelevant, and, sometimes, truistic or patently false, minimal propositions playing no role in the process of utterance understanding.

While the issue with disambiguation and saturation processes is how they are brought about, whether with or without pragmatic principles geared to uncovering the speaker's meaning, the issue with free enrichment is more fundamental. It is whether or not there really is any such process, so whether or not there are such things as constituents of the explicit content of the utterance which do not occur in any shape or form in the linguistic representation. Philosophers of language who insist on the psychological reality of the process include Recanati (1993, 2001) and Bach (1994, 2000). However, a current school of semantic thinking, represented by Stanley (2000, 2002), Stanley and Szabo (2000) and Taylor (2001), holds that if a contextually supplied constituent appears in the explicit content of an utterance then it must have been articulated in the logical form of the utterance, whether by an overt indexical or by a phonologically unrealised element (a covert indexical). In other words, the only pragmatic processes at work at this level are disambiguation and saturation, and there is a lot more saturation going on than the surface syntactic form reveals; any other process of pragmatic inference involved in understanding an utterance results in an *implicated* proposition.

What lies behind this denial of 'free' enrichment is a particular view of natural language semantics and its relation to linguistic communication (see Stanley 2002). The claim is that the truth-conditional content of an utterance is entirely determined by (a) its logical form, and (b) the (context-relative) meanings of its most basic components (words or covert elements), that is, it satisfies a strict principle of semantic compositionality. This is essentially the Gricean position on 'what is said' but with a great many more indexical elements requiring contextual instantiation. Relevance theorists have a rather different view of linguistic semantics, one which also complies with strict compositionality but which is not truth-conditional. Linguistic semantics is a system of mappings between elements of linguistic form and certain kinds of cognitive information and, as already discussed, the result of these mappings is standardly a subpropositional schema for the (pragmatic) construction of fully propositional representations. Truth-conditional semantics is a distinct enterprise and its proper object is not linguistic expressions but fully propositional entities, such as thoughts and communicated assumptions (semantic/pragmatic hybrids). On this view of linguistic semantics, then, the possibility of constituents in the proposition explicitly communicated which have not been articulated in the logical form of the linguistic expression does not raise any semantic problems.[2]

2.3 Pragmatic adjustments of conceptual encodings

Free enrichment is a process which involves the addition of a conceptual constituent to the decoded logical form; for example, 'it's snowing [IN ABERDEEN]'. There are other cases where it

seems that a better way of construing what is going on is that a lexical concept appearing in the logical form is pragmatically adjusted, so that the concept understood as communicated by the particular occurrence of the lexical item is different from, and replaces, the concept it encodes; it is narrower or wider (or some combination of the two) than the lexical concept from which it was derived. Consider an utterance of (6a) by a witness at the trial of X who is accused of having murdered his wife; the utterance is a response to a question about X's state of mind at the time leading up to the murder:

(6) a. He was upset but he wasn't upset.
     b. X WAS UPSET* BUT X WASN'T UPSET**

As far as its linguistically supplied information goes, this is a contradiction, but it was not intended as, nor understood as, a contradiction. The two instances of the word 'upset' were interpreted as communicating two different concepts of upsetness (as indicated in (6b) by the asterisks), at least one, but most likely both, involving a pragmatic narrowing of the encoded lexical concept UPSET; the second of the two concepts carries certain implications (e.g. that he was in a murdering state of mind) that the first one does not, implications whose applicability to X the witness is denying.

There are many other cases where any one of a wide range of related concepts might be communicated by a single lexical item; for instance, think of all the different kinds, degrees and qualities of feeling that can be communicated by each of 'tired', 'anxious', 'frightened', 'depressed', 'well', 'happy', 'satisfied', 'sweet', etc. In one context, an utterance of 'I'm happy' could communicate that the speaker feels herself to be in a steady state of low-key well-being, in another that she is experiencing a moment of intense joy, in yet another that she is satisfied with the outcome of some negotiation, and so on. The general concept HAPPY encoded by the lexical item 'happy' gives access to an indefinite number of more specific concepts, recoverable in particular contexts by relevance-driven pragmatic inference.

The examples considered so far have involved a narrowing or strengthening of the encoded concept, but there are others that seem to require some degree of widening or loosening. Consider what is most likely communicated by the highlighted lexical item in utterances of the following sentences:

(7) a. There is a *rectangle* of lawn at the back.
     b. This steak is *raw*.
     c. On Classic FM, we play *continuous* classics.
     d. Mary is a *bulldozer*.

The area of lawn referred to in (7a) is very unlikely to be truly a rectangle (with four right angles, opposite sides equal in length); rather it is approximately rectangular, and this holds for many other uses of geometrical terms: a 'round' lake, a 'square' cake, a 'triangular' face, etc. In (7b), the steak, perhaps served in a restaurant, is not really raw but is much less cooked than the speaker wishes; in (7c), the classical music played on the radio station is interspersed with advertisements and other announcements, so not strictly 'continuous', and so on. In each case, a logical or defining feature of the lexically encoded concept is dropped in the process of arriving at the intended interpretation: EQUAL SIDES in the case of 'rectangle', UNCOOKED for 'raw', UNINTERRUPTED for 'continuous', MACHINERY for 'bulldozer'.

While the existence of a pragmatic process of 'free' enrichment, as discussed in the previous subsection, is disputed by some truth-conditional semanticists, the process of pragmatic concept construction has not (yet) been challenged by semanticists or Gricean-oriented pragmatists, perhaps because it is a relatively new player on the scene.[3] Although this process does not bring about a structural change in the transition from linguistic logical form to proposition

explicitly communicated, as does free enrichment (expansion), it clearly does take us well away from encoded linguistic meaning and has no linguistic mandate, so marks yet another considerable departure from the Gricean semantic notion of 'what is said'.[4]

3 Relevance theory and the mutual adjustment of explicatures and implicatures

According to relevance theory, the pragmatic inferential system employs the following strategy in order to arrive at the intended interpretation of the utterance:

(8) Consider interpretations (disambiguations, saturations, enrichments, implicatures, etc) in order of accessibility (i.e. follow a path of least effort in computing cognitive effects); stop when the expected level of relevance is achieved.

Interpretive hypotheses are made rapidly, on-line, and in parallel. The mechanism that mediates the inferences from logical form to communicated propositions is one of 'mutual parallel adjustment' of explicatures and implicatures, constrained by the comprehension strategy. The result should consist of (sets of) premises and conclusions making up valid arguments, but the important point is that the process need not progress strictly logically from the accessing of premises to the drawing of conclusions. For instance, a particular conclusion, or type of conclusion, might be expected on the basis of considerations of relevance and, via a backwards inference process, premises constructed (explicatures and implicatures) which will make for a sound inference to the conclusion. The process may involve several backwards and forwards adjustments of content before an equilibrium is achieved which meets the system's current 'expectation' of relevance.

I'll illustrate the process with an example

which involves free enrichment. See Sperber and Wilson (1998) and, in particular, Wilson and Sperber (2000) for examples in which pragmatic concept construction plays a central role. Bob's utterance in (9) is a response to Ann's immediately preceding question. In such cases, expectations of relevance are quite constrained and specific since the question has indicated the sort of information that would be relevant (would have cognitive effects).

(9)   Ann: Shall we play tennis?
      Bob: It's raining.
      Explicature: IT'S RAINING AT LOCATION$_{A/B}$
      Implicated premise: IF IT'S RAINING IN LOCATION$_x$ THEN IT IS UNLIKELY THAT PEOPLE WILL PLAY TENNIS AT LOCATION$_x$
      Implicated conclusion: ANN AND BOB WON'T PLAY TENNIS AT LOCATION$_{A/B}$

In understanding Bob's utterance, the explicature constructed from the logical form has to be enriched with a location constituent in order that the implicated conclusion is properly warranted. In this case, the location is anchored to the place of utterance, though in a different context it might not be, so this is a matter of pragmatic inference.

The following step by step description of the pragmatic processes involved in understanding Bob's utterance in (10) is closely modelled on analyses given in Wilson and Sperber (2000):

(10) a.   Bob has uttered sentence with logical form: [it is raining] (*Output of linguistic decoding.*)
      b.   Bob's utterance is optimally relevant to Ann. (*Presumption of relevance.*)
      c.   Bob's utterance will achieve relevance by providing an affirmative or negative answer to Ann's question. (*Standard expectation created by the asking of a yes-no question.*)
      d.   If it is raining in a particular location then it is not likely that one can play

tennis in that location. (*Highly accessible assumption which might help to answer Ann's question.*)
      e.   It is raining at Ann and Bob's location. (*First accessible enrichment of Bob's utterance which could combine with (d) to yield an answer to Ann's question.*)
      f.   Ann and Bob can't play tennis at their location. (*Inferred from (d) and (e); satisfies (c); accepted as an implicature of Bob's utterance.*)
      g.   They can't play tennis at their location because it is raining at their location. (*Further highly accessible implicature inferred from (d) and (e), which, together with (f) and various other (weaker) implicatures, such as (h), satisfies (b), the general expectation of relevance.*)
      h.   Ann and Bob will have to find some other entertainment. They could go to the cinema, etc.

Bob has not given a direct yes/no answer to Ann's question; rather, Ann has to infer an implicated answer. The extra inferential effort required by Bob's indirect reply to Ann's question is offset by extra effects, specifically, the strongly communicated implicature in (10g) which supplies a reason for the negative answer to her question, and perhaps other weakly communicated implicatures, such as those in (10h).

Two caveats are in order here. First, I have given natural language paraphrases of explicatures and implicatures which, as always, are merely suggestive of the actual conceptual representations involved. Second, as the comments above about the mutual adjustment process indicate, the steps in the derivation are not to be thought of as sequential. Interpretive hypotheses about aspects of explicit and implicit content are made on-line and adjusted in parallel until both the hearer's expectation of relevance is met and a final stable state of sound inference is achieved.

It is clear from just this one example and the general comments about the relevance-theoretic derivation process, that we have here a considerable departure from the widely held Gricean view of how conversational implicatures are derived and, so, of their derivational relation to the explicit content of the utterance. According to that view, they are inferentially derived on the basis of the *antecedently determined* 'what is said' and arise as a response to a consideration of why the speaker is saying what she said, what she means (communicatively intends) by saying it. As will be seen in the next (and final) section, this difference of conception is central to two opposing views on the cognitive architecture of the pragmatic capacity.

4 How many pragmatic systems?

There is a variety of conceptually distinct pragmatic tasks. These may or may not involve distinct kinds of process, and distinct kinds of process may or may not involve distinct mechanisms (or architectural units). The following three positions on these relationships have actually been taken up by different pragmatists:

[1] The various different pragmatic tasks are performed by processes that comprise a single system, which takes decoded linguistic meaning as its input and delivers the propositions communicated (explicatures and implicatures).

[2] There is a crucial split between the processes involved in deriving explicit utterance content, on the one hand, and the processes of implicature derivation, on the other, with the two sets of processes each belonging to a distinct cognitive system, the output of the first (explicature or 'what is said') being the input to the second.

[3] There are distinct processes for at least some of the (conceptually) distinct pragmatic tasks (disambiguation, indexical reference assignment, recovery of unarticulated constituents, speech act assignment, etc) and each of these distinct

processes is performed by a distinct cognitive system.

The third position, which I won't explore here, has been adopted for purely practical reasons by some computationalists in attempts to provide an implementation of particular pragmatic tasks, and, on more theoretical grounds, by Asa Kasher (1991a, 1991b). The second position is the standard one (one system for the pragmatic processes involved in the recovery of the proposition expressed or explicature, and the other for implicature derivation). It is held by a range of people, whose outlooks otherwise diverge considerably: Grice, for whom conversational maxims were responsible for the derivation of implicatures, but not, it seems, for the pragmatic processes of disambiguation and indexical reference fixing required for a full identification of 'what is said'; the semantic theorists, Larson and Segal (1995, chapter 1), who assume there is a system for identifying the referents of indexicals which is distinct from a pragmatics system (for implicature generation); the post-Gricean pragmatist, Stephen Levinson (2000), who distinguishes a system of default rules for generating what he calls 'generalised' conversational implicature, which can contribute to the truth-conditional content of an utterance, hence to 'what is said', and a system of general communicative principles (probably relevance-based) for inferring particularised conversational implicatures; Recanati (1993, 1995, 2001, 2002a), who makes a fundamental distinction between *primary* pragmatic processes and *secondary* pragmatic processes.

I will focus on position [2] as it is developed in Recanati's work. Primary pragmatic processes are all those that contribute to 'explicature' (or 'what is said', in his nonGricean, nonminimalist sense of the term), whether obligatory processes like saturation or optional ones like free enrichment; secondary pragmatic processes are responsible for implicature derivation. Although both kinds of pragmatic processes are wholly dependent on context (in the widest sense), they are very different in other respects: the primary ones are associative and free from considerations of the speaker's intention, while the secondary ones are properly inferential and require representation of the speaker's intention; the two kinds of processes are also governed by distinct principles (a principle of 'highest accessibility' for the primary processes, Gricean type norms for the secondary processes) and the primary ones are prior, both logically and temporally, to the secondary ones. Indeed they are so fundamentally different as to belong to different levels of description: 'The determination of what is said takes place at a sub-personal level, . . . But the determination of what the speaker implies takes place at the personal level, . . .' (Recanati 2002a, p. 114).

In all these distinguishing respects, this view is at odds with that of the relevance-theoretic account which, as should be evident from the preceding section, takes the first of the three positions laid out above. There is a single pragmatic comprehension system, informed by a single overarching principle: 'Every utterance (more broadly, ostensive stimulus) carries a presumption of its own relevance' (see Sperber and Wilson 2002). The system operates in accordance with a comprehension procedure (given in (8) above) which is dedicated to the processing of communicative stimuli and distinct from the procedures of other systems (such as the general 'theory of mind' system). Recovery of the two kinds of communicated assumption, explicatures and implicatures, proceeds in parallel and is effected by a process of mutual adjustment which may involve processes of inference from implicature to explicature as well as from explicature to implicature. The function of this single pragmatics system is to recover speaker meaning, that is, what the speaker communicatively intended, but this is a sub-personal system and so does not require conscious reflection on what that intention is.

In the little space remaining, I will consider just two of the many differences between Recanati's binary position and the relevance-theoretic unitary position: (a) the question of the temporal order of processes of explicature and implicature derivation, and (b) the issue of kinds and levels of processing.

There is a reasonably clear sense in which explicatures are *logically prior* to implicatures: explicatures function as premises in sound patterns of inference in which (some, at least) implicatures are conclusions. But Recanati is also claiming that explicatures are *temporally prior*, they are the output of a system of primary pragmatic processes and the input to a system of secondary pragmatic processes which result in implicatures. If the relevance-theoretic view is right, however, there is no generalization to be made about which of the two kinds of communicated assumption is recovered first and functions as input to the recovery of the other; the parallel adjustment process entails that neither is wholly temporally prior to the other. An addressee may have quite specific expectations of relevance that, as it turns out, pertain to information which the speaker implicates, so that the pragmatic development of the linguistic logical form is, at least partly, made in order to provide inferential grounding for that implicature.

Setting aside the specifics of the relevance-theoretic view, there is a class of widely recognized implicatures, known as 'bridging' implicatures, which *have to* precede the full derivation of an explicature (see Clark, 1977, Levinson, 2000, Matsui, 2000). These are contextual assumptions that must be accessed, whether or not they are already known to the addressee, in order to identify a referent. So, for instance, to identify the referent of 'the beer' in (11a), the addressee has to access the implicature in (11b):

(11) a.   The picnic was awful. The beer was
            warm.
      b.   The beer was part of the picnic.

In the absence of any argument that denies the status of implicature to assumptions like those in (11b), they seem to present strong evidence in favour of a system of pragmatic interpretation which derives explicatures and implicatures in parallel.

Turning now to the issue of kinds of process and explanatory levels, consider the following statement by Recanati (2002, p. 114):

> As Grice emphasized, implicature-determination in the strict sense is a reflective process. Instead of merely retrieving what is said through the operation of unconscious, primary pragmatic processes, we reflect on the fact that the speaker says what he says and use that fact, together with background knowledge, to infer what the speaker means without saying it. As Millikan writes, 'the true communicator is in a position to tinker with the mechanisms of normal language flow, is sensitive to symptoms that the other is tinkering with these mechanisms, and can rise above these automatic mechanisms if necessary' (Millikan, 1984, p. 69). That is what happens in *special* cases. The retrieving of conversational implicatures, in particular, involves reflective capacities that are not exercised in what Millikan calls 'normal language flow'.

Leaving aside Millikan's own concerns and focussing just on Recanati's use of her views for his own purpose, there is a strong (and, to me, highly implausible) claim here that linguistic communication involving implicatures is special and abnormal, in some sense, that implicatures are only derived when something has gone awry with the normal automatic smooth processes of linguistic communication. With this claim in mind, let's consider some examples of utterances which clearly communicate an implicature, starting with the first example Grice gave when illustrating the role of his conversational maxims (Grice, 1975, p. 51):

(12) A: I am out of petrol.
   B: There is a garage round the corner. (*Gloss*: B would be infringing the maxim 'Be relevant' unless he thinks, or thinks it possible, that the garage is open, and has petrol to sell; so he implicates that the garage is, or at least may be, open, etc.)

Now, B could have given a more explicit response to A, one in which the information that petrol is currently being sold at a garage round the corner is part of what is said by the utterance. For instance, she could have uttered the sentence in (13):

(13) B': There is a garage round the corner which sells petrol and is open now.

According to the view just given, this utterance would have maintained the normal language flow while the one B actually gave, in (12), disrupts that normal flow. It is perhaps difficult to have a sure sense of what is meant by the notion of 'normal' language flow, but the exchange in (12) seems to be about as natural, normal and flowing a conversation as there is, while, arguably, the implicature-less one in (13) is somewhat awkward, being quite unnecessarily explicit (in the absence of any doubt about the functioning of the garage).

Furthermore, if there is any statistical basis to the use of the word 'normal', then Recanati's claim cannot be right, since the majority of our exchanges are implicature-laden. Note in this regard that, in (12), B has taken A to have implicated that she wants some petrol and his utterance is a response to that implicature. According to the relevance-theoretic single system view, the processes of explicature and implicature derivation proceed on-line, in parallel and in response to each other, without any major switch of processing mode, thereby reflecting what seems to be the normal communication flow of exchanges such as that in (12). This is what we would expect from a system which has evolved to solve the adaptive problem of figuring out a speaker's meaning, which may consist of just an explicature but, more often than not, consists of implicatures and explicature.

In the next example, the first part of B's utterance is a direct explicit response to A's question, but it raises a further (implicit) question 'what does B want?', which the second segment of B's utterance answers indirectly; B implicates that she wants some paper:

(14) A: Do you want something?
      B: Yes. # I've run out of paper.

Having processed B's utterance up to the point marked by #, A is very likely to have formed an anticipatory assumption schema [B wants _] for which the next section of B's utterance provides a completion. It so happens that the resulting proposition 'B wants some paper' is an implicature of the next part of B's utterance. Had the second unit been 'Some paper' or 'I want some paper', the answer would have been direct and the completed assumption schema would have been an explicature of the utterance. According to Recanati's view quoted above, the understood answer, that is the completed schema, 'B wants some paper', must be achieved by fundamentally different kinds and levels of processes in the two cases, and the one in which it is an implicature is in some way special, is brought about by a disruption in the linguistic communicative flow. However, this is not supported by intuitions about the two possibilities, and, in the absence of compelling arguments, it is difficult to see why we should adopt this view.

Moreover, if the idea that utterance comprehension processes include the formation of anticipatory hypotheses is correct, the binary view imposes a very odd requirement: particular hypotheses, such as the schema above, would have to be categorised as a feature of one kind of processing system (unconscious, subpersonal-level) in the case where it turns out

to be completed as an explicature, but part of a distinct one (conscious, personal-level) when it is an implicature. According to the relevance-theoretic view, such anticipatory hypotheses about where the relevance of an utterance is going to lie are a common occurrence and, given the single system of interlocking processes of explicature and implicature derivation, the problem of their having to switch from one sort of status to another does not arise.

There clearly are times at which the normal communicative flow is disrupted: certain instances of garden-path utterances, especially when exploited by speakers for particular, often humorous, effects; some cases of complex figurative use which require an effortful conscious search for an interpretation; other cases where there is some apprehended difficulty in satisfying oneself that the intended interpretation has been reached (it doesn't seem sufficiently relevant, for instance). The appropriate distinction within modes of processing and levels of explanation would seem to be between, on the one hand, a modular (sub-personal) pragmatic processor which, when all goes well, quickly and automatically delivers speaker meaning (explicatures and implicatures), and, on the other hand, processes of a conscious reflective (personal-level) sort which occur only when the results of the former system are found wanting in some way.

To conclude, these interesting issues in the study of linguistic communication have arisen only since pragmatics has moved from its place of origin in philosophy to its new location within cognitive science. Clearly, there is a long way to go before they are fully resolved and it seems very likely that empirical evidence from experiments on the time course of processing, from child development and from people with communicative deficits will play an important part in their resolution.

Notes

1 It has been suggested that the personal level, at least as conceived here, is not primarily a level of scientific description, since its explanations are not concerned with 'subsuming events under covering laws about how the world works'. The description of persons as 'experiencing, thinking subjects and agents' is characteristic of explanation in the philosophy of mind, though 'we do not rule out the possibility that these descriptions may also figure in scientific theories' (Davies, 2000, p. 93). For more on this contentious issue and on the relation between the personal and the sub-personal levels, see the special issue of *Philosophical Explorations*, volume 3 (1), January 2000.

2 There is now in the semantic/pragmatic literature quite a complex array of arguments for and against unarticulated constituents. Stanley (2000) and Stanley and Szabo (2000) have argued that, whenever there is thought to be a constituent of explicitly communicated content which has been recovered on wholly pragmatic grounds, it is really the value of a hidden indexical element in the linguistic logical form. In different ways, Bach (2000), Carston (2000), Breheny (2002) and Recanati (2002b) defend the existence of unarticulated constituents and the pragmatic process of free enrichment. Stanley (this volume) claims to have found a new problem for advocates of pragmatic enrichment. He argues that, as presented by relevance theorists and by Bach (2000), it is a process that over-generates, making false predictions about possible interpretations of utterances. This allegation remains to be addressed.

3 For further discussion of the role of ad hoc concept construction within the relevance-theoretic view of utterance understanding and its implications for the account of metaphor, see Carston (1997) and (forthcoming a, chapter 5), Sperber and Wilson (1998), Wilson and Sperber (2000), and Breheny (1999) and (forthcoming). For his related notions of 'analogical transfer' and 'metonymical transfer', pragmatic processes which contribute to the proposition explicitly communicated, see Recanati (1993, section 14.4) and (1995).

4 Many semanticists and pragmatists follow Grice in preserving a conception of 'what is said' which is minimally distinct from the semantics of the linguistic expression used. Bach (1994) aims for a wholly semantic notion, one which is free from any consideration of speaker intentions and allows for the contextual fixing of only 'pure' indexicals. In Carston (2002, chapter 2) and (2004), I have argued in some detail against there being any role for such a notion (intermediate as it is between linguistic expression type meaning and communicated propositions) in an account of the cognitive processes and representations involved in utterance interpretation.

References

Bach, K. 1994: Conversational impliciture. *Mind & Language*, 9, 124–162.

Bach, K. 2000: Quantification, qualification, and context: a reply to Stanley and Szabo. *Mind & Language*, 15, 262–283.

Bloom, P. 2002: Mindreading, Communication and the Learning of Names for Things. *Mind and Language* 17, 37–54.

Breheny, R. 1999: *Context-dependence and procedural meaning: the semantics of definites*. University College London PhD thesis.

Breheny, R. 2002: The Current State of (Radical) Pragmatics in the Cognitive Sciences. *Mind and Language* 17, 169–87.

Breheny, Richard, forthcoming: Maximality, negation and plural definites. Ms. Research Centre of English and Applied Linguistics, University of Cambridge.

Carston, R. 1997: Enrichment and loosening: complementary processes in deriving the proposition expressed? *Linguistische Berichte*, 8, Special Issue on Pragmatics, 103–127.

Carston, R. 2000: Explicature and semantics. *UCL Working Papers in Linguistics*, 12, 1–44. To appear in S. Davis and B. Gillon (eds.) forthcoming. *Semantics: A Reader*. Oxford: Oxford University Press.

Carston, R. 2002: *Thoughts and Utterances: the Pragmatics of Explicit Communication*. Oxford: Blackwells.

Carston, R. 2004: Relevance theory and the saying/implicating distinction. In L. Horn and G. Ward (eds.) *Handbook of Pragmatics*. Oxford: Blackwells.

Clark, H. 1977: Bridging. In P. Wason and P. Johnson-Laird (eds.) *Thinking: Readings in Cognitive Science*, 411–420. Cambridge: Cambridge University Press.

Davies, M. 2000: Interaction without reduction: The relationship between personal and sub-personal levels of description. *Mind and Society*, 1, 87–105.

Dennett, D. 1969: *Content and Consciousness*. London: Routledge & Kegan Paul.

Elton, M. 2000: The personal/sub-personal distinction: an introduction. *Philosophical Explorations* 3, 2–5.

Fodor, J. 1983: *The Modularity of Mind*. Cambridge, Mass.: MIT Press.

Fodor, J. 2000: *The Mind Doesn't Work That Way*. Cambridge, Mass.: MIT Press.

Grice, H.P. 1975: Logic and conversation. In P. Cole and J. Morgan (eds.) *Syntax and Semantics 3: Speech Acts*, 41–58. New York: Academic Press. Reprinted in H. P. Grice 1989, 22–40.

Grice, H.P. 1981: Presupposition and conversational implicature. In P. Cole. (ed.) *Radical Pragmatics*, 183–198. New York: Academic Press.

Grice, H.P. 1989: *Studies in the Way of Words*. Cambridge, Mass.: Harvard University Press.

Happé, F. and Loth, E. 2002: 'Theory of Mind' and Tracking Speakers' Intentions. *Mind and Language* 17, 24–36.

Kasher, A. 1991a: Pragmatics and the modularity of mind. In S. Davis (ed.) 1991. *Pragmatics: A Reader*, 567–582. Oxford University Press.

Kasher, A. 1991b: On the pragmatic modules: A lecture. *Journal of Pragmatics* 16, 381–397.

Langdon, R., Davies, M. and Coltheart, M. 2002: Understanding Minds and Understanding Communicated Meanings in Schizophrenia. *Mind and Language* 17, 68–104.

Larson, R. and Segal, G. 1995: *Knowledge of Meaning: An Introduction to Semantic Theory*. Cambridge, Mass.: MIT Press.

Leslie, A. 2000a: How to acquire a representational theory of mind. In D. Sperber (ed.) *Metarepresentations: a Multidisciplinary Perspective*, 197–223. Oxford: Oxford University Press.

Leslie, A. 2000b: 'Theory of mind' as a mechanism of selective attention. In M. Gazzaniga (ed.) *The New Cognitive Neurosciences*, 1235–1247. Cambridge, Mass.: MIT Press.

Levinson, S. 2000: *Presumptive Meanings: The Theory of Generalized Conversational Implicature*. Cambridge, Mass.: MIT Press.

Matsui, T. 2000: *Bridging and Relevance*. Amsterdam: John Benjamin.

Millikan, R. 1984: *Language, Thought, and Other Biological Categories*. Cambridge, Mass.: MIT Press.

Neale, S. 1990: *Descriptions*, Mass.: MIT Press.

Papafragou, A. 2002: Mindreading and Verbal Communication. *Mind and Language* 17, 55–67.

Recanati, F. 1993: *Direct Reference: From Language to Thought*. Oxford: Blackwell.

Recanati, F. 1995: The alleged priority of literal interpretation. *Cognitive Science*, 19, 207–232.

Recanati, F. 2001: What is said. *Synthese*, 128, 75–91.

Recanati, F. 2002a: Does Linguistic Communication Rest on Inference? *Mind and Language* 17, 105–126.

Recanati, F. 2002b: Unarticulated constituents. *Linguistics and Philosophy*, 25, 299–345.

Scholl, B. and Leslie, A. 1999: Modularity, development and 'theory of mind'. *Mind & Language* 14, 131–153.

Sperber, D. 1994a: Understanding verbal understanding. In J. Khalfa (ed.) *What is Intelligence?*, 179–198. Cambridge: Cambridge University Press.

Sperber, D. 1994b: The modularity of thought and the epidemiology of representations. In L. Hirschfeld and S. Gelman (eds.) *Mapping the Mind: Domain Specificity in Cognition and Culture*, 39–67. Cambridge: Cambridge University Press.

Sperber, D. and Wilson, D. 1986/95: *Relevance: Communication and Cognition*. Oxford: Blackwells.

Sperber, D. and Wilson, D. 1998: The mapping between the mental and the public lexicon. In P. Carruthers and J. Boucher (eds.) *Language and Thought: Interdisciplinary Themes*, 184–200. Cambridge: Cambridge University Press.

Sperber, D. and Wilson, D. 2002: Pragmatics, Modularity and Mind-reading. *Mind and Language* 17, 3–23.

Stanley, J. 2000: Context and logical form. *Linguistics and Philosophy*, 23, 391–434.

Stanley, J. 2002: Making it Articulated. *Mind and Language* 17, 149–68.

Stanley, J. and Szabo, Z.G. 2000: On quantifier domain restriction. *Mind & Language*, 15, 219–61.

Taylor, K. 2001: Sex, breakfast, and descriptus interruptus. *Synthese*, 128, 45–61.

Wilson, D. and Sperber, D. 2000: Truthfulness and relevance. *UCL Working Papers in Linguistics*, 12, 215–254.

PART ELEVEN

Compositionality and context

INTRODUCTION TO PART ELEVEN

COMPOSITIONALITY HAS ALREADY played a role in several parts of this book, for example in Frege's 'On Sense and Reference' and in Davidson's 'Truth and Meaning'. Roughly, a language is compositional, if the meanings of complex expressions are determined by the meanings of their semantic constituents (and their mode of composition). As I am writing these sentences, I understand what they mean. The great majority of my readers will, if everything goes right, also understand them. However, neither you, the reader, nor I, have ever heard or seen or otherwise come across these sentences before. How is this possible? It seems obvious that this ability is due to our knowledge (however unconscious) of the meanings of the words from which these sentences are made up, combined with knowledge (however unconscious) of how the meaning of complex expressions depends on the meanings of their parts[1] This explanation depends on the compositionality of language: if we are to work out the meaning of a complex expression from the meanings of its constituent parts, then the meanings of the parts must determine the meaning of the complex.

Ran Lahav, in his article, challenges the view that natural languages are compositional. He does this by considering adjectives. If English is compositional, then one might expect that an adjective like 'red' makes the same contribution to all the complex expressions in which it can occur: 'He got red in the face', 'red table', 'red telephone' etc. In particular, one might think that each time 'red' is used to qualify some noun, as in 'red table' or generally 'red *N*', it is the function of 'red' to restrict the range of applicability of the noun '*N*' to which it is attached. However, as Lahav argues, there is no systematic, uniform contribution that 'red' makes in all these contexts. A red watermelon is one with red pulp, i.e. red inside, while a red car may be a car that is red on the outside. A red crystal, again, is red both inside and out. However, we would hesitate to say that the word 'red' is simply ambiguous, i.e. that it means something different in 'red car' than in 'red watermelon', just as 'bank' means something different in 'The boat is moored on the left bank' than in 'They robbed a bank'.

We said that a language is compositional just if the meanings of its complex expressions are determined by the meanings of its constituent parts and their manner of composition. This can be made more precise by distinguishing various things we might mean by 'meaning'. In one sense, meanings attach to expression types, independently of context (what Kaplan calls 'character'). In this sense, indexicals like 'I' or 'now' have the same meaning on any occasion of use, and it is because of this constant meaning that 'I' refers to me when I use it, and to you when you use it.

---

[1] As Part Eight of this book demonstrates, the appearance of obviousness is mistaken, for there are those who deny that understanding involves knowledge.

Compositionality can also be thought of as a constraint on meaning in the sense of the *contents* that expressions have on particular occasions of use, i.e. the semantic properties which determine the truth value of sentences in which they occur. Thus, a complex expression is compositional in another sense just if the content it expresses on a given occasion depends only on the contents that its constituents express on that same occasion.

Compositionality in either of these senses is compatible with phenomena of context-dependence, as in the case of indexical expressions. To use one of Szabo's examples, the sentence, 'I am now at the north pole', expresses different propositions or contents on different occasions of use, depending on who uses it at what time. This is not a threat to compositionality, because even though we are dealing with the same constituents on the different occasions, the proposition expressed on an occasion still depends on the contents of the constituents on the occasions in question. Thus there is a perfectly straightforward way in which the contribution of 'red' might vary from context to context without a threat to compositionality, namely if the contribution it made were context-dependent in a way that resembles 'I', 'now' or 'yesterday'. Lahav argues at length that no such analysis can rescue compositionality, for the content of adjectives 'varies from one linguistic context to another in a way that cannot be analysed in terms of a general (not vacuously disjunctive) rule or function'.

Zoltán Gendler Szabó argues precisely in favour of the claim that recognizing a certain type of context dependence of adjectives will secure compositionality. Szabó's main target is a well-known example and argument from Charles Travis (see Travis 1996, 1997) involving the adjective 'green', but his proposal is also meant to meet Lahav's similar challenge to compositionality (see note 46 of the Szabó selection). Travis's example involves a leaf of a Japanese maple which is naturally russet in colour, but which has been painted green. Travis argues that the sentence 'The leaf is green' can be used to say something true of this leaf when sorting leaves for the purpose of providing colour samples, but that it can also be used to say something false of the very same leaf when we are trying to classify the leaf botanically. The argument is that the adjective 'green' does not make a uniform semantic contribution in all the contexts in which it can occur, a contribution that could be spelled out in the relevant clause of a compositional semantic theory.

Travis's example is different from Lahav's in that it involves, at least on the surface, a *predicative* use of the colour adjective, i.e. one where 'green' is apparently used to predicate a property directly of some object. Lahav's examples involve, at least on the surface, *attributive* uses: in 'red watermelon' or 'red car', the adjective is not predicated of an individual, but rather combined with a noun to form a complex noun-phrase. As Szabó explains, there are in fact two different approaches to adjectives that have these two types of uses: some regard the adjectives as fundamentally attributive. On this view, what 'good' does in 'is a good dancer' is just to modify the predicate 'is a dancer'– cases where there doesn't seem to be a noun to which 'good' is attached, are cases of ellipsis. Others regard these adjectives as fundamentally predicative and view apparent attributive uses as a special kind of predicative use. On this view, to call someone a 'good dancer' is simply to say that he or she is good and that he or she is a dancer. Szabó argues in favour of a predicative analysis (at least for the adjective 'good'). On this analysis, however, 'good' is also context-sensitive in the sense that its content will vary from one context to another. Often, any noun to which 'good' is attached will play a role in determining the content of 'good', but this need not be so.

Finally, Szabó argues that similar context-sensitive analyses can be given for a range of different adjectives, including colour adjectives, and that each of them respects compositionality.

Questions and tasks

1 Lahav frames his argument in terms of 'applicability conditions'. Why? Is this legitimate?
2 What exactly is Lahav's objection to the 'respectival analysis'?
3 About the 'enumerative analysis', Lahav says that all it 'manages to do is push the problem of noun-dependence one step further' (p. 407). What does Lahav mean, and has he identified a problem for the enumerative analysis?
4 Szabó's discussion concerning the predicative vs the predicate modifier analysis primarily uses the adjective 'good' as an example. Can his conclusions concerning 'good' be generalized to adjectives like 'red'?
5 What exactly is Szabó's analysis of the context-sensitivity of 'green'? Is something like Lahav's objection to the respectival analysis effective against Szabó's position?
6 What exactly is Szabó's objection to the intensional attributive analysis?

References and further reading

Davidson, Donald 1965: 'Theories of Meaning and Learnable Languages', in Y. Bar-Hillel (ed.), *Logic, Methodology and the Philosophy of Science*, Amsterdam: North-Holland Publishing Co.; reprinted in D. Davidson (1984), pp. 3–15.

Pagin, Peter 2005: 'Compositionality and Context', in G. Peter and G. Preyer (eds), *Contextualism in Philosophy*, Oxford: Oxford University Press.

Pelletier, Jeff 2003: 'Context dependence and compositionality', *Mind & Language* 2, pp. 148–61.

Predelli, Stefano 2005: 'Painted Leaves, Context and Semantic Analysis', *Linguistics and Philosophy* 28, pp. 351–74.

Recanati, François 2005: 'Literalism and Contextualism: Some Varieties', in G. Preyer and G. Peter (eds), *Contextualism in Philosophy*, Oxford: Oxford University Press, pp. 171–96.

Reimer, Marga 2002: 'Do Adjectives Conform to Compositionality?', *Philosophical Perspectives* 16, pp. 183–98.

Rothschild, Daniel, and Gabriel Segal Forthcoming: 'Indexical Predicates', *Mind & Language*.

Travis, Charles 1996: 'Meaning's Role in Truth', *Mind* 105, pp. 451–66.

Travis, Charles 1997: 'Pragmatics', in Bob Hale and Crispin Wright (eds), *A Companion to the Philosophy of Language*, Oxford: Blackwell, pp. 87–107.

Chapter 25

Ran Lahav

AGAINST COMPOSITIONALITY: THE CASE OF ADJECTIVES

It is often claimed that natural language is in general compositional, in the sense that the meaning of a complex expression is a function of the meanings of its constituent parts; or, to put this so-called principle of compositionality in other words, in the sense that an expression makes a uniform semantic contribution to all the compound expressions in which it is embedded. Thus formulated, the principle is rather vague, since its exact content depends on the sense of 'function of' or of 'uniform semantic contribution,' as well as on one's understanding of the notion of meaning. Indeed, the principle, which is usually traced back to Frege, appeared in the literature in a variety of versions.[1]

An intuitive paradigmatical example of this yet ill-defined principle, is the relationship between an adjective-noun expression and its constituent adjective and noun. The English adjective 'red,' for example, is said to make the same contribution to the meaning of the expression 'a red bird,' 'a red chair,' and any other English sentence in which the word 'red' appears; excluding, of course, idioms and metaphors, and perhaps some other special cases. However, it is exactly this seemingly obvious case of compositionality, namely that of adjectives, which I would like to question in the present paper. I will argue that an examination of how adjectives behave in natural language reveals that their semantic contribution to the meaning of the whole in which they are embedded varies non-systematically across linguistic contexts.

To see this, it is first necessary to make the notion of compositionality more precise. But since it is only adjectives that interest us here, it will suffice to characterize a notion of compositionality with respect to adjectives only, and in a sufficiently broad way so as to cover the majority of the common versions of the principle.

As to the notion of 'meaning' which appears in the principle, I will leave it an open question what meanings are. For the present purpose, we can use, instead of the problematic notions of meaning and semantic contributions, the notion of the *applicability conditions* of an adjective: the conditions that have to be satisfied by any object under any (correctly ascribed) noun in order for the adjective to correctly apply to that object; for example, the conditions under which an object is describable by 'red N,' for any noun N. After all, it is obvious that if two adjectives differ in their applicability conditions, then they also differ in their meaning (though perhaps not vice versa). Thus, instead of talking of 'a uniform semantic contribution,' we can interpret the principle broadly as requiring at least that every adjective has uniform applicability conditions in all the normal compound expressions in which it appears (excluding, of course special cases). Intuitively speaking, the idea is that the conditions that a table has to meet in order to be describable by 'red table' should be the same conditions that a house or a book has to meet in order to be describable by 'red house' or 'red book.' However, since the meaning of an expression may be context-dependent, the same should go for applicability conditions. The conditions that make something good or unique in one context should be allowed to be different from those that make something good or unique in another context, as long as there is a general rule for each adjective which specifies that context-dependency. Hence, by requiring that the applicability conditions of an adjective be uniform across all linguistic contexts, the principle should be understood as requiring that for every adjective there is a general function from contexts to applicability conditions. In that sense of a context-dependent notion of 'uniform,' the compositionality principle with respect to adjectives is the principle that every adjective has uniform applicability conditions across all compound expressions in which it is embedded. I take it that this formulation is broad enough to be accepted by most proponents of the different versions of the principle of compositionality. Intuitively, it says only that for any adjective there should be a general rule that specifies the conditions under which it can be applied to an object under a given noun.

One motivation for the compositionality principle for natural language is that it allows for a theoretically elegant account of the semantics of compound expressions. Another consideration is based on the argument that compositionality is necessary for the learnability of natural language.[2] However, in this paper I will not address directly any argument for compositionality. Instead, I will argue that as a matter of fact, adjectives behave in a non-compositional way. This will be, of course, an indirect challenge to such arguments. For, if the conclusion of an argument if false, then the argument cannot be sound.

Applicability conditions of adjectives

It is well known that the conditions under which many evaluative adjectives such as 'good' or 'beautiful' are applicable, depend on the noun to which the adjective is applied. What is beautiful for a girl is not beautiful for a tree, and what it is for a dog to be good differs from what it is for a couch or an apple to be good.[3] I do not refer here to another well known fact, that the applicability conditions of scalar adjectives, that is, ones which denote magnitudes such as 'long' or 'tall,' are scale-relative; that, for example, what is tall for a skyscraper is not tall for a man, and what is old for a turtle is not old for a car. What I have in mind is, rather, that different *types* of conditions, not just different magnitudes of the same condition, count towards the applicability of an adjective. A good knife, for example, is one that is sharp and is made of hard material, but a good man or a good apple is not sharper or blunter or made of a harder or softer material.

Several writers have pointed out isolated examples of other, non-evaluative adjectives whose applicability conditions are also noun-dependent. Quine pointed out that a red apple is red on the outside while a pink grapefruit is pink on the inside, and Partee took that example to be similar to the case of 'flat' which applies differently in 'flat tire,' 'flat beer' and 'flat note' (although it seems to me that it is more reasonable to regard the last two cases as mere metaphorical uses of 'flat').[4] What is not sufficiently appreciated, however, and sometimes even denied, is that virtually all adjectives behave in much the same way, and there seems to be no one fixed set of criteria determining their applicability to different objects. Keenan and Faltz, for example, explicitly claim that color and shape adjectives are noun-independent.[5] This, I think, is false, as the following examples will show. I should ask to be excused for the large number of examples that I give here. At the risk of being tedious, I intend them to demonstrate that the phenomenon of noun-dependence applies to adjectives in general, and not just to isolated special cases.

Consider the adjective 'red.' What it is for a bird to count as red is not the same as what it is for other kinds of objects to count as red. For a bird to be red (in the normal case), it should have most of the surface of its body red, though not its beak, legs, eyes, and of course its inner organs. Furthermore, the red color should be the bird's natural color, since we normally regard a bird as being 'really' red even if it is painted white all over. A kitchen table, on the other hand, is red even if it is only painted red, and even if its 'natural' color underneath the paint is, say, white. Moreover, for a table to be red only its upper surface needs to be red, but not necessarily its legs and its bottom surface. Similarly, a red apple, as Quine pointed out, needs to be red only on the outside, but a red hat needs to be red only in its external upper surface, a red crystal is red both inside and outside, and a red watermelon is red only inside. For a book to be red is for its cover but not necessarily for its inner pages to be mostly red, while for a newspaper to be red is for all of its pages to be red. For a house to be red is for its outside walls, but not necessarily its roof (and windows and door) to be mostly red, while a red car must be red in its external surface including its roof (but not its windows, wheels, bumper, etc.). A red star only needs to appear red from the earth, a red glaze needs to be red only after it is fired, and a red mist or a red powder are red not simply inside or outside. A red pen need not even have any red part (the ink may turn red only when in contact with the paper). In short, what counts for one type of thing to be red is not what counts for another. Of course, there is a feature that is common to all the things which count (non-metaphorically) as red, namely, that some part of them, or some item related to them, must appear wholly and literally redish. But that is only a very general necessary condition, and is far from being sufficient for a given object to count as red.

Color adjectives are not special in the noun-dependence of their applicability conditions. First, to mention them again, evaluative adjectives like 'good' or 'pretty' apply differently to different objects. Second, in the case of adjectives which, like color predicates, denote physical properties, the part of the object relevant to the applicability of the adjective varies across types of objects. A blunt knife, for example, has a blunt blade regardless of the bluntness of its handle, a flat foot is flat in its bottom surface, and a hot car has a hot engine (or, in other contexts, a hot interior) even though the rest of the car may be freezing cold. What is square in a square face are the contours of the chin, cheeks and forehead as they appear from the front, while a square house is square when looked at from above, and a square screwdriver has a square end. And third, there are many other adjectives that do not clearly fall under any particular category, which behave similarly. A slow animal is one which runs slowly, a slow student is one who grasps slowly, and a slow oven is one which cooks slowly. A tall man is tall regardless of whether he is standing or sitting or lying most of the time, while a tall building is tall only if it stands upright. A sad person is not distinguished by his intonation as is a sad voice, nor does he need to refer to tragic events as does a sad story. And a strong man is not unbreakable like a strong metal bar, and does not blow forcefully as a strong wind does. This is not to deny that there are intimate connections between the ways an adjective applies to different objects. It is only to say that despite the similarity, its applicability conditions differ considerably in different linguistic contexts.

Inapplicability of adjectives

Not only do adjectives apply differently to different objects, furthermore, many adjectives do not apply to many objects at all. Thus, for example, there is no conventional condition under which the expressions 'a straight house,' 'a soft car,' or 'a quiet stone' are applicable; not to mention the more obvious cases in which the noun is abstract while the adjective is not, such as 'a tall love' or 'a red idea,' or vice versa, 'a gradual rat' or 'an intense tree.' Notice, that the point is not that houses are never straight or that trees are never intense in the same way that trees never breath or talk. Rather, we have no agreed upon conception of what it would be for a house to count – or to fail to count – as straight, or for a rat to be gradual.

The fact that many adjectives lack conditions of applicability to some nouns, is well known.[6] But it is important to see that the reason for it is not that the meanings of the former are some-how inherently incongruent with the meanings of the latter, as in 'a square circle.' For we can easily imagine simple scripts in which a lin-guistic community associates non-metaphorical applicability conditions to many expressions which presently lack such conditions. In a com-munity where the front halves of cars are made of varying material, and the softness of the material is regarded as important for safety and as a major factor in the value of the car, the expression 'a soft car' would naturally and literally denote cars whose front halves are made of soft materials. And in a world in which rats are constantly changing in appearance, but some change more abruptly than others, the expression 'a gradual rat' may be naturally applied to the latter. (And don't object that the meaning of the gradualness of a rat in this case is different from what 'grad-ual' normally means, since as we saw, there is no one simple, fixed meaning common to all applications of an adjective to begin with.)

This implies that the reason that some adjec-tives do not have conditions of applicability to some nouns is not that there is some intrinsic incongruence between the individual meanings of the noun and the adjective, but simply because we have not had the occasion and inter-est to assign them applicability conditions. And this suggests again that the applicability condi-tions of an adjective are a patchwork of merely related, and not uniform, conditions.

Applicability conditions and compositionality

The noun-dependence of the applicability of adjectives suggests, I think, that adjectives have non-compositional semantics, in the sense that their applicability conditions (and thus their semantic contribution to the expression in which they are embedded) varies from one linguistic context to another in a way that cannot be analyzed in terms of a general (not vacuously disjunctive) rule or function. How-ever, the transition from noun-dependence to non-compositionality is not a trivial step, and prima facie there is a natural way to try to avoid it: to absorb the noun-dependence into the meaning, and thus into the applicability condi-tions of the adjective. This way, the applicability conditions of an adjective would be dependent upon the linguistic context, but would not vary across linguistic contexts.

One version of this idea, suggested by Partee, is to construe the meaning of an adjective as an enumeration of the different ways it applies to different types of objects.[7] This view can be called *the enumerative analysis of adjectives*. Alter-natively, one may try – as did Ziff, and later Fodor and Pylyshyn – to capture the factors that determine the applicability conditions by mak-ing the meaning of an adjective sensitive not to the type of object to which it applies, but to the respect in which the object is most interesting or salient.[8] The view can therefore be called *the respectival analysis of adjectives*.

The problem with these two analyses is that even if correct, they would not help the cause of compositionality. They only push the threat of non-compositionality one step back. For it can readily be seen that just as an adjective does not have noun-independent applicability conditions, neither do the expressions that are used in the proposed analyses. The analyses therefore leave us with the same noun-dependence with which we started.

1 The respectival analysis of adjectives

Let us first examine the respectival suggestion. As Fodor and Pylyshyn express the view: " 'Good NP' means something like NP *that answers to the relevant interests in NPs*: a good book is one that answers to our interest in books (viz. it's good to read); a good rest is one that answers to our interest in rests . . . the meaning of 'good' is syncategorematic and has a variable in it for relevant interests . . ."[9]

How should this analysis apply to other, non-evaluative adjectives? Perhaps it might be thought that 'red' means something like: red in the manner and in the parts whose color is most interesting or salient in this type of object. And 'square' means something like: approaching squareness to a larger extent than an average object of this type, with respect to its interesting or salient contours.

That the prospects of this position are not great can be seen from the simple observation that 'salient' and 'interesting' are themselves adjectives, and as such are noun-dependent. Consequently, although it is hardly deniable that a red house is indeed red in a salient respect or in a respect that interests us, the conditions which make the color of a house salient or interesting are different from the conditions which make the color of a crystal, pencil, or bird salient of interesting. The analysis therefore fails to provide applicability conditions that are uniform for different types of objects.

More specifically, according to the suggested analysis, the reason red houses are red outside is that the color of their external surface is most interesting or salient. Now, the sense in which a red house is more saliently or interestingly red outside than inside, is that the red covers most of its external appearance, and thus captures the eye when the house is seen from the outside. However, a red crystal is not saliently or interestingly red in that same way. What makes a red crystal red is not just the sensory conspicuousness of its redness, since a crystal whose surface only is red – or worse, which is painted red – is not really a red crystal. Its color is salient or interesting probably in that it determines its type or value. Red houses and red crystals are therefore saliently or interestingly red in different respects: the former in its sensory conspicuousness, while the latter in a more cognitive way, with respect to its geological significance. To try to explain the difference between the redness of houses and the redness of crystals in terms of salience or interest therefore only transfers the problem of the multiplicity of respects in which objects may be red to the multiplicity of respects in which objects may be salient or interesting.

One might object that the difference between the redness of houses and that of crystals is not a difference in the *respect* in which the redness is salient or interesting, but only in the *object* of interest or salience. It is simply a result of the fact that different parts interest us in houses and in crystals. But that would not do. We are interested in the color of the interior of a house, that is, in the colors of its rooms, no less than we are interested in the color of its external surface. Nevertheless the color of the inside of houses does not normally count towards the color of the house, whereas the color of the inside of crystals does.

Unlike the cases of houses and crystals, a red pen is red not because its redness is more conspicuous in its appearance, nor because of any geological or chemical interest in it, but because of our interest in its function: producing marks on paper. But on the other hand, a brush is not colorful even though its function is to lay colorful marks on surfaces, and neither is a potion whose function is to enhance the greenness of plants necessarily green.

The same phenomenon applies to other, non-color adjectives too. A square book is saliently or interestingly square in the sense of sensory conspicuousness; but a square house has many shapes that are not square, such as the shape of its external walls, which are much more conspicuous than its horizontal cross section. The squareness of a house depends, therefore, not on the pure sensory conspicuousness of its shape (unlike its color which is determined by pure sensory conspicuousness), nor on our interest in its function, but on some kind of architectural interest; which, it is worth noting, is not our everyday interest in houses. The strength of a wind is salient or interesting from the point of view of our interest in its effects, while the strength of a metal bar is salient or interesting from the point of view of our interest in its function, and a strong color is strong in the sense of some kind of sensory impression. Even the adjective 'good' does not mean answers our interests in that kind of object, as Ziff and later Fodor and Pylyshyn suggest, since we are normally interested also in properties which do not count towards the goodness of the object. A pornographic book might answer some of our interests in books although we would not regard it as a good book, and an ancient golden knife might answer our interest in cutlery although, being dull, it would not be regarded as a good knife.

More generally, just as there is no unitary respect in which all red objects are red, there is no reason to expect that there is a unitary respect in which all salient or interesting things are salient or interesting. For one thing, different types of interest and salience often conflict with each other, and these conflicts are resolved in different ways for different types of objects. Furthermore, in many cases it is not even clear that type of interest or salience it is which picks out the object's relevant respect. The contours which make a round face round, for example, are clearly not salient or interesting in any functional sense, nor are they more conspicuous in appearance than the profile's contours; and it is far from clear what type of salience or interest determines that a man is fat if his belly rather than his face or legs are fat.

Thus, analyzing adjectives in terms of interest or salience cannot help get rid of the problem of noun-dependence, since what counts as salient or interesting is different for different objects no less than what counts as red or square.

2 The enumerative analysis of adjectives

A similar problem applies to the second of the above mentioned analyses, in terms of enumerative meanings: it uses an expression that is no less noun-dependent than the analyzed adjective itself.

The basic idea of the enumerative analysis is that to apply an adjective to an object is to say that depending upon the type of object in question, a certain specified aspect of the object (e.g. its shape, or its function, its part, its environment) has some specified property.[10] The adjective 'red,' for example, is analyzed as meaning something like: having an external surface which is red if it is a non-transparent solid inanimate object, having a red inner volume if it is a fruit whose inside only is edible, etc.

Note that the adjective 'red' is analyzed here in terms of redness (of various parts of the object). But that should not be seen as a problem. For, the redness that is mentioned in the analysans can be construed as redness in some restricted, unitary sense, which does not vary from object to object. Specifically, since it seems that every red object is red in some surface and/or in some volume in it or pertaining to it, we can analyze all 'red' occurrences in terms of this restricted redness – redness in the sense in which a surface or a volume is red. Using the notion of *primitively red* for this sense of redness, a more precise formulation of the enumerative analysis of 'red' would be something like: having an external surface which is primitively red if it is a non-transparent solid inanimate object, having a primitively red inside if it is a fruit whose inside only is edible, etc.

The same should be applicable to other adjectives. To say that something is square, for example, is to say that the contours of its functional part are primitively square if it is a tool, that its contours as seen from above are primitively square if its is a building, and so on. And since the way in which an object's surface or volume is primitively red does not differ from object to object, it might seem that the analysis does indeed get rid of the noun-dependence of adjectives which threatens compositionality.

However, a closer look will reveal that this not the case. For there is another problematic expression that is used in the suggested analysans. If, as we saw, the idea is to explain away the noun-dependence by analyzing an adjective as meaning something like: having an aspect which is primitively A if the object is a B . . ., then the formulation of the analysans will necessarily consist of an expression denoting an aspect-of relation between the object and its aspect: 'the surface of an object,' 'an object *having* a blade which . . .,' 'its function is . . .,' 'the object's contours are . . .,' 'an object *whose* environment is. . . .' In fact, since, as we saw, many analysans must be rather complex, it is clear that in many of them several aspect-of expressions will be used, for example, '*having* walls *whose* external surface is . . .'

But now, the problem is that the applicability conditions of aspect-of expressions – 'of,' 'having' 'its' 'whose,' and their equivalents – are noun-dependent no less than the applicability conditions of the analyzed adjective itself. And if so, then what it is for one thing to be of another thing differs from object to object, no less than what it is for something to be describable by 'red' or 'square.' All that the proposed analysis manages to do is push the problem of noun-dependence one step further.

To see this, consider, for example, the expression 'has a primitively red external surface,' which is presumably supposed to be used in the analysis of 'red.' Since I am not concerned here with the compositionality of nouns such as 'surface,' we may grant, for the sake of the argument, that there are uniform conditions which make something count as a surface, or even as an external surface. The question arises, however, what it is that makes a given surface the surface of some given object, rather than that of another.

After all, there are many surfaces, and even *external* surfaces, in the world, including a great number of them in any given object. To take the example of a bird, the surface of the bird's beak, of its kidneys, of it feathers, and of its brain – not to mention surfaces in the bird's environment – are all surfaces, and even external ones. But although they are in the bird's body, they do not count as the external surfaces of the bird, but rather as those of its kidney, feather, brain. In virtue of what conditions is a given surface the surface of, say, the kidney, and not of the bird?

Now, the answer to that question should specify the *general* conditions for of-ness relations between any two items, and not only between birds and their surfaces. For, as we saw, an aspect-of expression is supposed to be used in virtually every analysis of an adjective. The analysis will therefore help the cause of compositionality only if aspect-of expressions behave more nicely than adjectives; which is to say, only if what it is for one object to be of another is not different for different types of objects, as is what it is for an object to be red or square.

But now, if we examine the conditions under which one object counts as being of, or being had by, another, we discover that what it is to have one type of object is different from what it is to have another type of object. And that should not be surprising. For although aspect-of expressions are, grammatically speaking, not adjectives but rather prepositions ('of') or verbs ('have'), they are similar to adjectives in their function, in that they express a predicate which applies to objects.

Consider, for example, what it is for something to be of a bird. For a surface or a bottom to count as being of a bird, it must be part of the bird's body; but a behavior or a nest or a mate of a bird need not. Furthermore, even being part of the bird's body is not a sufficient condition for the bird's surface or bottom, since not every surface or bottom in the bird's body is the bird's surface or bottom. As we saw, a surface or a bottom in a bird may be the beak's or the kidney's. As a matter of fact, if we allow science-fiction-like cases, it is not even enough for a feather or a leg to be part of the bird's body in order for them to count as the bird's feather or leg. Some birds may have body cells with tiny feathers, or corpuscles which move around in their blood stream with the help of tiny legs. Clearly, although these would be parts of the bird's body, they would not be the bird's feathers or legs. Note that it is not the fact that these object are too small or too deep inside the bird that disqualifies them from being the bird's. Lungs, for example, are the bird's lungs even though they are inside the bird's body, and so are body cells, even though they are microscopic.

Similarly, if a table is made of (a bird's) wings or (a zebra's) hide, that does not make any part of the table the table's wings or the table's hide. The wipers' motor in a car is not the car's motor, and a tail does not become my tail if I swallow it. Not every wall in a house is the house's wall, and not every shape in a face is the face's shape. In order for something to count as a leg or a head or a wall of an object, it has to serve a function specific for the object, or to be situated in the right place in it, or to be connected in the right way to other parts of the object, or in general to satisfy various conditions which vary from object to object. The situation is even worse for aspect-of relationship to aspects that are not parts. It is hard to see anything in common between the of-ness relationships in the case of the function of a knife, the job of a person, his birthday, his friend, and his weight.

It seems, therefore, that whether one object counts as being of another object depends on what type of object they are. And what this means is that the attempt to analyze adjective-noun expressions in terms of aspects of objects cannot eliminate the noun-dependence of applicability conditions. What it is for an object to be describable by 'red' differs for different objects no less than what it is for an object to have a primitively red surface, or primitively square contours.

Noun-dependence and natural language analysis

What all this suggests is that neither the enumerative nor the respectival analyses of adjectives can save compositionality from the problem of the noun-dependence of adjectives. What they both do is transfer the noun-dependence of the analyzed adjective to the noun-dependence of the expressions used in the proposed analysans, and thus leave us with the same threat to compositionality with which we started. Is there then some other way to save compositionality? A partial answer is that at the very least it seems that no analysis that captures the meaning of adjectives *by using natural language expressions* can do the job. For, any such natural language expression should comprise no aspect-of expression, no underspecified interest- or salience-adjectives, and more generally no adjective that applies non-primitively to an object. And as far as I can see, no plausible analysis is possible under these restrictions.

One might be tempted to think that an analysis of adjectives that uses only nouns and verbs might be possible. But this suggestion does not seem to work. One reason for this is that nouns and verbs are not sufficient to capture the meaning of many adjectives. How can one analyze what it is for an object to be red or square without using either adjectives or aspect-of expressions? Or course, you can *define* new nouns or verbs which will capture the meaning of an adjective, for example, define 'a redder' as meaning: an object which is red. But then, the applicability conditions of such newly defined expressions will inevitably inherit noun-dependence from the expressions used in their definition.

Another reason why this suggestion would not work is that at least many verbs are as noun-dependent as adjectives. For a hat to be ruined is for it to have unremovable stains or holes or wrinkles, unlike what it is for a clock or a city to be ruined. Giving someone a glass of water involves handing it without necessarily transferring ownership, unlike giving someone a house or an idea or a name. Opening a door is moving it to uncover an opening which it hides, while opening a box is moving only a part of it to uncover a hollow inside it, and opening a newspaper is spreading its pages, unlike opening a fruit or an eye or a wound.

It must be admitted that there are a number of verbs which at least on the surface do not seem to display noun-dependence. The verb 'walk,' so it seems, applies to anything that moves on its legs on the solid ground, and the verb 'eat' applies to anything that inserts food through its mouth into its digestive system. The same is true for many other verbs denoting human actions. However, it is important to note that what is common to the applicability conditions of such verbs is that they are defined in terms of various functionally characterized organs of the agent. Indeed, when we encounter expressions such as 'the tree walked,' or 'the tree talked,' the only way to make sense of them is to assume that the tree has the relevant organs, namely, legs in the first case and a mouth in the second. But if this is so, and the applicability conditions of such verbs are defined in terms of parts or aspects of the object, then we are back to the problem of noun-dependence of aspect-of expressions. Since the aspect-of relationship is not a uniform relationship, verbs which are defined in terms of it do not have uniform applicability conditions either. Thus, the recourse to verbs not only fails to help compositionality, it even makes it worse, by suggesting that noun-dependence applies to verbs too.

What remains of the suggestion to analyze adjectives by using only compositionally behaving expressions, is that the analysis can use only nouns, and the very few adjectives and verbs that might prove to be an exception to the noun-dependence rule. But those seem to be hardly enough resources for carrying out such a comprehensive analysis of all the adjectives and verbs in natural language. There does not seem to be

any way to analyze what it is for an object to be red or square without using adjectives, verbs, or aspect-of relationships.

Expelling noun-dependence from semantics

At this point, it might be tempting to think that if the noun-dependence of adjectives cannot be eliminated, then it can at least be made harmless to the principle of compositionality, by viewing it as belonging to the pragmatics of adjectives, and not to their semantics. An adjective such as 'red,' according to this idea, means something like what I called 'primitively red'; that is, red in the way that only a small number of objects are red, presumably red surfaces or red volumes. Strictly speaking, therefore, only surfaces and transparent bodies can be red. All other objects which in ordinary language we call 'red' – what we call 'red apples,' 'red books,' etc. – are not really red. We *call* them so for various pragmatical reasons, but strictly speaking, inaccurately and falsely. The case can be compared to that of the expression 'there are a thousand people in the audience.' The fact that we often use this expression for audiences that we know are only roughly of a thousand people, does not mean that 'a thousand' means roughly a thousand. It is therefore not part of the semantics of an adjective that we apply it differently to different objects, and so noun-dependence is not a counterexample to the principle of compositionality.

One problem with this suggestion is that if it is to be more than a vacuous trick, a reason has to be given for why so many sentences that we ordinarily take to be true should be viewed as being really inaccurate and false. The presumption should be that what speakers who are in command of the facts take to be true is true, unless shown otherwise. And I can see no good way of showing this in the case of adjectives. In particular, the familiar argument that compositionality is required for the learnability of language will not help here. The learnability of the problematic behavior of 'red' will not be explained merely by calling it pragmatics rather than semantics.

Furthermore, on the face of it, the suggestion seems rather implausible. When we use an expression such as 'there are a thousand people in the audience' in a way that is strictly speaking false or inaccurate, there must be room for greater accuracy. One can, for example, ask the speaker to be more precise. But there seems to be no parallel in the case of adjectives. If someone describes a car as red or a knife as sharp, then it makes no sense to ask him to be more precise about the way in which it is red or sharp (although it makes sense to ask him to be more precise about *magnitudes*: the exact shade of red, or the degree of sharpness). In fact, if after describing his knife as sharp the speaker adds 'more precisely, the sharpness of my knife is only in its blade, not in its handle,' then that will be accepted at most as a joke. And if there is no room for greater accuracy in the use of the adjective, then no inaccuracy has been there in the first place.

Moreover, when a sentence, such as 'there are a thousand people in the audience,' is used inaccurately and strictly speaking falsely, the hearer can complain that it was misleading. But again, there seems to be no parallel in the case of adjectives. If I tell someone that my knife is sharp, and the hearer, upon seizing the knife, disappointedly complains that I misled him into thinking that the handle of the knife is sharp too, we would ordinarily say that he simply does not understand what 'sharp knife' *means*.

For these reasons, it seems that the noun-dependence of the applicability of adjectives is due to their meaning, and not to the inaccurate way in which we apply them. Admittedly, I rely here on our ordinary linguistic intuitions, which need not be infallible. But until some good reason is given for rejecting them, the idea of banishing noun-dependence to pragmatics seems to be unacceptable.

Conclusion

All this is not intended to be a knock-down argument against the compositionality principle, but only to show that the common approaches which are often used to support it are unsatisfactory. This leaves open the possibility that the principle could be defended in some other way. But as far as I can see, that is possible, if at all, only at the price of ad hoc, unmotivated, or implausible claims.

Specifically, at least three defenses of the principle seem to be still open. First, it might be thought that adjectives in different contexts can be regarded as distinct words with different meanings, so that the lack of uniformity between their applicability is no longer embarrassing. 'Red' in 'red house' and 'red' in 'red apple' are simply two distinct words. Second, it might be thought that even though the uniform applicability conditions (and meaning) of an adjective cannot be satisfactorily analyzed by using natural language expressions, they might still be analyzable in theoretical terms. The common element between all the applicability conditions of an adjective would then be regarded as a theoretical posit, presumably some theoretically specifiable property. And third, the common element between the applicability conditions of an adjective can be construed as a primitive which is properly analyzable neither in theoretical nor in natural language terms.

It remains to be investigated whether any of these approaches, and possibly others, can work. But it seems to me that none of them is very appealing. The first position is especially implausible, since it seems to contradict the obvious fact that the meanings of an adjective across normal linguistic contexts are intimately related. And if the word 'red' in one context is a different word from 'red' in another, then it is unclear how this intimate semantic relationship can be explained. Furthermore, the position also seems to make the learnability of language – the speaker's ability to use his understanding of one 'red' to gain understanding of another 'red' – unexplainable by compositionality alone; which undermines one of the main motivations for the compositionality principle.

As to the other two alternatives for rescuing compositionality, they have the burden of explaining why, if adjectives do have uniform applicability conditions, these conditions systematically escape analysis in natural language terms. Furthermore, if compositionality is to help explain the learnability of natural language, then it has to be assumed that the speaker somehow uses the alleged uniform applicability conditions as criteria for the use of adjectives. But then it is rather mysterious why despite the speaker's mastery of such (alleged) uniform criteria, his natural language resources are systematically insufficient to provide a uniform characterization of these criteria. It seems more plausible that there simply are no such criteria.

Further discussion is needed to evaluate the plausibility of these positions. But the moral of the discussion is that in any case, compositional meanings of adjectives, even if there are such, can no longer be accounted for in a straightforward way, as simple, isolable semantic building blocks, as it might be tempting to view them. A much more complicated account is required. Indeed, it is my opinion that unless one is willing to believe in such bizarre monsters as adjectives that are individuated by their linguistic contexts, or primitive applicability conditions, adjectives should be construed as having a non-compositional semantics. While the applicability conditions and thus the meanings of an expression in different linguistic contexts ordinarily have a uniform context-independent element, they also have a surprisingly large component that differs non-systematically from context to context.

But there is another prima facie reason against those rather forced defenses of the principle of compositionality. Psychologically speaking, it seems quite clear what the cognizer does when applying an adjective in a newly encountered linguistic context: he uses analogies or similarity relationships to go from familiar linguistic contexts to new ones. One can figure out that, for example, a red box is red outside by making an analogy – and not a trivial one – to red houses and balls, but not to red crystals or watermelons. But now, it seems that nowhere in this psychological story is there any room for a uniform mental state which is the apprehension of the applicability conditions of 'red.' The speaker does not seem to use, psychologically speaking, any single criterion for applying 'red.' Now, of course, there is no automatic translation of psychological stories to semantic theories. But it seems that some strong parallel should exist between the two. And if so, then it seems reasonable to expect that what makes a red box or crystal or watermelon red is something that has to do with a network of similarity relationships to paradigmatical cases, and not with some unitary semantic unit. This is of course not a conclusive argument. But it suggests that an account of the semantics of adjectives based on family resemblance or similarity relationships, instead of on compositionally behaving fixed semantic building blocks, might prove better for dealing with the noun-dependence of adjectives.

Notes

1 See for example Frege, G., (1960), Montague, R., (1970), and Janssen, T. M. V., (1986).
2 Davidson, D., (1965); Leeds, S., (1979).
3 See for example Ziff, P., (1960), chapter 6, mainly on the adjective 'good;' Austin, J., (1962), chapter 7, on the adjective 'real.'
4 Quine, W. V. O., (1960); Partee, B., (1984), pp. 289–290.
5 Keenan, E. L., and Faltz, L. M., (1985), pp. 122–123.
6 Chomsky, N., (1965), chapter 4.
7 Partee, (1984), pp. 289–290.
8 Ziff, (1960), chapter 6; Fodor, J. and Pylyshyn, Z. W., (1988), pp. 42–43.
9 Fodor and Pylyshyn, (1988), pp. 42–43.
10 See Partee, (1984), p. 290, who expresses the idea

by suggesting that the meaning of an adjective is determined by an enumerative function whose values depend on the properties of the object to which the adjective applies.

References

Austin, J.: 1962, *Sense and Sensibilia* (Clarendon Press, Oxford).

Chomsky, N.: 1965, *Aspects of the Theory of Syntax* (M.I.T. Press, Cambridge).

Davidson, D.: 1965, 'Theories of Meaning and Learnable Languages', in Bar-Hillel, Y., (ed.), *Logic, Methodology and Philosophy of Science* (North Holland Publishing Company, Amsterdam), pp. 383–394.

Fodor, J. and Pylyshyn, Z. W.: 1988, 'Connectionism and Cognitive Architecture: A Critical Analysis', *Cognition* 28, pp. 3–71.

Frege, G.: 1960, 'On Sense and Reference', in Geach, P., and Black, M., (eds.), *Translations from the Philosophical Writings of Gottlob Frege* (Basil Blackwell, Oxford) [also contained in a new translation in this volume, pp. 49–55].

Janssen, T. M. V.: 1986, *Foundations and Applications of Montague Grammar* (Mathematisch Centrum, Amsterdam).

Keenan, E. L. and L. M. Faltz: 1985, *Boolean Semantics for Natural Language* (D. Reidel Publishing Company, Dodrecht).

Leeds, S.: 1979, 'Semantic Primitives and Learnability', *Logique et Analyse* 22, pp. 99–108.

Montague, R.: 1970, 'Universal Grammar', *Theoria* 36, pp. 373–398.

Partee, B.: 1984, 'Compositionality', in F. Landman and F. Veltman (eds.), *Varieties of Formal Semantics* (Foris, Dodrecht (GRASS vol. 3)), pp. 281–311.

Quine, W. V. O.: 1960, *Word and Object* (M.I.T. Press, Cambridge).

Ziff, P.: 1960, *Semantic Analysis* (Cornell University Press, Ithaca).

Chapter 26

Zoltán Gendler Szabó

ADJECTIVES IN CONTEXT

1 The context thesis

One of the fundamental assumptions of contemporary semantic theory is the principle of compositionality, the thesis that the meaning of a complex expression is determined by the meanings of its constituents and by the manner in which these constituents are combined. When challenged, defenders of the principle tend to appeal to the undeniable fact that competent speakers routinely understand complex expressions they have never heard before. This fact, they contend, can only be adequately explained if we assume that linguistic competence requires implicit grasp of a recursive system of semantic rules which assign meanings to complex expressions on the basis of the meanings of their constituents and the way those constituents are combined.

But this is much too quick. Nobody denies that the meaning of a complex expression *depends* on the meanings of its constituents and on its structure; the bite of compositionality is that it depends on *nothing else*. The appeal of the principle stems from the conviction that those who can understand a new expression must work out its meaning from facts they knew about the expression antecedently. And of course, the only candidate facts are lexical or syntactic. But this piece of reasoning neglects the possibility that the *context* in which someone encounters a new expression can provide additional clues relevant for interpretation. And if it does, there is no reason to assume that the lexical and syntactic facts *by themselves* fix the meaning of the new expression. So at the very least, attention to context undermines the unreflective assumption that compositionality is a trivial matter.[1]

Let us make our terminology more precise. The word 'meaning' is used in semantics to refer to all sorts of semantic values; in what follows, I want to focus on a particular semantic value often called 'content'. The *content* of a declarative sentence is the proposition it expresses and the contents of sub-sentential expressions are the semantic contributions of such expressions to propositions expressed by declarative sentences within which they occur as constituents. There is no general agreement concerning the nature of propositions; the only thing I will assume about them is that they determine truth-conditions, that is, that if two sentences express the same proposition they cannot differ in truth-value. Semantic theories typically aim at ascribing content to complex expressions in a compositional fashion, hence they are committed to the principle of compositionality of content.[2]

I take the *context* of utterance to be a wide and heterogeneous collection of facts concerning the linguistic and non-linguistic environment of a particular use of an expression. It includes facts about the time and the location of the utterance, facts about the speaker, the hearer, and the salient objects around them, facts about their shared background knowledge, about the form and content of the conversation they had before the utterance in question was made, and perhaps much more. There are several important foundational questions about contexts, but for the purposes of this paper I wish to remain more or less neutral with regard to these.[3] I will consider the context of an utterance simply as the sum total of *all* the non-lexical and non-syntactic facts relevant for determining what a speaker conveys by the utterance. Let us say that an expression is *context-dependent* if and only if it can have different contents when uttered in different contexts. A context-dependent complex expression none of whose constituents are context-dependent would then be a counterexample to the principle of compositionality of content. Is there such a counterexample?

There are many cases when we *seem* to be presented with context-dependent expressions, but in fact we are not. Such cases come in two varieties, which I will call *phonetic* and *pragmatic* illusions of context-dependence. Phonetic illusions of context-dependence occur when we have different expressions articulated in the same way. Consider the following two sequences of sentences:

(1) a. I should stop digging this hole in the bottom of this ship, but I cannot resist the temptation. Sinking boats can be entertaining.
     b. I should stop watching sea battles on video, but I cannot resist the temptation. Sinking boats can be entertaining.

According to their most plausible interpretations, (1a) is about my activity of sinking boats, while (1b) is about boats that are sinking. So it seems that the content of 'Sinking boats can be entertaining' varies depending on the larger linguistic context in which it is used. But this is not so. The illusion that we have expressions with multiple contents arises because our ordinary *notation* is ambiguous: ' 'Sinking boats can be

entertaining' ' refers to two different sentences.[4] The justification for the claim that we are dealing with two different expressions here is syntactic: the linear order of 'sinking' and 'boats' disguises glaring structural differences.

Pragmatic illusions of context-dependence may arise when utterances of an expression *convey* different things in different contexts. From this, one might be tempted to conclude immediately that the expression *says* different things in different contexts. But this does not follow. Consider these sequences:

(2) a. I could not solve the crossword puzzle, even after I wasted the whole weekend on it. The puzzle was extremely difficult.
     b. I solved the crossword puzzle in five minutes while cooking dinner and listening to the radio. The puzzle was extremely difficult.

It is quite plausible to take 'The puzzle was extremely difficult' as ironical in (2b), but not in (2a). Still, there is no good reason to postulate that this sentence expresses different propositions in these two cases; its content is invariably the proposition that the puzzle was extremely difficult. But since this proposition is in conflict with the content of the first sentence of (2b), a sensible hearer will conclude that in uttering the second sentence of (2b) the speaker did not mean to convey what he literally said. We have strong reasons to think that irony is a pragmatic matter: there is no foolproof conventional mark indicating that an utterance is ironical. Moreover, we couldn't even introduce such a conventional sign. For suppose we agreed that, say, a winking of the left eye signals that the utterance must be interpreted ironically; those who wanted to be *genuinely* ironical would certainly refrain from winking in making their remarks.

Despite the prevalence of phonetic and pragmatic illusions, cases of genuine context-dependence are not hard to come by. Consider (3) and (4), for example:

(3)   Some basketball players are giants.
(4)   I am now at the North Pole.

What (3) and (4) say is fixed in part by the context of utterance. If a giant is supposed to be a "legendary being of great stature and strength and of more than mortal but less than godlike power" then (3) is false, but if it is merely "a living being of great size", it is true.[5] Since the fact that 'giant' can have different contents is clearly marked in the lexicon, (3) is not a likely candidate for a pragmatic illusion of context-dependence. Saying that there are two words in English—'giant$_1$' and 'giant$_2$'—and that consequently we are dealing with a phonetic illusion of context-dependence in (3) would also be implausible.[6] Neither semantic intuition, nor etymology would support such a claim. A speaker who never heard 'giant' be used in referring to people of extraordinary size would probably still be able to figure out how to understand (3); by contrast a speaker who doesn't know that 'bank' can be used to refer to the edges of rivers will not know what to make of 'I closed my account in the bank.' 'Giant' is a *polysemous* expression, i.e. ''giant'' refers unambiguously to 'giant', but this lexical item has multiple closely associated contents.[7]

The case of (4) is even more straightforward: different people can say different things at different times uttering this sentence. I have never been in a position to use it to express a truth, but I might be in the future and others have been in the past. 'I' and 'now' are indexical expressions; their contents are fixed in accordance with a linguistic rule relative to the context of use. And the context-dependence of indexicals spreads to the sentences that contain them as constituents.

Neither polysemy nor indexicality is a threat to compositionality: (3) and (4) have multiple contents *because* they contain constituents whose contents depend on the context. To find a com-pelling counterexample to compositionality we would need a complex expression whose content changes with the context in which it is used even though the contents of all of its constituent expressions remain fixed. Whether or not there is such a counterexample, coming up with one is not a trivial matter. I will call the claim that there is no such counterexample the context thesis:

> Context Thesis: The content of an expression depends on context only insofar as the contents of its constituents do.

According to the context thesis the context-dependency of a complex expression must be indirect. Once one has fixed what content the simple constituents have in a given context, the way in which the content of the complex expression depends on the context is also fixed. In the next section, I will consider an argument against the context thesis, based on the semantic behavior of certain complex nominal expressions containing adjectives.

2 The color of a painted leaf

Charles Travis has argued that many different things might be said with the same words, even if the subject matter of the utterances remains the same:

> As an arbitrary example, consider the words 'The leaf is green', speaking of a given leaf, and its condition at a given time, used so as to mean what they do mean in English. How many distinct things might be said in words with all that true of them? Many. That emerges when we note that one might speak either truth or falsity in such words, if the leaf is the right way. Suppose a Japanese maple leaf, turned brown, was painted green for a decoration. In sorting leaves by colour, one might truly call this one green. In describing leaves to help identify their species, it might, for all the paint, be false to call it that. So

words may have all the stipulated features while saying something true, but also while saying something false. Nothing about what it is to be green decides whether the colour of a thing is the way it is with, or the way it is without the paint. What being green is is compatible with speaking either truth or falsity in calling the leaf green. For all that, the painted leaf is as it is sometimes, but not other times, said to be in calling it green.[8]

What the example shows is subject to debate. Let me start with what is relatively uncontroversial. First, the truth-value of an utterance of 'The leaf is green' made about the painted leaf depends on the context. Roughly, the utterance is true if it is made when one is sorting leaves for decoration, and false if it is made when one is trying to identify the species of the leaf. Second, the sequence of phonemes uttered in the two scenarios stand for the same unique sentence, i.e. ''The leaf is green'' refers unambiguously to the sentence 'The leaf is green'. Third, the words 'leaf' and 'green' are used in both cases "so as to mean what they do mean in English", which is presumably something fixed. Consequently, we have a single sentence which says different things in different contexts, even though the sentence is neither syntactically nor lexically ambiguous.

Is this a challenge to the context thesis? It depends. 'Meaning' is an elusive phrase and it is not entirely clear how Travis intends to use it here. If by 'meaning' we mean the conventions of use for an expression knowledge of which guarantees understanding then the fact that sentences with a fixed meaning can say different things is no surprise. Any sentence containing an indexical has a single meaning in this sense even though it can expresses a plethora of different propositions. But suppose 'meaning' is taken to mean the contribution an expression makes to the proposition expressed by sentences containing the expression. Then the claim that 'The leaf is green' can express different propositions even

though the words this sentence is constructed from have a fixed meaning is in direct conflict with the context thesis.

The obvious reply to this challenge is to reject the claim that the constituent expressions have identical contents in the two utterances. One idea would be to say that this is a case of referential indeterminacy: 'the leaf' can denote the leaf with or without the paint. There is some plausibility to this idea, given that we would be strongly inclined to call both of those entities leaves. No doubt, this line gives rise to some metaphysical puzzles (How come we have two leafs roughly at the same spatio-temporal location? Do we really create a new leaf in painting one? If we remove the paint is the leaf with paint destroyed?), but the solution is implausible independently of these puzzles. For if in some contexts 'the leaf' denotes what is below the paint, then presumably in those contexts 'The leaf is unpainted' is true. But this is unacceptable: there is no context in which one can hold up a painted leaf and say truthfully 'The leaf is unpainted'.

Clearly, it is better to locate the context-dependence in the adjective. One might say that there is no such thing as *the* content of 'green', just as there is no such thing as *the* content of 'giant' or *the* content of 'I'. What it is to be green varies with the context. But there are two problems with this reply. The first is that according to Travis the example was merely illustrative, and the phenomenon has nothing to do with specificities of 'green'. The second is that 'green' does not seem to be a polysemous or indexical word. Let us look at these problems in more detail.

According to Travis, the example of painted leaf can be easily generalized. In fact, he thinks the moral applies to "whatever else words speak of":

> The words 'is green', while speaking of being green, may make any of indefinitely many distinct contributions to what is said in words of which they are part. The above variation is illustrative. The same holds of any English

predicate. The fact that 'is green' speaks of being green does not alone decide what is required for a thing to be as it, on a speaking, says a thing to be. Similarly for whatever else words speak of.[9]

I think this is an overstatement. If one uses the sentence 'The number is even', talking about the number four, the sentence expresses a truth. One cannot construct some special scenario where due to some camouflage similar to the painting of the leaf 'The number is even' says something false.

There is a trivial way that the example can be generalized to practically all non-mathematical and non-logical cases. Take the sentence 'The book is a novel.' There are all sorts of borderline instances of novelhood, like longish short-stories, modern epics written in free verse, etc. Let the phrase 'the book' be used to denote some such entity. Then there are scenarios where the sentence is true according to the contextual norm, and others where it is false. This is not especially interesting, since it does not threaten the context thesis: intuitively, whenever the content of '. . . is a novel' is vague in this way, it is because the content of 'novel' is vague. What is challenging about the example of the painted leaf is that it is independent of problems of vagueness. Even if a brown maple leaf is painted the most paradigmatic green one can imagine, the problem whether the leaf is green remains.

If we neglect vagueness, however, Travis's example is not widely generalizable. There are indeed different scenarios where utterances of the sentence 'The ring is gold' are about the same object, but have different truth-values. If the ring contains silver besides pure gold the utterance can be true in ordinary circumstances and false in a laboratory. But speaking of a ring made of pure gold, 'The ring is gold' expresses a truth, no matter what the speaker thinks, or what the purpose of her statement is.

So, we can conclude that the kind of context-dependency that we see in 'The leaf is green' is

not universal: 'The number is even' or 'The ring is gold' are rather similar sentences that do not have it. Of course, it is equally obvious that the example is generalizable to many other adjectives, besides 'green'. It is quite easy to come up with parallel cases for 'The apple is red', 'The move is smart', 'The problem is interesting', or 'The soup is good'. The question is then, what is responsible for this limited phenomenon?

This brings us to the second problem concerning the suggestion that 'green' is a context-dependent adjective. One can articulate the intuition behind Travis' example thus: "Of course, the challenge can be countered by saying that 'green' expresses one content in one scenario and another content in the other. But intuitively, this is not the case. What it contributes to a proposition expressed by 'The leaf is green' in either scenario is the same: the property of being green. 'Green' is not a polysemous expression and it is not an indexical either. To stipulate that it is nevertheless context-dependent requires that we introduce context-dependence of a new, hitherto unknown sort. And this seems like an *ad hoc* maneuver."

If we look up 'green' in the *Webster Dictionary*, what we find—alongside the non-literal meaning specifications, which are irrelevant here— is the barely exciting information: something is green if it is "of the color green". This fact is indeed in conflict with both the assumptions that 'green' is polysemous and that it is an indexical. If 'green' were a polysemous word like 'giant', we would expect the dictionary to contain different numbered sub-entries specifying the different contents the word can have on different occasions of its use. If 'green' were an indexical like 'I', we would expect the dictionary to contain an informative clause which tells us how to select its content in a given occasion of its use. If 'green' is context-dependent, its context-dependence is of a different kind.

The question is whether a convincing story can be told about *how* the content of 'green' and other adjectives is supposed to depend on the context. If there is no such story, the sentence 'The leaf is green' refutes the context thesis and provides a genuine counterexample to the principle of compositionality of content. But I don't think the situation is as bad as all that. In the rest of this paper, I will present the outlines of an account of the semantics of a large class of context-dependent adjectives. And I will argue that this class includes 'green'.

3 Problems with 'good'

It is a curious fact that contemporary views on the semantics of adjectives evolved from a debate that started in moral philosophy. In their effort to articulate theories about what goodness consists in, philosophers turned to questions about the semantics of 'good'. 'Good' is an adjective with some peculiar characteristics, so any analysis of its content had to say something about the interpretation of adjectives in general as well as about the semantic features that distinguish 'good' from less problematic adjectives, like 'round' or 'tall'.

Like most adjectives, 'good' occurs in *predicative* as well as *attributive* positions. The former cases suggest that 'good' is a predicate, while the latter that it is a predicate-modifier. Which of these indications is to be taken seriously is a question that might affect the way in which we make sense of judgments to the effect that an act, a person, or a state of affairs is good.

There is a certain difficulty about pronouncements that 'good' is a predicate, or that it is a predicate-modifier. Categories like 'noun', 'verb', 'determiner', 'pronoun', 'adjective', or 'sentence' are syntactic, and categories like 'predicate', 'connective', 'quantifier', 'predicate-modifier', 'variable', or 'formula' are logical. These logical categories, though they are syntactic categories of certain formalized languages, are certainly not syntactic categories of English.[10] But what is it supposed to mean that an expression of English belongs to a syntactic category of some *other language*?

One natural way to understand such claims is to regard them as being about *logical forms*. I take the logical form of an expression e in a natural language L to be an expression e' in a suitable formalized language L$'$ which has the same *logical properties* as e. If L$'$ has a clear, well-understood semantics e' can be used to illuminate and explain the inferential behavior of e in L.[11] This means that an expression could have more than one logical form. If we can choose among the competing logical forms one that explains the inferential behavior of an expression in the most perspicuous way, we can call this *the* logical form of the expression.

To call 'good' a predicate (or to say that the semantic category for 'good' is that of predicate) is then to say that in the logical forms of English sentences containing the word 'good' we always find the same corresponding predicate. Similarly, to call it a predicate-modifier is to claim that in the logical forms of English sentences containing 'good' we always find the same corresponding predicate-modifier. These claims can be formulated as (5) and (6):[12]

(5) The logical form of 'good' is the predicate 'good (x)'

(6) The logical form of 'good' is the predicate-modifier '(good (F)) (x)' (Here 'x' is an individual variable and 'F' is a predicate variable.)

G.E. Moore (1903) claimed that 'good' is a predicate that expresses a simple property. Certainly, there is a *prima facie* plausibility in the idea that 'good' expresses goodness, like 'hard' hardness or 'green' greenness. If there is no reason to think otherwise, we can suppose that expressions in the same grammatical category have the same kind of contents.

A semantic analysis based on Moore's suggestion regards the predicative occurrences of 'good' as paradigm cases and treats sentences containing attributive occurrences as complexes built up from simpler sentences in which there are only predicative occurrences. According to Moore, something is a good book if and only if it is good and it is a book.[13] One way to implement these ideas is to say that the logical form of (7) is (7a), where the language of logical forms is a formalized extensional first-order language:

(7)   Sue is a good dancer.

(7a) `dancer (Sue) ∧ good (Sue)`

There is an argument due to Peter Geach (1956), which shows that this simple Moorean analysis cannot be the whole story about 'good'. The argument is based on the observation that inferences of a certain type are incorrectly predicted to be valid by the Moorean analysis. Let us call an inference a *transfer-inference*, just in case it fits the following pattern: its first premise is of the form '*a* is *AN*', its second premise has an entailment of the form '*a* is *M*' and its conclusion is of the form '*a* is *AM*'. Moore's analysis is in trouble with the following simple transfer-inference:[14]

(7)   Sue is a good dancer.
(8)   Sue is a pianist.
(9)   Sue is a good pianist.

(7a) `dancer (Sue) ∧ good (Sue)`
(8a) `pianist (Sue)`
(9a) `pianist (Sue) ∧ good (Sue)`

The second inference is trivially valid, but according to its most natural interpretation, the first inference is invalid; Sue might be a good dancer and a pianist without being a good pianist. The fact that 'good' fails to validate certain transfer inferences is regularly referred to in the literature as the *non-transparency* of this adjective.[15] The non-transparency of 'good' shows that at least one of the Moorean translations from the English sentences to the logical formalism must be incorrect.

Geach's suggestion was to give up the Moorean assumption that 'good' is a predicate and regard it instead as a predicate-modifier. On this approach, the attributive occurrences are the paradigm cases and the predicative occurrences must be explained away. To give an account of them, one has to assume that they are elliptical attributive occurrences. Thus the sentence 'These gloves are good' is usually to be understood as 'These gloves are good gloves'. Although this is a natural interpretation of the sentence, in certain situations it is incorrect. For example, if the sentence is uttered by someone who wants to clean the windows and is looking for some piece of cloth appropriate for that purpose, the suggested analysis would fail. In this situation the sentence is to be understood as saying 'These gloves are good pieces of cloth for cleaning the windows'. According to Geach something is good if and only if there is an appropriate noun N such that that thing is a good N.[16]

One way to build Geach's idea into a semantic analysis would be to assign (7b) to (7) as its logical form, where the language of logical forms remains extensional. Here the semantic value of a predicate-modifier is a function that maps predicate extensions to predicate extensions.

(7)   Sue is a good dancer.

(7b) `(good (dancer)) (Sue)`

This translation is not subject to the previous criticism. From the assumption that the complex predicate '`(good (dancer)) (x)`' applies to the bearer of the name '`Sue`' it does not follow that the complex predicate '`(good (pianist)) (x)`' applies to her. So Geach's move blocks the transfer-inference from (7) and (8) to (9).

In assigning (7b) as the logical form to (7), this analysis provides an implicit explanation why the inference is invalid. It goes like this: The inference is invalid, because '`(good (dancer)) (x)`' and '`(good (pianist)) (x)`' have different extensions, which, in turn, is true because '`dancer (x)`' and '`pianist (x)`' have different extensions. That is, Sue can be a good dancer and a pianist, and still fail to be a good pianist, *because* there are people who are dancers and not pianists or *vice versa*. Now, this explanation cannot be right. For, the inference would be invalid even if we added the assumption that all and only dancers are pianists. (Of course, if we add this, we can remove the premise 'Sue is a pianist'.)

(7)   Sue is a good dancer.
(10) All and only dancers are pianists.
(9)   Sue is a good pianist.

(7b) (good (dancer)) (Sue)
(10b) $\forall$x (dancer (x) $\leftrightarrow$ pianist (x))
(9b) (good (pianist)) (Sue)

Geach's analysis blocks one transfer-inference but it falls prey to another. Hence, it is not an adequate account of the non-transparency of 'good'.

Richard Larson has suggested a more promising theory about 'good' and a number of other problematic adjectives.[17] His idea is to return to Moore's idea that 'good' is a predicate in (7), but abandon the assumption that it is a predicate that applies to Sue.[18] What is being said to be good is Sue's dancing, not Sue herself. The logical form of the relevant reading of (7) could be captured as (7c):[19]

(7)   Sue is a good dancer.

(7c) Qe [dancing (e, Sue)] (good
      (e))

(Here, 'e' is an event variable and 'Q' is a generic quantifier. The different brackets in the notation are intended to express that 'dancing (e, Sue)' is in the restrictor of the generic quantifier and 'good (e)' is in its nuclear scope.)

A good paraphrase of (7c) would be 'Generally dancing events performed by Sue are good.' Given a Davidsonean analysis of adverbs, we get the same logical form for the sentence 'Sue

dances well'. *Prima facie*, this is good news: the relevant reading of 'Sue is a good dancer' seems indeed synonymous with 'Sue dances well'.

How does the introduction of event variables block the inference from 'Sue is a good dancer' to 'Sue is a good pianist'? Even if dancers and pianists were the exact same people, their dancing and piano-playing performances would still be distinct events. Consequently, it can easily be true that Sue's dancing performances are excellent, while her piano performances are terrible. That is, 'Qe [dancing (e, Sue)] (good (e))' might be true and 'Qe [piano-playing (e, Sue)] (good (e))' false.

But the problem of non-transparency is still with us. Imagine a world where dances are performed with a single aim: to persuade the gods to give rain for the crops. Furthermore, dancing is the only method people ever use to try to persuade the gods to give rain for the crops. In this world, not only are the dancers and the rainmakers the same people, dancing and rain-making are the very same events.[20] Now, suppose Sue is a shaman-dancer-rainmaker in this world. She had perfected her dancing and she is much admired for her graceful moves. Unfortunately, she is not particularly successful in making rain: year after year, despite her best efforts there is a terrible drought. It seems to me that under such circumstances we could say that Sue is a good dancer but not a good rainmaker. But now we have a problem:

(7)   Sue is a good dancer.
(11) All and only dances are rain-makings.
(12) Sue is a good rainmaker.

(7c) Qe [dancing (e, Sue)] (good
      (e))
(11c) $\forall$e (dancing (e) $\leftrightarrow$ rain
      making (e))
(12c) Qe [rainmaking (e, Sue)]
      (good (e))

The first inference is invalid,[21] but the corresponding inference run on the putative logical forms below is valid. So, Larson's logical forms cannot be correct either.

There is a standard way to get around the problem of non-transparency. The idea is that the logical forms should be drawn from an *intensional language*.[22] The interpretation of an intensional language distinguishes between (at least) two different semantic values of expressions: the extension and the intension. The extension of the expression is its ordinary semantic value (a truth-value for sentences, an object for names, a set of objects for one-place predicates, a function from sets to sets for predicate-modifiers, etc.); the intension of the expression is a function from possible worlds to its extension. One can have an intensional language where — although there are certain operators that are sensitive to the intensions of the expressions to which they are applied — quantification over possible worlds remains covert. Languages of modal logics are intensional languages of this type. Alternatively, one can have an intensional language, where reference to possible worlds is explicit. In these languages there are variables ranging over possible worlds.[23]

I think intensional languages of the second type are more perspicuous, so I will use this technique to present the intensional solution to the problem posed by the transfer-inferences.[24] The intensionalized version of Geach's proposal is (7d):

(7) Sue is a good dancer.

(7d) (good (dancer)) (Sue) (w)

In the logical form, 'w' is a variable that will be assigned the possible world with respect to which the sentence is evaluated. In most cases this is the actual world, so (7d) is true iff Sue is among the individuals that are good dancers in the actual sworld. But (7) can also occur as a constituent in a complex sentence with modal operators, which are translated as quantifiers binding the possible world variable.

Such a move blocks the transfer-inference from (7) and (10) to (9). Even if the predicates 'dancer (x)' and 'pianist (x)' have the same extensions in the actual world, they have different extensions in other possible worlds. Then the intensions of the complex predicates 'good (dancer) (x)' and 'good (pianist) (x)' are different functions, and therefore the expressions '(good (dancer)) (Sue)' and '(good (pianist)) (Sue)' have different intensions too. But then there is no reason why the sentences 'Sue is a good dancer' and 'Sue is a good pianist' should have the same truth-value in the actual world.

One might wonder whether the intensional move solves the problem. What if pianists and dancers are necessarily the same individuals? Doesn't intuition tell us that even under such circumstances Sue could be a good dancer and a bad pianist? It is hard to tell. Our intuitions might be confused here, for it is not clear whether the assumption that *necessarily* all and only pianists are dancers is conceptually coherent.[25] I will not pursue this line of objection for there is a more convincing one.

By assigning (7d) as logical form to (7), we implicitly commit ourselves to an explanation why the inference fails. The *reason* why Sue may be a good dancer and a pianist without being a good pianist even if all dancers are pianists and *vice versa* is that there is another possible world where someone (she, or someone else) is a dancer, but not a pianist, or a pianist, but not a dancer. This does not sound very convincing. How could the possibility that someone is a dancer, but not a pianist have anything to do with the question whether Sue has to be a good pianist, given that she is a good dancer and a pianist?

It is interesting to compare this with the following case. The inference from 'Sue is a prospective dancer' and 'All and only dancers are pianists' to 'Sue is a prospective pianist' is also invalid. Here the intensional explanation says that the *reason* why Sue may be a prospective dancer and a pianist without being a prospective pianist even if all dancers are pianists and vice versa is that there is another possible world where someone (she, or someone else) is a dancer, but not a pianist, or a pianist, but not a dancer. In this case the explanation is much more plausible. The failure of this inference can be explained by means of possibilities, because if someone is a prospective N, then she *may* become, or is *likely* to become an N. However, similar modal consequences cannot be drawn from the claim that someone is a good N.[26]

We are in a quandary. Extensional approaches to the adjective 'good' seem inadequate because they cannot account for its deep non-transparency. They all incorrectly predict that if the extensions of 'N' and 'M' are sufficiently closely tied, the inference from '*a* is a good N' to '*a* is a good M' goes through. The failure of the extensional accounts naturally suggests that we should regard 'good' as an intensional adjective. However, the explanation of non-transparency gained from the introduction of intensions appears to be the wrong one. The failure of the transfer inferences has nothing to do with modal considerations and so, by going intensional we avoid wrong predictions only through sacrificing explanatory value. A different approach is called for.

4 Ways of being good

On the surface the answer to the question why someone may be a good dancer and a bad pianist is quite obvious. Dancing and playing the piano are very different skills, so there is no reason why excellence in one should have anything to do with excellence in the other. In other words, if Sue is a good dancer then she is good *at dancing*, which is perfectly compatible with her being quite bad *at playing the piano*. So, goodness — at least in these cases — does not directly attach to Sue; it attaches to her only through one or another description that is true of her. Some of these descriptions, as that she is a dancer or that

she is a pianist, may specify certain roles, and she may be skillful, interesting, enthusiastic or well-paid in one of her roles, but unskillful, boring, indifferent or badly paid in another. Being good at dancing and being good at playing the piano are different *ways of being good*.[27] This seems to be the correct analysis of 'good' and many other adjectives.

As it stands, this explanation is in accordance with the analysis that regards 'good' as a predicate-modifier. However, theories that regard 'good' as a predicate-modifier tend to make a further step: they typically assume that the relevant roles are fully specified by the noun to which the adjective 'good' is attached. As Geach himself noted, there are cases in which this move is problematic.

The difficulties are exemplified by sentences in which one speaks about a good event, or a good thing to happen. Geach says that such sentences often do not have a fixed content, since " 'event', like 'thing', is too empty a word to convey either a criterion of identity or a standard of goodness."[28] This means that according to Geach, the reason why 'good event' does not have clear truth-conditions is that 'event' does not have a clear content. But, surely, the content of 'pebble' or 'differential-equation' are clear enough, and still, one does not know what to make of 'good pebble' or 'good differential-equation'.[29] The content of the sentence 'This is a good pebble' depends on the context of its use. In a certain situation, an utterance of this sentence might say that the pebble is good for playing marbles, in another that it is good for breaking a window.

So the noun N in a phrase '*a* is a good N' is often not sufficient in determining the role in which *a* is supposed to be good. Is it at least always necessary? Geach certainly thinks so, since he believes that in order to interpret '*a* is good', one always has to provide some suitable N that will yield the standards of goodness. I think this is implausible. Consider the scenario where students are performing an experiment in the laboratory. They are trying to produce some substance that can be used in a later experiment. The teacher points to a certain blue liquid and says to the students: 'This is good'. Is it really true that in order to interpret this, the students have to be able to come up with some noun N such that the blue liquid is a good N? It seems that even if they know close to nothing about what the blue liquid is, and hence the nouns they could come up with do not provide standards of goodness, they can know what the teacher's utterance said. The blue liquid was said to be good for the purposes of the experiment. Of course, Geach *might* reply that the noun (or, more precisely, the nominal expression) in question is something like 'stuff that can be used in a later experiment'. But why should we believe that the standards of goodness are provided by the content of this complex noun, rather than simply by the context in which the utterance was made?

Here is another problem with the predicate-modifier approach. Imagine a case when students are arguing about what to read next in their reading group. There are two candidates: a short book and a lengthy paper. One of the students points to the book and says: 'This is a good book'. Another, as a reply, points to the paper and says: 'This is good too'. What the second student said can be paraphrased roughly as 'This is good to read too'; it *cannot* be paraphrased as 'This is a good book too'. But standard accounts of ellipsis assume that the second sentence predicates something of the paper that is predicated of the book in the first. Given the predicate-modifier analysis of 'good', a suitable predicate is simply unavailable.[30]

All of this suggests strongly that the content of the noun 'N' does not play a direct semantic role in fixing the way in which a good N is said to be good. I suggest that we should return to the Moorean idea that the logical form of 'good' is a one-place predicate of individuals. Of course, there is a price for this: one certainly cannot hold a theory according to which the extension of 'good' is the class of good things. There may

be nothing in common to all of the good things. However, one can say that 'good' is an *incomplete* one-place predicate, one that is associated with a set of individuals only if additional information is provided. 'Good' can be completed in many different ways; for example under one completion it is associated with a set of those individuals who are good at dancing, under another with the set of those individuals who are good at playing the piano.

The analysis I am suggesting follows Moore in the sense that it regards the predicative occurrences of 'good' as the paradigm cases: 'good' is an incomplete expression, its semantic category is one-place predicate. I also accept Moore's analysis of the attributive occurrences: Sue is a good dancer if and only if Sue is good (as a dancer) and Sue is a dancer; Sue is a good pianist if and only if Sue is good (as a pianist) and Sue is a pianist. So the translation I suggest for (7) is (7e):

(7) Sue is a good dancer.

(7e) dancer (Sue) ∧ (good (R)) (Sue)

'R' is a variable standing for a certain role[31] in which something can be good. The value of this variable is fixed by the context in which (7) is used.[32]

Building variables into the lexical representation of 'good' may prompt the reaction that we are no longer discussing the *semantics* if 'good' and sentences containing 'good', we switched to the *pragmatics* of such expressions. The terms 'semantics' and 'pragmatics' are used in a variety of ways and in some of these senses this is undoubtedly true. But if we think that the minimal aim of semantics is to provide a systematic theory of the truth-conditions of assertive uses of well-formed declarative sentences then truth-conditional effects of context are properly regarded as lying within the domain of semantic theory. This, however, does not preclude the possibility that the mechanism used to determine the value of 'R' within a context is similar (or perhaps identical) to the mechanism applied in pragmatic implications.[33]

An advantage of this sort of semantics for 'good' is that it can account easily for the intuition that 'Sue is a good dancer' entails 'There is a way in which Sue is good' or 'Sue is good in some respect'. On the incomplete predicate analysis, the latter sentences can be regarded as existentially quantifying over the variable within the logical form of 'good' whose value is normally fixed by the context. It is not clear to me how one could account for these inferences on the alternative accounts.

Another advantage is that it accounts well for cases when something is said to be a good N, but the way it is good is not determined by 'N'. For example, consider a case when someone is looking for an appropriate object to prop up a television set. Upon finding a thick book, he might say 'This is a good book.' What his utterance says is, of course, that the book is good for propping up the television set, not that it is good *as a book*. Again, the predicate modifier approach has difficulties with capturing such intuitions.

One of the consequences of this analysis is the claim that in *some* contexts (7) could express something different from the proposition that Sue is good as a dancer and Sue is a dancer. And indeed, one can imagine a situation in which what is at question is her moral character, not her skill at dancing. Suppose some dancers are threatening to burn down the Met, because they are unhappy about their salary. Other dancers are trying to convince the members of the first group that burning down the Met would be a bad idea. Meanwhile the singers are having a drink in a bar, and they are discussing which of their colleagues are in which group. Most of them believe that Sue is the leader of those who are threatening to set the building on fire. One of the singers tries to defend Sue, and argues that unlike most of the dancers, she is actually in the second group, trying to save the building. The singer gives several reasons for this claim, and at the end of her argument she utters the sentence 'Sue is a good dancer', perhaps putting a strong emphasis on 'good'.[34]

But even if there are intricate examples where the proposition that Sue is a good dancer does not say that she is good at dancing, in normal contexts it does: 'good' within 'good N' normally has the content of 'good as an N'. This means that in order to accept (7e) as the logical form of (7), one has to slightly expand the notion of context informally introduced at the beginning of this paper. There I said that the content of previous utterances might play a role in determining the content of an expression. But this is not enough. Now I suggest that the content of certain expressions within the utterance may be part of the context that contributes to determining the content of other expressions within the *same* utterance. The content of 'good' in an utterance of (7) may depend, in part, on the content of 'dancer'.[35]

5 Varieties of incompleteness

The story about the semantics of 'good' told in the previous two sections has obvious implications for Travis's example concerning the color of the painted leaf. If it can be made plausible that the analysis given for 'good' — according to which its logical form is a contextually incomplete predicate — applies to other adjectives, including 'green', then we may have a semantic account of these expressions that does not violate the context thesis. If 'green' is an incomplete predicate, the context-dependence of 'The leaf is green' is attributable to the context-dependence of 'green'.

The resistance to the predicative analysis in the semantic literature is largely based on the non-transparency of most adjectives. Once it is acknowledged that the invalidity of these inferences can be attributed to contextual incompleteness, the resistance looses much of its force. The advantages of a uniform predicative approach to all adjectives are considerable. First of all it is uniform: it assigns the same kind of semantic value to all adjectives.[36] This is a theoretical gain for it keeps the syntactic and semantic structures close to one another. Second, assuming a broadly Davidsonean semantics for adverbs, we can account for similarities between adjectival and adverbial modification. Adjectives and adverbs can both be treated as predicates: the former as predicates of individuals, the latter as predicates of eventualities.[37] Proponents of a unified predicate-modifier approach have no similarly straightforward account to offer about modification in general.[38] Finally, there is some psycholinguistic evidence that the predicative use of adjectives is acquired (and, in the case of aphasia- and dysphasia-patients, re-acquired) first.[39] This suggests that the predicative use of adjectives is more basic.

Nevertheless, the predicative analysis cannot be universally applied to all adjectives. Some (e.g. 'utter', 'former', 'chief', 'final', etc.) have no predicative occurrences, so the assumption that they stand for incomplete predicates is extremely implausible. And 'Sue is a retired pianist' does not have the same content as 'Sue is retired (as a pianist) and Sue is a pianist'.[40] I suggest that we set the adjectives which do not support the inference pattern from '*a* is *AN*' to '*a* is *N*' aside, and accept for all the others an incomplete predicate analysis. In this way we maintain a uniform semantic analysis for the vast majority of adjectives.[41]

Contextual incompleteness in adjectives has different dimensions. The interpretation of *scalar* adjectives, like 'tall', 'heavy', 'fast', 'expensive' or 'old', requires a comparison class. Short basketball players are usually tall people, light whales are heavy animals and — for many of us — cheap airplane tickets to Europe are expensive gifts. The interpretation of *evaluative* adjectives, like 'lucky', 'delicious', 'time-consuming', 'simple' or 'fitting', requires that context provide an individual or group of individuals from whose perspective the evaluation is made. A particular event can be fortuitous for me, but not for others; an exercise can be simple for the expert and taxing for the novice, the outcome of an election may be lucky for one party, but not for the country. And of course, there are adjectives that belong to both of these categories; 'expensive' and 'time-consuming' would be good examples.

I suggest that different dimensions of incompleteness correspond to different sorts of variables in the logical form. The variables can receive their values from the context but also from linguistic material. In English, prepositional phrases tend to perform the latter job. For example, 'clever *at* doing cross-word puzzles' and 'time-consuming *as* a short-paper topic *for* graduate students' are wholly specified one-place predicates. Accordingly, I suggest that the logical form of 'clever' is '$(clever\ (R))\ (x)$', the logical form of 'time-consuming' is '$(time\text{-}consuming\ (C_1,\ C_2))\ (x)$', where '$R$' is a role-variable standing for a way of being clever, 'C_1' is a class-variable, standing for a class with respect to which something counts as time-consuming, and 'C_2' is another class-variable, standing for a class from whose perspective something counts as time-consuming.[42]

For predicates that are fully specified, transfer-inferences are valid. For example, from 'Sue is a clever dancer' and 'Sue is a pianist' it *does* follow that 'Sue is a clever pianist', *provided* that e.g. the context had already specified that 'clever' is to be understood as 'clever at solving crossword-puzzles' in both the first premise and the conclusion.[43] Of course, if only cleverness in solving crossword puzzles is concerned, it would be quite misleading to say that Sue is a clever dancer or a clever pianist. One should put it rather as 'Sue, who is a dancer (pianist) is clever'. The reason for this is that the sentence 'Sue is a clever dancer' strongly *suggests* that the kind of cleverness that is ascribed to Sue has something to do with the fact that she is a dancer.

So what should we say about 'green'? It is certainly not an evaluative adjective: no matter how much one believes in the possibility of an inverted spectrum, it is incorrect to say that a leaf is green for me. We use color terms as if color were an objective, observer-independent feature of the world. We have another construction, namely 'seems green' which is correctly used in cases when the speaker wants to express uncertainty with respect to veridicality of her subjective experience.

'Green' is probably a scalar adjective.[44] But setting degrees of greenness aside, one might be tempted to think that 'green' is a paradigm example of a contextually complete adjective. To be green is one of the most obvious examples of a feature that is *simple*. It is often difficult to decide whether something is green because of the condition of the object, the environment, or the nature of our perceptual mechanism; there are also borderline cases, when there might be no fact of the matter whether something is green. But all things that are green are green in the very same way.

I think this intuition is misleading. There are at least two ways in which an apple can be green: from the outside, or from the inside. In the former case, it can be ripe, in the latter it cannot.[45] There are at least three ways in which a book can be green: due to having a green dust jacket, a green cover, or green pages. And a corridor can be green in many ways: having green walls, or green ceiling, or green carpet, or green doors, etc.[46]

An object is green if some contextually specifiable (and presumably sufficiently large) *part* of it is green. The logical form of 'green' is '(green (C, P)) (x)', where 'C' is a class standing for a comparison class and 'P' is a variable standing for a certain part of the object.[47] It seems to me that the case of the painted maple leaf fits this pattern. If one is sorting leaves for decoration, what matters is the color of the outside, if one is trying to identify the species, what matters is what we find under the camouflage. This suggests that the context-dependency that appears in Travis's example is a relatively easily characterizable kind: it is a matter of different contextually specified values for the variable 'P'.

6 Conclusion

My strategy of defending the compositionality of content against Travis' challenge was to locate the source of the context-dependence of 'The leaf is green' in the adjective 'green'. I argued that the best semantics for 'green' postulates a variable within the logical form of this word. Since I also argued that — despite Travis' contention — this challenge couldn't be broadly generalized beyond sentences containing adjectives, the answer is to the point.

One might wonder whether in responding to similar challenges we have to postulate variables in other lexical items as well. I think we do. Consider, for example, the sentence 'Every leaf is green'. Arguably, many different things can be said with this sentence, depending on what the contextually relevant domain of quantification is supposed to be. And of course, one may have the *prima facie* intuition that none of the lexical items has a context-dependent content. Here again, I think the first intuition is misleading; a general account of domain restriction may demand that we postulate the presence of a domain variable within the logical form of 'leaf'.[48]

So, the strategy of defense of compositionality pursued here is likely to lead to a lexicon where many, perhaps most entries contain contextual variables. Whether the defense of compositionality I offered is ultimately convincing depends largely on the plausibility of such a lexicon. And that, in turn, depends on whether we can provide an account of how the values of these variables are to be determined in context. At the beginning of the paper I set foundational questions regarding the nature of context and our knowledge of its features aside. At the end, I concede that as long as these issues remain unresolved, the semantic proposal I gave remains questionable. But even if that is so, I hope that I succeeded in pointing out where the real issues lie regarding the compositional interpretation of adjectives.

Notes

1 As I understand the principle of compositionality, it says that the meaning of complex expressions — phrases, clauses and sentences — depends on two kinds of facts. Syntax tells us what the lexical constituents — words and smaller morphemes — occurring in a complex expression are and how they are combined; and the lexicon tells us what those constituents mean. According to the principle, such syntactic and semantic features of a complex expression are jointly sufficient to determine the meaning of that expression. But what does it take for certain features of an expression to *determine* what that expression means? It is customary in semantics to assume that the relevant determination relation is simply functional dependence. I believe this interpretation of the principle of compositionality is unreasonably weak. In Szabó (2000) I argue that the principle is best understood as the claim that there is *a single function across all possible human languages* that assigns the meanings of complex expressions to the meanings of their constituents and their syntactic manner of composition. This, however, will not matter for the purposes of the present discussion.

2 One might object to calling the content of an expression its "meaning". If we think that the meaning of an expression is a feature knowledge of which guarantees understanding of the expression then the proposition expressed by a sentence is not a good candidate for being the meaning of that sentence. (Intuitively, we all know what 'I am tired' means but we don't know what proposition it expresses on a given occasion unless we know who made the utterance.) Perhaps, we should follow David Kaplan and think of meanings as *characters*, i.e. functions from contexts to contents; cf. Kaplan (1977). Be that as it may, compositionality of content is at least as important in semantics as compositionality of meaning proper. Just as we can speak about understanding *expressions*, we can also speak about understanding *utterances* and the latter is presumably tied to grasping the proposition expressed by the utterance. So, insofar that it is plausible that we can understand not only sentences we never hear before but also particular utterances of such sentences, we have some intuitive support for the principle of compositionality of content.

3 There are two major traditions of thinking about context within semantics. There are those who follow Montague (1968) in representing contexts as *indices*, i.e. as an n-tuples of speaker, hearer, time, place, a series of salient objects, etc. And there are those who follow Stalnaker (1970) in thinking of contexts as *information states* which can be represented as sets of possible worlds (or sets of situations) compatible with the shared knowledge of the participants in the conversation.

4 I use the following conventions of quotation. An expression *e* between single quotes is a (possibly ambiguous) name for *e*. I also use the iterated single quote to name quotation names of expressions. Double quotes differ from iterated single quotes in appearance: in the case of iterated single quotes I leave a space between the inverted commas, in the case of double quotes I do not. Double quotes are strictly speaking not quotation devices: the expression between the double quotes is used, not mentioned. (Or perhaps, partly used, partly mentioned.) The following examples are illustrative:

(i) 'Cambridge' refers (ambiguously) to the cities Cambridge, England and Cambridge, Massachusetts.

(ii) ''Cambridge'' refers to an ambiguous quotation name which is used in (i).

(iii) According to a friend of mine, "Cambridge is a reasonably lively place." He probably has Cambridge, Massachusetts in mind.

These conventions are not supposed to be taken as an analysis of how quotation is ordinarily used in English. I have grave doubts about the coherence of our ordinary use quotation marks.

5 The definitions are from the *Webster Dictionary*.

6 Here and throughout the paper I use the Courier font with or without indices to indicate disambiguation.

7 Unfortunately, there is no terminological unity in linguistics concerning types of ambiguity. I prefer the following definitions. A linguistic type (a phoneme or a sequence of phonemes) is *ambiguous* if it has more than one content. If an ambiguous linguistic type stands for a single expression, it is *polysemous*; otherwise it is *homonymous*.

8   Travis (1994: 171–2).

9   Travis (1994: 172).

10   What makes a category syntactic is that we can determine which expressions belong to that category through morpho-syntactic means. Syntactic categories of formal languages can be 'read off' the rules which specify the class of well-formed formulas in the language.

11   One might wish to steer between an extremely weak and an extremely strong conception of logical form. According to the weak conception, the only criterion that we might use to evaluate the adequacy of a certain logical form is whether it gets all the inferences right. This would mean that we can assign the same logical form to any two sentences of English that are logically equivalent. But surely, we should not ascribe 'Snow is falling' and 'Snow is falling and snow is self-identical' the same logical form. The strong conception of logical form requires that an expression and its logical forms share all their semantically relevant properties. This would demand that semantic features, like [INANIMATE] be represented in logical form. But it is not clear whether we really want to ascribe different logical forms to 'It is here' and 'She is here'.

12   I use the Courier font for logical forms, which is the notation introduced in the previous section to indicate disambiguation; cf. fn. 6. Given that we use logical forms to *clarify* and *explain* the logical behavior of natural language expressions, the demand that the languages of logical forms be free of ambiguity seems reasonable. If I had the goal of absolute precision, I would use corner quotes whenever I mention logical forms containing free variables. Since I don't, I won't.

13   One of the many passages where Moore endorses this view is the following: "For 'good conduct' is a complex notion: all conduct is not good; for some is certainly bad and some may be indifferent. And on the other hand, other things, beside conduct, may be good; and if they are so, then, 'good' denotes some property, that is common to them and conduct . . ." Moore (1903: 2).

14   Cf. Geach (1956).

15   Hamann (1991: 666).

16   Geach endorses this view in the following passage: "Even when 'good' or 'bad' stands by itself as a predicate, and is thus grammatically predicative, some substantive has to be understood; there is no such thing as being just good or bad, there is only a being a good or bad so-and-so" Geach (1956: 65).

17   Larson (1998).

18   Larson believes that 'Sue is a good dancer' is ambiguous and one of its readings is more or less adequately captured by the original Moorean analysis: Sue is good and Sue is a dancer. I am skeptical about the existence of such a reading, for reasons that will become clear later. In any case, even if a Moorean reading exists, the interesting question is how to capture the other one.

19   The logical form I present is different from Larson's official logical forms in one respect. Larson assumes that the logical form of 'good' contains another argument place filled by a contextual variable 'C' whose values are comparison classes. This is necessary because a dancing event can be good relative a narrow class of dancing events but not so good relative to a broader comparison class. I have neglected this complication here.

20   One might deny that there could be a world where dancing events and rainmaking events coincide: such events could occur always simultaneously, but they would nevertheless be distinct events. I find this suggestion *ad hoc*. An anthropologist may observe dances, describe them in detail, and only later discover that their function is rainmaking. He would naturally think that he thereby found an alternative way to describe the very same events he had already observed.

21   I am assuming that whatever the semantics of the generic quantifier, it must validate such an inference.

22   Cf. Montague (1970a, esp. 201, 211–3), and Montague (1970b, esp. 242–3).

23   Cf. Lewis (1970, esp. 193–200).

24   In doing this, I don't want to prejudge the complicated issue of ontological commitment. Philosophers tend to like non-explicit quantification over possible worlds because they believe that it fails to carry ontological commitment to those entities. I am doubtful whether pushing explicit quantification into the meta-language can help the ontologically scrupulous, but I don't want to press the issue here. There is another typical motivation for using modal operators, rather

than explicit quantification. It has been argued that natural language lacks the expressive power of full-blooded quantification over possible worlds. This claim, however, had been challenged on empirical grounds by a number of philosophers and linguists.

25 But note the following objection: Arguably, 'sell' and 'buy' are expressions such that they are necessarily true of the very same events. Still, a particular transaction can be a good sell and a bad buy. So 'The transaction between Bill and Sam was a good buy' does not entail 'The transaction between Bill and Sam was a good sell.' But the argument is not fully convincing. A defender of the intensional approach may reply that selling and buying events must be distinguished. Alternatively, one might argue that although the events are the same, the actions of buying and selling are different, and that the logical forms of action verbs quantify over actions, rather than events.

26 This criticism of the use of the intensional machinery in blocking certain inferences has a predecessor in the literature. Sally McConnell-Ginet writes: "But the intensional machinery does not provide a good model of how we think about why those walking quickly might be different from those talking quickly, even though walkers and talkers are the same. The explanation lies not in the existence of an alternative situation (where individuals have different properties), but simply in the possibility of a different sorting of the individuals, given a refinement of the sorting principles." McConnell-Ginet (1982: 163).

27 The phrase 'way of being good' is borrowed from Thomson (1992).

28 Geach (1956: 68–9).

29 I thank Judith Thomson for bringing this problem to my attention. Her discussion of it can be found in Thomson (1994).

30 A defender of the predicate-modifier approach will have to say that this is not a case of genuine ellipsis. One could suggest, for example, that 'This is good too' is proxy for 'This is good read too'. This means that to interpret 'This is good too', one has to realize that if something is a good book then it is a good read.

31 'Role' is used here as a more or less technical term. An actor can be good in a given role. Stretching the

meaning of 'role' a little, one can say that a good dancer, or pianist is good in that role. Perhaps one can say that a good pencil is good in a role, but it certainly makes no sense to say that a good nap, a good sunset, or a good painting is good in some role. The variable 'ʀ' stands for some contextual information that specifies the incomplete predicate 'good'.

32 How is the value of such a variable determined in context? This is a question that cannot be reasonably addressed without taking a firm stand on foundational questions regarding the nature of contexts and the way the conversational participants know about it. I have no such comprehensive view to offer, so I will leave this issue open. My attitude here is similar to the attitude of those who argue that the demonstrative pronoun 'this' picks out some contextually determined object, but take no stand on whether the referent of the demonstrative is fixed by intentions, by demonstrations, by salience or some other means.

33 ". . . pragmatic factors may contribute to semantic interpretation without leading to the consequence that the idea of an independent semantic level should be given up. Pragmatic factors may trigger syntactic rules as well and in spite of this we would not like to say that there is no such thing as syntax and everything should be incorporated into pragmatics." Kiefer (1978: 161).

34 One might object that in this example I exploited an ambiguity. It seems plausible that 'good' has a special sense in which it means something like 'morally good', and it is this ambiguity, rather than some sort of context-dependence that properly accounts for the case. But I don't think it is right to say that in my example the defender of Sue declared her to be morally good. This is revealed by the fact that uttering 'Although morally reprehensible, Sue is a good dancer' (again, giving a strong emphasis to 'good') would not have been a contradictory assertion in the given context.

35 Fortunately, there do not seem to be cases when the content of a noun 'N' within a 'good N' depends on the content of 'good' in that phrase. This accounts for the strong intuition that within a noun phrase of the form $[_{NP}AN]$, the semantic status of the adjective and the noun are different. The

content of the adjective is influenced by the content of the noun, but not the other way around.

36 There are many who defend a double classification for adjectives; cf. Parsons (1972) and Siegel (1976).

37 Eventualities are events, states and processes.

38 Classic proponents of the uniform predicate-modifier approach include Montague (1970a) and Cresswell (1976).

39 Cf. Osgood (1971).

40 The fact that 'retired' has predicative uses is something of an anomaly. Note that 'Sue is a retired pianist' is hardly distinguishable from 'Sue is a former pianist', even though the former entails 'Sue is retired (as a pianist)' but the latter does not entail *'Sue is former (as a pianist)'. The difference between 'retired' and 'former' is probably due to the fact that 'retired' is derived from a participle, whereas 'former' isn't.

41 Is it legitimate to set these cases aside? The trouble, of course, is that it might turn out that a semantic account which covers these cases can account for those dealt with in the predicative analysis as well. Still, I think it would be bad methodology to assimilate all adjectives to the relatively few which fail to support the inference from 'a is AN' to 'a is N'. For then the fact that these inferences are valid for the vast majority of adjectives would have to be explained via *ad hoc* meaning-postulates. Those who insist on treating all adjectives as they would treat fairly exceptional cases are "generalizing to the worst case", just as Montague did when he assigned intensional types to all expressions.

42 It is important to notice that the prepositional phrase that can complete adjectives can modify different constituents of a sentence and that the results are not all equivalent. 'This mouse, for a mouse, is big' is equivalent to 'This mouse is big for a mouse', and 'This, for a mouse, is big' is equivalent to 'This is big for a mouse', but the first two sentences are not equivalent to the last two. The first two sentences entail that the object demonstrated is a mouse, the last two do not. Cf. Bartsch (1987: 16).

43 Bartsch (1987) notices that 'John's paper is stylistically good' entails 'John's paper is good' if we evaluate the premise and the conclusion within a context in which the same respects of goodness are relevant. (p. 5) Nevertheless, instead of the approach advocated here, she endorses a context-sensitive predicate-modifier account of the semantics of adjectives.

44 Languages may vary in how they categorize color adjectives, there might be even variation within the same language. For example, in Hungarian comparative forms of basic color adjectives are all acceptable, but comparative forms of complex color adjectives are not. Cf. Kiefer (1978: 154).

45 Could it be that in one of these cases the apple is not literally green? This is unlikely, for there seems to be no non-arbitrary way to decide which of the two cases are cases of non-literal greenness.

46 Lahav (1989) rejects the idea that the context sensitivity of 'red house' can be accounted for in this manner. He points out that we might be interested in the color of the inside of a house as much as we are interested in the color of its external surface, the color of the rooms does not normally count towards the color of the house. Although this observation is correct, it does not undermine the analysis. In some contexts it may well be correct to call a house red on account of its interior. The fact that such contexts are unusual is of no semantic concern.

47 In this regard, 'bald' behaves much like color adjectives. One can be bald on the top of one's head, in the front, in the back, none of which means that one is bald altogether.

48 We argue for this view in Stanley and Szabó (2000).

References

Bartsch, Renate 1987 "Context-dependent Interpretations of Lexical Items". In *Foundations of Pragmatics and Lexical Semantics*, J. Groenendijk, D. de Jongh and M. Stokhof (eds), 1–26. Dordrecht: Foris.

Cresswell, Max 1976 "The Semantics of Degree". In *Montague Grammar*, B. Partee (ed.), 261–292. New York: Academic Press.

Geach, Peter 1956 "Good and Evil". In *Theories of Ethics*, P. Foot (ed.), 64–74. Oxford: Oxford University Press.

Hamann, C 1991 "Adjectival Semantics". In *Handbuch der Semantik*, A. von Stechow (ed.). Berlin: Walter de Gruyter.

Kaplan, David 1977 "Demonstratives: An Essay on the Logic, Metaphysics, and Epistemology of Demonstratives and Other Indexicals". Reprinted in *Themes from Kaplan*, J. Perry and H. Wettstein (eds), 1989, 481–563. Oxford: Oxford University Press.

Kiefer, Ferenc 1978 "Adjectives and Presuppositions". *Theoretical Linguistics* 2: 135–73.

Lahav, Ron 1989 "Against Compositionality: The Case of Adjectives". *Philosophical Studies* 57: 261–79.

Larson, Richard 1998 "Events and Modification in Nominals". In *Proceedings From Semantics and Linguistic Theory (SALT) VIII*, D. Strolovitch and A. Lawson (eds), 145–168. Ithaca, NY: Cornell University Press.

Lewis, David 1970 "General Semantics". Reprinted in *Philosophical Papers, vol. 1.*, 189–229. Oxford: Oxford University Press.

McConnell-Ginet, Sally 1982 "Adverbs and Logical Form: A Linguistically Realistic Theory". *Language* 58: 144–184.

Montague, Richard 1968 "Pragmatics". Reprinted in *Formal Philosophy*, R. Thomason (ed.), 1974, 95–118. New Haven: Yale University Press.

—— 1970a "English as a Formal Language". Reprinted in *Formal Philosophy*, R. Thomason (ed.), 1974, 188–221. New Haven: Yale University Press.

—— 1970b "Universal Grammar". Reprinted in *Formal Philosophy*, R. Thomason (ed.), 1974, 222–246. New Haven: Yale University Press.

Moore, G. E. 1903 *Principia Ethica*. Cambridge: Cambridge University Press.

Osgood, Charles E. 1971 "Where do Sentences Come From". In *Semantics: An Interdisciplinary Reader in Philosophy, Linguistics and Psychology*, D. Steinberg and L. Jacobovits (eds), 497–529. Cambridge: Cambridge University Press.

Parsons, Terence 1972 "Some Problems Concerning the Logic of Grammatical Modifiers". In *Semantics of Natural Language*, D. Davidson and G. Harman (eds), 127–141. Dordrecht: Reidel.

Siegel, Muffy E. A. 1976 *Capturing the Adjective*. Ph.D. Dissertation, Amherst: University of Massachusetts.

Stanley, Jason and Szabó, Zoltán Gendler 2000 "On Quantifier Domain Restriction". *Mind and Language* 15: 219–61.

Stalnaker, Robert 1970 "Pragmatics". Reprinted in *Context and Content: Essays on Intentionality in Speech and Thought*, 31–46. Oxford: Oxford University Press.

Szabó Zoltán Gendler 2000 "Compositionality as Supervenience". *Linguistcs and Philosophy* 23: 475–505.

Thomson, Judith Jarvis 1992 "On Some Ways in Which a Thing Can Be Good". *Social Philosophy and Policy* 9: 96–117.

—— 1994 "Goodness and Utilitarianism". In *Proceedings of the American Philosophical Association* 67: 7–22.

Travis, Charles 1994 "On Constraints of Generality". In *Proceedings of the Aristotelian Society*. New Series 44: 165–88.

PART TWELVE

Rule-following and normativity

INTRODUCTION TO PART TWELVE

IN PART FIVE WE EXAMINED Quine's infamous critique of the analytic/synthetic distinction. Quine's main contention there was that the notion of analyticity cannot be rigorously explicated, except in terms of further notions which — he argued — stand as badly in need of elucidation as analyticity itself. These other notions included that of *synonymy*, and Quine's apparent suggestion that the notion of synonymy is incoherent or confused struck many commentators (e.g. Grice and Strawson in Chapter 12 above) as tantamount to the arresting claim that there is something wrong with the very notion of *meaning* itself. Quine's position threatens to imply that there is never a fact of the matter about what someone means by a linguistic expression.

Commentators disagree over whether Quine meant to defend such a radically subversive thesis. But that thesis is the very explicit conclusion of an argument which Saul Kripke (1982) excavated from various passages of Wittgenstein's later writings. According to Kripke, Wittgenstein's critique can be divided into negative and positive parts. On the negative side, he sketches a 'sceptical argument' whose conclusion is that there are 'no facts about meanings': i.e. sentences which appear to attribute meanings to speakers and linguistic expressions are never true, are never used to state facts. The positive part is a 'sceptical solution': an account of what it is, in that case, that speakers are really doing when they appear to attribute meanings to one another by uttering such sentences.

It is generally accepted that Wittgenstein himself did not go so far as to *endorse* the striking conclusion of the sceptical argument, and so the discussion is customarily characterized as a confrontation with a hypothetical subversive known as 'Kripke's sceptic'. The sceptic begins with the presumption that if there were facts about what speakers meant by expressions — e.g. if it were a fact that by the word 'green' Jones meant *green* — then it should be possible (either for Jones or someone else) to *know* about it. But on what basis can anyone do so? What properties of Jones make it the case that he means *green* rather than something else, and what counts as good evidence that he exhibits these properties?

For argument's sake, we're allowed to assume that we know everything about the speaker which we might expect theorists to consider relevant: in particular, it's assumed that we know everything about his past and present behaviour, and everything about his past and present mental states and processes. But according to the sceptic, no amount of such evidence ever justifies an attribution of meaning, and this is so because no matter how much such evidence we had, we could always find alternative, conflicting attributions of meaning to Jones which were equally well supported by it. Thus, e.g. consider the hypothesis that by 'green' Jones means *grue*, where 'grue' is defined as the colour of an object which is green before a given (arbitrarily chosen) future time, and blue at and after that time. Which of Jones's behavioural or psychological properties could we (or he) cite in justification of the claim that by 'green' he means *green* and not *grue*? Kripke (ibid., pp. 22–37) first considers behavioural properties. We may know that over decades of life as an English-speaker, Jones has applied the predicate to many thousands of green things, and has never applied it to anything of any other colour. But of course, this behavioural evidence supports the *grue* attribution just as well as it supports the *green* one.

The problem here is that understanding the word 'green' seems to be a *general* state – Jones's understanding engenders (or incorporates) an ability to apply the word correctly in an indefinite number of heterogeneous circumstances – whereas any behavioural evidence we can offer is specific, involving his activities in particular cases. With this in mind, we might suggest that Jones's linguistic understanding is constituted, not by his actual behaviour, but by his *dispositions* to apply expressions in certain ways. Behavioural dispositions would seem to be *general* in the requisite sense, and unless we presuppose Humean scepticism about induction, it seems reasonable to treat data about Jones's actual behaviour as perfectly good evidence for attributions of general dispositions. Kripke (ibid., pp. 26–37) considers this move in some detail, and offers two responses. First, he argues that behavioural dispositions do not, in fact, exhibit the same degree of generality as states of understanding: humans are *finite*, and so too are their dispositions. Many find this response unconvincing, and it is Kripke's second response that has attracted most attention. According to Kripke (and this is another quintessentially Wittgensteinian theme) the relation between a speaker's understanding of a term and his applications of it is *normative*. Jones's understanding of linguistic expressions *guides* or *prescribes* his applicatory behaviour, much as a person's understanding of a rule of a game or social institution can guide her behaviour in respect of it. There is such a thing as applying a term *correctly* or *incorrectly*, and understanding somehow involves grasp of this normative distinction. In contrast, behavioural dispositions are not normative. A characterization of a speaker's dispositions only *describes* her behaviour – it does not prescribe it. A speaker's actions may on occasion be out of step with her overall dispositions, but they cannot be *incorrect* in respect of those dispositions.

Kripke (ibid., pp. 41–52) next considers whether we might find evidence favouring the *green*-attribution somewhere in Jones's psychological/mental economy, but he argues that the prospects here are no better. Suppose (to begin with a quintessentially Wittgensteinian thought experiment) we assume that when Jones attends carefully to the meaning of the word 'green', this brings to his mind an *image* comprising a paradigmatically green-coloured patch (of the kind one finds in paint suppliers' brochures). Kripke's sceptic is happy to concede, for argument's sake, that Jones's understanding of the word might involve such an image; however images do not determine *general* contents any more than finite patterns of behaviour do: e.g. nothing about the image settles the question whether it is a representation of green or one of grue. It is tempting to reply that while it may be that nothing about the *image* settles which interpretation is correct, still some other aspect of Jones's psychology may have the requisite generality to do so, e.g. the fact that he intends the image to represent green, or intends it to represent a property of objects which will not change on grue-switchover day. But the sceptic is ready with two replies. First, if it is Jones's general semantic *intentions* that settle what he means by 'green', then the invocation of mental images was an epicycle here: we might as well have said at the beginning that a simpler intention of Jones's establishes that he means *green* rather than *grue*: i.e. his intention to apply the word to green things (and not to things of other colours). However – and this is the sceptic's second reply – the response merely pushes our question back one stage in any case: what evidence is there that Jones's intention is an intention to apply the word to green objects, rather than to objects exhibiting a grue-like alternative?

The conclusion of the sceptical argument is that 'there are no facts about meaning': sentences attributing meanings to speakers are never true. This invites the question what people are doing when they use such sentences. An obvious place to look for inspiration here is meta-ethics: anti-realists here hold that sentences which appear to attribute moral properties are in fact not used to state facts – are never true – but anti-realists offer different accounts of what, in that case, such sentences are used to do instead. E.g., *error theorists* maintain that users of the sentences in question make assertions – albeit assertions which are always false – while *non-factualists* maintain that the sentences are no more false than true, because their use is distinct from that of making assertions – e.g. in the moral case, it is suggested that they are used to express attitudes of moral approval and disapproval. According to the orthodox interpretation of Kripke, the 'sceptical solution' which he attributes to Wittgenstein (ibid., p. 55 ff.) is a version of this latter, 'non-factualist' kind of anti-realism. Since the sentences in question are not used to state facts, they do not have *truth conditions*; however Kripke/Wittgenstein suggests that they have '*assertion conditions*': i.e. there are conditions in which it is in some sense *proper* or *appropriate* to advance a sentence purporting to attribute a meaning to a speaker; and these are, roughly, the conditions in which the subject at issue uses the expression concerned in the same ways as other members of her speech community.[1]

After outlining Kripke's sceptical argument, Crispin Wright, in the first reading below, criticizes the sceptical solution. He argues that if the sceptical argument is successful, it is more powerful than Kripke seems to realize, and the sceptical solution cannot provide the kind of refuge he seems to intend. Whether a sentence is true depends on its meaning, so if there are, in general, no facts about meaning, it seems there can be, in general, no facts about whether sentences are true. Thus, if successful, the sceptical argument seems to imply a 'non-factualist' account not only of sentences appearing to attribute meanings to people, but of the *truth* of sentences in general. Further, this result threatens specifically to undercut the sceptical solution: if there are no facts about whether sentences are true, then sentences which appear to

---

[1] We describe this as the 'orthodox interpretation' because a number of influential commentators challenge it, arguing that Kripke's claim is not that attributions of meaning do not have truth conditions, but that they do not have the same kinds of truth conditions as other sentences. See Wilson 1994, 2006; Kusch 2006; and for a critical reaction, Miller forthcoming.

attribute assertion conditions to linguistic expressions can no more be fact-stating/ true than sentences which appear to attribute meanings to speakers.[2]

If the sceptical solution is untenable, then we had better hope there's something wrong with the sceptical argument. Wright's diagnosis of what is wrong is that Kripke overlooks an important way in which many first-person judgements about meaning are justified. Kripke assumes that knowledge of meaning must be *inferred* from 'knowledge of a different sort' – i.e. involving past behaviour or mental states or processes. The possibility thus neglected is that a subject's first-person knowledge of what she means by an expression is *non-inferential*. Indeed, Wright suggests, our pretheoretic 'intuitive conception' of first-person knowledge of ordinary propositional attitudes already presupposes just such a picture. We do not think that subjects come to know, e.g., what they intend to do by inferring it from data involving their behaviour and/or the mental states and processes which typically accompany the intentions. If anything, our default practice is the other way around: we grant that subjects can make non-inferential first-person attributions of attitudes that are probably true, and on the basis of those attributions we infer our interpretations of their behaviour and/ or collateral mental activity.

As Wright says, the suggestion that speakers enjoy non-inferential knowledge of their meanings and attitudes is a theme in Wittgenstein's later work; however, in contrast to some of Kripke's more fervently Wittgensteinian critics,[3] Wright does not think we can leave the matter there. According to Wright, it remains deeply puzzling how a state of understanding can simultaneously exhibit the properties which the 'intuitive conception' finds in it: that of being non-inferentially knowable to its subject, and that of having a thoroughly *general* content. In earlier work (independent of Kripke's) Wright defended an interpretation of Wittgenstein's remarks which is somewhat akin to Kripke's, and in the intervening years he has continued to argue in this vein. Wright does not hold that there are no facts about meaning, but on the basis of considerations involving the apparent tension between the two characteristics which he says the intuitive conception attributes to understanding, he argues that meanings cannot be *objective*. I.e., according to Wright, a speaker's linguistic behaviour is not guided by her grasp of facts about meanings whose constitutions are independent of that behaviour, and her judgements about what she means do not *track* such independent facts; rather, in a sense, the meaning facts are determined by speakers' behaviour and/or linguistic judgements.

This anti-objectivist conception of the metaphysics of meaning is not as radical a conclusion as that of Kripke's sceptic; however many critics regard it as too close for comfort. Wright seems to accept that the sceptical argument is powerful enough to undermine *most* accounts of meaning, most candidate answers to questions such as, 'in virtue of what does Jones mean *green* by "green"?' Thus, he seems to accept that, as Åsa Wikforss puts it in the second reading below, the sceptical argument is effective against 'all "pure use" theories that suggest accounting for meaning in terms of

---

[2] For detailed discussion of the question whether Kripke's position here (on the orthodox interpretation) is self-defeating, see Boghossian 1990 and Wright 1992, ch. 6 and appendix.
[3] See e.g. Baker and Hacker 1984, and McDowell 1984.

what the speaker does (and is disposed to do)'. And as she suggests, the range of 'pure use' theories extends far beyond the rather basic versions of behavioural dispositionalism considered by Kripke.

As we saw above, Kripe's best objection to dispositionalism is that it cannot accommodate the thesis that meaning is *normative* in the sense that a speaker's understanding of a term is akin to grasp of a *rule* which guides or prescribes her applications of it. As Wikforss says, the normativity thesis is widely accepted; and we note that Wright seems to accept it in the reading below, at least insofar as he endorses Kripke's argument against dispositionalism.[4] Wikforss, however, regards the normatively thesis as 'obscure' and implausible, and her project in the paper is to defend its rejection. Her main strategy is to consider four versions of the thesis (each one suggested by an interpretation of one or more of its advocates) and to criticize each one in turn. In some cases she concedes that features of the theoretical context at issue may be normative (albeit usually only in a conditional, 'hypothetical' sense) but she argues that on none of the versions she considers is the attribution of normativity to *meaning* justified.

[4] It's a good question whether the anti-objectivist conception of meaning which – we mentioned above – Wright develops in other work sustains the claim that meaning is normative in the requisite sense. One author who has persistently and vociferously argued that it does not (and that in consequence, it cannot be correct) is John McDowell. See e.g. his 1984 and 1992.

Questions and tasks

1   How convincing is Kripke's first objection to the suggestion that understanding consists in behavioural dispositions?
2   Do you agree with Wright that if the sceptical argument is effective against the factualist conception of meaning, then it also undermines the sceptical solution?
3   How plausible is the proposal that Wright considers part of our 'intuitive conception': that first-person knowledge of intentions is typically gleaned non-inferentially?
4   Which of the four versions of the normativity thesis criticised by Wikforss do you think is closest to the one endorsed by Wright? Is Wikforss's critique successful?

References and further reading

Baker, G., and P. Hacker 1984: *Scepticism, Rules and Language*, Oxford: Blackwell.

Bilgrami, A. 1993: 'Norms and Meaning', in R. Stoecker (ed.) *Reflcting Davidson*, Berlin: W. de Gruyter, pp. 121–44.

Boghossian, P. 1989: 'The Rule-Following Considerations', *Mind* 98, pp. 507–49; reprinted in A. Miller and C. Wright (eds), *Rule-Following and Meaning*, Chesham, UK: Acumen (2002).

Boghossian, P. 1990: 'The Status of Content', *Philosophical Review* 99, no. 2, pp. 157–84.

Hattiangadi, A. 2007: *Oughts and Thoughts: Rule-following and the Normativity of Content*, Oxford: Oxford University Press.

Kripke, S. 1982: *Wittgenstein on Rules and Private Language*, Oxford: Blackwell.

Kusch, M. 2006: *A Sceptical Guide to Meaning and Rules: Defending Kripke's Wittgenstein*, Chesham, UK: Acumen.

McDowell, J. 1984: 'Wittgenstein on Following a Rule', *Synthese* 58, pp. 325–63; reprinted in J. McDowell, *Mind, Value and Reality*, Cambridge, MA: Harvard University Press (1998).

McDowell, J. 1992: 'Meaning and Intentionality in Wittgenstein's Later Philosophy', *Midwest Studies in Philosophy* 17, pp. 40–52; reprinted in J. McDowell, *Mind, Value and Reality*, Cambridge, MA: Harvard University Press (1998).

McGinn, C. 1984: *Wittgenstein on Meaning*, Oxford: Basil Blackwell.

Miller, A. Forthcoming: 'Wittgenstein, Factualism, and Meaning', in D. Whiting (ed.) *The Later Wittgenstein on Language*, Basingstoke: Palgrave Macmillan.

Miller, A., and C. Wright (eds) 2002: *Rule-Following and Meaning*, Chesham, UK: Acumen.

Wedgewood, R. 2007: *The Nature of Normativity*, Oxford: Oxford University Press.

Wilson, G. 1994: 'Kripke on Wittgenstein and Normativity', *Midwest Studies in Philosophy*, vol. 19, pp. 366–90; reprinted in A. Miller and C. Wright (eds), *Rule-Following and Meaning*, Chesham, UK: Acumen (2002).

Wilson, G., 2006: 'Rule-following, Meaning and Normativity', in E. Lepore and B. Smith (eds), *The Oxford Handbook of the Philosophy of Language*, Oxford: Oxford University Press, pp. 151–74.

Wittgenstein, L. 1953: *Philosophical Investigations*, Oxford: Blackwell.

Wright, C. 1989: 'Wittgenstein's Rule-Following Considerations and the Central Project of Theoretical Linguistics', in A. George (ed.), *Reflections on Chomsky*, Oxford: Blackwell, pp. 233–64; reprinted in C. Wright, *Rails to Infinity: Essays on Themes from Wittgenstein's Philosophical Investigations*; Cambridge, MA: Harvard University Press (2001).

Wright, C. 1992: *Truth and Objectivity*, Cambridge, MA: Harvard University Press.

Wright, C. 2001: *Rails to Infinity: Essays on Themes from Wittgenstein's Philosophical Investigations*, Cambridge, MA: Harvard University Press.

Chapter 27

Crispin Wright

KRIPKE'S ACCOUNT OF THE ARGUMENT AGAINST PRIVATE LANGUAGE

Saul Kripke's *Wittgenstein on Rules and Private Language*† suggests interpreting Wittgenstein's argument against private language as a direct corollary of the considerations about rule following which immediately precede those passages in the *Investigations* (§243 and following) on which more traditional attempts to understand Wittgenstein's thought on privacy have tended to concentrate. For a long time I thought Kripke's interpretation of these matters more or less coincident with that at which I had arrived independently and which I had presented in my *Wittgenstein on the Foundations of Mathematics* and elsewhere.[1] A careful reading of Kripke's book has convinced me both that this is not the case and that the dominant impression given in my book of the relation between the private-language argument (PLA) and the rule-following considerations (RFC) is misleading.

The leading suggestion about the PLA in that book was that it is to be viewed as *part* of the considerations about rule following: an argument, essentially, that the sort of objectivity of meaning necessary if we are to think of the truth values of unconsidered, uninvestigated statements as determinate independently of any investigation we may carry out, can find no refuge in the situation of a single speaker and his idiolect. The RFC were then depicted as taking the argument outwards, as it were—arguing, first, that, within the sphere of communal practice, concepts and distinctions can be given currency, on the basis of which a "thinner" notion of correctness and incorrectness in linguistic usage can be rehabilitated than that sanctioned by objective meaning; but, second, that, as far as the propriety of objective meaning is concerned, the community at large ultimately fares no better than the would-be private linguist. With none of this, at least as a potentially fruitful framework for the investigation of Wittgenstein's later philosophies of mind and mathematics, do I now disagree. But it does seem to me now that the treatment in my book could be usefully supplemented in at least two respects.

First, I think the involvement of "anti-realist" premises in the arguments against objective meaning was there overemphasized; it seems to me that a more sensitive, sparing, and concept-specific use of such premises may be possible without compromise of the power of the argument. Second, more stress is wanted that Wittgenstein has a *differential* claim about private langauge: that the would-be private linguist and the community are not, in the end, in the same predicament. I shall not, in this paper, attempt to enlarge upon either of these claims.[2] The notable point is that an analogue of each is a prominent feature of Kripke's interpretation: the *skeptical argument* needs no anti-realist (verificationist) assistance; and the bearing of the *skeptical solution* on private language admits of no community-wide generalization.

Although I do not think that Kripke has

Wittgenstein right, my subject, except in the last section of the paper, is not the historical Wittgenstein but Kripke's Wittgenstein. I shall argue that, even if the main argument—the skeptical argument—which Kripke finds in Wittgenstein, is sustained, there is strong prima facie reason to doubt whether the accommodation with it—skeptical solution—which Kripke represents Wittgenstein as commending can really be lived with; whether, indeed, that accommodation is so much as coherent. And I shall canvass ways, unconsidered (or only very cursorily considered) by Kripke, for resisting the skeptical argument. The upshot will be that the RFC, as interpreted by Kripke, are flawed by a lacuna, and that, even if the lacuna were filled, the PLA could nevertheless not emerge in the manner that Kripke describes.

Because the gist of my remarks about Kripke's book is going to be largely critical, it is perhaps worth emphasizing my admiration of it. Whatever its relation to Wittgenstein's actual thought, and whether or not ultimately cogent, Kripke's dialectic is tremendously exciting. It will surely provide a great spur to improving our understanding of Wittgenstein's philosophy.

I The skeptical argument

Fundamental to Hume's moral philosophy, as to his views about causation, is a distinction between statements that are apt to express real matters of fact and certain sentences that, although possessed of standard features of the syntax of genuine statements—in particular, the capacity to serve as arguments for various types of statement-forming operator—are actually used not to state facts but rather to *project* various aspects of speakers' attitudes and affective responses. Moral discourse, and talk of causation, belong, for Hume, in the latter category. Moral judgments, so viewed, do not express our cognition of moral facts by which various moral sentiments in us are generated; rather they serve to project those moral sentiments upon the world. Likewise, those statements which the non-Humean takes to aver the existence of causal relations, from which certain observed regularities flow, serve for Hume to project an attitude that we take up toward those observed regularities.

It is familiar that this sort of distinction is pivotal to a whole class of important philosophical disputes. Realism not merely about ethics and causation, but also about aesthetics, theoretical science, pure mathematics, logical necessity, and Lockean secondary qualities may each be opposed by appropriate versions of Humean noncognitive "projectivism."

In this light, Kripke's Wittgenstein may be seen as first, by the skeptical argument, confounding the ordinary idea that our talk of meaning and understanding and cognate concepts has a genuinely factual subject matter, and then, via the skeptical solution, recommending an alternative projective view of its content. It is worth emphasis that the skeptical solution is independent of the skeptical argument: strictly, the option is open of simply accepting the latter as demonstrating the vacuity of all our talk of meaning, etc., with no prospect of its rehabilitation. (Similarly, a sympathizer might regard Hume as having demonstrated that we should simply drop all talk of causation.) Accordingly, it might seem as though one way of resisting the PLA, as Kripke interprets it, would simply be to take the skeptical medicine straight, eschewing the compensating sweetmeat of the skeptical solution afterwards. I shall return to that thought.

There are a variety of ways in which it might be argued that a region of discourse apparently apt for the stating of facts does not really perform that role. One way, the Humean strategy, would be to argue that from within the framework of a certain preferred epistemology, no reputable conception can be attained of the putative species of fact in question. Another general strategy would be to let the argument flow from a topic-neutral account of the ways in which the distinction between fact-stating and non-fact-stating declarative sentences comes out in their respective modes of employment in the language. But the strategy of argument which Kripke finds in Wittgenstein is different from both of these. Roughly, the conclusion that there are no facts of a disputed species is to follow from an argument to the effect that, even if we imagine our abilities idealized to the point where, if there were such facts to be known, we should certainly be in possession of them, we *still* would not be in a position to justify any particular claim about their character. So we first, as it were, plot the area in which the facts in question would have to be found if they existed and then imagine a suitable idealization, with respect to that area, of our knowledge-acquiring powers; if it then transpires that any particular claim about those facts still proves resistant to all justification, there is no alternative to concluding that the "facts" never existed in the first place.

The initial target class of putative facts comprises those which you might try to express by claims of the form "By E, I formerly meant so-and-so." The relevant idealization will involve your total recall of all facts about your previous behavior and previous mental history, it being assumed that facts about your former meanings must be located in one of those two areas if they are located anywhere. The argument will then be that, even in terms of the idealization, no such claim is justifiable. It follows that your previous life in its entirety is empty of such facts, and hence that there are none (cf. 21 and 39).

I have sometimes encountered in discussion the complaint that, whatever independent force Kripke's development of the argument may have, its use of skepticism betrays its claim to represent Wittgenstein's actual thought. In one way, this misconstrues the skeptical argument; in another way, however, it may have a point. The misunderstanding consists in a failure to see that Kripke's skeptic is a mere device, annexed to the demonstration of a projectivist thesis which might well be supported in other ways. (It is notable that the historical Wittgenstein, though undoubtedly hostile to classical forms of

skepticism, unmistakably displays projectivist leanings in certain of his remarks, e.g., on first-person ascriptions of sensation and when he compares mathematical statements to rules.) Classical forms of skepticism purport to discover inadequacies in our *actual* cognitive powers: the skeptic about induction, or other minds, or memory, holds that the best we can do, in attempting to arrive at justified opinions concerning statements in the relevant classes, always falls short of anything that ought really to be counted as justification. The skeptic whom Kripke finds in Wittgenstein, in contrast, is concerned to teach us something about the range of items that *exist to be known*. That said, there will still be a point to the complaint if it turns out that, despite these differences, the *techniques* utilized by Kripke's skeptic are importantly similar to those which feature in traditional skeptical arguments. Wittgenstein undoubtedly thought those arguments mistaken; it is hardly likely that he would have allowed himself to succumb to an argument which, even if tending toward a conclusion congenial to him, needed to rely upon epistemological principles that, if granted, would enormously strengthen the traditional skeptic's case. We shall consider the matter in due course.

Suppose it granted that there are indeed no facts that we can express by statements of the form, "By E, I formerly meant so-and-so." How exactly do destructive consequences follow about the notions of meaning and understanding in general? Kripke himself is fairly brief on the point (13), but it is not difficult to see. Remember that the argument will have involved an extensive idealization of your knowledge of your previous behavior and mental history: you will have been granted perfect recall of all such facts. If it turned out that you still could not justify any preferred claim of the form "By E, I formerly meant so-and-so," then how can you be better placed to justify a claim of the form "By E, I presently mean so-and-so"? For anything true of your mental life and behavior up to and including the present will be known to you tomorrow, in accordance with the idealization. And the argument will have shown that tomorrow you won't be able to justify any claim of the form "By E, I yesterday meant so-and-so." Hence you cannot be in a position to justify the present-tense counterpart of that claim today. The idealization also entails that nobody else is better placed than you to justify any such claim. It follows that nobody can justify any claim about what they, or anybody else, formerly meant or means. Hence, in the presence of the idealization, there can be no facts about what anybody means by any expression. And it is impossible to see how, consistently with that admission, there might yet be facts about what expressions, as it were impersonally, mean. The strategy of the skeptical argument thus appears sound and ingenious. Everything depends upon the details of its execution.

Simplifying the details somewhat, the execution runs essentially like this. Suppose you claim, on December 21 1984, that by 'green' you meant, on December 20 1984, *green*. The skeptic challenges you to justify your claim. You are idealized to have perfect recall of all your previous linguistic and nonlinguistic behavior, together with your entire mental life—the whole pageant of your thoughts, sensations, imaginings, dreams, moods, etc. (At this point in the argument there is, of course, no doubt entertained as yet about the supposition that you *presently* know what you mean by 'green'—the skeptic gets you to stand on the rug before he pulls it away; cf. 11/2.) Now no doubt you can cite a lot of behavior that is broadly consistent with your preferred account of your former understanding of 'green'. The skeptic will point out, however, that there are no end of alternative interpretations of your former meaning, all of which rationalize your behavior equally well. Perhaps, for example, by 'green' you formerly mean grue$_{1984}$; where an object is grue$_t$ at time k just in case k is earlier than the inception of January 1 in year t and the object is green, or k is some later time and the object is blue. Seemingly there

are indefinitely many grue-interpretations that can be used to make sense of your previous applications of 'green', all of which are incompatible both with the supposition that by 'green' you formerly meant green and with each other.

It might be objected that this is to consider only one kind of use of 'green', viz., simple ascriptions and withholdings, and that account will need to be taken of all sorts of other more sophisticated uses, including embeddings in descriptions of your own and others' propositional attitudes, which you previously will likely have made. But, of course, the point of the example is that 'green' will be assigned the same extension, up to and including the time of your dialogue with the skeptic, under indefinitely many grue-interpretations; so the skeptic should have no difficulty in rationalizing your previous uses both in extensional contexts and in all attributions of propositional attitudes whose possession, by yourself and others, can be explained in terms of the extension of the property of being green. And even if grue-interpretations don't work out in general, the decisive consideration is surely that your previous behavior with 'green' is *finite*; hence, it must be possible, it appears, with sufficient ingenuity, to come up with some interpretation of your previous understanding of 'green' which will be as unwelcome to you as the grue-interpretations. Finite behavior cannot constrain its interpretation to within uniqueness.

The arena of battle now shifts to the mental. Perhaps considerations uniquely determining your previous understanding of 'green' can be recovered from your previous thoughts, imaginings, etc. It is evident, however, that, if the search is to succeed, the relevant mental items must have a certain *generality*. It is no good remembering imagining certain green things, or green after-images that you may have experienced, or thoughts about what you would have said if asked to describe the color of that liqueur we had on such-and-such an occasion. For the constraints imposed by introducing such considerations cannot be stronger than if the images had been public objects or if the imaginary and hypothetical situations had actually taken place; and the effect of those transformations would merely be finitely to enlarge an inadequately finite pool of actual data. You have to come up with some mental episode that somehow has sufficient content to exclude *all* the unwanted interpretations of your former understanding of 'green', including all the grue-interpretations, at one go.

The only candidate, it appears, is some sort of general *thought*: you need to have entertained a thought that has something to say about each of the situations in which the difference between the true interpretation of your former understanding of 'green' and each of the successive grue-impostors successively comes to light. On the face of it, though, it is not far-fetched to suppose that you might very well have entertained such a thought. What if you remember having thought, say, "By 'green' I certainly don't mean any concept which, at some particular time, will continue to apply to an object only if that object changes color at that time." Does not that at least force the skeptic to work a bit harder at the concoction of unwelcome interpretations?

It wouldn't be all that satisfactory if this were the best you could do. After all, it is pretty much fortuitous whether any such thought ever occurred to you; and your knowledge about your former understanding of 'green' will not seem to you contingent on such an occurrence. What you will want to be able to say is that you know what you formerly meant by 'green' *whether or not* you happen to have had a convenient thought that can be used to scotch a particular line of unwelcome interpretation. But the skeptic, in any case, has a stronger, indeed a seemingly decisive reply. His challenge, after all, was general. No special interest attaches to the justifiability of claims about your former understanding of color predicates: the question was, can *any* claim of the form "By E, I formerly meant so-and-so" be justified? Clearly the challenge is not met if, in the attempt to justify one such claim, you presuppose your right to be sure of

another. But just such a presupposition is made by the attempted play with the general thought above. If, for example, by 'color' you had previously meant *schmolor* (20), where the concept of schmolor stands to all grue-type concepts exactly as color stands to blue, green, etc., then your having entertained that general thought is quite consistent with the skeptic's being correct in interpreting you as having meant grue1984 by 'green'.

The point is perfectly general. Thoughts you may have had about how, quite generally, you should be prepared to use an expression will suffice to meet the skeptic's challenge only if you presuppose their *proper interpretation*. But that is just to presuppose that the skeptic's challenge can be met with respect to the expressions that figure in those thoughts. Yet no category of mental item can be appropriate to the challenge except a general thought; only such a thought can have enough to say, can cover the indefinitely many potential situations in which you should wish to regard some determinate use of 'green' as mandated by the understanding that you believe you have long possessed of that expression.

It, therefore, appears that the only ploy that has any chance of accrediting your understanding of 'green' with an appropriately general normative role (11, 23, 24) totally fails to meet the skeptic's challenge. And now "it seems the whole idea of meaning vanishes into thin air" (22).

II The skeptical solution

Suppose that the skeptical argument is sound. Could we simply accept its conclusion and abandon all talk of meaning and understanding as founded upon error? Or must we seek some sort of rehabilitation of the concept of meaning, a skeptical solution? Kripke himself writes:

. . . I choose to be so bold as to say: Wittgenstein holds, with the skeptic, that there is no fact as to whether I mean [green or grue$_t$]. But if this is to be conceded to the skeptic, is this not the end of the matter? What *can* be said on behalf of our ordinary attributions of meaningful language to ourselves and to others? Has not the incredible and self-defeating conclusion, that all language is meaningless, already been drawn? (70/1)

There is, however, a certain awkwardness here. Suppose someone runs a similar skeptical argument about moral obligation, concluding that statements about what people morally ought, or ought not, to do, lack a factual subject matter. It would be, to say the least, an infelicitous expression of this result to say, "So undertaking, and refraining from, any particular projected course of action are always both morally permissible." For the conclusion of the argument would apply equally to judgments of moral permissibility: to claim that a course of action is morally permissible is just to say that it is not the case that it ought to be refrained from. It is natural to wonder, correspondingly, whether the conclusion of Kripke's skeptic is indeed "incredible and self-defeating" only if the notion of meaninglessness which Kripke uses in its formulation presupposes the notion of meaning as moral permissibility presupposes the notion of obligation. If that is so, the right conclusion is surely that such is not the way to formulate the conclusion of the skeptical argument. Once it is better formulated, such unhappy claims as that all language is meaningless, that nobody ever succeeds in understanding anybody else, etc., will presumably not be entailed.

If somebody wishes to reject the suitability of a certain class of concepts to figure in statements apt to be genuinely true or false, this rejection cannot coherently take the form, it appears, of *any* kind of denial of statements in which those concepts figure. What then is the proper way of formulating the conclusions of Kripke's skeptic? One influential view of the concepts of meaning and understanding, associated chiefly with the writings of W. V. Quine, is that their paramount function for us is as theoretical terms in a deeply entrenched but philosophically suspect scheme of explanation of human linguistic behavior and of nonlinguistic but language-related patterns of social activity. If we think of this scheme as issuing in a large class of only semi-articulated theories about particular individuals and groups of individuals, then one way of expressing the conclusion of the skeptical argument is that *scientific realism* about these theories is not an option; there are no facts, describable only by recourse to the concepts of meaning and understanding, which such theories might succeed in codifying. An immediate consequence of this perspective is that two quite different lines of response to the skeptical argument are apparently open. One is a kind of *instrumentalism*: a view which tries to retain the propriety of theorizing of the sort in question while granting its nonfactual status. The skeptical solution attempts just this. The other response is to regard theorizing of this sort as *discredited*, and to seek better approaches involving quite alternative systems of concepts. That, in general, is Quine's own response to the difficulties that he finds in meaning and other intentional notions. If it admits satisfactory development, then the skeptical solution—and with it Kripke's reading of the PLA—would seem to be *de trop*.

This picture of the role of the concepts of meaning and understanding in our ordinary thinking is, however, an oversimplification. It ignores the larger class of self-directed statements concerning meaning and understanding which we make—the class that Wittgenstein himself gives special attention to—and, still more importantly, it makes nothing of various platitudes that articulate our conception of the connections between meaning and truth. One such platitude is that the truth value of a statement depends only upon its meaning and the state of the world in relevant respects. Equivalently:

An utterance of S expresses a truth in a particular context if and only if what, in that context, S says is so, is so.

The obvious corollary is that, if we take the view that the skeptical argument discredits *all* talk of meaning, understanding, and cognate concepts—like the concept of what a sentence is used to say—it is not clear how much purchase we can retain on our ordinary notion of a statement's being true. A proponent of the Quinean view has the choice either to abandon the notion of truth altogether or to reconstruct it in a fashion that liberates it from conceptual ties with the discredited notion of meaning. The former course, however, is hardly an option unless we are prepared to abandon the idea that it is *ever* the case that language has a fact-stating function. (And if that were our view, why see the conclusion of the skeptical argument as calling into question the propriety of talk involving the concepts of meaning and understanding?) The reconstructive project, on the other hand, looks to be utterly daunting. (Indeed it is doubtful whether, in the present context, it is coherent to suppose that there can be such a project; for whatever reconstruction of truth, free of all play with meaning and cognate notions, were proposed, it is not clear why an analogue of the skeptical argument would not be available to rob any particular assignment of truth conditions to a sentence of all possible behavioral or psychological corroboration.)

So the strategy incorporated in the skeptical solution may seem more attractive. It is in any case more comfortable to think of any errors involved in our talk of meaning, or our moral language, as *philosophical*: as belonging to our picture of what is going on in those areas of linguistic practice, rather than as undermining the practices themselves. Thus, Kripke suggests (73 ff) that statements involving the notion of meaning have no *truth conditions*, properly so described, but only conditions of justified or warranted use:

> All that is needed to legitimize assertions that someone means something is that there be roughly specified circumstances under which they are legitimately assertable, and that the game of asserting them under such conditions has a role in our lives (77/8).

Kripke's interpretation of the PLA now follows elegantly from this reorientation. Without attempting to do justice to the detail of his exposition (81 ff, summarized 107/8), we find that the most natural account of the justification conditions of statement forms like:

(i)   Jones means addition by '+'.

and

(ii)   If Jones means addition by '+', then he will answer '125' when asked, "What is 47 + 78?"

involves essential reference to a community of practitioners with the symbols they mention. Very roughly, (i) will be considered justified if Jones performs satisfactorily often enough with '+' and marks his acceptance into the community of '+' users—those whose uses of '+' can generally be depended upon. And (ii) expresses a test for membership in that community, ratified by the responses of those already accredited with membership. Accordingly, such statement forms simply have no legitimate application to symbols whose use is essentially "private" and which cannot, in the nature of the case, competently be taken up by a community. So the concepts of meaning and understanding have no proper place in the description of an apparent linguistic practice of an individual, if that practice is one in which others could not competently share.

The elegance of Kripke's interpretation does not, however, long conceal its difficulties. One immediate difficulty is presented by the meaning-truth platitude. If the truth value of S is determined by its meaning and the state of the world in relevant respects, then non-factuality in one of the determinants can be expected to induce non-factuality in the outcome. (A rough parallel: If among the determinants of whether it is worth while going to see a certain exhibition is how well presented the leading exhibits are, then, if questions of good presentation are not considered to be entirely factual, neither is the matter of whether it is worth while going to see the exhibition.) A projectivist view of meaning is thus, it appears, going to enjoin a projectivist view of what it is for a statement to be true. Whence, unless it is, mysteriously, possible for a projective statement to sustain a biconditional with a genuinely factual statement, the disquotational schema '⌜ P ⌝' is true if and only if P' will churn out the result that *all* statements are projective.

Kripke's own remarks are confusing in this regard. He quotes with approval (73) Michael Dummett's suggestion that the central contrast between the picture of language and meaning proposed in the *Tractatus* and that of the *Investigations* resides in a shift from a conception of statement-meaning as truth-conditional to the view that the meaning of each statement is fixed by its association with conditions of justified assertion. But Dummett, at least as I read him, never intended that reorientation to involve a total rejection of the category of fact-stating discourse. It could not be so intended with any plausibility, since, as we have noted, the historical Wittgenstein thought that we are apt to be misled by the form of our discourse in certain selected areas into thinking that its role has to be that of stating facts. He could hardly have considered that we were likely to be so *misled* unless he thought that form of discourse to be very often associated with the activity of fact-stating. In any case, whatever intention Dummett, or Wittgenstein, may have had, it is doubtful that it is coherent to suppose that projectivist views could be appropriate quite globally. For, however exactly the distinction be drawn between fact-stating and non-fact-stating discourse, the projectivist will presumably want it to come by way of a *discovery* that certain statements fail to qualify

for the former class; a statement of the conclusion of the skeptical argument, for instance, is not *itself* to be projective. But can Kripke's exposition make space for this admission? According to Kripke, what is distinctive of fact-stating is the possession by one's statements of "real truth conditions" (whatever that may mean). And how can the judgment, "S has (real) truth conditions," be genuinely factual if—in accordance with the platitude and the considerations of a moment ago—"S is true" is not?

Another way of seeing that the situation cannot really be satisfactory is to inquire what status, once the skeptical argument is accepted, is supposed to be possessed by the sort of account adumbrated by Kripke of the assertion conditions of statements about meaning and understanding. Could it yesterday have been *true* of a single individual that he associated with the sentence "Jones means addition by '+' " the sort of assertion conditions Kripke sketches? Well, if so, that truth did not consist in any aspect of his finite use of that sentence or of its constituents; and, just as before, it would seem that his previous thoughts about that sentence and its use will suffice to constrain to within uniqueness the proper interpretation of the assertion conditions he associated with it only if he is granted correct recall of the content of those thoughts—exactly what the skeptical argument does not grant. But would not any truths concerning the assertion conditions previously associated by somebody with a particular sentence have to be constituted by aspects of his erstwhile behavior and mental life? So the case appears no weaker than in the skeptical argument proper for the conclusion that there *are* no such truths; whence, following the same routine, it speedily follows that there are no truths about the assertion conditions that any of us presently associates with a particular sentence, nor, *a fortiori*, any truths about a communal association. It follows that the premises, requisite for Kripke's version of the PLA, about the community-oriented character of the assertion conditions of statements concerning meaning and understanding are not genuinely factual, and the same must presumably be said of the conclusion, that the concepts of meaning and understanding have no proper application to a private linguist.

The skeptical solution seems to me, therefore, to be a failure. More: to sustain the skeptical argument is to uncage a tiger whose depredations there is then no hope of containing.

III Resisting the skeptical argument

Kripke himself considers two possible sources of error in the argument. The first is the assumption that facts about my former understanding of E must be constituted by aspects of my former behavior and mental life. Is not a more plausible candidate, a certain former *disposition*, the disposition to use E in certain sorts of way? Against this suggestion Kripke brings (26–37) two prima facie very telling sets of considerations to bear. First, the relevant sorts of disposition are, with respect to any particular expression, presumably finite, since all my capacities are finite; whereas, intuitively, we want the meaning of E to contribute toward the determination of its correct use in literally no end of potential cases. Second, meanings are, whereas dispositions are not, *normative*: I may, in certain circumstances, be disposed to use an expression in a way which is out of accord with my understanding of it and which, therefore, constitutes wrongful use of that expression; whereas I can scarcely be said to have a disposition to use an expression in a way out of accord with the way in which I am disposed to use it. Now there is, no doubt, scope for discussion about how decisive these two rejoinders are.[3] In particular, it need not be contradictory to suppose that someone may be disposed to act in a way in which he is not disposed to act—provided his dispositions are appropriately *stratified*. So much, at any rate, is certainly part of our ordinary concept of a disposition: almost all the dispositional properties about which we ordinarily speak are such that their display is

conditional on the absence of certain interfering factors, and there is no contradiction in the idea that such interference might be widespread and even usual. The matter is obviously one of some subtlety. Here I can do little more than record my own view that Kripke is ultimately right, at least as far as our intuitive conceptions of meaning and understanding are concerned. Understanding an expression is, intuitively, more like an ability than a disposition.[4] Roughly, it is the (fallible) ability to suit one's employment of the expression to certain constraints. Even at the most fundamental level, then, and when nothing interferes with the exercise of a disposition, there ought to be a distinction between what somebody's understanding of E requires of him and the use of that expression which he actually makes; it is just that, if nothing interferes with the exercise of the disposition, the use he makes *will be* the use required of him. You could put the point by saying that, intuitively, understanding generates *rule-governed* behavior; to suppose that it is at some fundamental level simply a matter of a disposition is to ignore the distinction between suiting one's behavior to a rule and merely behaving in such a way that, when the rule is construed as a descriptive hypothesis, it fits what one does.

A second response to the skeptical argument which Kripke discusses (41–50) is the idea that meaning green by 'green' "denotes an irreducible experience, with its own special *quale*, known directly to each of us by introspection." If there were such an experience "as unique and irreducible as that of seeing yellow or feeling a headache," then—in the presence of the relevant idealizations—it could simply be recalled in response to the skeptic's challenge and that would be that. Kripke's response to this proposal, drawing extensively on themes explicit in the *Investigations*, is surely decisive. Quite apart from the introspective implausibility of the suggestion, it is impossible to see how such an experience could have the *content* that understanding is conceived as having, could have, as it were, something to say about the correct use of E in indefinitely many situations. There might, indeed, be a distinctive experience *associated* with meaning so-and-so by E; but then, in order for recall of the experience to meet the skeptic's challenge, it would be necessary additionally to recall the association—and that would presuppose recall of one's former understanding of E, the possibility of which is exactly what is at issue.

There are, however, a number of other ways in which the skeptic's routine, seductive though Kripke's presentation makes it seem, is open to serious question. One concerns the play the skeptic makes with the *finitude* of previous linguistic behavior. There is no question, of course, but that the relevant behavior is finite and that it is thereby debarred from supplying a *conclusive* ground for affirming that your former understanding of E was, indeed, so-and-so. But to suppose that it follows that there is no rational basis for preference among indefinitely many competing hypotheses, all of which are consistent with your previous linguistic behavior, is tantamount to the supposition that Goodman's "new riddle of induction" admits of no solution. This point does not, of course, depend on the fact that we actually used a Goodman-type example in the development of the skeptical argument. Rather, Goodman's riddle is exactly the challenge to explain in what, if any, sense it is rational to prefer, on the basis of finite evidence, the sorts of general hypotheses which we invariably do prefer to any of the other indefinitely many alternatives whose formulation he illustrates. Of course, this assimilation is not in itself a satisfactory rejoinder to Kripke's skeptic. But it does at least show him up for a fairly familiar animal. And it teaches us that we ought not to regard the skeptical argument as, so to speak, establishing a theorem unless we think it right to despair of a solution to Goodman's riddle.[5]

What *is* unsatisfactory about the suggestion is that it gets the intuitive epistemology of understanding wrong. Recognition that a certain use of

an expression fits one's former (and current) understanding of it would not, it seems, except in the most extraordinary circumstances, have to proceed by inference to the best semantic explanation of one's previous uses of that expression. The kind of fact—if, against the skeptical argument, there can indeed be such a fact—which having formerly had a particular understanding of an expression is, is misrepresented by this response.

There is, however, a further response, focusing on the second stage of the skeptical argument, at the point where it is argued that, no matter how rich a battery of explicit thoughts you may formerly have entertained concerning your understanding of E, these thoughts will not turn the trick. Kripke's skeptic discounted the attempt to bring your previous general thoughts against unwelcome interpretations of your previous use of E, on the grounds that you thereby presuppose knowledge of the proper interpretation of those thoughts—which is, in detail, knowledge of the very putative species currently under suspicion. This can seem reasonable. On inspection, however, it cannot *always* be possible to justify a presumed genre of knowledge "from without" in the way the skeptic is here demanding. At any rate, it is obvious enough that, if we were to allow the propriety quite generally of this skeptical move, the results would be calamitous. Imagine, for example, a skeptic who questions a claim about my former perceptions, say, "Yesterday, I saw it raining." And suppose the ground rules are as for the dialogue with Kripke's skeptic; that is, I am to be permitted to adduce any relevant fact so long as I do not thereby presuppose that there is such a thing as knowledge of what I formerly perceived—since it is of belief in the very existence of the genre of knowledge that the skeptic is demanding justification. So I cannot simply claim to remember what I perceived: my ammunition will be restricted to my present *seeming-memories*, the presently available testimony of others, presently accessible putative traces, like damp ground, etc. and meteorological office and newspaper records. It ought to be a straight-forward, if tedious, exercise for the skeptic to accommodate all that without granting me the truth of my claim about my perception of yes-terday's weather. So I can know "all relevant facts" without knowing anything about what I formerly perceived. So there is no fact of the matter about what I formerly perceived. So, since the arguments will work just as well in the future when now is "then," there is no fact of the matter about what I *presently* perceive. So, since the argument applies to all of us, there is no such thing as perceptual knowledge. "There's glory for you!"

The trouble, evidently, is the assumption that knowledge of a former perception has to be *infer-ential*, that the ultimate grounds for such know-ledge must reside in knowledge of a different sort. That is true only if knowledge of what I am presently perceiving is inferential; otherwise, the skeptic may satisfactorily be answered simply by recalling what one formerly perceived. So, too, Kripke's skeptic persuades his victim to search for recalled facts from which the character of his former understanding of E may be *derived*. And that is fair play only if knowledge of a *pres-ent* meaning has to be inferential; otherwise the skeptic is satisfactorily answered simply by recalling what one formerly meant.

The claim, then, is that the methodology of the skeptical argument is appropriate, if ever, only to cases where it is right to view the putative species of knowledge in question as essentially inferential. And no ground for that supposition in the present case has so far been produced. But if it is to be possible simply to recall the character of former meanings, can the requisite presup-position, that knowledge of present meanings may be noninferential, really be made good? Kripke, in effect, confronts this suggestion when he considers the possibility (50/1) that meaning so-and-so by E might simply be an irreducible, *sui generis* state, a state "not to be assimilated to sensations or headaches or any 'qualitative' states, nor to be assimilated to dispositions, but a state of a unique kind of its own." His reply, only very briefly developed (52/3), is that it is utterly mysterious how such a state could have the requisite properties, in particular how, although a finite state realized in a finite mind, it could nevertheless have the potential infinity of con-tent that the normativity of meaning requires. How can there be a state which each of us knows about, in his own case at least, noninferentially and yet which is infinitely fecund, possessing specific directive content for no end of distinct situations?

This may be a good question. But Kripke's discussion contrives to leave the impression that it is rhetorical, that we have not the slightest idea what such a state might be. Whereas a little reflection shows that both these features—non-inferentiality and indefinite "fecundity"—are simply characteristic of our standard intuitive notion of *intention*. Normally, we are credited with a special authority for the character of our own intentions; asked about them, it is con-sidered that we ought to know the answer, and, saving lying and slips of the tongue, etc., that our answers should be given a special weight. Admit-tedly, this authority does not have to be taken to suggest noninferential knowledge; it might be, for example, that it derived from authority for the premises of an inference—say, certain occur-rent thoughts. But to think of self-knowledge of intention, in any case where the subject would be credited with authority, as invariably based on inference from associated occurrent thoughts is to caricature the ordinary notion. For one thing, each of us regularly carries out intentional acts without necessarily thinking about what we are doing at all. Usually these are routine activ-ities in which we are expert. It is perfectly proper to say of such activities that they are knowingly and intentionally performed and, indeed, that they are preceded by the appropriate intention. (If you were asked, in advance, whether you had the appropriate intention, you would unhesitat-ingly confirm that you did.) Notice also that we can in general make no ready sense of the question, "How do you know?" directed at an avowal of intention; if there were an inference in the offing, the question ought to admit of a straightforward answer. But the decisive consideration is this. Even when an intention is accompanied by certain occurrent thoughts relating to its content or the circumstances of the (envisaged) course of action, one's knowledge of the character of the intention is not to be thought of as achieved via reflection on the content of those thoughts. If it were, by what principle could I assure myself that *those* were the thoughts on which I should be concentrating, rather than some other recent (or, if I am clever enough, simultaneous) train? To come to know that you have a certain intention is not to have it dawn on you that you have an intention of *some* sort and then to recover an account of what the intention is by reflecting upon recent or accompanying thoughts. It is the other way round: you recognize thoughts as specifying the content of an intention that you have *because* you know what the intention is an intention to do.

What of the mysterious fecundity? Well, suppose I intend, for example, to prosecute at the earliest possible date anyone who trespasses on my land. Then there can indeed be no end of distinct responses, in distinct situations, which I must make if I remember this intention, continue to wish to fulfill it, and correctly apprehend the prevailing circumstances. But if we are at ease with the idea that my intention has a general content, noninferentially known to me, then there is no more a puzzle about the "infinity" of this content than there is a puzzle about the capacity of any universally quantified conditional, $(x)(Fx{\rightarrow}Gx)$, to yield indefinitely many consequences of the form, $Ga, Gb, \ldots$, when conjoined with corresponding premises of the form, $Fa, Fb, \ldots$.

I want to stress that this is merely to describe what seem to be features of our intuitive notion of intention. The notion is not unproblematic. It could be that it is radically incoherent. The fact remains that it is available to confront Kripke's

skeptic, and that, so far as I can see, the skeptical argument is powerless against it. The ordinary notion of intention has it that it is a characteristic of mind—alongside thought, mood, desire, and sensation—that a subject has, in general, authoritative and noninferential access to the content of his own intentions, and that this content may be open-ended and general, may relate to all situations of a certain kind. In order, then, to rebut the skeptical argument, it would have sufficed, at the point where the skeptic challenged you to adduce some recalled mental fact in order to discount the grue-interpretations, to recall precisely your former intention with respect to the use of 'green'. To be sure, any *specification* that you might give of the content of that intention would be open to unwelcome interpretation. But, if you are granted the intuitive notion of intention, you can reply that you do not in any case know of the content of an intention via a specification of it; rather, to repeat, you recognize the adequacy of the specification because you know of the content of the intention.

The point, in summary, is not that it is particularly *comfortable* to think of your former meaning of 'green' as consisting in your having had a certain general intention, construed along the lines of the intuitive conception, but rather that the skeptical argument has absolutely no destructive force against that proposal.

IV Kripke's Wittgenstein

I conclude with but the briefest indication of the most important difference, as I see it, between Kripke's Wittgenstein and Wittgenstein.

There is an evident concern in the *Investigations* with a large class of psychological predicates which, like intention intuitively conceived, *seem* to have a content that can somehow transcend that of any accompanying thoughts in the subject's mind. Examples are: recalling how a piece of music goes (without hearing it right through "in one's head"); deciding to have a game of bridge (without thinking through all the rules); realizing how to continue a series (without *per impossible*, thinking through the entire infinite expansion); grasping the meaning of an expression "in a flash" (without having all its possible uses run before one's mind); and so on. Each of these predicates, it seems, can come to be true of a subject quite abruptly, yet involves some sort of reference to things he need not, on that occasion, think about explicitly. Wittgenstein thought that we were greatly prone to misunderstand the "grammar" of these notions and to form quite false pictures of the nature of the connection that obtains between the psychological state of someone of whom such a predicate comes to be true and the "absent aspects" noted in the parentheses above. In particular, there need be *no* connection between the subjective content, properly so regarded, of such states and the detail of the "absent aspects".[6] Accordingly, the *normative* power of intention—the determinacy, when it is determinate, in the matter of whether a particular course of conduct fulfills a prior intention—cannot always be accounted for by reference only to the previous subjective content of the subject's psychological states. Wittgenstein's conclusion, however, is emphatically *not* that there is no such thing as the fulfillment of a prior intention—the conclusion, in effect, of Kripke's skeptic.

> Is it correct for someone to say: "When I gave you this rule, I meant you to . . . in this case"? Even if he did not think of this case at all as he gave the rule? *Of course it is correct.* For "to mean it" did not mean: to think of it (*Investigations* §692; my italics).

Rather, a satisfactory philosophy of intention has to validate our claim to noninferential authority for our present (and previous) intentions without succumbing to the mythology of infinite, explicit introspectible content. The intuitive conception of intention utilized against Kripke's skeptic above perennially tempts us toward this

mythology. But there has to be something right about it if—*pace* those who would wish to reanimate a dispositional account of meaning and intention—Kripke's skeptic is not to win the day.

It is this dilemma which is prominent in the last sections of part I of the *Investigations* (§ 591 to the conclusion), sections about whose evaluation there is so far little consensus. The insight that there is a problem here, of the most profound importance for the philosophies both of language and of mind—whether or not Wittgenstein solved it—is one of the principal lessons of the *Investigations*, and one which Kripke's book ought to make it easier to learn.

Notes

† Oxford: Basil Blackwell, 1981. All page references are to this text unless otherwise stated.

1 London: Duckworth, 1980. See also C. Leich and O. Holtzman, eds., *Wittgenstein: To Follow a Rule* (London: Routledge & Keagan Paul, 1981), pp. 99–106; and "Strict Finitism," *Synthese*, LI, 2 (May 1982): 203–282, pp. 248–252.

2 They are enlarged on in, respectively, "Rule-following and Constructivism," in C. Travis and B. Gelder, eds., *Inference and Understanding*, projected, and "Does Wittgenstein Have a Cogent Argument against Private Language?" in J. McDowell and P. Pettit, eds. *Context, Content and Thought*, forthcoming (New York: Oxford, 1985) [both papers are reprinted in C. Wright, *Rails to Infinity: Essays on Themes from Wittgenstein's Investigations*, Cambridge, MA: Harvard University Press].

3 See, e.g., Simon Blackburn, "The Individual Strikes Back", *Synthese*, LVIII, 3 (March 1984): 281–301, and Graeme Forbes, "Skepticism and Semantic Knowledge", *Proceedings of the Aristotelian Society*, LXXXIV (1983/4): 221–237.

4 Cf. G. P. Baker and P. M. S. Hacker, *Wittgenstein: Meaning and Understanding*, vol. 1 of *Essays on the Philosophical Investigations* (Oxford: Blackwell, 1983), ch. XVI.

5 Afficionados of Kripke's text might feel that he, in effect, answers this point (38). "Let no one—under

the influence of too much philosophy of science—suggest that the hypothesis that I meant plus is to be preferred as the *simplest* hypothesis. I will not here argue that simplicity is relative or that it is hard to define, or that a Martian might find the quus function simpler than the plus function. Such replies may have considerable merit, but the real trouble with the appeal to simplicity is more basic. Such an appeal must be based on a misunderstanding of the skeptical problem, or of the role of simplicity considerations, or both. Recall of the skeptical problem was not merely epistemic. The skeptic argues that there is no *fact* [my italics] as to what I meant, whether plus or quus. Now simplicity considerations can help us decide between competing hypotheses, but they obviously can never tell us what the competing hypotheses are. If we do not understand what two hypotheses *state*, what does it mean to say that one is 'more probable' because it is 'simpler'? If the two competing hypotheses are not genuine hypotheses, not assertions of genuine matters of fact, no 'simplicity' considerations will make them so."

I do not wish to suggest that canons of simplicity provide an appropriate response to Goodman's riddle. However, Kripke's point is general. Whatever criterion of preferability among competing hypotheses we come up with, its application can be appropriate only if we do genuinely have competing *hypotheses*, only if there is some "fact of the matter" about which we are trying to arrive at a rational view. Therefore—or so Kripke's thought presumably runs—we beg the question against the skeptic in appealing to any such criteria at this stage. But this surely gets everything back to front. It is only *after* the skeptical argument has come to its conclusion that the skeptic is entitled to the supposition that there is indeed no such fact of the matter. In the course of the argument, *he* cannot assume as much without begging the question. At the stage at which we might appeal to the sort of refined methodology which could be used to answer Goodman's riddle, there simply is not yet any basis for thinking that talk of meaning and understanding is not factual. For what is, I think, a better response to the point, see the sequel in the text.

6   For an excellent discussion of these examples, see Malcolm Budd, "Wittgenstein on Meaning, Interpretation and Rules," *Synthese*, LVIII, 3 (March 1984): 303–323.

Chapter 28

Åsa Wikforss

SEMANTIC NORMATIVITY

With the publication of Saul Kripke's book on Wittgenstein's rule-following discussions philosophy of language received a new slogan: "Meaning is Normative."[1] If I mean something by an expression, Kripke argues, then I *should* use it in certain ways; if I do not use the expression in the ways required, I have used it *incorrectly*, made a mistake. What makes Kripke's claim that meaning is normative particularly intriguing is his suggestion that it is a requirement which any theory of meaning must meet. That is, the claim is not actually part of a theory of meaning defended by Kripke, but rather is put forward as a pre-theoretical *litmus test* for other theories: Any theory which fails to allow for the required normativity can be rejected out of hand. Thus, all 'pure use' theories that suggest accounting for meaning in terms of what the speaker does (and is disposed to do), rather than in terms of what she should do, are to be dismissed. Since there are many versions of pure use-theories (causal-informational theories, conceptual role theories, Davidsonian use-theories,[2] etc.), it seems as if Kripke's normativity thesis, if correct, could be used to wipe out a good part of contemporary philosophy of language.[3]

It therefore is hardly surprising that Kripke's thesis has received so much attention. What is surprising is that despite extensive discussions of the topic it remains obscure exactly what the normativity thesis amounts to and why it should

be endorsed. The objective of this paper is to determine whether there is any reason to subscribe to the claim that meaning is essentially normative. Part of the difficulty is that there are many notions of normativity, and it is not clear how they are related.[4] My concern here will be exclusively with normativity in the sense that implicates an 'ought', a prescription. It is this notion of normativity that is relevant in the present context, since it is the alleged need for semantic 'oughts' that poses a threat to pure use theories. Thus, in his criticism of dispositionalism, Kripke writes: "A candidate for what constitutes the state of my meaning one function, rather than another, by a given function sign, ought to be such that, whatever in fact I (am disposed to) do, there is unique thing that I should do."[5]

My question, therefore, is simple: Is meaning essentially prescriptive? Is it the case that any acceptable theory of meaning must allow for semantic 'oughts', and that, for this reason, pure use theories can be ruled out *tout court*? The paper is divided into two main sections. In the first I examine four different versions of the idea that meaning is normative in order to determine whether any of them can be defended. My conclusion is that the examined theses all fail, either because the alleged normativity has nothing to do with normativity, or because it cannot plausibly be said that meaning is normative in the sense suggested. In the second section I offer some comfort to those who worry about giving up on semantic normativity. There are certain concerns that have typically driven people towards Kripke's thesis, concerns having to do with justification, communication, and naturalism. I argue that these concerns can be taken care of without appealing to semantic normativity. Contrary to received opinion, there is no reason to subscribe to the idea that meaning is an essentially normative notion.[6]

I Semantic normativity: four construals

1 Norms and truth

The most common suggestion is that the normative nature of meaning derives from the connection between meaning and truth. This is how Kripke tends to present it, and most commentators follow Kripke's lead in this. One example is found in Paul Boghossian's discussion of Kripke's normativity requirement:

> Suppose that the expression 'green' means *green*. It follows immediately that the expression 'green' applies *correctly* only to *these* things (the green ones) and not to *those* (the nongreens). The fact that the expression means something implies, that is, a whole set of *normative* truths about my behavior with that expression. . . .[7]

How are we to understand this alleged connection between truth and normativity? It should be clear that the connection is not immediate. That an expression is true of some things but not of others does not in itself imply that it should be used in any particular way, that there are "normative truths" about my behavior with that expression. If 'horse' means *horse*, then 'horse' is true of horses only, but it does not follow that I *should* apply the term to horses only.

In reply to this it is sometimes suggested that the 'should' in question derives from meaning

in combination with the speaker's intention to speak the truth. Thus, "If I wish to speak the truth, and if I mean *horse* by 'horse', then I should apply 'horse' to horses only." But it should be clear that this reasoning alone cannot show *meaning* to be normative. All it shows is that meaning may be one of the factors that are relevant to the truth of hypothetical imperatives concerning how I ought to act in order to reach certain goals. All sorts of factors can be relevant to such imperatives but this does not automatically make them normative (e.g. facts about the weather can go into determining whether or not I should take my coat, but this does not imbue these facts with normativity).[8]

To make the transition from truth to normativity a further assumption is needed. It must be argued that we somehow have an *obligation* to express ourselves truthfully. That an expression is true of certain things would then imply that the speaker ought to apply the expression only to those things that it is true of. This is the move that is standardly made in the literature. Boghossian, for example, suggests that "[t]o be told that 'horse' means *horse* implies that the speaker ought to be motivated to apply the expression only to horses. . . ."[9] Moreover, in order for this reasoning to demonstrate the normativity of meaning the 'ought' in question must be genuinely semantic; it must be an 'ought' which derives solely from semantic notions. Thus, regardless of whether we have some kind of epistemic or moral obligation to speak the truth, if *meaning* is to be normative, the normativity in question must be semantic in kind, not merely epistemic or moral.[10] The claim must be that expressing a false judgment is, ipso facto, a semantic error.

But it is far from clear how such a claim could be supported. Consider the case where I misperceive and utter 'That's a horse' of a cow. What semantic norm do I then violate? I see the animal, believe it to be a horse and, consequently, utter 'That's a horse'. Although I have made a false judgment, I have not broken any semantic norms. On the contrary, if 'horse' means *horse*, then my use of the word to express my belief that the animal is a horse was semantically 'correct'. What this shows is that we must distinguish between two quite different claims: The first is the claim that if I mean *horse* by 'horse' then applying the word to a non-horse is making a false statement. The second is the claim that if I mean *horse* by 'horse' then applying the word to a non-horse is violating a semantic norm. While the first claim is indisputable, it does not support the second claim.[11]

This is not to say that there is no sense in which expressing falsehoods could imply a violation of a linguistic rule. For instance, it has been suggested that there are certain rules that regulate assertion and that these rules are bound up with the notion of truth. An example of this is what John Searle calls the 'preparatory rule' (do not assert p unless you have adequate grounds for p) as well as the 'sincerity rule' (do not assert p unless you believe that p).[12] The liar, it might therefore be said, violates not only a moral rule but also a linguistic one. Notice, however, that these rules are not semantic but pragmatic. The normative force of such rules derives not from meaning alone but from their role in making our linguistic interactions go smoothly.[13] To conclude from the existence of these rules that *meaning* is an essentially normative notion is to commit a fallacy akin to Searle's well-known 'assertion fallacy', the fallacy of "confusing the conditions for the performance of the speech act of assertion, with the analysis of the meaning of words".[14]

Of course, one might challenge the idea that there is a strict division between semantics and pragmatics and argue that truth and linguistic correctness cannot be separated: To make a true judgment, one might argue, is to make a correct assertion; to make a false judgment is to make an incorrect assertion. It is not possible to fully address this challenge here. Two comments will suffice. First, the suggestion is prima facie very problematic. The link between Searle's assertion rules and truth is very weak. I can make a false judgment without either violating the sincerity rule (p can be falsely but sincerely asserted) or the preparatory rule (p can be false but justified).[15] Conversely, I can make a true judgment and violate both the sincerity rule (I do not believe p – I can lie without making a false judgment) and the preparatory rule (I do not have adequate grounds for p). That the link is this weak poses a serious difficulty for anybody who wishes to collapse truth and linguistic correctness, falsity and linguistic incorrectness. Second, if what underlies the idea that meaning is normative is the controversial claim that we reject the distinction between semantics and pragmatics, then it cannot be said that the commitment to normativity is a pre-theoretical constraint, independent of any particular theory of meaning. The normativity claim would no longer function as a theory-independent 'litmus test', but rather as part of a controversial theory of meaning.

The suggestion that the normativity of meaning derives from the connection between meaning and truth alone must therefore be rejected. This, I believe, throws new light on the claim descriptive theories, such as dispositionalism, cannot account for error, false judgments. The assumption behind this claim is that the distinction between true and false utterances is a normative distinction and that for this reason a purely descriptive theory of meaning must fail to account for error. Colin McGinn, for example, puts it:

> The general point here is that we can partition the totality of uses (actual or potential) into two sets, the correct and the incorrect, those that accord with the content of representation and those that do not; but this partitioning cannot be effected without employing a notion not definable simply from the notion of bare use, actual or dispositional, viz. the normative notion of using a representation as it ought to be used given its content.[16]

This objection fails, it should be clear, for the reasons given above. It simply is not true that in order to account for truth and falsity we need to distinguish between correct and incorrect use, between how the speaker ought to use her words and how she will use them. What we need to do, of course, is distinguish between what a word is true of and what it is not true of, but this is just the old problem of accounting for reference and has nothing to do with norms.[17]

There is therefore no principled reason why descriptive, 'pure use' theories must fail to account for error. Of course, there are descriptive theories that run into the problem of error, but it is important to see that this has nothing to do with their lack of normativity. Consider, for instance, the most common objection to dispositionalism, which runs as follows: "Simple dispositionalism identifies what I mean by 'horse' with what I would apply 'horse' to. This fails since 'horse' would then be true of everything to which I apply it and no error would be possible. To avoid simple dispositionalism, the dispositionalist must say that what I mean by 'horse' is identified with what I would apply 'horse' to under certain ideal circumstances. But these ideal circumstances cannot be specified in a non-question begging way, i.e. without employing semantic and intentional notions. Consequently, the dispositionalist cannot account for error."[18] Dispositionalism fails, that is, not because it cannot allow for semantic 'oughts' but because of the difficulties involved in giving a non-circular conditional analysis of dispositions. But this leaves a number of responses open to the dispositionalist. In particular, she can reject the assumption that simple dispositionalism can be avoided only by giving a conditional analysis of dispositions. The mistake, she can argue, is to assume that dispositions must be given a conditional analysis. All dispositions have exceptions in the sense that there are interfering factors that can prevent the manifestation of a disposition: Just as an object can be fragile and yet not break when dropped (if, say, a force

interferes preventing the object from breaking), so S can be disposed to apply 'horse' to horses and yet, on occasion, apply 'horse' to a cow. In neither case can a finite list of possible interfering factors be given and so no conditional analysis will be forthcoming, but in neither case does it matter. Rather, dispositions are to be understood categorically, as identical with certain underlying physical states. Thus, there is no problem of error.[19]

Whether responses such as these are ultimately compelling will have to be settled elsewhere. The important point here is that the problem of error has nothing in particular to do with normativity. The point might be put as follows: The standard diagnosis of why the problem of error arises is that it arises if a theory fails to allow for semantic normativity. But that is not the correct diagnosis. The correct diagnosis, rather, is that the problem of error arises for theories, such as simple dispositionalism, that construe the relation between meaning and use in such a way that any difference in use implies a difference in meaning. On these theories every apparent misapplication (S applies 'horse' to a cow), has to be construed as a meaning difference (S does not mean *horse* by 'horse' but *horse or cow*), and so no error is possible.[20] It should be clear, however, that there is no principled reason why a pure use theory should have to construe the relationship between meaning and use this way. What the pure-use theorist is committed to, plausibly, is the idea that meaning is fully determined by how S uses (and is disposed to use) her words. This can be put in the form of a supervenience claim: Any difference in meaning implies a difference in use. This claim does not, clearly, commit the pure use theorist to the quite different, problematic, claim that any difference in use implies a difference in meaning. The latter claim, again, does lead to the problem of error, whereas the former does not.[21]

The next question is whether there are other arguments supporting the view that meaning is normative. That is, accepting that we cannot motivate the normativity requirement by appealing to truth and reference alone, is there nevertheless an essential normativity which rules out descriptive accounts of meaning? Kripke, it seems, would give an affirmative answer. Boghossian puts it this way: "Kripke seems to think that even if there were a suitably selected disposition that captured the extension of an expression accurately, that disposition could still not be identified with the fact of meaning, because it still remains true that the concept of a disposition is descriptive whereas the concept of meaning is not."[22] And Boghossian sides with Kripke on this point, as do a number of other writers.[23] The question, then, is why we could not give a descriptive account of meaning, once it is granted that we could give a descriptive account of truth and reference. What would be left out? On this issue, there is less of a consensus. Let us examine three of the most common suggestions.

2 Linguistic errors

One suggestion is that semantic normativity does not concern correctness in the sense of truth, as on the standard view, but a correctness which is distinctively linguistic. This suggestion can be found in McGinn's critical discussion of Kripke's book. Kripke's notion of correctness, McGinn argues, does not concern *factual* correctness (stating a truth about the world) but instead concerns "*which word* is linguistically appropriate to the facts." McGinn continues: "Thus, for example, suppose I truly believe that this object is red; the question of linguistic correctness is then which word expresses this belief: is 'red' the word I ought to use to state the fact in which I believe?"[24] This suggests the following picture. When I make a statement, such as "That's a horse", two types of mistake can be made. First, I can make a factual mistake, as when I misperceive. Second, I can make a linguistic mistake, as when I use the word 'horse' to express my belief that the animal is a cow. I have then not made a

factual mistake (my belief is correct) and yet my statement is linguistically incorrect.

How are we to understand McGinn's notion of 'linguistic incorrectness'? McGinn is not very clear on this. He suggests that Kripkean normativity is "a matter of meaning now what one meant earlier" and that linguistic incorrectness consists in going against one's own prior intentions, in "using the same word with a different meaning from that originally intended."[25] Thus, if at time t1 I intended 'horse' to mean *horse* and at t2 use 'horse' to mean *cow*, then I have made such a mistake. However, if this is a mistake at all, it is clearly not a semantic one. If at t2 I use 'horse' with a different meaning than at t1, then I have simply changed my intentions and the word has a different meaning.

To give some content to McGinn's notion of a linguistic mistake we need something stronger. There are two ways of making it stronger. First, it can be argued that the normativity in question concerns what I *should mean* by my words. We can then make room for a genuine notion of a linguistic mistake: If I should mean *horse* by 'horse', and I mean *cow* by 'horse' uttering "That's a horse" of a cow then I have made such an error. This, it is clear, gives us a construal of Kripke's normativity requirement which would rule out pure use theories. We can, again, use dispositionalism to illustrate this. Meaning, on the dispositionalist picture, is determined by the dispositions S in fact has, and there is no question of having the 'right' or 'wrong' dispositions. In this sense dispositionalism undermines the distinction between how a word *should* be used and how it *is* used. Indeed, at points this is precisely how Kripke formulates his objection to dispositionalism. The fundamental problem, he says, is whether my actual dispositions are 'right' or not, whether there is "anything which mandates what they *ought* to be?"[26]

The problem is that it is hard to see how this type of normativity could be essential to meaning. Semantic normativity, as standardly characterized, is the idea that *if* S means *horse* by 'horse' then she should use this word in certain ways. This, clearly, does not imply that S *should mean horse* by 'horse'. To get the latter implication one would have to add constraints on what S is free to mean by her words. However, since these additional constraints go beyond semantic normativity they cannot be derived from meaning itself. No doubt there are all sorts of reasons why one ought to have certain meaning dispositions rather than others. For instance, if I wish to make myself easily understood when in an English speaking community, I ought to be disposed to apply 'horse' to horses, not to cows. But the 'ought' here derives from my desire to communicate with ease, not from meaning alone, and it is therefore not an objection to a particular theory of meaning that it fails to account for such 'oughts'.[27]

There is a second way of making McGinn's notion of error stronger. McGinn is quite right, it might be argued, to say that there is a notion of error over and above false judgments: Meaning errors. Such errors occur when we misapply a word, not because we have made some kind of empirical error, but because we have an incomplete understanding of the meaning of our own words, of our own concepts. For instance, S means *horse* by 'horse', but has only partially understood the meaning of her own word (she thinks that donkeys fall under the concept *horse*) and so she misapplies it. A pure use theory, however, is not able to allow for the possibility of incomplete understanding, since this possibility violates the supervenience claim. Thus, if S could have incomplete understanding of her concepts, there could be a difference in concepts which would not be reflected in individual use. This is well illustrated by certain versions of externalism. For instance, Tyler Burge has argued that because meaning and thought content is determined by the speaker's social (and physical) environment, individual speakers will typically have an incomplete grasp of their own concepts, and this undermines the idea that meaning and thought-content supervene on

individual use.[28] This is the point of Burge's famous thought experiment concerning the concept arthritis: Two speakers can use (and be disposed to use) the expression 'arthritis' in the same way, and yet not share the same concept.

Let's grant, then, that pure use theories cannot allow for meaning errors or conceptual errors of this sort.[29] The question is why the possibility of making meaning errors should be essential to meaning. An appeal to Burge is of no help to answer this question, it is clear, since one cannot use Burge's account of incomplete understanding to reach any type of modal conclusions about the nature of meaning and concepts. Burge does not argue that it is necessary that we be able to make meaning errors, but merely that in a linguistic community some speakers (but not all) typically have an incomplete grasp of the community concepts. Indeed, it is hard to see what such an argument would look like. It certainly cannot be claimed that meaning errors are essential to the possibility of false judgments.[30] To be able to mistake a cow for a horse, I need not also be able to think that "horse" applies to cows. We must not confuse the gap between what S thinks is true and what is true, with the gap between what S thinks a word means and what it does mean. While we must allow for the former gap, there is no reason why we should have to allow for the latter gap.

I am therefore skeptical of the claim that meaning errors of this sort could be shown to be essential to meaning. Let us consider a third construal of the idea that meaning is normative.

3 Intentions and internal relations

A common suggestion is that the normativity of meaning derives from the normative nature of intentions.[31] This suggestion is based on a famous quote from Kripke:

> The point is not that, if I intend to accord with my past meaning of '+', I *will* answer '125', but that, if I intend to accord with my past

meaning of '+', I *should* answer '125'. Computational error, finiteness of my capacity, and other disturbing factors may lead me not to be *disposed* to respond as I *should*, but if so, I have not acted in accordance with my intentions. The relation of meaning and intention to future action is *normative*, not *descriptive*.[32]

How are we to understand the suggestion that the relation between intention and future action is normative? It is clear that there are norms associated with intentions. For example, if I intend to get rich I should spend less. These norms are similar to Kant's hypothetical imperatives in that they specify some contingent means of reaching a given goal: 'If you desire x you should do y', where 'should' has the content of 'it would be prudent to do y'. Failing to do y, then, does not necessarily imply failing to meet one's goal since there may be other means to the same end (I could win the lottery). It should be clear, however, that this cannot be what Kripke is after. Kripke's 'imperative' (if I intend *addition* by '+' I *should* answer '125' to '68 + 57') does not specify a contingent means to an end. It is not an empirical hypothesis that if I intend to add I should answer '125' in order to act in accordance with my intention, and there is no other, equally good way, of adding (say, by answering '135' instead).

Instead, what Kripke appears to have in mind when saying that the relation between intention and future action is normative is the idea that the relation between an intention and its fulfillment is, as Wittgenstein liked to put it, 'internal' and not 'external'.[33] For instance, if I intend to eat an apple, then it is not merely an empirical question what will fulfill my intention; rather, I *have* to eat an apple (and not, say, a pear) to fulfill this intention. Similarly, if I intend to add, then it is not an empirical question what I should do in order to fulfill my intention; rather, I *must* add (e.g. I *must* answer '125' to the query '68 + 57'). Kripke is explicit about this. In a footnote anticipating the discussion of normativity he writes: "Wittgenstein's view that the relation between

the desire (expectation, etc.) and its object must be 'internal', not 'external', parallels corresponding morals drawn about meaning in my text below (the relation of meaning and intention to future action is 'normative, not descriptive' . . .)."[34]

The trouble with this approach is that the fact that the relation between an intention and its fulfillment is *internal* does not show that it is *normative*. If I intend to eat an apple and I eat a pear instead, then my intention is not fulfilled, but there is no implication that by eating the pear I have failed to do what I *should* do. Similarly, to say that the relation between intending to add and answering '125' to '68 + 57' is internal is not to say that I ought to answer '125', but just that if I do not do so my intention is not fulfilled, that is, *I am not adding*. This is not at all a prescriptive claim but a constitutive one. In other words, the claim "If you intend to add you should answer '125' to '68 + 57' in order to fulfill your intention" does not lay down any sort of prescription but specifies *what it is to add*, to do that which you intended.[35] So the alleged normativity has nothing to do with normativity.

There is therefore no reason a pure use theorist, such as the dispositionalist, should have difficulties accounting for the distinction between internal and external relations. The dispositionalist does suggest that to have the intention to add (to mean *addition* by '+') is to be disposed to give certain responses, and it is, of course, an empirical contingency that a person will behave in a certain way. But this is just to say that it is an empirical contingency that a given person has a certain disposition. It does not follow from this that it is an empirical contingency that in order to fulfill one's intention to add one must answer '125'. That is, the claim that meaning addition by '+' is to have a certain disposition, does not in itself imply a denial of the claim that only she who answers '125' to '68 + 57' is adding. Consequently, the dispositionalist cannot be accused of obliterating the distinction between internal and external relations.

This takes us to a fourth, and final, construal of the idea that meaning is normative.

4 Rationality constraints

Philosophers with a Davidsonian bent are prone to emphasizing the normative nature of meaning and content. John McDowell, for example, argues that "our dealings with content must be understood in terms of the idea that mental activity is undertaken under the aspect of allegiance to norms."[36] To support this claim McDowell appeals to Davidson's idea that normative interconnections are "necessary to make intelligible the presence of content in our full picture of mental life . . ."[37] Such interconnections, McDowell argues further, cannot be accounted for within a purely individualistic, functionalistic, framework. Rather, meaning and content must be construed as determined by our shared social rules.

McDowell's suggestion, in other words, is that we can derive the normativity of content and meaning from Davidson's view of rationality as constitutive of intentionality.[38] The appeal to rationality considerations provides the missing link between epistemic normativity and semantics. This suggestion is taken seriously by some descriptivists who set out to argue against Davidson's appeal to rationality constraints. Such a move is uncalled for, however. It is quite possible to stick to the Davidsonian view of intentionality and yet deny that meaning is normative. In fact, this is precisely what Davidson does. Davidson has repeatedly argued against the idea that meaning is bound up with rules and insisted that meaning is determined simply by what the individual does and is disposed to do (hold true). To take a famous example, when Archie Bunker utters "Let's have some laughter to break up the monogamy" he is not, according to Davidson, making an error but merely using familiar words with a new meaning.[39] Davidson's account of meaning is therefore a prime example of a pure use theory.

This may appear puzzling at first. How can one hold both that rationality is constitutive of intentionality, and that norms are not essential to meaning (in particular if, like Davidson, one takes meaning and belief to be inextricably connected)? But there is nothing puzzling about it. Davidson's appeal to rationality considerations is not at all prescriptive. His claim is not that we should be rational, but that rationality is constitutive of what it is to be a language user, a thinker.[40] And constitutive claims of this sort, as argued above, do not have any implications for how S ought to use her words.[41] The claim is not "If S means *horse* by 'horse' she should . . .", but rather that *unless* S uses (is disposed to use) 'horse' in such a way that a reasonable set of horse-beliefs can be attributed to her, 'horse' does not mean *horse* in her language. In fact, it is precisely *because* Davidson takes rationality to be constitutive of intentionality that he denies that meaning is normative. The reason we should not interpret Archie Bunker's utterance standardly, in accordance with the community norms, is that this would violate the principle of charity: It would imply ascribing an inexplicable, crazy belief to Archie (the belief that laughter can break up the monogamy).[42]

It is therefore quite possible to endorse a pure use theory of meaning and yet subscribe to Davidson's view that rationality is constitutive of intentionality. Thus, yet another argument for the normativity of meaning dissolves.

II Living without norms

I have suggested that none of the ordinary construals of Kripke's normativity thesis can be supported. This shows that we should question the (almost) universal commitment to Kripke's thesis. It does not, admittedly, suffice to show that meaning is not normative since there may be another construal of the normativity requirement, yet to be formulated, which is in fact compelling. I doubt it, however. I think nothing is lost and much gained by giving up on normativity, and I will end by suggesting how we can live without normativity. There are certain anxieties that typically drive people towards Kripke's thesis and I will argue that those anxieties can be alleviated without semantic normativity. The anxieties I have in mind concern three issues: Justification, communication, and naturalism.

1 Justification

In the course of spelling out his normativity objection, Kripke sometimes appeals to the notion of *justification*. After stating the dispositionalist reply to the skeptic, Kripke responds that "this reply ought to appear to be misdirected, off target."[43] The reason for this, according to Kripke, is that the skeptic's demand that it be shown that the answer '125' (to the query '68 + 57') is justified can never be satisfied by an appeal to dispositions. I may know that '125' is the response I am disposed to give, but, Kripke asks, how does any of this "indicate that — now *or* in the past — '125' was an answer justified in terms of instructions I gave myself, rather than a mere jack-in-the-box unjustified and arbitrary response?"[44]

How are we to understand the notion of justification appealed to here? It is not, it should be clear, the ordinary notion of a rationalization. To rationalize my linguistic use ("That's a horse") we need to appeal to what I believe (I believe the animal is a horse) and what I mean ('horse' is true of horses only), but there is no need to appeal to a rule. That is, an appeal to descriptive facts is enough to rationalize my use and no norm need be involved. So Kripke's notion of justification is not that of a rationalization. Rather, he has something stronger in mind. The idea is that in using my words I must be *guided* by a general rule, an 'inner instruction', telling me how to apply the word in the particular case. Kripke says for instance that the meaning fact "should *tell* me what I ought to do in each new instance."[45] If I mean *horse* by 'horse',

therefore, I must be guided by a rule telling me how to apply the word (such as, "Apply 'horse' only to horses").

But why should we find this claim at all compelling? Why are not rationalizations enough to avoid the conclusion that my use is "unjustified and arbitrary"? If my word 'horse' is true of horses only, there is nothing arbitrary about me applying 'horse' to an animal I take to be a horse. There is no need to refer to a guiding rule in Kripke's sense.

What is worse, it is not even clear that we can make *sense* of the suggestion that speaking a language essentially involves being guided by rules telling us how to apply our words. The rule in question is supposed to be essential to what it is to mean *horse* by 'horse', to have the concept *horse*. But how can I understand the rule "Apply 'horse' only to horses", how can it guide my actions, unless I already have the concept horse? And if I already have this concept then this cannot in turn be explicated in terms of a further rule, on pain of a regress. Either, therefore, the rule guiding my use of 'horse' presupposes that I have the concept *horse* already, and so the rule is not essential to content as such, or we get an infinite regress of rules. Consequently, it cannot be essential to content that we are guided by rules in Kripke's sense.[46]

Not only, therefore, is it the case that we do not need to appeal to guiding rules in order to justify our linguistic use, it is also unclear how rules of that sort could be essential to meaning.

2 Communication

One important motivation for appealing to rules is the idea that this is required in order to account for communication.[47] Without rules, it is argued, we get linguistic anarchy: People could use their words in any way they like and so the important connection between language and communication is lost. The result is a 'Humpty Dumpty'-theory of meaning.

But this worry too is unfounded. The

assumption is that the only possible constraints on use are norms. As should be clear from the discussion above, however, there is an alternative picture that constrains use in a much more powerful way. According to this picture, there is a constitutive relation between use and meaning such that in order to mean *horse* by 'horse' you must use (be disposed to use) your words in certain ways. The 'must' here, again, is not an 'ought' in disguise; it is not the 'must' of a prescription, but the 'must' of an internal relation. The claim is that there is an internal relation between meaning and use such that how S uses (is disposed to use) her words determines what she means by them. The theory is therefore fully descriptive, and yet linguistic anarchism is avoided. To take a famous example: Humpty Dumpty can mean *a nice knock-down argument* by 'glory', if he likes, but only if he uses (is disposed to use) 'glory' accordingly.[48]

So, instead of appealing to norms constraining use, one can make the relationship between use and meaning constitutive and thereby avoid linguistic anarchism. In fact, I think anybody who takes seriously the idea that there is an intrinsic relationship between meaning and communication should does it this way. As long as the constraints on use are merely prescriptive the connection between meaning and use is too loose to secure communication. This is so since prescriptive constraints allow for a creature to be a language user and yet not use her words in ways that are intelligible to others (because she consistently violates all her semantic prescriptions). Thus, on such a view, S could mean *horse* by 'horse' and yet use 'horse' in any way she likes.[49] By making the link between meaning and use constitutive, this kind of scenario is avoided.

3 Naturalism

One of the reasons Kripke's normativity requirement had such an impact on the philosophical community was that it seemed to pose a new threat to naturalism. If meaning is normative, if it implies an 'ought', then the problems of giving a naturalistic account of ethics could be transposed to semantic naturalism. And some people liked this: They liked the idea of having a knock-down argument against naturalistic theories of meaning and content.[50] So, the question is, if we reject semantic normativity are we stuck with naturalism (assuming this is something we would rather not be)?

No. What follows from the rejection of semantic normativity is not that *naturalism* is home safe, but that *descriptivism* is. We must not conflate these two notions. Of course, naturalism is a notoriously unclear notion. Early this century it denoted theories that avoided an appeal to the supernatural (such as Aristotelianism), today it often signifies some form of reductive theory about the mind, one which not only shuns an appeal to other-worldly entities but also to any intentional or psychological notions.[51] In addition, there is the famous 'naturalistic fallacy' of trying to derive an 'ought' from an 'is'. How all these notions of naturalism are related is a topic in itself, but let me say the following.

A descriptive theory of meaning, again, is a theory which claims that meaning is to be accounted for in terms of what S does and is disposed to do, without any appeal to prescriptions. I have suggested that this claim is best understood as one about meaning determination: Meaning is determined by, supervenes on, what S does and is disposed to do. A naturalist theory, as the term 'naturalism' is most commonly used today, is one that attempts to account for meaning in purely non-intentional and non-semantic terms. Such a theory is reductive in the sense that it avoids appealing to intentional notions, but it may or may not take the form of providing a reductive *analysis* of meaning, i.e. it may or may not be an account which provides necessary and sufficient conditions for meaning.[52] Given these characterizations, it is clear that a theory may be descriptive but not naturalistic. That is, one might hold that meaning is determined by use, but resist the suggestion that use can be given a fully non-intentional characterization.[53] Conversely, a theory may be naturalistic and prescriptive. Such a theory would grant that meaning essentially involves prescriptions, but suggest that we can give a naturalist reduction of these prescriptions.[54] Naturalism of the latter sort would be akin to ethical naturalism, which attempts to show that we can, after all, derive an ought from an is.

What follows, then, if Kripke's normativity requirement is rejected is that a crucial obstacle to descriptive theories has been removed, and this does mean that the naturalist has less to worry about – naturalist theories of meaning can no longer be rejected on the grounds that such theories must fall prey to the naturalistic fallacy. However, naturalism goes beyond descriptivism, and the question therefore remains whether naturalism is acceptable.[55] And to answer that question we have to consider all the old objections to naturalism. For instance, there is still Davidson's claim that because rationality is constitutive of intentionality we should not expect a naturalistic reduction of meaning and content. This remains a challenge to naturalism, notice, even if we deny that Davidson's claim has anything to do with prescriptions. The challenge derives from the idea that rationality is constitutive of the intentional, but not of the physical, and that therefore psychology is governed by different constitutive principles than the physical sciences.[56] Moreover, the worry that a purely naturalistic account of meaning cannot allow for error, survives even if semantic normativity is rejected. To account for error, as suggested above, the function from meaning to use must be construed in such a way that not every difference in use is a difference in meaning. This requires distinguishing those differences in use which do imply a difference in meaning from those that do not, and it is a serious question whether this can be done within a purely naturalistic framework. So plenty of weapons remain for those who wish to go on a crusade against naturalism.

We can conclude, therefore, both that the standard versions of Kripke's normativity requirement should be rejected, and that the types of worries that have driven people towards Kripke's thesis, can be resolved without appealing to semantic norms. For these reasons, I suggest we simply give up the uncritical commitment to semantic normativity and start afresh.

Notes

1 Kripke, 1982.
2 That Davidson's account of meaning qualifies as a pure use theory will be argued below, in section 1.4.
3 See Boghossian (1989). Of course, Kripke's (or "Kripkenstein's") goal is to wipe out all theories of meaning. But people have been much less taken by Kripke's meaning skepticism than with the normativity thesis, and my focus here is on the latter.
4 For instance, there is normative in the sense of evaluative, and normative in the sense of prescriptive, and it is not obvious that the former reduces to the latter. For a discussion of this see Bernard Williams (1985). See also von Wright's discussion of the distinction between *Tunsollen* and *Seinsollen*, norms for actions and 'ideal rules' (von Wright, 1963, pp. 14–15).
5 Kripke, 1982, p. 24.
6 It should be noted that there are other dissenting voices. In particular, Akeel Bilgrami has argued that the assumption that meaning is normative must be rejected (Bilgrami, 1992 and 1993). See also Coates (1986), Glüer (1999), Glüer & Pagin (1998–1999), and Horwich (1995).
7 Boghossian, 1989, p. 513.
8 See Bilgrami (1993) for this point.
9 Boghossian, 1989, p. 533. See also Ebbs, 1997, p. 18. Ebbs derives the normativity of meaning from the idea that we must aim at truth in making assertions. Similar reasoning can be found in Millikan (1990, pp. 350–351).
10 Of course, there is the suggestion, associated with Davidson, that epistemic notions are central to semantic notions and that, therefore, semantic normativity derives from epistemic norms. I discuss this suggestion in section 1.4 below.

11 For a related point see Bilgrami (1993, pp. 142–143).

12 Searle, 1969, chapter 3. See also Grice, 1989.

13 Grice is very clear on this. He groups the various rules for assertion under a general principle – the "Cooperative Principle" – the purpose of which is to make for ease of communication (Grice, 1989, p. 26).

14 Searle, 1969, p. 141. That the belief in semantic normativity derives from a conflation of semantics with pragmatics is suggested by Rosen (1997).

15 This point is made by G.E. Moore in his discussion of Wittgenstein's 1930–1933 lectures: "It is obvious that you may use language just as correctly when you use it to assert something false as when you use it to assert something true" (1954, p. 80).

16 McGinn, 1989, p. 160.

17 Jerry Fodor shows awareness of this. Responding to Boghossian's claim that any candidate for a theory of meaning must be such as to ground the normativity of meaning, Fodor writes: "The trouble is that requiring that normativity be grounded suggests that there is more to the demand of a naturalized semantics than that it provide a reduction of such notions as, say, *extension*. But what could this 'more' amount to? . . . I am darkly suspicious that the Kripkensteinian worry about the normative force of meaning is either a non-issue or just the reduction issue over again; anyhow, that it's not a *new* issue" (1990, pp. 135–136).

18 For a version of this objection to dispositionalism see Kripke (1982, p. 30), and Boghossian (1989, pp. 537–538).

19 This strategy for solving the problem of error can be found in C.B. Martin and John Heil (1998).

20 The problem of error is therefore sometimes called the 'disjunction problem'. See Fodor, 1988, p. 102.

21 See Pagin (1997) for a discussion of the idea that meaning supervenes on use. Pagin makes very clear that the relationship between meaning and use need not be 'one-one', such that any difference in use is a difference in meaning (1997, pp. 23–24).

22 Boghossian, 1989, p. 532.

23 See Blackburn, 1984, p. 291; Brandom, 1994, p. 29; McDowell, 1984, p. 329; Wright, 1984, pp. 771–772 [p. 449 above].

24 McGinn, 1984, p. 60.

25 Ibid., p. 147.

26 Kripke, 1982, p. 57.

27 See Bilgrami (1992, pp. 110–111), for a discussion of this.

28 Burge, 1979.

29 Of course, this does not rule out pure use theories that take meaning to be determined by community-wide use, rather than by individual use. Nor need it rule out pure use theories that take the notion of 'use' to include causal interaction with the external environment. My focus here, however, is on the type of pure use theory that seems most vulnerable to this kind of objection.

30 This claim is made by Bar-On (1992).

31 See for instance McDowell (1991) and Wright (1984 and 1987).

32 Kripke, 1982, p. 37.

33 The special relationship between in intention and its fulfilment is a central topic in Wittgenstein's middle period writings. See for instance *Philosophical Remarks*, p. 111.

34 Kripke, 1982, p. 25. Wright suggests the same: "Intentions have a normative power in the sense that an intention determines whether a particular course of conduct *fulfils* it" (1984, p. 777) [Sic: but see p. 453 above].

35 To this it might be objected that, surely, one could be adding and not answer '125', as when one miscalculates. But that would miss the point here. The point is not that necessarily if you do not answer '125' to '68 + 57' you are not adding, but merely that internal relations are not prescriptive and that, therefore, the fact that the relation between intending to add and answering '125' is internal does not show that it is normative. It is then a further question whether it should be said (as Kripke seems to do) that only she who answers '125' has fulfilled the intention to add.

36 McDowell, 1986, p. 11.

37 Ibid., p. 12.

38 For a more recent version of this idea see Zangwill (1998).

39 Davidson, 1986.

40 It might be thought that rationality is trivially a prescriptive notion since it implies prescriptions of the sort "If S believes that p, S should believe that q". This is mistaken. Spelling out rationality in terms of prescriptions is not at all trivial but presupposes a controversial view of belief as a matter

of choice (since ought implies can). Anybody who rejects that view of belief will also deny that rationality is to be understood in terms of prescriptions.

41 See Glüer (1997) for a discussion of the distinction between constitutive rules and norms.

42 See Bilgrami (1992, pp. 102–104), for a discussion of the relationship between Davidson's principle of charity and semantic normativity. Although Bilgrami uses a different argument than the one above, he too concludes that Davidson's appeal to rationality constraints does not imply semantic normativity.

43 Kripke, 1982, p. 23.

44 Ibid., p. 23.

45 Kripke, 1982, p. 24. See also Gampel (1997) and Zalabardo (1997) who both argue that meaning must function as a guiding rule. Gampel puts it: "[m]eaning is like a rule, being essentially capable of serving to guide and justify linguistic use" (1997, p. 229). See Glüer & Pagin (1998–1999) for a critical discussion of the idea that rules of meaning are guiding rules.

46 This, I believe, is the point of Wittgenstein's rule-following remarks: Construing meaning in terms of rule guidance would lead to a regress and so we must give up the assumption that speaking a language involves being guided by semantic rules. This interpretation runs counter to the received view of Wittgenstein, but fits neatly with his insistence that our use of language is not justified by a rule but more like a primitive response. He says, for example: " 'What made you call this color 'red'?' . . . Nothing *makes* me call it red; that is, *no reason*. I just looked at it and said 'It's red' " (Wittgenstein, 1958, p. 148).

47 See for example Dummett, 1986.

48 Of course, if one is to secure communication it is essential that the constitutive relation between meaning and use is spelled out in such a way that communication is made possible. For instance, some form of regularities over time should be required. For this reason I think we should be skeptical of Davidson's more recent views (see Davidson, 1986) according to which meaning is highly contextualized such that the meaning of my words may change from context to context. See Wikforss (1996) for an extended discussion of this question.

49 Perhaps not quite in any way she likes, since the prescriptivist can hold that S must have some minimal competence with the expression in question in order to be subject to the relevant prescriptions (see Burge, 1979, for example). This just shows, however, that the prescriptivist needs to add constitutive constraints (constraints defining minimal competence) and that it is these constraints, rather than the prescriptions, that secure the possibility of communication.

50 See for example McDowell, 1984 and 1994.

51 See Burge (1992) who distinguishes between naturalism in the sense of 'physicalism', the claim that there are no mental, non-physical entities (a version of Aristotelianism within philosophy of mind) and naturalism in the sense of a methodological demand that mentalistic discourse must be explained, reduced, or eliminated in favour of a discourse which is acceptable in the natural sciences. An example of a theory which is naturalistic in the first sense but not the second, is Davidson's anomalous monism.

52 See Tye (1992) for a discussion of this. As an example of a naturalist theory which does not provide necessary and sufficient conditions Tye quotes Fodor (1990, p. 96).

53 For example, the theories of Davidson and Peacocke are both descriptive, but neither is reductive since they do appeal to intentional notions in their account of meaning (although Peacocke's theory may be more naturalistic than Davidson's). See Davidson (1984) and Peacocke (1992).

54 An example would perhaps be Millikan who accepts Kripke's normativity requirement but attempts to show how it is compatible with naturalism of the teleological sort (Millikan, 1990).

55 See Bilgrami (1992) for a related point. Bilgrami emphasizes that one can resist naturalistic reductionism on other grounds than that norms cannot be given a naturalistic reduction.

56 Davidson is quite clear on this. Physical concepts, he says, "have different constitutive elements" than psychological concepts, and for this reason we cannot insist on a law-like connection between the physical and the psychological (1980, p. 239).

References

Bar-On, Dorit (1992). 'On the Possibility of a Solitary Language', *Nous* 26, 1.

Bilgrami, Akeel (1992). *Belief and Meaning: The Unity and Locality of Mental Content*, Oxford: Blackwell.

Bilgrami, Akeel (1993). 'Norms and Meaning', in R. Stoecker (ed.), *Reflecting Davidson*, Berlin: W. de Gruyter.

Blackburn, Simon (1984). 'The Individual Strikes Back', *Synthese* 58.

Boghossian, Paul (1989). 'The Rule-Following Considerations', *Mind* 98.

Brandom, Robert (1994). *Making It Explicit*, Cambridge: Harvard University Press.

Burge, Tyler (1979). 'Individualism and the Mental', in P. French, T. Uehling and H. Wettstein (eds.), *Midwest Studies in Philosophy 6: Studies in Metaphysics*, Minneapolis: University of Minnesota Press.

Burge, Tyler (1992). 'Philosophy of Language and Mind: 1950–1990', *Philosophical Review* 101.

Coates, Paul (1986). 'Kripke's Skeptical Paradox: Normativeness and Meaning', *Mind* 95.

Davidson, Donald (1963). *Essays on Actions and Events*, 1980, Oxford: Oxford University Press.

Davidson, Donald (1986). 'A Nice Derangement of Epitaphs', in *Lepore*.

Dummett, Michael (1986). ' "A Nice Derangement of Epitaphs": Some Comments on Davidson and Hacking', in *Lepore*.

Ebbs, Gary (1997). *Rule-Following and Realism*, Cambridge, MA: Harvard University Press.

Fodor, Jerry (1987). *Psychosemantics*, Cambridge, MA: MIT Press.

Fodor, Jerry (1990). *A Theory of Content*, Cambridge, MA: MIT Press.

Gampel, E.H. (1997). 'The Normativity of Meaning', *Philosophical Studies* 86.

Gibbard, Allan (1994). 'Meaning and Normativity', *Philosophical Issues* 5.

Glüer, Kathrin (1999). 'Some Considerations about the Normativity of Meaning and Rationality', *Acta analytica* 14(23).

Glüer, Kathrin (1997). 'Dreams and Nightmares', Talk presented at Karlovy Vary Symposium, September.

Glüer, K. & Pagin, P. (1998–1999). 'Rules of Meaning and Practical Reasoning', *Synthese* 117.

Grice, Paul (1989). *Studies in the Way of Words*, Cambridge: Cambridge University Press.

Horwich, Paul (1995). 'Meaning, Use and Truth', *Mind* 104.

Kripke, Saul (1982). *Wittgenstein. On Rules and Private Language*, Cambridge: Harvard University Press.

Lepore, Ernest (ed.) (1986). *Truth and Interpretation: Perspectives on the Philosophy of Donald Davidson*, Oxford: Basil Blackwell.

Martin, C.B. and Heil, John (1998). 'Rules and Powers', *Philosophical Perspectives* 12.

McDowell, John (1984). 'Wittgenstein on Following a Rule', *Synthese* 58.

McDowell, John (1994). *Mind and World*, Cambridge, MA: Harvard University Press.

McGinn, Colin (1984). *Wittgenstein on Meaning*, Oxford: Basil Blackwell.

McGinn, Colin (1989). *Mental Content*, Oxford: Basil Blackwell.

Millikan, Ruth (1990). 'Truth Rules, Hoverflies, and the Kripke-Wittgenstein Paradox', *Philosophical Review* XCIX.

Moore, G.E. (1954). 'Wittgenstein's Lectures in 1930–1933', Reprinted in J. Klagge and A. Nordmann (eds.), *Philosophical Occasions*, 1933, Cambridge: Hackett Publishing Company.

Pagin, Peter (1997). 'Is Compositionality Compatible with Holism?', *Mind and Language* 12.

Peacocke, Christopher (1992). *A Study of Concepts*, Cambridge, MA: MIT Press.

Pettit, Philip and McDowell, John (1986). *Introduction to Subject, Thought, and Context*, Oxford: Clarendon Press.

Rosen, Gideon (1997). 'Linguistic Normativity: Reply to Åsa Wikforss', Paper presented at the APA Central Division Meeting, April.

Searle, John (1969). *Speech Acts*, Cambridge: Cambridge University Press.

Tye, Michael (1992). 'Naturalism and the Mental', *Mind* 101.

Wikforss, Åsa Maria (1996). *Linguistic Freedom: An Essay on Meaning and Rules*. Dissertation submitted to Columbia University.

Williams, Bernard (1985). *Ethics and the Limits of Philosophy*, Cambridge, MA: Harvard University Press.

Wittgenstein, Ludwig (1958). *The Blue and Brown Books*, Oxford: Blackwell.

Wittgenstein, Ludwig (1964). In R. Rhees (ed.), *Philosophical Remarks*, Oxford: Blackwell.

von Wright, G.H. (1963). *Norm and Action*, London: Routledge and Kegan Paul.

Wright, Crispin (1984). 'Kripke's Account of the Argument against Private Language', *Journal of Philosophy* 81 [Chapter 27 above].

Wright, Crispin (1987). 'On Making Up One's Mind: Wittgenstein on Intention', in Weingarter and Schurz (eds.), *Proceedings of the XIth International Wittgenstein Symposium*, Vienna: Holder-Pichler-Tempsky.

Zalabardo, Jose L. (1987). 'Kripke's Normativity Argument', *Canadian Journal of Philosophy* 27.

Zangwill, Nick (1998). 'Direction of Fit and Normative Functionalism', *Philosophical Studies* 91.

PART THIRTEEN

Metaphor

INTRODUCTION TO PART THIRTEEN

THE TASK OF DEFINING METAPHOR is similar to Socrates' task of defining justice in Plato's *Republic* or knowledge in the *Theaetetus*. We are quite familiar with the phenomenon, we can easily recognize paradigm examples, but it is much harder to say what it is that all the instances of metaphor have in common. Here are some examples:[1]

(1)   When you think life is a waltz, it's a five-step.
(2)   He is Kramer from Seinfeld. [said of an actual person]
(3)   My legs turned to jelly.
(4)   Her calves are poetry.
(5)   Is metaphor the dreamwork of language?

It is uncontroversial that metaphorical utterances are frequent, and that they can be used, with more or less success, to communicate something. It seems also clear that in communicating with metaphor, language users rely on something like the literal meaning of the words used, but that producing and understanding metaphorical utterances goes beyond the application of simple lexical knowledge. Clearly, one needs to rely on some further background knowledge in order successfully to use sentences like (1) and (2): one needs to know something about waltz and five-step in order to understand (1), and one needs to know something about the character Kramer, if one is to understand (2). But even if one doesn't have the requisite background knowledge (e.g. if one merely knows that a waltz is a dance and that Kramer is a character in a sitcom), one will recognize that (1) and (2) must be intended in a figurative way. Despite there being a difference between understanding a metaphor and not understanding it, there seems to be a certain measure of discretion in interpretation.

There seems to be a distinctive way in which metaphorical communication exploits the literal meaning of words. For there are other forms of non-literal communication which also build on literal meaning and background assumptions, but which clearly aren't classifiable as metaphor. If I say ironically 'He is a fine friend'. or exaggeratedly 'You never listen to me', I clearly do not mean to commit myself to the proposition literally expressed by my words, and I do convey a non-literal message. If I say 'He has beautiful handwriting', in a letter of reference for a philosophy lectureship, while I may commit myself to the literally expressed proposition, I communicate a further, non-literal implicature, which again depends on the literal meaning (see Part Ten above). In each case I also rely on certain background information, such

[1] Thanks to Emma Wallin for help with the examples.

as the fact that it is obvious that he is not a fine friend, or that the letter of reference is expected to contain information that is more relevant. None of these is an example of metaphor. What is the distinctive mechanism by which metaphorical communication proceeds? How does the content of the metaphorical message build upon the literal meaning of the words used?

One possible answer is that the words used have, in addition to their literal meaning, a metaphorical meaning. This is at least plausible for metaphorical utterances like 'The argument has a hole in it', or 'She didn't lose any sleep over it'. It does seem that the phrase 'to lose sleep over something' has, in addition to a literal meaning, a metaphorical meaning, a meaning that is part of the lexicon. Similarly, perhaps, those who understand the sentence, 'the argument has a hole in it', understand it on the basis of lexical knowledge of a non-literal sense of 'hole', one according to which arguments can have holes. On this view, metaphor would be a special case of ambiguity: some words have several meanings, some literal, some metaphorical, and we decide, on the basis of the context, which of the meanings is relevant for a given utterance. Unlike non-metaphorical ambiguity, the several meanings of metaphorical words are related in a characteristic way: one is a literal meaning; the other, metaphorical meaning is *somehow* derived from the literal meaning.

The trouble is that the two examples just given are examples of so-called 'dead' metaphors, i.e. metaphors that are already established in their use and can therefore plausibly be known in advance. While dead metaphors can plausibly be taken to be special cases of ambiguity, this is far less clear for live metaphors like the ones in (1)–(5). Nevertheless, one might think that dead metaphors provide a model. One might think that the relationship between literal and metaphorical meaning is the same in both cases, so that in the case of live metaphors, while the metaphorical meaning is not yet established, it can perhaps nevertheless be worked out in some way from the literal meaning and the context of utterance. Thus, expressions would have, in addition to their literal meaning a potential for metaphorical meaning, which in some contexts is activated. The question is then how exactly the metaphorical meaning can be decoded on the basis of the literal meaning and the context.

This is the sort of model Davidson opposes quite vehemently in his article. On his view, metaphors do not mean anything over and above their literal meaning. Thus, when I use (2) to say about someone that he is Kramer from Seinfeld, I am saying something that is obviously (some would say necessarily) false, and this is the only thing I am saying. This may appear crazy, because it seems undeniable that I am trying to convey something over and above the obvious falsehood, and that this is the point of my utterance. However, Davidson does not seem to deny that there is this non-literal point of metaphorical utterances. What he is denying is that this point amounts to saying something, or to meaning something. His point is not just terminological (see p. 487). He believes that whatever it is that we communicate with metaphors, it is not a 'cognitive content', not some fact or truth. He argues in detail against a number of theories that make the assumption that there is some cognitive meaning that the successful interpreter will need to decipher.

Davidson's objections, as well as his positive suggestions, are examined in detail by Max Black. He takes his departure from the observation that arguably, Davidson himself makes a serious claim by his opening metaphorical remark that metaphor is the dreamwork of language. One could disagree with this, for example if one believed that metaphor was sometimes the waking work of language. Such a disagreement would obviously not concern the literal meaning but whatever is metaphorically conveyed. This suggests that metaphors do after all convey the contents of beliefs and that these contents are capable of being evaluated as true or false. Black subjects Davidson's objections to detailed scrutiny and offers an objection to Davidson's own, positive proposal.

Questions and tasks

1   What does Davidson mean when he says that 'metaphor belongs exclusively to the domain of use' (p. 478)?
2   What is Davidson's argument against the view that metaphor is a kind of ambiguity?
3   What is Davidson's argument against the view that the metaphorical meaning of a live metaphor is 'immortalized' in the literal meaning of that metaphor when it 'dies', i.e. becomes a dead metaphor?
4   What is Davidson's argument against the view that the meaning of a metaphor is the meaning of a corresponding simile?
5   Davidson claims that 'all similes are true and most metaphors are false' (p. 484). Is he right? Is the second part of this claim compatible with what he says in note 10?
6   Davidson imagines someone shrugging off his claim that there is no metaphorical meaning 'as no more than an insistence on restraint in using the word "meaning" '. He says that 'this would be wrong' (p. 487). Is Black guilty of this mistake? What is left of Davidson's thesis when restraint in using the word 'meaning' is relaxed?
7   What is Black's objection to Davidson's positive thesis?

References and further reading

Black, Max 1962: 'Metaphor', in *Models and Metaphors: Studies in Language and Philosophy*, Ithaca, NY: Cornell University Press, pp. 25–47.

Black, Max 1993: 'More about Metaphor', in A. Ortony (ed.), *Metaphor and Thought*, Cambridge: Cambridge University Press, pp. 19–41.

Camp, Elizabeth 2006: 'Contextualism, Metaphor and What Is Said'. *Mind & Language* 21, pp. 280–309.

Camp, Elizabeth Forthcoming in 2009: 'Metaphor', in L. Cummings (ed.), *The Pragmatics Encyclopedia*, London: Routledge.

Camp, Elizabeth, and Marga Reimer 2006: 'Metaphor', in E. Lepore and B. Smith (eds), *The Oxford Handbook of Philosophy of Language*, Oxford: Oxford University Press, pp. 845–63.

Cohen, T. 2005: 'Metaphor', in J. Levinson (ed.), *The Oxford Handbook of Aesthetics*, Oxford: Oxford University Press, pp. 366–76.

Cooper, David 1986: *Metaphor*, Oxford: Blackwell.

Davies, Martin 1982: 'Idiom and Metaphor', *Proceedings of the Aristotelian Society* 83, pp. 67–85.

Fogelin, Robert 1988: *Figuratively Speaking*, New Haven, CT: Yale University Press.

Grice, H. Paul 1975: 'Logic and Conversation', in P. Cole and J. L. Morgan (eds), *Speech Acts*, vol. 3: *Syntax and Semantics*, pp. 41–58; reprinted in P. Grice, *Studies in the Way of Words*, Cambridge, MA: Harvard University Press (1989), pp. 22–57.

Guttenplan, Sam 2005: *Objects of Metaphor*, Oxford: Oxford University Press.

Kittay, Eva F. 1987: *Metaphor: Its Cognitive Force and Linguistic Structure*, Oxford: Oxford University Press.

Lakoff, George, and M. Johnson 1980: *Metaphors We Live By*, Chicago: Chicago University Press.

Moran, Richard 1997: 'Metaphor', in C. Wright and B. Hale (eds), *A Companion to Philosophy of Language*, Oxford: Blackwell, pp. 248–68.

Recanati, François 2001: 'Literal/nonliteral', *Midwest Studies in Philosophy* 25, pp. 264–74.

Searle, John 1979: 'Metaphor', in John Searle, *Expression and Meaning: Studies in the Theory of Speech Acts*, Cambridge: Cambridge University Press.

Stern, Josef 2000: *Metaphor in Context*, Cambridge, MA: MIT Press.

Stern, Josef 2006: 'Figurative Language', in M. Devitt and R. Hanley (eds), *The Blackwell Guide to the Philosophy of Language*, Oxford: Blackwell, pp. 168–85.

Tirrell, Lynn 1991: 'Reductive and Nonreductive Simile Theories of Metaphor', *Journal of Philosophy* 88, pp. 337–58.

White, Roger 1996: *The Structure of Metaphor: The Way the Language of Metaphor Works*, Oxford: Blackwell.

Wilson, Deirdre, and Robyn Carston 2006: 'Metaphor, Relevance and the "Emergent Property" Issue'. *Mind & Language* 21, pp. 404–33.

Chapter 29

Donald Davidson

WHAT METAPHORS MEAN

Metaphor is the dreamwork of language and, like all dreamwork, its interpretation reflects as much on the interpreter as on the originator. The interpretation of dreams requires collaboration between a dreamer and a waker, even if they be the same person; and the act of interpretation is itself a work of the imagination. So too understanding a metaphor is as much a creative endeavour as making a metaphor, and as little guided by rules.

These remarks do not, except in matters of degree, distinguish metaphor from more routine linguistic transactions: all communication by speech assumes the interplay of inventive construction and inventive construal. What metaphor adds to the ordinary is an achievement that uses no semantic resources beyond the resources on which the ordinary depends. There are no instructions for devising metaphors; there is no manual for determining what a metaphor 'means' or 'says'; there is no test for metaphor that does not call for taste.[1] A metaphor implies a kind and degree of artistic success; there are no unsuccessful metaphors, just as there are no unfunny jokes. There are tasteless metaphors, but these are turns that nevertheless have brought something off, even if it were not worth bringing off or could have been brought off better.

This paper is concerned with what metaphors mean, and its thesis is that metaphors mean what the words, in their most literal interpretation, mean, and nothing more. Since this thesis flies in the face of contemporary views with which I am familiar, much of what I have to say is critical. But I think the picture of metaphor that emerges when error and confusion are cleared away makes metaphor a more, not a less, interesting phenomenon.

The central mistake against which I shall be inveighing is the idea that a metaphor has, in addition to its literal sense or meaning, another sense or meaning. This idea is common to many who have written about metaphor: it is found in the works of literary critics like Richards, Empson, and Winters; philosophers from Aristotle to Max Black; psychologists from Freud and earlier to Skinner and later; and linguists from Plato to Uriel Weinreich and George Lakoff. The idea takes many forms, from the relatively simple in Aristotle to the relatively complex in Black. The idea appears in writings which maintain that a literal paraphrase of a metaphor can be produced, but it is also shared by those who hold that typically no literal paraphrase can be found. Some stress the special insight metaphor can inspire and make much of the fact that ordinary language, in its usual functioning, yields no such insight. Yet this view too sees metaphor as a form of communication alongside ordinary communication; metaphor conveys truths or falsehoods about the world much as plainer language does, though the message may be considered more exotic, profound, or cunningly garbed.

The concept of metaphor as primarily a vehicle for conveying ideas, even if unusual ones, seems to me as wrong as the parent idea that a metaphor has a special meaning. I agree with the view that metaphors cannot be paraphrased, but I think this is not because metaphors say something too novel for literal expression but because there is nothing there to paraphrase. Paraphrase, whether possible or not, is appropriate to what is *said*: we try, in paraphrase, to say it another way. But if I am right, a metaphor doesn't say anything beyond its literal meaning (nor does its maker say anything, in using the metaphor, beyond the literal). This is not, of course, to deny that a metaphor has a point, nor that that point can be brought out by using further words.

In the past those who have denied that metaphor has a cognitive content in addition to the literal have often been out to show that metaphor is confusing, merely emotive, unsuited to serious, scientific, or philosophic discourse. My views should not be associated with this tradition. Metaphor is a legitimate device not only in literature but in science, philosophy, and the law; it is effective in praise and abuse, prayer and promotion, description and prescription. For the most part I don't disagree with Max Black, Paul Henle, Nelson Goodman, Monroe Beardsley, and the rest in their accounts of what metaphor accomplishes, except that I think it accomplishes more and that what is additional is different in kind.

My disagreement is with the explanation of how metaphor works its wonders. To anticipate: I depend on the distinction between what words mean and what they are used to do. I think metaphor belongs exclusively to the domain of use. It is something brought off by the imaginative employment of words and sentences and depends entirely on the ordinary meanings of those words and hence on the ordinary meanings of the sentences they comprise.

It is no help in explaining how words work in metaphor to posit metaphorical or figurative meanings, or special kinds of poetic or metaphorical truth. These ideas don't explain metaphor, metaphor explains them. Once we understand a metaphor we can call what we grasp the 'metaphorical truth' and (up to a point) say what the 'metaphorical meaning' is. But simply to lodge this meaning in the metaphor is like explaining why a pill puts you to sleep by saying it has a dormative power. Literal meaning and literal truth conditions can be assigned to words and sentences apart from particular contexts of use. This is why adverting to them has genuine explanatory power.

I shall try to establish my negative views about what metaphors mean and introduce my limited positive claims by examining some false theories of the nature of metaphor.

A metaphor makes us attend to some likeness, often a novel or surprising likeness, between two or more things. This trite and true observation leads, or seems to lead, to a conclusion concerning the meaning of metaphors. Consider ordinary likeness or similarity: two roses are similar because they share the property of being a rose; two infants are similar by virtue of their infanthood. Or, more simply, roses are similar because each is a rose, infants, because each is an infant.

Suppose someone says 'Tolstoy was once an infant'. How is the infant Tolstoy like other infants? The answer comes pat: by virtue of exhibiting the property of infanthood, that is, leaving out some of the wind, by virtue of being an infant. If we tire of the phrase 'by virtue of', we can, it seems, be plainer still by saying the infant Tolstoy shares with other infants the fact that the predicate 'is an infant' applies to him; given the word 'infant', we have no trouble saying exactly how the infant Tolstoy resembles other infants. We could do it without the word 'infant'; all we need is other words that mean the same. The end result is the same. Ordinary similarity depends on groupings established by the ordinary meanings of words. Such similarity is natural and unsurprising to the extent that familiar ways of grouping objects are tied to usual meanings of usual words.

A famous critic said that Tolstoy was 'a great moralizing infant'. The Tolstoy referred to here is obviously not the infant Tolstoy but Tolstoy the adult writer; this is metaphor. Now in what sense is Tolstoy the writer similar to an infant? What we are to do, perhaps, is think of the class of objects which includes all ordinary infants and, in addition, the adult Tolstoy and then ask ourselves what special, surprising property the members of this class have in common. The appealing thought is that given patience we could come as close as need be to specifying the appropriate property. In any case, we could do the job perfectly if we found words that meant exactly what the metaphorical 'infant' means. The important point, from my perspective, is not whether we can find the perfect other words but the assumption that there is something to be attempted, a metaphorical meaning to be matched. So far I have been doing no more than crudely sketching how the concept of meaning may have crept into the analysis of metaphor, and the answer I have suggested is that since what we think of as garden variety similarity goes with what we think of as garden variety meanings, it is natural to posit unusual or metaphorical meanings to help explain the similarities metaphor promotes.

The idea, then, is that in metaphor certain words take on new, or what are often called 'extended', meanings. When we read, for example, that 'the Spirit of God moved upon the face of the waters', we are to regard the word 'face' as having an extended meaning (I disregard further metaphor in the passage). The extension applies, as it happens, to what philosophers call the extension of the word, that is, the class of entities to which it refers. Here the word 'face' applies to ordinary faces, and to waters in addition.

This account cannot, at any rate, be complete, for if in these contexts the words 'face' and 'infant' apply correctly to waters and to the adult Tolstoy, then waters really do have faces and Tolstoy literally was an infant, and all sense of metaphor evaporates. If we are to think of words in metaphors as directly going about their business of applying to what they properly do apply to, there is no difference between metaphor and the introduction of a new term into our vocabulary: to make a metaphor is to murder it.

What has been left out is any appeal to the original meaning of the words. Whether or not metaphor depends on new or extended meanings, it certainly depends in some way on the original meanings; an adequate account of metaphor must allow that the primary or original meanings of words remain active in their metaphorical setting.

Perhaps, then, we can explain metaphor as a kind of ambiguity: in the context of a metaphor, certain words have either a new or an original meaning, and the force of the metaphor depends on our uncertainty as we waver between the two meanings. Thus when Melville writes that 'Christ was a chronometer', the effect of metaphor is produced by our taking 'chronometer' first in its ordinary sense and then in some extraordinary or metaphorical sense.

It is hard to see how this theory can be correct. For the ambiguity in the word, if there is any, is due to the fact that in ordinary contexts it means one thing and in the metaphorical context it means something else; but in the metaphorical context we do not necessarily hesitate over its meaning. When we do hesitate, it is usually to decide which of a number of metaphorical interpretations we shall accept; we are seldom in doubt that what we have is a metaphor. At any rate, the effectiveness of the metaphor easily outlasts the end of uncertainty over the interpretation of the metaphorical passage. Metaphor cannot, therefore, owe its effect to ambiguity of this sort.[2]

Another brand of ambiguity may appear to offer a better suggestion. Sometimes a word will, in a single context, bear two meanings where we are meant to remember and to use both. Or, if we think of wordhood as implying sameness of meaning, then we may describe the situation as one in which what appears as a single word is in fact two. When Shakespeare's Cressida is welcomed bawdily into the Grecian camp, Nestor says, 'Our general doth salute you with a kiss.' Here we are to take 'general' two ways: once as applying to Agamemnon, who is the general; and once, since she is kissing everyone, as applying to no one in particular, but everyone in general. We really have a conjunction of two sentences: our general, Agamemnon, salutes you with a kiss; and everyone in general is saluting you with a kiss.

This is a legitimate device, a pun, but it is not the same device as metaphor. For in metaphor there is no essential need of reiteration; whatever meanings we assign the words, they keep through every correct reading of the passage.

A plausible modification of the last suggestion would be to consider the key word (or words) in a metaphor as having two different kinds of meaning at once, a literal and a figurative meaning. Imagine the literal meaning as latent, something that we are aware of, that can work on us without working in the context, while the figurative meaning carries the direct load. And finally, there must be a rule which connects the two meanings, for otherwise the explanation lapses into a form of the ambiguity theory. The rule, at least for many typical cases of metaphor, says that in its metaphorical role the word applies to everything that it applies to in its literal role, and then some.[3]

This theory may seem complex, but it is strikingly similar to what Frege proposed to account for the behaviour of referring terms in modal sentences and sentences about propositional attitudes like belief and desire. According to Frege, each referring term has two (or more) meanings, one which fixes its reference in ordinary contexts and another which fixes its reference in the special contexts created by modal operators or psychological verbs. The rule connecting the two meanings may be put like this: the meaning of the word in the special contexts makes the reference in those contexts

to be identical with the meaning in ordinary contexts.

Here is the whole picture, putting Frege together with a Fregean view of metaphor: we are to think of a word as having, in addition to its mundane field of application or reference, two special or supermundane fields of application, one for metaphor and the other for modal contexts and the like. In both cases the original meaning remains to do its work by virtue of a rule which relates the various meanings.

Having stressed the possible analogy between metaphorical meaning and the Fregean meanings for oblique contexts, I turn to an imposing difficulty in maintaining the analogy. You are entertaining a visitor from Saturn by trying to teach him to use the word 'floor'. You go through the familiar dodges, leading him from floor to floor, pointing and stamping and repeating the word. You prompt him to make experiments, tapping objects tentatively with his tentacle while rewarding his right and wrong tries. You want him to come out knowing not only that these particular objects or surfaces are floors but also how to tell a floor when one is in sight or touch. The skit you are putting on doesn't *tell* him what he needs to know, but with luck it helps him to learn it.

Should we call this process learning something about the world or learning something about language? An odd question, since what is learned is that a bit of language refers to a bit of the world. Still, it is easy to distinguish between the business of learning the meaning of a word and using the word once the meaning is learned. Comparing these two activities, it is natural to say that the first concerns learning something about language, while the second is typically learning something about the world. If your Saturnian has learned how to use the word 'floor', you may try telling him something new, that *here* is a floor. If he has mastered the word trick, you have told him something about the world.

Your friend from Saturn now transports you

through space to his home sphere, and looking back remotely at earth you say to him, nodding at the earth, 'floor'. Perhaps he will think this is still part of the lesson and assume that the word 'floor' applies properly to the earth, at least as seen from Saturn. But what if you thought he already knew the meaning of 'floor', and you were remembering how Dante, from a similar place in the heavens, saw the inhabited earth as 'the small round floor that makes us passionate'? Your purpose was metaphor, not drill in the use of language. What difference would it make to your friend which way he took it? With the theory of metaphor under consideration, very little difference, for according to that theory a word has a new meaning in a metaphorical context; the occasion of the metaphor would, therefore, be the occasion for learning the new meaning. We should agree that in some ways it makes relatively little difference whether, in a given context, we think a word is being used metaphorically or in a previously unknown, but literal way. Empson, in *Some Versions of Pastoral*, quotes these lines from Donne: 'As our blood labours to beget / Spirits, as like souls as it can, . . . / So must pure lover's soules descend. . . .' The modern reader is almost certain, Empson points out, to take the word 'spirits' in this passage metaphorically, as applying only by extension to something spiritual. But for Donne there was no metaphor. He writes in his *Sermons*, 'The Spirits . . . are the thin and active parts of the blood, and are a kind of middle nature, between soul and body.' Learning this does not matter much; Empson is right when he says, 'It is curious how the change in the word [that is, in what we think it means] leaves the poetry unaffected.'[4]

The change may be, in some cases at least, hard to appreciate, but unless there is a change, most of what is thought to be interesting about metaphor is lost. I have been making the point by contrasting learning a new use for an old word with using a word already understood; in one case, I said, our attention is directed to language, in the other, to what language is about.

Metaphor, I suggested, belongs in the second category. This can also be seen by considering dead metaphors. Once upon a time, I suppose, rivers and bottles did not, as they do now, literally have mouths. Thinking of present usage, it doesn't matter whether we take the word 'mouth' to be ambiguous because it applies to entrances to rivers and openings of bottles as well as to animal apertures, or we think there is a single wide field of application that embraces both. What does matter is that when 'mouth' applied only metaphorically to bottles, the application made the hearer *notice* a likeness between animal and bottle openings. (Consider Homer's reference to wounds as mouths.) Once one has the present use of the word, with literal application to bottles, there is nothing left to notice. There is no similarity to seek because it consists simply in being referred to by the same word.

Novelty is not the issue. In its context a word once taken for a metaphor remains a metaphor on the hundredth hearing, while a word may easily be appreciated in a new literal role on a first encounter. What we call the element of novelty or surprise in a metaphor is a built-in aesthetic feature we can experience again and again, like the surprise in Haydn's Symphony No. 94, or a familiar deceptive cadence.

If metaphor involved a second meaning, as ambiguity does, we might expect to be able to specify the special meaning of a word in a metaphorical setting by waiting until the metaphor dies. The figurative meaning of the living metaphor should be immortalized in the literal meaning of the dead. But although some philosophers have suggested this idea, it seems plainly wrong. 'He was burned up' is genuinely ambiguous (since it may be true in one sense and false in another), but although the slangish idiom is no doubt the corpse of a metaphor, 'He was burned up' now suggests no more than that he was very angry. When the metaphor was active, we would have pictured fire in the eyes or smoke coming out of the ears.

We can learn much about what metaphors

mean by comparing them with similes, for a simile tells us, in part, what a metaphor merely nudges us into noting. Suppose Goneril had said, thinking of Lear, 'Old fools are like babes again'; then she would have used the words to assert a similarity between old fools and babes. What she did say, of course, was 'Old fools are babes again', thus using the words to intimate what the simile declared. Thinking along these lines may inspire another theory of the figurative or special meaning of metaphors: the figurative meaning of a metaphor is the literal meaning of the corresponding simile. Thus 'Christ was a chronometer' in its figurative sense is synonymous with 'Christ was like a chronometer', and the metaphorical meaning once locked up in 'He was burned up' is released in 'He was like someone who was burned up' (or perhaps 'He was like burned up').

There is, to be sure, the difficulty of identifying the simile that corresponds to a given metaphor Virginia Woolf said that a highbrow is 'a man or woman of thoroughbred intelligence who rides his mind at a gallop across country in pursuit of an idea'. What simile corresponds? Something like this, perhaps: 'A highbrow is a man or woman whose intelligence is like a thoroughbred horse and who persists in thinking about an idea like a rider galloping across country in pursuit of . . . well, something.'

The view that the special meaning of a metaphor is identical with the literal meaning of a corresponding simile (however 'corresponding' is spelled out) should not be confused with the common theory that a metaphor is an elliptical simile.[5] This theory makes no distinction in meaning between a metaphor and some related simile and does not provide any ground for speaking of figurative, metaphorical, or special meanings. It is a theory that wins hands down so far as simplicity is concerned, but it also seems too simple to work. For if we make the literal meaning of the metaphor to be the literal meaning of a matching simile, we deny access to what we originally took to be the literal meaning of the metaphor, and we agreed almost from the start that this meaning was essential to the working of the metaphor, whatever else might have to be brought in in the way of a non-literal meaning.

Both the elliptical simile theory of metaphor and its more sophisticated variant, which equates the figurative meaning of the metaphor with the literal meaning of a simile, share a fatal defect. They make the hidden meaning of the metaphor all too obvious and accessible. In each case the hidden meaning is to be found simply by looking to the literal meaning of what is usually a painfully trivial simile. This is like that—Tolstoy like an infant, the earth like a floor. It is trivial because everything is like everything, and in endless ways. Metaphors are often very difficult to interpret and, so it is said, impossible to paraphrase. But with this theory, interpretation and paraphrase typically are ready to the hand of the most callow.

These simile theories have been found acceptable, I think, only because they have been confused with a quite different theory. Consider this remark by Max Black:

> When Schopenhauer called a geometrical proof a mousetrap, he was, according to such a view, *saying* (though not explicitly): 'A geometrical proof is *like* a mousetrap, since both offer a delusive reward, entice their victims by degrees, lead to disagreeable surprise, etc.' This is a view of metaphor as a condensed or elliptical *simile*.[6]

Here I discern two confusions. First, if metaphors are elliptical similes, they say *explicitly* what similes say, for ellipsis is a form of abbreviation, not of paraphrase or indirection. But, and this is the more important matter, Black's statement of what the metaphor says goes far beyond anything given by the corresponding simile. The simile simply says a geometrical proof is like a mousetrap. It no more *tells* us what similarities we are to notice than the metaphor does. Black mentions three similarities, and of course we could go on adding to the list forever. But is this list, when revised and supplemented in the right way, supposed to give the *literal* meaning of the simile? Surely not, since the simile declared no more than the similarity. If the list is supposed to provide the figurative meaning of the simile, then we learn nothing about metaphor from the comparison with simile—only that both have the same figurative meaning. Nelson Goodman does indeed claim that 'the difference between simile and metaphor is negligible', and he continues, 'Whether the locution be "is like" or "is", the figure *likens* picture to person by picking out a certain common feature. . . .'[7] Goodman is considering the difference between saying a picture is sad and saying it is like a sad person. It is clearly true that both sayings liken picture to person, but it seems to me a mistake to claim that either way of talking 'picks out' a common feature. The simile says there is a likeness and leaves it to us to pick out some common feature or features; the metaphor does not explicitly assert a likeness, but if we accept it as a metaphor, we are again led to seek common features (not necessarily the same features the associated simile suggests; but that is another matter).

Just because a simile wears a declaration of similitude on its sleeve, it is, I think, far less plausible than in the case of metaphor to maintain that there is a hidden second meaning. In the case of simile, we note what it literally says, that two things resemble one another; we then regard the objects and consider what similarity would, in the context, be to the point. Having decided, we might then say the author of the simile intended us—that is, meant us—to notice that similarity. But having appreciated the difference between what the words meant and what the author accomplished by using those words, we should feel little temptation to explain what has happened by endowing the words themselves with a second, or figurative, meaning. The point of the concept of linguistic meaning is to explain what can be done with words. But the supposed

figurative meaning of a simile explains nothing; it is not a feature of the word that the word has prior to and independent of the context of use, and it rests upon no linguistic customs except those that govern ordinary meaning.

What words do do with their literal meaning in simile must be possible for them to do in metaphor. A metaphor directs attention to the same sorts of similarity, if not the same similarities, as the corresponding simile. But then the unexpected or subtle parallels and analogies it is the business of metaphor to promote need not depend, for their promotion, on more than the literal meanings of words.

Metaphor and simile are merely two among endless devices that serve to alert us to aspects of the world by inviting us to make comparisons. I quote a few stanzas of T. S. Eliot's 'The Hippopotamus':

The broad-backed hippopotamus
Rests on his belly in the mud;
Although he seems so firm to us
He is merely flesh and blood.

Flesh and blood is weak and frail,
Susceptible to nervous shock;
While the True Church can never fail
For it is based upon a rock.

The hippo's feeble steps may err
In compassing material ends,
While the True Church need never stir
To gather in its dividends.

The 'potamus can never reach
The mango on the mango-tree;
But fruits of pomegranate and peach
Refresh the Church from over sea.[8]

Here we are neither told that the Church resembles a hippopotamus (as in simile) nor bullied into making this comparison (as in metaphor), but there can be no doubt the words are being used to direct our attention to similarities between the two. Nor should there be much inclination, in this case, to posit figurative meanings, for in what words or sentences would we lodge them? The hippopotamus really does rest on his belly in the mud; the True Church, the poem says literally, never can fail. The poem does, of course, intimate much that goes beyond the literal meaning of the words. But intimation is not meaning.

The argument so far has led to the conclusion that as much of metaphor as can be explained in terms of meaning may, and indeed must, be explained by appeal to the literal meanings of words. A consequence is that the sentences in which metaphors occur are true or false in a normal, literal way, for if the words in them don't have special meanings, sentences don't have special truth. This is not to deny that there is such a thing as metaphorical truth, only to deny it of sentences. Metaphor does lead us to notice what might not otherwise be noticed, and there is no reason, I suppose, not to say these visions, thoughts, and feelings inspired by the metaphor are true or false.

If a sentence used metaphorically is true or false in the ordinary sense, then it is clear that it is usually false. The most obvious semantic difference between simile and metaphor is that all similes are true and most metaphors are false. The earth is like a floor, the Assyrian did come down like a wolf on the fold, because everything is like everything. But turn these sentences into metaphors, and you turn them false; the earth is like a floor, but it is not a floor; Tolstoy, grown up, was like an infant, but he wasn't one. We use a simile ordinarily only when we know the corresponding metaphor to be false. We say Mr S. is like a pig because we know he isn't one. If we had used a metaphor and said he was a pig, this would not be because we changed our mind about the facts but because we chose to get the idea across a different way.

What matters is not actual falsehood but that the sentence be taken to be false. Notice what happens when a sentence we use as a metaphor,

believing it false, comes to be thought true because of a change in what is believed about the world. When it was reported that Hemingway's plane had been sighted, wrecked, in Africa, the New York *Mirror* ran a headline saying, 'Hemingway Lost in Africa', the word 'lost' being used to suggest he was dead. When it turned out he was alive, the *Mirror* left the headline to be taken literally. Or consider this case: a woman sees herself in a beautiful dress and says, 'What a dream of a dress!'—and then wakes up. The point of the metaphor is that the dress is like a dress one would dream of and therefore isn't a dream-dress. Henle provides a good example from *Antony and Cleopatra* (2. 2):

> The barge she sat in, like a burnish'd throne
> Burn'd on the water.

Here simile and metaphor interact strangely, but the metaphor would vanish if a literal conflagration were imagined. In much the same way the usual effect of a simile can be sabotaged by taking the comparison too earnestly. Woody Allen writes, 'The trial, which took place over the following weeks, was like a circus, although there was some difficulty getting the elephants into the courtroom'.[9]

Generally it is only when a sentence is taken to be false that we accept it as a metaphor and start to hunt out the hidden implication. It is probably for this reason that most metaphorical sentences are *patently* false, just as all similes are trivially true. Absurdity or contradiction in a metaphorical sentence guarantees we won't believe it and invites us, under proper circumstances, to take the sentence metaphorically.

Patent falsity is the usual case with metaphor, but on occasion patent truth will do as well. 'Business is business' is too obvious in its literal meaning to be taken as having been uttered to convey information, so we look for another use; Ted Cohen reminds us, in the same connection, that no man is an island.[10] The point is the same. The ordinary meaning in the context of use is odd enough to prompt us to disregard the question of literal truth.

Now let me raise a somewhat Platonic issue by comparing the making of a metaphor with telling a lie. The comparison is apt because lying, like making a metaphor, concerns not the meaning of words but their use. It is sometimes said that telling a lie entails what is false; but this is wrong. Telling a lie requires not that what you say be false but that you think it false. Since we usually believe true sentences and disbelieve false, most lies are falsehoods; but in any particular case this is an accident. The parallel between making a metaphor and telling a lie is emphasized by the fact that the same sentence can be used, with meaning unchanged, for either purpose. So a woman who believed in witches but did not think her neighbour a witch might say, 'She's a witch', meaning it metaphorically; the same woman, still believing the same of witches and her neighbour but intending to deceive, might use the same words to very different effect. Since sentence and meaning are the same in both cases, it is sometimes hard to prove which intention lay behind the saying of it; thus a man who says 'Lattimore's a Communist' and means to lie can always try to beg off by pleading a metaphor.

What makes the difference between a lie and a metaphor is not a difference in the words used or what they mean (in any strict sense of meaning) but in how the words are used. Using a sentence to tell a lie and using it to make a metaphor are, of course, totally different uses, so different that they do not interfere with one another, as say, acting and lying do. In lying, one must make an assertion so as to represent oneself as believing what one does not; in acting, assertion is excluded. Metaphor is careless of the difference. It can be an insult, and so be an assertion, to say to a man 'You are a pig'. But no metaphor was involved when (let us suppose) Odysseus addressed the same words to his companions in Circe's palace; a story, to be sure, and so no assertion—but the word, for once, was used literally of men.

No theory of metaphorical meaning or metaphorical truth can help explain how metaphor works. Metaphor runs on the same familiar linguistic tracks that the plainest sentences do; this we saw from considering simile. What distinguishes metaphor is not meaning but use—in this it is like assertion, hinting, lying, promising, or criticizing. And the special use to which we put language in metaphor is not—cannot be—to 'say something' special, no matter how indirectly. For a metaphor *says* only what shows on its face—usually a patent falsehood or an absurd truth. And this plain truth or falsehood needs no paraphrase—its meaning is given in the literal meaning of the words.

What are we to make, then, of the endless energy that has been, and is being, spent on methods and devices for drawing out the content of a metaphor? The psychologists Robert Verbrugge and Nancy McCarrell tell us that:

> Many metaphors draw attention to common systems of relationships or common transformations, in which the identity of the participants is secondary. For example, consider the sentences: *A car is like an animal, Tree trunks are straws for thirsty leaves and branches.* The first sentence directs attention to systems of relationships among energy consumption, respiration, self-induced motion, sensory systems, and, possibly a homunculus. In the second sentence, the resemblance is a more constrained type of transformation: suction of fluid through a vertically oriented cylindrical space from a source of fluid to a destination.[11]

Verbrugge and McCarrell don't believe there is any sharp line between the literal and metaphorical uses of words; they think many words have a 'fuzzy' meaning that gets fixed, if fixed at all, by a context. But surely this fuzziness, however it is illustrated and explained, cannot erase the line between what a sentence literally means (given its context) and what it 'draws our attention to' (given its literal meaning as fixed by the context). The passage I have quoted is not employing such a distinction: what it says the sample sentences direct our attention to are facts expressed by paraphrases of the sentences. Verbrugge and McCarrell simply want to insist that a correct paraphrase may emphasize 'systems of relationships' rather than resemblances between objects.

According to Black's interaction theory, a metaphor makes us apply a 'system of commonplaces' associated with the metaphorical word to the subject of the metaphor: in 'Man is a wolf' we apply commonplace attributes (stereotypes) of the wolf to man. The metaphor, Black says, thus 'selects, emphasizes, suppresses, and organizes features of the principal subject by implying statements about it that normally apply to the subsidiary subject'.[12] If paraphrase fails, according to Black, it is not because the metaphor does not have a special cognitive content, but because the paraphrase 'will not have the same power to inform and enlighten as the original. . . . One of the points I most wish to stress is that the loss in such cases is a loss in cognitive content; the relevant weakness of the literal paraphrase is not that it may be tiresomely prolix or boringly explicit; it fails to be a translation because it fails to give the insight that the metaphor did.'[13]

How can this be right? If a metaphor has a special cognitive content, why should it be so difficult or impossible to set it out? If, as Owen Barfield claims, a metaphor 'says one thing and means another', why should it be that when we try to get explicit about what it means, the effect is so much weaker—'put it that way', Barfield says, 'and nearly all the tarning, and with it half the poetry, is lost.'[14] Why does Black think a literal paraphrase 'inevitably says too much—and with the wrong emphasis'? Why inevitably? Can't we, if we are clever enough, come as close as we please?

For that matter, how is it that a simile gets along without a special intermediate meaning? In general, critics do not suggest that a simile says one thing and means another—they do not suppose it *means* anything but what lies on the surface of the words. It may make us think deep thoughts, just as a metaphor does; how come, then, no one appeals to the 'special cognitive content' of the simile? And remember Eliot's hippopotamus; there there was neither simile nor metaphor, but what seemed to get done was just like what gets done by similes and metaphors. Does anyone suggest that the *words* in Eliot's poem have special meanings?

Finally, if words in metaphor bear a coded meaning, how can this meaning differ from the meaning those same words bear in the case where the metaphor *dies*—that is, when it comes to be part of the language? Why doesn't 'He was burned up' as now used and meant mean *exactly* what the fresh metaphor once meant? Yet all that the dead metaphor means is that he was very angry—a notion not very difficult to make explicit.

There is, then, a tension in the usual view of metaphor. For on the one hand, the usual view wants to hold that a metaphor does something no plain prose can possibly do and, on the other hand, it wants to explain what a metaphor does by appealing to a cognitive content—just the sort of thing plain prose is designed to express. As long as we are in this frame of mind, we must harbour the suspicion that it *can* be done, at least up to a point.

There is a simple way out of the impasse. We must give up the idea that a metaphor carries a message, that it has a content or meaning (except, of course, its literal meaning). The various theories we have been considering mistake their goal. Where they think they provide a method for deciphering an encoded content, they actually tell us (or try to tell us) something about the *effects* metaphors have on us. The common error is to fasten on the contents of the thoughts a metaphor provokes and to read these contents into the metaphor itself. No doubt metaphors often make us notice aspects of things we did not notice before; no doubt they bring surprising analogies and similarities to our attention; they do provide a kind of lens or lattice, as Black says, through which we view the relevant phenomena. The issue does not lie here but in the question of how the metaphor is related to what it makes us see.

It may be remarked with justice that the claim that a metaphor provokes or invites a certain view of its subject rather than saying it straight out is a commonplace; so it is. Thus Aristotle says metaphor leads to a 'perception of resemblances'. Black, following Richards, says a metaphor 'evokes' a certain response: 'a suitable hearer will be led by a metaphor to construct a . . . system.'[15] This view is neatly summed up by what Heracleitus said of the Delphic oracle: 'It does not say and it does not hide, it intimates.'[16]

I have no quarrel with these descriptions of the effects of metaphor, only with the associated views as to *how* metaphor is supposed to produce them. What I deny is that metaphor does its work by having a special meaning, a specific cognitive content. I do not think, as Richards does, that metaphor produces its result by having a meaning which results from the interaction of two ideas; it is wrong, in my view, to say, with Owen Barfield, that a metaphor 'says one thing and means another'; or with Black that a metaphor asserts or implies certain complex things by dint of a special meaning and *thus* accomplishes its job of yielding an 'insight'. A metaphor does its work through other intermediaries—to suppose it can be effective only by conveying a coded message is like thinking a joke or a dream makes some statement which a clever interpreter can restate in plain prose. Joke or dream or metaphor can, like a picture or a bump on the head, make us appreciate some fact—but not by standing for, or expressing, the fact.

If this is right, what we attempt in 'paraphrasing' a metaphor cannot be to give its meaning, for that lies on the surface; rather we attempt to evoke what the metaphor brings to our attention. I can imagine someone granting this and shrugging it off as no more than an insistence on

restraint in using the word 'meaning'. This would be wrong. The central error about metaphor is most easily attacked when it takes the form of a theory of metaphorical meaning, but behind that theory, and statable independently, is the thesis that associated with a metaphor is a definite cognitive content that its author wishes to convey and that the interpreter must grasp if he is to get the message. This theory is false as a full account of metaphor, whether or not we call the purported cognitive content a meaning.

It should make us suspect the theory that it is so hard to decide, even in the case of the simplest metaphors, exactly what the content is supposed to be. The reason it is often so hard to decide is, I think, that we imagine there is a content to be captured when all the while we are in fact focusing on what the metaphor makes us notice. If what the metaphor makes us notice were finite in scope and propositional in nature, this would not in itself make trouble; we would simply project the content the metaphor brought to mind on to the metaphor. But in fact there is no limit to what a metaphor calls to our attention, and much of what we are caused to notice is not propositional in character. When we try to say what a metaphor 'means', we soon realize there is no end to what we want to mention.[17] If someone draws his finger along a coastline on a map, or mentions the beauty and deftness of a line in a Picasso etching, how many things are drawn to your attention? You might list a great many, but you could not finish since the idea of finishing would have no clear application. How many facts or propositions are conveyed by a photograph? None, an infinity, or one great unstatable fact? Bad question. A picture is not worth a thousand words, or any other number. Words are the wrong currency to exchange for a picture.

It's not only that we can't provide an exhaustive catalogue of what has been attended to when we are led to see something in a new light; the difficulty is more fundamental. What we notice or see is not, in general, propositional in character. Of course it *may* be, and when it is, it usually may be stated in fairly plain words. But if I show you Wittgenstein's duck-rabbit, and I say, 'It's a duck', then with luck you see it as a duck; if I say, 'It's a rabbit', you see it as a rabbit. But no proposition expresses what I have led you to see. Perhaps you have come to realize that the drawing can be seen as a duck or as a rabbit. But one could come to know this without ever seeing the drawing as a duck or as a rabbit. Seeing as is not seeing that. Metaphor makes us see one thing as another by making some literal statement that inspires or prompts the insight. Since in most cases what the metaphor prompts or inspires is not entirely, or even at all, recognition of some truth or fact, the attempt to give literal expression to the content of the metaphor is simply misguided.

The theorist who tries to explain a metaphor by appealing to a hidden message, like the critic who attempts to state the message, is then fundamentally confused. No such explanation or statement can be forthcoming because no such message exists.

Not, of course, that interpretation and elucidation of a metaphor are not in order. Many of us need help if we are to see what the author of a metaphor wanted us to see and what a more sensitive or educated reader grasps. The legitimate function of so-called paraphrase is to make the lazy or ignorant reader have a vision like that of the skilled critic. The critic is, so to speak, in benign competition with the metaphor maker. The critic tries to make his own art easier or more transparent in some respects than the original, but at the same time he tries to reproduce in others some of the effects the original had on him. In doing this the critic also, and perhaps by the best method at his command, calls attention to the beauty or aptness, the hidden power, of the metaphor itself.

Notes

1 I think Max Black is wrong when he says, 'The rules of our language determine that some expres-

sions must count as metaphors' ('Metaphor', 29). There are no such rules.

2 Nelson Goodman says metaphor and ambiguity differ chiefly 'in that the several uses of a merely ambiguous term are coeval and independent' while in metaphor 'a term with an extension established by habit is applied elsewhere under the influence of that habit': he suggests that as our sense of the history of the 'two uses' in metaphor fades, the metaphorical word becomes merely ambiguous (*Languages of Art*, 71). In fact in many cases of ambiguity, one use springs from the other (as Goodman says) and so cannot be coeval. But the basic error, which Goodman shares with others, is the idea that two 'uses' are involved in metaphor in anything like the way they are in ambiguity.

3 The theory described is essentially that of Paul Henle, 'Metaphor'.

4 W. Empson, *Some Versions of Pastoral*, 133.

5 J. Middleton Murray says a metaphor is a 'compressed simile' (*Countries of the Mind*, 3). Max Black attributes a similar view to Alexander Bain, *English Composition and Rhetoric*.

6 M. Black, 'Metaphor', 35.

7 N. Goodman, *Languages of Art*, 77–8.

8 T. S. Eliot, *Selected Poems*.

9 Woody Allen, 'Condemned'.

10 T. Cohen, 'Figurative Speech and Figurative Acts', 671. Since the negation of a metaphor seems always to be a potential metaphor, there may be as many platitudes among the potential metaphors as there are absurds among the actuals.

11 R. R. Verbrugge and N. S. McCarrell, 'Metaphoric Comprehension: Studies in Reminding and Resembling', 499.

12 M. Black, 'Metaphor', 44–5.

13 Ibid., 46.

14 O. Barfield. 'Poetic Diction and Legal Fiction', 55.

15 M. Black, 'Metaphor,' 41.

16 I use Hannah Arendt's attractive translation of '*σημαωνει*'; it clearly should not be rendered as 'means' in this context.

17 Stanley Cavell mentions the fact that most attempts at paraphrase end with 'and so on' and refers to Empson's remark that metaphors are 'pregnant' ('Aesthetic Problems of Modern Philosophy', 79). But Cavell doesn't explain the endlessness of

paraphrase as I do, as can be learned from the fact that he thinks it distinguishes metaphor from some ('but perhaps not all') literal discourse. I hold that the endless character of what we call the paraphrase of a metaphor springs from the fact that it attempts to spell out what the metaphor makes us notice, and to this there is no clear end. I would say the same for any use of language.

Chapter 30

Max Black

HOW METAPHORS WORK: A REPLY TO DONALD DAVIDSON

1.—*Perplexities about metaphors.*[1] To be able to produce and understand metaphorical statements is nothing much to boast about: these familiar skills, which children seem to acquire as they learn to talk, are perhaps no more remarkable than our ability to tell and to understand jokes. How odd then that it remains difficult to explain what we do (and should do) in grasping metaphorical statements. In a provocative paper, "What Metaphors Mean,"[2] Donald Davidson has recently charged many students of metaphor, ancient and modern, with having committed a "central mistake." According to him, there is "error and confusion" in claiming "that a metaphor has, in addition to its literal sense or meaning, another sense or meaning." The guilty include "literary critics like Richards, Empson, and Winters; philosophers from Aristotle to Max Black; psychologists from Freud and earlier to Skinner and later; and linguists from Plato to Uriel Weinreich and George Lakoff." Good company, if somewhat mixed. The error to be extirpated is the "idea that a metaphor has a special meaning" (p. 32).

If Davidson is right, much that has been written about metaphor might well be consigned to the flames. Even if he proves to be wrong, his animadversions should provoke further consideration of the still problematic modus operandi of metaphor.

2.—*The commonsense of metaphors.* Before addressing Davidson's main contentions, I shall list some assertions, all of which I believe to be true, about a paradigmatic instance of metaphorical statement. It will be convenient to use the remark (R) with which Davidson opens his paper: "Metaphor is the dreamwork of language."[3]

I believe that all of the following assertions are true of R and that corresponding assertions would apply to many other metaphorical statements.

1   The *thought* that metaphor is the dreamwork of language (that R, for short) might have occurred to Davidson, and probably did, before he committed it to paper.[4]

1.1   If this happened, Davidson *affirmed* that R and he did not merely entertain the thought or use R as an example of metaphor.[5]

1.2   Thereby he expressed a distinctive *view* of metaphor, his topic.[6]

1.21   Davidson had won some new *insight* into what metaphor is.

2   When he wrote out R at the start of his paper, he was *making* that remark—and not quoting the sentence or, as some logicians say, "mentioning" it.[7]

2.1   In so doing, he was writing *in earnest*, not joking or pretending or playacting.

2.11   He *meant* what he wrote.[8]

2.2 In making the remark he was *saying* something, not merely doing something else such as nudging his reader to find similarities between metaphors and dreamwork.[9]

2.3 A reader could understand or misunderstand Davidson's remark.[10]

3 In Davidson's use of R, the word "dreamwork" was being used metaphorically, and the remaining words literally.[11]

3.1 Davidson was not using R as he would have done had he intended R to be taken literally.[12]

4 In making the remark, R, Davidson chose words precisely appropriate to his intention.[13]

4.1 He said and intended to say that metaphor *is* the dreamwork of language.

4.11 Davidson would not have been satisfied to say instead that metaphor is *like* linguistic dreamwork; or that the one can be *compared* to the other; or that in metaphorizing[14] we are regarding one thing *as if* it were another.

5 In affirming R, Davidson was implying and intimating various unstated remarks.[15]

5.1 He was implying, but not explicitly saying, that metaphor and dreamwork have some similar or analogous properties.[16]

5.2 He was using "dreamwork" to *allude* to certain Freudian doctrines.[17]

5.3 Davidson was *suggesting* various unstated contentions, left to the reader to develop at discretion, for example, that a metaphor has a latent as well as a manifest content.

5.4 He might reasonably be taken to be suggesting also various *evaluations* of metaphor consonant with the parallel Freudian doctrines about dreams.

6 A reader could *disagree* with Davidson's remark (e.g., by objecting that the under-

lying analogy was "too thin"—or by saying "Metaphor is sometimes *waking* work").[18]

6.1 Reasons could be offered for and against R.[19]

7 R, or any other metaphorical remark, might be criticized as inept, misleading, obscure, unilluminating, and so forth.[20]

7.1 A metaphorical statement, such as R, can fail or succeed.[21]

Summary: A metaphorical statement, such as R, can be affirmed (1.1) in private thought (1) and hence need not be addressed to another person. In either case the statement expresses a view of its topic (1.2) and some putative insight (1.21). When a statement is seriously communicated (2, 2.1), its user, if expressing himself precisely, means just what he says or writes (2.11). The author of a metaphor *says* something (2.2), although he will also typically be alluding to (5.1), suggesting (5.3), and evaluating (5.4) other things. When a statement is metaphorical, the sentence used, part only of which consists of a word or words used metaphorically (3), is not intended to be taken literally (3.1). In appropriate and precise formulation, a metaphorical statement cannot be replaced by literal statements of resemblance or comparison, or by allied *as*-if statements (4.11, 2.2), but will usually imply these and other unstated implications (5, 5.1). Metaphors can be understood or misunderstood (2.3) and can be rejected or endorsed (6.1). Metaphorizing may fail or succeed (7.1).

In thus setting out the commonsense of the production and understanding of metaphorical remarks, I have abstained from using the verb "to mean" except in one instance (2.11) where it can be replaced. Yet, it would be natural to add further comments about what Davidson *meant* by his metaphorical remark and what he would properly be taken by a competent reader as intending to mean. At a pretheoretical commonsensical level, one would suppose that Davidson could hardly have thought R (1) without meaning something by the words that occurred to him, and it is hard to understand how he could have affirmed R (1.1) unless he meant something by that remark (2.11). Nor could he have acquired insight into the nature of metaphor (1.2 and 1.21) otherwise. I have also claimed that he was *saying* various things, many of them implicitly (2.2, 4.1, 5, and 5.1).

The propositions I have formulated concerning a reader's ability to disagree with R (6) and to offer reasons for such disagreement (6.1) further strengthen the case for thinking that the producer of a metaphor such as R is usually making some *assertions*. Davidson denies this. But it is time to see precisely what he is claiming.

3.—*Davidson's contentions.* A careful reading of Davidson's essay will show that he is concerned to argue three main propositions, the first two of which reject a crucial part of what I have called the "commonsense" of metaphor, while the third states his own position.

(A) The producer of a metaphorical statement says nothing more than what is meant when the sentence he uses is taken literally.

(B) The sentence used in making a metaphorical statement has in context nothing more than its literal meaning.[22]

(C) A metaphor producer is drawing attention to a resemblance between two or more things.[23]

4.—*Some comments on these contentions.* On (A): Davidson uses "says" throughout in a more restricted way than would fit my own usage of "affirmed" (for which see no. 6). He would of course not deny that a metaphor producer "says," or perhaps even "affirms," something in the weak sense of uttering the words in question seriously. What he does emphatically wish to deny is that in such utterances any *truth-claims* are made. Sometimes he makes this point by denying that a metaphorical statement has "a specific

cognitive content," one that "its author wishes to convey and that the interpreter must grasp if he is to get the message" (p. 46 [p. 487 above]). Anyone who "attempts to state the message, is then fundamentally confused ... because no such message exists" (p. 47 [p. 488]). If such a message were "said" or asserted by the author, his words would have to be taken as "standing for, or expressing, [some alleged] fact" (p. 46 [p. 487]). If we are led by a metaphor to appreciate some fact, as may happen, that is because the metaphor works like "a picture or a bump on the head." In Davidson's usage, then, to "say" something metaphorically would be to express some supposed *fact* or facts; the theory that a metaphor ever does so is just "false" (p. 46 [p. 487]).

One might suppose that since Davidson regards the sentence used in a metaphorical statement as preserving its ordinary literal meaning, he might take its user to be asserting at least one supposed fact—in our prime example, the alleged fact that metaphor is literally dreamwork. But of course there is no such fact, as Davidson himself emphasizes, "For a metaphor *says* only what shows on its face—usually a patent falsehood or an absurd truth ... given in the literal meaning of the words" (p. 43 [p. 485]): what metaphorical statements, taken literally, assert is nearly always plainly false and absurd. Thus, (A) should be understood to mean that a metaphor producer is "saying" *nothing at all*. What, then, is a metaphor producer doing? We shall see when we come to examine (C).

On (B): Davidson devotes much of his paper to attacking the view, supposedly held by contemporary theorists, that some of the words used in a metaphorical remark change their senses when so used. He says that the "central mistake" is "the idea that a metaphor has, in addition to its literal sense or meaning, another sense or meaning" (p. 32 [p. 477]). He denies vigorously that in the metaphor "the Spirit of God moved upon the face of the waters" it is proper to "regard the word 'face' as having *an extended meaning*" (p. 34 [p. 479], my italics). He thinks that "according to [the current and erroneous] theory a word has a *new meaning* in a metaphorical context" (p. 37 [p. 481], my italics) and adds, provokingly, "the occasion of the metaphor would, therefore, be the occasion for learning the new meaning." In comparing and contrasting metaphors and lies, he claims that "the difference . . . is not a difference in the words used or what they mean (*in any strict sense of meaning*) but in how the words are used" (p. 43 [p. 485], my italics).[24]

Much of this vigorous polemic is beside the point. I know of no theorist who claims that the words used in metaphorical remarks thereby acquire some new meaning in what Davidson calls, as we have seen, the "only strict sense of meaning."[25] I would guess that the strict sense he has in mind is the "Literal meaning . . . [that] can be assigned to words and sentences apart from particular contexts of use" (p. 33 [p. 478]). Well, certainly, when Wallace Stevens called a poem a pheasant, he was not permanently changing the standard dictionary sense of "pheasant," a feat almost never accomplished by a single use of a familiar word. One may indeed agree with Davidson that awareness of the "ordinary [literal] meaning"[26] is necessary if the metaphor is to be recognized and understood.

The question to be considered, then, is not the idle one of whether the words used in a metaphorical remark astonishingly acquire some permanently new sense but rather the question whether the metaphor maker is *attaching* an altered sense to the words he is using in context. Did Stevens mean by "pheasant" something having a tail and able to fly, thereby committing himself to the absurd idea that a poem literally is a bird? Or was he rather using his remark to *say* something about poetry (the question addressed in proposition (B) above)?

The use of a sentence having a familiar standard sense or meaning in order to say something unusual is too familiar to arouse perplexity. When a chess master says, while watching a match, "No pie from that flour"—or rather makes the corresponding Russian remark[27]—

what he means could be of no interest to a baker. So, *pace* Davidson, I see no reason on general grounds to be suspicious of the claim that metaphor makers are indeed saying various things, without thereby inducing any permanent change in the standard meaning of the words used metaphorically.

On (C): A sympathetic interpretation of Davidson's positive conception of how metaphors work would be to regard him as supporting the view, advanced by some other writers,[28] that anybody making a metaphorical remark is performing a distinctive speech-act, whose force could be more perspicuously expressed by some such formula as "I (hereby) draw your attention to a likeness between (say) metaphor and dreamwork." I think he might accept this, or something like this, given his reiterated emphasis on how a metaphor producer is *using* words to "nudge," "intimate," "provoke," and so on rather than to say anything. To be sure, Davidson's many remarks about the *effects* of a metaphor (acting like "a bump on the head") might suggest that he is more interested in what Austin would have called the perlocutionary effects of metaphorical discourse than in any postulated illocutionary force of metaphorical utterance. Either way, there are serious objections.

1. On the speech-act approach, it is hard to make sense of what happens when somebody expresses a thought *to himself* (see proposition 1 in my list of commonsensical truths about metaphor, above). Any clear cases of speech-acts that come readily to mind involve communication with an audience: it makes little sense to think of promising *oneself* something, or warning, advising, pronouncing judgment, and so on, to oneself. What then, on Davidson's view is a soliloquizing thinker, using metaphorical language, supposed to be doing? Nudging and provoking himself to pay attention to some covert likeness? But surely he has already done so? What then is the point of saying to himself that metaphor *is* dreamwork? Is he perhaps pretending to talk to himself, as if he had not already

been seized by an unobvious resemblance between the two things in question?

2. There seems, in Davidson's view, just as little point also in drawing *another* person's attention to a likeness between two things, since, according to him, "all similes are true ... because everything is like everything" (p. 41 [p. 484]). If the hearer agrees with Davidson that "all similes are trivially true" (p. 42 [p. 484]), how is he supposed to be prodded by Davidson's dreamwork remark? Is he to attend to the "trivial" similarity between the two things mentioned?

3. If Davidson's view were correct, there would be a readily available and more perspicuous way of expressing a metaphorical thought, whether to oneself or to another person, which would bypass the difficulties listed above that attend any commitment to metaphorizing as speech-act. Why not simply say "Metaphor *is like* dreamwork"? Given that the two things mentioned do not, at first blush, look very much alike, such a remark should do all the nudging, provoking, and intimating that Davidson attributes to the usual metaphorical form. If so, we shall have to explain why all of us have an inveterate and, as I think, justified impulse to say in such cases that A is B and not merely that A is like B (see propositions 4.1 and 4.11 above). The only plausible reply that occurs to me would be to assimilate metaphor to hyperbole (as in "There are hundreds of cats in the garden")—as an exaggerated and somewhat hysterical style of talk to be eschewed by careful thinkers.

4. I believe, therefore, that Davidson's position reduces to a reformulation of the ancient and, as one might have hoped, discredited, theory that I have in the past called a "comparison view."[29] I still think that my earlier conclusion that "a comparison view ... suffers from a vagueness that borders on vacuity"[30] holds against any such view and specifically against Davidson's latest, though unacknowledged, espousal of it.[31]

5. The gravest objection to Davidson's vigorously argued standpoint then is that, while rejecting current views, it supplies no insight into how metaphors work and fails to explain why the use of metaphors seems to so many students of metaphor an indispensable resource.

5.—*The case against assigning meaning to metaphors.* I have been arguing in the last section that Davidson's view of how metaphors work is not as he seems to think a new and illuminating view of the topic but is rather, if I am not mistaken, one that treats metaphors as perversely cryptic substitutes for literal similes. I have claimed that this way of looking at metaphors does not explain how strong metaphors work to express and promote insight. Now somebody who is more sympathetic to Davidson's position than I am might retort that the alternative current views are in no better shape. It seems advisable, therefore, to complete this examination of Davidson's paper by evaluating his specific objections to what might be called, for short, any *semantic* interpretation of metaphor (of which my "interaction view" would be a special case).

So far as I can see, Davidson presents five objections, reproduced below with a brief reply appended to each.

First objection: "There are no instructions for devising metaphors; there is no manual for determining what a metaphor 'means' or 'says'; there is no test for metaphor that does not call for taste" (p. 31 [p. 477]).

First reply: That the meaning of a live or active metaphor cannot count as part of its standard meaning, and is therefore to be found neither in dictionaries or encyclopedias, is a point that has often been made by students of metaphor. Thus I have said in the past that the producer of such a metaphor "is employing conventional means to produce a nonstandard effect, while using only the standard syntactic and semantic resources of his speech community. Yet the meaning of an interesting metaphor is typically new or 'creative', *not inferrible from the standard lexicon*."[32] This point leaves untouched the contention at issue, that a metaphor *producer* means something, possibly novel, by his metaphorical statement.

Second objection: "It is no help in explaining how words work in metaphor to posit metaphorical or figurative meanings" (p. 33 [p. 478]). Davidson contends that "simply to lodge [the] meaning in the metaphor is like explaining why a pill puts you to sleep by saying it has a dormitive power" (p. 33 [p. 478]). He contrasts such pseudoexplanation with the "genuine explanatory power" of an appeal to "Literal meaning and literal truth conditions [that] can be assigned to words and sentences apart from particular contexts of use" (p. 33 [p. 478]).

Second reply: One must agree that it would be pointless and obfuscating to invoke some ad hoc "figurative" sense, not otherwise specified, to explain "how metaphor works its wonders" (p. 33 [p. 478]). Nevertheless, it would help us to understand how a particular metaphorical utterance works in its context if we could satisfy ourselves that the *speaker* is then attaching a special extended sense to the metaphorical "focus" (selecting, as I have explained elsewhere, some of the commonplaces normally associated with his secondary subject, in order to express insight into his primary subject). This view is not open to the charge of invoking fictitious entities.

We may compare explanations of ironic talk: it really does help us to understand what somebody means by saying of a colleague's contribution to a college meeting, "X is so *amusing!*" to realize, as we immediately do, that "amusing" here has a sense contrary to its standard sense. Throughout his essay Davidson seems fixated on the explanatory power of standard sense; but when such an explanation is plainly defective, there can be no objection in principle to invoking what the speaker means when speaking metaphorically.

Third objection: The view "that in metaphor certain words take on new, or what are often called 'extended,' meanings [as when somebody calls Tolstoy an infant] ... cannot, at any rate, be complete," for if in such a context the word "infant" applies correctly to the adult Tolstoy, then "Tolstoy literally was an infant, and all sense of metaphor evaporates" (p. 34 [p. 479]).

Third reply: Recognition of an "extended" nonce meaning is not intended to be a "complete" explanation of how metaphor works. There is no implied claim, either, that in such use a word "applies correctly." If Davidson's objection were sound, then to perceive that an ironical speaker meant by "amusing" something like "unfunny" would be to make all sense of irony "evaporate." Irony remains irony, even when understood; and so does metaphor.

Fourth objection: "If a metaphor has a special cognitive content, why should it be so difficult or impossible to set it out?" (p. 44 [p. 486]). Davidson challenges my old contention that a literal paraphrase "inevitably says too much—and with the wrong emphasis."[33] "Why," he asks, "inevitably? Can't we, if we are clever enough, come as close as we please?" (p. 44 [p. 486]).

Fourth reply: Why not, if we are clear about coming "close" and do not mistake an explication for a translation? I supplied a partial answer to Davidson in the passage preceding the one that he reproduces: "the set of literal statements so obtained will not have the same power to inform and enlighten as the original. For one thing, the implications previously left to a suitable reader to educe for himself, with a nice feeling for their relative priorities and degrees of importance, are now presented explicitly as having equal weight."[34] I went on to say that explication or elaboration of a metaphor's grounds (such as I later supplied in "More About Metaphor," pp. 443–45, using the example of "Marriage is a zero-sum game") can be extremely valuable "if not regarded as an adequate cognitive substitute for the original."

The point is of general application. Toynbee's remark, in connection with American nuclear policy: "No annihilation without representation," could no doubt be spelled out to render his allusion to the familiar slogan boringly explicit. I suppose any sensitive reader would feel that something of the force and point of the original remark would then have been lost. As in aposiopesis, a metaphor leaves a good deal to be supplied at the reader's discretion. To say something with suggestive indefiniteness is not to say *nothing*.

Fifth objection: "Much of what we are caused to notice [by a metaphor] is not propositional in character" (p. 46 [p. 487]).

Fifth reply: Agreed. But it is going too far to claim that in understanding a metaphor "What we notice or see is not, *in general*, propositional in character" (p. 47 [p. 487], my italics). A metaphor may indeed convey a "vision" or a "view," as Davidson says, but this is compatible with its also *saying* things that are correct or incorrect, illuminating or misleading, and so on.

6.—*Verdict*. If a "semantic" conception of metaphor is open to no more serious objections than those advanced by Davidson (lack of recipes for producing metaphors, absence of explanatory power in the theory, incompleteness of the semantic view, difficulty of paraphrasing a metaphor's cognitive content, presence of nonpropositional insight in metaphorical thought), its advocates have no cause for alarm and may rest unabashed in their imputed "error and confusion." The verdict must be "nonproven."

In my opinion, the chief weakness of the "interaction" theory, which I still regard as better than its alternatives, is lack of clarification of what it means to say that in a metaphor one thing is thought of (or viewed) *as* another thing. Here, if I am not mistaken, is to be found a prime

reason why unregenerate users of appropriate metaphors may properly reject any view that seeks to reduce metaphors to literal statements of the comparisons or the structural analogies which *ground* the metaphorical insight. To think of God *as* love and to take the further step of identifying the two is emphatically to do something more than to *compare* them as merely being alike in certain respects. But what that "something more" is remains tantalizingly elusive: we lack an adequate account of metaphorical thought.[35]

Notes

1 I shall use "metaphor" throughout this paper as a concise way of referring to metaphorical *statements*.

2 Donald Davidson, "What Metaphors Mean," *Critical Inquiry* 5 (Autumn 1978): 31–47. All further references in text [page references to the version reprinted in this volume are in square brackets].

3 The full sentence is: "Metaphor is the dreamwork of language and, like all dreamwork, its interpretation reflects as much on the interpreter as on the originator" (p. 31 [p. 477]). I shall use "R" sometimes to refer to Davidson's *remark*, sometimes to refer to the *sentence* he used.

4 This rather obvious point deserves emphasis, since most students of metaphor overemphasize the quasi-performative aspects of metaphorical utterance. The uses of metaphorical statements are not confined to the role they play in communication with others. R, unlike such a clear performative as "I promise . . .," makes sense in private thought. It would seem to me farfetched to regard such private utterance as a degenerate case of communication, like a chessplayer "playing with himself."

5 Alternatively, one might say that he *committed* himself to R. I use "affirmed" here in a sense sufficiently broad to permit a command or a question to be affirmed, in order not to beg the question whether somebody affirming a metaphor can be making truth-claims.

6 Probably most of those who agree would find it hard to spell out what having a view amounts to.

7 We lack a convenient label for such straightforward, primary uses of language.

8   Or: *intended* that he should be taken as speaking in *propria persona*, straightforwardly (4.1) and seriously.

9   I intend "saying" here to mean much the same as J. L. Austin's "constating," i.e., the presenting of claims that might be disputed (see 6 and 6.1). We shall see that Davidson emphatically disagrees with 2.2.

10   Of course, a promise or a bet can be misunderstood, so accepting 2.3 need not commit one to accepting 2.2.

11   I call these the *focus* and the *frame* of the sentence respectively. See "Metaphor," chap. 3 of my *Models and Metaphors* (Ithaca, N.Y., 1962), p. 28. See also my "More about Metaphor," *Dialectica* 31 (1977): 431–57.

12   If only because R, taken literally, is plainly false, as Davidson points out in similar cases.

13   I am assuming that Davidson, like other careful writers, would not say "Metaphor *is* dreamwork" unless he intended to say just that and not something else. In the propositions 4 and 4.11, I am urging that the categorical use of the copula in a metaphor of the form "A *is* B" serves a distinctive purpose (though, to be sure, a somewhat obscure one). Thus I regard 4.11 as an important weapon against theorists who wish to reduce metaphor to simile or comparison.

14   I shall use this word to refer both to the production of metaphorical statement (whether in thought, speech, or writing) and also to the comprehension of another person's metaphor.

15   It would be arbitrary to restrict a metaphor's content to what is *explicitly* expressed by it. I take the metaphor's author to be committed (4.11) to its implications.

16   It is tempting to say that R implies that metaphor is *like* dreamwork. But the latter assertion implies that metaphor is *not* dreamwork! Only different things can be sensibly compared.

17   Here and in 5.3 I am trying to acknowledge, however inadequately, the aspects of a metaphor's working that cannot plausibly be subsumed under implicit "*saying*."

18   Thus using one metaphor to oppose another, as can sometimes happen.

19   The truth of this and the preceding assertion, 6, supports my own view that metaphors can imply truth-claims (see 2.2).

20   I shall not discuss here the vexed question whether metaphors can be true or false.

21   Anybody inclined to agree with Davidson that "there are no unsuccessful metaphors" (p. 31 [p. 477]) might be asked to consider Hegel's metaphor of the solar system as a syllogism whose three terms are the sun, the planets, and the comets (from Julien Benda, *Du style d'idées* [Paris, 1948], p. 143).

22   I have expressed these propositions in my own words. Davidson's most explicit statement of his own view is: "a metaphor doesn't say anything beyond its literal meaning (nor does its maker say anything, in using the metaphor, beyond the literal)" (p. 32 [p. 478]). Also: "Metaphor runs on the same familiar linguistic tracks that the plainest sentences do" (p. 43 [p. 485]).

23   "A metaphor makes us attend to some likeness, often a novel or surprising likeness, between two or more things" (p. 33 [p. 478]). Davidson also says, more picturesquely, that a metaphor "nudges us into noting" a likeness which it "intimates" (p. 38 [p. 482]); it "invites" us to make comparisons (p. 40 [p. 484]); a metaphor "inspires or prompts [an] insight" (p. 47 [p. 488]). I suppose it is the metaphor maker who literally invites, prompts, provokes, or nudges the receiver. "A simile tells us, in part, what a metaphor merely nudges us into noting" (p. 38 [p. 482]). As for what a simile tells us, "In the case of simile, we note what it literally says, that two things resemble one another; we then regard the objects and consider what similarity would, in the context, be to the point" (p. 40 [p. 483]). Davidson here, and throughout, apparently overlooks the fact that a simile can be *figurative*. Thinking of a similarity as a literal statement of mutual resemblance between two things will fail to explain why many similes are not immediately reversible. In ordinary usage, "An atom is like a solar system" does not always imply that "A solar system is like an atom."

24   Davidson does, however, agree with Paul Henle, Nelson Goodman, "and the rest in their accounts of what metaphor accomplishes, except that I think it accomplishes more and that what is additional is different in kind [from meaning anything or saying anything]" (p. 33 [p. 478]). I shall examine what Davidson thinks a metaphor "accomplishes"

in my comments on proposition (C) below. He is, by the way, mistaken in saddling the writers under attack with thinking of "metaphor as primarily a vehicle for conveying ideas, even if unusual ones" (p. 32 [p. 478]). Aristotle et al. can answer for themselves; but no moderately attentive reader of my own writings on metaphor could suppose that I ever maintained that metaphorical statements are *primarily* used "for conveying ideas." I have argued merely that such statements can and usually do have a "cognitive content," or do "carry a message," by virtue of implying assertions with truth-value. Like all of Davidson's opponents, I have stressed that much more than the expression of propositional truth is at work in metaphorical discourse.

25 Webster gives four main senses of "mean"; I wonder how many of these Davidson would regard as "strict"? Alas for Ogden and Richards' efforts to display the endemic ambiguities of the word.

26 "The ordinary meaning [of a metaphor] in the context of use is odd enough to prompt us to disregard the question of literal truth" (p. 42 [p. 485]).

27 "No pie from that flour!" (nothing will come of it) was Tal's comment after the fourth game of the Karpov-Korchnoi match in Baguio apropos of Karpov's use of a dubious opening variation (*Chess Life and Review*, January 1979, p. 44).

28 See, for instance, Dorothy Mack, "Metaphoring as Speech Act," *Poetics* 4 (1975): 211–56; and Ina Loewenberg, "Identifying Metaphors," *Foundations of Language* 12 (1975): 315–38. Ted Cohen's "Metaphor and the Cultivation of Intimacy," *Critical Inquiry* 5 (Autumn 1978): 3–12, might also be read as sympathetic to this approach.

29 See my "Metaphor," *Models and Metaphors*, pp. 35–37, where citations from earlier defenders of such a view are supplied.

30 Ibid., p. 37.

31 Davidson echoes my older criticisms of the view that "equates the figurative meaning of the metaphor with the literal meaning of a simile" when he says that the literal meaning is "usually a painfully trivial simile . . . trivial because everything is like everything, and in endless ways" (p. 39 [p. 482]). He doesn't seem to notice that the objection applies equally to his own position, even if one continues to insist that a metaphor does not *say* anything but rather provokes and intimates, etc., something like the perception of symmetrical similarities.

32 "More about Metaphor," p. 436, italics added.

33 "Metaphor," *Models and Metaphors*, p. 46.

34 Ibid.

35 I have made some preliminary suggestions in sect. 8, "Thinking in Metaphors," of "More about Metaphor," pp. 446–48.

PART FOURTEEN

Language and vagueness

INTRODUCTION TO PART FOURTEEN

THE PARADOX OF VAGUENESS, sometimes called 'paradox of the heap' or 'sorites'[1] has ancient pedigree. We are here including three articles on this topic because in recent years the problem of vagueness has been the focus for a lot of interesting work in the philosophy of language.

Here is an example of the pattern of argument called 'soritical reasoning': On a building site down the road, there is a heap of sand. Let's call it H. Now, suppose we remove a single grain of sand from H. We still have a heap, though a heap with one grain fewer. Let's call this H_{-1}. We can repeat the procedure and remove another grain, and another grain etc., resulting in H_{-2}, H_{-3}, etc., until we get to H_{last}, i.e. what remains of H when all grains but one have been removed. Now, heaps of sand seem to be 'tolerant' to removal of single grains: it seems undeniable that for any n, if H_{-n} is a heap then $H_{-(n+1)}$ is also a heap. For how could one grain make the difference between a heap and a non-heap? The problem now is that the assumption of tolerance seems to take us to the absurd conclusion that even H_{last} is a heap, i.e. that a single grain of sand constitutes a heap. This conclusion seems to depend merely on two premises: the premise that H is a heap, and the tolerance assumption:

(H) H is a heap
(T) For every n, if H_{-n} is a heap then $H_{-(n+1)}$ is
     also a heap.[2]

The reasoning involves only two rules of inference: universal instantiation and *modus ponens*. How can we avoid the conclusion that H_{last} is a heap? Unless we want to deny (H), i.e. that H is a heap in the first place, it looks like we have only two options: we can either say that the tolerance principle is not, after all, true or alternatively, reject one of the inference rules. Neither of these options is particularly attractive, and in either case we would have some explaining to do, namely why (T) seems undeniable, or what exactly is wrong with the inference rules.

As Achille Varzi explains in the first part of his paper, some philosophers have indeed taken the second of these options. On one version of this view, predicates like 'is a heap' express vague properties, properties that can be possessed to a greater or lesser degree. Accordingly, the truth of claims about whether something is a heap or not comes in degrees. Or, in Varzi's terms: on this view, the extension of 'is a heap' is a

---

[1] 'Sorites' is the ancient Greek word for heap.
[2] Exercise: Show how exactly the conclusion that H_{last} is a heap can be derived from the fact that H is a heap together with (T), using only two rules of inference: universal instantiation and *modus ponens*.

'fuzzy set', i.e. a set being a member of which is a matter of degree. It is often said that this degree-theory of vagueness is a theory which locates vagueness in the world rather than in language. According to it, the world itself contains objects and properties without sharp boundaries.

Such views contrast with 'semantic' views of vagueness, which locate vagueness exclusively in language. Thus, instead of saying that vague predicates have imprecise or fuzzy extensions, one might insist that the potential extensions of predicates are all completely precise, and that any imprecision resides in the relationship between vague predicates and their candidate precise extensions. 'Supervaluationism' is a view of this kind, and Varzi argues that it is superior to degree-theory. According to supervaluationism, a vague predicate, such as 'is a heap' is associated with a number of precise extensions, each of which represents one of the ways in which one could make the predicate precise while respecting all the pre-theoretically clear cases of heaps and non-heaps. A statement that some object is a heap is then true just if the object is a member of all candidate precise extensions, and it is false if it is in none of them. In borderline cases, the object will be a member of some but not other candidate precise extensions. In these cases, the statement lacks a truth value, i.e. it is neither true nor false.[3] Intuitively, and at first sight, this seems to be correct: some collections of grains seem to be borderline cases in the sense that it is neither true nor false to say that they are heaps.

This is the point to which Timothy Williamson objects in the first section of his article: he claims that to say that it is neither true nor false that he is thin (Williamson is taking himself to be a borderline case of a thin person) leads straight-forwardly to a contradiction. On Williamson's own view, vague predicates do have precise extensions. Thus, the tolerance principle (T) above is false because there is a last grain removal of which will make the difference between a heap and a non-heap:

($\neg$T) There is a number n, such that H_{-n} is a
heap and $H_{-(n+1)}$ is not a heap.

This, of course, seems incredible. How would we find out what this last grain is, and how, if we cannot find out, is it that the predicate 'is a heap' has acquired such a precise extension? For it seems plausible that it is the way we use a predicate that determines what it means, and *a fortiori* what its extension is. So how could the predicate have a precise extension if we are unable to draw a sharp line between the heaps and the non-heaps? If meaning supervenes on language use, how could meaning draw a line that we language users are unable to draw?

Williamson takes this type of objection very seriously and answers it with care. He claims that his view does not conflict with the view that meaning supervenes on language use. Crudely speaking, his line of response is to say that there are already some natural boundaries, namely the boundaries drawn by natural properties, such as the natural property of being a heap or being thin. If our language use is sufficient to

---

[3] This kind of view has been defended, for example, in Fine 1975 and Keefe 2000. Excellent overviews are provided in Keefe 2008, Sainsbury 2009 and Sorensen 2008.

determine that the predicate 'is a heap' expresses such a natural property, then it will determine also a precise extension. Williamson also explains why, while there is a last grain, we can never know which grain it is. This is because of a general principle concerning knowledge: the 'margin for error principle'.[4]

People very often think that Williamson's theory is simply incredible, for it is incredible that there should be a last grain that makes the difference between a heap and a non-heap. It may come as a surprise to these people, that supervaluationists, like Varzi, also believe that ($\neg T$) is true, i.e. it's true that there is a number n, such that H_{-n} is a heap and $H_{-(n+1)}$ is not a heap. Remember that supervaluationists claim that it is true to say that some object is a heap, just if the object is a member of every candidate extension of 'heap'. Supervaluationists also generalize this approach: any statement involving a vague predicate is true just if it is true according to every admissible way of making the vague predicate precise. Apply this to the claim 'there is a number n, such that H_{-n} is a heap and $H_{-(n+1)}$ is not a heap'. This is true according to every way of making 'heap' precise, because on every such way, there is a last grain that makes the difference.

What, then, is the difference between supervaluationism and Williamson's view? Consider a borderline case of a heap, call it B. Williamson will say that the statement that B is a heap is either true or false, even though we cannot know which. Supervaluationists will say that the statement is neither true nor false. Supervaluationists also have a different explanation why the tolerance principle (T), despite being false, nevertheless seems true: When removing grains one by one, we never come to a point at which we could say truly: 'now it is a heap', and after removing a further grain 'now it no longer is a heap'. None of the objects in the series H, H_{-1}, H_{-2}, . . ., is such that one could truly say that it is a heap and its successor is not. This would suggest to anyone ignorant of the special supervaluationist semantics of vague predicates, that ($\neg T$) must be false and (T) true. It also explains why it is not possible to find a counterexample to (T), despite its falsity.

Like Williamson and Varzi, Delia Graff Fara[5] claims that (T) is false and ($\neg T$) true. However, her explanation of why we nevertheless have a strong inclination to believe (T), is different from Williamson's and Varzi's. On this point, she is in broad agreement with 'contextualists' like Kamp (1981), Raffman (1996), Soames (1999) and Shapiro (2006). On the contextualist view, vague predicates, like 'is a heap' or 'is rich' are context-dependent in a special way that creates the impression of tolerance. Many predicates are context-dependent in the sense that their extension varies with the context of utterance (compare Part Eleven above). To give a simple example, the extension of the predicate 'is my uncle' depends on who utters it. A more interesting example is the predicate: 'is an object I am not currently considering'. Obviously, because of 'I', the extension here again depends on who utters it. But it will also

---

[4] Williamson's view is called the 'epistemic view of vagueness' or 'epistemicism', and is elaborated in greater detail in Williamson 1994. An earlier defense of epistemicism is by Roy Sorensen (1988). See also Sorensen's more recent 2001.

[5] Graff Fara's paper was originally published under the name 'Delia Graff' in 2000. Since then, she has changed her name to 'Delia Graff Fara'.

depend on the time of utterance, and what the utterer is considering at that time: anything the utterer is considering is excluded from the extension, everything else is in it. Now, someone might set out to find objects that are in the extension of the predicate. This is an impossible quest. As soon as the person turns their attention to any object, that very act of considering the object will exclude it from being a member of the extension. The person, if naïve, might conclude: 'I can't find anything that is in the extension, and frankly, I don't see how I possibly could. So the extension of the predicate is probably empty'. If the extension were empty, this would mean that there is no object this person fails to consider at that moment. But that must be wrong! What went wrong in the naïve reasoning is that the boundary of the extension of the predicate shifted during the search. It shifted in such a way that objects we were considering were never inside it.

Contextualists think that our inclination to accept tolerance principles for vague predicates, and in particular (T), is due to a similar fallacy: the reason we can't find the last grain that makes the difference between a heap and a non-heap is that the boundary will never be where we are looking. For the boundary, as with other context-sensitive predicates like the one discussed above, shifts as we shift our attention. Suppose we are 'force-marched' through the series H, H_{-1}, H_{-2}, . . ., having to say about each collection whether it is a heap or not, starting with H. We would carry on saying 'yes' for a long time, until, at H_x, we come dangerously close to H_{last}. At this point the boundary will suddenly switch to the other side, outside our field of attention. (Raffman 1996 calls this a 'Gestalt switch'.) If we were force-marched through the series in the opposite direction, we would surely keep saying 'no' until a while after H_x. This is, according to contextualism, because there is a constraint on how the extension of the predicate varies with the context. Graff Fara calls this the 'similarity constraint'. It makes sure that the boundary between the heaps and the non-heaps never runs between two members of the series that are salient in the conversation (or rather whose similarity is salient).[6]

Thus Graff Fara, along with other contextualists, explains the seductiveness of tolerance constraints with the special way in which the extensions of vague predicates shift their boundaries: the boundary never being where we are looking. Can she also explain why we cannot find the boundary once we are fixing our attention to one particular use of a vague predicate, in a particular context of utterance?

At this point it will be useful to distinguish two different versions of contextualism. According to what I want to call the 'indexicalist version', the context-dependence of vague predicates is modelled directly on indexical expressions. Consider the predicate 'is my uncle'. It will express different properties in different contexts of use – the property of being my uncle, when I utter it, the property of being your uncle if you utter it. Accordingly, the sentence, 'Barack Obama is my uncle', will express different propositions depending on the context of utterance, namely depending on the property expressed by the predicate in the context. If the context-dependence of vague

---

[6] Exercise: What exactly does Graff Fara's similarity constraint say? How does it differ from Soames' analogous constraint, and what difference does this make?

predicates is exactly analogous, then 'is a heap' will express different properties depending on the context of use, each of them with a precise extension. This version of contextualism will be in a very similar position to epistemicism, in that it has to explain two points: How do vague predicates *in context* acquire these precise extensions? and Why can't we find out where the precise boundaries are? Indexical contextualists might at this point avail themselves of the epistemicist's explanations. Or they might look for new ones.

Graff Fara's paper seems sometimes to stop short of committing her to contextualism in this definite sense. Her more recent work (2008), like that of another prominent contextualist, Raffman (2005), makes clear that neither of them wants to commit herself to the indexicalist version of contextualism. But how else could contextualism be fleshed out? Let's consider a different example of context-dependence, namely the predicate 'is hungry'. The indexicalist way to think of the contribution of 'is hungry' is to say that it expresses different properties at different times, namely at any time t, it expresses the relational property of being hungry at t. On this view, the sentence 'DGF is hungry' will express different propositions at different times. There is also a different, non-indexical way of construing context-dependence here: 'is hungry' might be seen as expressing always the same property, and the sentence, 'DGF is hungry', always the same proposition. On this view, some propositions do not have absolute truth values, for the proposition that DGF is hungry will presumably change its truth value over time. Now, a non-indexical contextualist about vagueness might model the context dependence of vague predicates on the non-indexical view of 'is hungry'. Thus, the *property* expressed by a vague predicate does not change with the context of use.[7] If that is the view, then just like in the case of hungriness, vague properties vary in extension with some contextual parameter. At this point, an interesting question is whether the extensions that properties have in context are precise.[8] If they are, the two questions faced by the epistemicist can again be raised: How does language use determine these precise extensions? and Why can't we find out where the boundaries of these extensions are? If the extension of a vague predicate in context is not precise, then how is it that tolerance principles like (T) can be straightforwardly false (in any context)?

---

[7] I am here speaking merely of the form of context-dependence that the contextualist uses to explain the seductiveness of tolerance constraints. The non-indexical contextualist about vagueness may very well have an indexical view of other forms of context-dependence exhibited by vague predicates, such as the dependence of contextually determined comparison classes.
[8] Exercise: What does Graff Fara say about this?

Questions and tasks

1   Construct a soritical argument that purports to show that even a 100-year-old man is young.
2   Varzi argues that the supervaluationary account is superior to degree-theories. Is he right?
3   What is Williamson's objection to supervaluationism in section I, and does Varzi have an answer?

4   Explain how Williamson's margin for error principle explains why we can't find the grain removal of which will turn the heap into a non-heap.

5   Graff Fara mentions several ways in which predicates like 'is rich' or 'is tall' are context-dependent. One of them is dependence on a contextually determined comparison class. How, if at all, is this context-dependence relevant to the sorites paradox?

6   On pp. 532–3, Graff Fara lists three questions. Work out how she answers, or how she should answer, each of them.

7   In what sense is Graff Fara committed to the claim that there are sharp boundaries?

References and further reading

Fara, Delia Graff 2008: 'Profiling Interest Relativity', *Analysis* 68, pp. 326–35.

Fine, Kit 1975: 'Vagueness, Truth and Logic', *Synthese* 54, pp. 235–59; reprinted in *Vagueness: A Reader*, Rosanna Keefe and Peter Smith (eds), Cambridge: MIT Press (1996), pp. 119–50.

Kamp, Hans 1981: 'The Paradox of the Heap', in U. Mönnich (ed.), *Aspects of Philosophical Logic*, Dordrecht: Reidel, pp. 225–77.

Keefe, Rosanna 2000: *Theories of Vagueness*, Cambridge: Cambridge University Press.

Keefe, Rosanna 2008: 'Vagueness: Supervaluationism', *Philosophy Compass* 3, pp. 315–24.

McGee, Vann, and Brian McLaughlin 1995: 'Distinctions without a Difference', *Southern Journal of Philosophy* 33, pp. 203–51.

Raffman, Diana 1996: 'Vagueness and Context-Sensitivity', *Philosophical Studies* 81, pp. 175–92.

Raffman, Diana 2005: 'How to Understand Contextualism about Vagueness: Reply to Stanley', *Analysis* 65, pp. 244–8.

Sainsbury, Mark 1996: 'Concepts without Boundaries', in Rosanna Keefe and Peter Smith (eds), *Vagueness: A Reader*, Cambridge, MA: MIT Press, pp. 251–64.

Sainsbury, Mark 2009: *Paradoxes*, 3rd edn, Cambridge: Cambridge University Press.

Shapiro, Stewart 2006: *Vagueness in Context*, Oxford: Oxford University Press.

Soames, Scott 1999: *Understanding Truth*, New York: Oxford University Press.

Sorensen, Roy 1988: *Blindspots*, Oxford: Clarendon Press.

Sorensen, Roy 2001: *Vagueness and Contradiction*, Oxford: Oxford University Press.

Sorensen, Roy 2008: 'Vagueness', in Edward N. Zalta (ed.), *The Stanford Encyclopedia of Philosophy* (Fall 2008 edn), http://plato.stanford.edu/archives/fall2008/entries/vagueness

Stanley, Jason 2003: 'Context, Interest-Relativity and the Sorites', *Analysis* 63, pp. 269–80.

Williamson, Timothy 1994: *Vagueness*, London: Routledge.

Chapter 31

Achille C. Varzi

VAGUENESS, LOGIC AND ONTOLOGY

Introduction

Remember the story of the most-most? It's the story of that club in New York where people are the most of every type. There is the hairiest bald man and the baldest hairy man; the shortest giant and the tallest dwarf; the smartest idiot and the stupidest wise man. They are all there, including honest thieves and crippled acrobats. On Saturday night they have a party, eat, drink, dance. Then they have a contest. "And if you can tell the hairiest bald man from the baldest hairy man—we are told—you get a prize."

The story is from Saul Bellow's *Herzog*, a novel published almost forty years ago but still very modern in its philosophical provocations.[1] It is a funny and provoking story because so is the idea of a contest like that of the most-most. There is no sharp boundary demarcating the category of bald men, no precise number of hairs separating the bald from the hairy. Hence it makes no sense to suppose that one can identify the hairiest bald man. It does not even make sense to suppose that such a person exists, as if the difficulty were merely epistemic. Some people are clearly bald and some are clearly hairy, but between these two sorts of people there exist a variety of borderline cases: baldish guys, men wearing toupees, hirsute beatniks with a shiny spot on the top of their heads. Our concept of baldness and our linguistic practices do not specify any

precise, general criterion for saying in each case whether we are dealing with a bald man or with a hairy one. 'Bald' and 'hairy' are vague concepts and their ranges of application have vague boundaries.

Shall we distinguish three categories, then? Some people are clearly bald (Picasso), some are clearly hairy (the count of Montecristo), and some are borderline cases. That's a third category of its own, and we may suppose that the New York club includes the most of each of these three categories.

Unfortunately things are not so easy. Two boundaries aren't any better than one. And if it is impossible to identify the hairiest bald man (i.e., to draw a boundary between bald and non-bald), it is also impossible to identify the first *clear instance* of a bald man (i.e., to draw a boundary between clearly-bald and borderline-bald). The vagueness of these concepts does not reduce to the existence of borderline cases: it is the absence of a sharp boundary in their range of application that makes them vague. Imagine we find ourselves in a room with the count of Montecristo and suppose we start plucking his hairs, one at a time. At the beginning of the process the count is pretty hairy. At the end he will be bald. But when exactly will he cease to be hairy? When will he begin to be bald? These are questions that we could not answer even if we were omniscient.

Increasing the number of intermediate

categories won't do, either. We could distinguish between borderline cases and borderline borderline cases, or borderline borderline borderline cases, but things would only get worse. Multiplying the number of relevant boundaries amounts to making an even stronger commitment to precision than that of the members of the most-most club. And this is a serious problem because it gives rise to a genuine logical puzzle. Gradually, but ineluctably, we find ourselves in a situation that appears to be contradictory. On the one hand, we find it natural to agree with the following two statements:

(1) Upon removing 1 hair, the count of Montecristo is still hairy.
(2) For every n: if the count of Montecristo is still hairy upon removing n hairs, then he is still hairy upon removing n + 1 hairs.

(What difference can a single hair make?) On the other hand, we certainly want to deny the statement

(3) Upon removing all hairs, the count of Montecristo is still hairy.

Yet (3) follows logically from the conjunction of (1) and (2). (This can be shown by repeated applications of the rules of universal instantiation and *modus ponens*.) Hence, either we reject one of the premises, (1) or (2), contrary to our intuitions about the meaning of 'hairy'; or we find ourselves forced to give up some elementary logical principles so as to block the inference to (3). Either way, the picture is worrisome.

Vagueness and the normativity of logic

This dilemma was known, in some form or other, already to the ancient world. (The first version of the paradox is attributed to Eubulides of Miletus.[2]) More important, it was well known

also to Gottlob Frege, one of the fathers of modern symbolic logic. For Frege the rigorous delimitation of every concept was one of the fundamental provisos for the possibility of applying the rules of logic:

> A definition of a concept (of a possible predicate) must. . . . unambiguously determine, as regards any object, whether or not it falls under the concept (whether or not the predicate is truly assertible of it). Thus there must not be any object as regards which the definition leaves in doubt whether it falls under the concept. . . . We may express this metaphorically as follows: the concept must have a sharp boundary.[3]

Indeed, beginning with Frege and for a very long time, logicians have been assuming that vagueness may bring logical disaster in its wake. Vague concepts have been regarded as illegitimate, at least to the extent that logic is understood as a normative discipline (rather than a descriptive discipline, like psychology). And this, in turn, has been taken to imply that vagueness should be eliminated altogether from the realm of logic.

The trouble is that this way of proceeding is itself very problematic. For vagueness is an extremely pervasive phenomenon. As Michael Dummett put it, it gets into everything, like dust.[4] Perhaps the concepts employed in mathematics and some concepts used in the so-called exact sciences are exempted from its grasp. But the vast majority of the concepts that we use in ordinary discourse are vague. And this is not only true of adjectives like 'bald' and 'hairy' and 'short' and 'wise'. The same goes for concepts that find expression in many other grammatical categories such as nouns (how many grains of sand does it take to make a *heap*?), verbs (how slowly can you *run*?), adverbs (how *fast* can you drive?), and so on. So the problem is: on the one hand, vagueness leads to a logical paradox; on the other hand, if we applied Frege's criterion and protected logic by eliminating all those words and those concepts which exhibit some degree of vagueness, then we would end up with a language that is so poor as to be utterly useless. Moreover, it is not even clear whether the criterion is actually applicable. It would be applicable (at least in principle) if there existed a sharp boundary between the vague and the non-vague. But even this may turn out to be an unwarranted presumption: some concepts are clearly vague (*bald*) and some are clearly not vague (*circular*), but there are concepts that appear to lie at the borderline. Is there a precise moment at which a person ceases to be *alive*? Is there an exact moment at which a woman becomes a *mother*? Are these concepts vague or are they precise?

Even without taking such problematic cases into account, the vagueness of our concept of vagueness can be appreciated by construing a paradoxical argument that makes 'vague' similar to such predicates as 'bald' and 'hairy', as Roy Sorensen has pointed out.[5] Consider, for example, the following series of concepts: 'either bald or with less than 1 hair on his head', 'either bald or with less than 2 hairs on his head', . . ., 'either bald or with less than 500.000 hairs on his head'. (We may suppose that 500.000 is approximately the number of hairs on the head of the count of Montecristo at the time when he enters the room in our earlier experiment.) Evidently, the first term of this series is vague: it is as vague as 'bald', since both are clearly true of hairless people, and for all other people they are exactly alike. Moreover, there is no point in the series where we encounter a vague predicate followed by a sharp one: what difference can a single hair make? So we find it natural to agree with the following two statements:

(4)   The adjective 'either bald or with less than 1 hair on his head' is vague.

(5)   If the adjective 'either bald or with less than n hairs on his head' is vague, then so is 'either bald or with less than n + 1 hairs on his head'.

On the other hand, we certainly want to deny the statement

(6)   The adjective 'either bald or with less than 500.000 hair on his head' is vague.

For the last term of our sequence is clearly not vague. It is, in fact, just as precise as the predicate 'with less than 500.000 hairs on his head', and this is true of all men with less than 500.000 hairs on their heads and false of all others. As before, however, the statement which we want to deny follows logically from those which we want to assert. And if we take this situation as a sign of vagueness, we must conclude that 'vague' is just as vague a concept as 'bald' and 'hairy'.

The moral is that it is impossible to draw a line between vague and precise concepts just as it is impossible to draw a line between bald and hairy people. Hence the strategy advocated by Frege is ultimately inapplicable. Nor can we just assume that the precise languages postulated by classical logic are idealizations to be realized in the future, for our argument shows that vagueness dies hard. If we actually try to stipulate it away, our stipulations will themselves be made in less than perfectly precise terms and the regimented language will inherit some of that vagueness. So if vagueness is incompatible with classical logic, classical logic is ultimately inapplicable to ordinary thought and language. So much for the normativity of classical logic.

Vague reference

The pervasiveness of vagueness goes even farther than this. We have focused on conceptual vagueness—the vagueness exhibited by general terms such as adjectives, nouns, or verbs. But there can be vagueness also in the case of singular terms, i.e., names or descriptive phrases purporting to refer to individual objects or events rather than concepts or classes. Perhaps the referents of 'Bill Clinton' or 'the mayor of New York' are well defined. But what about such terms as 'Everest',

'Toronto', or 'that cloud in the sky'? Surely the referents of such terms are to some extent indeterminate. And this sort of indeterminacy does not reduce to ambiguity: it bears the mark of vagueness—for example, it gives rise to paradoxical arguments parallel to those defined by (1)–(3) and (4)–(6). You are on the top of Mount Everest and you begin descending. After each step you ask yourself whether you are still on the mountain. At the beginning you have no doubts, and you have no doubts at the end, when you find yourself in the center of Katmandu. But of course there is no point where you can confidently assert: Here is where Everest ends. So again you find yourself in a predicament. You are inclined to agree with the following two assertions:

(7)   After 1 step I am still on Everest.
(8)   For every n: if I am still on Everest after *n* steps, then I am on Everest after *n* + 1 steps.

while denying their logical consequence:

(9)   At the end of the descent I am still on Everest.

One might argue that in this case the vagueness lies in the predicate 'I am still on', or perhaps in the relational predicate 'after n steps I am still on', but it is easy to reformulate the argument using precise predicates instead. For instance, we can imagine a purely geometric version of the paradox in which the region of space occupied by Mount Everest is compared with a sequence of precisely demarcated spatial regions, each slightly larger than its predecessor, starting from a small region which comprises the peak of the mountain and ending with a very large region that extends all the way to downtown Katmandu. At which point of the sequence shall we say that region R_n has a smaller volume than the volume of Mount Everest while the next region, R_{n+1}, has an equal or greater volume?

Evidently the problem is that the term 'Everest' does not refer to a precise chunk of reality. It does not refer to a volume of matter sharply demarcated from its surrounding and it therefore makes no sense to compare the region it occupies with a series of precise regions. Simply, 'Everest' is a vague term. And so are 'Toronto', 'that cloud in the sky', and many other names and descriptions that we use in ordinary discourse.

Indeed, even an apparently innocuous proper name such as 'Bill Clinton' is arguably vague: What exactly are the spatial boundaries of its referent? Surely they comprise Clinton's heart, and surely they do not comprise my left foot. But what about the candy that Clinton is presently chewing: Is it part of Clinton now? Will it be part of Clinton only after he has swallowed it? After he has started digesting it? After he has digested it completely? And exactly when did Clinton come into existence? Exactly when will it be correct to say that Bill Clinton does not exist any longer?

Ontological vagueness vs semantic vagueness

Vagueness is such a pervasive phenomenon that one can hardly overestimate the threat that it represents to traditional logical and philosophical theories. There is, in addition, dispute concerning the nature of this phenomenon, and different conceptions lend themselves naturally to different ways of coping with it. Consider our statement to the effect that the referent of a vague term t is not sharply demarcated. This very statement is ambiguous and admits a *de re* reading, as in (10a), or a *de dicto* reading, as in (10b):

(10) a.   The referent of t is such that it is indeterminate whether certain chunks of reality lie within its boundaries.
     b.   It is indeterminate whether certain

chunks of reality lie within the boundaries of the referent of t.

On the first reading the indeterminacy is ontological: vague terms refer to vague objects, objects which lack precise spatial or temporal boundaries. For example, 'Everest' is vague insofar as the boundaries of Everest do not sharply divide the matter composing it from the matter outside it. In Michael Tye's words:

> Everest's boundaries are fuzzy. Some molecules are inside Everest and some molecules outside. But some have an indefinite status: there is no objective, determinate fact of the matter about whether they are inside or outside.[6]

Likewise, on this view there is no objective fact of the matter about whether certain water droplets are inside a cloud, whether a certain drop of rain fell on Downtown Toronto, whether the candy is part of Clinton. Mountains, clouds, neighborhoods, houses, forests, deserts, islands, and perhaps even people, on this view, are all genuinely vague denizens of reality. Like the figures of an impressionist painting, they do not fit in the standard topological picture according to which every object has an interior surrounded by an exterior. Like old soldiers, "they just fade away".[7]

On the second reading—the *de dicto* reading—the indeterminacy exhibited by a vague term is exclusively semantic, or cognitive at large. It lies in the representation system (our language, our conceptual apparatus), not in the represented entity, and to say that the referent of a term is not sharply demarcated is to say that the term vaguely designates an object, not that it designates a vague object. When we say 'Everest' (or when the founder of the Indian Geodetic Office baptizes a certain piece of land, at the border between Tibet and Nepal, 'Everest') we simply do not specify exactly which piece of land we are referring to. The referent of our term is vaguely fixed. If we wish, we can add that it is ultimately

the vagueness of the relevant sortal concept (the concept *mountain*, in this case) that is responsible for the way in which the referent of 'Everest' is vaguely fixed. But it is not the stuff out there that is vague. Each one of a large variety of slightly distinct chunks of reality has an equal claim to being the referent of our newly introduced name. And each such thing is precisely determinate. To use a different example, from Henryk Mehlberg,

> The term 'Toronto' is vague because there are several methods of tracing the geographical limits of the city designated by this name, all of them compatible with the way the name is used. It may be interpreted, for instance, either as including some particular tree on the outskirts of the city or as not including it. The two areas differing from each other with respect to the spot where this tree is growing are two distinct individual objects; the word 'Toronto' may be interpreted as denoting either of these objects and is for that reason vague.[8]

This opposition between ontological and semantic vagueness applies also in the case of names and descriptions for other sorts of entity. An expression such as 'Sebastian's walk' is a vague event designator: there is indeterminacy concerning the exact spatiotemporal location of the designated event. On the ontological conception this means that the event itself is vague, that its spatial and temporal boundaries are genuinely fuzzy. On the semantic conception, by contrast, 'Sebastian's walk' is vague only insofar as it vaguely designates an event. It's not that there is this event, Sebastian's walk, with imprecise boundaries. There are plenty of things going on inside and outside Sebastian as he moves along the sidewalk, each with a precise location in space and time, and many of them qualify as legitimate referents of the phrase 'Sebastian's walk'. The phrase itself is too vague to discriminate among them.

Finally, we can introduce an opposition between ontological and semantic interpretations also in the case of conceptual vagueness, i.e., the vagueness exhibited by predicates such as 'bald' and the like. These are predicates whose extensions do not have sharp boundaries, and the assertion that the extension of a predicate P lacks sharp boundaries can be given a *de re* reading, as in (11a), or a *de dicto* reading, as in (11b):

(11) a. The extension of P is such that it is indeterminate whether certain objects fall within its boundaries.

   b. It is indeterminate whether certain objects fall within the boundaries of the extension of P.

The *de re* reading yields ontological vagueness. A predicate such as 'bald' would then designate a fuzzy set, a set whose membership function allows for borderline values: some people, such as Picasso, are definitely in this set; others, such as the count of Montecristo, are definitely out; and others have an indefinite status: there is no objective, determinate fact of the matter about whether they are in or out. By contrast, the *de dicto* reading corresponds to a purely semantic conception of vagueness. The set of bald people is not a vague set at all. There are exactly 2^n sets of people (where n is the number of all people at the present time), each with its perfectly precise membership function, but it is indeterminate which of those sets can do duty for the extension of the predicate 'bald'. There are several good candidates but the predicate itself is too vague a description to successfully pick out a unique one of them.

Ways out

At this point one can look at the available options. How can vagueness be reconciled with logic without forgoing the normative value of the latter?

A popular stance is to take the ontological turn and to abandon classical logic in favor of some kind of "fuzzy logic".[9] To the extent that the referents of our names and the extensions of our predicates can have hazy boundaries, the truth conditions of our statements can also be blurred; some statements will be definitely true, some will be definitely false, and some will have a truth value which is somewhat intermediate between true and false. For example, after removing a few thousand hairs from the count's scalp, the statement

(12) The count of Montecristo is still hairy

will no longer be fully true because the count will no longer be a clear member of the fuzzy set of hairy people (and not yet a clear member of the fuzzy set of bald people). And after a few hundred steps your statement

(13) I am still on Everest

will no longer be fully true because the land under your feet will no longer be a clear part of the vague mountain called 'Everest'. Typically one allows for an infinity of intermediate truth values, to do justice to the intuition that there is no limit to the degree to which a statement can be truer than others. For example, (13) will be slightly truer if uttered after n steps than after n + 1 steps. It is actually customary to allow for a continuum of intermediate truth values, to do justice to the intuition that vagueness goes hand in hand with lack of discontinuity. (One can utter (13) at any point between the nth and the (n + 1)th step.) And once an infinity of truth values is available, one can easily block the paradox involved in reasoning as in (1)–(3) or (7)–(9). In each case the second premise of the argument—the one expressing the intuition that vague predicates and vague names are, in Crispin Wright's phrase, tolerant to marginal change[10]—will not be fully true. And a piece of reasoning which relies on repeated applications of a rule of inference (modus ponens) to premises which are not fully true is a piece of reasoning that is not fully sound. Its soundness decreases as the number of applications increases.

This is a popular account but it is not without its own problems. In fact I think its problems are much worse than the troubles the account is supposed to handle. For one thing, there is something bizarre in the idea that the imprecision of certain boundaries is to be explained away by reference to an infinity of perfectly precise degrees of truth (membership, parthood). To what degree, exactly, is it true that the count of Montecristo is still hairy upon removing 10,000 hairs? To degree 0.8? Perhaps to degree 0.81? Or maybe 0.8123456? To what degree is a certain borderline molecule part of Mount Everest? Practically one can ignore such details, but the theory itself requires precise answers in each case. Second, there is the embarrassing presupposition that a point exists where one goes from full truth to partial truth, and from partial truth to full falsehood. At what point, during the process that we have envisaged, does the count of Montecristo cease to be a clear case of a hairy person? What is the last step after which it is no longer true (i.e., fully true) that you are on Mount Everest? Evidently the assumption of a boundary separating the clear cases from the borderline cases is just as problematic as the assumption of a boundary separating the true from the false. Finally, the very idea that the vagueness of our words lies in the vagueness of the world—that vague words refer to vague objects and sets—is deeply puzzling. For what would the relevant objects and sets be? *What* exactly is the vague mountain corresponding to the name 'Everest'? How could we be so precise as to designate it?

I think these are serious difficulties that every ontological conception of vagueness is bound to face, and I am not at all optimistic about the possibility of overcoming them. Besides, the costs are very high: one is to give up classical logic as well as classical set theory and mereology. Accordingly, I will now focus on an alternative way out, which is based not on the ontological (*de re*) conception of vagueness but on the semantic (*de dicto*) conception. I will argue that such a conception is superior to the ontological conception and I will show how it can, if properly understood, provide a way out of the Fregean dilemma. To repeat, then: on this view there is no such thing as a vague mountain. Rather, there are many things where we conceive the mountain to be, each with its precise boundary, and when we say 'Everest' we are just being vague as to *which* thing we are referring to. Likewise, there is no such thing as a vague set: to say that a predicate is vague is to say (at the very least) that its extension is incompletely specified, and where there is incomplete specification of extension there is indeterminacy between various ways of picking out a precise extension.

Such a conception of vagueness is, I think, intuitive as it stands. It is a natural correlate of the idea that vagueness could in principle be removed by careful stipulations, which is exactly what Frege thought we should always do to prevent logical chaos. It could be removed, that is, if our stipulations could be made in precise terms. More importantly, however, the semantic conception of vagueness is intuitive because it combines very naturally with a supervaluationary account of the sort advocated by Kit Fine, David Lewis, and others.[11] For to the extent that vagueness can in principle be removed, it can be removed in many different ways. (There are many objects and sets that we could choose to assign to 'Everest' and 'bald'.) Thus, when evaluating a statement involving vague expressions it is natural to consider the many possible ways in which those expressions can be made precise. If the statement is true under all such "precisifications", then we may take it to be true *simpliciter*; the unmade semantic stipulations don't matter. In other words, it makes no difference what those expressions could mean had their semantic values been defined more precisely: what the statement says is true regardless (or super-true, as Fine has it). Likewise, if the statement comes out false under every precisification then we may regard it as false (or super-false) in spite of its vagueness. It is only when the statement comes out true under some precisifications and false under others that there is trouble. In such cases, the statement suffers a truth-value gap. In Lewis's words:

> Whatever it is that we do to determine the "intended" interpretation of our language determines not one interpretation but a range of interpretations. . . . What we try for, in imparting information, is truth of what we say under all the intended interpretations.[12]

To illustrate, although 'Everest' is vague, it is nevertheless true that after 1 step you are still on Everest because this statement is true regardless of how we suppose the referent of 'Everest' to be made precise. Likewise, it is false that you are still on Everest at the end of your descent. On the other hand, there is no way we can settle the issue when it comes to the intermediate regions, since the land under your feet may turn out to be inside Everest or outside it depending on how we carve out a precise referent for 'Everest'. In those cases nothing will settle the issue for us, and the statement that you are still on Everest will fail to receive a definite truth value. This also allows us to explain why, for example, we can confidently assert that Mount Everest is in Asia and deny that it is in Europe, though we must suspend judgment when it comes to saying whether Everest is mostly in Tibet: the truth value of such a statement depends crucially on how much land one includes in the referent of 'Everest'. And, of course, we can by the same pattern explain why we feel doubtful when it comes to evaluating the statement that the count of Montecristo is still hairy after the removal of, say, 10,000 hairs: the truth value of such a statement depends crucially on how we imagine the extension of 'hairy' to be precisified. Still, the count is clearly hairy at the beginning of the process and bald at the end, since every

precisification must agree with that. (The predicates 'hairy' and 'bald' are vague, but certain facts about them are perfectly clear and every precisification must comply with these facts.)

Why supervaluationism is a better account

The supervaluationary account is attractive because it reflects a deep, preanalytical intuition concerning vagueness as it arises in ordinary language. We speak vaguely because in ordinary circumstances the vagueness of our words does not matter. We know that what we say would be true if we were speaking precisely, no matter how we imagine this precision to be reached, and therefore we don't care. The unmade semantic stipulations don't affect the truth of what we say.

To be sure, one could now object that just as fuzzy logic fails to overcome the presumption that there exist sharp boundaries—boundaries demarcating the borderline cases, if anything—so does supervaluationism. After all, supervaluationism says that the truth value of a vague statement is a function of the truth values of its precisifications, and this presupposes that the set of precisifications is itself precise. It presupposes, for example, that there exists a unique set of precisely demarcated areas which qualify as all and only the admissible referents of 'Everest', and a unique set of precisely demarcated sets which qualify as all and only the admissible extensions of 'hairy'. This sounds counterintuitive. However, this counterintuitiveness does not constitute a genuine threat for the account. Surely, intuitively it is impossible to draw a sharp line around the set of the admissible precisifications of a term, or of a set of expressions. If a certain piece of land a counts as an admissible referent of 'Everest', then so does any slightly larger piece of land obtained from a by adding a tiny hunk of matter along the border. (What difference can a tiny hunk of matter make?) If a certain set of people X counts as an admissible extension of 'hairy', then so does any set obtained from X by removing a single hair from the head of any member of X. (What difference can a single hair make?) But this only means that the notion of a precisification is itself vague. It means that the semantic machinery of super-valuationism suffers itself from the phenomenon of vagueness. And bad news as this may be, it comes as no surprise. We already know that the language in which the theory is formulated—the semantic metalanguage—is itself vague because we already know that 'vague' is vague. And if the semantic notion of vagueness is vague, so is the semantic relation of precisification. (This is, after all, the reason why we cannot hope to eliminate vagueness by means of *actual* stipulations.) So, by treating vagueness as a semantic phenomenon supervaluationism is bound to suffer from higher-order vagueness. But this higher-order vagueness is itself a semantic phenomenon and supervaluationism does not, therefore, succumb to the objection raised above against the ontological conception of vagueness.

One could argue that there is another problem with the semantic notion of a precisification. For isn't there a hidden presumption in the very idea that a vague term is one which *can* be precisified in many ways? Consider again Mount Everest and let Alpha be any precisely demarcated, mountain-shaped piece of land culminating in Everest's peak. After a few hundred steps during your descent it is indeterminate whether you are still on Everest, but it is not indeterminate whether you are still on Alpha, for 'Alpha' has a very precise meaning. Hence—one could argue—Mount Everest must be distinct from Alpha by Leibniz's law (specifically by the principle of the indiscernibility of identicals). That is, when we say 'Everest' we cannot be talking about Alpha, not even in principle. And by generalization it follows that we cannot be talking about *any* precisely demarcated piece of land. By a similar pattern, one could argue that

no precise set would serve as a precisification of a vague predicate such as 'bald'. So if this line of reasoning were correct, then the supervaluationary account would be illegitimate and we would be forced to reconsider the basic issues.[13]

The reasoning, however, is incorrect.[13] To put it briefly, the use of Leibniz's law is fallacious in this context. It involves a fallacy analogous to a familiar one arising in the presence of intensional operators. We know that the two statements in (14) have different truth values:

(14) a.   It is contingent that 10 is greater than the number of planets.
     b.   It is contingent that 10 is greater than 9.

Yet this is not enough to conclude that 9 and the number of the planets have different properties (hence that they are distinct, by Leibniz's law) unless we also assume the equivalence between statements of the forms (15a) and (15b):

(15) a.   It is contingent that 10 is greater than t
     b.   t is an x such that it is contingent that 10 is greater than x.

And, of course, this equivalence holds when 't' is replaced by '9' (a rigid designator) but not when it is replaced by 'the number of planets'.[14] Likewise, if 'Alpha' picks out a precisely demarcated piece of land, then the two statements in (16) may have different truth values:

(16) a.   It is indeterminate whether after n steps you are on Everest.
     b.   It is indeterminate whether after n steps you are on Alpha.

This is not enough to conclude that Everest and Alpha have different properties (different spatial properties, in this case) unless we also assume the equivalence between statements of the forms (17a) and (17b):

516 Achille C. Varzi

(17) a.   It is indeterminate whether after n steps you are on t

    b. t is an x such that it is indeterminate whether after n steps you are on x,

where 't' can be replaced by 'Everest' or by 'Alpha'. And clearly enough we have no reason to make such an assumption. The equivalence holds when 't' is a precise designator such as 'Alpha', just as the equivalence between the two statements in (15) holds when 't' is a rigid designator. But when 't' is a vague designator such as 'Everest' the equivalence holds only on a *de re* conception of vagueness. On the *de dicto* conception (17b) is bound to be false even when (17a) is true.

One could also formulate this defense of supervaluationism with the help of an analogy. As Lewis has pointed out, supervaluational precisifications are a bit like possible worlds, with super-truth playing a role analogous to necessary truth, i.e. truth in every possible world. The analogy between the operators 'it is contingent that' and 'it is indeterminate whether' is then immediate and the familiar diagnosis of the opposition in (15) extends directly to (17).[15] We cannot infer that Everest and Alpha are distinct, but only that it is indeterminate whether Everest is Alpha. And this is perfectly coherent with supervaluationism.

Indeed, from this point of view the objection under examination can be turned into a fatal objection against ontological vagueness. This is the gist of a nice little argument going back to Gareth Evans.[16] Let me reproduce it in a slightly modified version, as follows. Suppose, toward a *reductio*, that the vagueness of 'Everest' is *de re* and suppose that Beta is any object for which the identity statement

(18) Everest = Beta

is indeterminate. If indeed there are molecules such that it is neither definitely true nor definitely false that they are inside Everest, it should

not be hard to find such an object. For example, our earlier Alpha could do. Now, the indeterminacy of (18) implies the truth of

(19) It is indeterminate whether Everest = Beta.

On the other hand, it is evident that in spite of all vagueness Everest is determinately identical to itself. Everything is identical to itself, whether its boundaries are sharp or not. Hence the statement

(20) It is indeterminate whether Everest = Everest.

must be false. But then Leibniz's law allows us to conclude that Everest and Beta are in fact distinct. This would be a fallacious move if the vagueness of 'Everest' were understood *de dicto*, as we have just seen. But it is not fallacious if this vagueness is understood *de re*. For in that case (19) and (20) imply, respectively:

(19′) Beta is an x such that it is indeterminate whether x = Everest.

(20′) Everest is an x such that it is indeterminate whether x = Everest.

And in the case of statements such as these Leibniz's law is perfectly applicable. We must therefore conclude that (18) is not indefinite but false, contrary to our initial supposition. We must also conclude, by reasoning in a similar fashion, that on the ontological conception of vagueness *every* statement of the form

(21) Everest = x

is false, except when 'x' is replaced by 'Everest'. In other words, we must conclude that there are no circumstances under which a statement of this form will be indeterminate. The world is full of vague objects but each such object has identity conditions that are absolutely precise. And this is very strange indeed. Leibniz's law leaves supervaluationism unaffected but it has, apparently, fatal consequences on the alternative, ontological conception.

The paradox dissolved

These considerations offer some support in favor of the supervaluationary account and against the ontological account. But let us now go back to our starting point and let us see how supervaluationism deals with the paradoxical arguments illustrated by (1)–(3) and (7)–(9). For that is a necessary test: we don't have a way out of Frege's dilemma—the incompatibility of vagueness with the normativity of logic—unless we have an account of this sort of paradoxical argument. So what are we to make of such paradoxical patterns of reasoning within the supervaluationary framework?

The answer is that supervaluationally these patterns are (somewhat surprisingly) valid but unsound. They are valid because supervaluationism turns out to be perfectly compatible with classical logic after all. This follows from the fact that supervaluational truth is defined entirely in terms of truth under a precisification, and precisifications yield classical models.[17] On the other hand, the arguments under examination are unsound because in each case the second premise is not true. In fact it is false (i.e., super-false), for it comes out false on every precisification of the relevant vague terms. No matter how 'hairy' is precisified, there is bound to be a number n such that the count of Montecristo is still hairy upon removing n hairs but not upon removing n + 1 hairs. So the statement

(2)   For every n: if the count of Montecristo is still hairy upon removing n hairs, then he is still hairy upon removing n + 1 hairs.

is bound to be super-false. Likewise, on every precisification of 'Everest' there is bound to be a number n such that after n steps you are still on Everest but after n + 1 steps you are not. So your statement

(8)   For every n: if I am still on Everest after n steps, then I am on Everest after n + 1 steps.

is bound to be super-false. Hence any argument using such statements as premises is bound to be unsound. The conclusion may well follow but it need not be true.

Now, this blocks the paradox but—one could object—the price is unacceptable. For to deny such statements as (2) or (8) is to violate the intuition that the relevant vague terms are tolerant to marginal change. And that intuition is non-negotiable, isn't it?

The answer is that the intuition is non-negotiable but also misleading. Vague expressions such as 'hairy' and 'Everest' are indeed tolerant to marginal change, but not because they verify such statements as (2) or (8). Rather, they are tolerant to marginal change insofar as it is impossible for anybody to exhibit a specific *counterexample* to such statements as (2) or (8).[18] In other words, they can satisfy a semantic condition of the form (22a) without satisfying the corresponding condition in (22b):

(22) a.   'Every n is such that . . . n . . .' is false
      b.   Some n is such that '. . . n . . .' is false.

Of course, this is a distinction without a difference in the ordinary semantics for classical logic. That is why we have a natural impulse to demand a counterexample whenever a generalized statement is denied. It is also a distinction without a difference if vagueness is understood ontologically, at least insofar as such a conception is to provide a basis for the semantics of fuzzy logic. (In fuzzy logic the truth value of a universal generalization is typically defined as the greatest lower bound of the truth values of its instances, so if the generalization gets the lowest possible value—false—there must be at least one instance that gets that value as well.) However, in the presence of semantic vagueness the distinction becomes significant and the impulse to demand a counterexample for every false generalization leads to confusion and paradox. The paradox arises precisely because the impossibility to come up with an n that falsifies schematic conditionals of the form (2') or (8')

(2') If the count of Montecristo is still hairy upon removing n hairs, then he is still hairy upon removing n + 1 hairs.

(8') If I am still on Everest after n steps, then I am on Everest after n + 1 steps.

induces us to think that the corresponding universal generalizations, (2) and (8), are true. And that is illegitimate.

This sort of reply is often greeted with a gaze of suspicion, if not incredulity. However, this explanation is the right one—and the only possible one—if we agree on the *de dicto* understanding of vagueness. For let us focus again on a concrete example, say 'Everest'. (The case of 'hairy' is similar.) On the one hand, if Everest is not a vague object then it must have sharp boundaries, for every object has sharp boundaries somewhere. Hence the statement that there is no cut-off number n, i.e., the statement in (8), must be false. On the other hand, 'Everest' is vague, which means that it is impossible to pick out a specific object and, consequently, to specify an actual cut-off number n. For there are only three possibilities, and none of them corresponds to a value of n which falsifies the conditional in (8'): (i) If n is relatively low, then the antecedent and the consequent of the conditional are both true on all admissible precisifications. (ii) If n is relatively high, then the antecedent and the consequent of the conditional are both false on all precisifications. (iii) If n is a borderline number of steps (and this may well be a vague issue), then there will be precisifications which verify the antecedent and the consequent as well as precisifications which falsify the antecedent and the consequent, but there will also be precisifications where the antecedent comes out true but the consequent comes out

false, thereby yielding a truth-value gap in the supervaluation. Thus (8') is false. In short, supervaluationally it is false that there exists no number n of steps that marks the boundary of Everest, but there is no number n of steps such that it is true of it that it marks the boundary. This is the only reasonable thing to say if all objects are sharp but 'Everest' is vague. And it is precisely the answer delivered by the supervaluationary account. To reject it is to fall for a *de re* account of vagueness, hence for an ontology of vague entities.

I conclude that the supervaluationary account is indeed superior to the ontological account and provides us with a powerful way out of the Fregean dilemma. Vagueness is not incompatible with the normativity of logic, but only with the presumptions underlying the ordinary semantics for classical logic.[19]

Notes

1 See Bellow [1964], pp. 295–296.
2 For a history of the paradox and its numerous variants, see Sainsbury & Williamson [1997] and Keefe & Smith [1997].
3 Frege [1903], §56.
4 Dummett [1995], p. 207.
5 In Sorensen [1985].
6 Tye [1990], p. 535.
7 The phrase is from Sylvan & Hyde [1993], p. 19.
8 Mehlberg [1958], p. 257.
9 Fuzzy logic can be traced back to Zadeh's fuzzy set theory [1965]. A representative application to vagueness is Machina [1976].
10 See Wright [1975].
11 See e.g. Fine [1975] and Lewis [1986].
12 Lewis [1993], p. 22.
13 In Collins & Varzi [2000] a different line of argument is considered to the effect that *some* vague terms cannot be precisified. However, the terms in question are rather special, so I will ignore that complication in the present context.
14 The *locus classicus* is Smullyan [1948].
15 See Lewis [1988].

16 See Evans [1978]. Similar arguments can be found in Salmon [1981], pp. 243–246, Wiggins [1986], and Pelletier [1989].

17 See Fine [1975] for details.

18 This line of response is detailed in McGee and McLaughlin [1995]. My own account is in Varzi [1999].

19 The last two sections of this paper draw in part from material originally presented in Varzi [2001].

References

Bellow, S., 1964, *Herzog*, New York, Viking Press.

Collins, J., and Varzi, A. C., 2000, 'Unsharpenable Vagueness', *Philosophical Topics* 28: 1–10.

Dummett, M., 1995, 'Bivalence and Vagueness', *Theoria* 61: 201–216.

Evans, G., 1978, 'Can There Be Vague Objects?', *Analysis* 38: 208.

Fine, K., 1975, 'Vagueness, Truth and Logic', *Synthese* 30: 265–300.

Frege, G., 1903, *Grundgesetze der Arithmetik, begriffsschriftlich abgeleitet*, Band II, Jena, Pohle; partial Eng. trans. in *Translations from the Philosophical Writings of Gottlob Frege*, ed. by P. T. Geach and M. Black, Oxford: Blackwell, 1952, pp. 21–41.

Keefe, R., and Smith, P., 1997, 'Introduction: Theories of Vagueness', in R. Keefe and P. Smith (eds.), *Vagueness: A Reader*, Cambridge (MA) and London: MIT Press, pp. 1–57.

Lewis, D. K., 1986, *On the Plurality of Worlds*, Oxford: Blackwell.

Lewis, D. K., 1988, 'Vague Identity: Evans Misunderstood', *Analysis* 48: 128–130.

Lewis, D. K., 1993, 'Many, but Almost One', in J. Bacon, K. Campbell, and L. Reinhardt (eds.), *Ontology, Causality, and Mind*, Cambridge: Cambridge University Press, pp. 23–38.

Machina, K., 1976, 'Truth, Belief, and Vagueness', *Journal of Philosophical Logic* 5: 47–78.

McGee, V., and McLaughlin, B., 1995, 'Distinctions Without a Difference', *Southern Journal of Philosophy* 33 (Suppl.): 203–252.

Mehlberg, H., 1956, *The Reach of Science*, Toronto: Toronto University Press.

Pelletier, F. J., 1989, 'Another Argument Against Vague Objects', *Journal of Philosophy* 86: 481–492.

Sainsbury, M., and Williamson, T., 1997, 'Sorites', in B. Hale and C. Wright (eds.), *A Companion to the Philosophy of Language*, Oxford: Blackwell, pp. 458–484.

Salmon, N. U., 1982, *Reference and Essence*, Oxford: Blackwell.

Smullyan, A. F., 1948, 'Modality and Description', *Journal of Symbolic Logic* 13: 31–37.

Sorensen, R. A., 1985, 'An Argument for the Vagueness of "Vague" ', *Analysis* 27: 134–137.

Sylvan, R. & Hyde, D., 1993, 'Ubiquitous Vagueness without Embarrassment', *Acta Analytica* 10: 7–29.

Tye, M., 1990, 'Vague Objects', *Mind* 99: 535–557.

Varzi, A. C., 1999, *An Essay in Universal Semantics*, Dordrecht: Kluwer.

Varzi, A. C., 2001, 'I confini del Cervino', in V. Fano, M. Stanzione, and G. Tarozzi (eds.), *Prospettive della logica e della filosofia della scienza. Atti del sesto convegno triennale*, Cosenza: Rubbettino, pp. 431–445.

Wiggins, D., 1986, 'On Singling Out an Object Determinately', in P. Pettit and J. McDowell (eds.), *Subject, Thought, and Context*, New York: Oxford University Press, pp. 171–182.

Williamson, T., 1994, *Vagueness*, London: Routledge.

Wright, C., 1975, 'On the Coherence of Vague Predicates', *Synthese* 30: 325–364.

Zadeh, L., 1965, 'Fuzzy Sets', *Information and Control* 8: 338–353.

Chapter 32

Timothy Williamson

VAGUENESS AND IGNORANCE

No one knows whether I'm thin. I'm not clearly thin; I'm not clearly not thin. The word 'thin' is too vague to enable 'TW is thin' to be recognized as true or as false, however accurately my waist is measured and the result compared with vital statistics for the rest of the population. Is this ignorance? Most work on vagueness has taken for granted the answer 'No'. According to it, there is nothing here to be known. I am just a borderline case of thinness; 'TW is thin' is neither true nor false. Doubt will be cast on the coherence of this view. There are standard objections to the alternative that 'TW is thin' is either unknowably true or unknowably false. Doubt will be cast on them too. For all we know, vagueness is a kind of ignorance.

I

Why doubt the majority view? Well, suppose that 'TW is thin' is neither true nor false. If I were thin, 'TW is thin' would be true; since it isn't, I'm not. But if I'm not thin, 'TW is not thin' is true, and so 'TW is thin' false. The supposition seems to contradict itself. Yet on the majority view it is true.

To generalize the argument, consider a language L with negation (~), disjunction (∨), conjunction (&) and a biconditional (↔). Extend L to a metalanguage for L by adding a truth predicate (T) for sentences of L and quotation marks ('...') for naming them. The falsity of a

sentence of L is identified with the truth of its negation. Thus the supposition at issue, the denial of bivalence for a sentence of L, is equivalent to the denial that either it or its negation is true:

(1) $\sim[T ('P') \vee T ('\sim P')]$

Two instances of Tarski's disquotational schema for truth are:

(2a) $T('P') \leftrightarrow P$
(2b) $T('\sim P') \leftrightarrow \sim P$

The argument uses (2a) and (2b) to substitute their right-hand sides for their left-hand sides in (1):

(3) $\sim[P \vee \sim P]$

It then applies one of De Morgan's laws to (3), giving

(4) $\sim P \& \sim \sim P$

This is a contradiction, whether or not the double negation is eliminated. Thus (1) reduces to absurdity. In effect, one uses Tarski's schema to equate bivalence ($T('P') \vee T('\sim P')$) with the law of excluded middle ('P ∨ ~ P'), and then argues from the incoherence of denying the latter to the incoherence of denying the former.[1]

The argument does not purport to show that bivalence must be asserted, only that it must not be denied. Whether bivalence must be asserted will depend on whether the law of excluded middle must be asserted, an issue which has not been addressed. Even so, the argument may seem to prove too much. Can every denial of bivalence be reduced to absurdity? However, the argument applies not whenever bivalence is denied, but only when it is denied of a particular sentence. It does not touch intuitionism in mathematics, for example. Although intuitionists deny the general principle of bivalence, they are forbidden to give particular counterexamples, just because the inference from (1) to (4) is intuitionistically valid.[2] They sometimes refrain from asserting the bivalence of a particular sentence, but they never deny it. This does not undermine their denial of the general principle, for 'Not every sentence is bivalent' does not intuitionistically entail 'Some sentence is not bivalent'. Vagueness is a different matter. Vague sentences are supposed to be obviously not bivalent in borderline cases, and the usual way of evoking this sense of obviousness is by vivid descriptions of particular examples. If it is obvious that not all vague sentences are bivalent, it is obvious that 'TW is thin' is not bivalent. So if one must not deny the bivalence of 'TW is thin', does vagueness give any reason to deny bivalence in general?[3]

The core of the argument is its use of Tarski's disquotational schema for truth; everything else is relatively uncontroversial.[4] At first sight, it looks vulnerable to an obvious objection. If P is neither true nor false, should not T('P') be simply false? But then the left-hand sides of (2a) and (2b) but not their right-hand sides would be false; on a strong reading of the biconditional this would make (2a) and (2b) not true. This is just what one might say in the case of reference failure. Consider, for example, a context where 'this dagger' fails to pick anything out. One might hold that no sentence in which 'this dagger' is used is true in the context. Thus neither 'This dagger is sharp' nor 'This dagger is not

sharp' is true, so 'This dagger is sharp' is neither true nor false. By the same principle, the Tarskian biconditional ' "This dagger is sharp" is true if and only if this dagger is sharp' would not be true in the context, for it uses as well as mentions 'this dagger'. The argument has no force in the case of reference failure; why should it have any force in the case of vagueness?

On the suggested treatment of reference failure, 'This dagger is sharp' says nothing that could have been true or false, and even counterfactuals such as 'If the servants had been assiduous, this dagger would have been sharp' are neither true nor false (of course, the sentence type 'This dagger is sharp' could have been used in a different context to say something true or false). According to the parallel treatment of a vague sentence in a borderline case, 'TW is thin' says nothing that could have been true or false, and even conterfactuals such as 'If he had dieted, TW would have been thin' are neither true nor false.[5] Such consequences are unwelcome. Unlike 'This dagger is sharp', 'TW is thin' could have said something true without saying something different. Most simply, 'TW is thin' means that TW is thin; on the suggested treatment, ' "This dagger is sharp" means that this dagger is sharp' is neither true nor false, for 'this dagger' is used, not mentioned, on its second occurrence. But since 'TW is thin' means that TW is thin, what it is for 'TW is thin' to be true is just for TW to be thin. Similarly, since 'TW is not thin' means that TW is not thin, what it is for 'TW is not thin' to be true, and so for 'TW is thin' to be false, is just for TW not to be thin.[6] The difference between reference failure (as treated above) and vagueness favours the Tarskian biconditionals in the latter case.[7] In doing so, it undermines the thought that 'TW is thin' is neither true nor false, i.e. (1), by vindicating the argument from it to (4).

We can consistently deny bivalence of a sentence with reference failure precisely because in doing so we abjure the use, embedded or unembedded, of that sentence in that context. If we are not willing to abjure the use, embedded or unembedded, of a vague sentence in the context of borderline cases, we cannot consistently deny its bivalence. According to a sceptical view, rigour demands that we should abjure such uses because vagueness is itself a kind of reference failure. Adjectives refer, if at all, to sharply defined properties, but a vague one like 'thin' fails to single out such a property and so fails to refer; sentences of the form '*a* is thin' say, strictly, nothing, whether or not *a* is a borderline case. Since almost all our utterances involve vague terms, this view makes almost all of them mere noise. They are not even failed attempts to express thoughts, since parallel considerations would suggest that almost all our concepts are equally contentless.[8] The only consistent expression of such a view is in silence.[9]

Once we are permitted to use 'thin', we can argue that 'TW is thin' says something that would have been true in various circumstances, because I would have been thin. Then ' "TW is thin" is true if and only if TW is thin' says something too. But if it says anything, it is true. For, given that 'TW is thin' means that TW is thin, what more could it take for 'TW is thin' to be true than for TW to be thin?

To deny bivalence for vague sentences while continuing to use them is to adopt an unstable position. The denial of bivalence amounts to a rejection of the practice of using them. One is rejecting the practice while continuing to engage in it. Rapid alternation between perspectives inside and outside the practice can disguise, but not avoid, this hypocrisy.

II

If one cannot deny bivalence for vague sentences, can one deny something like it? There is a standard move at this point. Instead of saying that 'TW is thin' is neither true nor false, one says that it is neither *definitely* true nor *definitely* false. Definite truth does not itself obey the disquotational schema, otherwise nothing would

have been gained. It takes less for 'TW is thin' not to be definitely true than for TW not to be thin. Since it does not take less for 'TW is thin' not to be true than for TW not to be thin, truth is not the same thing as definite truth. On pain of the argument in section I, this new position does not involve a denial of bivalence. Indeed, the principle of bivalence does not mention definiteness; it merely says that a sentence is either true or false. On the face of it, the claim that a sentence is neither definitely true nor definitely false has no more to do with bivalence than the claim that it is neither necessarily true nor necessarily false, or that it is neither obviously true nor obviously false.[10] To pursue indirect connections would be premature.

Before one can assess the claim that vague sentences are neither definitely true nor definitely false in borderline cases, one needs to know what it means. That the adverb 'definitely' has been given a clear relevant sense is less than obvious. If 'definitely true' were just a circumlocution for 'true', no problem would arise, but the view under consideration requires the two expressions to have quite different senses. Can 'definitely' be explained in other terms, or are we supposed to grasp it as primitive? No doubt 'TW is thin' is definitely true if and only if TW is definitely thin, but what is the difference between being thin and being definitely thin? Is it like the difference between being thin and being very thin? Again, 'TW is thin' is presumably not definitely true if and only if TW is not definitely thin; what is the difference between not being thin and not being definitely thin?[11]

Let it be obvious that 'TW is thin' is neither definitely true nor definitely false. In reporting this obvious truth, the philosopher has no right to stipulate a theoretical sense for 'definitely'. Rather, it must be used in a sense expressive of what is obvious. Yet what is *obvious* is just that vague sentences are sometimes neither knowably true nor knowably false. The simplest hypothesis is that this is the *only* sense in which the vague sentences are neither definitely true nor definitely false. Bivalence and classical logic hold. Either I'm thin and 'TW is thin' is true or I'm not thin and 'TW is thin' is false; we have no way of knowing which. Although this is not at all the standard view of what 'definitely' means, the obscurity of the standard view gives us reason to explore alternatives. The epistemic view is usually held to be inconsistent with obvious facts, but the leading candidate for such a fact—the failure of bivalence—has already disappeared. The rest of the paper explores the epistemic view.[12]

III

Many descriptions of vagueness rule out the epistemic view from the start. A term is said to be vague only if it can have a borderline case, and a case is said to be borderline only if our inability to decide it does not depend on ignorance. But to assume that the cases ordinarily called 'borderline' are borderline in this technical sense is just to beg the question against the epistemic view. For example, 'TW is thin' would ordinarily be called a 'borderline' case, but one should not assume without argument that our inability to decide the matter does not depend on ignorance. Of what fact could we be ignorant? There is an obvious answer: we are ignorant either of the fact that TW is thin or of the fact that TW is not thin (our ignorance prevents us from knowing which). If that is a bad answer, it has yet to be explained why. That it uses the word 'thin' is just what one would expect in the light of section I. There is no general requirement that vague words be definable in other terms.

Those wholly predictable opening moves against the epistemic view mismanage a deeper objection. It can be made using the idea that vague facts *supervene* on precise ones. If two possible situations are identical in all precise respects, they are identical in all vague respects too. For example, if x and y have exactly the same physical measurements, x is thin if and only if y is thin. More generally:

(*) If x has exactly the same physical measurements in a possible situation s as y has in a possible situation t, x is thin in s if and only if y is thin in t.[13]

The objection to the epistemic view can now be formulated. Let my exact physical measurements be m. According to the epistemic view, I am either thin or not thin. By (*), if I am thin, necessarily anyone with physical measurements m is thin. Similarly, if I am not thin, necessarily no one with physical measurements m is thin. Thus either being thin is a necessary consequence of having physical measurements m, or not being thin is. Suppose that I find out, as I can, what my physical measurements are. I would then seem to be in a position either to deduce that I am thin or to deduce that I am not thin. But it has already been conceded that no amount of measuring will enable me to decide whether I am thin.[14]

The basis of this objection to the epistemic view is not that one can know all the relevant facts in a case ordinarily classified as 'borderline' but that one can know a set of facts on which all the relevant facts supervene, without being able to decide the case. Unlike the first claim, the second does not beg the question against the epistemic view. The epistemic theorist has as much reason as anyone else to accept supervenience claims like (*). However, the objection commits a subtler fallacy.

The kind of possibility and necessity at issue in supervenience claims like (*) is metaphysical. There *could not be* two situations differing vaguely but not precisely. Suppose that I am in fact thin. By (*), it is metaphysically necessary that anyone with physical measurements m is thin. If I know that I have physical measurements m, in order to deduce that I am thin I must *know* that anyone with physical measurements m is thin. The plausibility of the objection to the epistemic view thus depends on something like the inference that since the supervenience generalizations are metaphysically necessary, they can be known *a priori*. The inference from metaphysical necessity to *a priori* knowability may be a tempting one: but, as Kripke has emphasized, it is fallacious. Indeed, metaphysical necessities cannot be assumed to be knowable in any way at all, otherwise all mathematical truths could be assumed knowable. It is integral to the epistemic view that metaphysically necessary claims like 'Anyone with physical measurements *m* is thin' can be as unknowable as physically contingent ones like 'TW is thin'.

One should not be surprised that the known supervenience of *A*-facts on *B*-facts does not provide a route from knowledge of *B*-facts to knowledge of *A*-facts. A more familiar case is the supervenience of mental facts on physical facts. Suppose, for the sake of illustration, that bravery is known to supervene on the state of the brain. Then if *s* is a maximally specific brain state (described in physical terms) of brave Jones, it is metaphysically necessary that anyone in brain state *s* is brave. Clearly, however, there is no presumption that one could have found out that Jones was brave simply by measuring his brain state and invoking supervenience. 'Anyone in brain state *s* is brave' cannot be known *a priori* Perhaps one can know it *a posteriori*, because one can find out that someone is brave by observing his behaviour, then combine this knowledge with knowledge of his brain state and of the supervenience of mental states on brain states. 'Anyone with physical measurements *m* is thin' cannot be known *a posteriori* in a parallel way, for no route to independent knowledge of someone with physical measurements *m* that he is thin corresponds to the observation of brave behaviour.

The epistemic view of vagueness is consistent with the supervenience of vague facts on precise ones. The next section considers a different objection to the epistemic view, and makes another application of the concept of supervenience.

IV

A common complaint against the epistemic view of vagueness is that it severs a necessary connection between meaning and use. Words mean what they do because we use them as we do; to postulate a fact of the matter in borderline cases is to suppose, incoherently, that the meanings of our words draw lines where our use of them does not. The point is perhaps better put at the level of complete speech acts, in terms of sentences rather than single words. The meaning of a declarative sentence may provisionally be identified with its truth conditions, and its use with our dispositions to assent to and dissent from it. The complaint is that the epistemic view of vagueness sets truth conditions floating unacceptably free of our dispositions to assent and dissent.

So far, the complaint is too general to be convincing. If our dispositions to assent to or to dissent from the sentence 'That is water' do not discriminate between H_2O and XYZ, it does not follow that the truth conditions of the sentence are equally undiscriminating. What needs to be emphasized is that there is no sharp natural division for the truth conditions of 'He is thin' to follow corresponding to the sharp natural division between H_2O and XYZ followed by the truth conditions of 'That is water'. The idea is that if nature does not draw a line for us, a line is drawn only if we draw it ourselves, by our use. So there is no line, for our use leaves not a line but a smear.

Before we allow the revised complaint to persuade us, we should probe its conception of drawing a line. On the face of it, 'drawing' is just a metaphor for 'determining'. To say that use determines meaning is just to say that meaning *supervenes* on use. That is: same use entails same meaning, so no difference in meaning without a difference in use. More formally:

(#) If an expression *e* is used in a possible situation *s* in the same way as an expression f is used in a possible situation t, *e* has the same meaning in *s* as f has in t.

There are various problems with (#), such as its

neglect of the environment as a constitutive factor in meaning and its crude notion of 'used in the same way'. However, some refinement of (#) will be assumed for the sake of argument to be correct. For the epistemic view of vagueness is quite consistent with (#) and its refinements. Although the view does not permit simple-minded reductions of meaning to use, it in no way entails the possibility of a difference in meaning without any corresponding difference in use. Had 'TW is thin' had different truth conditions, our dispositions to assent to and dissent from it would have been different too.

Our use determines many lines. Of these one of the least interesting is the line at which assent becomes more probable than dissent. It is no more plausible a candidate for the line between truth and falsity than is the line at which assent becomes unanimous. The study of vagueness has regrettably served as the last refuge of the consensus theory of truth; the theory is no more tenable for vague sentences than it is for precise ones. We can be wrong even about whether someone is thin, for we can be wrong both about that person's shape and size and about normal shapes and sizes in the relevant comparison class. These errors may be systematic; some people may characteristically look thinner or less thin than they actually are, and there may be characteristic misconceptions about the prevalence of various shapes and sizes. To invoke perfect information or epistemically ideal situations at this point is merely to swamp normal speakers of English with more measurements and statistics than they can handle. Perhaps an epistemically ideal speaker of English would be an infallible guide to thinness, but then such a speaker might know the truth value of 'TW is thin'. If one sticks to actual speakers of English, there is no prospect of reducing the truth conditions of vague sentences to the statistics of assent and dissent, whether or not one accepts the epistemic view of vagueness.

The failure of simple-minded reductions is quite consistent with supervenience. There may

be a subtler connection, perhaps of a causal kind, between the property of thinness and our use of 'thin'. Even if everything has or lacks the property, the reliability of our mechanism for recognizing it may depend on its giving neither a positive nor a negative response in marginal cases. The cost of having the mechanism answer in such cases would be many wrong answers. It is safer to have a mechanism that often gives no answer than one that often gives the wrong answer. From such a mechanism, one might be able to work back to the property, through the question 'Which property does this mechanism best register?'.[15]

It might be objected that if a mechanism sometimes gives no response, there will be distinct properties p and q such that both are present when it responds positively, both are absent when it responds negatively, but sometimes one is present and the other absent when it does not respond, and that since it is equally good at registering p and q, and no better at registering any other property, the question 'Which property does this mechanism best register?' has no unique answer. This objection ignores the statistical nature of reliability. The mechanism cannot be expected to register any distal property infallibly; since its functioning depends on the state of the subject as well as on the state of the environment, no distal property will be present whenever there is a positive response and absent whenever there is a negative one.[16] Reliability is a matter of minimizing a non-zero probability of error; for all that has been shown, just one property may do that.[17]

A subject whose primary access to a property is through a recognitional mechanism may not be helped to detect it by extra information of a kind which cannot be processed by that mechanism, even if the new information is in fact a reliable indicator of the presence of the property—for the subject may not know that. My exact measurements may in fact be a sufficient condition for thinness, and knowledge of the former still not enable us to derive knowledge of the latter; for all that, thinness may be the property best registered by our perceptual recognitional capacity for thinness.

The foregoing speculations should not mislead one into supposing that a causal theory of reference is essential to an epistemic view of vagueness. They illustrate only one way in which our use of a vague expression might determine a sharp property. A comprehensive account of the connection between meaning and use would no doubt be very different. Since no one knows what such an account would be like, the epistemic view of vagueness should not be singled out for its failure to provide one. No reason has emerged to think that it makes such an account harder to provide. At the worst, there may be no account to be had, beyond a few vague salutary remarks. Meaning may supervene on use in an unsurveyably chaotic way.

V

The charge against the epistemic view of vagueness might be revised. If the view does not force what we mean to transcend what we *do*, perhaps it forces what we mean to transcend what we *know*. The new charge is as obscure as the old one, but may be worth exploring.

A cautious answer is that the epistemic view of vagueness allows us to know what we mean. No gap need open between what we mean and what we think we mean, for both are determined in the same way, perhaps that described in section IV. We know that 'TW is tall' as we use it means that, and is true if and only if, TW is tall. If we cannot know whether TW is tall, who but the verificationist thought that actual knowledge of truth conditions requires possible knowledge of truth value?

It may be replied that the epistemic view makes us ignorant of the sense of a vague term, not just of its reference. Of course we do not know where all the thin things are in physical space; the point is that we should not even know where they all are in conceptual space. We

should be using a term that does in fact determine a line in conceptual space without being able to locate that line. We should understand it partially, as one partially understands a word one has heard used once or twice. But in the latter case the word's meaning is backed by other speakers' full understanding, whereas no one is allowed full understanding of the vague term. The objection to the epistemic view is that it attributes partial understanding to the speech community as a whole. It is not entitled to say that we know what we mean. It attributes to the community incomplete knowledge of a complete meaning; would it not be more reasonable to attribute complete knowledge of an incomplete meaning?

The objection is based on the Fregean model of the sense of a term as a region in conceptual space: to grasp a sense is to know where its boundary runs. Individual points in this space are located by means of precise descriptions such as 'having exact physical measurements m'. Thus the demand that one know which points are in the region marked off by a vague term such as 'thin' is simply the demand that one know truths such as 'Anyone having exact physical measurements m is thin' or 'No one having exact physical measurements m is thin'. The unreasonableness of that demand was already noted in section III; the metaphysical necessity of such truths does not justify the demand to know them. The metaphor of conceptual space adds no force to the demand. Rather, its function is illicitly to collapse distinctions between concepts whose equivalence is metaphysically necessary but not *a priori*. If a proposition is identified with a region in a space of possible worlds, cognitively significant distinctions are lost in a familiar way; exactly the same happens when the objection identifies a sense with a region in conceptual space.

On the epistemic view, our understanding of vague terms is not partial. The measure of full understanding is not possession of a complete set of metaphysically necessary truths but complete induction into a practice. When I have heard a word used only once or twice, my understanding is partial because there is more to the community's use of it than I yet know. I have not got fully inside the practice; I am to some extent still an outsider. It does not follow that if we had all understood the term in the vague way I do, all our understandings would have been partial, though they would still have determined complete intensions.[18] In that counterfactual situation, we should all have been insiders. To know what a word means is to be completely inducted into a practice that does in fact determine a complete intension.

That rather minimalist answer to the objection is enough. However, a more speculative line of thought may be mentioned. If meaning supervenes on use, might it also supervene on knowledge? The idea can be developed. Let the *verification conditions* of a sentence be those in which its truth conditions knowably obtain, and its *falsification conditions* be those in which its truth conditions knowably fail to obtain. A kind of supervenience claim quite consistent with the epistemic view of vagueness is:

(@) If two sentences have the same verification conditions and the same falsification conditions, they have the same truth conditions.

(@) claims a supervenience of truth conditions on verification and falsification conditions. It no more identifies truth conditions with verification conditions than it identifies them with falsification conditions. In general, (@) is probably too strong. For example, there may be a sentence whose truth conditions cannot be known to obtain and cannot be known not to obtain; it would have the same verification conditions and falsification conditions as its negation, but not the same truth conditions. However, ordinary vague sentences are not like that. (@) might hold for them. In fact a formal version of (@) can be proved for a simple modal logic in which 'necessity' is interpreted as knowability, truth

does not entail knowability, and the underlying propositional logic is classical.[19]

(@) will not satisfy reductionist aspirations, for the truth conditions are used in characterizing the verification and falsification conditions. But that is a problem for the reductionist aspirations, not for the epistemic view of vagueness. What the consistency of (@) with the epistemic view shows is that the latter does not force what we mean to transcend what we know, if the purport of the charge is that the epistemic view would not allow truth conditions to supervene on the conditions in which they can be known to obtain or not to obtain.

VI

Little has been said to explain our ignorance in borderline cases. Of course, ignorance might be taken as the normal state: perhaps we should think of knowledge as impossible unless special circumstances make it possible, rather than as possible unless special circumstances make it impossible. However, we may be able to do better than that in the case at hand.

Consider again the supervenience of meaning on use, at least for a fixed contribution from the environment. For any difference in meaning, there is a difference in use. The converse does not always hold. The meaning of a word may be stabilized by natural divisions, so that a small difference in use would make no difference in meaning. A slightly increased propensity to call fool's gold 'gold' would not change the meaning of the word 'gold'. But the meaning of a vague word is not stabilized by natural divisions in this way. A slight shift in our dispositions to call things 'thin' would slightly shift the meaning of 'thin'. On the epistemic view, the boundary of 'thin' is sharp but unstable. Suppose that I am on the 'thin' side of the boundary, but only just. If our use of 'thin' had been very slightly different, as it easily could have been, I would have been on the 'not thin' side. The sentence 'TW is thin' is true, but could easily have been false.[20] Moreover, someone who utters it assertively could easily have done so falsely, for the decision to utter it was not sensitive to all the slight shifts in the use of 'thin' that would make the utterance false.

The point is not confined to public language. Even idiolects are vague. You may have no settled disposition to assent to or dissent from 'TW is thin'. If you were forced to go one way or the other, which way you went would depend on your circumstances and mood. If you assented, that would not automatically make the sentence true in your idiolect; if you dissented, that would not automatically make it false. What you mean by 'thin' does not change with every change in your circumstances and mood. The extension of a term in your idiolect depends on the whole pattern of your use in a variety of circumstances and moods: you have no way of making each part of your use perfectly sensitive to the whole, for you have no way of surveying the whole. To imagine away this sprawling quality of your use is to imagine away its vagueness.[21]

An utterance of 'TW is thin' is not the outcome of a disposition to be reliably right: it is right by luck. It can therefore hardly be an expression of knowledge. Contrapositively, an utterance of 'TW is thin' is an expression of knowledge only if I am some way from the boundary of 'thin', that is, only if anyone with physical measurements very close to mine is also thin. More generally, for a given way of measuring difference in physical measurements there will be a small but non-zero constant c such that:

(!)   If x and y differ in physical measurements by less than c and x is known to be thin, y is thin.

Similar principles can be formulated for other vague terms. Vague knowledge requires a margin for error.

Given (!), one cannot know a conjunction of the form 'x is thin and y is not thin' when x and y differ in physical measurements by less than c. To

know the conjunction, one would have to know its first conjunct; but then by (!) its second conjunct would be false, making the whole conjunction false and therefore unknown. Since such conjunctions cannot be known, the unwary may suppose that they cannot be true. 'Thin' will then look as though it is governed by a tolerance principle of the form: if x and y differ in physical measurements by less than c and x is thin, y is thin. One can now construct a sorites paradox by considering a series of men, the first very thin, the last very fat, and each differing from the next in physical measurements by less than c: by repeated applications of the tolerance principle, since the first man is thin, so is the last man. Fortunately, 'thin' is not governed by the tolerance principle: it is governed by the margin for error principle (!), which generates no sorites paradox.[22]

The plausibility of (!) does not depend on the epistemic view of vagueness. Its rationale is that reliable truth is a necessary (perhaps not sufficient) condition of knowledge, and that a vague judgement is reliably true only if it is true in sufficiently similar cases. This point does not require the judgement to be true or false in every case. But once our uncertainty has been explained in terms of the independently plausible principle (!), it no longer provides a reason for not asserting bivalence, for bivalence is quite compatible with (!).

VII

The most obvious argument for the epistemic view of vagueness has so far not been mentioned. The epistemic view involves no revision of classical logic and semantics; its rivals do involve such revisions. Classical logic and semantics are vastly superior to the alternatives in simplicity, power, past success, and integration with theories in other domains. In these circumstances it would be sensible to adopt the epistemic view in order to retain classical logic and semantics even if it were subject to philosophical criticisms in which we could locate no fallacy; not every anomaly falsifies a theory.[23] Although that second line of defence exists, there is no need to occupy it if the argument of this paper is correct, for we can locate the fallacies in philosophical criticisms of the epistemic view of vagueness.

Notes

1   Tarski derives bivalence (which he calls 'the principle of excluded middle') from his definition of truth (rather than the disquotational schema) as Theorem 2 of his 1931 'The concept of truth in formalized languages'; see his *Logic, Semantics, Metamathematics*, tr. J.H. Woodger (2nd ed., Indianapolis: Hackett, 1983): 197. The proof uses the law of excluded middle (in the present sense).

2   The intuitionist is assumed here to equate 'true' with 'provable' rather than with 'proved'.

3   The sorites paradox might move some to deny that all sentences of the form 'n grains make a heap' are bivalent, but not to deny bivalence for any particular n (although for some n they would refrain from asserting it). If the argument in the text is sound, the supposedly obvious assumptions which might drive one to this view are false.

4   A general setting for the argument is as follows. There is a partial ordering $\leq$ of the semantic values assigned to sentences (e.g. truth values) under which they form a lattice, i.e. each pair of values has a greatest lower bound (glb) and a least upper bound (lub), greater values being thought of as 'truer'. If $|P|$ is the semantic value assigned to P, $|P \& Q| = \text{glb} \{|P|, |Q|\}$, $|P \lor Q| = \text{lub} \{|P|, |Q|\}$ and if $P \leq Q$ then $|\sim Q| \leq |\sim P|$. These assumptions are met by standard classical, supervaluational, intuitionist and many-valued treatments and others. Now suppose that $|P| = |T('P')|$ and $|\sim P| = |T('\sim P')|$. Then $|P| = |T('P')| \leq \text{lub} \{|T('P')|, |T('\sim P')|\} = |T('P') \lor T('\sim P')|$; similarly, $|T('\sim P')| \leq |T('P') \lor T('\sim P')|$. Thus $|\sim [T('P') \lor T('P')]| \leq |\sim P|$ and $|\sim [T('P') \lor T('\sim P')]| \leq |\sim\sim P|$, so $|(1)| \leq \text{glb} \{|\sim P|, |\sim\sim P|\}\} = |(4)|$. Thus what is needed is a defence of Tarski's schema which assigns the same semantic value to each side of the bicondi-

tional; this is supplied in the text. Two further assumptions are that P has a negation whose falsity is equivalent to the truth of P and that a contradiction is indeed absurd. The former is clearly correct for 'TW is thin', which is enough for the argument. As for the latter, if the denial of bivalence for vague sentences is obviously correct, it does not involve a contradiction (someone might answer the question 'Is TW thin?' with 'He is and he isn't', but it would take a bold man to revise logic on the basis of that idiom).

5   A standard analysis of 'If he had dieted, TW would have been thin' is assumed, on which it results from feeding 'He [or TW] dieted' and 'TW is thin' into a counterfactual conditional.

6   A homophonic truth theory is thus not essential to the argument; the translatability of P and $\sim$P into the metalanguage is enough, as Tarski noted. Incidentally, it is not claimed that a Tarskian theory tells the whole truth about truth, just that it tells an essential part of the truth. Without a disquotational schema, it is doubtful that one has a truth predicate at all.

7   The supervaluational treatment of vagueness, most systematically expounded by Kit Fine in 'Vagueness, truth and logic', *Synthese* 30 (1975): 265–300, may seem an obvious counterexample to the argument in the text from failure of bivalence to failure of excluded middle. However, Fine allows a Tarskian truth predicate 'true$_T$'; he argues that it is conceptually prior to the ordinary truth predicate 'true', because 'x is true' is to be defined by 'Definitely (x is true$_T$)'; 'true' is not subject to the Tarskian schema (296–7; compare S. Kripke, 'Outline of a theory of truth', *Journal of Philosophy* 72 (1975): 690–716, at 715). Since Fine's account validates the law of excluded middle, it validates bivalence for the primary notions of truth and falsity. Where the present approach differs is in its claim that the ordinary notion of truth is subject to the Tarskian schema and is therefore not to be defined in Fine's way. The 'definitely' operator is discussed in section II. In *The Logical Basis of Metaphysics* (London: Duckworth, 1991) Michael Dummett argues that the ordinary notion of truth for a vague language is the non-Tarskian one because only it is 'objective' in the sense that 'every sentence determinately either does or does not possess it'

(74). This condition is not self-evident, not least because it is inconsistent with second-order vagueness. The disquotational schema is endorsed for a vague language by K. Machina. 'Truth, belief and vagueness', *Journal of Philosophical Logic* 5 (1976): 47–78, at 75; C.A.B. Peacocke, 'Are vague predicates incoherent?', *Synthese* 46 (1981): 121–41, at 136–7 (both within theories of degrees of truth); R.M. Sainsbury, 'Concepts without boundaries' (inaugural lecture at King's College London, 1990).

8   Even the intention to express some thought or other harbours vagueness.

9   The classic expression of a sceptical view is section 56 of Frege's *Grundgesetze der Arithmetik*, vol. II. The more limited sceptical view that observational predicates are vague in such a way as to be incoherent is discussed in my *Identity and Discrimination* (Oxford: Blackwell, 1990): 88–103; in effect section VI below explains how the incoherent principle 'If *x* and *y* are indiscriminable by the naked eye, *x* is thin if and only if *y* is thin' could look true while being false.

10   For a contrary view see Dummett (op. cit.): 74–82.

11   There are views on which 'definitely' makes a difference only in the scope of negation and in similar contexts. I also assume that the reference of 'TW' is unproblematic.

12   The epistemic view probably goes back to the Stoic logician Chrysippus, a man with some claim to have discovered the classical propositional calculus: see J. Barnes, 'Medicine, experience and logic', in J. Barnes, J. Brunschwig, M.F. Burnyeat and M. Schofield, eds., *Science and Speculation* (Cambridge: Cambridge University Press, 1982) and M.F. Burnyeat, 'Gods and heaps', in M. Schofield and M.C. Nussbaum, eds., *Language and Logos* (Cambridge: Cambridge University Press, 1982). More recently, it has been defended in J. Cargile, 'The sorites paradox', *British Journal for the Philosophy of Science* 20 (1969): 193–202; R. Campbell, 'The sorites paradox', *Philosophical Studies* 26 (1974): 175–91; R.A. Sorensen, *Blindspots* (Oxford: Clarendon Press, 1988): 217–52; P. Horwich, *Truth* (Oxford: Blackwell, 1990): 81–7; T. Williamson (op. cit.): 103–8. It is critically discussed in M. Heller, *The Ontology of Physical Objects* (Cambridge: Cambridge University Press, 1990): 89–106. D. Sperber and D. Wilson,

'Loose talk', *Proceedings of the Aristotelian Society* 86 (1985/6): 153–71, retain classical logic and semantics while explaining vague utterances in pragmatic terms. 'He is bald', said of a man with just one hair on his head, being false but relevantly informative; a generalization of this view from 'bald' to 'heap' might need to postulate ignorance.

13   More accurately, one's thinness may depend on the physical measurements of one's comparison class as well as on one's own. This does not affect the point about to be made.

14   Exercise: how does this argument fare against the supervaluational approach?

15   A more teleological question would be 'Which property did this mechanism evolve to register?'. Considerations like those in the text would still apply.

16   Why consider distal properties rather than proximal ones? This is a general but not unanswerable question for causal theories of reference; it is not a special problem for the epistemic view of vagueness.

17   If several properties tie for first place, the obvious candidate is their conjunction (even if it is not itself one of them).

18   My deference to speakers with fuller understanding may be excluded from the counterfactual situation. Think of an intension as a function from possible worlds to extensions.

19   See my 'Verification, falsification and cancellation in KT', *Notre Dame Journal of Formal Logic* 31 (1990): 286–90. The result is consistent with the doubt expressed about ($@$), since it cannot automatically be lifted to extensions of the language.

20   The point is not that I might easily not have been thin. In the relevant counterfactual situations, my physical measurements are just what they actually are, but 'thin' means something slightly different from what it actually means.

21   What goes for words in your idiolect also goes for your concepts.

22   (!) might be thought to generate a sorites paradox not for 'thin' but for 'known to be thin', given that (!) is known, that each man in the series is known to differ from the next in physical measurements by less than *c*, and that the very thin man is known to be thin. However, analysis of the argument shows it to require the KK principle that what is

known is known to be known. But since 'known to be thin' is itself vague, it too obeys a margin for error principle, which in turn implies that one can know x to be thin without being in a position to know that one knows that x is thin. Thus the KK principle fails The failure of the KK principle (i.e. the S4 axiom) in the modal logic KT is essential to the result cited at n. 19.

23 For another argument for the epistemic view see *Identity and Discrimination* (op. cit.): 107.

Chapter 33

Delia Graff Fara[*]

SHIFTING SANDS: AN INTEREST-RELATIVE THEORY OF VAGUENESS

[. . .] [M]y main aim in this paper is to give an account of why vague *expressions* seem boundaryless to us. I'll begin by giving a semantic explanation of the phenomenon I want to account for, but will ultimately propose that the semantic explanation has psychological underpinnings. On the account I'll propose, the semantics of vague expressions renders the truth conditions of utterances containing them sensitive to our interests, with the result that vagueness in language has a traceable source in the vagueness of our interests. In the course of providing this account, I'll also explain why our interests can be vague, why it is they can seem tolerant—and hence boundaryless—in a way that leaves their coherence intact. Before proceeding in section III with my own proposal, however, I want to discuss some of the going solutions to the sorites paradox in order to focus ideas.

II Three questions

Not all solutions to the paradox proposed by philosophers are designed to address just the same set of questions. In this section I want to set out some of the different questions the sorites paradox raises and to say which of those questions others have focused on and which of those questions will be my focus here.

I'll say that we have an instance of the sorites paradox when we are confronted with a group of sentences having the following form, each of which seems individually plausible:

(A) Fa

(B) $(\forall x)(\forall y)(Fx \mathbin{\&} Rxy \rightarrow Fy)$

(C) $\neg Fz$

(D) $(\exists b_1 \ \ldots \ b_n)(Rab_1 \mathbin{\&} Rb_1 b_2 \mathbin{\&} \ \ldots \ \mathbin{\&} Rb_{n-1} b_n \mathbin{\&} Rb_n z)$

Here 'F' is to be a vague predicate; a is to be a clear case of the predicate; z is to be a clear non-case; and 'R' is to be replaced with some relation that renders sentences (B) and (D) plausible. So 'F' might be replaced with 'is a tall man'; it might be that a is some professional basketball player and z is some professional jockey; in which case 'R' could stand in for the relation 'is 1 mm taller than', or maybe just 'is the predecessor of in s', where s is some appropriately constructed sorites series. Sentences with the form of (D) then say that *there is* a sorites series of the relevant kind with a as the first member and z as the last.

Since (appropriate instances of) (A–D) seem individually plausible but jointly inconsistent, a first question to address is: what has to give, one or more of (A–D), or their inconsistency? I follow most philosophers in giving up the truth of (B), the sorites sentence.[4] But as soon as one prepares to give up the truth of sorites sentences, a number of new problems arise:

1.   *The Semantic Question.* If the universal

generalization '$(\forall x)(\forall y)(Fx \text{ \& } Rxy \rightarrow Fy)$' is not true, then must this classical equivalent of its negation be true?

The "sharp boundaries" claim: $(\exists x)(\exists y)(Fx \text{ \& } Rxy \text{ \& } \neg Fy)$

(a) If the sharp boundaries claim is true, how is its truth compatible with the fact that vague predicates have borderline cases? For the sharp boundaries claim seems to deny just that.

(b) If the sharp boundaries claim is *not* true, then given that a classical equivalent of its negation is not true either, what revision of classical logic and semantics must be made to accommodate that fact?

2. *The Epistemological Question.* If '$(\forall x)(\forall y)(Fx \text{ \& } Rxy \rightarrow Fy)$' is not true, why are we unable to say which one (or more) of its instances is not true—even when, say if the F in question is 'is a tall man', all the heights of the possible values of x and y are known?

3. *The Psychological Question.* If the universally generalized sorites sentence is not true, why were we so inclined to accept it in the first place? In other words, what is it about vague predicates that makes them seem tolerant, and hence boundaryless to us?

Fine's supervaluationism

Let's first consider an account of the sorites based on a supervaluational treatment of vagueness, like that developed by Kit Fine (1975), according to which a sentence is true (false) just in case it is classically true (false) for all admissible ways of drawing precise boundaries for the vague expressions in the language. On Fine's view, borderline cases lead to truth-value gaps; that is, to be a borderline case of a predicate is to be in neither its extension nor its anti-extension. Although his supervaluation semantics renders sorites sentences false and sharp-boundaries claims true, supervaluationism still affords the following answer to question 1(a) above:

Although sharp-boundaries claims are true, this is compatible with a predicate's having borderline cases—construed as extension gaps—since sharp-boundaries claims for vague predicates, though true, have no true instances.

As it stands, however, Fine's account provides no answers to the Epistemological and Psychological Questions posed above: why are we unable to say which instances of a given sorites sentence are not true; and why were we so inclined to accept the sorites sentence in the first place? With regard to the Epistemological Question, on a truth-value gap approach to vagueness, sorites sentences will typically have a range of untrue instances. Suppose we have an appropriately constructed sorites series for a given vague predicate F, one on which each member of the series is R-related to the next. If we restrict the range of variables to just the members of such a series, then on Fine's account 'Fx & Rxy $\rightarrow$ Fy' will have no truth-value just when either of the values of 'x' and 'y' is in the extension gap of F. (Whenever, that is, 'Rxy' is true). Thus to know which instances of the sorites sentence are untrue is just to know exactly which things on the series are in the extension gap of F. This is something we evidently do not know, and we have no explanation why. Fine's sophisticated treatment of higher-order vagueness does not in any way remedy this situation.[5]

With regard to the Psychological Question, Fine recognizes that there is at least some pressure to explain why, if sorites sentences for vague predicates are false, we are nevertheless so attracted to them. His remarks here are brief, however. I quote those remarks in full:

> I suspect that the temptation to say that [a sorites sentence] is true may have two causes. The first is that the value of a falsifying n appears to be arbitrary. This arbitrariness has nothing to do with vagueness as such. A similar case, but not involving vagueness, is: if n straws do not break a camel's back, then nor do (n + 1) straws. The second cause is what

one might call truth-value shift. This also lies behind LEM. Thus $A \vee \neg A$ holds in virtue of a truth that shifts from disjunct to disjunct for different complete specifications, just as the sentence 'for some n a man with n hairs is bald but a man with $n + 1$ hairs is not' is true for an n that shifts for different complete specifications. (Fine 1975: 286)

It is odd that Fine should cite the *arbitrariness* of the falsifying n as a cause of our temptation to say that a sorites sentence is true. In many cases, we readily acknowledge that a sentence with similar form is not true, or that a "slippery slope" argument is not a good one, despite the arbitrariness of the bad step. That is why the claim "That's the straw that breaks the camel's back" has such metaphorical weight. If I tug your ear once, you may not get angry. If I keep tugging your ear, when it is has long ceased to be funny, you will eventually get angry. There will be some arbitrariness in *which* of the tugs pushes you over the edge, but that in no way leads me to believe that if n ear tugs do not provoke your wrath, then neither will $n + 1$.

The second cited cause of our temptation to accept sorites sentences is a "truth-value shift." Here Fine must mean that we do not recognize sorites sentences as false because their falsity holds in virtue of a falsity that shifts from instance to instance for different complete specifications. One important worry here is that, especially for someone who rejects bivalence, an explanation of why we don't think a sentence is false should not count as an explanation of why we do think that sentence is true. A further but related worry is that the explanation seems tantamount to the claim that we are tempted to accept sorites sentences because we do not recognize supervaluational semantics to be correct. The claim raises a serious methodological question. The project of providing an adequate semantic theory of natural languages is an empirical enterprise. What are we to take as the data of our enterprise? Which are the

phenomena against which we measure our theory for adequacy or correctness? What observed phenomena could prove a theory wrong? One of the main motivations for and attraction of the supervaluationist's theory is that it manages to verify sentences that express "penumbral connections"—such as 'If Jim is taller than Eric, then Jim is tall if Eric is'—where truth-functional theories that admit truth-value gaps do not. But why is our inclination to regard true existential and disjunctive claims as having a corresponding 'which one?' question that has a correct answer given any less weight? Fine seems to think that overall best fit with our intuitions is the best we can hope for in a semantic theory, even when sometimes the fit is not at all good at certain places.[6] Acceptance of bivalence would be one way to accommodate both the penumbral intuition as well as the clear intuition that true existential claims have a true instance. Fine does not consider the question whether acceptance of bivalence might yield an overall best fit.

When I say that Fine's account of vagueness provides an answer only to the first of the three questions I set out above, I do not mean to suggest that the account should for that reason be rejected. Rather, I want to point out that the account addresses some issues but not others, and to emphasize that without supplementation it cannot be regarded as a complete solution to the sorites.

Williamson's epistemicism

Timothy Williamson is another philosopher who thinks that sorites sentences are false, and that sharp-boundaries claims are true. Unlike Fine, however, Williamson accepts bivalence, and so must answer the Semantic Question I posed by accounting for borderline cases in a different way from those philosophers who posit extension gaps for vague predicates. Williamson proposes instead that borderline cases of vague predicates are those things of which it's *unknowable* whether or not they're in the predicate's extension. Williamson aims to make this sort of ignorance plausible by arguing that just as we may have inexact knowledge of the number of people in a crowded stadium, or of the location of what was the top card in a deck after the deck is cut, we may also have inexact knowledge of the meanings of expressions in our own language.[7] We know enough about the meaning of 'is a tall man' to know that any seven-foot tall man is in its extension; we don't know enough to know what the *least* height is that's sufficient for a man to be in its extension.

Williamson's account is well suited to provide an answer to the Epistemological Question I posed precisely because it gives an epistemological answer to the Semantic Question.[8] Given a bivalent semantics for vague predicates, sorites sentences will have exactly one untrue instance.[9] On Williamson's view, inexact knowledge explains why we don't know which instance that is. Still, no answer to the Psychological Question is forthcoming. Even if we accept Williamson's epistemicism, and so come to accept that sorites sentences are false, it still remains a mystery why we were so attracted to them in the first place.

In further developments of his view, Williamson does address the question why we can't even *imagine* discovering the precise location of the boundary for a vague predicate, whereas we could easily imagine discovering the precise number of people in a crowd, or the precise location of a certain card in a deck.[10] Given the sense of *unimaginability* that turns out to be at issue, however, these further developments have no bearing on the present question. The sense in which precise boundaries for vague predicates are argued to be unimaginable is this: when we imagine a sorites series for a vague predicate F, although there is a point in the imagined series that marks the transition from the Fs to the non-Fs, we cannot know where in the imagined series that point is. The source of our ignorance in the face of an imagined series is, as before, inexact knowledge of meaning. So, as before, although we do have an account of why we don't know

where the boundary of F's extension is in an appropriately constructed series (whether imagined or not), we have no account of why we *believe*, of every particular point in the series, that the boundary is not there—why we believe of every point in the series that it does *not* mark the transition from the Fs to the non-Fs, or indeed from the definitely-Fs to things with any other status.

Degrees of truth

I'll have little to say here about approaches to vagueness that adopt *degrees* of truth, but at least a few words are in order. One attraction of degree-theories, I would guess, is that it seems that they provide answers to both the Psychological and Epistemological Questions, while theories that admit of just two or three truth-values do not. Although the details may vary, any proponent of degrees of truth can say that we are inclined to accept sorites sentences as true because each instance of a sorites sentence has at worst a very high degree of truth; we are unable to say exactly which instances of a sorites sentence are less than perfectly true because that would involve locating a boundary in a sorites series between a thing of which F is perfectly true and a thing of which it is only slightly less than perfectly true. The answers seem smooth enough. But in the absence of some substantial philosophical account of what degrees of truth are, we have no reason to accept that it should be both natural and common to mistake high degrees of truth for the highest degree of truth, or to mistake a small difference in degree of truth for no difference in degree of truth.

Context-dependent theories

My purpose in discussing the theories of Fine and Williamson is to contrast them with theories that are designed specifically to address what I'm calling the Psychological Question. A growing number of linguists and philosophers appeal to the *context-dependence* of vague predicates in order to do just that.[11] Hans Kamp, for example, was prompted to reject the supervaluational semantics for vague predicates he developed in "Two Theories about Adjectives" (Kamp 1975) precisely because it remains mysterious on that account why vague predicates seem tolerant to us. On the semantic account of vagueness he later developed in "The Paradox of the Heap" (Kamp 1981), it turns out that vague predicates really are tolerant in the sense that every instance of a sorites sentence really is true. In other words, on the semantics Kamp came to favor, the sentence 'if *x* is tall and *x* is just 1 mm taller than *y*, then *y* is tall' is true, in any context, for any values of '*x*' and '*y*'.[12] In order to block unwanted conclusions, he proposes a radical revision of classical semantics, one that involves the notion of an *incoherent context*, and according to which a false universal generalization may have none but true instances, and on which a false conclusion may sometimes be inferred from true premises by only valid rules of inference. Though I think revisions this radical should be avoided if at all possible, I am in complete sympathy with Kamp's motivation. Since like Sainsbury I take apparent tolerance and boundarylessness—rather than borderline cases—to be the defining features of vagueness, I want an account that is geared to address the Epistemological and Psychological Questions I posed, since in effect, answering both of these questions requires us to explain why vague predicates seem tolerant to us, even though sorites reasoning shows us that they cannot be. I am happy to wait and see what story about borderline cases, and the characteristic hedging responses they provoke, might naturally flow from such an account.

III The bare-bones solution

My solution to the sorites is going to unfold in layers. The first layer is what I call the "bare-bones" account. It is most closely allied with those solutions to the paradox that appeal to

the context-dependence of vague expressions,[13] especially those offered by Kamp (1981) and Soames (1999: chap. 7),[14] but is more neutral than these theories in a number of respects, perhaps most notably the question whether to accept bivalence. Discussion of another crucial respect in which the account is neutral will be postponed until the end of this section.

I'll begin by drawing attention to one commonly noted feature of vague expressions, namely that we can use them with *different standards* on different occasions. Sometimes the variation in standards can be traced to an implicit comparison class. For example, the sentence 'John is rich' might be uttered on one occasion to mean that John is rich *for a philosopher*, while it might be uttered on some different occasion to mean that John is rich *for an executive at Microsoft*. There has not been a great deal of attention paid in philosophical discussions of vagueness to the phenomenon of implicit comparison classes. The inattention is understandable, since making comparison classes explicit does nothing to resolve vagueness: the predicate 'tall for a basketball player' is no less vague than 'tall'. If the variation in the standards of use for vague expressions were always attributable to some variation in implicit comparison class, there would be little point in discussing that variation in the context of the present essay.

But it is not the case that the variation of the standards in use for a vague expression is always attributable to some implicit comparison class. Here is one example that lends some support to the claim. Suppose I am a casting agent auditioning actors for parts in a play. On one day I'm casting for someone to play the role of Yul Brynner, who had absolutely no hair. On a different day I'm casting for someone to play the role of Mikhail Gorbachev, who has some hair, but very little on top. When I turn away auditioners citing as a reason that they are not bald, I may be using different standards for 'bald' on the different days. I may say "Sorry, you're not bald" to an actor when he auditions to play Yul Brynner, and may then say, to that very same man when he auditions on the following day to play Gorbachev, "Yes you look the part; at least you're bald." My sense is that the variation in standard here is not due to a variation in implicit comparison class, since the comparison class implicitly at work in the two cases is the very same one—in each case, I meant 'bald for a man'.

Further argument for the claim that not every variation in standards is attributable to some variation in comparison class requires me to say a bit more about the workings of comparison classes. One point that's often either ignored or missed in discussions of the semantics of adjectives and their implicit or explicit relativization to comparison classes is that being tall for a basketball player, for example, is not just a matter of how your height compares with some *average* height for basketball players. If by some freak and tragic accident all the tall players are killed, so that the average height of basketball players suddenly drops by a fairly large margin, it does not automatically become true to say of the tallest surviving player that he is tall for a basketball player. We can even lament the fact that none of the surviving players is tall for a basketball player.

Looked at another way, if by some freak and tragic accident it comes to be that all and only basketball players are golfers, it does not thereby become true to say that anyone who's tall for a golfer is tall for a basketball player. Whether one is tall for a certain kind depends on what the *typical* height is for things of that kind, and what the typical height is for a kind is not just some function of the heights of its presently existing instances.

What the preceding considerations are intended to show is that relativization to comparison classes is not an extensional phenomenon.[15] Comparison classes do not work just by contributing sets; for one, they need to form a kind. That is why it sounds strange to say that my computer is tall for a thing on my desk, even though it is in fact the tallest thing on my desk. Because the things on my desk don't form a

kind, we have no notion of what a *typical* height is for a thing on my desk.[16]

My argument that not every variation in standards of use for vague expressions can be attributable to a variation in implicit comparison class can now proceed. I'll give an example of a variation in the standards of use for the adjective 'blue' where the only candidate comparison class does not form a kind. The example is a simple one. Suppose I want you to hand me a certain book. If the book in question is colored a very light grayish blue, and it's sitting among a bunch of other books, all of which are colored a very light grayish red, I may say, "Hand me the blue one." If, on the other hand, the book I want is sitting with a bunch of richly colored cobalt blue books, I may say, "Hand me the gray one." I take it that it would be true to say, in the first case, that the book I wanted was blue and, in the second case, that the book I wanted was gray. I also take it that 'gray' and 'blue' are mutually exclusive.

The variation in standards here obviously has something to do with the color of the books in the immediate surroundings of the one I want. But it cannot be that there is an implicit comparison class—one which would have been made explicit by using the expression 'blue for a book in its immediate surroundings'—because the books *in the immediate surroundings* do not form a kind, and so there is no notion of what a *typical* color is for things in that category. Also note that, in large measure, it is *up to me* whether I say 'gray' or 'blue'. I have some leeway and my choice is not completely dictated by the color of the other books lying around.

As a side point, let me add that the reason it sounds strange to say "That's blue for a book" is not that *books* (all of them) don't form a kind. They do. Rather, it sounds strange because, although books form a kind, they come in such a wide array of colors, none of them more standard than the rest, that we have no notion of what a typical color is for a thing of that kind.

Returning to the main thread: we have some

leeway in our standards of use for vague predicates; the variation in standards of use is not always attributable to a variation in comparison class; but still, we cannot use these predicates any old way we like.[17] What are the constraints? First, there are what we may call *clear-case* constraints. For each predicate, there will be only a limited range of cases which it will be permissible to count as positive instances. We can never use the word 'green' in such as way as to apply to the color of the sun. For each predicate there will also be a class of things which it will be mandatory to count as positive instances. No matter what standard is in place for 'blue', the predicate applies to the color of a clear afternoon sky. There will also be *relational* constraints for some predicates: whatever standard is in place for 'tall', anything the same height as or taller than something that meets the standard itself meets the standard. A further sort of constraint will *coordinate* the standards in use for related predicates: whatever standards are in use for 'rich' and 'poor', nothing can meet both, and it must be possible for something to meet neither. These three constraints together describe what the typical supervaluationist means by an "admissible" precisification of a vague predicate.

A fourth sort of constraint is what I call a *similarity* constraint. It is as follows: whatever standard is in use for a vague expression, anything that is *saliently* similar, in the relevant respect, to something that meets the standard itself meets the standard; anything saliently similar to something that fails to meet the standard itself fails to meet the standard. Put another way, if two things are saliently similar, then it cannot be that one is in the extension of a vague predicate, or in its anti-extension, while the other is not. If two things are similar in the relevant respect, but *not* saliently so, then it may be that one is in the extension, or in the anti-extension, of the predicate while the other is not. One reason for requiring that the similarity be a *salient* one is to block the absurd conclusions that would otherwise follow by sorites reasoning,

since any two dissimilar things can be connected by a similarity chain.

The proposed constraints, then, fall into four categories: (i) Clear-Case Constraints, (ii) Relational Constraints, (iii) Coordination Constraints, and (iv) Similarity Constraints. Let me stress that these four types of constraint are being offered simply as *constraints*. It is not being suggested that they uniquely determine what standard of use for a vague expression must be in place in any given situation. I am merely claiming that the only standards of use that can be in place are ones that satisfy all the proposed constraints. It is also not being suggested that these constraints have any special *semantic* status—that they are constraints which would be known, even implicitly, by any competent speaker. In fact, in the next section I'll deny that the Similarity Constraint is purely semantic, and will propose instead that it is in part a consequence of the vagueness of our interests.

I take it that the first three constraints I proposed are uncontroversial. But it is probably not obvious what the justification is for the fourth constraint. For the moment I want to provide justification for the fourth constraint by showing that it conforms neatly to our use. Suppose we're in an airport, and there are two suspicious-looking men I want to draw your attention to. I'm describing them so that you can pick them out of the crowd. But I can't point—that would be too conspicuous. You ask me, "Are they tall?" If the men are not much over five-foot, eleven inches, then (depending on the heights of the people in their immediate surroundings) I may have some leeway in choosing to answer "yes" or "no." But if, in addition, the two men are pretty much the same height—one is just noticeably shorter than the other—then the option is not available to me to say that one is tall but the other is not. Because the similarity of their heights is so perceptually salient—and now that you've asked me whether they're tall, also conversationally somewhat salient—I may not choose a standard that one meets but the other doesn't.

Another example, one that's slightly more far-fetched, is the following. Imagine an eccentric art collector who reserves one room for her paintings that contain just red pigments, and reserves another room for her paintings that contain just orange pigments. One day she is presented as a gift a painted color spectrum ranging from primary red on one end to orange on the other. She resolves to cut the canvas in half. Now if she cuts without thinking, perhaps in a state of mad excitement because she is so eccentric, she will most likely cut in just the right place—by which I mean that once the halves are re-framed and hung, she will still be able to truly proclaim that her paintings containing just red pigments are in one room, and that her paintings containing just orange pigments are in another. Although the right-hand edge of the painting in the red room is extremely similar to the lefthand edge of the painting in the orange room, their similarity is not *salient*, so the boundary between red and orange may occur between them. If the decision about where to cut is labored, in contrast, the collector will likely find herself unable to locate the boundary between the red and the orange, the pigments on either side of any proposed cut being too similar—and when the decision is labored, *saliently* similar—for one to go in the red room and the other in the orange.

I think we can come up with lots of examples of this kind.[18] A teacher might divide up her third-grade class into two groups, according to height. One group is to constitute the A-league basketball team, the other, the B-league team. Even if the heights of the children form a relatively smooth curve, it seems that she can truly say, once the division has become established, that the tall students are on the A-league team and the rest are on the B-league team. It would be true to say this given the division she's actually made, and it would have been true to say this even if, for auxiliary reasons, she had made the division at a slightly different point.

The preceding examples are intended to provide support for the Similarity Constraint by

illustrating that when, but only when, one can manage to abstract from or ignore the extreme similarity between two objects—that is, when but only when their extreme similarity is not *salient*—the property one expresses in using a vague predicate is one which could be possessed by just one member of the pair. I concede that, despite the examples, the Similarity Constraint may still seem mysterious, even to those who at this point find it somewhat plausible. In the next section I'll give a fuller story about the notion of *salient similarity* adverted to in the Similarity Constraint, which I hope will have the double effect of making it seem both more plausible and less mysterious.

For now, however, I want to continue with discussion of the bare-bones account. In particular, I want to explain why, if the Similarity Constraint is descriptively correct, it provides the resources for answering the Epistemological and Psychological Questions. We have a universally generalized sorites sentence, for example the following:

$$(\forall x)(\forall y)(x \text{ is tall } \& y \text{ is just 1 mm shorter than } x \rightarrow y \text{ is tall})$$

In answer to the Epistemological Question, we may say that although it cannot be the case that every instance of such a universal generalization is true, the reason that we are unable to say just which instance or instances of it are not true is that when we evaluate any given instance, for any particular x and y that differ in height by just 1 mm, the very act of our evaluation raises the similarity of the pair to salience, which has the effect of rendering true the very instance we are considering. We cannot find the boundary of the extension of a vague predicate in a sorites series for that predicate, because the boundary can never be where we are looking. It shifts around. In answer to the Psychological Question, we may say that it is no wonder that we were so inclined in the first place to regard the universal generalization as true, given that any instance of it we consider is in fact true at the time we consider it.

The astute reader will no doubt have immediately noticed that my answers here presuppose bivalence in the sense that they do not follow from the Similarity Constraint *alone*, in absence of further semantic principles, unless bivalence is true. Let me explain. According to the Similarity Constraint for a given vague predicate F, when two things are not only very similar in the respect relevant for predications of F, but also saliently so, then if one is in the extension of F so is the other, and if one is in the anti-extension of F so is the other. This leaves open the possibility, if there are truth-value gaps, that saliently similar things may both be in the extension gap of F, which in turn leaves open the possibility, in absence of further semantic principles, that an instance of a sorites sentence involving such a pair will itself be neither true nor false. My answers to the Epistemological and Psychological Questions required, in contrast, that such instances would not be merely valueless but true, as they would be given only bivalence and the Similarity Constraint.[19]

While it is true that I am an adherent of bivalence, it is not the case that the bare-bones solution is available only to those who accept bivalence. For example, a supervaluationist who is sympathetic to the account I've presented might hold (just as he does for the other three constraints I've discussed) that the Similarity Constraint acts as a constraint not only on the actual, partial extensions of vague predicates, but also on the precisifications of them that are operative in his truth-definition. To see how this would work, let us suppose that *a* and *b* are saliently similar in respect of height, and that *a* is the taller of the two. Given the Similarity Constraint, they are either both in the extension of 'tall', both in the anti-extension of 'tall', or both in its extension gap. Whichever one of these obtains, the conditional '*a* is tall $\to$ *b* is tall' turns out to be supervaluationally true. For given the Similarity Constraint on precisifications, there

will be no admissible way of drawing precise boundaries for 'tall' that divides the two. That is, on every admissible precisification of 'tall', either *a* and *b* are both in the extension of 'tall', or they are both out. Thus in every admissible precisification, the conditional '*a* is tall $\to$ *b* is tall' is classically true, and hence the conditional is supervaluationally true. Thus the very answers to the Epistemological and Psychological Questions that follow from the Similarity Constraint, given acceptance of bivalence, are also available to the sympathetic supervaluationist.

I am not the first to propose that something like what I'm calling the Similarity Constraint is both descriptively correct and of use in solving the sorites. Kamp (1981) and Soames (1999), for example, also propose that the similarity of two objects can in special circumstances prevent the extension-boundaries of a vague predicate from occurring between them. Kamp and Soames differ from me, however, in respect of what those special circumstances are. The difference might be paraphrased as follows: while I propose that similar things cannot be divided by an extension-boundary for a vague predicate when their *similarity* is salient, Kamp and Soames propose that similar things can't be divided by an extension boundary for a vague predicate when it is salient that one of them is in the extension or that one of them is in the anti-extension of the predicate. The repeated use of the word 'salient' here should not be given too much weight, however; it was merely intended as a useful way of bringing out the contrast. A more accurate way of expressing the similarity constraint these two adopt is as follows: if *a* and *b* are sufficiently similar and 'Fa' is "taken for granted by the participants in the discourse," then 'Fb' is true (Kamp); if *a* and *b* are sufficiently similar and *a* is "explicitly characterized" as falling under F, and "other conversational participants accept this," then 'Fb' is true (Soames).

A key difference between Kamp's and Soames's version on the one hand, and mine on the other, occurs in a situation in which it is part of the background of a conversation (in either Kamp's or Soames's sense) that *a* falls under F, but the similarity of *a* and *b* is *not* salient. In such a situation, given Kamp's and Soames's proposed constraint, *b* is in the extension of F, while given my proposed constraint it need not be. My proposal seems preferable in its handling of cases discussed above, like that of the eccentric art collector, or of the third-grade teacher who must divide her class into two basketball teams. Suppose that the collector is in her orange room, and is explaining to a guest that she hangs her paintings containing just orange pigments in that room, and that her paintings containing just red pigments are hung in another. Suppose also that they are examining the redder edge of the orange half of the spectrum, and that enough conversation has taken place so that it is now part of the background of the conversation, in whatever sense, that 'orange' is being used in such a way so as to apply to that redder edge. The similarity of that edge to the more orange edge of the other half in her red room is not at all salient. We may suppose that it has been years since the art collector has been in her red room or even thought about the fact that there is another half of the spectrum hanging there. The guest is not even aware of the existence of another half. Given my constraint, what the collector says to her guest can be true. Given Kamp's and Soames's constraint, it cannot.

Let's put this difference aside however. What's of greater interest here, given that Kamp and Soames each reject bivalence and that neither adopts supervaluation semantics, is how they put their own versions of the similarity constraint to use in solving the sorites paradox in a way that explains our initial temptation to regard sorites sentences as true. On this question they diverge. On Kamp's view, every instance of a sorites sentence is in fact true, in *any* context. The result is achieved by adopting a semantics for the conditional that is not truth-functional. A con-

ditional is on this view true in a context *c* just in case either its antecedent is false in *c*, or its consequent *would* be true in the context that would result from *c* by incorporating the antecedent of the conditional into the background of *c*. This approach, combined with Kamp's version of the similarity constraint—whenever *a* and *b* are similar and 'F*a*' is part of the background, 'F*b*' is true—has the effect of verifying, in every context, every instance of a sorites sentence.[20]

Soames, in contrast, adopts a straightforward truth-functional semantics for the connectives, that given by the strong Kleene truth tables, according to which a conditional with a valueless antecedent and consequent is itself valueless. Now if vague predicates have extension gaps, both Soames's version and my version of the similarity constraint allow for the possibility that similar objects may both be in the extension gap of a vague predicate, even if their similarity is salient. Thus if Adam is just 1 mm taller than Bert, and this extreme similarity between their heights is not only known but salient, it may still be, given the strong Kleene tables, that the sentence 'If Adam is tall, then Bert is tall' has no truth value. The answer I offered to the Psychological Question is therefore not available to Soames.[21] For I had proposed that our inclination to accept sorites sentences and our inability to say just which instance or instances of them are not true is explained by the fact that any instance we consider is, as we consider it, in fact true. Soames, also concerned to answer the Psychological Question, proposes instead that the explanation for our initial attraction to sorites sentences is that we *mistake* them for true *metalinguistic* principles, namely, those principles that give expression to his version of the similarity constraint.[22]

Soames's explanation requires for its force that the truth of these metalinguistic principles is something widely known. I gather that Soames is thinking of his version of the similarity constraint as being a feature of the *meaning* of a vague predicate, and that therefore we would know, at least implicitly, that similarity constraints are true in virtue of our being competent speakers. Whether similarity constraints have this sort of semantic status is something which should be open to question, however. As I further develop my own view in the next section, I'll suggest that this is precisely not the case—that similarity constraints are empirical truths, made true, at least in part, because we have the kinds of interests that we do.

My reason for discussing the views of Kamp and Soames here is not merely to explain how my own view compares with others related to it, but also, in so doing, to emphasize that something very much like, if not exactly like, the bare-bones solution to the sorites is available to those with a variety of semantic and logical commitments and that, in particular, it is neutral with respect to the question of bivalence.

I should mention two other philosophers whom I think of as being in the bare-bones camp, even though their views go well beyond the skeletal account offered here. Unfortunately, my remarks must be briefer than I would like. Diana Raffman employs something like a similarity constraint for vague predicates in her solution to the sorites paradox. On her view, there is a true object-language principle, which she calls 'IP*', expressed as follows for the specific case of the predicate 'looks red': "for any n, if patch #n looks red then patch #(n + 1) looks red, *insofar as #n and #(n + 1) are judged pairwise*" (Raffman 1994: 47). On Raffman's view, as on Soames's our inclination to accept sorites sentences is explained by a proposed tendency to mistake them for distinct but related claims—in Raffman's case, for the true claim IP*.[23] In one way, my own Similarity Constraint seems more closely related to Raffman's version than to either of Kamp's or Soames's, in that it seems that on Raffman's view the *salience* of a given similarity (in her case, perceptual salience) is doing the crucial work.

Jamie Tappenden's (1993) view is a more dis-

tant relative, but still, something like a similarity constraint plays a central role in his account of the sorites. Tappenden, who also admits truth-value gaps, proposes that if two objects are sufficiently similar (whether or not that similarity is salient) then the standards in use for a vague predicate F must not be such as to place one of the objects in the extension of F and the other in its anti-extension. (Extension/Gap and Gap/Anti-Extension pairs of assignments are both fine.) Given also his acceptance of the strong Kleene tables, the inadmissibility of using such standards amounts to the inadmissibility of using a vague predicate in such a way as to render a sorites sentence for it *false*. This privileged status, *inadmissible to falsify*, is argued to support a special kind of speech act which Tappenden calls "articulation." The point of articulating a sentence is to get someone to stop or refrain from using a vague predicate in an inadmissible way, where one way to use a vague predicate inadmissibly is to use it in a way that does not conform to Tappenden's version of the similarity constraint. Tappenden explains our inclination to accept sorites sentences by claiming that since, though untrue, they are articulable, we may be warranted in uttering them; we mistake our good reason for uttering sorites sentences as reason to believe them.[24] One problem for the account is that sharp-boundaries claims (also not true according to Tappenden) turn out to have the same privileged status as sorites sentences. Something other than *articulability* is required to explain the difference in our attitudes toward such sentences.

I want to conclude this section with some remarks about the respects in which the bare-bones account is bare-boned. I have emphasized that the account is neutral on the question of bivalence. It has also been silent about how exactly to cash out the notion of *salience* that has been used so freely. We should probably think of the occurrences of 'salient' and its cognates as they've occurred here as just a peg on which to hang some more substantive theory, which I aim to provide. The account presented so far is also bareboned in another respect: it is neutral about how the variation in standards of use for vague predicates should be characterized semantically. In particular, it has been left open just how much of this variation should be thought of as arising from *context-dependence*. Let me explain. When I say that the standards of use for a predicate like 'tall' can vary, I mean that the extension of 'tall' can change from occasion to occasion, *even if the heights of everything remain stable*. When I say that the standards for 'expensive' can vary, I mean that the extension of the predicate can vary, *even if the costs of everything remain stable*. Given that the extensions of vague predicates can vary in this way, we might want to say that every such variation points to a change in context. One idea might be that 'tall' always expresses an intrinsic property, one which whether a thing has it depends only on that thing's height. Another idea might be that 'tall' always expresses a relational property, one which whether a thing has it depends only on how that thing's height compares to the height of certain other things. Either way, if the extension of 'tall' can vary even as the heights of *everything* remain stable, this could only be because 'tall' was context-dependent—because it expressed different properties on different occasions.

We should not assume off the bat, however, that 'tall' does express a property possession of which depends *only* on heights. It is possible that the predicate could express the same property from occasion to occasion, and that the reason the extension may change as the heights of things do not change is that the property expressed context-invariantly by 'tall' is a property which is such that whether a thing has it depends not only on heights, but on other things as well. I will go on to propose that despite the constant changing of standards of use for vague predicates that is dictated by the Similarity Constraint, there is much less context-dependence than one might have initially thought would be a consequence of the bare-bones view.

IV Vague expressions are interest-relative

The second layer of my solution to the sorites rests on a certain view about what predications involving vague expressions mean. Let me illustrate the view by means of examples. I propose that

> That car is expensive

is to be analyzed as meaning:

> That car costs a lot,

which in turn is to be analyzed as meaning:

> That car costs significantly more than is typical.

Similarly, 'John is tall' is to be analyzed as meaning 'John has a lot of height', which is in turn to be analyzed as meaning 'John has significantly more height than is typical'. This sort of analysis is extended also to cases involving explicit relativization to a comparison class as follows: 'Mickey is old for a mouse' is to be analyzed as meaning 'Mickey has a lot of age for a mouse', which is in turn to be analyzed as meaning 'Mickey has significantly more age than is typical for a mouse'.

I do not want to try to get too specific about exactly what sense of 'analysis' is being assumed here. Suffice it to say, for the time being, that when I say that 'John is tall' is to be *analyzed* as meaning that John has significantly more height than is typical, I intend to be making a claim about what type of property it is that we attribute to John when we say that he is tall. In particular, I intend to be claiming that the property thereby attributed to John is not an intrinsic property, but rather a relational one. Moreover, it is not a property the possession of which depends only on the difference between John's height and some norm, but also on whether that difference is a significant one. I take it that whether or not a difference is a significant difference does not depend only on its magnitude, but also on what our interests are. (Exactly whose interests are at issue is a delicate question, which I'll try to ignore as much as possible.) The central claim of this section, indeed of the paper, is that if this interest-relative analysis is correct, then the Similarity Constraint, and the bare-bones solution along with it, drops out as a consequence.

I should first say a few words about my analysis of 'a lot' as meaning 'significantly more than is typical'. There is actually quite a bit more complexity to the issue. Sometimes 'a lot' can mean 'significantly more than is typical', but other times it can mean 'significantly more than is wanted or needed'. And also it can mean 'significantly more than is expected'. I feel sure that even these options are not exhaustive. It seems to me we need the 'typical' meaning for a case like the following. I am throwing a huge party. I know that there are going to be at least one hundred people coming. I have already done some shopping for the party, in particular, I have already stocked my refrigerator with beer. My friend Linda comes over to help with the preparations, and upon opening my refrigerator proclaims, "Wow! That's a lot of beer." Now, I have a normal size refrigerator—there are at most one hundred bottles in there. This is not enough beer for the huge party I'm throwing, and Linda knows this. Still, it is appropriate for her to say that there is *a lot* of beer in the refrigerator, because it is significantly more beer than one typically finds in a refrigerator.

The reason we cannot end the story there, however, is that analyzing 'a lot' as meaning 'significantly more than is typical' is not going to work for other sorts of cases. For example, it is both typical and expected that supermarkets will always have *a lot* of milk in stock. If 'a lot' just meant 'significantly more than is typical', then we could not say of our local supermarket that it has a lot of milk in stock, since the amount of milk it has in stock is a completely typical

amount for supermarkets to have. Here I think that when we say that the supermarket keeps a lot of milk in stock, we mean something like: it stocks significantly more milk than will be wanted or needed by shoppers on any given day. We cannot extend this proposal back to the beer case, however, since as I said, it is going to be a huge party, and I do not have *enough* beer for it.

What about a case like this: we're driving through Iowa, and suddenly we come upon a huge field of corn. We can see that the field stretches for miles. I say, "Wow, that's a lot of corn." Now it is not the case that I mean here that that's significantly more corn than is typical. We are in Iowa after all. Nor do I mean that it's significantly more than is wanted or needed. It's a big country, and we need a lot of corn. My exclamation, "Wow, that's a lot of corn" is my way of expressing some surprise—there is significantly more corn than I expected to come upon at that moment.

I want to stress that, despite these considerations, I am not wedded to the idea that 'a lot' is ambiguous. Perhaps it could be argued that the 'typical' meaning for 'a lot' really is sufficient, given some pragmatic considerations, to handle cases of the types I've discussed. The crucial feature of what I've said for my purposes here, is that 'a lot' means '*significantly* more than some norm'. Clearly, there is more than one kind of norm. It seems equally clear that the different uses of 'a lot' discussed above should in some way or another be accounted for as resulting from a difference in the kind of norm involved. Whether 'a lot' should therefore be deemed either ambiguous or context-dependent is a highly theoretical and largely theory-internal question which it seems to me could be plausibly answered either way.

Nevertheless, if vague expressions are to be analyzed as I've proposed, then we should expect that, like 'a lot', they could be used in ways that involve different norms on different occasions. Consider the expression 'old for a dog'. Here we have a vague adjective explicitly relativized to a comparison class. On my proposal, the expression is to be analyzed as meaning 'has significantly more age than is typical for a dog'. (Henceforth, 'typical' is to be understood as making reference to some or other norm.) Suppose that Fido is fourteen years old and Rover is twenty years old. Someone who says that Rover is old for a dog may be making a remark about his extreme longevity, while someone who says that Fido is old for a dog may be merely remarking that he is in his old age. This is to be explained, on my view, by a variation in norm. Rover, the twenty-year-old, has significantly more age than is the norm for a dog to attain; while Fido, the fourteen-year-old, has significantly more age than some different kind of norm for a dog, one that's much harder to articulate, but which perhaps concerns the peak age of good health.

There are also norms of expectation. This is what explains why it can be appropriate for me to say, when I see my young nephew for the first time in months at a family gathering, "Derek, you're so *tall*." It can be appropriate for me to say this even though I know that my nephew has always been and still is short for his age. What I am saying is that he has significantly more height than I expected him to have, given what his height was the last time I saw him.

Let us now shift our attention away from that feature of my proposal which has it that predications involving vague expressions involve reference to some norm, and turn our attention to the feature I am most concerned with, namely, that in claiming that someone is tall for a ten-year-old, for example, we are claiming that he has *significantly* more height than some norm for ten-year-olds. I want now to proceed with my central claim that if this is correct, the Similarity Constraint drops out as a consequence. The argument rests on the idea that two things that are qualitatively different in some respect, even when they are known to be different, can nonetheless be the *same for present purposes*. What I claim

is that if two things are the same for present purposes, in respect of height say, then one can have *significantly* more height than is typical if and only if the other does. Given my proposed analysis of 'tall', it follows that when two things are in respect of height the same for present purposes, one is in the extension of 'tall' if and only if the other is. What's required, if the Similarity Constraint is to follow, is that two things come to be the same for present purposes when they are not only very similar, but when also their similarity is in some sense salient—in particular, when it is being actively considered.

Often it is appropriate to say of distinct but very similar things that they are the same for present purposes. For example, suppose a small child is watching me make a pot of coffee and, thinking she is being helpful, points out that a couple of grains have spilled from my coffee scoop. She assumes that the coffee scoop is a measuring device rather than a tool for convenient transfer, and so mistakenly concludes that this is an exact science. When she then wonders why I don't bother to replace the grains I've spilled, I might explain to her that there is no need because the two amounts are the same for present purposes. Assuming that it is indeed *true* that the two amounts are the same for present purposes, this cannot entail that for present purposes: it is true that the two amounts are the same. It is false that the two amounts are the same, and my purposes cannot alter that fact. To say that the two amounts of coffee are the same for present purposes is to say that as far as my coffee-making purpose is concerned, the two amounts might as well be the same; my coffee-making purpose permits me to behave as if the two amounts were the same, since the purpose is in no way thwarted by my behaving as if they were the same.

Although my coffee-making purpose permits me to behave as if the two amounts are the same, what really makes the two amounts the same for present purposes is that my interests on the whole *require* me to behave as if the two amounts were the same. The reason for the requirement is that in addition to having an interest in getting a decent amount of coffee made, I also have in interest in doing this efficiently. Because of my interest in efficiency, there is some cost associated with measuring out the coffee grains precisely, and also some cost associated with taking the time to replace a few spilled grains. The cost of discriminating between the two amounts of coffee at hand clearly outweighs the benefits of discriminating between them, since even though I always prefer greater caffeine intake to less, I would be unlikely to notice, much less care a lot about, the differential effect if any these two amounts would have on me. From this point on, I will say that two things are the same (in a certain respect) for present purposes when the cost of discriminating between them (in that respect) outweighs the benefits. In saying this, I am not making a claim about what we *mean* when we say that two things are the same for present purposes. I think we just mean by this that for present purposes, it is fine to ignore the difference between the two things. Rather, I am claiming that what makes it fine to ignore the difference, is that the cost of discriminating outweighs the benefits.[25]

Crucially, there can only be a cost to discriminating between two things if they are in some sense both "live options." When I make my coffee in the morning and spill a few grains from the scoop, there is a cost to discriminating between the two amounts at hand. That is, there is a cost to taking the time to count and replace the grains I've spilled. The cost outweighs the benefits, so the two amounts are the same for present purposes. It does not follow, however, that any pair of amounts of coffee grains that differ to the same degree are also the same for present purposes. If it is not a live option that I'll use either of some pair of amounts, then there is no cost associated with discriminating between them, and hence they are *not* the same for present purposes.

Being the same for present purposes can be seen to

play exactly the same role here as *being saliently similar* was playing in the bare-bones account. Thus I am cashing out the notions of "similarity" and "salient similarity" in the following way: to say that two things are similar enough to be subject to the Similarity Constraint is to say that were they live options, the cost of discriminating between them would outweigh the benefits. To say that they are *saliently* similar is to say that they are indeed live options, that the cost of discriminating between them *does* outweigh the benefits—that is, that they are in fact the same for present purposes. Given my analysis of 'tall', for example, as meaning 'has *significantly* more height than is typical', and given also that if two things are in respect of height the same for present purposes one can have significantly more height than is typical if and only if the other does, the Similarity Constraint for 'tall' drops out as a consequence.

One potential problem that immediately arises is that if it can be true that two people are in respect of height the same for present purposes *whenever* their heights are at most 1 mm apart, that is, if there can be enough live options, then we could have it that whenever the heights of two people are at most 1 mm apart, one is in the extension of 'tall' if and only if the other is. (I'll just assume, for the sake of the objection, that the distribution of heights forms a sufficiently smooth curve.) Given the transitivity of the biconditional, this would have precisely the consequence we're trying to avoid, namely, that Michael Jordan is in the extension of 'tall' if and only if I am. Yet I am clearly not tall. To avoid this result, we need at least one pair of people whose heights are at most 1 mm apart yet whose heights are not the same for present purposes.

This is in fact a worry I should have mentioned when presenting the bare-bones version of my solution. The worry stated as it would have arisen there is that if we could get ourselves into a situation where the similarity in height of any two people that differed by at most 1 mm was a salient similarity, then by my Similarity

Constraint it would follow that given any two people at all, one would be in the extension of 'tall' if and only if the other was. If every similarity in height is salient, then there is no place for the boundary between the tall and the not-tall to be. But this seems to be exactly the situation we are in when we are discussing the sorites paradox, and imagining that we are confronted with a series of people each of whom is just 1 mm taller than the next. The worry here is a serious one, for given also the Clear-Case Constraint, it may seem that my account is not merely false, but contradictory. For I am a clear case of 'not-tall'. So by the Clear-Case Constraint I am in the anti-extension of 'tall'. Given enough salient similarities, it would follow by the Similarity Constraint that Michael Jordan is in the anti-extension of 'tall', and hence not tall. But Michael Jordan is a clear-case of 'tall', and so by the Clear-Case Constraint, he is in the extension of 'tall', and therefore tall. Contradiction.

One way around this problem would be to argue that there cannot be enough salient similarities. When we are confronted with a sorites series for 'tall', although it is salient that each adjacent pair in the series is very similar, it is not the case that each adjacent pair in the series is such that it is salient that they are similar. There are too many pairs for us to actively entertain each similarity.

Another way around the problem we are facing would proceed by noting that the presented *reductio* of the bare-bones account contained a crucial mistake. It assumed that on any given occasion, there will be a standard in use for a vague predicate that satisfies all of my constraints. But that is not quite right. Rather, it is that the only standard that can be in use for a vague predicate is one that satisfies all four constraints. In a situation where there are too many salient similarities, no standard could satisfy all four constraints. There is no contradiction in that. Thus the problem of too many salient similarities might be avoided by saying that in such a situation, the vague predicate at issue fails to express any property at all. In such a situation, no proposition is expressed by an utterance of a sentence containing the given vague predicate.

I actually think that once *being saliently similar* is cashed out as I've described, the first way around the problem proves to be the correct one. Whichever of the wide variety of purposes we may have in conversations where we have occasion to use vague expressions like 'tall', 'old', 'expensive', and the like, it will simply be a brute fact that that there will be a least height, age, or cost of which it is true to say that it is significantly greater than is typical—at least, that is, if it is true to say of any height, age, or cost at all that it is significantly greater than is typical. Any lesser amount simply cannot be the same for whatever purposes are in place. Even if there is some cost associated with any discrimination we might make between similar heights, ages, etc., the cost of making the discrimination nowhere does not outweigh the benefits of making it somewhere. The boundary between those differences that are significant and those that are not will try to locate itself, so to speak, at a place where there is least resistance.

I take it, returning to the example we began with, that when I desire some coffee it is just a brute fact that there is a least amount of coffee of which it is true to say that it will satisfy my desire. Anything less will not do. I know that many philosophers will protest; they will say, "But how could it be that your desire for coffee is like *that*?" I say, given that a teaspoon of coffee is not enough to satisfy my desire, how could it *not* be like that! Moreover, I have an explanation for why my desire seems that it is not like that. There should be nothing surprising or doubtful in the suggestion that we have inexact knowledge (in Williamson's sense) of the satisfaction conditions of our desires. I have never bothered to figure out exactly how the enjoyment I get from coffee maps on to the different amounts of it I might drink. And even were I to try to ascertain this, it would be close to impossible to ensure a controlled experiment, since it will always be that factors other than the amount I drink affect my enjoyment. But it is not merely that I have inexact knowledge of the satisfaction conditions of my desire for coffee on a given occasion; it is also that the satisfaction conditions of my desire may subtly shift, so as to be satisfied by different amounts of coffee as different options become available to me and the costs of discriminating between different pairs of amounts change. That, I claim, is the essence of a vague desire, and it explains why we are inclined to accept sorites sentences such as the one that opened the essay, namely, 'When my purpose is just to make some coffee to drink, then for any n, if n grains of coffee are enough for my purposes, then so are n − 1'. [. . .]

VI The semantic question

As an adherent of classical logic and bivalence, I believe that sorites sentences are false and that "sharp boundaries" claims are true. On any sorites series for a vague expression, I believe that somewhere in the series (not where we're looking) there is an object that possesses the property expressed by an utterance involving a vague expression right next to an object that lacks that property. I am reluctant, however, to call the proposed boundary between the property possessor and the property lacker a *sharp* boundary, since as I have stressed, this is but a metaphor, and I have as much right to the metaphor as does the proponent of gaps or degrees. I would cash out the metaphor in the following way: the boundary between the possessors and the lackers in a sorites series is not sharp in the sense that we can never bring it into focus; any attempt to bring it into focus causes it to shift somewhere else. This essay has been devoted to developing and defending this idea, and to explaining why it provides the means for saying why we cannot find boundaries in a sorites series, and why we tend to believe of any given point in the series that the boundary is not there.

I have not, however, in any way addressed what I called the Semantic Question concerning the sorites paradox. That question was: if so-called "sharp boundaries" claims are true, how is that compatible with a vague predicate's having borderline cases? For "sharp-boundaries" claims seem to deny just that. If there are no truth-value gaps or degrees of truth between truth and falsity, then what is it for something to be a borderline case?

When trying to answer the question what is it for something to be a borderline case of a vague predicate, I think it important to begin by saying just what phenomenon it is we are trying to account for. Some philosophers, such as Fine, just define borderline cases as those things of which a predicate is neither true nor false. Timothy Williamson regards it as better to proceed by giving examples. The first approach will not do, since there are coherent accounts of vagueness incompatible with it. Williamson's approach will not do either, since it seems impossible to find examples about which people can agree.

We are prompted to regard a thing as a borderline case of a predicate when it elicits in us one of a variety of related verbal behaviors. When asked, for example, whether a particular man is nice, we may give what can be called a *hedging* response. Hedging responses include: "He's niceish," "It depends on how you look at it," "I wouldn't say he's nice, I wouldn't say he's not nice," "It could go either way," "He's kind of in between," "It's not that clear-cut," and even "He's a borderline case." If it is demanded that a "yes" or "no" response is required, we may feel that neither answer would be quite correct, that there is "no fact of the matter."

In asking what it is for something to be a borderline case of a predicate, I think we should ask what might prompt one of this array of responses. There is no justification for assuming at the outset that it is always the same cause in every case. In fact, I think that hedging responses may have a variety of causes, which for the most part are to be counted as one or another form of ignorance.[29] The interest-relative theory of the meaning of vague expressions not only makes sense of this, but predicts it.

If asked to judge whether or not a certain car is *expensive* (for a car), what we must judge is whether or not that car costs a lot for a car, whether, that is, its cost is significantly more than it is typical for a car to cost. There is a lot of room for ignorance here. For one, we may have no idea of what the typical cost of a car is, or we may have merely inexact knowledge (in Williamson's sense) of what the typical cost of a car is. We may also have inexact knowledge of what our own interests are, of what exactly it would take for the difference between the car's cost and the typical cost to be a difference that is significant to us.

There are also more distinctly semantic (or if you prefer, pragmatic) sources of the ignorance which better explain why a hedging response might be provoked. It is convenient to place these under the heading 'ignorance of the context'. If the comparison class has been left implicit, for example, we may not know which comparison class is intended by our questioner. Even if it is clear that the comparison class is cars, rather than, e.g., essential possessions, we may still be unsure of which of the many norms of cost for a car is under consideration—are we to judge whether the car costs significantly more than a car *ought* to cost? Or are we to judge whether the car costs significantly more than the average car costs? Or are we to judge whether the car costs significantly more than anyone should be willing to pay for a car? Perhaps we are to judge whether the car costs significantly more than what cars used to cost when the price of cars was (as it seems to us now) more reasonable. The answers to these questions do not stand or fall together.

Yet another example is this: if we are joining in on a conversation already underway about whether the given car is expensive, there is room for even more ignorance, since in assessing whether the car costs significantly more than is typical for a car to cost, we may still feel unsure

of what the right answer is to the question significant to whom? Are the interests of one but not the other of the conversants at issue? Is it both of their interests? Is it the interests of anyone who might want to buy the car? If the parties are in disagreement about whether the car is expensive, the reason we, as a third party to the conversation, might feel inclined to say, "There's no fact of the matter" (whatever that means) is closely related to the reason that some feel inclined to say that "there's no fact of the matter" about whether abortion is wrong. How the question is answered will depend on the interests or values of the person answering it, and we feel uncomfortable or unsure in giving the interests or values of one person special weight.

If ignorance, and especially "ignorance of the context," explains why we give hedging responses when we do, then a rejection of bivalence to account for borderline cases is unwarranted. Even if the idea that the truth-conditions of utterances containing vague expressions are both context-dependent and also sensitive to our interests in the way outlined here turns out not to be sustainable, my hope is that I have at least demonstrated that if we pay more careful attention to the way we actually use vague expression, there proves to be more room than is commonly thought within the space of classical logic and semantics to account for the many phenomena of vagueness.

Notes

*   [Editors' note: Formerly Delia Graff.] A kernel of the ideas in this essay first showed up in my "second-year paper" written at M.I.T. in 1994–5. Discussions with George Boolos during that year and the next had an enormous impact on my thinking on this and related topics. Diana Raffman's presentation of her work during her visit to M.I.T. that same year also had significant influence on my ideas about vagueness. I'm definitely in her debt. Discussions with Robert Stalnaker of the ideas that eventually showed up in another precursor of this essay—chapter three of my

dissertation—really helped me to get clearer on exactly how context-dependence was (then) playing a role in my account of the sorites. Numerous discussions over the years about vagueness and context-dependence with Michael Fara, Michael Glanzberg, Richard Heck, Jason Stanley, and Timothy Williamson have been invaluable. Thanks finally to Christopher Hill and Timothy Williamson for helpful comments on the final draft.

4   I make an exception, however, for phenomenal versions of the sorites paradox—cases where 'F' is an observational predicate, e.g., 'looks red', and 'R' is an observational sameness relation, e.g., 'looks the same as'. With phenomenal versions of the sorites, I believe we should give up sentence (D). That is, if *a* clearly looks red and *z* clearly does not, I deny that *a* and *z* can be connected by a looks-the-same-as chain. See my "Phenomenal Continua and the Sorites" (Graff 2001) for a defense.

5   See §5 of Fine (1975) for his semantics for higher-order vagueness. The question at issue there is what is the correct semantics for the *definitely* operator we use to express vagueness—where to say that Herbert is neither definitely tall nor definitely not tall is to say that he is a borderline case. On the provisional semantics Fine proposes for the definitely operator, a sentence with an initial definitely operator (I'll use 'D' as an abbreviation) is always either true or false, with the result that "higher-order" predicates such as '*x* is borderline tall' turn out to have no extension gap, and are therefore not vague. The more sophisticated semantic treatment of the definitely operator offered to accommodate the vagueness of higher-order predicates allows for sentences such as 'John is definitely tall' or 'John is borderline tall' also to lack a truth-value. What remains unchanged on the revised account, however, is that a sentence *A* will be true if and only if '*DA*' is true. Thus even on the revised account, the extension of a predicate '*Fx*' will be the same as that of '*D''Fx*', for any number *n* of iterations of the definitely operator. Similarly, the extension of '¬*Fx*' will be the same as that of '*D''*¬*Fx*' for any *n*. What I'm claiming we have no explanation for, on this account, is why we are unable to find the boundaries of these extensions. Sainsbury (1991b: §II) makes similar remarks.

6   See Fine (1975: 286).

7   See chaps. 7 and 8 of Williamson (1994).

8   One gets the impression that philosophers who are concerned about vagueness feel that those who accept bivalence are under some special obligation to provide an answer to the Epistemological Question. But I can't see why this should be so.

9   I'm assuming here that the domain is restricted to the members of some appropriately constructed sorites series.

10   See Williamson (1997), esp. §2.

11   Representative examples are Hans Kamp (1981), Manfred Pinkal (1984), Jamie Tappenden (1993), Diana Raffman (1994, 1996), Kees van Deemter (1996), Scott Soames (1999: chap. 7), and myself (1997).

12   See §III below for further discussion of Kamp's view.

13   See n. 11 above for references.

14   And even more so with the theory developed and defended in my dissertation (Graff 1997).

15   This must be distinguished from the frequently discussed point that adjectives such as 'tall', like 'good', are not intersective, in the sense that being in the extension of 'tall man' is not just a matter of being in the intersection of the extensions of 'tall' and 'man', since if it were, then from John's being both a tall man and a basketball player it would follow that he is a tall basketball player. In principle, adjectives could be non-intersective while still being extensional, and with few exceptions, are often treated this way. Wheeler (1972) and Cresswell (1976) serve as examples.

16   Well, it might be that as a matter of coincidence the things on my desk at a given time happen to form a kind. The point is that there is no kind which is such that something is a member of it at a time *in virtue of* its being on my desk at that time. When I say that we therefore have "no notion" of what a typical height is for a thing on my desk, I mean that there is *no* typical height for a thing on my desk, and we cannot make sense of the idea of there being one.

17   The fact that the variation in standards is subject to constraints is one indication that we should not merely liken such variations to Donnellan-style cases of misdescription. Alice Kyburg and Michael

Morreau (2000) offer a nice discussion of this point.

18 I must express a special debt to Diana Raffman's (1994) work for inspiring examples like these.

19 Well, even that is not completely accurate. I am also presupposing that we have some relatively standard interpretation for the conditional, though not necessarily a material interpretation.

20 We should be wary of this result—that the collection of conditionals 'F(i) → F(i + 1)' 'can be jointly true—given also that Kamp wants to maintain modus ponens as a valid rule of inference, and also that he does not adopt a nihilist position along the lines of that advocated by Peter Unger (1979). In order to avoid the apparent incompatibility of such a combination of views, Kamp proposes a nonstandard conception of validity. I refer the reader to Kamp (1981) for details. See esp. 260f.

21 Soames and I do give the same answer to the Epistemological Question, however. We both say that we cannot discover exactly which instance or instances of a given sorites premise are not true, because that would require locating the boundary (or boundaries) in a sorites series for the given vague predicate. But this is something we cannot do, since the boundary (or boundaries) can never be where we're looking.

22 See Soames (1999: 215).

23 See Raffman (1994: 47) and Raffman (1996: n. 18).

24 See Tappenden (1993: §5). I should add that Tappenden's account, though it does offer an answer to the Psychological Question, furnishes us with no answer to the Epistemological Question.

25 Some care would be required in further explicating what is meant by 'discriminate'. When I spill a few coffee grains, of course I know that the amount in the coffee scoop before the spill is not the same as the amount in it afterwards. My knowledge of the difference is not sufficient for me to count as discriminating between the two amounts, however, at least not in the sense intended here. If we take it that to discriminate between the amounts is to behave as if they were different, then we might lay down by stipulation that knowing is not behaving. Alternatively we might stipulate that the only behaviors under consideration are those directed at furthering my more or less immediate interests. I

feel tempted here to echo remarks of Kripke's in *Naming and Necessity* by protesting that I am not offering a theory. It is not that I think that theories are bad in principle. I just want to acknowledge that some refinement or supplementation is definitely needed.

29 I want to mention one source of hedging responses which does not stem in any way from ignorance and which also seems to have little to do with vagueness as such—namely, a desire to avoid unwanted conversational implicatures. What I have in mind is this: suppose you feel confident that a given stretch of road is not straight for a road; nevertheless, if it is not winding either, you may feel uncomfortable in asserting or unwilling to assert without qualification that the stretch of road is not straight (for a road), or if asked whether it is straight you may feel most inclined to hedge. In this case, it is not that you don't have a firm belief one way or the other about whether the stretch of road is straight. It is rather that in asserting without qualification that the stretch of road is not straight you would implicate that it is winding. We might account for the implicature by saying that typically your assertion that a certain stretch of road is not straight would have no point unless its departure from straightness were significant. I say that hedging with this sort of source has nothing to do with vagueness as such because it arises with precise expressions as well. You may know that x is taller than y, but still feel uncomfortable saying so without qualification, because in so doing you would (perhaps falsely) implicate that x is *significantly* taller than y, else your assertion would have little point.

References

Cresswell, M. 1976. "The Semantics of Degree." In *Montague Grammar*, ed. B. Partee. New York: Academic Press.

Fine, K. 1975. "Vagueness, Truth and Logic." *Synthese* 30: 265–300.

Frege, G. 1903. *Grundgesetze der Arithmetik, Begriffsschriftlich Abgeleitet*, vol. II. Jena: Pohle. Translation of selections taken from Geach and Black (1980).

Geach, P., and M. Black, eds. 1980. *Translations from the Philosophical Writings of Gottlob Frege*, 3d ed. Oxford: Blackwell. First edition published in 1952.

Graff, D. 1997. "The Phenomena of Vagueness." Ph.D. thesis. Cambridge, Mass.: Massachusetts Institute of Technology.

———. 2001. "Phenomenal Continua and the Sorites." *Mind* 110.

Heim, I. and A. Kratzer. 1998. *Semantics in Generative Grammar*. Oxford: Blackwell.

Hyde, D. 1994. "Why Higher-Order Vagueness Is a Pseudo-Problem." *Mind* 103: 35–41.

Kamp, H. 1975. "Two Theories about Adjectives." In *Formal Semantics of Natural Language*, ed. E. L. Keenan. Cambridge: Cambridge University Press.

———. 1981. "The Paradox of the Heap." In *Aspects of Philosophical Logic*, ed. U. Mönnich. Dordrecht: D.-Reidel.

Kennedy, C. 1999. *Projecting the Adjective: The Syntax and Semantics of Gradability and Comparison*. New York: Garland Press.

Klein, E. 1980. "A Semantics for Positive and Comparative Adjectives." *Linguistics and Philosophy* 4: 1–45.

Kripke, S. 1975. "Outline of a Theory of Truth." *Journal of Philosophy* 72: 690–716.

Kyburg, A., and M. Morreau. 2000. "Fitting Words: Vague Language in Context." *Linguistics and Philosophy* 23 (6): 577–97.

Montague, R. 1970. "English as a Formal Language." In *Linguaggi nella Società e nella Tecnica*, ed. B. Visentini et al. Milan: Edizioni di Comunità. Reprinted in Thomason (1974).

———. 1973. "The Proper Treatment of Quantification in Ordinary English." In *Approaches to Natural Language*, ed. J. Hintikka, J. Moravcsik, and P. Suppes. Dordrecht: Reidel. Reprinted in Thomason (1974).

Pinkal, M. 1984. "Consistency and Context Change: The Sorites Paradox." In *Varieties of Formal Semantics*. Proceedings of the Fourth Amsterdam Colloquium, Sept. 1982, ed. F. Landman and F. Veltman. Groningen-Amsterdam Studies in Semantics. Dordrecht: Foris Publications.

Raffman, D. 1994. "Vagueness without Paradox." *Philosophical Review* 103 (1): 41–74.

———. 1996. "Vagueness and Context-Relativity." *Philosophical Studies* 81: 175–92.

Sainsbury, R. M. 1991a. "Concepts without Boundaries." King's College London Dept. of Philosophy. Inaugural lecture delivered 6 Nov. 1990.

———. 1991b. "Is There Higher-Order Vagueness?" *Philosophical Quarterly* 41 (163): 167–82.

Soames, S. 1999. *Understanding Truth*. New York: Oxford University Press.

Tappenden, J. 1993. "The Liar and Sorites Paradoxes: Toward a Unified Treatment." *Journal of Philosophy* 90 (11): 551–77.

Thomason, R. H., ed. 1974. *Formal Philosophy: Selected Papers of Richard Montague*, New Haven, Conn.: Yale University Press.

Tye, M. 1994. "Why the Vague Need Not Be Higher-Order Vague." *Mind* 103: 43–45.

Unger, P. 1979. "There Are No Ordinary Things." *Synthese* 41: 117–54.

van Deemter, K. 1996. "The Sorites Fallacy and the Context-Dependence of Vague Predicates." In *Quantifiers, Deduction, and Context*, ed. M. Kanazawa, C. Piñon, and H. de Swart. Stanford, Calif.: CSLI Publications.

von Stechow, A. 1984. "Comparing Semantic Theories of Comparison." *Journal of Semantics* 3: 1–77.

Wheeler, S. C. 1972. "Attributives and Their Modifiers." *NOUS* 6: 310–34.

Williamson, T. 1994. *Vagueness*. London: Routledge.

———. 1997. "Imagination, Stipulation and Vagueness." In *Philosophical Issues*, vol. 8: *Truth*, ed. E. Villanueva. Atascadero, Calif.: Ridgeview.

Wright, C. 1975. "On the Coherence of Vague Predicates." *Synthese* 30: 325–65.

PART FIFTEEN

Fictional discourse

INTRODUCTION TO PART FIFTEEN

FICTION GIVES RISE to many challenging problems. Some of these problems concern the meaning of fictional names, and these problems have already made an appearance in earlier parts of this collection (i.e. in Parts Two, Three and Four). But fiction also raises a range of problems that are independent of the issue of fictional names. The articles here reproduced are not specifically concerned with fictional names, though these inevitably come under discussion as well. We shall use this introduction to separate some of the issues raised by fictional discourse and to indicate which of these are addressed in the three articles.

One problem, or complex of problems, with fiction concerns the reference of fictional names, such as 'Ulysses', 'Sherlock Holmes' or 'Barbarella'. Do these names refer to, or designate anything? As Russell noticed, if they refer to anything, what they refer to wouldn't be real people (this offended Russell's 'robust sense of reality' [above, p. 82]). Let us suppose for a moment that they do not refer to anything, i.e. that they are 'empty'. This puts pressure on the Millian view that the meaning of names in general (and of fictional names in particular) is exhausted by the fact that they designate some object (see Part Two above). On this view, if a name does not refer to anything, there is no contribution it can make to the proposition expressed by sentences containing it. Thus sentences containing these empty names fail to express propositions. This may be problematic if we want to say that fictional sentences, such as

(1)   Barbarella is an interplanetary traveller.

have meaning, and can be understood. At least, that is, if a sentence's being understood or being meaningful requires expressing a proposition. Thus, the view that fictional names do not refer to or designate anything might be taken to support the thesis that names do, after all, have a meaning that goes beyond their reference. An example would be Frege's view that the fictional name 'Ulysses' has a sense, even though it lacks reference (see p. 52 above), and that accordingly, the sentence 'Ulysses landed at Ithaca', while lacking reference (i.e. failing to have a truth value), nevertheless expresses a thought or proposition.[1] Both the Millian and Frege, however, have trouble with existential statements involving fictional names:

---

[1] It should be noted, that both the Millian and the Fregean say that (1) fails to express a truth. Now, there are those, like Lewis and Predelli below, who deny this. And there undeniably are contexts where (1) would seem to express something true, or at least where (1) would contrast favourably with, for example, 'Barbarella is a pipe-smoking detective'. However, let us put these contexts aside for a short while – they will be our next focus of attention.

(2)   Barbarella does not exist.

(2) seems to express a truth. But how could it, if 'Barbarella' lacks a referent?[2]

So perhaps the view that fictional names lack referents requires us to look for a view of names that differs from both Millianism and Frege's. One such view (which came under discussion in Part Four above) would treat names as being synonymous with descriptions. Thus, if 'the D' was a description capturing the main attributes purportedly ascribed to Barbarella in the fiction, then we might maintain that 'Barbarella' means the same as 'the D', and that definite descriptions should receive a Russellian treatment (see Part Three above). On Russell's view of definite descriptions, 'the D exists', is true just if there is a unique D (which exists).[3] Presumably, this is false, for there is no person with the attributes purportedly ascribed to Barbarella in the fiction. If we treat 'The D does not exist' as an external negation[4] of 'The D exists', then it is true just if there is no unique D (which exists). Thus, interpreted as synonymous with 'The D does not exist', (2) comes out true, as it should. However, this comes at the price of denying that fictional names are singular terms.[5]

What if we drop our supposition that fictional names do not refer to or designate anything? Do we have to go against our robust sense of reality? What kind of thing would they refer to? And if they do refer, how would sentences like (2) ever come out as true? The ('Meinongian') conclusion that some things don't exist would seem inevitable. Nevertheless, some theorists, among them Amie Thomasson below, have claimed that fictional names do, at least in some contexts, refer to or designate something, something that exists. But in order to understand the motivation for this claim, we need to look at a second complex of issues, ones that arise independently of questions about empty names.

Let us consider a sentence that does not contain any fictional names like 'Holmes' or 'Barbarella', but which is nevertheless relevant to some fiction, such as:

(3)   The home of a brilliant pipe-smoking detective is in Baker Street, London[6]

or

---

[2] There are a number of options the Millian and the Fregean have here. Frege, for example, thought that (2) expressed the thought that the name 'Barbarella' has no reference. See Salmon 1998 for an excellent exposition of these issues, and see Sainsbury 2005, chapter 6, for a strikingly simple account of (2) from a position that is 'in-between' Millianism and Frege's position.

[3] The last bit 'which exists' seems superfluous, and so thought Russell. Why?

[4] Exercise: Show two ways in which 'There is exactly one D and it exists' can be negated. Are both of them coherent interpretations of 'The D does not exist'? For detailed discussion, see again Salmon 1998.

[5] Another price is the problem Lewis mentions, namely a difficulty raised by Kripke: if by coincidence something actually is the D, then we have to conclude that that thing is Barbarella, and that Barbarella does exist.

[6] I am assuming that 'Baker Street, London' is not an empty fictional name but rather refers to the relevant street in London.

(4)   There is a blond angel called 'Pygar'.[7]

There seem to be situations where (3) and (4) can be used to state a truth, namely when we are discussing the Holmes stories or the film *Barbarella* from an internal perspective. If in actual fact no pipe-smoker, let alone a brilliant detective, ever lived in Baker Street, then there will also be contexts, namely those where we are discussing reality rather than fiction, where (3) can be used to state a falsehood. Similarly, if there is in fact no blond angel called 'Pygar', then (4) will presumably state a falsehood in any actual reality-invoking context. If sentences (3) and (4) do indeed express a truth in some contexts and a falsehood in others then that calls for explanation: does the sentence express different propositions in different contexts? If so, is this a form of ambiguity? Or is it a form of indexicality? In either case, which expressions in the sentences are responsible for the ambiguity or indexicality?

David Lewis's answer would be that (3) and (4) are ambiguous. For example, some utterances of (4) are abbreviations for 'In the fiction *Barbarella*, there is a blond angel called "Pygar" ', while others are not. The implicit 'In the fiction of *Barbarella*, . . .' is according to Lewis an intensional operator. He spends most of his paper elaborating the semantics of operators of the form 'In the fiction of *F*, . . .'. Predelli's article challenges Lewis's analysis and makes an alternative proposal, according to which the variation in truth value of sentences like (3) and (4) between fiction- and reality-invoking contexts is not due to a change in the proposition expressed. Rather, the variation is owed to the fact that the proposition expressed in both contexts is evaluated with respect to different circumstances in each context. Thus, the dispute between Lewis and Predelli can be seen as concerning the second complex of problems, which arose independently of the issue of fictional names.

We distinguished the problem of fictional names from the problem of apparent contextual variation of the truth value of sentences like (3) and (4). The two problems also interact. Thus, sentence (1) could be used in internal discourse about the fiction of *Barbarella*, in which case it would be intuitively considered true. But there are also contexts where we can truly say things like

(5)   Barbarella was created by Jean-Claude Forest.

---

[7] Some alert readers might pause here and wonder whether (4) was rightly characterized above as a sentence that does not contain a fictional name. Does it not contain the fictional name 'Pygar'? It does indeed contain the fictional name within quotation marks, which indicates that the name is merely being mentioned, not used. What is used is not the fictional name 'Pygar', but the quotation-name ' "Pygar" '. The latter is not fictional and not empty. It refers to a name. If you are not convinced, replace (4) by 'There is a blond Angel whose name begins with "Py" and ends in "gar" '.

[11] Some will deny this. Thus, for example, Sainsbury would claim that while in some contexts uttering (3) will be correct in a certain sense (and uttering its negation would be incorrect in that sense), correctness in this sense merely amounts to fidelity to the fiction and not to truth (Sainsbury 2005, p. 203).

Amie Thomasson thinks that in such contexts, the name 'Barbarella' refers to some-thing, namely to an 'abstract artefact', an abstract object created by the author of the Barbarella fiction. Now, it seems that in contexts of this sort, i.e. where (5) expresses a truth, sentence (1) cannot be uttered truly, for abstract artefacts don't travel between planets. Similarly, sentence (5) seems to express a falsehood within the sort of internal discourse where (1) is intuitively true, for according to Jean-Claude Forest's fiction, Barbarella is not created by Jean-Claude Forest.

We are now again faced with the problem of apparent contextual variation in truth value. We will have to decide whether to take these appearances at face value, i.e. whether to take them to reflect the truth values of the propositions expressed in each case. Thomasson does not take them at face value. In other words, despite appearances to the contrary, (1) expresses a false proposition concerning an abstract artefact. In that case, we need to explain away the appearances, for example by explaining how, even though a false proposition is expressed, we have the impression that something true was being said.

If we do take impressions at face value, i.e. regard (1) as true in the internal context and false in external discourse, then we have to explain how this variation arises: is (1) ambiguous? If so, is this because the name 'Barbarella' is ambiguous? If it is not ambiguous, then is there indexicality? I.e. does some expression ('Barbarella'?) change its value according to the context of use?

Questions and tasks

1   How does Lewis try to solve the difficulty raised by Kripke, mentioned in our note 5? Does he succeed?

2   Intensional operators are operators that operate on intensions. What is the intension that the intensional operator 'In the Holmes stories, . . .' operates on in the sentence, 'In the Holmes stories, Sherlock Holmes lived at 221B Baker Street'?

3   According to Thomasson, fictionalizing discourse and internal discourse involve pretence. According to Lewis's theory, no pretence is involved, rather, in fic-tionalizing discourse and internal discourse, we genuinely assert propositions that involve a fiction operator. What are the most significant differences between these two approaches?

4   Explain how Predelli's example sentence (6) is supposed to support his proposal.

5   Predelli claims that the contents expressed by utterances within internal fic-tional discourse have to be evaluated for truth with respect to a possible world other than the world of utterance. How does this position differ from the pretence account of such contexts preferred by Thomasson?

6   Thomasson regards fictionalizing and internal discourse as involving pretence: we pretend to assert certain things. She distinguishes between a *de dicto* and a *de re* construal of the pretence. On the *de dicto* construal, could what a narrator pretends to assert become true by coincidence?

References and further reading

Braun, David 2005: 'Empty Names, Fictional Names, Mythical Names', *Noûs* 39, pp. 596–631.

Currie, Gregory 1990: *The Nature of Fiction*, Cambridge: Cambridge University Press.

Evans, Gareth 1982: Ch. 10 of *The Varieties of Reference*, Oxford: Oxford University Press.

Everett, Anthony 2005: 'Against Fictional Realism', *Journal of Philosophy* 102, pp. 624–49.

Everett, Anthony 2007: 'Pretense, Existence, and Fictional Objects', *Philosophy and Phenomenological Research* 74, pp. 56–80.

Frege, Gottlob 1892: 'Über Sinn und Bedeutung', *Zeitschrift für Philosophie und philosophische Kritik*, NF, 100: 25–50. Translation in this volume, pp. 49–55.

Friend, Stacie 2007: 'Fictional Characters', *Philosophy Compass* 2, pp. 141–56.

Lamarque, P., and S. H. Olsen 1994: *Truth, Fiction and Literature*, Oxford: Clarendon Press.

Lewis, David 1983: 'Postscripts to "Truth in Fiction" ', in David Lewis, *Philosophical Papers*, vol. 1, Oxford: Oxford University Press, pp. 276–80.

Parsons, Terence 1980: *Nonexistent Objects*, New Haven, CT: Yale University Press.

Reimer, Marga 2001: 'The Problem of Empty Names', *Australasian Journal of Philosophy* 79, pp. 491–506.

Sainsbury, Mark 2005: Ch. 6 of *Reference without Referents*, Oxford: Oxford University Press.

Sainsbury, Mark 2009: *Fiction and Fictionalism*, London: Routledge.

Salmon, Nathan 1998: 'Nonexistence', *Noûs* 32, pp. 277–319.

van Inwagen, Peter 1977: 'Creatures of Fiction', *American Philosophical Quarterly* 14, pp. 299–308.

Walton, Kendall 1990: *Mimesis as Make-Believe: On the Foundations of the Representational Arts*, Cambridge, MA: Harvard University Press.

Chapter 34

David K. Lewis

TRUTH IN FICTION

We can truly say that Sherlock Holmes lived in Baker Street, and that he liked to show off his mental powers. We cannot truly say that he was a devoted family man, or that he worked in close cooperation with the police.

It would be nice if we could take such descriptions of fictional characters at their face value, ascribing to them the same subject-predicate form as parallel descriptions of real-life characters. Then the sentences "Holmes wears a silk top hat" and "Nixon wears a silk top hat" would both be false because the referent of the subject term—fictional Holmes or real-life Nixon, as the case may be—lacks the property, expressed by the predicate, of wearing a silk top hat. The only difference would be that the subject terms "Holmes" and "Nixon" have referents of radically different sorts: one a fictional character, the other a real-life person of flesh and blood.

I don't question that a treatment along these Meinongian lines could be made to work. Terence Parsons has done it.[1] But it is no simple matter to overcome the difficulties that arise. For one thing, is there not some perfectly good sense in which Holmes, like Nixon, is a real-life person of flesh and blood? There are stories about the exploits of super-heroes from other planets, hobbits, fires and storms, vaporous intelligences, and other non-persons. But what a mistake it would be to class the Holmes stories with these!

Unlike Clark Kent *et al.*, Sherlock Holmes is just a person—a person of flesh and blood, a being in the very same category as Nixon.

Consider also the problem of the chorus. We can truly say that Sir Joseph Porter, K.C.B., is attended by a chorus of his sisters and his cousins and his aunts. To make this true, it seems that the domain of fictional characters must contain not only Sir Joseph himself, but also plenty of fictional sisters and cousins and aunts. But how many—five dozen, perhaps? No, for we cannot truly say that the chorus numbers five dozen exactly. We cannot truly say anything exact about its size. Then do we perhaps have a fictional chorus, but no fictional members of this chorus and hence no number of members? No, for we can truly say some things about the size. We are told that the sisters and cousins, even without the aunts, number in dozens.

The Meinongian should not suppose that the quantifiers in descriptions of fictional characters range over all the things he thinks there are, both fictional and non-fictional; but he may not find it easy to say just how the ranges of quantification are to be restricted. Consider whether we can truly say that Holmes was more intelligent than anyone else, before or since. It is certainly appropriate to compare him with some fictional characters, such as Mycroft and Watson; but not with others, such as Poirot or "Slipstick" Libby. It may be appropriate to compare him with some non-fictional characters, such as Newton and

Darwin; but probably not with others, such as Conan Doyle or Frank Ramsey. "More intelligent than anyone else" meant something like "more intelligent than anyone else in the world of Sherlock Holmes." The inhabitants of this "world" are drawn partly from the fictional side of the Meinongian domain and partly from the non-fictional side, exhausting neither.

Finally, the Meinongian must tell us why truths about fictional characters are cut off, sometimes though not always, from the consequences they ought to imply. We can truly say that Holmes lived at 221B Baker Street. I have been told[2] that the only building at 221B Baker Street, then or now, was a bank. It does not follow, and certainly is not true, that Holmes lived in a bank.

The way of the Meinongian is hard, and in this paper I shall explore a simpler alternative. Let us not take our descriptions of fictional characters at face value, but instead let us regard them as abbreviations for longer sentences beginning with an operator "In such-and-such fiction. . . ." Such a phrase is an intensional operator that may be prefixed to a sentence ϕ to form a new sentence. But then the prefixed operator may be dropped by way of abbreviation, leaving us with what sounds like the original sentence ϕ but differs from it in sense.

Thus if I say that Holmes liked to show off, you will take it that I have asserted an abbreviated version of the true sentence "In the Sherlock Holmes stories, Holmes liked to show off." As for the embedded sentence "Holmes liked to show off," taken by itself with the prefixed operator neither explicitly present nor tacitly understood, we may abandon it to the common fate of subject-predicate sentences with denotationless subject terms; automatic falsity or lack of truth value, according to taste.

Many things we might say about Holmes are potentially ambiguous. They may or may not be taken as abbreviations for sentences carrying the prefix "In the Sherlock Holmes stories. . . ." Context, content, and common sense will usually

resolve the ambiguity in practice. Consider these sentences:

> Holmes lived in Baker Street.
>
> Holmes lived nearer to Paddington Station than to Waterloo Station.
>
> Holmes was just a person—a person of flesh and blood.
>
> Holmes really existed.
>
> Someone lived for many years at 221B Baker Street.
>
> London's greatest detective in 1900 used cocaine.

All of them are false if taken as unprefixed, simply because Holmes did not actually exist. (Or perhaps at least some of them lack truth value.) All are true if taken as abbreviations for prefixed sentences. The first three would probably be taken in the latter way, hence they seem true. The rest would probably be taken in the former way, hence they seem false. The sentence

> No detective ever solved almost all his cases.

would probably be taken as unprefixed and hence true, though it would be false if taken as prefixed. The sentence

> Holmes and Watson are identical.

is sure to be taken as prefixed and hence false, but that is no refutation of systems of free logic[3] which would count it as true if taken as unprefixed.

(I hasten to concede that some truths about Holmes are not abbreviations of prefixed sentences, and also are not true just because "Holmes" is denotationless. For instance these:

> Holmes is a fictional character.
>
> Holmes was killed off by Conan Doyle, but later resurrected.

Holmes has acquired a cultish following.

Holmes symbolizes mankind's ceaseless striving for truth.

Holmes would not have needed tapes to get the goods on Nixon.

Holmes could have solved the A.B.C. murders sooner than Poirot.

I shall have nothing to say here about the proper treatment of these sentences. If the Meinongian can handle them with no special dodges, that is an advantage of his approach over mine.)

The ambiguity of prefixing explains why truths about fictional characters are sometimes cut off from their seeming consequences. Suppose we have an argument (with zero or more premises) which is valid in the modal sense that it is impossible for the premises all to be true and the conclusion false.

$$\frac{\psi_1, \ldots, \psi_n}{\therefore \phi}$$

Then it seems clear that we obtain another valid argument if we prefix an operator "In the fiction f . . ." uniformly to each premiss and to the conclusion of the original argument. Truth in a given fiction is closed under implication.

$$\frac{\ln f, \psi_1, \ldots, \ln f, \psi_n}{\therefore \ln f, \phi}$$

But if we prefix the operator "In the fiction f . . ." to some of the original premises and not to others, or if we take some but not all of the premises as tacitly prefixed, then in general neither the original conclusion ϕ nor the prefixed conclusion "In the fiction f, ϕ" will follow. In the inference we considered earlier there were two premises. The premiss that Holmes lived at 221B Baker Street was true only if taken as prefixed. The premiss that the only building at 221B Baker Street was a bank, on the other hand, was true only if taken as unprefixed; for in the stories there was no bank there but rather a rooming

house. Taking the premises as we naturally would in the ways that make them true, nothing follows: neither the unprefixed conclusion that Holmes lived in a bank nor the prefixed conclusion that in the stories he lived in a bank. Taking both premises as unprefixed, the unprefixed conclusion follows but the first premiss is false. Taking both premises as prefixed, the prefixed conclusion follows but the second premiss is false.[4]

Our remaining task is to see what may be said about the analysis of the operators "In such-and-such fiction. . . ." I have already noted that truth in a given fiction is closed under implication. Such closure is the earmark of an operator of relative necessity, an intensional operator that may be analyzed as a restricted universal quantifier over possible worlds. So we might proceed as follows: a prefixed sentence "In fiction f, ϕ" is true (or, as we shall also say, ϕ is true in the fiction f) iff ϕ is true at every possible world in a certain set, this set being somehow determined by the fiction f.

As a first approximation, we might consider exactly those worlds where the plot of the fiction is enacted, where a course of events takes place that matches the story. What is true in the Sherlock Holmes stories would then be what is true at all of those possible worlds where there are characters who have the attributes, stand in the relations, and do the deeds that are ascribed in the stories to Holmes, Watson, and the rest. (Whether these characters would then *be* Holmes, Watson, and the rest is a vexed question that we must soon consider.)

I think this proposal is not quite right. For one thing, there is a threat of circularity. Even the Holmes stories, not to mention fiction written in less explicit styles, are by no means in the form of straightforward chronicles. An intelligent and informed reader can indeed discover the plot, and could write it down in the form of a fully explicit chronicle if he liked. But this extraction of plot from text is no trivial or automatic task. Perhaps the reader accomplishes it only by figuring out what is true in the stories—that is, only by exercising his tacit mastery of the very concept of truth in fiction that we are now investigating. If so, then an analysis that starts by making uncritical use of the concept of the plot of a fiction might be rather uninformative, even if correct so far as it goes.

A second problem arises out of an observation by Saul Kripke.[5] Let us assume that Conan Doyle indeed wrote the stories as pure fiction. He just made them up. He had no knowledge of anyone who did the deeds he ascribed to Holmes, nor had he even picked up any garbled information originating in any such person. It may nevertheless be, purely by coincidence, that our own world is one of the worlds where the plot of the stories is enacted. Maybe there was a man whom Conan Doyle never heard of whose actual adventures chanced to fit the stories in every detail. Maybe he even was named "Sherlock Holmes." Improbable, incredible, but surely possible! Now consider the name "Sherlock Holmes," *as used in the stories*. Does the name, so used, refer to the man whom Conan Doyle never heard of? Surely not! It is irrelevant that a homonymous name is used by some people, not including Conan Doyle, to refer to this man. We must distinguish between the homonyms, just as we would distinguish the name of London (England) from the homonymous name of London (Ontario). It is false at our world that the name, "Sherlock Holmes," as used in the stories, refers to someone. Yet it is true in the stories that this name, as used in the stories, refers to someone. So we have found something that is true in the stories but false (under our improbable supposition) at one of the worlds where the plot of the stories is enacted.

In order to avoid this difficulty, it will be helpful if we do not think of a fiction in the abstract, as a string of sentences or something of that sort. Rather, a fiction is a story told by a storyteller on a particular occasion. He may tell his tales around the campfire or he may type a manuscript and send it to his publisher, but in either case there is

an act of storytelling. Different acts of storytelling, different fictions. When Pierre Menard retells *Don Quixote*, that is not the same fiction as Cervantes' *Don Quixote*—not even if they are in the same language and match word for word.[6] (It would have been different if Menard had copied Cervantes' fiction from memory, however; that would not have been what I call an act of storytelling at all.) One act of storytelling might, however, be the telling of two different fictions: one a harmless fantasy told to the children and the censors, the other a subversive allegory simultaneously told to the *cognoscenti*.

Storytelling is pretence. The storyteller purports to be telling the truth about matters whereof he has knowledge. He purports to be talking about characters who are known to him, and whom he refers to, typically, by means of their ordinary proper names. But if his story is fiction, he is not really doing these things. Usually his pretence has not the slightest tendency to deceive anyone, nor has he the slightest intent to deceive. Nevertheless he plays a false part, goes through a form of telling known fact when he is not doing so. This is most apparent when the fiction is told in the first person. Conan Doyle pretended to be a doctor named Watson, engaged in publishing truthful memoirs of events he himself had witnessed. But the case of third-person narrative is not essentially different. The author purports to be telling the truth about matters he has somehow come to know about, though how he has found out about them is left unsaid. That is why there is a pragmatic paradox akin to contradiction in a third-person narrative that ends ". . . and so none were left to tell the tale."

The worlds we should consider, I suggest, are the worlds where the fiction is told, but as known fact rather than fiction. The act of storytelling occurs, just as it does here at our world; but there it is what here it falsely purports to be: truth-telling about matters whereof the teller has knowledge.[7] Our own world cannot be such a world; for if it is really a fiction that we are dealing with, then the act of storytelling at our world was not what it purported to be. It does not matter if, unbeknownst to the author, our world is one where his plot is enacted. The real-life Sherlock Holmes would not have made Conan Doyle any less of a pretender, if Conan Doyle had never heard of him. (This real-life Holmes might have had his real-life Watson who told true stories about the adventures he had witnessed. But even if his memoirs matched Conan Doyle's fiction word for word they would not be the same stories, any more than Cervantes' *Don Quixote* is the same story as Menard's. So our world would still not be one where the Holmes stories—the *same* Holmes stories that Conan Doyle told as fiction—were told as known fact.) On the other hand, any world where the story is told as known fact rather than fiction must be among the worlds where the plot of the story is enacted. Else its enactment could be neither known nor truly told of.

I rely on a notion of trans-world identity for stories; this is partly a matter of word-for-word match and partly a matter of trans-world identity (or perhaps a counterpart relation) for acts of storytelling. Here at our world we have a fiction f, told in an act a of storytelling; at some other world we have an act a′ of telling the truth about known matters of fact; the stories told in a and a′ match word for word, and the words have the same meaning. Does that mean that the other world is one where f is told as known fact rather than fiction? Not necessarily, as the case of Menard shows. It is also required that a and a′ be the same act of storytelling (or at least counterparts). How bad is this? Surely you would like to know more about the criteria of trans-world identity (or the counterpart relation) for acts of storytelling, and so indeed would I. But I think we have enough of a grip to make it worthwhile going on. I see no threat of circularity here, since I see no way of using the concept of truth in fiction to help with the analysis of trans-world identity of acts of storytelling.

Suppose a fiction employs such names as

"Sherlock Holmes." At those worlds where the same story is told as known fact rather than fiction, those names really are what they here purport to be: ordinary proper names of existing characters known to the storyteller. Here at our world, the storyteller only pretends that "Sherlock Holmes" has the semantic character of an ordinary proper name. We have no reason at all to suppose that the name, as used here at our world, really does have that character. As we use it, it may be very unlike an ordinary proper name. Indeed, it may have a highly non-rigid sense, governed largely by the descriptions of Holmes and his deeds that are found in the stories. That is what I suggest: the sense of "Sherlock Holmes" as we use it is such that, for any world w where the Holmes stories are told as known fact rather than fiction, the name denotes at w whichever inhabitant of w it is who there plays the role of Holmes. Part of that role, of course, is to bear the ordinary proper name "Sherlock Holmes." But that only goes to show that "Sherlock Holmes" is used at w as an ordinary proper name, not that it is so used here.[8,9]

I also suggest, less confidently, that whenever a world w is not one of the worlds just considered, the sense of "Sherlock Holmes" as we use it is such as to assign it no denotation at w. That is so even if the plot of the fiction is enacted by inhabitants of w. If we are right that Conan Doyle told the Holmes stories as fiction, then it follows that "Sherlock Holmes" is denotationless here at our world. It does not denote the real-life Sherlock Holmes whom Conan Doyle never heard of, if such there be.

We have reached a proposal I shall call ANALYSIS 0: *A sentence of the form "In fiction f, φ" is true iff φ is true at every world where f is told as known fact rather than fiction.*

Is that right? There are some who never tire of telling us not to read anything into a fiction that is not there explicitly, and Analysis 0 will serve to capture the usage of those who hold this view in its most extreme form. I do not believe, however, that such a usage is at all common. Most of us are content to read a fiction against a background of well-known fact, "reading into" the fiction content that is not there explicitly but that comes jointly from the explicit content and the factual background. Analysis 0 disregards the background. Thereby it brings too many possible worlds into consideration, so not enough comes out true in the fiction.

For example, I claim that in the Holmes stories, Holmes lives nearer to Paddington Station than to Waterloo Station. A glance at the map will show you that his address in Baker Street is much nearer to Paddington. Yet the map is not part of the stories; and so far as I know it is never stated or implied in the stories themselves that Holmes lives nearer to Paddington. There are possible worlds where the Holmes stories are told as known fact rather than fiction which differ in all sorts of ways from ours. Among these are worlds where Holmes lives in a London arranged very differently from the London of our world, a London where Holmes's address in Baker Street is much closer to Waterloo Station than to Paddington.

(I do not suppose that such a distortion of geography need prevent the otherworldly places there called "London," "Paddington Station," ... from being the same as, or counterparts of, their actual namesakes. But if I am wrong, that still does not challenge my claim that there are worlds where the stories are told as known fact but where it is true that Holmes lives closer to Waterloo than to Paddington. For it is open to us to regard the place-names, as used in the stories, as fictional names with non-rigid senses like the non-rigid sense I have already ascribed to "Sherlock Holmes." That would mean, incidentally, that "Paddington Station," as used in the stories, does not denote the actual station of that name.)

Similarly, I claim that it is true, though not explicit, in the stories that Holmes does not have a third nostril; that he never had a case in which the murderer turned out to be a purple gnome; that he solved his cases without the aid of divine revelation; that he never visited the moons of Saturn; and that he wears underpants. There are bizarre worlds where the Holmes stories are told as known fact but where all of these things are false.

Strictly speaking, it is fallacious to reason from a mixture of truth in fact and truth in fiction to conclusions about truth in fiction. From a mixture of prefixed and unprefixed premises, nothing follows. But in practice the fallacy is often not so bad. The factual premises in mixed reasoning may be part of the background against which we read the fiction. They may carry over into the fiction, not because there is anything explicit in the fiction to make them true, but rather because there is nothing to make them false. There is nothing in the Holmes stories, for instance, that gives us any reason to bracket our background knowledge of the broad outlines of London geography. Only a few details need changing—principally details having to do with 221B Baker Street. To move the stations around, or even to regard their locations as an open question, would be uncalled for. What's true in fact about their locations is true also in the stories. Then it is no error to reason from such facts to conclusions about what else is true in the stories.

You've heard it all before. Reasoning about truth in fiction is very like counterfactual reasoning. We make a supposition contrary to fact—what if this match had been struck? In reasoning about what would have happened in that counterfactual situation, we use factual premises. The match was dry, there was oxygen about, and so forth. But we do not use factual premises altogether freely, since some of them would fall victim to the change that takes us from actuality to the envisaged counterfactual situation. We do not use the factual premiss that the match was inside the matchbox at the time in question, or that it was at room temperature a second later. We depart from actuality as far as we must to reach a possible world where the counterfactual supposition comes true (and that might be quite far if the supposition is a fantastic one). But we do not make gratuitous changes. We hold fixed the features of actuality that do not have to be changed as part of the least disruptive way of making the supposition true. We can safely reason from the part of our factual background that is thus held fixed.

By now, several authors have treated counterfactual conditionals along the lines just sketched. Differences of detail between these treatments are unimportant for our present purposes. My own version[10] runs as follows. A counterfactual of the form "If it were that ϕ, then it would be that Ψ" is non-vacuously true iff some possible world where both ϕ and Ψ are true differs less from our actual world, on balance, then does any world where ϕ is true but Ψ is not true. It is vacuously true iff ϕ is true at no possible worlds. (I omit accessibility restrictions for simplicity.)

Getting back to truth in fiction, recall that the trouble with Analysis 0 was that it ignored background, and thereby brought into consideration bizarre worlds that differed gratuitously from our actual world. A fiction will in general require some departures from actuality, the more so if it is a fantastic fiction. But we need to keep the departures from actuality under control. It is wrong, or at least eccentric, to read the Holmes stories as if they might for all we know be taking place at a world where three-nostrilled detectives pursue purple gnomes. The remedy is, roughly speaking, to analyze statements of truth in fiction as counterfactuals. What is true in the Sherlock Holmes stories is what would be true if those stories were told as known fact rather than fiction.

Spelling this out according to my treatment of counterfactuals, we have ANALYSIS 1: *A sentence of the form "In the fiction f, ϕ" is non-vacuously true iff some world where f is told as known fact and ϕ is true differs less from our actual world, on balance, than does any world where f is told as known fact and ϕ is not true. It is vacuously true iff there are no possible worlds where f is told as known fact.* (I postpone consideration of the vacuous case.)

We sometimes speak of the world of a fiction. What is true in the Holmes stories is what is true,

as we say, "in the world of Sherlock Holmes." That we speak this way should suggest that it is right to consider less than all the worlds where the plot of the stories is enacted, and less even than all the worlds where the stories are told as known fact. "In the world of Sherlock Holmes," as in actuality, Baker Street is closer to Paddington Station than to Waterloo Station and there are no purple gnomes. But it will not do to follow ordinary language to the extent of supposing that we can somehow single out a single one of the worlds where the stories are told as known fact. Is the world of Sherlock Holmes a world where Holmes has an even or an odd number of hairs on his head at the moment when he first meets Watson? What is Inspector Lestrade's blood type? It is absurd to suppose that these questions about the world of Sherlock Holmes have answers. The best explanation of that is that the worlds of Sherlock Holmes are plural, and the questions have different answers at different ones. If we may assume that some of the worlds where the stories are told as known fact differ least from our world, then these are the worlds of Sherlock Homes. What is true throughout them is true in the stories; what is false throughout them is false in the stories; what is true at some and false at others is neither true nor false in the stories. Any answer to the silly questions just asked would doubtless fall in the last category. It is for the same reason that the chorus of Sir Joseph Porter's sisters and cousins and aunts has no determinate size: it has different sizes at different ones of the worlds of H.M.S. Pinafore.[11]

Under Analysis 1, truth in a given fiction depends on matters of contingent fact. I am not thinking of the remote possibility that accidental properties of the fiction might somehow enter into determining which are the worlds where that fiction is told as known fact. Rather, it is a contingent matter which of those worlds differ more from ours and which less, and which (if any) differ least. That is because it is a contingent fact—indeed it is *the* contingent fact on which all others depend—which possible world is our actual world. To the extent that the character of our world carries over into the worlds of Sherlock Holmes, what is true in the stories depends on what our world is like. If the stations of London had been differently located, it might have been true in the stories (and not because the stories would then have been different) that Holmes lived nearer to Waterloo Station than to Paddington Station.

This contingency is all very well when truth in fiction depends on well-known contingent facts about our world, as it does in the examples I have so far given to motivate Analysis 1. It is more disturbing if truth in fiction turns out to depend on contingent facts that are not well known. In an article setting forth little-known facts about the movement of snakes, Carl Gans has argued as follows:

> In "The Adventure of the Speckled Band" Sherlock Holmes solves a murder mystery by showing that the victim has been killed by a Russell's viper that has climbed up a bell-rope. What Holmes did not realize was that Russell's viper is not a constrictor. The snake is therefore incapable of concertina movement and could not have climbed the rope. Either the snake reached its victim some other way or the case remains open.[12]

We may well look askance at this reasoning. But if Analysis 1 is correct then so is Gans's argument. The story never quite says that Holmes was right that the snake climbed the rope. Hence there are worlds where the Holmes stories are told as known fact, where the snake reached the victim some other way, and where Holmes therefore bungled. Presumably some of these worlds differ less from ours than their rivals where Holmes was right and where Russell's viper is capable of concertina movement up a rope. Holmes's infallibility, of course, is not a countervailing resemblance to actuality; our world contains no infallible Holmes.

Psychoanalysis of fictional characters provides a more important example. The critic uses (what he believes to be) little-known facts of human psychology as premises, and reasons to conclusions that are far from obvious about the childhood or the adult mental state of the fictional character. Under Analysis 1 his procedure is justified. Unless countervailing considerations can be found, to consider worlds where the little-known fact of psychology does not hold would be to depart gratuitously from actuality.

The psychoanalysis of fictional characters has aroused vigorous objections. So would Gans's argument, if anyone cared. I shall keep neutral in these quarrels, and try to provide for the needs of both sides. Analysis 1, or something close to it, should capture the usage of Gans and the literary psychoanalysts. Let us find an alternative analysis to capture the conflicting usage of their opponents. I shall not try to say which usage is more conducive to appreciation of fiction and critical insight.

Suppose we decide, *contra* Gans and the literary psychoanalysts, that little-known or unknown facts about our world are irrelevant to truth in fiction. But let us not fall back to Analysis 0; it is not our only alternative. Let us still recognize that it is perfectly legitimate to reason to truth in fiction from a background of well-known facts.

Must they really be facts? It seems that if little-known or unknown facts are irrelevant, then so are little-known or unknown errors in the body of shared opinion that is generally taken for fact. We think we all know that there are no purple gnomes, but what if there really are a few, unknown to anyone except themselves, living in a secluded cabin near Loch Ness? Once we set aside the usage given by Analysis 1, it seems clear that whatever purple gnomes may be hidden in odd corners of our actual world, there are still none of them in the worlds of Sherlock Holmes. We have shifted to viewing truth in fiction as the joint product of explicit content and a background of generally prevalent beliefs.

Our own beliefs? I think not. That would

mean that what is true in a fiction is constantly changing. Gans might not be right yet, but he would eventually become right about Holmes's error if enough people read his article and learned that Russell's viper could not climb a rope. When the map of Victorian London was finally forgotten, it would cease to be true that Holmes lived nearer to Paddington than to Waterloo. Strange to say, the historical scholar would be in no better position to know what was true in the fictions of his period than the ignorant layman. That cannot be right. What was true in a fiction when it was first told is true in it forevermore. It is our knowledge of what is true in the fiction that may wax or wane.

The proper background, then, consists of the beliefs that generally prevailed in the community where the fiction originated: the beliefs of the author and his intended audience. And indeed the factual premises that seemed to us acceptable in reasoning about Sherlock Holmes were generally believed in the community of origin of the stories. Everyone knew roughly where the principal stations of London were, everyone disbelieved in purple gnomes, and so forth.

One last complication. Suppose Conan Doyle was a secret believer in purple gnomes; thinking that his belief in them was not shared by anyone else he kept it carefully to himself for fear of ridicule. In particular, he left no trace of this belief in his stories. Suppose also that some of his original readers likewise were secret believers in purple gnomes. Suppose, in fact, that everyone alive at the time was a secret believer in purple gnomes, each thinking that his own belief was not shared by anyone else. Then it is clear (to the extent that anything is clear about such a strange situation) that the belief in purple gnomes does not "generally prevail" in quite the right way, and there are still no purple gnomes in the worlds of Sherlock Holmes. Call a belief *overt* in a community at a time iff more or less everyone shares it, more or less everyone thinks that more or less everyone else shares it, and so on.[13] The proper background, we may conclude,

comprises the beliefs that are overt in the community of origin of the fiction.

Assume, by way of idealization, that the beliefs overt in the community are each possible and jointly compossible. Then we can assign to the community a set of possible worlds, called the *collective belief worlds* of the community, comprising exactly those worlds where the overt beliefs all come true. Only if the community is uncommonly lucky will the actual world belong to this set. Indeed, the actual world determines the collective belief worlds of the community of origin of the fiction and then drops out of the analysis. (It is of course a contingent matter what that community is and what is overtly believed there.) We are left with two sets of worlds: the worlds where the fiction is told as known fact, and the collective belief worlds of the community of origin. The first set gives the content of the fiction; the second gives the background of prevalent beliefs.

It would be a mistake simply to consider the worlds that belong to both sets. Fictions usually contravene at least some of the community's overt beliefs. I can certainly tell a story in which there are purple gnomes, though there are none at our collective belief worlds. Further, it will usually be overtly believed in the community of origin of a fiction that the story is not told as known fact—storytellers seldom deceive—so none of the worlds where the fiction is told as known fact can be a collective belief world of the community. Even if the two sets do overlap (the fiction is plausible and the author palms it off as fact) the worlds that belong to both sets are apt to be special in ways having nothing to do with what is true in the fiction. Suppose the story tells of a bungled burglary in recent times, and suppose it ends just as the police reach the scene. Any collective belief world of ours where this story is told as known fact is a world where the burglary was successfully covered up; for it is an overt belief among us that no such burglary ever hit the news. That does not make it true in the story that the burglary was covered up.

What we need is something like Analysis 1, but applied from the standpoint of the collective belief worlds rather than the actual world. What is true in the Sherlock Holmes stories is what would be true, according to the overt beliefs of the community of origin, if those stories were told as known fact rather than fiction.

Spelling this out, we have ANALYSIS 2: *A sentence of the form "In the fiction f, ϕ" is non-vacuously true iff, whenever w is one of the collective belief worlds of the community of origin of f, then some world where f is told as known fact and ϕ is true differs less from the world w, on balance, than does any world where f is told as known fact and ϕ is not true. It is vacuously true iff there are no possible worlds where f is told as known fact.* It is Analysis 2, or something close to it, that I offer to opponents of Gans and the literary psychoanalysts.

I shall briefly consider two remaining areas of difficulty and sketch strategies for dealing with them. I shall not propose improved analyses, however; partly because I am not quite sure what changes to make, and partly because Analysis 2 is quite complicated enough already.

I have said that truth in fiction is the joint product of two sources: the explicit content of the fiction, and a background consisting either of the facts about our world (Analysis 1) or of the beliefs overt in the community of origin (Analysis 2). Perhaps there is a third source which also contributes: carry-over from other truth in fiction. There are two cases: intra-fictional and inter-fictional.

In the *Threepenny Opera*, the principal characters are a treacherous crew. They constantly betray one another, for gain or to escape danger. There is also a streetsinger. He shows up, sings the ballad of Mack the Knife, and goes about his business without betraying anyone. Is he also a treacherous fellow? The explicit content does not make him so. Real people are not so very treacherous, and even in Weimar Germany it was not overtly believed that they were, so background does not make him so either. Yet there is a moderately good reason to say that he is treacherous: in the *Threepenny Opera*, that's how

people are. In the worlds of the *Threepenny Opera*, everyone put to the test proves treacherous, the streetsinger is there along with the rest, so doubtless he too would turn out to be treacherous if we saw more of him. His treacherous nature is an intra-fictional carry-over from the treacherous natures in the story of Macheath, Polly, Tiger Brown, and the rest.

Suppose I write a story about the dragon Scrulch, a beautiful princess, a bold knight, and what not. It is a perfectly typical instance of its stylized genre, except that I never say that Scrulch breathes fire. Does he nevertheless breathe fire in my story? Perhaps so, because dragons in that sort of story do breathe fire. But the explicit content does not make him breathe fire. Neither does background, since in actuality and according to our beliefs there are no animals that breathe fire. (It just might be analytic that nothing is a dragon unless it breathes fire. But suppose I never *called* Scrulch a dragon; I merely endowed him with all the standard dragonly attributes except fire-breathing.) If Scrulch does breathe fire in my story, it is by inter-fictional carry-over from what is true of dragons in other stories.

I have spoken of Conan Doyle's Holmes stories; but many other authors also have written Holmes stories. These would have little point without inter-fictional carry-over. Surely many things are true in these satellite stories not because of the explicit content of the satellite story itself, and not because they are part of the background, but rather because they carry over from Conan Doyle's original Holmes stories. Similarly, if instead of asking what is true in the entire corpus of Conan Doyle's Holmes stories we ask what is true in "The Hound of the Baskervilles," we will doubtless find many things that are true in that story only by virtue of carry-over from Conan Doyle's other Holmes stories.

I turn finally to vacuous truth in impossible fictions. Let us call a fiction *impossible* iff there is no world where it is told as known fact rather than fiction. That might happen in either of two ways. First, the plot might be impossible. Second, a possible plot might imply that there could be nobody in a position to know or tell of the events in question. If a fiction is impossible in the second way, then to tell it as known fact would be to know its truth and tell truly something that implies that its truth could not be known; which is impossible.

According to all three of my analyses, anything whatever is vacuously true in an impossible fiction. That seems entirely satisfactory if the impossibility is blatant: if we are dealing with a fantasy about the troubles of the man who squared the circle, or with the worst sort of incoherent time-travel story. We should not expect to have a non-trivial concept of truth in blatantly impossible fiction, or perhaps we should expect to have one only under the pretence—not to be taken too seriously—that there are impossible possible worlds as well as the possible possible worlds.

But what should we do with a fiction that is not blatantly impossible, but impossible only because the author has been forgetful? I have spoken of truth in the Sherlock Holmes stories. Strictly speaking, these (taken together) are an impossible fiction. Conan Doyle contradicted himself from one story to another about the location of Watson's old war wound. Still, I do not want to say that just anything is true in the Holmes stories!

I suppose that we might proceed in two steps to say what is true in a venially impossible fiction such as the Holmes stories. First, go from the original impossible fiction to the several possible revised versions that stay closest to the original. Then say that what is true in the original is what is true, according to one of our analyses of non-vacuous truth in fiction, in all of these revised versions. Then nothing definite will be true in the Holmes stories about the location of Watson's wound. Since Conan Doyle put it in different places, the different revised versions will differ. But at least it will be true in the stories that Watson was wounded elsewhere than in the left big toe. Conan Doyle put the wound in various places, but never there. So no revised version will put the wound in the left big toe, since that would change the story more than consistency demands.

The revised versions, like the original fiction, will be associated with acts of storytelling. The revised versions, unlike the original, will not actually be told either as fiction or as known fact. But there are worlds where they are told as fiction, and worlds where they are told as known fact.

Even when the original fiction is not quite impossible, there may be cases in which it would be better to consider not truth in the original fiction but rather truth in all suitably revised versions. We have a three-volume novel set in 1878. We learn in the first volume that the hero had lunch in Glasgow on a certain day. In the third volume, it turns out that he showed up in London that same afternoon. In no other way does this novel purport to be a fantasy of rapid transit. The author was just careless. We could without vacuity apply our analyses directly to the novel as written. Since the closest worlds where it is told as known fact are worlds with remarkable means of travel, the results would astonish anyone—for instance, our forgetful author—who had not troubled to work out a careful timetable of the hero's movements. It would be more charitable to apply the analyses not to the original story but instead to the minimally revised versions that make the hero's movements feasible by the means of travel that were available in 1878. At least, that would be best if there were ways to set the times right without major changes in the plot. There might not be, and in that case perhaps truth in the original version—surprising though some of it may be—is the best we can do.

Notes

1 In "A Prolegomenon to Meinongian Semantics," *Journal of Philosophy* 71 (1974): 561–80, and in "A

Meinongian Analysis of Fictional Objects," *Grazer Philosophische Studien* 1 (1975): 73–86.

2   I have also been told that there has never been any building at that address. It doesn't matter which is correct.

3   For instance, the system given in Dana Scott, "Existence and Description in Formal Logic," in *Bertrand Russell: Philosopher of the Century,* ed. by Ralph Schoenman (London: Allen & Unwin, 1967).

4   Thus far, the account I have given closely follows that of John Heintz, "Reference and Inference in Fiction," *Poetics* 8 (1979).

5   Briefly stated in his addenda to "Naming and Necessity," in *Semantics of Natural Language,* ed. by Gilbert Harman and Donald Davidson (Dordrecht: Reidel, 1972); and discussed at greater length in an unpublished lecture given at a conference held at the University of Western Ontario in 1973 and on other occasions. My views and Kripke's overlap to some extent. He also stresses what I have called the ambiguity of prefixing and regards the storyteller as engaged in pretence. The conclusions he draws from the present observation, however, differ greatly from mine.

6   Jorge Luis Borges, "Pierre Menard, Author of the Quixote," in *Ficciones* (Buenos Aires, 1944; English translation, New York: Grove, 1962).

7   There are exceptions. Sometimes the storyteller purports to be uttering a mixture of truth and lies about matters whereof he has knowledge, or ravings giving a distorted reflection of the events, or the like. Tolkien explicitly purports to be the translator and editor of the Red Book of Westmarch, an ancient book that has somehow come into his possession and that he somehow knows to be a reliable record of the events. He does not purport to be its author, else he would not write in English. (Indeed, the composition of the Red Book by several hobbits is recorded in the Red Book itself.) I should say the same about a first-person historical novel written in English in which the narrator is an ancient Greek. The author does not pretend to be the truthful narrator himself, but rather pretends to be someone of our time who somehow has obtained the Greek narrator's story, knows it to be true, and passes it on to us in translation. In these exceptional cases also, the thing to do is to consider those worlds where the act of story-telling really is whatever it purports to be—ravings, reliable translation of a reliable source, or whatever—here at our world. I shall omit mention of these exceptional cases in the remainder of this paper.

8   A rather similar treatment of fictional names, different from mine in that it allows the actual and purported meanings of "Sherlock Holmes" to be the same, is given in Robert Stalnaker, "Assertion," in *Syntax and Semantics* 9, ed. by Peter Cole, (New York: Academic Press, 1978).

9   Many of us have never read the stories, could not produce the descriptions that largely govern the non-rigid sense of "Sherlock Holmes," yet use this name in just the same sense as the most expert Baker Street Irregular. There is no problem here. Kripke's causal picture of the contagion of meaning, in "Naming and Necessity" (*op. cit.*), will do as well for non-rigid senses, as for rigid ones. The ignoramus uses "Sherlock Holmes" in its standard non-rigid sense if he has picked it up (in the right way) from someone who knew the governing descriptions, or who picked it up from someone else who knew them, or. . . . Kripke's doctrines of rigidity could not be defended without the aid of his doctrine of contagion of meaning; contagion without rigidity, on the other hand, seems unproblematic.

10   Given in *Counterfactuals* (Oxford: Blackwell, 1973).

11   Heintz (*op. cit.*) disagrees; he supposes that for each fiction there is a single world to be considered, but a world that is in some respects indeterminate. I do not know what to make of an indeterminate world, unless I regard it as a superposition of all possible ways of resolving the indeterminacy—or, in plainer language, as a set of determinate worlds that differ in the respects in question.

12   Carl Gans, "How Snakes Move," *Scientific American,* 222 (1970): 93.

13   A better definition of overt belief, under the name of "common knowledge," may be found in my *Convention* (Cambridge, Mass.: Harvard University Press, 1969), pp. 52–60. That name was unfortunate, since there is no assurance that it will be knowledge, or even that it will be true. See also the discussion of "mutual knowledge*" in Stephen Schiffer, *Meaning* (Oxford: Oxford University Press, 1972), pp. 30–42.

Chapter 35

Stefano Predelli

TALK ABOUT FICTION

1 Introduction

Suppose that we are discussing Milos Forman's movie *Amadeus*, and that I say:

(1) Salieri commissioned the *Requiem*.

My utterance is apparently true: in the movie, the composer Antonio Salieri is the mysterious figure who anonymously commissions the Mass for the Dead. Imagine now that I utter (1) during a debate on the history of sacred music in 18th century Vienna. My utterance appears to be false: the *Requiem* was probably commissioned by Count Walsegg, surely not by *Kapellmeister* Salieri.[1] This raises an interesting semantic problem. For how can an utterance of an indexical-free sentence such as (1) be true when it occurs in a conversation about a movie, yet be false when it is part of my comment on the history of music? And, more generally, how can an utterance of (1) be true at all, given that Salieri did *not* commission the *Requiem*?

In this paper, I propose an answer to these questions, which I believe to be preferable to the dominant position on the issue. I summarize the traditional view of discourse about fiction in the next section. In section three, I present certain independently motivated results on the semantic behavior of indexical expressions. In the concluding section, I employ these results in my solution of the problem under study.

2 The Replacement View

English contains indexical expressions, such as 'I', 'here', 'now', and 'actually'.[2] As is well known, an adequate semantic theory for an indexical language must evaluate sentence-types with respect to a context, i.e., it must take as its input pairs made up of a sentence-type and a context.[3] Consider for example the sentence

(2) It is cold today.

It is to be expected that one could not reach any semantically interesting result with respect to (2) taken in isolation. On the other hand, we should be able to derive from a correct semantic theory that, for instance, the pair made up of (2) and of a context containing July 4th as its temporal co-ordinate, is true iff it was cold on Independence Day.

Take now an example of an actual utterance, my utterance of (2) on December 25. Utterances are objects for which semantic questions may arise, such as the questions of content and truth. Intuitively, my utterance said that it is cold on Christmas day, and is true if and only if that is indeed the case. It would then be desirable to test our formal semantic apparatus by applying it to the utterance at issue, and by verifying whether its output matches our intuitive verdict. Some preliminary adjustments, however, prove necessary, since our formal theory has not been designed to take utterances as its input. What is needed is a *representation* of my utterance in a format which is tractable from the point of view of formal semantics, i.e., as a pair made up of a sentence-type and a context.

In the case of my utterance of (2), this preliminary step appears to be straightforward and uncontroversial. The correct representation of my utterance consists in the pair made up of the sentence-type instantiated by the token I emitted, and of the context corresponding to the situation in which my emission took place. I call these elements, respectively, the *uttered sentence* and the *context of utterance*. Let me now refer to the view according to which *any* utterance is to be semantically represented as the pair made up of the uttered sentence and of the context of utterance, as the *Naive View*. Against the Naive View, it may be pointed out that, in some cases, the uttered sentence should *not* occur in an utterance's semantic representation. Take for instance my utterance of

(3)   I am,

said in reply to your question 'Are you tired?' It may be alleged that a correct representation of my utterance should not involve (the sentence-type instantiated by) (3), and that it should rather consist in the pair made up of the context of utterance with the sentence-type (instantiated by)

(4)   I am tired.

This challenge to the Naive View prescribes that, in certain cases, we replace the uttered sentence with another sentence, in order to obtain a perspicuous representation of the utterance at issue. I thus refer to positions of this kind as *Replacement Views*.

The theory which has most frequently been suggested as a solution of the problem presented at the beginning of my essay is a Replacement View. I shall call it the *Replacement View of Discourse About Fiction*, or RV for short. Although different versions of the RV have been proposed, it may here suffice to summarize the reasoning that fuels them in the following way. Recall my two utterances of (1) described at the beginning of this essay. Since no semantic theory may assign contrasting truth-values to one and the same input, these utterances are to be assigned distinct representations. But, so the RV continues, it is hopeless to concentrate our efforts on the attempt to determine what context must occur within the appropriate representations of my utterances, given that no indexical expression plays any interesting role in them. The only promising distinction between the representations of the utterances in the story, the RV concludes, is one between the sentence-types occurring in those representations. In particular, notwithstanding the fact that, while discussing the movie, I produced a token of the type instantiated by (1), the RV insists that a distinct sentence-type must occur in the pair most perspicuously representing my utterance. A typical candidate for this role is the sentence-type

(5)   It is true in the movie *Amadeus* that Salieri commissioned the *Requiem*.

On the other hand, the RV continues, my utterance during my comments on the history of music is to be taken at face value, and a semanticist interested in its evaluation may safely focus on the uttered sentence-type and on the appropriate context.

This strategy also allows us to explain the apparent truth of my remark on Forman's movie. Since a perspicuous representation of my utterance is alleged to contain a sentence such as (5), it is to be expected that a sufficiently ingenious treatment of the locution 'it is true in the move *Amadeus* that', occurring in that sentence, may yield the desired truth-value. In his stimulating paper 'Truth in Fiction', David Lewis has suggested a treatment of expressions such as 'in fiction f (it is true that)' as intensional operators, along the following lines:

. . . a prefixed sentence "In fiction f, φ" is true . . . iff φ is true at every possible world in a certain set, this set being somehow determined by the fiction f.[4]

Let us assume that we have at our disposal a tenable theory of the relationships between a piece of fiction and the class of worlds it determines. No matter what the details of such a theory are, and how it handles certain tricky examples, it seems clear that the sentence 'Salieri commissioned the *Requiem*', which occurs in (5) within the scope of the intensional operator under discussion, is true at every possible world determined by the movie *Amadeus*. Thus, so the RV concludes, an utterance, whose representation involves the sentence-type (5), may well be true even though Salieri did not actually commission the *Requiem*.

Although the RV produces the intuitively correct results, I do not think that one should accept its fundamental premise. In particular, I believe that formidable difficulties face the defender of that view, when he is pressed for details as to the exact nature of the relationship allegedly holding between (1) and (5). In fact, I suspect that the only "evidence" for the claim that my utterance about the movie is to be represented by a pair containing a sentence quite different from the one I uttered, consists in one's desire to "get the semantics right".[5] But I do not intend to provide direct arguments against the RV. In the following sections, I argue that, if we accept the possible-world account of fiction presupposed by the RV, we have at our disposal a more satisfactory way of dealing with the problem under study. The conceptual apparatus I employ in my solution is not developed as an *ad hoc* device, whose sole motivation stems from our desire to obtain the intuitively correct results with respect to utterances about fiction. To the contrary, so I shall argue, it is independently needed as a natural explanation for a variety of otherwise puzzling linguistic phenomena.[6]

3 Contexts

As I explained in the previous section, when we apply our favorite semantic theory to instances of actual utterances, we must represent them as pairs made up of sentence and a context. According to the Naive View, a faithful representation of an utterance always contains the context of utterance. In many interesting cases, however, this suggestion proves inadequate. The list of such cases is surprisingly rich and varied, but a few examples will suffice here. Imagine that a book on the history of World War II, written in 1996, contains the following passage:

> It is May 1940. Germany outflanks the Maginot line. Now, nothing stands between Hitler's troops and Paris.

The indexicals occurring in this fragment, namely 'now' and (at least according to some views) the verbs' tenses, are not to be evaluated with respect to the context of utterance (inscription). For instance, the last sentence in the above passage does not intuitively convey the blatantly false information that German troops are on their way to Paris in 1996. One obtains the correct results by applying an adequate semantic theory to the pair consisting of the uttered sentence and of a context which, unlike the context of inscription, contains 1940 as its temporal co-ordinate. Or take the utterance of a reporter in Los Angeles, who says

> Let us turn to the weather in New York. Here, the winds are blowing at 50 mph.[7]

If we desire to be faithful to our pre-theoretic intuitions about the content and truth-value of the reporter's utterance, we must be able to derive from the semantic theory at our disposal the result that the second part of that utterance talks about the weather in New York. But, assuming that the referent of 'here' with respect to a context *c* is the location co-ordinate of *c*, we are in a position to reach the desired conclusion only if we focus on a representation which includes a context containing New York, rather than Los Angeles, as its location. And, in the attempt to vividly narrate certain events in American history, I may say:

It is 1940 and I am President Roosevelt. I know that America must enter the war.

Of course, I am not expressing a trivially false information concerning my identity and my views on American foreign policy. The correct result is obtained by interpreting the above fragment with respect to a context containing Roosevelt and 1940, i.e., with respect to a context whose agent and time differ from the utterer and the time of utterance.[8]

There is, I believe, sufficient intuitive support for my suggestion that the foregoing examples should be semantically evaluated by taking into consideration a context distinct from the context of utterance. It is pretheoretically natural to point out that the author of the book on World War II was writing, so to speak, "from the point of view of her subject matter", and that I was, in a sense, pretending to be in Roosevelt's shoes. By the same token, one may assimilate my comments about *Amadeus* to these examples, and point out that, roughly speaking, I was talking "from the point of view of the story". When one tries to cash out this vague insight within the apparatus that I have suggested, one may conclude that my utterances about the movie, not unlike the other examples presented in this section, are to be represented by pairs containing a context other than the context of utterance. But the contextual parameter which differentiates the context of utterance from the semantically relevant context is, in this case, the possible-world co-ordinate. The context with respect to which we are to evaluate my utterance does not contain the possible world in which my utterance took place, i.e., the actual world, but the world of the story.

There is an interesting argument which may suggest that such a conclusion is on the right track. Suppose that, while talking about the movie, I say

(6)   Although Mozart thought that the mysterious figure was his father's ghost, the actual commissioner of the *Requiem* was Salieri.

Given how things are described in the movie, this utterance is true. But in order to obtain the correct semantic behavior for the expression 'the actual commissioner', one ought to evaluate (6) with respect to a context which, unlike the context of utterance, contains the fictional world of *Amadeus* as its possible-world parameter. With respect to such context, 'the actual commissioner of the *Requiem*' denotes Salieri, and the sentence 'the actual commissioner of the *Requiem* was Salieri' comes out true; with respect to the context of utterance, on the other hand, 'the actual commissioner of the *Requiem*' denotes Count Walsegg, and 'the actual commissioner of the *Requiem* was Salieri' is evaluated as false.

4 The solution

Whether an utterance is true or not depends not only on the semantic properties of that utterance, but also on the way things are, on how the world happens to be. We may then say that an utterance is true with respect to a certain state of the world, but false with respect to a certain other state of affairs.[9] However, we do not expect a "hyphenated" verdict from the application of our semantical machinery to the utterances under study. We are not only interested in truth-with-respect-to-such-and-such-circumstances, but also, and foremost, in truth *simpliciter*. But such a notion of unrelativized truth is easily definable, once we recognize that a certain circumstance may be taken, in a sense, as privileged. Since we are here thinking of circumstances of evaluation as possible worlds, the circumstance which, *as a first approximation*, we may single out as important for the definition of unrelativized truth is the actual world.

I called the suggestion of taking the actual world as the privileged circumstance "a first approximation". For suppose that we are interested in evaluating the possible utterance of

(7)   Bill Clinton is the President in 1995

which I *would* have performed today, had it been the case that George Bush won the 1992 election. Would that utterance of mine have been true, or would I have been speaking falsely? Clearly, my counter-factual utterance has the same truth-conditions as my actual utterance of the above sentence, i.e., the one is true with respect to a possible world iff the other is. Thus, were we to single out the same privileged circumstance in both cases, we ought to conclude that both utterances share the same unrelativized truth-value. But this conclusion is intuitively incorrect. Unlike my actual utterance of (7), my counter-factual utterance of that sentence is intuitively false *simpliciter*, since it is false with respect to what would have been the actual world, had Bush been able to defeat his opponent. It is thus imperative that we refine our criteria for choosing the circumstance relevant to the determination of unrelativized truth-value.

Contexts play an interesting role at this stage, since to each context there corresponds a possible world. We may then say that a context containing a possible world w *determines* the circumstance w.[10] Compare now the contexts for the two utterances of (7) described above. These contexts differ with respect to (at least) the possible-world parameter. In the case of my actual utterance, the actual world occurs in the relevant context. However, in the case of the utterance I would have made, had the Republican candidate won the 1992 election, the world of the context is one in which Bush rules the country in 1995. In other words, the context for my counter-factual utterance contains the world which I would have picked out, had I used the

expression 'the actual world' in that utterance. This conclusion may be generalized. Thus, we may add to our semantic theory the following definition of unrelativized truth:

(a representation of) an utterance $\langle t, c \rangle$ is true *simpliciter* iff it is true with respect to the possible world of the context c.[11]

In section three, I argued that the Naive View is wrong in holding that any utterance must be represented by a pair, made up of the uttered sentence and the context of utterance. I also claimed that my utterance of (1), occurring during our discussion on the movie, is a counter-example to the Naive View. There is sufficient evidence that such a representation involves a context which, unlike the context of utterance, contains the world of the movie as its possible world co-ordinate. It follows from this thesis, together with the definition of truth presented above, that my cinematographic remark is true *simpliciter* iff it is true at the world of *Amadeus*, i.e., iff it is true in the movie that Salieri commissioned the *Requiem*. The intuitively correct truth-conditions are thus obtained without replacing the uttered sentence with any other locution. On the other hand, as the RV recognizes, my utterance of (1) as a factual remark is to be taken at face value, and is thus false *simpliciter*, given that the *Requiem* was actually commissioned by Count Walsegg, and not by Salieri.

Notes

1 On the history of the *Requiem*, see Robbins Landon 1988, Chapter VII.
2 In this paper, I *assume* an indexical treatment for the occurrences of 'actually' and 'actual' in the examples discussed below. For a defense of the indexical interpretation of these expressions, see Salmon 1987.
3 From a formal point of view, we may think of contexts as sequences of the items needed for the evaluation of the indexical expressions occurring

in the language under study. For the purpose of this paper, it suffices to represent contexts as made up of an agent, a time, a location, and a possible world. I shall refer to the items in a context as the context's *co-ordinates* or *parameters*.

4 Lewis 1978, 39.

5 Notice that the situation with respect to (1) seems to be importantly different from that of (3). It may be argued that, although there are *syntactical* reasons for holding that (3) is to be replaced by (4), there are no analogous motivations for replacing (1) with (5). For such a criticism of the RV, see Bertolet 1984.

6 I shall thus simply *assume* that we can make sense of the idea of a class of possible worlds being *determined* by a fiction. For the sake of simplicity, I will even go as far as pretending that a piece of fiction, such as the movie *Amadeus*, determines exactly one possible world. This pretense will not have crucial repercussions with respect to the example under study, and a more adequate metaphysical picture will hopefully be consistent with the theory I present.

7 This example is similar to an analogous case discussed in Crimmins 1992. The point Crimmins makes is, however, entirely different from mine.

8 I have discussed these examples in Predelli 1996, where I defend the distinction between the context of utterance and what I call the *context of interpretation*.

9 It is a matter of controversy exactly how rich a circumstance of evaluation is supposed to be. David Kaplan (and others, including myself) are sympathetic to a rather "thick" view of circumstances: "A circumstance will usually include a possible state or history of the world, a time, and

perhaps other features as well". (Kaplan 1977, 502). But even those who find this view unpalatable agree that a circumstance must include at least a possible world. This "thin" conception of a circumstance suffices for the purpose of this essay.

10 Had we agreed to take circumstances of evaluation as, say, world-time pairs, we would of course conclude that a context containing a time t and a world w determines the circumstance {w, t}.

11 See also Kaplan 1977, 547.

. . .

References

Bertolet, Rod: 1984, 'On A Fictional Ellipsis', *Erkenntnis* 21, 189–194.

Crimmins, Mark: 1992, *Talk About Beliefs*, The MIT Press, Cambridge, MA.

Field, Hartry: 1973, 'Theory Change and the Indeterminacy of Reference', *The Journal of Philosophy* 70, 462–481.

Kaplan, David: 1977, 'Demonstratives', in Joseph Almog, John Perry, and Howard Wettstein (eds.), *Themes From Kaplan*, Oxford University Press, Oxford and New York, 1989.

Lewis, David: 1978, 'Truth in Fiction', *American Philosophical Quarterly* 15, 37–46.

Predelli, Stefano: 1996, 'Never Put Off Until Tomorrow What You Can Do Today', *Analysis* 56(2), 85–91.

Robbins Landon, Howard Chandler: 1988, *1791. Mozart's Last Year*, Schirmer Books, New York.

Salmon, Nathan: 1987, 'Existence', in J. Tomberlin (ed.), *Philosophical Perspectives I: Metaphysics*, Ridgeview, pp. 49–108.

Chapter 36

Amie L. Thomasson

SPEAKING OF FICTIONAL CHARACTERS

Fiction has persisted as a philosophical problem because (as in the case of most classic philosophical problems) there are apparent inconsistencies in our ordinary ways of speaking of and thinking about the subject. We want to say, for example, in one breath that Frankenstein's monster was a creation of Dr. Frankenstein, in another that he was a creation of Mary Shelley. We want to say that Sherlock Holmes is a detective, but also that he is a fictional character that thus cannot be called upon to solve crimes. We want to say that Emma Woodhouse doesn't exist, but in other contexts we want to confirm that there are such fictional characters as Emma and her sister Isabella, while there is no such character as Emma's pesky kid brother. It is because of these surface-level inconsistencies in what we want to say that a philosophical account of fictional discourse is needed. But since there are apparent inconsistencies, any consistent theory must give up appearances somewhere. I think it is at least in part for this reason that no theory has won universal acceptance by giving us all we (pre-theoretically) wanted.

But, that much being acknowledged, how can we *best* understand fictional discourse in a way that avoids apparent inconsistencies like the three mentioned above? Does the best understanding of fictional discourse involve allowing that fictional names ever refer to fictional characters? If so, in which contexts, and what sorts of things are these fictional characters referred

to? Those are the questions I will address below.

Perhaps the leading way of revising problematic talk about fiction in order to avoid the apparent inconsistencies involves taking at least some of our talk about fiction to involve pretense or make-believe of some sort – but how much of our talk about fiction involves pretense?[1] How can we determine, of any piece of discourse, whether or not it involves pretense?[2] Kendall Walton considers the same question, and offers this answer:

> How do we know whether to look for an implied unofficial game [of make-believe] at all, rather than taking a given statement to be ordinary? There is no easy recipe . . . There is, I suppose an initial presumption that statements concerning fiction are to be regarded as ordinary in the absence of good reasons to construe them otherwise . . . Beyond that, a principle of charity is operative. Understanding an utterance in a way that would make it an absurd or blatantly false or trivial or stupid thing to say is to be avoided if an alternative is available . . . (1990, 409–10)

This seems a plausible enough start: To depart from literal readings, we need a clue, e.g. that what the speaker is saying would otherwise be absurd, blatantly false, or self-contradictory. Thus the surface-level inconsistencies in talk about fiction alone (combined with the charitable principle that people aren't just stupid and continually contradicting themselves) suggest that *something* not quite literal and straightforward is going on *somewhere* in our talk about fiction. Any further departure must be similarly motivated – that is, we should be as *minimally* revisionary as we can in shifting from understanding speakers literally to taking their statements to be pretense involving. Another reasonable criterion[3] is that the speaker(s) must at least potentially be capable of recognizing and accepting that they were pretending – pretense being, as Searle (1979, 65) puts it, an intentional verb, such that "One cannot truly be said to have pretended to do something unless one intended to pretend to do it".

1 Pretense theories

So, which sorts of fictional discourse should be reconstrued as implicitly involving some kind of pretense? There are at least four sorts of fictional discourse to consider:

(1) Fictionalizing discourse (discourse *within* works of fiction)
(2) Internal discourse by readers about the content of works of fiction (without explicitly prefixing it with "according to the story")
(3) External discourse by readers and critics about the characters as fictional characters, the circumstances of their creation, their historical relation to other literary figures, etc.
(4) Nonexistence claims, e.g. that Sherlock Holmes does not exist.

Certainly it is plausible that, in writing a work of fiction, the fictionalizing discourse of the storyteller involves a pretense (shared with readers) that she is telling a true story about real people.[4] It's also plausible that internal discourse by readers about the content of the story invokes the

same pretense, and can be understood as discussing what is true *according to the story* (with the pretense obviating the need to explicitly state this prefix). In fact, although those who accept fictional characters are frequently accused of taking fictional discourse too seriously, missing the pretense involved, or "not really getting it" (Yablo 1999), realists and anti-realists about fictional characters alike appreciate the element of pretense involved in writing works of fiction and discussing their content, when we speak of the characters as if they were real people, and argue about their psychological characteristics, backgrounds, or likely next moves. Taking these contexts to involve pretense enables us to avoid apparent contradictions of the first two sorts, since it is merely part of the pretense invoked by the relevant stories that Frankenstein's monster was a creation of Dr. Frankenstein, and that Sherlock Holmes is a detective. By refiguring one side of the apparent contradiction as involving pretense, these inconsistencies may be avoided.

But many have gone further, accepting the idea (best developed in the work of Kendall Walton) that not just *some*, but *all* talk involving fictional names contains an element of pretense. Thus, if we think of the first major question for any theory of fictional discourse to address as: Do fictional names (ever) refer?, the pure pretense theorist answers with an emphatic "no". On such views, claims that the character of Frankenstein's monster was made up by Mary Shelley, and that Sherlock Holmes is not a detective but a fictional character, must involve pretense just as surely as the earlier claims. The apparent conflict between the claim that Frankenstein's monster was a creation of Dr. Frankenstein and the claim that he was a creation of Mary Shelley's is resolved by revising *both* claims as implicitly pretenseful – the first involving the (standard) pretense that the story *Frankenstein* is true, the second involving an 'ad hoc' game of make-believe in which "to author a fiction about people and things of certain kinds is fictionally to create such" (Walton 1990, 410–11). Similarly, the apparent conflict between saying that Sherlock Holmes is a detective, and that he is a fictional character, is to be resolved by noting that the first half involves the (standard) pretense that the story is true, and the second invokes an *ad hoc* game of pretense according to which there are two kinds of 'people', real people and fictional characters (Walton 1990, 423).[5]

The first thing to notice is that this approach does double the revisionary work necessary to avoid the apparent conflicts; from the point of view of solving the basic problems of fictional discourse, this is removing the ceiling to change a light bulb. The second thing to notice is that the additional revisions are made in cases where it intuitively does not seem that any pretense is going on, and it would be hard to convince the relevant speakers that they are invoking a game of make-believe. If two police officers discussing a case say "This is such a tough one, we need Sherlock Holmes to help us solve it", they do indeed seem engaged in a pretense that Holmes is a real detective who could be called upon in times of need. But the point of a humorless colleague's remark "There's no such person as Holmes, it's just a fictional character", seems to be precisely to step *outside* of these forms of pretense and assert the real truth about Holmes. Indeed, a pure pretense theorist must take all literary historians' and critics' apparently serious claims about fictional characters, their origins, history, development, etc., to involve new, ad hoc, games of make-believe – whether these are claims that Shakespeare's character Hamlet was modeled on the 13th century character Amleth of Saxo Grammaticus' *Historia Danica*, that the play *Waiting for Godot* has five characters, or that if Arthur Conan Doyle's medical practice had been busier, the character of Sherlock Holmes might have never been created. Yet none of these seem, pre-theoretically, to involve pretense or games of make-believe, and such additional revisions are not necessary to prevent speakers from saying something self-contradictory or blatantly false, nor could the speakers normally be brought to recognize that they were invoking a pretense – so those grounds for attributing pretense to a piece of discourse do not apply here.

If reading claims *within* and internal claims *about* works of fiction as pretense-involving is enough to resolve the apparent inconsistencies, and if literary scholars and others who make claims about the historical situation in which a character was created, its influence on the future of literary history, its fame or appearance in other works of art, do not take themselves to be invoking a pretense, that should provide us with at least initial motivation for considering more minimally revisionary theories that accept that not *all* of our talk involving fictional names involves pretense, and that at least *sometimes* these names may be used seriously to refer.

But before turning to those theories, it is natural to ask why (given the above) so many people are persuaded by pure pretense theories of fictional discourse. One reason may be that, by denying that fictional names ever refer to anything, they seem to sit well with the intuitions that Sherlock Holmes, Emma Woodhouse, and the like *don't* exist.[6] Anyone who accepts that fictional names at least sometimes *do* refer owes us an explanation of why we then think of singular nonexistence claims involving fictional names as *true*.

The second (and I think major) reason involves metaphysical qualms that admitting such things as fictional characters to our ontology (as referents of fictional names) is simply implausible, or at least excessively profligate.[7] Thus, some might suppose that we *do* have grounds for attributing pretense even to external talk about fictional characters since (even if it's not *blatantly* false or absurd) it is so *implausible* to think that there are fictional characters that we should avoid saddling speakers with this commitment if at all possible. I will return below (in sections 2.2 and 2.3 respectively) to discuss each of these issues.

2 Referential theories

More minimally revisionary theories of fiction have been developed, e.g., by Saul Kripke, Nathan Salmon, Stephen Schiffer, John Searle, Peter van Inwagen, and myself, which typically accept that fictionalizing and internal fictional discourse involve some kind of pretense, but allow that, at least in external critical discourse, fictional names may refer to fictional characters. According to theories of this sort, the fictional characters referred to are not nonexistent people; instead, they are generally held to be entities in some sense created by our story-telling practices.[8] On the view I have defended (1999, 2002), they are (existent) abstract artifacts, created by the creative activities of the author or authors telling a certain story, within a certain tradition. Thus apparent inconsistencies like the first two are resolved more simply by reconfiguring *one* side of each statement: according to the pretense invoked by the story, Frankenstein's monster was a creation of Dr. Frankenstein, but really it is a fictional character created by Mary Shelley; and according to the pretense invoked by the story, Sherlock Holmes is a detective, but really Holmes is a fictional character who thus cannot be called upon to solve crimes.

But, while realist theories are inspired by the idea that in, external discourse, fictional names refer to fictional characters, there is more controversy about whether one should take fictional names also to refer in fictionalizing contexts, internal contexts, and in the context of nonexistence claims.

2.1 Fictionalizing and internal discourse[9]

Although all of the realist theories mentioned above accept that there is *some* pretense involved in claims in fictionalizing and internal contexts, difficult issues remain about exactly what form the pretense takes. There are (at least) two different forms pretense can take. 1) It can be *de re*, as

when children pretend, of a lump of mud, that it is a pie, or 2) It can be *de dicto*, as when children pretend that there is a monster in the closet (though there is no one, and no thing, of which they pretend that it is the monster). So one question that arises naturally for anyone who accepts that sentences within works of fiction (inscribed by the author) involve a mere pretense of asserting various things, is whether the pretense involved in fictionalizing contexts is *de re* or *de dicto*. Anyone who wants to accept (as I do) that works of fiction may genuinely be about real or historical places or figures (such as London and Gladstone) will want to accept that at least some of the sentences in works of fiction involve *de re* pretense, referring back to London or Gladstone, and pretending to assert various things about them (that Holmes lived in it, or met him). But what about the sentences using the fictional name "Holmes" as opposed to a real name like "London" or "Gladstone"?

There are at least two options: 1) The pretense in later sentences of fictional works is *de re*, so the fictional names here refer to fictional characters, of which the sentences of the novel pretend to assert various things, i.e., of Sherlock Holmes, they pretend to assert that he smokes a pipe (just as of Gladstone, they pretend to assert that he was met by a clever detective). (If internal discourse is treated similarly, readers' sentences such as "Sherlock Holmes smokes a pipe" may be read as saying, of Sherlock Holmes, that he is such that, according to the story's pretense, he smokes a pipe). Or, 2) The pretense in these cases is *de dicto*, so that fictional names in these contexts do not refer back to some entity outside the scope of the pretense; instead they involve merely the pretense that there was some man, such that he was called "Holmes", smoked a pipe, solved crimes, etc. (Internal claims may be read similarly as asserting that according to the story's pretense, there was a man called "Holmes" who smoked a pipe.)

Which view of fictionalizing discourse should we take? There are actually plusses and minuses on both sides. Elsewhere (1999), I have defended the former view, suggesting that, while the first use of the name must be a sort of performative bringing the character into existence, later references by the author within the novel simply refer back to the character and ascribe it certain properties (by pretending to assert more things about it). I was drawn to this view by its power to simplify and unify our account of fictional discourse. It provides us with a uniform understanding of the form of pretense involved in writing fiction, whether the author is referring to extant individuals, characters of other stories, their own characters later in that story or in a sequel – in all cases, the author makes a *de re* reference to an extant individual and ascribes it new properties. It also provides us with a straightforward account of what it is for a character to appear in another story: simply that the new author refer back to it (*de re*), and ascribe it new properties.

Nathan Salmon also defends the view that, ultimately, the fictional names in a story refer to fictional characters (the abstract artifacts), though he emphasizes that this does not mean that the *author* was referring to anyone or even *using* (as opposed to pretending to use) the name at all. As he puts it "Once fictional characters have been countenanced as real entities, why hold onto an alleged use of their names that fails to refer to them? It is like buying a luxurious Italian sports car only to keep it garaged" (1998, 298). He accepts this view for a different reason: On a Millian account, it seems that if we deny that fictional names refer within works of literature, then the sentences within literary works could not express propositions. And if these don't express propositions, then neither do meta-fictional sentences about the content of works of literature, for on the Millian account, if "Sherlock Holmes plays the violin" does not express a proposition, neither does "According to the story, Sherlock Holmes plays the violin" (297). So, another advantage of accepting that the fictional names in works of literature refer to

fictional characters is that it provides an easy solution to the problem of how sentences within works of fiction and about their content can be meaningful and express propositions.

But this reading of fictionalizing claims, combined with the ontological view that the fictional characters referred to are abstract artifacts, leads to some odd conclusions. For then we must take works of literature to invoke the pretense, of some abstract object, that it is a detective, is a man, solves crimes, etc. The strangeness can be somewhat mitigated by noticing that this is a pure *de re* reference back to a character, so the content of the pretense is not that something is both an abstractum and a man.[10] It can also be somewhat mitigated by noting that similar cross-category ascriptions are made all the time about real people in discussions of theatrical performances, where we may say *de re*, of an actor, that we are to pretend that he is a cat, or an angel, or even (in Pirandello's *Six Characters in Search of an Author*) a fictional character, (in a morality play) [the property of] Charity, or (in a children's play about mathematics) the number three. Nonetheless, it remains a somewhat awkward consequence.

Thus other realists about fictional characters, such as Searle, Kripke, Schiffer, and van Inwagen, have held that fictional names, when they appear in fictionalizing discourse, do not refer (or attempt to refer) to anything.[11] In this case, it is natural to take the sentences in works of fiction[12] to be involved in pretense of *de dicto* form[13] – so that the sentences of the Holmes stories do not pretend of Holmes (the fictional character, an abstract artifact) that he was a detective; instead, the pretense has the form: There once was a man, such that he was called "Holmes", was a detective, was very clever, etc. It is then in virtue of such (*de dicto* pretenseful) inscriptions that later readers, critics, and historians may make *de re* reference back to Sherlock Holmes, the fictional character, and say things of that character such as that it was created by Arthur Conan Doyle, is the most famous character of Victorian literature, etc. Such views are intuitively plausible, and seem to better capture the psychology of writing,[14] as well as the idea that writing a work of literature is performative or creative, *enabling* future reference to characters rather than *making* reference to them.

But such views face their own difficulties. One is that which moved Salmon in the other direction: If fictional names in works of literature don't refer, are not at least those inclined to a Millian theory of reference also forced to say that the sentences of these works – and thereby also any meta-fictional sentenses that report the content of works of literature – fail to express propositions?[15] But if we take the *de dicto* option, then (following Currie, 1990) we may take fictional names, where they occur in works of literature, not to function as genuine names at all (and thus not as empty names), but rather as labels making anaphoric reference back to a variable bound by a quantifier within the scope of the pretense, e.g. pretending that: There once was a man, such that he was called "Holmes", and he smoked a pipe, he solved crimes, etc. (perhaps also implicitly: *and* he is the one to whom this name-use chain traces back).[16] While the quantifier may not always be explicitly expressed in works of literature (except nice old-fashioned works that begin "Once upon a time, there was . . .") one could hold that this is the implicit form of the author's pretense, even when she simply launches in with a name.[17]

This sort of solution does require that we treat fictional names and real names differently when they appear in works of fiction (assuming that real names there refer *de re* to actual people and places). It also complicates the story about the conditions under which an extant character may appear in a new story or sequel, since (to avoid the cross-category pretense problem arising in a new context) we shouldn't say that the new author refers *de re* to the old character and ascribes it new properties by pretending to assert new things about it. We could instead perhaps say that the new author refers *de re* back to the

prior literary work, and pretends of it that it was true, and thus that there was a man, such that the sentences of the prior work referred to him, and he also did these things I'm about to describe . . .[18] This enables us to retain the idea that the literary works (including sequels) are not involved in *de re* pretenses about abstract artifacts, while allowing that *de re* connections to earlier literary works are the basis for outside readers and critics to truly claim that one and the same fictional character appears in both works.

If those replies are defensible, perhaps one should accept that fictional names do not refer to fictional characters in fictionalizing discourse, although their use in fiction enables these names to refer to characters in external contexts. In any case, what is most important is to note that theories that accept that fictional names at least *sometimes* refer to fictional characters can avoid the apparent contradictions of the first two types (e.g. between claims that Frankenstein's monster was a creation of Dr. Frankenstein, and that he was a creation of Mary Shelley; and between claims that Sherlock Holmes is a detective, and that he is a fictional character that thus cannot be called upon to solve crimes) in a far less revisionary way than you can if you think fictional names *never* refer.

2.2 Nonexistence claims

But there is one issue for realists we have not discussed, and one apparent contradiction we have not yet resolved. Do fictional names refer in the context of singular nonexistence claims? It seems that a realist about fictional characters must treat claims like "Emma Woodhouse doesn't exist" as *false* (since on this theory, Emma is a fictional character which *does* exist); thus a central problem facing any realist about fictional characters is often thought to be accounting for the "sense in which it might truly be said that Holmes does *not* exist" (Brock 2002, 2).[19]

But in fact the problem is even more complicated than this, for as we have seen, the 'common sense' belief that it is true to say "Emma Woodhouse doesn't exist" is also in apparent conflict with the common sense view that there is such *a fictional character* as Emma Woodhouse, whereas there is no such character as Emma's pesky kid brother Fred.[20] Thus any adequate theory must be able to explain not only the sense in which "Emma Woodhouse doesn't exist" is *true*, but also the sense in which "The fictional character Emma Woodhouse doesn't exist" is false (since this character, unlike the character Fred, *does* exist).

Direct reference theorists have tended to take one of two approaches to handle nonexistence claims: the 'gappy proposition' view developed, e.g., by Braun 1993, Reimer 2001, and Adams, Fuller and Stecker 1997; or Keith Donnellan's metalinguistic account. According to the first view, nonexistence statements involving empty names express incomplete or 'gappy' propositions, so, e.g., "Holmes doesn't exist" expresses the gappy proposition $<<\{ \ \}, \text{existing}>, \text{negation}>$, held by some (Braun 1993) to be true.[21] On the second view, direct reference theorists should handle nonexistence claims metalinguistically, such that:

> If N is a proper name that has been used in predicative statements with the intention to refer to some individual, then 'N does not exist' is true if and only if the history of those uses ends in a block. (Donnellan 1974, 25)[22]

On this view, a name use chain ends in a 'block' when, for example, it ends with the introduction of a name into a work of fiction (or a mistake, an act of imagination, etc.) (Donnellan 1974, 23–4).

But while they attempt to account for the sense in which "Emma Woodhouse doesn't exist" is true, neither of these views (in their basic form) can account for the sense in which it is nonetheless false to say that the *fictional characters* Emma and Holmes do not exist (since these characters, unlike the character of Fred, *do* exist).

If we took fictional names to always be empty, and thus nonexistence statements involving these names to always express gappy propositions, we could not make such distinctions (all would be true, e.g., on Braun's 1993 view). Similarly, if we accepted that all claims of the form "N doesn't exist" are true whenever the name use chain ends with the introduction of a name in a work of fiction, imagination, or through a mistake, we could not distinguish between true and false nonexistence claims about fictional characters, considered as such (all would be true).

What seems to make the difference between true and false claims of existence involving fictional names is whether the intended referent of the name is some *person* or the relevant *fictional character*. Acknowledging this needn't involve a shift to descriptive theories of reference, for in fact, we have independent reason to mitigate *pure* direct reference theories by accepting that speakers' broad intentions regarding what ontological kind of object is the intended referent must play *some* role in determining which object, if any, is referred to by their use of a term.[23] This is essential at the level of reference-fixing in order to disambiguate among the many possible referents *which* is to be the referent of the name. Otherwise, as has often been noted (e.g. Devitt and Sterelny 1999, 79–81), direct reference theories suffer from the *qua* problem: since one may have causal contact with many things in attempting to ground the reference of a name (a person, group of people, spatial or temporal part of a person, property of that person, etc.), without some disambiguating concept of the *sort* of thing to be named, it is left radically indeterminate what, if anything, the term refers to. It is also plausible that it is essential for reference to be successfully passed from one person to another (without a reference shift or failure of reference) that the name-learner have an appropriate basic ontological conception of what ontological sort of thing is to be referred to by the name (if it succeeds in referring at all).[24] So a name use chain must be initiated and maintained by people who have some intention regarding whether, e.g., the referent of the name is to be a real person or a fictional character, and the success conditions for establishing and maintaining a chain of reference will differ accordingly: in the case of intended reference to a person, the name-use chain must end at some individual human being who is baptized; in the case of intended reference to a fictional character (as I have argued elsewhere (1999, Chapter 4)), the name use chain must lead back to the spatio-temporal foundations of the character in copies of the story. We may then refer to a fictional character *via* a copy of the story just as we can refer to Bach's Third Violin Concerto via a performance of it or a written copy of the score.

Given the importance of speakers' ontological intentions, could we then say that if the speaker intends to refer to a person with her use of the name "Holmes", then (on her use) the name "Holmes" is empty, and her claim "Holmes doesn't exist" expresses a (true) gappy proposition; whereas if she intends to refer to a fictional character, then her use of the name refers to a fictional character, and her claim "Holmes doesn't exist" expresses a complete (but false) proposition? Surely this isn't quite right. If a speaker intends to refer to a person with the name "Holmes", presumably she doesn't realize that there is no such person, and thus would not *assert* "Holmes doesn't exist". In fact, the same seems to be true in the case of a speaker who intends to refer to a fictional character – if she thinks there is such a character to refer to, presumably she will *not* make a claim of its non-existence. While speaker intentions seem to be relevant to what (ontological) kind of thing, if anything, is referred to in their use of a term, using speakers intentions in *this* way makes nonsense of what a speaker could be trying to assert with a nonexistence claim of either sort.

This gives us reason to reconsider some sort of metalinguistic view, for it suggests that nonexistence claims presuppose and implicitly comment on a *separate* range of prior uses of the name by speakers with, perhaps inappropriate, intentions to refer to a thing of a certain ontological kind. Nonexistence claims involving fictional names are generally made where the speaker suspects that some mistake has been made, e.g. where past speakers have intended to use the name (in predicative statements) to refer to a person, as when child has exclaimed "Santa Claus is coming tonight!" and we correct him by saying "Santa Claus doesn't exist". In making a nonexistence claim, the speaker does not *herself* intend to use the name "Santa Claus" to refer to a person; rather, she indicts prior uses of it that (she thinks) were made with that intention.

As we have seen, the realist about fictional characters cannot *directly* adopt Donnellan's metalinguistic solution, for, if the realist about fictional characters is right, not all name use chains that end in "blocks" (as Donnellan originally described them) are cases where the name in question fails to refer. But once we accept that the intentions of speakers (regarding what broad ontological sort of thing their term should refer to, if it refers at all) are relevant to determining whether or not their use of a term refers, we can see how to generalize Donnellan's suggestion to avoid the above problem:

> If N is a proper name that has been used in predicative statements with the intention to refer to some entity of ontological kind K, then 'N does not exist' is true if and only if the history of those uses does not meet the conditions for referring to an entity of kind K.

Thus the statement "Moses doesn't exist" (given that the implicit appeal is to predicative statements of the form "Moses led the Israelites out of Egypt", etc.) is true if, e.g., the history of the use of the name in those contexts does not lead back to the 'baptism' of a person, but merely to some story. Where N is a fictional name, whether "N does not exist" is true or not depends entirely on whether or not, in the prior predicative statements presupposed, speakers intended to refer to a person or to a *fictional character*. If prior speakers intended to refer to a person by using the name (e.g. "I think I'll hire Sherlock Holmes to solve this case"), then their use is just like the uses of "Moses" above, and (in the context of those presupposed uses) "Holmes does not exist" is true.

Additional evidence for the view that nonexistence claims implicitly comment on a prior range of uses (which the speaker supposes to be misguided) comes from the fact that we do not normally make nonexistence claims involving fictional names in the context of literary discussions, where it is assumed that everyone understands that it is fictional characters that are under discussion. In a literary discussion of Hamlet in a literature classroom, where predications are being made such as that "Shakespeare modeled Hamlet on a 13th century character of Saxo Grammaticus", it would be bizarre to suddenly assert, "Hamlet doesn't exist!" – for the prior uses of the name here only intended to refer to a fictional character, and there is every reason to think they succeed at that, via a name use chain that leads back to the Shakespearean text.

On the other hand, nonexistence claims *may* be sensibly made in the context of literary discussion if what is being denied is that there is such a *character*. If a literature professor writes on a student paper "your discourse about Austen's underdevelopment of the character of Fred is surprising, since there is no such character in the novel – your character 'Fred' doesn't exist", the implicit appeal is to the student's predications such as "Fred is the least well-developed of Austen's characters". But for the name "Fred" to refer to a fictional character, the name use chain for "Fred" in which the student participates must leads back to appearance of the name "Fred" in a work of literary fiction. If, instead, it leads back only to the inventive mind of a classmate who deliberately misinformed his lazy peer, then the professor justifiably indicts the student's prior uses of the term, and utters a

truth when she says "your character 'Fred' doesn't exist".

Thus on this reading, given their different presuppositions, claims like "Emma Woodhouse doesn't exist" are perfectly consistent with claims like "There is such a fictional character as Emma Woodhouse". Taking the metalinguistic route also enables us to avoid the paradox of nonexistence claims, since fictional names there do not refer (or attempt to refer) to fictional characters – so we need not actually refer to an object in order to deny its existence. Instead, such claims are made true (or false) based on whether or not (in other predicative uses) the name succeeds in referring to an object of the type presupposed.[25]

2.3 Ontological qualms

I have argued that the best view of fictional names is one that accepts that, at least sometimes, they refer to fictional characters. The main motivation underlying the common desire to avoid this view and accept a pure pretense or paraphrase theory is based in the worry that positing fictional characters is simply implausible or too profligate. Indeed if it really was wildly implausible to say that there are fictional characters, that could provide a justification for attributing pretense to all discourse about fictional characters – even the external discourse of literary criticism.

However, I think that the ontological qualms that drive many people to deny that fictional names ever refer are based in a misguided sense of what sort of things fictional characters would be, and what it would 'take' to have fictional characters to refer to. So I'll close by briefly addressing the ontological issue of what fictional characters are, why it is not at all implausible to accept that there are some, and why doing so does not amount to engaging in ontological profligacy.

The feeling that it is simply implausible to say that there are fictional characters may come from

either (or both) of two sources: 1) The conviction that it is true to say that Holmes, etc., don't
exist, and 2) The sense that accepting fictional
characters would mean accepting bizarre and
problematic entities. I have discussed (1) above,
arguing that the realist about fictional characters
can make perfectly good sense of the truth of
nonexistence claims, while also accounting for
the truth of claims that there are such fictional
characters. Thus, here we need only address (2),
the worry that has lingered ever since the
Russell-Meinong debate, that accepting fictional
characters will require accepting ill-behaved
objects such as nonexistent or imaginary people
– things apt to infringe the principle of noncon-
tradiction, the law of the excluded middle, or
other cherished principles, and lacking in clear
identity conditions.

I have argued elsewhere (1999 (Chapter 1),
and 2003), however, that the best view of what
fictional characters are (if there are any, as I think
there are), is that fictional characters are abstract
cultural artifacts, relevantly similar to other
social and cultural entities including particular
laws of state (the U.S. Constitution, the Miranda
Laws), works of music (Nielsen's Symphony
No. 4, Op. 29, "The Inextinguishable"), and the
works of literature in which fictional characters
appear (Tolstoy's *War and Peace*). These things are
all abstract in the sense that they lack any particular spatio-temporal location, but unlike the
Platonist's abstract entities, they are artifactual –
created (not discovered) at a certain time, e.g.
through the author's activities in writing a work
of fiction, and are contingent (not necessary)
entities that might have never been created. This
sort of view automatically calms any qualms
about accepting nonexistent objects, imaginary
people, or even platonistic abstracta into one's
ontology, since fictional characters are actually
existing cultural artifacts (not non-existent or
imaginary people), and they are created entities,
not occupants of an eternal realm of timeless
independent abstracta.

I have also argued (1999, Chapter 7) that

– given a suitable approach to fictional discourse
– we can accept fictional characters (so conceived) without abandoning the principle of
non-contradiction or the law of the excluded
middle. Finally, I have argued (1999, Chapter 5)
that an artifactual view of fictional characters
does enable us to draw out identity conditions
for them that are at least as good as those we have
for other sorts of medium-sized cultural objects,
including works of literature themselves. So
understood, accepting fictional characters is no
more implausible than accepting works of literature or other abstract cultural artifacts such as
symphonies, laws, and marriages.[26]

The central worry that remains, then, is that,
even if it is not implausible and does not require
us to accept bizarre entities into our ontology,
positing fictional characters remains ontologically profligate and so is to be avoided if at all
possible. Yet the idea of parsimony and its converse, profligacy, need to be reexamined more
carefully. I have argued elsewhere (2001, 2003,
and (unpublished) Chapter 8) that one does not
gain a more parsimonious theory by denying
entities of a given kind if one accepts the existence of entities that (according to ordinary
usage) logically entail that there are entities of
the kind in question. Thus, for example, according to normal usage of the phrase "pair of
gloves", the existence of a matching right glove
and left glove is logically sufficient for there to be
a pair of gloves. If someone accepted that there is
a left glove and right glove, and that these match,
but denied that there is a pair of gloves, we
would hardly know how to interpret what they
are trying to say, since, according to the ordinary
use of terms, a situation in which there are
matching left and right gloves *just is* a situation in
which there is a pair of gloves. Such a claim
seems to violate the ordinary rules for using our
word "pair", but not to yield a theory that is
more parsimonious in the sense of having
'fewer' entities (as, say, it is more parsimonious
for a detective to posit one murderer than two, or
for a physicist to posit three kinds of funda-

mental particle rather than seven). Indeed the very idea that we could 'count up' the individual gloves *and* the pair (to accuse the friend of pairs of accepting *more* entities than the foe) seems to be based on a category mistake.[27]

Much the same seems to go for many of our cultural artifacts.[28] For there to be a marriage, it is logically sufficient that there be certain laws accepted laying out sufficient conditions for a legal marriage to occur (e.g. that an unmarried, competent and sincere man and woman sign a marriage license in the presence of a judge and witnesses), and that those conditions be fulfilled. What sense could we make of someone who accepted that there were such laws, people, and events, but denied that there were marriages? Perhaps he or she might have some artificially inflated idea of what a 'real' marriage would have to be (a union of souls, perhaps, or a union blessed by God), and think that this higher condition was never met. But this would not tell against there being marriages in the more minimal everyday sense. If we restrict ourselves to discussing marriages in that sense, surely it is not a more parsimonious view to accept the existence of the relevant laws and practices but deny the marriages – again, this is only a distortion of ordinary usage, not a view on which there are 'fewer things' in the world.

The same sorts of consideration apply to our ordinary ways of talking about fictional characters. If we pay attention to the way authors, readers, and critics use the term "fictional character", it is clear that it is no part of the success conditions for using that term that there be some separate practice-independent object to refer to. According to our ordinary ways of talking about such things, as Stephen Schiffer 1996 has pointed out, pretenseful uses of a fictional name in statements such as "Sherlock considered the evidence" in a work of literature automatically license us to refer to "the fictional character, Sherlock" in literary discussions. Thus for there to be a fictional character in a certain situation, all it takes is that there be a work of literature in which the relevant sorts of pretenseful statements are made involving a fictional name. Given such a work of literature, nothing more is required, no extra ingredients are needed, to 'get' a fictional character, just as *nothing more is required* for there to be a pair of gloves than for there to be a matching left glove and right glove, and nothing more is required for there to be marriages than that certain legal principles be accepted and their criteria fulfilled. In each case, the existence of the former entities (according to our ordinary understanding of terms like "pair", "marriage", and "fictional character") is guaranteed by the existence of the latter entities.

So what sense can we make of those who would accept the existence of such works of literature, but deny the existence of fictional characters? Perhaps they have an artificially inflated idea of what would be required for there to be a fictional character (e.g. that that there be some nonexistent person) – if so, it is they who are taking fictional discourse and its commitments too seriously. In any case, those who accept the existence of the relevant sorts of literary work, but deny that of fictional characters, only distort the ordinary rules for using the term "fictional character" without yielding a genuinely more parsimonious ontology; if we accept such works of literature, we need not fear that it would be profligate to accept that there are fictional characters in the only sense that most people ever expected there to be.[29]

Once we see that fictional characters (according to the criteria ordinarily associated with the use of the term) are 'minimal' relative to certain kinds of literary work, and are no odder than marriages, mortgages, literary works, and other cultural artifacts, it is clear that it is not at all implausible to accept that there are fictional characters, so conceived, and so we lack the motivation needed to attribute pretense to apparently serious external discourse about fictional characters. That, in turn, should enable us to simply consider the evidence and options in finding the most plausible, and least revisionary, way of resolving the apparent inconsistencies in fictional discourse – even if the best such theory is (as I have argued) one that allows that fictional names, at least sometimes, refer.

Notes

1 Other popular approaches of course involve paraphrasing some of the discourse involved (where such paraphrases need not involve pretense). Much of what I say below could easily be rewritten in a way that applies to traditional paraphrase theories, but to simplify matters I will stick with the pretense case.

2 This of course lies behind debates about whether to accept pretenseful or 'fictionalist' accounts of a whole range of entities beyond fictional characters – including mathematical entities, possible worlds, etc. So if we can say anything interesting here, it may have implications there.

3 I think, however, that Walton would not accept this criterion.

4 Gregory Currie argues that in fact the best way to understand fictionalizing discourse is not as involving a *pretense* of assertion, but rather as involving the author's intention that the audience make-believe the content of the story (1990, 24–31), in virtue of their recognizing that very intention. For our purposes above, nothing much hangs on this variation.

5 Stuart Brock's 2002 'fictionalist' theory of external discourse involving fictional names proposes a different pretenseful way of handling 'external' literary-critical claims: they are considered elliptical for claims about what is true *according to* the realist's theory of fiction so, e.g., "Scarlett O'Hara is a fictional character" is elliptical for the longer sentence "according to the realist's hypothesis, Scarlett O'Hara is a fictional character" (Brock 2002, 9).

6 Reimer 2001 invokes this as a reason for rejecting Salmon's 1998 referential account. Of course pretense theorists also owe us an account of how these sentences can be true, given that the name involved fails to refer. Walton's method is to treat sentences such as "Sherlock Holmes doesn't exist" as first invoking a pretense to refer, and then (with

'doesn't exist') betraying that pretense. (1990, 422)

7 Adams et al. 1997, 129 reject referential views on grounds of such 'implausibility'.

8 Van Inwagen is not committal about whether or not characters are created; they are mere 'theoretic entities of literary criticism'.

9 Many thanks to David Barnett for very helpful discussion of issues in this section, which led me to rethink my former position.

10 Salmon emphasizes this point (1998, 316n.45).

11 van Inwagen (2003, n. xxiv) rejects Salmon's view, but it is not clear if he accepts the *de dicto* pretense view of fictionalizing discourse described above.

12 Or rather, those that do not refer back *de re* to extant people or places.

13 Searle 1979, 71 does this fairly explicitly, although some of the other above-mentioned authors are less committal.

14 David Braun (unpublished) plausibly suggests that authors' thoughts and intentions determine whether their inscriptions refer to fictional characters. If so, it seems plausible that in many cases at least they do not intend to refer to abstract artifacts, but rather merely to pretend that there were such and such people, doing such and such things.

15 Another option is (with Kripke, unpublished, lecture 2, and van Inwagen, 2003, n. 19 and n. 24) to deny that such statements express propositions at all – they merely pretend to. Yet even if we deny that they express a proposition, still we face the question of how such sentences could be *meaningful* or what sort of meaning they convey, and here the above options are still relevant. Another option (following Braun 1993) would be to take these statements to express *gappy* propositions, e.g. $\langle \{ \}$, being a detective).

16 Robert Howell 1979, 133 argues that any adequate theory of fiction must preserve the contrast between those statements in works of fiction that seem to be making *de re* reports on individual people, and those that only seem to be making generic existential claims. This distinction might be preservable even on the *de dicto* pretense view above by including the final parenthetical clause in analyzing statements that have the surface form of *de re* claims in works of fiction (but not the others). Kripke (unpublished, Lecture 1) suggests a similar

clause to the parenthetical one above when he says that fictional works typically pretend that the criteria for the reference of the names involved (whatever those are) are fulfilled.

17 This is roughly Currie's view (1990, 147–50). He argues that uses of fictional names in works of fiction do not refer *de re* back to any object, but rather "each fictional name is replaced by a variable bound by an existential quantifier" (1990, 150). To capture the apparent uniqueness, he argues that we must also assume that there is a fictional author who knows of and reports on the activities described (1990, 153–4). He also concludes that only stories *as a whole* express propositions, since there are quantifiers that have the whole story as their scope (1990, 155).

18 A similar idea is developed in Voltolini (unpublished), who takes character identity to be based in continuation of the same game of pretense.

19 Various solutions have been proposed, including the idea (which, following Parsons 1980, I advocated in my 1999) that such claims implicitly engage in 'restricted quantification', such that, when we say "Emma Woodhouse doesn't exist", we are implicitly restricting the quantifier to cover only (real) people, not fictional characters, and asserting that, among those, none is Emma. Kripke (unpublished, lecture 6, 20) similarly treats such nonexistence claims as saying that there is no such *person* as Emma. Salmon holds the view that, in nonexistence statements, fictional names function as disguised improper definite descriptions (1998, 303–4), so such assertions as "Emma doesn't exist" are to be read as "Emma-as-she-is-described-in-the-story doesn't exist".

20 Kripke's example (unpublished) is the fictional character Moloch, which turns out not to exist (i.e. there is no such *character*).

21 Reimer 2001, and Adams et al. 1997 treat these gappy propositions as not truth-evaluable, and thus seek other ways of explaining our intuitions that such nonexistence statements are true.

22 This 'handling' though is presented explicitly only as a view of the *truth conditions* for these utterances, not of what these statements mean or what propositions they express.

23 I have argued the parallel point for general terms in

my 2003 and (forthcoming). David Braun similarly suggests that the intentions of authors determine whether or not their statements refer to characters (unpublished).

24 Donnellan 1974, 24 suggests that if the name use of "Homer" traced back to a scholar who mistakenly thought all the relevant poems were written by a single person, "Homer" would not refer – again suggesting that some correct ontological conception (person versus group) is necessary to avoid reference failure. Kripke's examples (e.g. 1972, 92–6) of possible reference shifts (despite the maintenance of a causal-historical chain) also suggest that some further conditions are needed to secure reference.

25 Braun 1993, 455 argues against metalinguistic ways of handling nonexistence claims on grounds that it would make the following two sentences putatively express the same proposition:

If Vulcan does not exist, then "Vulcan" does not refer.

If "Vulcan" does not refer, then "Vulcan" does not refer.

But the latter is necessary, while the first is contingent (since the name could have been used to refer to something else). (Kripke (unpublished, lecture 6, 22–6) offers similar objections to metalinguistic analyses of nonexistence claims.) But if we consider the name not just as sounds or marks, abstractly conceived, but the name-as-actually-used (in a certain tradition, to make certain predicative statements), then many problems fall away. Used in a certain community as a purported rigid designator, if the name fails to refer, then (following Kripke 1972, 158) it is necessarily non-referring, and so the first sentence, too, is necessarily true. (Compare Braun 1993, 467n.13)

Another objection (raised by both Braun 1993 and Kripke (unpublished)) is that it would prevent negative existentials that use different names (in different languages) from expressing the same proposition, which seems wrong. Nonetheless, (as Braun notes, ibid.) Donnellan 1974, 29 attempts to account for the intuition that they can by reference to the fact that the use of the two names is historically connected.

There are still some legitimate worries about whether it makes sense to think of such claims as really being about the name rather than a named individual. But I think the impression of inappropriateness can be mitigated if we put it less formally – in any nonexistence claim, there does seem to be a presupposition of some prior uses of the name and an implicit indictment of them. So while it seems inappropriate to treat an adult telling a child that Santa Claus doesn't exist as talking about the name "Santa Claus", it doesn't seem so far off if we take her as saying, "look really, all this talk about Santa Claus you've been hearing all of your life—it just comes out of a story". Consider the similar discussion in Peter Bichsel's 1975 novel *Die Jahreszeiten*. One character, Kieninger, seemingly describes an Annemarie of his acquaintance – Annemarie always goes to the cinema on Tuesday, has her free day on Monday, etc. The narrator, disbelieving Kieninger, replies "But Annemarie is nothing more than a pretty name". (46, my translation)

26 Some would, while accepting the analogy, deny the existence of such cultural artifacts – e.g. van Inwagen (forthcoming, 23) asks, when people go through a ceremony or perform a speech act, do we have reason in general to think "an object called a 'marriage' or a 'promise' thereby comes into existence"? For a reply to this, see §5 of my 2001, and Chapter 9 of my manuscript *Ordinary Objects* (unpublished).

27 The 'pair of gloves' category mistake example is Ryle's 1949, 22 ff.

28 In my 2001 I make a similar argument against those who, like van Inwagen 1990, accept the existence of particles arranged tablewise by artisans, but deny the existence of tables and other medium-sized composite objects.

29 Otherwise put, it is a category mistake to think that those who accept the sufficient foundations for fictional characters (works of literature of certain kinds in certain contexts) but deny the existence of fictional characters have a more parsimonious ontology than do those who accept fictional characters as conceived above. The connection between category mistakes, counting, and parsimony is drawn out more fully in my (unpublished).

References

Adams, F., G. Fuller and R. Stecker 1997, "The Semantics of Fictional Names", *Pacific Philosophical Quarterly* 78, pp. 128–148

Bichsel, P. 1975, *Die Jahreszeiten*, Hamburg: Luchterhand

Braun, D. 1993, "Empty Names", *Noûs* 27: 4, pp. 449–469

Braun, D. (unpublished), "Empty Names, Fictional Names, Mythical Names", presented at APA Central Division symposium on Fictional Names, April 2003

Brock, S. 2002, "Fictionalism about Fictional Characters", *Noûs* 36:1, pp. 1–21

Currie, G. 1990, *The Nature of Fiction*, Cambridge: Cambridge University Press

Devitt, M. and K. Sterelny 1999. *Language and Reality* (second edition). Cambridge, Massachusetts: MIT Press

Donnellan, K. S. 1974, "Speaking of Nothing", *Philosophical Review* 83:1, pp. 3–31

Howell, R. 1979, "Fictional Objects: How they are and how they aren't", *Poetics* 8, pp. 129–177

Kripke, S. 1972, *Naming and Necessity*, Oxford: Blackwell

Kripke, S. (unpublished), The John Locke Lectures for 1973

Parsons, T. 1980, *Nonexistent Objects*, New Haven: Yale University Press

Reimer, M. 2001, "The Problem of Empty Names", *Australasian Journal of Philosophy* 79:4, pp. 491–506

Ryle, G. 1949, *The Concept of Mind*, Chicago: University of Chicago Press (originally London: Hutchinson)

Salmon, N. 1998, "Nonexistence", *Noûs* 32:3, pp. 277–319

Schiffer, S. 1996, "Language-Created Language-Independent Entities", *Philosophical Topics* 24:1, pp. 149–167

Searle, J. 1979, *Expression and Meaning: Studies in the Theory of Speech Acts*, Cambridge: Cambridge University Press

Thomasson, A. L. 1999, *Fiction and Metaphysics*, Cambridge: Cambridge University Press

Thomasson, A. L. 2001, "Ontological Minimalism", *American Philosophical Quarterly*, 38:4, pp. 319–331

Thomasson, A. L. 2003, "Fictional Characters and Literary Practices", *British Journal of Aesthetics*, 43: 2, pp. 138–157

Thomasson, A. L. (forthcoming), "The Ontology of Art", in Peter Kivy, ed., *The Blackwell Guide to Aesthetics*, Oxford: Blackwell

Thomasson, A. L. (unpublished), *Ordinary Objects*. Book manuscript in progress

Van Inwagen, P. 1977, "Creatures of Fiction", *American Philosophical Quarterly*, 14, pp. 299–308

Van Inwagen, P. 1983, "Fiction and Metaphysics", *Philosophy and Literature*, 7, pp. 67–77

Van Inwagen, P. 1990, *Material Beings*, Ithaca, New York: Cornell University Press

Van Inwagen, P. 2003. "Existence, Ontological Commitment, and Fictional Entities", in Michael Loux and Dean Zimmermann, eds., *The Oxford Handbook of Metaphysics*, Oxford: Oxford University Press

Voltolini, A. (unpublished), *How Ficta Follow Fiction* (book manuscript)

Walton, K. 1990, *Mimesis as Make-Believe*, Cambridge, Massachusetts: Harvard University Press

Yablo, S. 1999, Review of Amie Thomasson, *Fiction and Metaphysics*, *Times Literary Supplement, November 5*

Index

Printed in Great Britain
by Amazon